Humphrey Burton read Music and History at Cambridge University
and entered the BBC as a sound studio manager in 1955. In 1958 he
joined the ground-breaking TV arts magazine, *Monitor*. He has won
many international awards, including three from the British Academy,
four Emmies and the Italia Prize (for *The Making of West Side Story*).
Twice in charge of Music and Arts for BBC Television, Burton was also
a founder member of London Weekend Television, where he edited
and presented the ITV arts series *Aquarius*. He is still active in the
fields of radio and television. To celebrate his seventieth birthday in
March 2001 he conducted a charity gala performance of Verdi's
Requiem at the Royal Albert Hall in aid of prostate research.

Burton worked with Yehudi Menuhin on many radio and television
programmes, including a 20-part radio series for Classic FM. He was
also a frequent collaborator with Leonard Bernstein, and later wrote
his biography, also published by Faber. He was awarded a CBE in the
Millennium Honours.

Yehudi in London, 1945

MENUHIN
A Life

HUMPHREY BURTON

faber and faber

by the same author
LEONARD BERNSTEIN

First published in 2000
by Faber and Faber Limited
3 Queen Square London WC1N 3AU
This paperback edition first published in 2001

Photoset by Agnesi Text, Hadleigh
Printed in England by Clays Ltd, St Ives plc

A CIP record for this book
is available from the British Library

ISBN 0–571–20679–4

2 4 6 8 10 9 7 5 3 1

Contents

List of Illustrations

LIST OF ILLUSTRATIONS

Plates

Except where individually credited, all photographs come from the Menuhin Archive or private family albums and reproduction is strictly prohibited. Every effort has been made to trace the owners of copyright. If omissions have occurred, please advise the publisher.

Introduction

I first met Yehudi Menuhin in 1959. I shall call him Yehudi throughout the narrative, by the way; his personality inspired that kind of intimacy and 'Menuhin', alone, comes over too pompously – although I prefer it as the title for the book as a whole. This is not a personal memoir; indeed I pop up again only in the sources listed at the end, but I knew Yehudi quite well for forty years. I was a greenhorn television director, working for the *Monitor* arts programme on BBC TV, when he came into the studio to talk about his beloved Bartók and the solo violin Sonata he had commissioned. His wife Diana sat in on the session, I remember, peeling lichees between takes and doing her embroidery. Later I was to film him standing on his head to demonstrate yoga techniques, improvising with Ravi Shankar, playing the Bach Double with a fourteen-year-old Chinese boy at the UN General Assembly, conducting the *Eroica* at the Barbican. I even waved a football rattle when he conducted the Toy Symphony at a birthday gala.

The impetus for this biography came from a radio series I made for Classic FM in 1996, Yehudi's eightieth birthday year. At the time I suggested to him that our interviews, with their emphasis on his musical life, and their many illustrations from his recorded performances, could be worked up into a book. Initially he was enthusiastic but the project had to go on hold because of a potential clash of interests with an expanded version of his excellent autobiography, *Unfinished Journey*. Two years later I took up the idea again and this time Yehudi agreed wholeheartedly, as did his wife Diana, allowing me access to his personal archive of press cuttings, concert programmes and correspondence – with no strings attached. So this is not an 'official' biography: no editorial control was asked for or ceded: his only request was that I would let him see the proofs of my endeavours. Alas, that proved impossible; his death in March 1999 took everybody by surprise since as both conductor and musical diplomat he still seemed, at eighty-two, to be firing on all eight cylinders – he was never one for small cars.

Yehudi knew from our radio interviews – he came to the studio on half-a-dozen occasions and talked for two hours at a time – that my primary consideration was his music-making over more than seventy years. Yet he had also been completely frank about personal matters during our studio conversations, notably about his divorce, and I felt it would be wrong to try to separate his life from his music; his transformation from Jewish immigrants' son in a Bronx tenement block to British baron in Belgravia makes an extraordinary story. I hope specialist writers will follow with detailed assessment of the recordings, the technique and the pedagogic achievement. My aim has been simply to set out the facts, not the least surprising of which is that for the first twenty-two years of his life Yehudi was said to be nearly a year younger than he really was (see chapter 1). I have avoided cluttering the narrative with footnotes and reference numbers; readers who like to know sources will find the details at the back of the book along with a chronology and the titles of books I have consulted. I decided not to provide complete lists of recordings and videos; they go out of date too quickly.

Yehudi himself published four books about the violin and violin-playing and there are two books of conversations with him, all replete with personal anecdotes, but there has been no chronological account of his life since Robert Magidoff's biography, completed in 1954 when Yehudi was still in his thirties. It was well reviewed at the time and I have consulted it frequently, but I do not accept its basic premise that Yehudi's playing deteriorated from its childhood perfection as soon as he began consciously to question what he was doing. Other commentators suggest it was the Second World War that brought on a decline, or the shock of failing at marriage, or the sight of the survivors of Belsen. I have listened carefully to the recordings and I hear very little falling off in the quality of his performances, certainly not until his late fifties and sixties when a physical deterioration in his right arm prompted him to explore other channels, notably symphonic conducting, through which he could express his boundless love of music. By providing a short list of recommended recordings at the end of each chapter I hope readers will be tempted to explore the vast repertoire of violin music he has left us, much of it transferred to CD. Many of these recordings (and of his conducting work) can be borrowed from public libraries.

As I sat down to write these lines this morning Radio 3 was broadcasting Schumann's Violin Concerto in the pioneer recording Yehudi made (with Barbirolli conducting the New York Philharmonic) back in 1938. It is superb playing and reminded me of another undervalued aspect of Yehudi's life, his commitment to restoration and re-evaluation. As he grew older he moved away from campaigns in the purely violinistic field (he had also championed an *Urtext* Paganini concerto and 'new' concertos by Mendelssohn and Vivaldi) to take in world music, notably that of India, and then world political issues such as apartheid, civil liberties in the USSR and the rights of cultural minorities. At the end of our last interview, in 1996, I asked him to sum up what he stood for. Giving a voice to the voiceless, was his reply, and I perceived he was no longer thinking in musical terms at all. Nevertheless music is what holds this book together, just as music was, for all his political initiatives, the central force that inspired him and – as the Schumann Concerto reminded me – continues to move us, through his genius, from beyond the grave.

HUMPHREY BURTON
19 MAY 2000

PART ONE
Childhood
1916–1930

Fifteen-month-old flag-waver Yehudi Mnuchin

1 Origins

Baby Yehudi with his parents

FOR THE BENEFIT of astrologers, and others who believe such details to be significant, Yehudi Mnuchin (his family name until he was three years old) was born around one in the morning. The date was 22 April 1916, although for the first two decades of his life all publicity material stated that he was born nine months later, on 22 January 1917 and his birthday was celebrated publicly on that day.

Thus throughout Yehudi's time as a child prodigy, people were led to believe that he was nearly a year younger than his real age, a clumsy subterfuge on his father's part (but played along with by Yehudi in his teens) for which there is no reasonable explanation. His father, Moshe Menuhin, who changed the family name when he took American citizenship in 1919, claimed in his autobiography *The Menuhin Saga* that in order for Yehudi to qualify 'at age five' for entrance to kindergarten he had been obliged, when seeking to enrol him in January 1921, to 'up' his age by three months – but this merely adds to the confusion since from his first public appearance Yehudi was said to have been born a year *later*, i.e. in 1917, rather than in 1916 as Moshe's explanation has it.

Many are the myths that surround a world-famous artist when his father is an instinctive publicist. Moshe was a short, wiry fellow, combative, sharp, radical, passionately pro-Arab and blessed (or cursed, depending on one's attitude to the exploitation of child prodigies) with the outlook of an eager salesman looking for ways to increase the novelty value of his product. Or perhaps – returning to the question of the wrong date – he simply hated birthdays. Moshe's father had died on his son's fourth birthday. He had no memories of the man, but he had not forgotten the day of his death. He recalled pedalling his tricycle (a birthday present, no doubt) around the still warm corpse, and being severely scolded for it by his family.

Yehudi was born in New York, at the Mount Lebanon Hospital in the Bronx. He never loved the city that was to applaud his musical achievements for seven decades and he left it when he was still in his cot, first for Elizabeth, New Jersey, an ugly town just across the Hudson River which his father labelled 'Elizabethdump', and then, when only an infant of twenty-one months, to the promised land of milk and honey, California, where his parents could enjoy the kind of climate they had known in their teens when they had lived – and first met – in Palestine. Moshe and his wife Marutha made an intriguing, unlikely couple: the man more Jewish than Russian (even though he strove to distance himself from his religious inheritance); the woman defiantly uncaring about Jewish rituals and determinedly Russian – and oriental Russian at that, in her love of fantastic stories and her pleasure in exotic, oriental clothes and furnishings. She boasted of her unauthenticated Circassian origins and her Tartar blood even though the Tartars were bloodthirsty, marauding warriors who slaughtered Jews whenever the opportunity arose. In her son's phrase, she wore her separateness like a badge.

Moshe was born in 1893 in the White Russian town of Gomel, now in the Belorussia, then part of the Tsarist empire, to an Orthodox Jewish family which could trace its line back to a famous Hasidic rabbi, Rebbe Levi Yitzhak of Berditchev. In his autobiography Moshe writes vividly about the oppressive atmosphere in the Pale of Settlement, 'heavy with a sense of exile, persecution, and fear and hatred of *goyim*, the non-Jews'. His father was 'a well-to-do dry-goods merchant'. His mother was a Schneerson by birth and thus linked to the powerful Lubavitch Hasidic dynasty. Widowed young, she was left to bring up four children. From the moment his mother remarried, to a rich grain-dealer with five children of his own, Moshe felt increasingly estranged from the enclosed ghetto society. He was only ten when his mother took him to Odessa and put him on a boat for Palestine to live with his grandfather in Jerusalem. 'Had it not been for the civilizing, healing atmosphere surrounding that saintly man,' he wrote later, 'I would inevitably have been condemned to the hopeless, bitter hostility against the world, especially the Gentile world, that underlay the attitudes of so many Russian Jews.'

Marutha Sher, Yehudi's mother, also came from a broken home: her father had gone off to America when she was still quite small. She was born near the Black Sea resort town of Yalta in the Crimean peninsula, where the Tartars flourished, and was apparently the only child among seven to have survived infancy. Her mother, a strong personality who later provided the funds for Yehudi's first violin, was the focus of her life. They moved to Palestine when Marutha was fifteen. Moshe was by then a student at the recently founded and fanatically nationalistic Herzlia Gymnasium. He became aware of Marutha because he had lodgings in the house next door:

The first time I saw her, she was climbing on to the dangerously steep roof of her home . . . she seemed so fearless, so reckless on that roof, that I was numbed – and then filled with admiration for a girl who could behave like a boy yet looked so sweet and feminine . . . Marutha literally stopped the traffic when she went out. Jews and Arabs, young and old, turned to watch this attractive girl with blue eyes and blond hair, so aloof and elegant, yet so modest and mature. Gradually as I got to know her Marutha became my sole confidante for the discussion of the serious matters of life. Our daily walks and talks offered me a unique opportunity of practising my English and discussing America, the land of my dreams . . . our companionship rapidly became indispensable to me . . . She broadened my horizons and saved me from becoming self-obsessed and narrow-minded.

All the same, when Moshe graduated, aged nineteen, he put career before matters of the heart and applied for a scholarship to study mathematics at New York University. Being a spiritual Zionist if not a political one, his plan was to take a degree and then return to Palestine to serve his country. But the allure of the United States was clearly very strong: when he was only fourteen he inherited $200 from his beloved Jerusalem grandfather and attempted emigration; indeed he had got as far as France before being turned back by American consular officials. His elder brother Louis had already taken the plunge and was sending back enthusiastic reports from California.

Armed with letters of recommendation, Moshe arrived in New York in November 1913. His first taste of America was a strawberry ice-cream soda. (Strawberry ice-cream was to become his son's favourite dish after playing concerts.) Thanks to his contacts he was fixed up within hours with lodgings (on Clinton Street, East Broadway) and with a job teaching Hebrew at the Talmud Torah, uptown on Lexington at 111th Street. Four hours a day, five days a week, $80 a month: he must have done his work well since he held on to the job all through his college years. Before the end of his first month he had enrolled at New York University, out in what was then the fresh air of the Bronx. Marutha was forgotten until one day he bumped into the son of the Sher family's landlord (who had also come over to the US) and learned that she was currently living with her father in Chicago. He wrote, declaring his love. She responded, and for the next six months, according to Moshe, they exchanged letters every day. In Palestine they had never so much as kissed but the postal friendship developed to the point that Marutha, now seventeen, resolved to take her life into her own hands and thwart her father, who would never have approved of her marrying a penniless student. She took a train to New York. The young couple embraced for the first time in their lives at Grand Central Station and Moshe escorted her to the lodgings he had rented for her at the home of a Jewish laundryman, just across the road from his campus digs at Gould Hall. (He had soon quit the East Side; it reminded him unpleasantly of the oppressive atmosphere of the Russian ghetto from which he had escaped a decade earlier.)

On 7 August 1914, just days after the outbreak of the First World War in Europe, the couple got married. The clerk at the first Marriage License Bureau they visited asked Moshe's age. 'Twenty-one in November,' came the reply. 'In that case you must have your parents' consent.' 'My father's dead; my mother's in Russia and there's a war going on.' The clerk was not to be moved. 'What's the hurry?' he asked. They rushed out to the elevated railway and clattered up to the Bronx, where Moshe lied about his age (a recurring theme, it seems) in order to obtain the licence. Given their own youthful impulsiveness, they could hardly have been surprised when twenty-three years later their son Yehudi told them of his engagement to a girl he had met only three weeks earlier and had wooed by telephone from a distant hotel room.

Moshe plighted his troth with a thin lover's-knot gold ring his sister Shandel had given him on the eve of her own wedding in Palestine. It was an arranged marriage and she was miserable; she had had an unhappy love affair that ended with her lover's suicide. 'Marry for love,' she had whispered to Moshe. 'Give this ring to your sweetheart in my name. One must love to live.' When her wedding ceremony ended, she drank a full bottle of carbolic acid and died in agony. (Many years later Marutha gave the ring to Yehudi's first wife, Nola, and when that marriage failed, Moshe asked for the ring to be returned.) The rabbi told him that no matter how great the ring's sentimental significance it was not appropriate for a wedding. Moshe was obliged to borrow $2 from the teacher colleague who was acting as witness and dash out into the street to buy the genuine article.

Moshe still had a year of study ahead of him. Marutha got a part-time job teaching Hebrew and for the first months of their marriage they shared the kitchen of their laundryman landlord. They started hunting for a modest apartment and Marutha found the ideal place in the University Heights district. According to Moshe, the landlord was very persuasive: 'You'll love it here. The atmosphere! The exclusiveness! No Jews allowed!' Without hesitation Marutha said, 'My dear man, we *are* Jews!' 'But you don't look like Jews so you are still welcome.' Moshe concluded his account rather grandly, 'As we left, Marutha made a vow: "If ever I have a son, his name will be YEHUDI. Let him stand or fall by his name."' So having a child was clearly on her mind, despite their precarious financial circumstances. It's uncertain, however, why she rejected such easily identifiable Old Testament names as Abraham or Isaac in favour of Yehudi, which means quite simply 'the Jew', a sort of Everyman soubriquet. The more familiar form is Yehuda. Her penchant for being different prompted Marutha to adopt the genitive form.

Another apartment, with a landlord more sympathetic to Jews, was rented at 50 Buchanan Street and they made a home for themselves, decorated with exotic oriental rugs and sofas laden with cushions. They took in lodgers and were blissfully happy. Moshe recalled that they used to walk along the aqueduct on University Avenue holding hands and singing songs, or hike to Van Cortland Park or even to distant Yonkers. Bread was 5c. a loaf, milk 4c. or 5c. a quart, mackerel 5c. apiece, and meat 10–15c. a pound. Marutha had learned to cook and bake and she enjoyed running up long dresses for herself made of white cheesecloth, good practice for the clothes she made for her daughters all through their childhood.

Yehudi's younger sister, Yaltah, who is no great fan of her mother, has suggested that the strong-willed Marutha believed her destiny was to give birth to a genius. A year after their marriage Marutha duly became pregnant. To celebrate the forthcoming event, Moshe bought books by his favourite author Sholem Aleichem and night after night he taught his wife Yiddish as they laughed and cried over the colourful tales of the Russian ghetto. When her labour pains began, they took a taxi for the first time in their lives to reach the hospital. Marutha sent Moshe home and the child was born some twelve hours later – 'a perfect little boy', according to the doctor who delivered him. He was breastfed for nine months and walked and talked, so his father claimed, exceptionally early. Marutha was obliged to take him with her to school when she resumed her teaching job and she 'nursed him', as Moshe put it, in the cloakroom during the breaks between classes. Twelve years later, on a 1929 visit to New York, Yehudi's parents drove him back to University Heights. It was the day after a concerto performance at Carnegie Hall and Moshe hired a car to drive them up to the Bronx. There stood the house, 50 Buchanan Street, unchanged:

Under the stairs was the place where Yehudi's baby carriage had been kept, a clothes line swinging just where it did when his little clothes used to flutter on it. They visited the grocery store where Marutha didn't have 5c. to pay for a loaf and Yehudi was shown the viaduct where night after night his parents had sung by the hour, laughing away hardships and hunger while they started to equip themselves for life.

Yehudi's birth precipitated Moshe's decision not to return to Palestine after graduation in 1917, nor to continue the postgraduate studies in education that he was already pursuing at NYU in Washington Square. Instead he found a full-time job in the field of education, in charge of a newly founded Hebrew School serving the Jewish community in Elizabeth, New Jersey. He was developing a new approach to teaching in a field that hitherto had been devoted to preserving Orthodox Judaism. The arrival of the Mnuchins in Elizabeth, a grim town of oil refineries and freight-train marshalling yards, caused something of a sensation, she with her boldly 'bobbed' hair – not the style adopted by conventional Jewish wives – and he with his dynamism and his progressive outlook on Zionism. He encouraged his pupils to speak Hebrew as well as write it. She taught the children to sing and recite poetry, even to act in Hebrew and English plays. Hanukkah, the first major religious celebration under their leadership, was a great success, Moshe reported, but however happy the pupils and parents might have been with this unconventional approach, there was a groundswell of opposition from the synagogue elders that made Yehudi's parents decide to move on.

The climate of East Coast America was unsympathetic, and it was not only a question of miserable winter weather. Politically, young Mnuchin was out of sympathy (and remained so ever after) with New York's Jewish Establishment, which tended to be orientated towards the creation in Palestine of a Jewish national home – a concept reinforced in November of that year by British government support as outlined in the Balfour Declaration. On New Year's Eve he and his wife attended an evening of depressingly bombastic speeches. A snowstorm delayed their return home from New York City until four in the morning. The depressed Moshe had a vision of California and began planning their escape. A cable was despatched to his brother Louis. Their beloved upright piano, bought on the never-never and lovingly played by Marutha when the housework was done and baby Yehudi was asleep, was crated up and sent off by freight train. Early on the morning of 1 February the furniture was sold to a dealer for a derisory $18 and as soon as Moshe received his salary arrears, paid in cash later that day, they were off.

When they got to New York their worldly goods, hitherto wrapped up in nothing more secure than a bundle of sheets, had to be repacked in a hastily purchased secondhand trunk which was immediately despatched direct to Oakland Pier to await their arrival. Such was the impetuosity of their departure that Moshe found he did not have enough cash saved for their trip. A friendly ticket clerk at Grand Central put together a roundabout travel routing which brought the price down to $150 dollars for the family and at 10 p.m. they set off on their six-day odyssey, carrying with them (Moshe is specific about these symbols of their great journey) a baby chair, a potty, a shovel and a broom. The infant Yehudi was put to sleep on a blanket with a bottle of warm milk as his companion, only to be rudely awakened when their cheap-rate itinerary forced a change of trains in the middle of the night. When they arrived in Oakland (via Kansas City, Chicago and Los Angeles) they were hungry and exhausted and Moshe didn't have enough cash left to phone his brother. It was only thanks to the Travelers Aid Society that he was contacted, turning up some hours later with a horse and buggy that transported them on a long moonlit ride to Louis's rented farm in Hayward, south-west of Oakland on the eastern side of San Francisco Bay. Next morning they awoke to find themselves looking over a green valley: it was spring and their new life had begun.

The chicken farm proved a less than idyllic home. Louis had decided to take the opposite course to his young brother and was soon to return to Palestine to fight for the Zionist cause. There were frequent quarrels but Louis lent Moshe $200 with which he rented an apartment in South Berkeley, closer to the big city. Marutha had been offered a job teaching at a Jewish Sunday school and Moshe was drawn to the idea of postgraduate study at the university. But he needed an income. With the help of letters of introduction from his NYU education professor to San Francisco's Jewish community leaders – Moshe was to prove adept at enlisting powerful supporters – he built on his teaching experience in Elizabeth and opened a Hebrew School in the vestry of the Orthodox Synagogue, on Webster and McAllister Streets. Seventy children enrolled in the first week and soon there were three late-afternoon classes, with the students divided according to age and knowledge of Hebrew, five days a week. Later he added a Sabbath hour on Saturday morning for Bible stories and prayers. Orthodox Jews cannot travel on the Sabbath, so Moshe would tactfully descend from the jitney with which he concluded his train and ferry journey from Berkeley and walk the last ten blocks. It was a lot of work for the tiny salary of $65 per month.

Moshe was an avid chronicler of the early manifestations of his son's musical gifts, but the very first 'incident' in Yehudi's life, dating from the family's stay in Berkeley, concerns the painful banality of tonsilitis. A specialist said the boy's tonsils would have to be removed. Moshe had no money to pay for surgery, but it emerged that the specialist sometimes operated free of charge. The ailing Yehudi was wheeled to the West Berkeley dispensary in his folding pushchair (a distance of about a mile, Moshe carefully noted) where his father was subjected to a humiliating grilling from a social worker: 'Don't you think that somebody who makes $65 a month should be able to pay $10 to the dispensary for taking care of his baby?' But the Mnuchins simply didn't have $10. They had to promise to pay when they could and the operation went ahead but there was no post-operative care: they simply wheeled Yehudi straight back home again. Yehudi's own earliest memory dates from this time:

I was two years old and being given a piggy-back by my father. My mother was there too, and as we walked through the quiet tree-lined avenue . . . she fed me cherries.

Soon afterwards came the first indication of the boy's musical gifts. The Mnuchins were friendly with a Jewish couple whose little daughter Lily became a playmate for Yehudi. 'One evening', Moshe writes,

as we were putting him to sleep, he asked for Lily. We told him in Hebrew (Hebrew being his mother's tongue): '*Lily halchah lishun*' ('Lily's gone to sleep'). He turned on his side and began to sing '*Lily halchah lishun*', starting on the lowest note he could manage and continuing up the scale, in perfect pitch, until he reached the highest note he could hit. He paused and then began to descend the scale down, down until he reached the note on which he'd started. Then he fell asleep. Marutha and I looked at each other in astonishment. Every evening from then on, Yehudi sang himself to sleep with his own lullaby.

Their friend Reuben Rinder, cantor of the Temple Emanuel Synagogue, was called in to admire this uncanny phenomenon. 'I tried the old piano to see where he got his idea of how the notes ought to sound,' he reported, 'but the piano was out of tune while Yehudi's intonation was perfect.' Two years later it was Rinder who asked another friend, the violin teacher Louis Persinger, to audition Yehudi.

Marutha received another sign that Yehudi was especially sensitive to music when she began studying with a cellist from the San Francisco Orchestra, Arthur Weiss. Whenever she practised at home she would hear Yehudi billing and cooing to himself as she drew her bow across the strings. There is no mention in Moshe's chronicle of any previous interest in classical music (readily available though it was in New York) but in 1918 he and his wife started attending Sunday afternoon symphony concerts at the Curran Theater. And two-year-old Yehudi went with them, smuggled in a carry-cot up to the cheap seats in the balcony with a supply of hot milk and biscuits on hand in case he became obstreperous – though of course, being Yehudi, he didn't; on the contrary: 'He listened to the music with rapt attention.' Disarmingly, Marutha would say later that they took him with them because they couldn't afford a babysitter, but the more likely explanation is that they believed passionately in sharing all experiences and wanted to expose their boy to the finest influences. 'Before long,' according to Moshe, whose memories of this distant period need to be taken with several pinches of salt,

not only the public but also members of the orchestra and the conductor, Alfred Hertz, knew about the strange baby with a passion for music. If ever we missed a concert, people made enquiries when we reappeared with Yehudi the next Sunday.

Yehudi himself was too young to remember any specific musical performance but a powerful recollection of the repeated experience remained with him, to be distilled in his own autobiography:

Seated on my mother's knee in the gallery, I am looking over a shadowy cliff, as through a telescope the wrong way round, at the bottom of which the musicians in a pool of light are miniature but distinct, their busy concentration down there producing sounds to ravish soul and sense.

Moshe's career nose-dived briefly when San Francisco was brought to its knees by the terrible Spanish flu epidemic which took more lives in a few months than had been lost in the world war that had just ended. Just when Moshe needed extra cash to pay for the transportation of the upright Matushek piano that had finally been delivered from Elizabeth, the Hebrew School was forced to close and he was obliged to take a temporary job in a timber yard in Alameda where his fellow workers berated him for working too hard. When life returned to normal he organized an expansion of his original Hebrew School into a chain of seven strung across the city; he obviously had real administrative flair in the teaching field. His salary was raised to $150 a month and the family moved to a rented apartment at 732 Hayes Street. Marutha was at last able to satisfy her yearning to sleep in the open as she had done in Palestine. Abutting the windows, Yehudi recalled, was 'a flat roof upon which an awning was pitched, and there, if the weather was in any way suitable, we slept'.

Professionally the next two years were a period of strain for Moshe as he fought a long battle for control of his schools with the newly arrived rabbi, Wolf Gold. But for Yehudi life with his mother seems to have been idyllic. When Moshe could get away they indulged their love of Sunday picnic excursions into the countryside, their greatest pleasure being the visits they made to their friends the Kavin family who ran a chicken farm in Petaluma, a village known in those days as 'The Egg Basket of the World'. Yehudi recalled sitting in the back of the farmer's Dodge with the two Kavin girls, looking through the small round back windows at the road running away from them:

As we drove along, my father sang old Hasidic songs. The motion of the automobile, California's landscape and my father's singing curiously blended into one sensation that has left a lasting impression on me. Aba sang with a joy and abandon that seemed to give him release from all his cares.

'Aba' was the family name for Yehudi's father; his mother was first 'Imma' and later 'Mammina'. In this narrative their regular first names, Moshe and Marutha, are deployed throughout.

Two other childhood impressions were carried over into adulthood like Proust's afternoon madeleine. When he was three Yehudi was taken to see the Pantages Vaudeville Company, which, like San Francisco's symphony orchestra, performed at the Curran Theater. He was enchanted by the first professional violin recitalist he ever heard, one Carichiarto, a swarthy fellow who, according to Yehudi, played quite beautifully. But he confessed that no single experience of the theatre 'more lastingly marked me than a performance by Anna Pavlova . . . I remember being absolutely carried away; hardly less transporting was the mere sight of her luggage . . . six or seven great wardrobe trunks' – the very image of the travelling artist that Yehudi himself was all too soon to become. Pavlova's programme included 'The Californian Poppy', a dance inspired by a favourite sweet-smelling orange flower which, as Pavlova did at the end of her ballet, closes in on itself as it droops. Yehudi dreamed of Pavlova for months and she inspired a particularly purple passage in his memoirs:

Sown in a sensibility fashioned by my mother, the seed Pavlova planted, a conception of beauty and grace perfected by the discipline of the dance, was to come to flower in adult life in my wife, Diana.

His second wife, Diana Gould, had been a ballet dancer.

On 18 September 1919, Moshe made the final break with his Russian past and his Palestinian upbringing by becoming an American citizen. At the Superior Court the officiating judge proposed a change in the family name:

Americans cannot pronounce the 'ch' in 'Mnuchin' as it is in Hebrew, and cannot hook up the two consonants 'm' and 'n' without a vowel in between. May I suggest that you spell your name Menuhin?

Nine months to the week after that day of celebration, on 20 May 1920, the Menuhins' first daughter was born. They called her Hephzibah, Hebrew for 'the desired one'. She and her brother were to form one of the finest violin and piano duos of the twentieth century. A few weeks before his sister came into the world, young Yehudi had been given a toy violin for his fourth birthday. He had smashed it to the ground, complaining bitterly, 'It won't sing! It won't sing!'

2 The Prodigy

Yehudi aged six

1921–3: early studies with Sigmund Anker; 1923–6: studies with Louis Persinger and first public appearances; support from Sidney Ehrman; 1926: January: first New York recital; March: first concerto performance in San Francisco; November: first Civic Auditorium concerto appearance; December: departure for Europe.

YEHUDI MENUHIN was the best-known prodigy of the twentieth century, but there are many gaps and inconsistencies in our knowledge of his early childhood and certain errors in the dating of events were unwittingly introduced by Yehudi himself. He wrote that he was given a violin soon after his fourth birthday, but it was more than a year before he started lessons with a reputable teacher. In his autobiography, *Unfinished Journey,* he related that the idea of becoming a violinist had come to him at the age of three, when he was sitting on a parent's knee at a symphony concert in the Curran Theater:

I let my gaze slide past the conductor . . . to focus on the concertmaster, Louis Persinger. Once in a while he would have a solo passage. I learned to wait for those moments when the sweet lovely sound of the violin floated up to the gallery, thrilling, caressing and more entrancing than any other. I asked my parents if I might have a violin for my fourth birthday and Louis Persinger to teach me.

The request must have struck a chord in his father's memory. As a boy back in Russia he had fallen in love with the klezmer violinists who, as he put it, made their instruments *sing*. His grandfather, who encouraged him in the singing of Hasidic songs, was shocked by the thought of a violinist in the family:

An ordinary common Jew can fiddle at weddings but not a Hasidic rabbi's grandson! Singing? Ah, that is different. The angels in heaven sing. Singing is man's way of merging with God.

Moshe disobeyed and took three lessons from the laundrywoman's violinist husband. But then the grandfather caught him and the desire to play the fiddle went underground, to surface twenty years later in his aspirations for his son.

In his account of Yehudi's awakening talent, Moshe confirmed that when they went to concerts the infant showed a particular interest in the violin and would become excited when a solo violinist was featured. Fritz Kreisler, Jascha Heifetz, Mischa Elman and the veteran Eugène Ysaÿe all played in San Francisco during Yehudi's infancy. Such appearances might seem a more realistic source of inspiration than Yehudi's own account, given that the concertmaster (the 'leader' in English parlance) is hardly an obvious focus of attention: he remains seated even when playing solos and he shares a music stand with a colleague so he is never visually prominent. But what both father and son forgot is that when Yehudi was a small boy Louis Persinger switched roles from concertmaster to soloist two or three times a season. In 1920 he performed concertos by Mendelssohn, Saint-Saëns, Bruch and Beethoven; in 1921 a Bach concerto and in 1922 Lalo's *Symphonie espagnole*; in 1923 he again played the Beethoven and Mendelssohn concertos. So it probably *was* Persinger who triggered young Yehudi's ambition. It was in any case hardly unusual for a

Russian-Jewish boy to want to play the violin. A later twentieth-century joke had it that the immigrants from Russia who arrived in Israel without a violin case could only have been pianists. (As it happens, the upright piano installed in the Menuhin household never attracted young Yehudi. He disparaged the instrument all his life.) The three-year-old's obsession came to the ears of a fellow teacher at Moshe's Hebrew School and on his fourth birthday he was presented with a toy violin. 'Yehudi picked it up,' wrote Moshe,

believing that by some magic he could extract pure sounds from it. When the results were unsatisfactory he smashed the toy to pieces and trampled on it. He burst into mad anger, as if insulted by the gift.

'I shall never forget the disappointment of that imitation violin,' Yehudi wrote in his own memoirs.

Made of metal, with metal strings, cold to the touch, with a sound as horribly tinny as its construction, this travesty of my longings enraged me for, as far as I can recall, the first time in my life.

There was a happy ending: in a letter to her mother in Palestine, Marutha described her son's tantrum and Grandmother Sher responded by sending a money order. Yehudi never met his benefactor – she died shortly afterwards – but her photograph hung on the wall in the room where he practised and Yehudi swore he once caught her winking her approval as he played the slow movement of Bach's E major Concerto. The amount of her gift varies with the telling: Moshe put it at as little as $25 but much later (in 1976) Yehudi remembered it as $800 and by 1996, presumably in a further attempt to reflect the contemporary purchasing power of the gift, his memory of the figure had risen to $1000. The point of the story is that there was enough cash not only to purchase a real half-size fiddle and bow but also for the down payment on the first family car, an open four-door Chevrolet. Yehudi loved them both.

More than a year passed, however, between the toy episode and his first lessons, so Moshe's report that Grandmother Sher responded 'by return mail' must be treated with some caution. The next firm date Moshe provided is 21 January 1921, when Yehudi, aged four and three-quarters, was taken to the city's best kindergarten, the Lowell, to be enrolled. This was the origin of what might be described as 'the false birthday syndrome':

When the Registrar, with a slight smile, told us that they could not accept pupils before their fifth birthday, I took the hint and said it was Yehudi's fifth birthday that very day, and our son was accepted forthwith.

The false date was retained but at some point very soon after – certainly by Yehudi's first recital – Moshe dropped his son's age by nine months: as already noted, 22 January 1917 was wrongly given as Yehudi's date of birth until his early twenties. Yehudi described the Lowell as

a regular American school with several hundred pupils. The teachers seemed to humdrum along and there was a not too pleasant smell of children's feet. I was only to go for the morning and when I got back my mother asked me what I had learned. I said, 'Well, I didn't really learn anything, but there was a window high up on the wall and I could see a branch of a tree and I was intensely waiting for a bird to land on it. No bird came but that was my refuge from the room and the teacher.' 'Well,' she said, 'obviously you're not meant for school.'

In another account of the school episode, Yehudi said he was upset by the sight of a teacher hitting a child. According to Moshe's memoirs, his son asked the kindergarten to telephone his parents and the boy himself came on the line demanding to be taken home. That they capitulated so readily to a typical first-day reaction, which most parents would have resisted, suggests that Marutha had all along wanted to teach her children herself. At the outset this cannot have been because of Yehudi's special musical talent since the decision was taken before he started to study the violin. Later on, tutors were hired to supplement her efforts and neither of Yehudi's sisters ever went to school. (Yaltah, the younger of the two, was born on 7 October 1921.) Instruction at home was not, after all, such an outlandish idea since Moshe had studied modern education methods and both parents had had several years' practical teaching experience back in New York and New Jersey.

Despite Marutha Menuhin's burning ambition to be the mother if not of the true Messiah then of a very significant figure, there's no proof that Moshe and Marutha wanted to develop a child genius *per se*. But they were pioneers, both by nature and by their Palestinian upbringing, and they saw themselves as young Americans playing their part in the brave new world of 1920s California. Yehudi was later to provide the focus for home education by his insistence on studying the violin, but initially his parents seem to have been relatively cautious about providing him with instruction since they waited until after his fifth birthday before taking the plunge. Their first approach to a teacher, via the good offices of their cantor friend Reuben Rinder, was to the concertmaster Louis Persinger. He turned them down without an audition. Marutha set about finding a teacher in the neighbourhood. 'The first one we saw', Yehudi remembered,

was rather uninspiring. He had a sign at the top of the stairs leading to his small and dilapidated house: VIOLIN LESSONS GIVEN. He proved to be a broken-down old man defeated by drudgery and smelling unpleasantly of tobacco and wine. We didn't take to him, neither my mother nor I. But we found another man who was fairly famous in San Francisco, Sigmund Anker.

Lessons commenced on 31 May 1921. In his memoirs Yehudi stated, wrongly, that the following November, immediately after he had failed to win a competition, his mother made a second and this time successful approach to Louis Persinger, who has been widely credited as Yehudi Menuhin's first significant teacher. In fact Yehudi stayed with Anker another eighteen months, his last lesson being on 14 May 1923.

Sigmund Anker (1892–1958) was born in Austria. He had emigrated to San Francisco before the First World War and played in the city's new Symphony Orchestra before developing a flourishing teaching practice. He had at least thirty violin pupils and organized a string orchestra for children aged between seven and fourteen; it took part in Anker's concerts and even gave radio broadcasts. Yehudi played in it for a time. In his brochures Anker naturally claimed credit for having given Yehudi his first lessons and taught him the rudiments of music. 'After a brief period of study,' he wrote,

Yehudi had already mastered several of the most difficult compositions, which could only be done by having had correct instruction. The fundamental work is most essential, as is recognized in Menuhin's playing.

Anker received a consistently bad press from Yehudi, who described him as a Svengali with the techniques of a drill sergeant, transforming boys and girls into virtuosi by the batch.

His business in life was to groom the young to brilliant performances of Sarasate and Tchaikovsky and he had neither capacity nor ambition for anything more subtle . . . he knew nothing of the process of violin playing, or if he did, lacked the skill to pass on his knowledge . . . his method was to set up a target – correct intonation, full round tone, or whatever – and whip his pupils towards it by unexplained command. 'Vibrate,' he would shout, 'vibrate' – with never a clue as to how it was done.

Yehudi's account of his first steps on the violin was written more than fifty years after the event and reads like a compendium of the basic errors committed by all untutored beginners.

Merely holding the violin, at arm's length, very tightly, seemed problem enough; where did one find a second pair of arms to play it? . . . Where the left hand, in the 'golden mean' position, should form spirals round the neck of the instrument (as the right hand does, around the bow) mine pinioned it between thumb and the base of my first finger. Where the digits should arch softly over the fingerboard, each muscularly independent of the others, mine – all but the smallest, which drooped behind – cleaved to one another like three parade ponies, moving *en masse* from one positional rung to another up the chromatic ladder as if they found safety in numbers. Where the violin should lie on the collarbone, secured there by the head's natural but delicate weight, I clamped it tight. Where the right hand . . . and the bow function rather as the wheel and axis of a gyroscope, the former rotating in order to keep the latter on a true course, I sawed a straight line and, on every downstroke, swerved or 'turned the corner' (to make matters worse the bow was too long for me). At crucial points where the sound should have vibrated freely, it was hopelessly grounded.

Despite Anker's weekly lessons, Yehudi claimed to have taught himself by trial and error. After six months, he wrote,

for no reason I can explain, the violin began to lose its foreignness, my grip relaxed, my body discovered the freedom to forget itself, and I could enjoy what I was doing.

Was it an inexplicable miracle or was his teacher doing a better job than Yehudi allowed? Six years later, when Yehudi was famous, the *San Francisco Examiner* published a letter from Anker in which he claimed (with some justification) a measure of responsibility for his former pupil's meteoric success. Anker stated that, exactly six months after lessons began, Yehudi played his first concert. The date was 26 November 1921, the location a small hall at 630 18th Avenue, and the work a short piece ('a tuneful little selection' was Anker's phrase) called *Remembrance*. (This must have been the *Souvenir* in D (1904) by the Czech composer František Drdla.) There is no review extant of what was probably just a regular teacher's display event. For the record, Moshe gave 10 December as the début date and the venue as the Fairmont Hotel. Anker's scrapbook contains the first podgy press photo, announcing a matinée concert at the Imperial on 24 December.

In *Unfinished Journey* Yehudi wrongly recalled his début as a competition held at the Fairmont Hotel in which he had the disconcerting experience, never to be repeated, of coming second rather than first. He thought he played *Remembrance*, and a girl of twelve named Sarah Kreindler came first, playing Sarasate's flashy *Gypsy Airs*. Yehudi had to make do, so he remembered, with the consolation prize of an illustrated book about another child prodigy, Mozart, which was donated by the family friend, Cantor Reuben Rinder. There surely was such a competition and Sarah was certainly one of Anker's brightest pupils, but it was not Yehudi's début. To complicate matters further, Yehudi's first biographer gave a different account of this defeat in which the competition took place several years later, for a gold medal, Yehudi's selection being Beethoven's celebrated but technically undemanding Minuet in G.

According to Anker's account of his pupil, on 11 February 1922, when Yehudi was still only five, he played a minuet by Paderewski before a larger audience at a Pacific Music Society concert in the Fairmont Hotel. Two months later, his mother accompanied him, at the same location, in a piece called *Redowa de Wallenstein*. Marutha acted as one of the hostesses at this recital. She had given up studying the cello with Dr Weiss after the birth of her second daughter, Yaltah, the previous October, but when her day's work was done, Yehudi remembered, she still liked to play Chopin on their upright piano. The Waltz in C♯ minor was her favourite.

In June 1922 Yehudi was heard on KUO, the new radio station of the *San Francisco Examiner* (the programme was 'given for kiddies of the children's hospitals and orphanages') and on 9 November came his first appearance at the Civic Auditorium, playing Accolay's A minor Violin Concerto (with piano accompaniment) in the Annual Music Week sponsored by the Pacific Music Society. Here for the first time there exists a considered response to the boy's playing, written by the *Examiner*'s Redfern Mason, one of San Francisco's most respected music critics.

BOY VIOLINIST WINS LAURELS

. . . the performers ranged from tots to young people who are at the parting of the ways. And the youngest of them all was the most wonderful. He was a little fellow five years old [*recte* six], so young that he did not know what fear was but only wonder at what might be the meaning of that many-headed God – the audience. His name is Yehudi Menuhin; he has learned the fiddle for a year [*recte* eighteen months] and already he plays it with prophecy of the master that is to be . . . Yehudi had memorized [the concerto] and he played it with the artless sincerity of one listening to an inward voice. The tone had an infantile guilelessness and a beauty that brought to my mind Wordsworth's 'Heaven lies about us in our infancy'.

Since it was reviewed by a professional critic, it would be accurate to label this appearance Yehudi's public début – at the age of six and under the tutelage of Sigmund Anker. Until now a concert at Oakland on 29 February 1924, in which Yehudi played de Bériot's *Scène de ballet* (also with piano accompaniment) has always been cited as his public début but there appears to be no reason – apart from the size of the audience – to deny that honour to the concert reviewed above.

Three months later (on 10 February 1923) Yehudi performed de Bériot's Concerto No. 9, another warhorse for aspiring soloists. 'Musician, aged 5, charms hearers' was the headline of the report in the *San Francisco Journal*. In fact he was only two months short of seven. The *Chronicle* described him as

the latest child prodigy discovered in San Francisco . . . a straight-limbed, sturdy, normal little boy of six [the correct age for once; the false birth date allowed three months of accuracy each year] with round, bulging pink cheeks, the most laughing blue eyes and rollicking ways who loves to shoot down the hill 'ninety miles an hour' on his scooter.

He was said to be 'almost smaller than the half-sized violin which he hugs to his breast so eagerly when his parents permit him to play it'. The virtuoso-to-be was

a regular little boy and huskier than the average. He is not the accepted type of child genius with pale cheeks and burning eyes . . . He is only allowed to practise one hour a day, much to his regret. Some of his idle time is spent in reading James G. Macy's *Young People's History of Music*, in doing his lessons in the Fourth Reader, doing addition and subtraction, and practising up his multiplication tables so that when he enters the public school next fall [he never did] he can skip several of the lower grades . . . Best of all, Yehudi likes to look forward to that rosy future. 'I am going to be the greatest violinist in the world. I've heard Jascha Heifetz and Mischa Elman. They are wonderful, wonderful, but', the six-year-old young man adds firmly, 'I shall play even better when I am a big man!'

The newspaper feature was accompanied by a photograph of Yehudi playing the violin and 'giving instruction' to his two-year-old sister Hephzibah.

Some might think the boy's high opinion of himself to be disagreeably cocky, others that it was no more than the truth. It's unclear whether it was spoken directly to the journalist or filtered through Moshe's publicity-conscious pen. The self-assessment was certainly reinforced by an unsigned review of the same concert in the *San Francisco Journal* (11 February 1923):

The Valentine program given by the Pacific Musical Society yesterday afternoon, through its Junior Auxiliary, developed far more than pleasing numbers. It presented a youngster of five years [nearly seven] whose violin instruction has been of only one year's duration [1¼ years] and who played the de Bériot Concerto No. 9 with the poise and temperament of a veteran.

He is Yehudi Menuhin . . . The child is so small that he had to be guided on the platform, and his attack of the first note made the audience 'sit up' with wonderment. The three movements of the long concerto were played without hesitation and with an accuracy and expressiveness to marvel at! He was stormed with applause at the close of his number, which calls for many of the violin's technical peculiarities, such as double stopping, octaves and harmonics; the whole number was given with the utmost purity.

The family nicknamed the de Bériot the 'Yosemite Concerto' because the previous summer they had made a two-day two-hundred-mile trip to Inspiration Point in the Yosemite valley. A flavour of the pioneer spirit Moshe relished and no doubt glamorized can be detected in his description of the holiday:

We lived there in a tent, gathered wood for our stove, and cooked in the open. Yehudi, of course, had his little violin and worked on the de Bériot. The valley resounded with the luscious melodies and other campers would gather round our tent to listen to his playing. Marutha often invited them to join us for a hearty breakfast of pancakes . . .

Moshe omits from this rosy account an incident to which Yehudi himself attributed some significance. At the end of the breakfast picnic the boy got up and strolled away to look at the mountain tops freshly revealed after the morning mists had cleared. His mother called him back. Even alfresco, one did not get down from the table without asking permission. The requisite words stuck in the boy's throat and he could not bring himself to speak. Moshe failed to negotiate a compromise over his son's first challenge to authority. The guests slipped awkwardly away while the family sat speechless for several hours until the stubborn Yehudi muttered something that was deemed facesavingly adequate. 'My first challenge to authority was over,' Yehudi remembered. 'There have been others since, none so unequal.' Marutha was said to have brooded over the incident, 'spreading a pall of gloom over the household . . . [everyone] moved about in shrouds'.

Other weekend excursions in the open Chevvy took them out of town to Concord, Santa Rosa and Mount Tamalpais. They never drove faster than 15 m.p.h. Moshe denounced any driver who overtook them as 'a reckless man who had no sense of family responsibility'. In the summer of 1923 they headed south sixty miles to the beautiful Santa Cruz mountains. They rented a pair of cottages near the town of Los Gatos, where a decade later they were to make their permanent home. The landlord was an eccentric former priest, a neighbour of theirs in San Francisco, who ran a community he called 'The Holy City'. California was already famous for its cranks: 'Father' Riker ('Ricker' according to Yehudi's book) also owned a prosperous trucking company entitled 'The Perfect Christian Divine Way'. The Menuhins were not converted but they took even their holidays very seriously: 'We settled down for a few weeks of hiking, playing, reading, writing, arithmetic, and of course violin practice.'

In 1923 the expanding family moved into a larger home. In *Unfinished Journey* Yehudi stated the move was in 1921, the year of Yaltah's birth and his first violin lessons. However a *Chronicle* article of February 1923 states they were still living at 733 Hayes Street and elsewhere Yehudi said the move was made three months after his lessons with Persinger began, i.e. in the autumn of 1923. By then Yehudi's potential as a performer would have been sufficiently evident for them to buy a residence appropriate for their future needs. The handsome two-storey wooden house, 1043 Steiner Street, still stands on one of San Francisco's attractive hillsides. It boasted a double living room, normally divided by sliding doors into dining and living rooms but capable when opened up of seating sixty guests at an informal concert – an astonishingly grandiose concept for a young couple of limited means with three very small children. But the Menuhins loved entertaining – Yehudi remembered a many-leafed table around which twenty people would sit down for dinner – and they needed somewhere for young Yehudi to play for their friends.

There was a small room off the kitchen where the boy did his daily practice. Marutha did not oversee his work so much as overhear it while she prepared the meals. At the back there was a yard with some trees and a swing. They built a deck on which they erected a large tent and there the entire family slept, in divided sections, apparently all the year round, because the ingenious Moshe let out the upstairs bedrooms to lodgers. Yehudi remembered two old Russian ladies in the larger front room overlooking the street, and a succession of students in the back room overlooking the garden. In the basement Moshe created a large garage where he rented parking spaces (memories differ as to whether it was for three, five or even seven cars) to pay off the $5000 mortgage on the new house at $50 dollars per month. As he took on more administrative responsibilities, Moshe's monthly salary rose to $250 and later $350; he was developing a solid career in the education of the children of the San Francisco Jewish community. But his son was on his way to riches undreamed of in Moshe's relatively modest scheme of things. Yehudi's progress under Anker was phenomenal. He had just turned seven (and was being presented as only six) when he performed the first movement of the Mendelssohn Violin Concerto with what was described as 'a freedom and tenderness hardly believable' at an end-of-season pupils' concert held in the Fairmont Hotel in May 1923. 'His genius', declared the *San Francisco Journal*, 'is almost uncanny as he plays with the security and balance of an adult not only in the notes but with an understanding spirit.'

Yet despite the rave reviews, the Menuhins decided – no doubt prompted by Yehudi himself – to drop Sigmund Anker in favour of Louis Persinger. Perhaps, as Yehudi hinted in his memoirs, Marutha was incensed by her son's failure to win a gold medal in competition with Sarah Kreindler. Yet Anker's self-defence has the ring of truth: 'Had I given him a poor foundation the child could not play today what he does.' And Moshe wrote that he had nothing against Anker:

On the contrary we were deeply grateful to him; his teaching had been of inestimable value . . . however Anker *was* hurt, and for a long time considered us ungrateful. Again and again, Marutha and I were to incur similar misunderstandings but we had to act strongly in the best interests of our children.

Questioned in 1998 about his hostility towards Sigmund Anker, Yehudi could not explain how he had come to misreport the length of his time with Anker nor why he discounted his first teacher's contribution to his development. His loyalty to the memory of Anker's successor led him to assert in his autobiography that in October 1921, when his mother was away giving birth to Yaltah, it was Louis Persinger who came round to the house every day to tune his violin – despite the fact that Persinger's lessons did not begin until July 1923.

Persinger was then in his mid-thirties. He was born in 1887, the son of a railway signalman. His precocious musical talent led to a public début in Colorado when he was only twelve. At thirteen he was sent to Leipzig, where he studied violin, piano and conducting. His teacher was the great Artur Nikisch who in 1914 engaged him as concert-master of the Berlin Philharmonic. That was after three years of violin study in Brussels with the equally renowned Eugène Ysaÿe. Although Persinger played many concerto performances, including an American début in 1912 with the Philadelphia Orchestra under Leopold Stokowski, his temperament (and perhaps the influence of his wife, whose person-ality Yehudi remembered as being more forceful than Persinger's) led him away from a soloist's career. In 1916 he became concertmaster of the San Francisco Orchestra, a post he held for a decade. Subsequently he concentrated on chamber music and teaching.

Persinger was a handsome and gentle spirit, as may be seen from the many photographs with his pupil. He had only recently taken up teaching and as a consequence had no well-tried 'method' to impose. According to Yehudi he 'allowed me to beget my own in my own time . . . He demonstrated and I imitated, winning achievement by ear, with-out detour through the conscious mind.' What Persinger did pass on was his musicianship, which was of a high order, and he gave Yehudi a personal and devoted attention rare among the great teachers, who normally seek to avoid the charge of favouritism among dozens of pupils. But Yehudi was no ordinary student. The duration of Persinger's lessons lengthened, and their frequency increased, starting twice weekly and ending with instruction every day when they were on tour together. It is hard to avoid the conclusion that Persinger projected on to Yehudi the dreams of glory that for one reason or another he had abandoned for himself.

Persinger recalled the first time Yehudi played for him. He did not specify the work performed; the crucial point was that he stopped the boy long before the end:

I shall never forget the fury that lit up his eyes at my interruption. It was an insult to him and his art. But I had heard enough . . . His feeling for rhythm was splendid, his ear absolutely true. There was more besides – a potentiality for greatness.

Persinger might have had no experience of teaching young children but he had the right instinct where Yehudi was concerned. Their first lesson, at Persinger's studio in Hyde Street, was a defining moment for Yehudi. Rather than seeking to impress the boy and his mother with a show of flashy pyrotechnics, Persinger chose to play music of total seriousness, a work befitting the genius he had already detected.

According to Yehudi the lesson began with a few preliminaries: 'I was told to play some little thing and was advised on this and that.' Persinger had his violin out:

He was already playing, I think – and he asked us to listen to the *Adagio* of the G minor Sonata by Bach for violin alone. He played it gloriously and we were both of us deeply moved by the music's profound sense of tragedy, of dignity, of nobility. We knew then exactly where I wanted to go: I wanted to play like that. And that was the lesson and we left.

An expanded account of the first lesson can be found in *Unfinished Journey*:

We sat spellbound until the last note died away and stillness filled the room to overflowing; then went home, still transported to another plane of existence, drunk on Bach. I knew this sublimity was what I must strive for.

Perplexingly, the biographer Robert Magidoff placed this solemn moment of dedication not at the first lesson but the following year, when Yehudi was eight, adding that as a consequence of Yehudi's exalted reaction Persinger acceded to his entreaties to be allowed to study Bach. Whether he was seven or eight at the time, the first Bach work he played was the E major Violin Concerto. (It was while practising its *Adagio* movement that Yehudi received the approbatory wink from his deceased grandmother.)

Thus was the young Menuhin introduced to a great violin tradition which extended back through Persinger's teacher, Ysaÿe, to Vieuxtemps and Wieniawski. For the next three years Persinger guided him through a steady flow of substantial works by what he described as 'violin composers' – Spohr, Lipiński and de Bériot – and the flashy salon pieces, such as Bazzini's *Ronde des lutins*, which were then an essential part of every violinist's repertoire. Yehudi was a prize pupil to be shown off at every opportunity. '[Efrem] Zimbalist came to my studio the last time he was out here and heard him play a couple of concertos,' Persinger told *Musical America* in September 1924.

He was quite amazed by the boy's brilliancy and said that he had never encountered a youngster anywhere who showed such promise. He said he had everything necessary to become one of the great ones, and the nearest approach to anything of the sort he could remember was Heifetz when he heard him at nine years of age.

Yehudi was then eight. Zimbalist later advised him on the purchase of his first Stradivarius.

Jascha Heifetz, fifteen years his senior, was a strong influence on the young Yehudi, who collected his recordings and heard him in the flesh as early as 1922. His playing represented a kind of perfection, both emotional and technical. Yehudi was also impressed (but not to the point of imitation) by his aristocratic, ramrod-stiff bearing on the platform. Heifetz was a master of *portamento*, he remembered: 'He could slide in any which way, either thick or thin or fast or slow or from below or from above, always infallibly in tune.' One childhood summer Yehudi took a wind-up gramophone and the Heifetz recording of the fiendishly difficult *Ronde des lutins* on a fortnight's holiday in the Santa Cruz mountains, determined not just to master it but to return to San Francisco playing it even faster than his idol. The older artist provided a consolation as well as a challenge; Yehudi often played himself to sleep with the Heifetz recording of the Tchaikovsky *Sérénade mélancolique*. He was, he said, 'a little Jewish boy with the cares of the world on his shoulders'.

Persinger took his star pupil to meet another renowned violinist, Mischa Elman, who was as volatile on the platform as Heifetz was impassive. Yehudi remembers him as

a very feeling, sentimental, warm-hearted man . . . he had the most beautiful tone, rich and golden and irresistible and he moved on the stage in the freest way I've ever known. Once I saw him and his beautiful Stradivarius perform a total circle, quite uninhibited.

He met Elman's father some years later at a New York violin dealer's. According to Yehudi, Elman *père*

kept saying things that got on my little stupid boy's nerves: 'You know I'm Mischa Elman's father.' 'Fine,' I replied, 'fine, delighted.' Then he repeated it and I finally said, 'And what else did you do for him?' Very naughty; very, very naughty!

Even as a boy Yehudi relished the violinistic freemasonry displayed by Mischa Elman. Persinger had been singing the praises of another recent visitor, Pablo Casals. 'Casals?' snorted Elman. 'Oh, but he's just a cellist!' (Thirty years later Menuhin was to join forces for memorable evenings of chamber music with Casals, then living in exile in the Pyrenees town of Prades.)

With talk already in the air of his future career as a soloist, Yehudi was also curious to inspect the lifestyle of an international virtuoso but he was unimpressed by Elman's room at the St Francis Hotel: 'dim and dismal, facing a noisy street, not at all like home'. The *idea* of home was important to the Menuhins. When their travels with Yehudi began,

Moshe and Marutha always packed memories of their Steiner Street house, such as treasured books and favourite photos. In hotels and even on railway trains they reserved a family suite, with a kitchen. Only once or twice in the first twenty years of his life did Yehudi eat out in a public restaurant.

Even had they not been exceptionally gifted as musicians, Yehudi and his sisters would have been brought up as free spirits – within a cocoon. Yehudi rarely rebelled against the ordered existence that his parents created to further his vocation. Instead of playing in the street with neighbours, he played the violin at home, alone; he complained when he had to stop practising for meals or bed. He called it

a very healthy routine. We got up early in the morning to get the practice done before eleven o'clock. When my sisters were old enough we always went out to the park above our house, ran around, played a form of tag or hide and seek which we improvised; (later on I played a bit of tennis in the park); returned home for lunch, had a sleep and then lessons in arithmetic or reading or languages, two hours more work, then supper and to bed by seven o'clock.

He had few friends but his life was so full of music that he did not know what he was missing.

As far as I remember, I never voiced the nihilistic doubts that seemed to challenge my family's whole way of life . . . Trusting myself more readily to music than to words, I had a means of expression which took care of most needs and in the violinist's daily solitude found the more reason for confiding myself to it. Finally, our life was so ordered that it was itself an argument against the delusions of anarchy.

Yet there were occasional signs of childhood unrest, among them a perfectly natural fear of the dark which he quelled, so he told his first biographer, by reminding himself of his mother's fierce Cherkess (Circassian) ancestry. Boys of Cherkess blood must be fearless and resolute, and not let down their mamas! Then came a fear that his parents might soon die, since they were approaching the desperately vulnerable age of thirty. He would lie in bed at night straining to hear signs of life, reassured when the sound of laughter floated across from the neighbouring bedroom where Moshe was reading aloud from one of the twenty volumes of Sholem Aleichem he had bought for Marutha. In the day the sense of order created by Marutha would just occasionally be disrupted by a demonstration of the rebelliousness already noted. His first outing to a movie – aged five – was marred, if the biographer Magidoff is to be believed, by his eccentric resolve to put out his tongue at the first acquaintance he met on his way to the cinema. The hapless recipient of this vulgarly defiant gesture was none other than the old family friend, Cantor Reuben Rinder, who claimed to be amused; Marutha most definitely was not and a disgraced Yehudi went home without his treat.

The boy would occasionally put his foot in things with an almost malicious glee – a characteristic that did not diminish with the years. He endangered his father's administrative job with the Hebrew Schools by innocently explaining to the local rabbi, Moshe's boss, that the corned beef they ate at home was pinker than his and had a layer of fat around the edges . . . Ham was off-limits for a conventional Jewish family, which the Menuhin household decidedly was not. On another occasion he ruined a match-making ploy on which his mother was engaged by blithely informing their lodger that he'd been invited to join them for supper solely as a potential husband for a visiting family friend.

In extreme old age, just before her hundredth birthday, Marutha Menuhin could still remember her approach to Yehudi's education:

My ambition was to keep him not aware of himself. He was very gentle, very unassuming. At the age of three I took him out on the street for a walk and he said, 'Oh Mammina, look at the shoes on that man; they're all worn out on the left side; it's not good for the feet.'

'Well, did you tell him this?'

'Yes, I told him to fix them.'

I said, 'Well, maybe he has no money. How about giving him the money and he'll buy some shoes?'

'Oh yes, thank you.'

And off he went. Yehudi is a true gentleman of the old world.

Marutha taught him to read music when he was only five (in parallel with Anker's lessons, one must presume) and later supervised his musical education. She sat in on his violin lessons and was never far away when he was practising. 'If I happened to make nice sounds she would comment; if I scraped half-heartedly she would tell me I was no better than a shoemaker and urge me towards a big tone.' She insisted that nothing should be allowed to alter her son's simple regime. 'Everything had to be taken in its stride,' Yehudi remembered,

even on concert days. I had my afternoon nap – which might be a little longer on those days – but in the morning we would still go to the park and after the concert straight to bed. Even had we won the lottery, family life wouldn't have changed, nor would she have permitted luxury of any kind.

According to Yehudi, his father was in full agreement with this policy:

Concerts were necessary, at first as a test of achievement, later as a means of support, but at no time during my youth were they allowed to challenge the emphasis on family life and on the children's primary duty to study and to learn.

Time was too valuable to be wasted on the idle curiosity of the outside world:

Hence there were no interviews with newspapers [untrue]; hence requests to play for some society's special occasion or in some rich lady's salon were equally refused [true]; and hence we grew up naturally, shielded from the world of inquiry which would have turned us into self-regarding freaks if it could. I can't thank my parents enough for having had the common sense to regard us as normal children.

Yehudi wrote with no irony. Only rarely would he concede in later life that he had suffered from a lack of childhood friendships, peer-group rivalry and school discipline.

Persinger was in charge from the summer of 1923, when Yehudi had just turned seven, until December 1926, when the family sailed to Europe for the first time with the intention of taking Yehudi to study with Persinger's master Eugène Ysaÿe. Those three and a half years saw the boy develop from promising newcomer to national treasure. From the early Persinger months the event Yehudi best remembered was not a concert but an informal occasion at the festive season of December 1923. 'Every a year a huge Christmas tree from the Sierras was put up in the civic auditorium and decorated with tinsel, and thus festively caparisoned the great hall was delivered over to the children of the city and their parents.' An audience of three thousand was entertained by a dozen youngsters, among them a chubby young fellow of eight named Yehudi Menuhin.

Two months later Yehudi appeared in public in a more formal way. His previous performances, under Anker, had been at his teacher's open days, concerts given before audiences of families and friends, although with the occasional press notice from a helpful music critic; there would have been no question of a fee. Persinger arranged Yehudi's first public appearance at an out-of-town location, the Oakland Auditorium, across the bay from San Francisco. The occasion was a children's concert promoted by the San Francisco Symphony Orchestra. There was no pre-publicity and no press reaction so one may hazard the guess that Persinger, who was still the orchestra's concertmaster at that time and was billed to play a solo at the concert, slipped in an unscheduled appearance by his amazing pupil. Yehudi must have made a strong impression because in the printed programme for the orchestra's regular concerts on 7 and 9 March the following special notice was inserted: 'Do not fail to hear Yhudi [sic] Menuhin, the six-year-old [sic] violinist who is to appear at the Young People's Symphony Concert . . . next Wednesday afternoon . . . his artistry is almost beyond belief.' The injunction was repeated a few days later, describing him as 'Yhudi Menuhen, the six-year-old wonder violinist'. On Wednesday, 12 March 1924, Yehudi appeared at the Exposition Auditorium (the former name of the Civic Auditorium). The concert was conducted by Alfred Hertz and attended by six thousand school children (or eight thousand, depending on the report one consults).

But Yehudi did not play with the orchestra. Sandwiched between Grieg's *Norwegian Dance* and Grainger's *Molly on the Shore*, the boy – this time the programme book spelt his name 'Yhudi Menuhun' – played de Bériot's *Scène de ballet* with Louis Persinger at the piano, following it as an encore with the *Gypsy Airs* (*Zigeunerweisen*) by Sarasate. Yehudi's 'graceful bowing, pure intonation, fluent execution and exquisite phrasing', reported Redfern Mason in the *San Francisco Examiner* (13 March 1924), 'are not alone the remit of the wonderful instruction of his teacher Louis Persinger, but come from an inborn genius with which the child is endowed.' Mason noted that Persinger not only played little Yehudi's accompaniments but 'tuned his violin and, in a word, played Godfather to him . . . Louis knows what a wonderful thing is a child.'

Yehudi contributed to the confusion surrounding the date of his début. He stated it correctly in the first edition of his autobiography, but in the revised edition, published in 1996, he changed it without explaining why. His first professional engagement, one reads there, was on 28 February 1922, 'when I was seven'. But this cannot be correct; he was born in April 1916, so he would have been only five on the date quoted. The chronology may be summarized as follows: Yehudi first played in public when he was five and a pupil of Sigmund Anker. He made his professional début when he was seven – a try-out at a children's concert in Oakland was followed two weeks later by an appearance at the Civic Auditorium. (His first concerto performance with an orchestra was exactly two years later, when he was nine. On

12 March 1926 he played Lalo's *Symphonie espagnole* with the San Francisco Symphony Orchestra at the Curran Theater.)

In the interview with Louis Persinger which appeared in *Musical America* for September 1924 he expressed admiration for Moshe's and Marutha's caution concerning their son's development.

Yehudi's appearances . . . were sensational and brought offers of engagements in Los Angeles, Fresno, Sacramento, etc., but all have been refused. [Moshe claimed to have been offered $10,000 for Yehudi to appear in vaudeville.] His parents take the sensible view that he must not overdo it at present. The best thing about the youngster is that he is totally unspoiled, has a wonderful sense of humour and does not overrate his own importance in the world.

He spoke also of the spontaneous beauty of his pupil's playing, describing it as

coming from a deep, mysterious and miraculous well . . . he seemed to absorb everything I taught him the way a sponge absorbs water. His progress both as to the musical and technical side was very rapid. We began our study of a new work, after its general characteristics were made clear to him, by going over it phrase by phrase. I would play the phrase, he would repeat it as exactly as possible, and the manner in which he grasped things as he went along was a constant source of joy and surprise to me. In Yehudi's case there was no danger in this method, for his conception and playing were too fresh and too true to be an imitation of anything.

'It was not only a question of spontaneity,' Persinger continued.

His reasoning powers were extraordinary, quite aside from his musical gifts. To correct a fault you needed only to draw attention to it once or twice. Sometimes, when a point was a trifle elusive, I appealed to his strong sense of humour and got it over to him that way. As I would occasionally turn from the piano while illustrating the musical structure of a new work to him, I would be startled to see the intense look in his eyes. Always beautiful and expressive, they at times seemed to be looking far away and above the earth. Yehudi acquired skill so quickly and memorized so rapidly that one of the chief problems was to restrain him. He showed a tendency at times to 'run away' with passage work, to hasten over a slow movement without plumbing its depths, and his fingers occasionally tended to 'kick in' on the vibrato – at first he had a funny little wiggle that passed as such – and for a time his bow was much too long for his arm.

The tendency to skate over the surface was noted by no less an authority than the regular conductor of San Francisco's orchestra when Yehudi played the Mendelssohn Violin Concerto in an audition for a valuable scholarship. 'Midway through the *Andante*,' Yehudi remembered, the adjudicator, Alfred Hertz, a bearded, brass-loving German of Bismarckian girth, rose to challenge the fast tempo I had set myself. I explained that I wanted to get to the lovely third movement before my time ran out as I feared that only *allegro* fireworks could ingratiate me with my judges, that the prize would be laid in forfeit before I showed my stuff, that there wasn't a moment to waste.

Yehudi wrote that he was seven at the time of this test but he was nearer nine. Hertz reassured him that he could take his time and he duly won the bursary. A newspaper report said it provided two years of tuition. Magidoff quoted $20 per month for two years. According to Yehudi in *Unfinished Journey* it was for one year only; Moshe said it was $30 not $20. Since Persinger claimed never to have taken a penny from the Menuhins, one wonders where the money went. It was the only competition Yehudi ever won.

After a year and a half of study Persinger suggested that Yehudi should give a full-length solo recital. Marutha gave her blessing (Moshe was at pains to point out that all such decisions were taken by his wife) and a professional concert manager, Alice Seckels, was contracted to manage the event, which took place at the Scottish Rite Auditorium in San Francisco on 30 March 1925. The concert was advertised under a banner headline written by Moshe: 'San Francisco's own genius'. It was a sell-out, but to dampen down excitement on the day, Marutha kept to her routine for as long as possible. Supper was at six, in the kitchen as usual, with the lodger Ezra Shapeero joining them for a gossip. Then Yehudi would have been sent up to his room to prepare for the next morning's lessons. Only at the last moment was he instructed to change out of his old sweater and cotton shorts and don the quaint white silk blouse and velvet trousers that Marutha had decreed should be his concert garb.

The programme included the Mendelssohn Violin Concerto, which he had first learned under Sigmund Anker, and Paganini's *Moto perpetuo* – accompanied by Persinger at the piano. Critics and professional musicians thronged the hall. Afterwards a musician of his acquaintance spoke excitedly to Redfern Mason of the *Examiner*: 'Let your pen fly; you cannot overdo it. This is not talent; it is genius.' And thus encouraged, Mason duly delivered another column of purple prose:

All the fiddlers in town were there, mature artists and people who have to be shown, and Yehudi brought them, metaphorically speaking, to their knees. His recital was not a success; it was a triumph. He began with the Vieuxtemps *Fantasia appassionata*, and as the fluent periods unfolded, people looked at one another in wonder. It did not seem possible that this authoritative melody could come from the fingers of a mere child. When he played the Mendelssohn Concerto their surprise deepened into an astonished wonder. The conception of what the music meant was so ripe, the manner of its production so artistic that, if the player had been invisible, they would have thought they were listening to the playing of a proved master. I thought of Joachim [the German prodigy; he was only twelve when he studied with Mendelssohn], who, when a lad, left his boat in the bathtub, dried his hands, to play this same work for Mendelssohn himself, and was publicly embraced by the composer. I think Mendelssohn would have done the same to Yehudi if he had heard him last night.

Perhaps this was the concert that elicited an oft-repeated anecdote concerning Yehudi's innocence. The lodger Ezra Shapeero remembered going into Yehudi's bedroom to kiss him goodnight after a particularly fine recital. Obviously trying to take advantage of the occasion, Yehudi wheedled,

'Now do me a big favour?'
    Wondering what was on the boy's mind, Shapeero consented.
'Then please fix the handle bar on my tricycle first thing in the morning.'

The genial Louis Persinger seems to have lost patience with his star pupil only once. The young Menuhin frequently expressed the wish to learn the Mount Everest of the violin repertoire, the Beethoven Concerto. Persinger resisted for a long time but eventually relented, on condition that Yehudi first study the Mozart A major Concerto (K. 219). Yehudi immediately tried to withdraw from a family trip to the seaside that afternoon but after taking his temperature and finding it normal his mother insisted on sticking to her plans. For the following two days Yehudi worked away at the Mozart so assiduously (as he thought) that at his next lesson he was able to play it from memory. But for once Persinger was not impressed. The boy's studies had been superficial. He must have been skating over the notes in his rush to get the Mozart behind him on his way to the Beethoven. In a gesture so shocking that Yehudi never forgot it, the teacher slammed down his score in the middle of the slow movement, music characterized by a spider's web filigree of grace notes. In front of Yehudi's mother, Persinger angrily told the boy to go home: 'Use your good mathematical head and figure out for yourself the exact rhythms. I don't want to see you again until you have given thought to every note in every movement!'

Marutha was furious with Yehudi. 'Failing was a relatively venial sin but to fail while craving success marked me out as a common *arriviste*. To skimp one's duty,' Yehudi explained, 'to hope that a slipshod second best would pass muster, was to betray the endurance, the self-discipline, the standards of the Cherkess.' Yehudi was sent to his room when he got home and in the evening Marutha instructed Moshe to give him a good spanking with a leather strap. Moshe omitted any mention of the episode in his memoirs but Magidoff made quite a meal of it in his biography:

Miserably, Moshe took the belt off his trousers, and Yehudi understood. He remembers bearing no resentment. Indeed watching the anguish on his father's face, he pitied him and tried to make it easier for him. He went up to the narrow bed and bent over it. Moshe swung the belt with a fierce gesture, but let it fall slowly and there was little pain. He swung again and then once more and rushed out of the room. Marutha followed. Yehudi did not see her face, but in a groping, childish way, he knew that she, too, was suffering.

Magidoff rather undermined the pathos by implying that Marutha was taking revenge on her son for the humiliation he had caused her. According to Yehudi's own account, his mother thought everything should be experienced once, including a beating, but he was the only one who was 'game' for the experiment; his father was no disciplinarian. Fortunately his love of Mozart was not affected by this half-hearted exposure to corporal punishment. In his book Yehudi used the belting episode as the springboard for a paean of praise for Mozart's A major Concerto. In his childhood, he wrote, he felt a greater affinity with Mozart than with any other composer:

In order to penetrate his music and communicate it to the listener, I did not have to transpose myself – I could play him and remain myself, with no need to feel big, powerful and grown up; I did not even have to imagine myself in love.

Despite his conciliatory words he must have had something of a block about the K.219 Concerto because in his youth he never played it in public.

Marutha was as cross with Persinger as she was with Yehudi. By the next lesson a chastened Yehudi had mastered Mozart's hemidemisemi-quavers for Persinger's approbation but the steely Marutha insisted that the teacher apologize to the pupil for having spoken so sharply to him. Menuhin remembered Persinger taking him to the front platform of a San Francisco tramcar in order to utter a few unobserved words in mitigation of his scolding. Her Circassian honour salved, Marutha rejoined them for a courtesy call at the Clift Hotel, where Yehudi played the Mozart to another visiting musical dignitary, Ossip Gabrilowitsch. This legendary Russian pianist and conductor, then in charge of the Detroit Orchestra, listened intently and finally embraced Yehudi without saying a word. Yehudi took to him instantly; he was, after all, the son-in-law of his favourite author, Mark Twain.

The excitement engendered by Yehudi's recital at the Scottish Rite Auditorium confirmed his arrival as a major figure in San Francisco's musical life. He was not yet ten years old but his education was clearly going to involve expensive teaching, travel abroad and the purchase of a good violin and bow, representing *in toto* a cash outlay far beyond the resources Moshe could ever command as a Hebrew School supervisor. Several Jewish philanthropists began to take an interest in young Yehudi, among them Dr Samuel Langer, an influential member of the board of the Jewish Educational Society who had become a family friend through Moshe's work as Hebrew Schools supervisor. Langer was head of a Jewish orphanage in San Francisco. He wanted to apply some of the organization's funds for the benefit of Yehudi's education but his chairman, a Rolls-Royce-driving lawyer in his fifties named Sidney Ehrman, wouldn't hear of depriving the orphans. When he was introduced to the Menuhins after the recital Ehrman offered instead to provide a $500 bursary specifically for Yehudi.

Accounts differ as to what happened next. Magidoff has it that Marutha insisted on declining all offers of financial help, including Mr Ehrman's. Yehudi's memoirs take a similar line:

He offered my parents a sum of money, but like all good fairy stories a few reverses had to be undergone before the happy ending. Aba and Imma turned down the cash on the grounds that they didn't need other people's money to bring up their children.

But Moshe's autobiography refutes what he calls 'this absurd yarn'. It stems, he adds, from a vicious source (Magidoff again?) whose motive was to defame Marutha. According to Moshe, writing fifty years after the event, his wife accepted Ehrman's offer without hesitation: 'It was to the many concert promoters, waving tens of thousands of dollars before us, that we declared "No!"'

Ehrman was impressed by Marutha:

I found her emotional, sensitive, proud and stubborn. And logical in what she had to say. She was not sure she wanted her son to make music his career, for she was afraid that the chaotic and glamorous life of a prodigy might spoil him, distort his vision and wreck his life. 'I would rather', she said, 'that he grew up to be a shoemaker, so long as he remained a complete and honest man. I am afraid of too rigid a concentration on his career, for without such concentration I see no way for him to [achieve(?) – word omitted in the original text] greatness. I am afraid of the disorganization of our family life, the separations, the problems connected with the schooling of the boy and his sisters.'

Ehrman talked her round: his offer was intended to cover the entire family, he told her, to keep them together. Marutha soon took to calling him 'Uncle' and Yehudi himself always spoke warmly about him. Apart from his own father 'no man has had a greater title to my filial affection than Uncle Sidney', he wrote, 'not even my revered masters Enesco and Persinger'. One wonders why Yehudi inspired such affection and generosity: it was perhaps because Sidney Ehrman had been a violinist himself in his youth; he owned a Guadagnini violin which he eventually gave to Yehudi. Ehrman died in 1972, at the age of a hundred and two.

The improvement in the family's circumstances brought about by Ehrman's generosity prompted a new regime at home. It was important to have bedrooms for the girls, so out went the lodgers, with the exception of the faithful student, Ezra Shapeero, who was like an elder brother to the children. In came tutors for Yehudi and his sisters, among them Rebecca and Josephine Godchaux, who taught them French; Professor Arnold Perstein of the University of California, who taught English literature; and John Paterson, a violinist in the city's orchestra, who taught harmony and counterpoint. Paterson's wife became Yaltah's first piano teacher; Hephzibah was already studying piano with Judith Blockley.

In the summer of 1925, when Yehudi was nine, Louis Persinger told the family that he had decided to resign from the orchestra and move for the winter season to New York, where a wealthy patron had offered to help him concentrate on the string quartet he had recently formed. The Menuhins were in a quandary. Moshe's job kept him in San Francisco, supervising the seven Hebrew Schools he had helped to set up. But there could be no substitute for Persinger so far as Yehudi's violin playing was concerned and so, with the beneficent Sidney Ehrman's money acting as a safety net, Marutha decided to return to New York with the three children. It was the first time since their marriage eleven years previously that the parents had been separated.

Marutha and the children were to travel for sixty hours on the *Overland Limited,* followed by a twenty-hour trip from Chicago to New York on the *Twentieth Century Limited* – train names that Yehudi was never to forget. At Oakland station Moshe thrust a bottle of smelling salts into his son's hand. As the only man in the party, he said, it would be Yehudi's task to take care of his mother. As they steamed across the continent Yehudi looked out of the window, checking their progress against a map of the United States thoughtfully provided by Dr Langer.

In New York Marutha rented an apartment on 114th Street, close to Morningside Park. Sammy Marantz, a favourite pupil when the Menuhins had taught in Elizabeth, came over from New Jersey whenever he could to help out with the children. Most days Yehudi walked with his mother and sisters across town and south for forty blocks to take his lessons with Persinger at the home of a *grande dame* named Cecilia Casserly. She lived on Lexington Avenue in an elegant duplex on the corner of East 61st Street. Persinger's quartet also rehearsed there, so Yehudi heard chamber music for the first time. He noted with a certain awe that the apartment boasted a minstrels' gallery.

Yehudi went to school at last. His mother enrolled him for courses of sight singing, ear training and harmony at the Institute of Musical Art, then in the process of being transformed into what is now the Juilliard School. At nine he was the youngest pupil they had ever accepted; his fellow students were all of college age. Yehudi had a sweet, unfaltering soprano voice, according to one of his teachers, Dorothy Crowthers, but by his own account he was no good at harmony, being unable to memorize the names of chords. It was part and parcel of a rather depressing autumn. He missed his father and he was homesick for clean and quiet San Francisco. His first impressions of the city of his birth were not flattering:

terrifying canyon streets with the darkness of November closing in upon them . . . noise, dirt and stench of the subway . . . haunted, tormented New Yorkers fighting for their lives against winter and wages and the pressure of constant scurrying crowds.

Persinger suggested that while they were in New York his pupil should give a recital 'in a big concert hall, in a big way' (Yehudi's description). Three thousand miles away in San Francisco, Moshe and

Sidney Ehrman both thought the proposal was premature. Ehrman didn't oppose the cash expenditure (several thousand dollars would be at risk) but thought Yehudi should be brought along more gradually. Moshe then consulted Dr Langer, who took the opposite view, arguing that Yehudi's development as an artist need not be artificially retarded. Langer wired Max Rosenberg, another of Yehudi's admirers in the Jewish community. Rosenberg was on holiday in India but within twenty-four hours he sent his approval. Presumably Moshe told this story at such length and with such circumstantial evidence in order to disprove the allegation that he was an over-eager exploiter of his son's genius.

Before he could give a concert in the New York spotlight, Yehudi had to have a better violin. His benefactor this time was not Ehrman but a teacher colleague of Moshe's named Rosenthal who shared the $800 bill with the aforementioned philanthropist Max Rosenberg. No doubt with Persinger's approval, Marutha bought Yehudi his first Italian violin, a seven-eighths size instrument dated 1696 by the Milanese violin-maker Giovanni Grancino. According to a San Francisco newspaper it was the only undersized Grancino in existence, constructed for an Italian court gala musical festival.

Yehudi recollected the purchase in *The Violin*, a book published in 1996. 'I acquired my first beautiful Italian violin at the age of eight [actually nine]. It was a seven-eighths Grancino, not a full-size instrument.' At the Sotheby's sale of his collection, on 16 November 1999, Lot 92 was identified as the violin purchased in New York. But surprisingly it was no longer assigned the Grancino pedigree: it is listed as 'Milanese School, first half of the eighteenth century'. From enquiries to the Menuhin Estate I learned that when the violin was assessed for insurance purposes in the mid-1990s the experts' conclusion was that the earlier ascription to Grancino could not be sustained. But nobody informed Yehudi that the instrument for which he held an intense sentimental regard had been downgraded. (His full-size Grancino, bought two years later, made £100,000; it is only four millimetres longer but is a much better example of Grancino's art.)

There is a somewhat puzzling pendant to this story of the violin purchase: a few weeks after Yehudi arrived in New York, another San Francisco newspaper reported that Mrs John Casserly, 'a wealthy patroness of music and art', had given Yehudi what it described as a Stradivarius violin:

The boy played at a reception in Mrs Casserly's home, which was attended by forty prominent New York musicians, among them the Damrosches [Walter, conductor, and Frank, head of the Juilliard] and Louis Persinger. The Stradivarius was given the boy after a reception in the home of Mischa Elman.

No further mention of this gift has been uncovered: presumably Yehudi had played somebody else's Strad at the party and Moshe, still in San Francisco, had got the wrong end of the stick.

The acquisition of the Grancino violin stimulated a touching dream involving Fritz Kreisler:

Kreisler walks on to the stage of Carnegie Hall. The ovation swells, then dies abruptly when people, among them myself, seated in the front row, notice something peculiar. He is carrying two identical violins. From the edge of the platform he extends one to me and says in a solemn voice that easily carries through the hall, as if this constituted his recital: 'Take it, my child. It is yours to keep.'

Kreisler was the third of Menuhin's idols, along with Heifetz and Elman. The Kreisler sound, he wrote, 'was all subtle emphasis, innuendo and dropped hints', an elusive mix which in his teens Yehudi was to find much harder to emulate than the dazzling but more superficial texture of a Heifetz recording.

Yehudi's first New York concert was booked for Sunday, 17 January 1926, at the Manhattan Opera House. (This was Oscar Hammerstein I's building of 1906, long since turned over to concerts and not to be confused with the grander Metropolitan Opera.) The event was promoted by a respected New York manager, Loudon Charlton, but it seems not to have been particularly well handled since it failed to cover its costs – this despite heroic last-minute publicity efforts by Moshe, who had talked his way into being granted leave of absence, ostensibly in order to study the work of Hebrew Schools in other American cities. Advance ticket sales were poor and Moshe spent long days rounding up potential supporters and addressing envelopes to the donors on the mailing list of the Federation of Jewish Charities, helpfully provided by his former colleague at the New York Board of Jewish Education. The programme included the first movement of the Paganini Concerto in D, a Handel sonata (No. 6 in E minor) and Lalo's *Symphonie espagnole*, as well as a handful of lighter pieces and *Nigun* by Ernest Bloch.

In the 1920s a Sunday-night recital was by definition a low-key affair. The *New York Times* ignored it altogether; other papers sent only their second- or third-string reviewers, one of whom reflected that 'the natural wonder that a youth of such tender years should play in public was swallowed up after a few phrases in wonder that he was able to do it so well'. Another reported that 'this chubby, tow-headed boy has the *savoir faire* of eight times his eight years'. (Yehudi was nine and three-quarters.) A third could do no better than 'truly astonishing'. It was a far cry from Redfern Mason's colourful reportage in San Francisco. The fathers of the great Heifetz and Elman were said to be sitting in the front row but Yehudi thought this was probably a journalist's invention, intended to impart a higher significance to the occasion; as he remembered it, the only musician present was Walter Damrosch, who was soon to give him his first concerto engagement in New York. Most reviews referred to Moshe's assurance that Yehudi was not being exploited as a prodigy; he had given his recital merely to get experience in playing in public. Yet if Moshe's publicity for his son's next appearance in San Francisco is to be believed, the concert had the makings of a legend: the audience was said to have stormed the platform at the end of the recital.

Stagehands and police had to drive the crowd from the boy in the interest of his safety. He played encore upon encore, exhausting his repertoire ere the lights were extinguished. Next morning the critics went wild with enthusiasm.

The family returned to San Francisco via Los Angeles, where they were shown the homes of Douglas Fairbanks and Mary Pickford. (Marutha had to be told who they were.) Back home Yehudi informed a journalist that he had been more interested in the dinosaurs at the Museum of Natural History than the audience at the Manhattan Opera House. Symphony concerts were now being regularly broadcast in San Francisco and a new radio receiver, presumably a gift from the Ehrmans, was awaiting the family at 1043 Steiner Street. They tuned in to a jazz broadcast: 'The children listened and laughed at the strange music, so different from their usual musical companions.'

What Moshe publicized as his son's 'annual concert' took place on 4 March 1926 in the same venue as the previous year, the Scottish Rite Auditorium (later converted into a cinema) on Van Ness Avenue. The main works on the programme were the Lalo and Paganini concertos he had played two months previously in New York. Moshe's interest in concert management dates from this time, sharpened by what he saw as the deficiencies of the administration of Yehudi's recent New York recital. He hired a prominent local concert promoter, Selby C.

Oppenheimer, whose artists' list included Beniamino Gigli and Walter Gieseking. Moshe prepared his own list of VIPs, kept tight control of free seats, supervised the publicity and ended up with a sell-out event that was also, because of Yehudi, an artistic triumph.

'One listens to him playing', wrote the *Chronicle*'s critic, Alexander Fried,

in the same spirit in which one gazes upon the Niagara Falls, or the Grand Canyon, or a sunset at the Golden Gate. There is nothing to be said about the ineffable wonder. He played the difficult cadenzas in the Paganini . . . at a pace that left mature violinists bewildered and speechless. Double-stops passages, harmonics, *spiccati*, all the most difficult technical feats of violin mastery are to him as the spinning of tops to ordinary children.

Fried had equal praise for his rich expressive tone – and for the accompanist Louis Persinger,

who also tuned the lad's instrument. In the face of a continual series of ovations, the child was as calm as a veteran. What built the world in six days has contrived the genius of Yehudi. He walks on the waves.

But he was not allowed to ride a bicycle. Uncle Sidney Ehrman presented him with one but Alfred Hertz, who happened to be dining with the family that day, counselled most strongly against it: zooming down the precipitous streets of San Francisco might cause the boy to have a dangerous fall. Equally concerned for the boy's hands, Moshe was just as terrified of ball games. Baseballs were disallowed but after pressure from Ehrman Yehudi was at least allowed to play catch – with a tennis ball.

Only a week after the recital, Yehudi made his début with a symphony orchestra. On 12 March 1926 he played three movements of Lalo's *Symphonie espagnole* – the *Allegro*, *Andante* and *Rondo*; the other two movements were regularly omitted in those days. The concert, at the Curran Theater, was repeated two days later. Persinger conducted the San Francisco Symphony Orchestra, rather to Alfred Hertz's displeasure. 'We thought it not unreasonable,' Moshe noted, 'it being for Yehudi's good to have his teacher in charge.' Persinger had, after all, been the orchestra's Assistant Conductor for a decade and Hertz, who was by now a good friend of the Menuhin family, later conducted several concerto performances given by Yehudi in San Francisco.

The 'famous boy wonder' was the talk of the town, prompting

43

another field day among the headline writers: 'Yehudi Menuhin holds his hearers with magic violin'; 'Baby maestro jams Curran Theater'; 'Yehudi's ride to triumph'. 'The auditorium', wrote Alexander Fried,

presented a rare spectacle as the nine-year-old soloist came out for his prodigious display. There was not an empty seat to be seen, boxes overflowed with eager standees, the theater orchestra pit was full to the brim, heads peeped at every open exit. Yehudi's achievement was as miraculous as in his recent recital. It was stunning to observe his mature phrasing and his brilliant employment of *mezza voce*, delicate nuances and fine adjustments of tempi that go a long way to make up the bone and sinew of interpretation. Slight roughnesses there still are, technically and musically, but from every outward evidence he is in the best possible hands.

The boy received a fee of $500 for two performances. Diplomatically he donated it (at his parents' suggestion) to the orchestra's benevolent fund; there had been a $36,000 deficit when the season began. Five hundred dollars was already a substantial sum, but when his fame spread to Europe, the remuneration was to increase tenfold. Incidentally, Menuhin remembered Hertz as the conductor of that first concert, whose year he wrongly gave in *Unfinished Journey* as 1925. He added that, after the performance, 'Hertz lifted me off my feet with his embrace, pressing my face into his beard, which felt like a moist whisk broom.' There is no reason to doubt this memory since Hertz was present to conduct the remainder of the concert.

Yehudi's development proceeded at an almost alarming pace; every month saw him adding new concertos to his repertoire. In the summer of 1926 it was announced that he had been booked to open the San Francisco Symphony's autumn season of fund-raising 'pop' concerts with a performance of the Tchaikovsky Concerto. But a problem arose with Louis Persinger whose chamber-music activities led him that autumn to Santa Barbara, nearly four hundred miles down the California coast, from where he would be obliged to drive to and from San Francisco for Yehudi's lessons. It was not a satisfactory arrangement for the long term and Yehudi himself must have been intuitively aware that he was ready for change, for a move up to a truly international level of teaching.

The family spent several weeks that summer holidaying at the Ehrmans' luxurious estate on the western shore of Lake Tahoe. Yehudi developed a crush on their daughter Esther, despite the fact that she was nearly twice his age, and he was also fond of her brother, young Sidney, who was then a Debussy-loving student at Berkeley. (When he left to study in England he gave Yehudi his desk.) In between the horse-back riding and the motorboat excursions, there were family conferences with 'Uncle' Sidney to determine the boy's next move. Europe had become a factor in the equation. For American musicians in search of a rounded education, a period of European study was obligatory. But with whom should it be? The previous season Yehudi had encountered the genius of the Romanian George Enesco. He made his San Francisco début (in March 1925) in a double role, as the soloist in the Brahms Violin Concerto and as conductor of his own First Symphony. 'Before a note was sounded he had me in thrall,' Yehudi remembered. It was a *coup de foudre*.

His countenance, his stance, his wonderful mane of black hair – everything about him proclaimed the free man, the man who is strong with the freedom of gypsies, of spontaneity, of creative genius, of fire.

These would have been exceptionally perceptive observations for a boy of eight. Menuhin was writing fifty years after the event.

For the moment, however, Enesco as teacher was not an option. Persinger wanted his pupil to study with his own much revered master, Eugène Ysaÿe, a giant among violinists in every sense, to whom Chausson had dedicated his *Poème* and César Franck his immortal Violin Sonata. With Ehrman's new, extended guarantee of financial support, Moshe negotiated a half-year's absence from his job as Hebrew Schools supervisor: the entire family would make the trip across the Atlantic, travelling first to Paris, fountain of liberty and Mecca for all Americans, and then on to Ysaÿe's home in Brussels. A leap in the dark? It was typical of Moshe and Marutha to reverse the conventional settlers' flow, quitting the new home country, California, in order to head east for Europe. But they were far from rejecting the US. Less than a year previously, on 15 December 1925, Moshe had written to the *San Francisco Examiner* in patriotic vein to refute the story that his son was a recent immigrant from a Far Eastern country (i.e. the USSR):

Yehudi and his parents are very proud of their native and adopted country; indeed they think that were it not for the opportunities that this country gave them to obtain a cultural education and were it not for the freedom of action allowed the peaceful, private citizen, Yehudi could never have reached the point where he is today, whether he will turn out to 'climb to the topmost ladder of fame' or just be a good boy to the joy of his parents and friends.

One thing we are sure of, that Yehudi will never deny his American nativity.

[On this Moshe was to be proved wrong.] Yehudi Menuhin is an American product. The misfortune about us Americans [Moshe had taken US citizenship only six years previously] is that we associate superficiality, smallness, 'Babbitism', with the term American, and everything big, deep, unique, experimental with Europe. There is another America in the making of which we ought to take more cognizance instead of being pathological and sensitive.

He might have added that Yehudi slept with a portrait of Abraham Lincoln over his bed. When the critic Redfern Mason visited the Menuhins' Steiner Street home he noted Lincoln next to Socrates, Dionysus, Mendelssohn, Chopin and a group of rustic fiddlers, all images cut by Yehudi from newspapers, 'a sort of pictorial synthesis of his ideals'. Only a print of the prophet Samuel was a gift from his father, 'the child Samuel, he who heard the voice of God calling him in the night watches'. Prophetically, for it was seventeen years before they actually met, Moshe told Mason that he hoped Yehudi would go to Hungary to study with Béla Bartók.

In preparation for the great transatlantic adventure, French had to be mastered. One morning Rebecca Godchaux read Yehudi a poem that emphasized the language's euphony. After the lesson, Marutha insisted her son should commit it to memory that very evening. A face-off similar to the confrontation in Yosemite National Park ensued. Yehudi got sleepy; the syllables failed to stick but 'a Cherkess never leaves anything unfinished' and it was past midnight before he was allowed to go to bed. Next afternoon he could recite it perfectly – an early demonstration of his remarkable fluency with foreign languages. He already spoke Hebrew and English; guided by his mother, who at mealtimes insisted on talking only the language under study for a month at a time, he was to add German and Italian to his accomplishments – with study of the best literature added for good measure.

On 16 November 1926 Yehudi played for the first time with an orchestra at the vast Civic Auditorium, which had been built for the 1915 exhibition celebrating San Francisco's rebirth after the disastrous earthquake. The work chosen, Tchaikovsky's Violin Concerto, was more ambitious than the Lalo *Symphonie espagnole*. Before the performance the Menuhins dined with the Ehrmans. On the drive to the hall, Moshe recalled, Yehudi sat up front with Barney the chauffeur. Then he went out on stage.

'His innocent childish eyes surveyed a kingdom of ten thousand souls,' wrote Alexander Fried.

In his pudgy hands were a small bow and violin, his magic wand and royal scep-
tre. At his feet sat in perfect silence the greatest crowd the huge hall can hold;
behind him in equal reverence were Alfred Hertz and the eighty seasoned artists of
the San Francisco Symphony Orchestra . . .

Nine-year-old [*recte* ten and a half] Yehudi is still a marvellous child; soon he
will be a marvellous youth and then a marvellous man . . . The lad, looking smaller
than ever in his vast surroundings, filled them with his personality and his genius.
The tremendous audience, much as it knew what to expect, was amazed and
inflamed at his performance . . . Yehudi's uncanny fingers dealt easily with the
tough notes and his heart plunged boldly into the depths of the composer's imagination . . . the deafening applause did not relent until Louis Persinger came to the
platform to accompany him in a series of extra solo numbers.

Yesterday was Yehudi Menuhin's last San Francisco concert appearance in a
long time. He will leave soon for the East, whence eventually he will continue to
Belgium to take up his studies with the famous Eugène Ysaÿe. His principal task
is to allow the years to catch up with his achievements. His technique can be but
little more finished but his repertory and tone naturally need years to increase to
mature dimension. It will be an interesting scene when he first draws his bow
before the veteran French master.

And so it was, though not quite in the manner Fried might have predicted. The critic Redfern Mason matched Alexander Fried's hyperbole
paragraph for paragraph. What a concert it must have been!

Playing with his eyes closed, Yehudi evoked a song from that wonder box which
is the fiddle that floated birdlike above the orchestral accompaniment. Rapt in
what he was doing, the boy seemed oblivious of the presence of the listening
multitude. His is the gift of complete concentration. At the same time he has not
the aloofness of Heifetz, and, though his soul may be in the heaven of sound, the
physical body of him is as firmly rooted on earth as is that of Fritz Kreisler himself
. . . When they were not playing, the violinists of the orchestra watched him with
a sort of admiring despair.

A wild outburst of applause greeted the conclusion of the *Allegro*, and Yehudi
ducked, boylike, his face beaming with happiness. He handed his instrument to
Piastro [the leader] to tune and then poured forth the tenderness and sorrow of the
Canzonetta. There is a Judaic strain in this and an atavistic something in the lad
seemed to sense in it, for he played it as if the genius of Jewry were crying out within him. The broad strains of the passage which leads up to the finale seemed to
awaken the latent man in him, and he launched into the vertiginous *Vivacissimo*
with a gay alacrity and, when at last the instrumental *tour de force* was ended the
audience went as mad as only a San Francisco audience can go mad when it is
moved to the depths.

Redfern Mason had earlier sat in on the rehearsal. He reported
what he described as 'a momentary tangle. Yehudi had coolly pointed
with his bow to Alfred Hertz's score. "Let us start from there. That is

where the trouble is." Hertz and the orchestra roared.' Yehudi's abiding memory of that concert was more sentimental than musical. 'After the first movement I was groping in my pocket for a handkerchief when Esther [Ehrman], seated next to my mother in the first row, stood up and gave me hers.' He felt, he said, like a medieval knight receiving the gift of his lady's glove at a jousting. At the farewell luncheon party given by Dr Langer before the family set off for Europe on 25 November, Esther gave him a Chinese puzzle ring which he kept for many years thereafter in its 'shrine', his violin case.

Persinger presented him with a framed photograph, inscribed 'To dear Yehudi, hoping he will one day develop into a great artist – one who will prove to be not only the *master* but also the worldly *servant* of the Beautiful.' He added an enchanting poem which is worth quoting for the benefit of all teachers and pupils:

> Yehudi, Don't Forget To Write
>> When
> The Octaves Get Out Of Tune,
> Or The Trills Begin Too Soon!
>> And
> The D String Sounds Like A Throaty Squawk,
> While The G Refuses To Talk!
>> To Say Nothing About
> The Fingers Sliding Around Like A Cat In The Mud
> And The E String Sounding Like One Slick Soap Sud!
>> Or
> The Bow Scratching Near The Bridge So Hard
> That It Would Ruin The Poor Ears Of Any Bard,
>> And
> The Rhythms Getting All Tangled Up
> Like The Uncut Tail Of A Spaniel Pup!
>> While
> The A String's Unholy, Juicy Rantings
> Resemble The Pup's Mustard Plaster Pantings!
>> Yes
> Yehudi, Young Man, That Will Be The Proper Time
> (Just To Somewhat Complete My Rhyme!)
>> When
> I Hope You'll Take Your 'Pen In Hand'
> And Tell Me The News About Your Four-String Band!
>> And
> If You Don't Return From Old Europe, Yahooty,
> With A Lot Of Fresh Musical Booty,

You'll
Certainly Astonish Me,
Your Devoted
L.P.

Yehudi responded in a note that was later reproduced in the San Francisco newspapers:

Sweet master,
  As the train is going eastward, within me are growing sentiments. For as soon as we parted last night I felt that lonely sensation, that one which I had a year ago for my father. Indeed, Mr Persinger, you are my father of music. I have never felt you so near to me as I do now. Wherever life brings me, whether east, west, north or south, I will always hear your sweet voice. That voice which oft-times corrected me, and if I would be without it, only God would know the kind of life I would lead.
  Your loving pupil,
  Yehudi Menuhin

Recommended Recordings
(Each chapter will conclude with a brief list of relevant CDs.)

Tchaikovsky: *Sérénade mélancolique*
Jascha Heifetz (violin)
RCA 09026 61743–2 (1954, reissued 1998)
This is the music with which Yehudi sang himself to sleep when he was a small boy.

Various composers: 'Concertos from my childhood'
with Itzhak Perlman (violin)
EMI 7243556750 2 6
This Itzhak Perlman CD contains recordings of Accolay's Concerto No. 1 in A minor and the *Scène de ballet* by de Bériot, two works played by Yehudi in his childhood.

Lalo: *Symphonie espagnole*
Paris Symphony Orchestra, conducted by George Enesco
EMI 5 65960 2 or BID LAB 046
The work with which Yehudi made his concerto début. This is the first of Yehudi's four recordings of the Lalo, made in 1933.

3 'Keep your eyes on the stars'

With his sisters in Paris, 1927

1927: February: European début with two concerto concerts in Paris; summer: with Enesco in Romania; November: triumphant Beethoven Concerto in New York; 1928: October: Hephzibah's recital début, aged eight; December–March: first US tour; 1929: January: gift of 'Prince Khevenhüller' Stradivarius from Harry Goldman.

GEORGE GERSHWIN was not the first American musician to be impressed by the Klaxon horns of Parisian taxicabs. Two years earlier, Yehudi Menuhin spent his first night on French soil at the Hôtel Pas de Calais in the Rue des Saints Pères. 'The narrow street', he wrote, was still noisy with taxis, their Klaxons fitted with rubber bulbs which, when squeezed, emitted an almost animal sound and filled the night with croaks and gasps of varying pitch and intensity, as if a friendly garrulous zoo had been let loose beneath my window . . . I lay awake listening to the jolly hubbub and anxiously wondering if, after a whole fortnight without practice, I could still play the violin.

To journey abroad was a great adventure for the children but it must have been a headache for Moshe and Marutha. Backed by Sidney Ehrman's financial guarantee, they rented an apartment on the Rue de Sèvres near the Latin Quarter, not far from St Sulpice, but Moshe was unsure how to proceed. Yehudi had been saying for over a year that he wanted to study with George Enesco, who lived in Paris when he was not on tour. But the teacher whose name was in the frame was the Belgian Eugène Ysaÿe, who lived in Brussels. Ysaÿe had inspired Louis Persinger when he was not much older than Yehudi was now; he was Fritz Kreisler's idol, and had been described by Carl Flesch, another great violin teacher, as the most outstanding musician he ever heard. Yehudi must play for Ysaÿe, his parents decided; they must stick to the plan announced before they left San Francisco.

Marutha travelled with him to Brussels. When they rang on Ysaÿe's door next morning there was a long pause before it was finally opened by a young woman clad only in a dressing-gown. Yehudi had never before seen a woman in a state of undress; that she was Ysaÿe's student (and future wife) didn't allay the boy's sense of impropriety – or his mother's. They were shown upstairs, where Ysaÿe greeted them without getting up from his sofa. There was a disagreeable odour hanging in the air. Yehudi didn't know it at the time but the venerable Belgian, aged sixty-eight, was suffering from a gangrenous foot and could no longer stand. The greetings concluded, Yehudi played the first movement of the *Symphonie espagnole*, the work Persinger had performed for his own audition with Ysaÿe, twenty-five years earlier. The old man took up his Guarnerius, Yehudi remembered, and provided him with an impeccable accompaniment of *pizzicato* chords. When the first movement was over Ysaÿe said, 'You have made me happy, little boy, very happy indeed.' But then he asked Yehudi to play an A major arpeggio in four octaves. Yehudi floundered. Except where they figured in specific musical compositions, arpeggios had no place in Yehudi's daily routine. Persinger had once written out a whole page of exercises in scales and thirds but, to the best of his rueful recollection, Yehudi had never studied them, abhorring what he called 'abstraction of technique'. Ysaÿe sounded a warning: 'You would do well to practise.' Nevertheless he invited Menuhin to become his student. Marutha temporized; she would first have to speak to her husband. They were barely out of the house before Yehudi was expressing his lack of sympathy for the old man and repeating to his mother his passionate demand to study with Enesco.

Would he have benefited from a spell in Brussels? On balance, probably not. Ysaÿe was undoubtedly a world-class musician. He was a composer, led a distinguished quartet and for many years had been the conductor of a leading American symphony orchestra. The list of his violin pupils was tremendously impressive. But he was a sick man. And if the critic Alexander Fried was right, Yehudi was at a stage when he needed more help with interpretation than with technique. It's true that eight years later, at the end of his teens, Yehudi went through a technical crisis which forced him to work out consciously what he'd done instinctively as a boy. But at the age of ten he seemed to be possessed of a sixth sense that drew him back to Paris, one of the world's most important musical centres in the 1920s, and to George Enesco, then forty-six and at the height of his fame.

They had no letter of introduction but as if by providence Enesco was giving a Paris recital that very week at the Salle Gaveau and naturally the Menuhins attended and afterwards went backstage. Marutha told her son that he must take his future in his own hands. 'Unsupported by parents or sisters, a very scared child indeed, I stationed myself in the artists' room.' But Moshe remembered it differently, reporting the conversation as if he had been present:

Yehudi said, 'I should very much like to study with you, Mr Enesco.'
  'But I don't give private lessons.'
  'But I *must* study with you – *please* let me play for you.'
  'That's impossible, my dear child. I leave Paris in the morning.'
  'Could I play for you before you go?'
  'I'd like nothing better. But you'll have to come to my house at 5.30.'

The dialogue, culled from the memoirs of Menuhin father and son, is reproduced in good faith – some such green-room exchange must surely have taken place – and next morning Yehudi duly presented himself for a pre-dawn audition at Enesco's home, 26 Rue de Clichy. 'Enesco sat down at the piano,' Moshe remembered, and asked Yehudi to play anything he felt like. Neither looked at any printed music, though we had brought a good many pieces with us. Enesco accompanied Yehudi from memory and through natural improvisation. It sounded as if they had been playing together for years.

Yehudi was accepted, as a pupil, as he had always known in his bones he would be. But Enesco truly was leaving that day for a tour, so lessons would have to wait for a couple of months. As for payment, the selfless Romanian later told Moshe that he had no right to accept anything: 'Yehudi has as much to offer me as I have to give him.'

Paris in winter was a wonderland for Yehudi and his sisters, so different from the hilly streets of San Francisco. Marutha quickly created a daily routine as similar to that back home as possible. The first excursions were along the Rue de Sèvres to the Hôtel Lutétia, but soon they were venturing as far as the Bois de Boulogne, where the children filled their pockets with shiny chestnuts. A born entrepreneur, Moshe wasn't content to wait for Enesco's return. Early in January 1927 an audition was arranged with the conductor Paul Paray, then an up-and-coming conductor aged forty who had been in charge of the Concerts Lamoureux since 1923. On 12 January Paray wrote to Moshe:

I have heard your young son. He is prodigious. I would be very happy to have him play with the Concerts Lamoureux as soon as possible, and *twice*: on Sunday 6 February with Lalo's *Symphonie espagnole* and on Saturday 12 February with the Tchaikovsky Concerto.

Not the least astonishing aspect of this invitation is that Paray was able to reorganize his concert programmes at such short notice.

Yehudi, aged ten and temporarily without a teacher, had to prepare himself for these concerts. Moshe wrote that the unsupervised daily grind 'brought out a high degree of self-discipline and responsibility in him . . . We realized that it was vital that he should have periods when he could be alone and thus be forced into self-development, self-guidance and self-criticism.' Physically, too, he was growing fast and he clearly needed a larger violin. Armed with an open cheque book from Sidney Ehrman and after many visits to other Paris *luthiers*, the family selected a 1690 Grancino at Tournier's on the Rue de Rome – full-sized this time, and at $3000 nearly four times as expensive as the seven-eighths Grancino purchased in New York a year earlier. The instrument was still in Menuhin's possession at the time of his death; at the Sotheby's auction of his violins on 16 November 1999 it was sold for £100,000.

Yehudi's first appearance at the Concerts Lamoureux on 6 February 1927 was a *succès fou*. The *San Francisco Chronicle*'s specially cabled report began:

Not since the days when the child Mozart, seated on a pile of music on a piano stool, amazed his hearers has Paris been so astonished by a juvenile performer as when Yehudi Menuhin, a 10-year-old San Francisco boy, appeared today as the violin soloist with the famous Lamoureux Orchestra . . . From the first notes the audience was convinced it was listening to a phenomenal virtuoso, regardless of age, while the boy's demeanour, combining poise and professional ease with delightful boyish earnestness, charmed as much as the rich tones and surprising technique of the artist. Paray, who is not given to emotional displays, embraced the boy and kissed him on both cheeks . . .

Le Petit Parisien was equally ecstatic about Yehudi's manifold virtues:

. . . sentiment, soul, tenderness, purity of tone, accuracy, a *staccato* and bowing that are extraordinary . . . and with all these gifts there is a perfect steadiness and simplicity . . . this little Mozart reminds us of the beautiful days of Ysaÿe and Kreisler.

Moshe claimed to be puzzled by his son's new success. Disingenuously, one can't help feeling, since he had arranged the audition and allowed the concert to take place, he told the correspondent of the *Chicago Tribune* that Yehudi had been brought to Paris

to escape too much attention of the wrong kind, too much publicity, too much stressing of the remarkable earning powers of a ten-year-old child . . . we felt he could stay and develop quietly here, and later in Germany, until at sixteen or seventeen he should be ready to go on the concert stage. Instead, due to this appearance, the doorbell and telephone bell have been ringing enough to drive us wild. French newspapers and French impresarios have swarmed in steadily ever since, talking money, money, money.

One of the offers was said to be worth $10,000. Moshe told another reporter that, after studying with Enesco, his son would go to Brussels for lessons with Ysaÿe, implying that that avenue had not yet been completely rejected, whatever Yehudi's wishes. (The plan was never mentioned again.) To the *Chicago Tribune* he confided that although the family's departure from America had been in part prompted by Louis Persinger's undue reverence for Yehudi, teacher and pupil would be reunited 'when the concert tours begin'. (It isn't clear whether he was talking about five years hence, after Yehudi's proposed studies in Germany. Moshe was perhaps already contemplating an American tour with his son, such as he undertook less than two years later, in the winter of 1928.)

'Yehudi hasn't been spoiled yet', Moshe continued.

He doesn't know the phrase they use about him in America: 'wonder of the century'. He's still just as interested in French pastry as he is in his violin . . . we must keep him that way as long as possible. He shan't give another concert in Paris after the one already arranged for this weekend.

And he didn't. But first there was the Tchaikovsky Concerto to prepare, the work with which he had said farewell to San Francisco three months earlier. The Salle Gaveau was packed – *archibondée*, to use the charming French word – with hundreds of disappointed Parisians left outside on the *trottoir*. Drama accompanied Yehudi's performance: a string snapped on the new Grancino. 'To judge by the concerted gasp of the spectators,' reported the *Chicago Tribune*,

their hearts broke with it. . . . the calmest person in the house was the soloist. After receiving back his violin from the concertmaster's repairing hands, he continued the movement from the point of the accident and set a new example for composure and sang-froid.

In a letter to Dr Langer, Yehudi gave his own account of this unnerving incident:

The funniest thing hapened [*sic* – as with all errors in the letter's orthography] on the third page, the E string broke. Lukily the violinist next to the Concertmaster happened to have the string with him and it was changed quikly. But for the rest of the movement I had to play on an 'out-of-tune' violin. However I did my best. At the end of the Concert, Monsieur Paray . . . presented me with a magnificent copper plate, all carved out so it assumed the shape of a beautiful woman, sitting on a rock and playing the flute, and on the side is a flower wreath of flowers . . . The copper plate is framed in a beautiful square frame of wood, on the back of which is a rectangular piece of gold on which is engraved:

à

YEHUDI MENUHIN
en-souvenir de son
premier concert à Paris
Février 6ème 1927
L'Orchestre Lamoureux

Yehudi's letter continued with praise for the conductor: 'With one rehearsal he understood every little point that I did in the Tchaikovsky. He is an amiable man, a dear fellow, adorned with the qualities of youth.' Paray accompanied Yehudi at the piano for his encores: the *Ronde des lutins* by Bazzini and Bloch's *Nigun*. Paray's feeling that night was, he said, one of the purest emotions of his life.

Moshe's feelings must also have been running high. His son's Paris triumph compelled him to consider his own position. He was only thirty-three. He had spent the last eight years building up the Hebrew Schools in San Francisco and his career prospects were good. He'd been granted leave of absence for the European trip but after only three months he decided to resign and devote himself entirely to his son's education and career. When Enesco agreed to teach Yehudi, Moshe wrote of becoming 'partners in the business' of Yehudi's career while they enjoyed hot chocolate and brioches in a café in the Rue de Clichy. Inevitably an element of sacrifice was involved for a man brought up to believe that the father's traditional role was to be the family breadwinner. But his son was a sort of genius, a miracle. And there was the compensating (and glamorous) prospect of becoming a member of the international musical world. As a consequence of his father's decision, Yehudi's centre of gravity also changed:

I moved at this point from the feminine to the masculine department of the family. Until 1927 the violin had been in my mother's stewardship, but between Ysaÿe and Enesco it was transferred to Aba's.

Hephzibah and Yaltah remained in Marutha's care.

One morning in March a *pneumatique* express letter arrived from Enesco; his tour was over and the long-awaited lessons could begin – with the Brahms Concerto. For Yehudi, Enesco was 'the sustaining hand of providence, the inspiration that bore me aloft'. Pablo Casals described the young Enesco as the most prodigiously gifted musician since Mozart. Born in Moldavia, a far-flung province of the Habsburg Empire, he had been, like Yehudi, a boy prodigy, studying the violin in Vienna before moving to Paris, where he was taught composition by Gabriel Fauré. Now forty-six, Enesco thought of himself primarily as a composer. His *Romanian Rhapsodies*, composed in his teens, were deservedly popular, his later works less so, and he made his living as a conductor and violin virtuoso. He divided his time between Paris, his concert tours and his summer home in Sinaia, Romania.

Yehudi worshipped Enesco and wrote about him with unqualified rapture: 'What I received from him – by compelling example, not by word – was the note transformed into vivid message, the phrase given shape and meaning, the structure made vivid.' When Enesco did employ words, 'they were not cut-and-dried injunctions, nor ready-made solutions, but suggestions, images, which bypassed reason to infuse the imagination with a completer understanding'. Enesco was not a teacher in the conventional sense of somebody who prescribes a course of instruction with defined goals, regular examinations and public concerts. He was particularly sensitive to the need to find an appropriate style for each composition under study:

He rarely indulged in theorizing about music, directing my attention instead to the passage or phrase at hand. He invariably found the right word, image, or symbol to help me understand. In driving a point home he frequently referred to the life of the composer, urging me to read books about him and his works. In criticizing me and correcting my faults, Enesco never caused pain or humiliation, remaining at all times urbane and friendly, however harsh the import of his criticism. He united in his person the primeval forces of nature along with a most exquisite sense of style, the melodic singlemindedness of folksongs and the most refined traditions of the great masters. No matter how rarified the music he played, it became in his hands earthy, full of vitality and vigour. This quality in Enesco seemed to answer my inner needs and bound me to him.

Lessons were undertaken whenever Enesco was in town – perhaps on five successive days and then none for a fortnight. Each lesson would be extended over an entire afternoon. Enesco taught like a conductor taking a rehearsal with a soloist, accompanying at the piano, often singing the principal orchestral parts when a concerto was being studied, always coaching the work in terms of music rather than technique. Yehudi says he played 'more or less as a bird sings, instinctively, uncalculatingly, unthinkingly'. Neither of them gave much thought to theory so what came across was Enesco's conception of the work:

For years and years afterwards, I could hear his voice, sometimes in words, mostly in music, telling me about what I was playing, and as my experience grew these remembered counsels gained in validity . . . everything I do carries his imprint yet.

When Enesco was in San Francisco the following season, he was asked about the content of Yehudi's lessons. 'I taught him', he replied,

that real art comes from inside not from outside. Technically he had been well taught by Persinger – you could not improve upon it. He has worked on all kinds of vibrato – the vibrato of amiable conversation; the vibrato of passion, of exasperation. He will need all of them. When he plays Mendelssohn and Bruch he can give free rein to the oriental something which is in every Jew. But that won't do with Bach and Beethoven and Mozart. They are emotional, too, but in a restrained, classical way.

In support of Moshe's and Marutha's educational beliefs Enesco added that Yehudi read good books: 'That is part of the essential education of an artist.'

Moshe now had the responsibility of writing down the teacher's observations in a thick notebook. He sat in on the lessons, pretending to read the newspapers but actually keeping an ear open for phrases that could be discussed over a café brioche on the way home and provide useful reminders when the boy was at home practising. One day in spring 1927 a lesson was interrupted by a surprise visit from Maurice Ravel. He brought with him the manuscript of his new Sonata for violin and piano. The first public performance was announced for May and he wanted to try it out before entrusting it to Durand for publication. With Ravel at the piano, Enesco sight-read the entire piece, stopping occasionally to work on a tricky passage. He then laid the music aside and proceeded to perform the Sonata, including its gorgeous, bluesy slow movement, from memory. That was a feat even Yehudi could not emulate. Enesco owned fifty-eight volumes of Bach, all of which he had memorized, and as if that weren't enough he could play *Tristan und Isolde* by heart at the keyboard, singing every role as he did so. In short, he was unique.

The long walk to the lessons led across the Seine, along to the Place de l'Opéra, and then up to Montmartre, passing the Gare St Lazare on the way. It seemed to Yehudi that the Paris pavements were made of harder stone than those of San Francisco or New York. They gave him backache and he remembered his pleasure in being able to lean against a wall in Enesco's studio while he was learning the César Franck Sonata. Later that spring he and his father would travel out to what was then the little village of Bellevue, near Meudon, where Enesco had a cottage. Yehudi liked to take an early train so that there would be time for a country walk, enjoying 'the smell of damp earth, the rich vegetation of the Ile de France, the bird calls ringing through the woods'. The Franck Sonata, which he also studied there, became so imbued with the spirit of the place that he had only to hear it 'to see again the room on the upper floor, Enesco at the upright piano, and beyond the open window, the smiling French countryside'.

While Yehudi's life now revolved around Enesco, his sisters Hephzibah and Yaltah shared the daily routine imposed by Marutha: lessons at home, walks in the park, early bed – seven o'clock for the girls, half past for their brother. At weekends, there were tourist trips out into the country, to Versailles, Rambouillet and Fontainebleau.

The children's favourite way of letting off steam was to run through the streets of Paris wheeling wooden hoops. The girls would be dressed in identical coats, with sailor's collars, and all three children wore workmen's flat caps which made them look like a juvenile vaudeville act. The girls received piano lessons from Enesco's accompanist, Marcel Ciampi. He had been reluctant to take on such young children but with the formidable Marutha in attendance he agreed to let them audition for him. Hephzibah, seven in May, had been studying in San Francisco for three years and was already well on the way to emulating her brother's prodigious career. Yaltah, five, was not to be denied a hearing and her equally precocious talent prompted Ciampi to exclaim: 'Mais le ventre de Madame Menuhin est un véritable conservatoire.' ('Madame Menuhin's womb is a veritable conservatoire.')

There were darker aspects to the Menuhins' first sojourn in Paris. The bedrooms of their apartment looked over a courtyard where one night a man was murdered. Yehudi was woken by the gunshot, heard screams and shouts, witnessed the blood on the cobblestones the next morning and suffered from nightmares for weeks thereafter. Magidoff's biography suggested there was tension within the family too. Marutha insisted on living economically, despite or rather because of Uncle Sidney's blank cheque. Moshe had taken a calculated gamble; the omens were good but there was no certainty that Yehudi would prove to be a regular breadwinner. From conversations overheard between his parents he would have come to realize that a heavy load of responsibility rested on his young shoulders. But there is nothing of this in his own memoirs. Blessed with a selective memory, he preferred to recall the friendships he made during his first Parisian spring – all with adults, be it said, rather than with children of his own age. There was Madame Simon, a friend of the Godchaux family in San Francisco, who lived in a grand house on the Avenue du Bois de Boulogne and had a splendid collection of china dolls. Etienne Gaveau was a celebrated piano manufacturer (a son of the firm's founder) and something of a dandy. For 'a nominal charge' (Moshe's phrase) he loaned them a pair of uprights for Hephzibah and Yaltah to practise on and he gave the family free entry to his box for concerts at the Salle Gaveau. Yehudi remembered him best for his beautifully trimmed, white-tufted beard, so different from the long wispy appendages of the rabbis he had occasionally met with his father back home.

The most important of these new family friends, Jan Hambourg, was another well-to-do son of a famous father. Then in his mid-forties, Hambourg was an accomplished violinist who had studied with Ysaÿe. He preferred to lead the life of a Parisian dilettante and having married a rich American he could afford it. He owned two fine violins, an Amati and a Peter Guarnerius, and he followed an unchanging routine, which Yehudi witnessed several times: every day except Sunday he would don a wine-coloured velvet jacket, select a fiddle and play one of Bach's six works for unaccompanied violin of which, in 1934, he published his own performing edition. Yehudi's passion for the complete works of Bach, already enflamed by the sight of them on Enesco's bookshelf, was confirmed by this encounter. Yet Moshe was rather tart about Hambourg. Referring to his years of study with Ysaÿe, he commented slyly that 'unhappily it did not show in his playing, but he became a real connoisseur of food, art, music and violins'. Jan and his wife Isabelle had no children of their own and lavished kindnesses on the Menuhin children, even taking them to noted Paris restaurants – Jan was a member of the Société Gastronomique – to introduce them to the marvels of French cuisine. When Yehudi claimed never to have eaten in a restaurant during the first twenty years of his life he drew a veil over his excursions with the Hambourgs: he remained a lover of good food all his life. Incidentally, it was *chez* Hambourg that Yehudi was to meet the American novelist Willa Cather, who became a firm favourite of the family, a frequent correspondent of Marutha's and the self-appointed moral adviser for Yehudi throughout his teens.

Finally there was another American, Mrs Cora Koshland, a *grande dame* who back home lived in a San Francisco replica of the Petit Trianon. She was visiting Paris while on her annual European vacation in order to supervise the preparation of a new Ark she had commissioned for the synagogue where she worshipped (the reform Temple Emmanu-El), as a memorial to her late husband. George Dennison and Frank Ingerson were two artist–craftsmen she had engaged to research the religious symbols that would be part of the Ark's design. They hailed from Los Gatos in the Santa Cruz mountains and were to become neighbours and firm friends of the Menuhin family.

Enesco went back to Romania every summer – he was romantically linked with Princess Maruka Cantacuzène, a close friend of Queen Marie – and in 1927 he invited the Menuhins to join him. They took the Orient Express from Paris and thanks to Uncle Sidney travelled in some style: Yehudi practised in one compartment while Marutha taught the girls French in another and Moshe read the newspapers in a third. For their exercise the children would jog up and down the train's corridor. At scheduled stops Moshe led them out on to the platform and instructed them to breathe in the fresh air. They didn't bring their hoops but they would run alongside the stationary train, a strange trio for the other passengers to smile at, the girls dressed in the peasant clothes Marutha had run up in Paris in anticipation of their summer vacation. She always preferred to live modestly and Enesco had booked them into the annexe of a hotel, a pleasant self-catering *pension* which lacked only one essential feature: a bath. Yaltah remembers the entire village coming to gawp when an enormous cast-iron model was delivered from Bucharest. In Paris the pressures of study permitted only one visit a week to Les Halles but in Sinaia the holiday regime was relaxed enough for them to make daily excursions to the market. Marutha was suspicious of Balkan hygiene, however, and therefore avoided all meat except chicken.

Since Enesco was close to the Romanian royal family (it was the colourful Queen Marie who had presented him with the collected works of J. S. Bach) the Menuhins paid a visit to the royal castle of Peles. They passed the monastery founded by an ancestor of Enesco's princess partner. Entering a park, they could see in the distance the gables of a fairy-tale castle reminiscent of mad King Ludwig's Neuschwanstein. A carriage drove past them, drawn by two dashing ponies, and Yehudi recognized its solitary passenger as the new boy king, Michael. (King Ferdinand, his grandfather, had died on 19 July.) As it disappeared round a bend he threw a stone at it. It was an action he never forgot – a sign of the dawning social consciousness that had already made itself felt back in Paris, where he had expressed outrage at the lowly salaries of the musicians in the Orchestre Lamoureux. He could not remember why he had reacted so fiercely. Indeed it is rather odd, given his fondness in later years for kings and queens, among them Romania's Michael.

It may have been a resentment at the unconscious haughtiness of the boy – or a childish envy that he had the run of the place, a stableful of ponies, toys and servants. Later on we were shown the throne room, where King Michael alone had the right to be seated. I ran up to the throne and planted myself on it. An outraged guard ordered me to climb down, and Aba [Moshe] was rushing up to get me, his face pale with fright . . . I was ashamed of my resentment and envy and spoke about it only to Hephzibah, with whom I was beginning to share my thoughts.

Enesco had recently built a house for himself and his princess mistress outside Sinaia. He called it Villa Luminisch, 'Villa of Light', and there were spectacular sunsets to be seen from his first-floor studio, which looked out over a valley towards a mountain range. Princess Canta-cuzène lived on the ground floor and to avoid disturbing her Enesco's visitors went up a spiral staircase housed in a turret. Yehudi's tempo of study that summer might have been relaxed, but according to Moshe his repertoire had significantly expanded by the end of his first season under Enesco's guidance to include music by Bach and Tartini, two concertos by Mozart, the Chausson *Poème*, and, above all, the great concertos of Brahms and Beethoven. Enesco also introduced Yehudi to a work for violin and piano by Szymanowski called *Myths*, a sort of Polish *L'après-midi d'un faune*, composed in 1915. Moshe recorded that Enesco

asked Yehudi to look out of the window at the villagers gathering in the harvest and to imagine the buzzing of the bees and the whining of the mosquitoes. Then [as Yehudi played the Szymanowski] he imitated the sound of bees and mosquitoes with uncanny brilliance.

In the later summer of 1927 Queen Marie, a grand-daughter of Queen Victoria, was in mourning for her husband of thirty-five years. She invited Yehudi to play at her court, but Marutha was determined that Yehudi should lead a low-key existence, and she turned down the invitation. So, at Enesco's suggestion, the Queen came to hear him at Villa Luminisch. She sat downstairs with her friend Princess Canta-cuzène and eavesdropped for two hours on a lesson, the studio door having been left ajar. Afterwards Moshe and Yehudi were taken down to be presented. Enesco bowed and kissed the Queen's hand; Yehudi offered only a handshake as a greeting. Enesco observed that it was the first time Yehudi had met a queen. 'Oh no,' said the precocious eleven-year-old (or so the family legend would have it), 'in America all women are queens – but we do not kiss their hands or bow to them.' His head was not chopped off for such a treasonable utterance; instead the Queen gave him a signed copy of her own collection of fairy tales. The inscription read: 'To little Yehudi, hoping he will behave better when we meet in America.'

Yehudi was more impressed by his meeting with Romanian gypsies. When still on the Orient Express, speeding east across Europe, he had a feeling of going home – to a second home, that is, the mysterious Orient from which his mother claimed, through her Circassian blood, to be descended. In Sinaia they were quite close to the Black Sea and Yalta, Marutha's home town in the Crimea. (Her second daughter, Yaltah, was named for it.) At home in San Francisco Marutha would relax in Turkish silk trousers, drawn in at her slender waist by a silver belt. In Sinaia she took to wearing embroidered folk blouses bought for her by Moshe in the local market. The family went for long walks in the ravishing countryside, often on footpaths said to be reserved for the royal family. Beyond the rich summer houses of the courtiers and the *haute bourgeoisie*, the city noises gave way to a Mahlerian sound-world of cowbells and shepherds playing their pipes in the high hills. Gypsies formed part of the Oriental mystique, Yehudi's inheritance from his mother, and one evening – at a midnight festival, according to Moshe – Yehudi was taken to hear them play on the veranda of a café. The young Romanies danced round a fire in a mood of total aban-donment inspired by the *furioso* improvisations of their violinists.

Moshe was pleased to discover that many gypsy melodies are sec-ond cousins to the Jewish songs he had learned in his ghetto childhood, cross-fertilized during centuries of tribal wanderings. To Yehudi, so strictly educated and emotionally so hemmed in by the stiff-upper-lip conventions his mother had imposed on him, it was a revelation that one could make music in such a completely uninhibited way. The inter-action between gypsy folk music and the classical music of the West (and later of India) became a life-long interest. The technique of the gypsies was another marvel: 'It astonished me that they could fetch such extraordinary sounds from such primitive instruments, using bows that were saplings strung with unbleached horsehair.' The gypsy band-leaders were invited to the Menuhin *pension* for a longer 'jam session'. When Yehudi played his violin for them he chose not Ravel's *Tzigane*, as one might have expected (Moshe listed it as part of Yehudi's new repertoire, so he certainly knew it) but Tartini's 'Devil's Trill' Sonata, which Yehudi felt to be the classical work that came nearest to the gypsy spirit (and probably could be performed to better effect than the Ravel if he was playing without piano accompaniment).

What would one have given to be present that evening, especially to have seen Moshe's face when his son impetuously presented the gypsy's leader with one of the three extremely expensive, gold-mounted Sartory violin bows he had brought with him from Paris! In return the gypsies kept the Menuhins supplied with baskets of wild strawberries for the remainder of their stay. Yehudi also learned to perform some Romanian folk dances, and by happy chance Mrs Cora Koshland was there to capture his dashing performance on her film camera. She had arrived in style, having hired a trio of Chrysler cars, solid open four-door vehicles in which she proceeded to explore the Romanian hinterland, the Menuhin family accompanying her *en masse*.

Anti-Semitic demonstrations in Romania earlier in the year had led to pogroms and rioting in the streets. Yehudi missed them but Moshe was not so lucky. The Jews, he was told, were responsible for the country's spiralling rate of inflation. In a Sinaia municipal park he witnessed the tail end of a bloody clash between Jewish and Gentile students. When he went to Bucharest to cash his letter of credit he was shadowed by a plain-clothed security man whom he was convinced the government (at Enesco's prompting) had assigned to look after him. So swiftly had the value of Romanian currency dropped that he had to buy a suitcase to carry the wads of notes back to Sinaia. The money was needed to pay the bills: the vacation was over. Enesco was leaving for a concert tour and the Menuhins were to return not to Paris – Enesco's plans took him away too often – but to America, before returning again to Europe to begin a spell of study with Adolf Busch.

Conscious that Yehudi was absorbing too much of his own romantic style, Enesco had recommended that Yehudi should study with the German violinist, who was a master of the classical school. He reportedly said, 'Learn all you can and then forget it.' For her part, Marutha might well have decided that after a year's absence her children needed to see their Californian home again before contemplating another long stay in Europe. The decisive factor in the return to America was an invitation from Walter Damrosch for Yehudi to play a concerto with the New York Symphony Orchestra at Carnegie Hall in November. (The Symphony Orchestra's merger with the Philharmonic occurred the following March.) The arrangements were made by Yehudi's new lawyer, Dr Edgar Leventritt, and by his new agents, the New York firm of Salter and Evans, who already had four great artists on their books: the singers Amelita Galli-Curci, Elisabeth Rethberg, Tito Schipa and Lawrence Tibbett.

There was a tussle about what Yehudi should play in New York. The New York Symphony Orchestra proposed a Mozart concerto but Yehudi wanted to make his New York orchestral début with Beethoven's Concerto – he'd been studying it all summer with Enesco. Walter Damrosch, the Orchestra's chief conductor, thought the Beethoven was too risky; even one lapse in such a well-known work would lead to unfavourable reviews. Fritz Busch was to conduct the concert and he was dismissive of Yehudi's proposal: 'Man lässt ja auch Jackie Coogan nicht den Hamlet spielen.' ('One doesn't cast Jackie Coogan [Hollywood's best-known child actor] as Hamlet.') Yehudi stood firm: he would have more *fun* playing the Beethoven and he didn't care if it did jeopardize his career.

The decision was left until Yehudi's arrival in New York; first it was time to take leave of George Enesco. It was a sad parting as Enesco had become very close to him. Yehudi and his father drove out of Sinaia as usual in a horse-drawn buggy with a hood that could be pulled up over the travellers like the cover of a baby's pram. It was always an adventure for Yehudi to take this trip, and never more than on this occasion. Rain was threatening and thunder could be heard echoing round the mountains. But it was still dry, so Yehudi sat up front with the coachman. He remembered watching the wooden coach wheels running over the glistening stones as they forded a stream *en route* for the Villa Luminisch. When they arrived Enesco asked him to perform the *Chaconne* from Bach's D minor Partita. While Yehudi was playing the storm broke with a vengeance: 'Lightning split the sky from end to end of the valley, illuminating woods and valleys again and again with fierce and sudden brilliance.' The storm made a sensational accompaniment to the Bach. As soon as the boy concluded the fifteen-minute work, one of the most arduous in the repertoire, Enesco asked him to play it again, and then a third time, always with the storm as accompaniment. He was driving home the lesson that for a concert artist stamina is as important as technique. Moshe wrote that the storm seemed to inspire his son, adding that the weather calmed down as Yehudi reached the end of the work for the third time. 'My boy,' Enesco commented, 'always remember this raging storm and the peace that came after it. The *Chaconne* is a storm that ends in peace.'

Before they left Moshe took Enesco on one side and expressed his concern that Yehudi no longer seemed to be pushing himself – he practised honestly for the requisite hours but did not plead to be allowed to continue. Enesco told him not to worry about his son's relaxed attitude to work. 'It is God's gift to him: it will see him through life.' To Yehudi he gave a touching word of advice: 'Keep your eyes on the stars, my boy.'

The return to New York, the city of his birth, was very different from his departure, almost exactly twelve months earlier. Then he had been a gifted boy; now he was a celebrity. A posse of photographers came on board the SS *Rochambeau* as it arrived at the mouth of the Hudson. Yehudi and his sisters were made to pose for pictures that appeared next day in most of the New York newspapers. One portrait of Yehudi had the unfortunate caption, 'This little girl has been called the greatest child musician since Mozart.' Laurence Evans and Jack Salter, his new agents, met the family at the pier and presented Yehudi with a heavy black-and-white silk scarf: 'Never having possessed anything as grand as this I was terribly pleased and impressed.'

The family established its base at the Colonial Hotel on Eighty-first Street in Manhattan and Moshe summoned his first press conference. Even Marutha was persuaded to speak, evidently with her tongue in her cheek: 'I would just as soon Yehudi became a farmer as a great musician,' she began, explaining that they had seen 'too many musicians who are bloated with conceit, self-willed and unhappy'. When people applauded Yehudi at concerts she told her son they were clapping his pretty blouse or some other trivial matter. Moshe was at pains to deny any charge of exploitation: 'We thought he is so fond of playing in public and is apparently so little affected by it either nervously or emotionally that he begs to be allowed to play, much as any other child might beg for a new toy.' Speaking to a new audience to whom he could expound his educational theories, already familiar to San Francisco's press corps, Moshe moved into top gear:

Our children have never been to school – we decided to spend all our energies on educating them ourselves. We began by exposing them to everything available by way of cultural influences – good music, pictures, the best literature . . . Today Yehudi is deep in reading *Les misérables*. He has read all of Molière's comedies and a great variety of French authors in the original. He also likes to read history and has just finished H. G. Wells's *Outline*, which delighted him.

No scepticism can be discerned in the newspaper reports of Moshe's claims on behalf of his son. New York's hardboiled reporters swallowed them hook, line and sinker.

Now Yehudi had to set aside his French books and persuade Fritz Busch that, at the age of eleven, he was competent to perform the Beethoven Concerto. The German conductor was making his first appearance in New York. A dignified old-fashioned European who detested hype and publicity, he spoke hardly any English and was less than happy when he was required to attend a hot and crowded press conference and photocall. It had not been Busch's idea to hire Yehudi, after all, and in his mind the main work on the programme was the world première of his brother Adolf's Symphony in E minor, Op. 38. The new work was hardly a strong box-office attraction, however; only Yehudi's charismatic presence ensured a Carnegie Hall sell-out, repeated two days later at the New York City Center, then known as the Mecca Auditorium.

Busch was Music Director of the Dresden Opera, and it was a young Dresden concert manager, Kurt Wienhold, who persuaded him to allow Yehudi to audition the Beethoven for him at his hotel. (Wienhold was later to become Yehudi's American manager.) Louis Persinger had arrived from California to coach Yehudi, but when he headed for the piano, Busch stopped him and himself sat down at the keyboard. Here was an additional test for the boy, to follow the German maestro's tempo rather than to adopt the speed he had so often practised with Persinger. Busch's scepticism increased when Yehudi took off his overcoat, revealing ludicrously short flannel trousers stopping well above his knees – Marutha intended to keep him a boy as long as possible. Another point against him: he had to ask Persinger to tune his violin. Then Busch struck up the closing bars of the orchestral exposition and Yehudi played his first entrance, those vaulting, magical broken octaves that rise to such stratospheric and eloquent heights. The scepticism vanished in a moment: 'Yehudi played so gloriously,' Busch wrote in his memoirs, 'and with such complete mastery, that by the second orchestral *tutti* I was already won over. This was perfection.'

He signalled to Persinger to take over the accompaniment and retreated to a corner, evidently very moved. He listened for a time and then suddenly stopped the play-through. Throwing his arms around the boy he announced, 'Mein lieber Knabe, you can play anything with me, any time, anywhere!' And they started work on the interpretation then and there. As he was putting away his violin to leave, Yehudi said he could also play the Brahms Concerto. Busch expressed disbelief that such small hands could encompass a notoriously difficult passage in tenths. Fresh from his coaching with Enesco, Yehudi played the passage flawlessly. A few days later Busch wrote to the Berlin Philharmonic recommending that they engage Yehudi for the following spring season to play both the Beethoven and the Brahms in a single concert with a Bach concerto thrown in for good measure.

After the first orchestral rehearsal the musicians gave Yehudi a standing ovation. And Busch decided to reorganize the programme. He switched the Concerto to the second half, arguing that 'not a creature in Carnegie Hall would have had ears for any music whatever after Yehudi had played the last bars of the rondo'. At the concert (on 25 November 1927) Yehudi was dressed in velvet knickerbockers with a white sport blouse and white socks. When he arrived on the platform he handed his fiddle to the concertmaster to check the tuning – he still had difficulty in tightening the pegs. 'While the opening *tutti* was in progress', wrote the *New York World* the next day,

the boy stood quietly . . . just before his entry he adjusted a good-sized black pad which dangled from his violin . . . from the first broken octaves it was at once apparent that Yehudi Menuhin was an authentic artistic genius. It was the beautiful mature musical instinct of the young virtuoso that made this reviewer sit up and marvel . . . There were blemishes which I think were imposed on the boy from without. One is an indulgence in an overstressed vibrato, the other [is] over-sentimental phrasing when the music becomes strongly emotional. He played often out of tune but he seems fully aware of that, for he kept handing his violin to the concertmaster to be tuned whenever the music allowed him a moment's rest.

Another reviewer suggested the slight slips of intonation might have been caused by 'the profuse perspiration which beset the tiny virtuoso'.

During the first movement the audience burst into applause at the end of the cadenza, threatening to stop the performance, 'but supported by Busch and the orchestra, Yehudi returned them to Beethoven (he had been playing Joachim's cadenza) with all the authority and presence of mind of a veteran performer'. Bursting into applause at that particular moment in the Concerto reveals the New York audience in an unflattering light; at its conclusion the cadenza yields imperceptibly to a simple but ravishing restatement of the principal melody, accompanied by the orchestral strings, *pizzicato*. It is one of the most sublime passages in all music and any applause would have ruined the atmosphere.

A comic moment occurred when Yehudi was acknowledging the ovation at the end of the performance. Busch had sent him on alone for a solo bow and the orchestra, themselves vigorously applauding, stayed sitting when the boy asked them to share in the tumultuous reception. Uncertain as to what do next he caught sight of Louis Persinger backstage. (Magidoff wrote 'in the wings' but there are no wings at Carnegie Hall, just a doorway near the back of the stage.)

Yehudi rushed towards his teacher and led him out centre stage, laughing, pointing at him and applauding. Members of the audience thought he must be Moshe and shouted, 'Bravo, Papa Menuhin!' (To share his triumph with Louis Persinger was a generous but arguably misplaced tribute, since the most recent coach of the Beethoven had been George Enesco.) The crowds did not disperse until Yehudi returned for the last time dressed in his street clothes, complete with his Parisian flat cap.

The evening was a turning-point in Yehudi's development. Olin Downes of the *New York Times*, the most influential of the city's music critics, remembered that he arrived at the concert in sceptical mood, 'convinced that a child could play the Beethoven no more effectively than a trained seal . . . I left with the conviction that there is such a thing as a great artist who begins at an early age.' He rewrote his review twice. 'A boy of eleven', he informed his readers, 'proved conclusively his right to be ranked with the outstanding interpreters of this music.' The technique, he noted, 'was not only brilliant but finely tempered . . . governed by innate sensitiveness and taste'. In the *Herald Tribune* Lawrence Gilman wrote that Yehudi's performance 'takes away the breath and leaves you groping tirelessly among the mysteries of the human spirit'. Irving Weil of the *New York Journal American* described him as a 'rather fat little youngster in blouse and knickers and bare knees – but a miracle none the less'. Yehudi himself wrote in his memoirs that these two New York concerts were 'successful beyond our wildest dreams, vindicating so much that had gone before, promising so much for the future'.

His reward was marvellously mundane. When Walter Damrosch came round afterwards to add his bravos, he was followed into the artists' room by a family friend carrying a large dish of ice-cream which had been promised to the prodigy if he delivered the goods. Yehudi skipped past Damrosch crying, 'So I did play well!' Ice-cream, particularly strawberry ice-cream, became part of the Menuhin myth, and contributed not inconsiderably to Yehudi's teenage tubbiness. During their previous stay in New York his mother had imposed exercise with Swedish dumb-bells. He was to justify his taste for ice-cream by declaring it a symbol of his parents' joint affection for him.

I lived within the bosom of my family, not in the world, and I was acutely conscious of the smallest differences between my parents, so that everything they did jointly gladdened me as no ovation ever could. If ever the performance brought happiness to my mother, the entire family basked in it, especially my father, who was then in seventh heaven.

Poor Adolf Busch's Symphony was virtually forgotten in all the furore. 'Suffice it to say,' wrote the *New York Times,* 'that it is enormously sober and indubitably competent, as safe as Brahms and as sane as the diatonic scale.' The *Journal's* verdict was even more succinct: 'very long, very loud and completely futile'. Adolf Busch is remembered today as a fine violinist and an important teacher; two summers later Yehudi was to become his most renowned pupil.

On 12 December 1927 Yehudi appeared again at Carnegie Hall, this time in a recital at which he performed some of the works he had been studying with Enesco, among them the Bach *Chaconne,* the Chausson *Poème* and Mozart's Concerto, K.271A, a work of dubious authenticity. The *Herald Tribune's* headline read, 'Many on stage kiss him after his superb playing of an exacting program'. The *Boston Globe* reported that 'folks chased right up to the platform and kissed him on both cheeks'. Once again the hall was packed, with so many extra chairs squeezed on to the concert platform – three hundred, according to one estimate – that there was hardly room for the performers.

Olin Downes described it as 'an uncommonly critical and representative audience', containing many professional string players who had come to hear for themselves whether previous reports had been exaggerated. 'Their enthusiasm was obvious and unmistakable: demonstrations waxed as the evening waned.' When Downes left to meet his deadline Yehudi was still playing encores to a public in thrall to his mastery. The critic was not without reservations: at two hours in duration before the encores, the programme was, he wrote, unnecessarily long and unwisely chosen. Wieniawski's *Tarantella* [the *Scherzo-tarantelle*] was 'excessively cheap music' and taken much too fast. Nor did he admire the choice of the Mozart Concerto – 'a very dull opening movement' – although he conceded that Yehudi's reading of the finale was

brilliant in the extreme and evoked a special demonstration . . . There were slight imperfections of detail but his performance revealed all kinds of brilliant technic [a favourite Teutonically derived noun in Downes's critical apparatus], including short trills of the most exceptional closeness, evenness and finish . . . Everything potentially was there, and he was happy, playing with entire sincerity and enormous enthusiasm. This was not a child repeating a lesson but a child with every emotional and intellectual quality intense within him and communicating his reactions to the audience . . . In some places there was impure intonation, caused not

by the performer but by a string that tightened . . . the amount of tone drawn from
a rather poor instrument of three-quarters size was astonishing.

In fact Yehudi was playing on the slightly larger Grancino acquired in
Paris; nevertheless Downes's comment did not go unnoticed and four-
teen months later Yehudi was to become the possessor of a world-class
Stradivarius.

Leonard Liebling in the *New York American* praised Yehudi's rhythmic firmness 'which several times kept his piano partner [Persinger]
from falling by the wayside'. One reviewer, Richard Stokes of the
World, sounded a note of warning to set beside that of Ysaÿe's regarding the unpractised arpeggios; he did not like the way Yehudi held his
fiddle, which, dangerously in his opinion, was 'permitted to slope
down from the shoulder instead of being flung aloft as in the Auer system, while the tone is dependent wholly upon strength of bowing
instead of partly on the fingers of the left hand'. But this was a rare
criticism of what had plainly been a sensational evening: 'At the end,'
wrote Stokes, 'he was still rippling off scales with dizzy speed, turning
melodies on the fine lathe of his bow and whipping chords from the
strings with the crack of a lash.'

A true expert in the audience was the great violin pedagogue
Leopold Auer, then eighty-two. Asked by another reviewer, Samuel
Chotzinoff, for his reaction to Yehudi, 'The old man glares from under
his fur coat and snaps out, "Marvellous!"' Praise indeed from the
teacher of Elman and Heifetz.

A few days later Yehudi Menuhin was included in the annual 'Roll-
call of Honor' organized by the *Nation* magazine, alongside the scientist Albert Einstein, the poet Edna St Vincent Millay and the intrepid
airman Colonel Lindbergh, who had flown solo across the Atlantic.
(Yehudi had been invited to play for him in Paris but his parents, keeping
a low profile, had declined.) Yehudi's citation read: 'for proving that
musical genius of the highest quality still lives in this mechanistic age'.

The planned return to San Francisco had to be postponed when
Marutha fell ill. She went to hospital the day after Yehudi's recital and
underwent an operation. For the four weeks of his wife's recuperation
Moshe did the cooking at the Colonial Hotel and looked after the
children. Family life was to be kept simple even if great riches were
suddenly within their grasp. The entire Western world wanted to hear
Yehudi, it seemed. In 1928 alone Moshe claimed to have turned down

offers for engagements worth the phenomenal sum of $200,000 – many millions in today's equivalent. 'Yehudi's extraordinary gift,' wrote Olin Downes, was being 'wisely protected from undue exploitation.' Moshe told the press that he and Marutha had now accepted that

Yehudi's job in life is to be a musician. If he has a touch of genius – and I am compelled to believe he has – our task is to surround him with such a sane, helpful atmosphere that his capacities will unfold as plants unfold in a healthy environment.

Sitting down with Louis Persinger, Evans and Salter and their music-loving lawyer Edgar Leventritt, Moshe worked out a pattern for Yehudi's development that eschewed anything that smacked of sensationalist profiteering, yet did not cut Yehudi off totally from the public arena, since he so clearly enjoyed playing in public and could command massive audiences wherever he went. From January 1929 onwards, a year hence, he would tour the United States for two months every season in concerts arranged by Evans and Salter. Even in its first year this national tour proved to be much longer (and more lucrative) than originally envisaged. Warming to his new role as an impresario, Moshe reserved West Coast bookings for himself and also conducted his own negotiations with the Victor Talking Machine Company for Yehudi's first recordings, planned for later that year.

What do we know of Yehudi's inner thoughts during this climactic New York visit, so different from the idyllic months he had enjoyed in Romania? Taking his post-prandial rest on the day after his Beethoven Concerto triumph, he remembered being too excited to snooze.

I couldn't feel the weight of my limbs. Perhaps this is what people call growing pains: the body, heretofore taken for granted, seems to escape one's control so that muscles stiffen involuntarily and lose the knack of relaxing . . . More than twenty years were to pass before I began to understand the functioning of joints and muscles, or its importance to violin playing . . . I can now feel the weight of a single finger and appreciate in the shoulder muscles the smallest movement of an arm. But if it has taken a lifetime to solve the puzzle, from that November afternoon, I knew there was a puzzle to solve.

In a complex passage of his autobiography, written nearly half a century later, Yehudi recognized that he had touched spiritual heights in his performance of the Beethoven Concerto, but that he could not take a short-cut to emotional maturity:

My devoted, careful parents saw to it that I wasn't confined to what I could easily do; they saved me from musical idiocy . . . giving me books, languages and countryside, family life, and much besides; but there is no such thing as instant biography. Maturity, in music and in life, has to be earned by living. Having started from the top, after a fashion, and in one respect only, I had to construct my maturity from an unusual angle.

In a very American analogy, he saw himself as a balloon, floating with no visible support at the fiftieth floor of a skyscraper. His task, he said, was to put down threads from the balloon and surreptitiously build from the bottom up, without ever living down there.

Music swamped his emotional life. Esther Ehrman was his Dulcinea but she was ten years older and soon to be married to Claude Lazard of the banking family. Rosalie Leventritt, daughter of his lawyer, was his New York girlfriend during the family's extended stay but it was not, one must hasten to add, a physical relationship: Yehudi at eleven was not sexually precocious. Dorothy Crowthers, his instructor when he had taken lessons at the Juilliard School two winters earlier, contributed a profile of her pupil to the magazine *Musical America*.

'Have you heard the story of Vieuxtemps and mood?' asked the little violinist. 'He used to smoke a big cigar and hold it near the f-holes of his violin so that when he played the Bach *Chaconne* he would smell the smoke and think of a cathedral.' Yehudi's conversation is refreshingly devoid of the personal pronoun, I. He does not speak of his art or his concerts unless questioned, preferring to discuss such dissimilar topics as Wagner and his operas, of which he is eager to hear more performances, dogs, which he adores, some of the new scientific inventions which interest him, and anything with an element of humour in it. If one were to present a list of the things Yehudi likes best, it would be a delightfully heterogeneous mixture such as this: Beethoven, Bach and of course Handel, Haydn and Mozart; St Bernard dogs; icy weather; the new Cadillac cars; French pastry; the measured tread of the knights in *Parsifal*; San Francisco; ice-cream, playing ball and climbing rocks.

There was no mention of Handel or Haydn among the works studied with Enesco, so we must assume those composers to be new enthusiasms, possibly inspired by the family's friendship in New York with Sam Franko, a distinguished American violinist and composer who had studied with Vieuxtemps. It may have been Franko from whom Yehudi collected the engaging anecdote about the cathedral-redolent cigar. Yehudi had included Franko's *Irish Lament* among his encores at the Carnegie Hall recital. The reference to *Parsifal* is more of a puzzle; Wagner's sacred music-drama was given only on Good Fridays at the Metropolitan Opera, but perhaps there was a performance elsewhere in the city in the winter of 1926–7.

The enforced stay in New York had its compensations. Early in

January the Menuhins attended a recital given by Jascha Heifetz. They probably met him afterwards: at all events Heifetz commented that

The parents of little Yehudi Menuhin are wise in retiring the youngster for the rest of the season. A very few appearances a year serve to give the child poise and an incentive to work, but too many spoil him.

Meanwhile journalists were invited to sit in on the boy's lessons with Persinger. He was reported to be worried about his trills, complaining that they were 'nervous', rather than 'healthy'. For one passage Persinger suggested he play 'like a butterfly on a bush – flutter – flutter'. Yehudi duly made the music flutter. 'It's as though you raised an eyebrow,' Persinger commented.

As soon as she was well enough to travel, Marutha was taken by ambulance from the hospital directly to the Pullman car that was to be their home for the return journey to San Francisco. Outside their Steiner Street house, which had been let to friends during their fourteen months of absence, they found a shiny new Buick, a gift from the Ehrmans. When the weather improved they were to use it for explorations in the Santa Cruz mountains, prospecting for a possible estate to purchase with their new-found riches – Moshe frequently talked to the press about his desire to live on a farm. For the time being he satisfied his ambition for the open-air life with the construction of a sun porch at number 1043. 'The house is school, conservatory, play house and home to us – all in one.'

Yehudi plunged straight in to concert-giving. The date chosen for his homecoming recital, only a week after arriving in San Francisco, was 22 January and Moshe was quite shameless about exploiting it as Yehudi's eleventh birthday. There was even a leading article in one of the city's newspapers: 'It may be a rich heirloom of memory for one to say in after years that he assisted in honoring the boy at this San Francisco recital . . . his eleventh birthday.' Yehudi was driven to the Civic Auditorium with the Ehrmans in their Rolls-Royce. He sat next to Esther and held her hand all the way to the hall: the fragrance of her perfume allegedly sustained him through the entire concert. The ever loyal Redfern Mason was among the ten thousand at the Civic Auditorium:

Yehudi did not disappoint his friends: his playing rose to the high top gallant of their hopes. [It must be remembered that San Francisco was a nautical city.] Anything further removed from the infant prodigy of tradition could not be imagined. Louis

Persinger tuned his fiddle. Yehudi gave his audience a boyish smile and launched into the impassioned music which Tartini dreamed he heard the devil play for him . . . it was a miracle of youthful divination. During the Bach *Chaconne* musicians looked at one another with a sort of admiring hopelessness as those twin melodies unfolded, the undersong as clearly delineated as the air which was in the ascendant . . . His absorption reminds one of the absolute concentration of animals watching their prey . . . The Mozart was manifestly a joy to him . . . one divined how much importance has been to him the association with his master George Enesco . . . In the Chausson *Poème* the vernacular is more of our own day and here it was that Yehudi's fiddle sang with an emotion as nearly contemporary as is, shall I say, the poetry of Lamartine, that meditative dreamer whose poetry Yehudi's sister loves to recite? . . . Last came the lovely folksongs of Russia . . . Yehudi's technique never faltered . . . [After the concert] 'A little child shall lead them' – the words of Isaiah – came into my mind as I watched the multitude surge up to the platform. Something admirable in that, but not unmixed with something less than admirable – a sort of musical 'tuft' hunting.

In the programme book for the recital Yehudi's biographical note stated baldly that he had begun lessons with Persinger when he was four years old. Redfern Mason had a pertinent comment: 'We thanked Louis Persinger . . . and we thanked too Sigmund Anker, who taught the boy in his laborious beginnings of an art of which he is today a past master.' Anker's angry letter of correction to the *Examiner*, already quoted, appeared soon afterwards.

Moshe noted that the recital brought in the huge sum of $10,000. It was evident that the Ehrmans' generosity would no longer be a *sine qua non* of their activities. Uncle Sidney, wrote Moshe, 'was always ready to provide anything that was beyond our means, but it looked as though we would be able to support ourselves from this point on'. The plans outlined in New York were confirmed: Yehudi would stay with Persinger all year and Persinger would accompany him on his first American concert tour. Then in March 1929 the family would again go to Europe, this time so that Yehudi could study with Adolf Busch.

A month later, on 23 February 1928, Yehudi played the Beethoven Concerto with the San Francisco Symphony under Alfred Hertz. The *Chronicle*'s critic, Alexander Fried, reported that technically the performance 'lacked by a hair's breadth the perfection of his recent recital'. On that occasion Fried had written that Yehudi's technical accomplishments were 'unsurpassed by any living fiddler, even in this day of supreme virtuosi, and he plays with a tone and cultured art worthy of his craftmanship'. The Beethoven Concerto, Fried correctly observed, was the sternest test yet of the mettle of Yehudi's sensibility, and on that score 'he was triumphant'. The proprietorial Redfern Mason was more down to earth in his allusions:

No sickly hothouse plant, this Yehudi of ours, but a boy who can play ball with as much vim as a Tom Sawyer. He evokes the soul of the violin with the zest of a kid handling a baseball bat.

The orchestra, Mason noted, was as enthusiastic as the public: 'They did what they only do for artists of the first rank: they gave him a *Tusch* [a standing ovation].'

In Persinger's final year as Yehudi's teacher he would arrive each week with a carefully annotated score for study and under his guidance Yehudi rapidly expanded his repertoire, learning more than thirty works. Among them were the Brahms D minor Sonata, Beethoven's 'Kreutzer' Sonata, the Glazunov Concerto and several works by Vivaldi, edited for him by Sam Franko. Moshe stated he never paid Persinger a fee but in the light of the family's new affluence, liberal expenses must have been in order. Persinger was still based with his quartet in Santa Barbara and once a week made the exhausting round-trip car drive to spend a day with Yehudi. The pupil was always respectful but could not entirely conceal his preference, indeed his reverence, for Enesco. Eventually the mild Persinger flared up, exclaiming that he never wanted to hear Enesco's name again. Marutha overheard the outburst and tactfully removed the photographs of Enesco that decorated the living-room wall.

In September 1928 Persinger gave another interview about his famous pupil to *Musical America*:

Yehudi has been trained to control himself. But he gets most awfully excited; the pupils of his eyes expand until they are the size of a dime; and after a concert he seems dazed and doesn't recognize people who come back to congratulate him.

Even when he did recognize them he could be pretty dismissive. One well-wisher said he played better than Paganini. 'Have you *heard* Paganini?' came the reply. He continued to receive lessons in algebra from his father. At other teaching sessions they discussed history and political issues. When Yehudi was reported by a newspaper to have socialistic tendencies, Moshe denied it vehemently. His son was, he wrote, 'a liberal and a humanitarian at heart who can suffer vicariously to others'. Moshe himself was sufficient of a celebrity by now to think it necessary to inform the San Francisco reading public of his and twelve-year-old Yehudi's intellectual position: 'Our philosophy is the *Manchester Guardian* school in England and *The Nation* in America.' 'We have not changed our circumstances in the slightest degree,' he told the *Jewish Tribune*. 'We actually had to borrow money to square our budget. The children have had a healthy, normal home atmosphere,' he continued, sublimely indifferent to what other families might consider 'normal'. 'A staff of eight teachers was engaged to tutor the children . . . each came two to four times a week.'

Apart from Persinger and John Paterson, Yehudi's music theory teacher, there were now two teachers for French, two piano teachers for the girls, two teachers for English and one for German, whose job was to prepare them for concerts in Berlin and education in Basel, Adolf Busch's home. In anticipation of the return to Europe, Rebecca Godchaux's French lessons were stepped up. Yehudi became especially proficient, Moshe boasted, in the maxims of La Rochefoucauld, while the blonde Hephzibah was such an expert on the exceptions to the rules in French grammar that she was nicknamed 'Madame Larousse'.

Yehudi's understanding of harmony had evidently improved since his days at the Juilliard. (In Paris he had received lessons from the Director of the Conservatoire.) John Paterson reported that sometimes his pupil gave the impression of being lost in daydreams, yet when tested he was always able to repeat the teacher's idea and add a couple of examples of his own. He studied the instruments of the orchestra and learned about the unusual clefs employed by transposing instruments such as clarinets and horns. 'He found harmonic analysis unusually easy, so that he was able to catalogue in his mind any new chord combination he would come across.' Were it not for his innate charm, Yehudi might have been perceived as a bit of a swot.

Marutha ruled the roost with iron authority. 'During breakfast and supper good records are put on. The noon meal is kept for family round-table talk . . . Usually little Hephzibah tells us some of the delightful French stories which she loves to read.' Exercise after the lunchtime rest was compulsory. It could take the form of hiking, running, handball, tennis or even driving – Yehudi was already having unofficial lessons with Sidney Ehrman's English driver, who let him practise his gear shifts on the family's second car, a Packard. Yehudi claimed to be able to drive as well as he played the violin by the time he was fourteen.

In April 1928 it was announced that Moshe Menuhin had signed a nine-year contract with the Victor Talking Machine Company, shortly to be merged with RCA to form the powerful RCA Victor. Yehudi's first recording was already in the can. A church across the bay in Oakland was hired to serve as a studio and two engineers from the company's headquarters in Camden, New Jersey, drove across the continent with the electric recording equipment in the back of their Buick. Yehudi was very impressed by a bullet hole in the car's windscreen. The engineers told him they'd been fired on in Wild West Texas, though a stray pebble might actually have done the damage. On 15 March, four violin works were recorded; the two shortest, Fiocco's *Allegro* and Ries's *La Capricciosa*, went on to a double-sided 10-inch record which was released at the end of June, while the slightly longer works, Achron's *La Romanesca* and Monasterio's *Sierra Morena* (published in Mischa Elman's *Favourite Encore Album* and publicized at the time as the *Serenata Andaluza*) came out in September on a double 12-inch original red-seal disc. Moshe reported laconically that 'the royalties were substantial'. Yehudi remembered best that as a reward for his hard work at the session he was taken that very day to see the first talking picture, *The Jazz Singer*, starring Al Jolson.

A second recording session was held at Camden the following year, on 12 February. Yehudi was by then playing on a full-size Stradivarius and twice as much music (almost thirty minutes – something of a record, according to Moshe) was put on to discs in five and a half hours, including a truncated but incredibly pure version of the slow movement of the Mozart G major Concerto (K.216) and Bloch's stirring *Nigun*, which at six and a half minutes was the longest of his recordings to that date by almost two minutes. It took up both sides of a disc. In Oakland there had been no way for Yehudi to listen to his own recordings because the wax masters had to be taken back to New Jersey. Even at the second session, at Camden, there was no instant playback. This wasn't possible unless the producer ordered two identical waxes – an expensive process – and was prepared to sacrifice one of them. Instead the Menuhins stayed overnight and appraised the finished records the following day. Yehudi was feeling 'rather grand and important' because he was invited to sit in with the Chairman and the Board of Directors. No objections were raised by the company to the works by Saenger, Samazeuilh or Serrano – three of the rather kitsch composers selected: 'Musical demands were simpler in those days,' wrote Yehudi, 'and in any case the marketability of pieces would have over-ridden any aesthetical qualms.' The boardroom lunch that followed the playback was the most exciting aspect of the trip for Yehudi: 'I ate my first oyster, one of the Chesapeake Bay monsters, which was larger than the biggest steak I had ever seen!' That oysters are forbidden in the Orthodox Jewish diet might well have added to his enjoyment.

Louis Persinger was the discreet, wellnigh anonymous accompanist on the records. Later that year another pianist, who would eventually became Yehudi's favourite musical partner for nearly half a century, made her début in San Francisco. This was Hephzibah, the elder of his sisters. Musical studies were allowed but Marutha had genuinely tried to discourage her from thinking of music as a career, believing a woman's place was in the home. (The almost equally gifted Yaltah was to experience even greater hostility when she expressed a desire to follow suit.) But on 25 October 1928, half an hour after her normal bedtime, Hephzibah appeared in public at the Scottish Rite Auditorium, where three and a half years previously Yehudi had given his first recital. She was now eight years old and to her parents it seemed proper, as the critic Alexander Fried reported in the *Chronicle*, that she should have the same privilege of a concert at the same age. In another colourful piece, Fried called the little girl a budding piano genius,

dwarfed by the magnitude of a scowling, black grand piano, perched on a high bench, her hair streaming in flaxen curls down her back and about her pudgy arms, her foot mounted on a stool to wield a special high pedal.

The programme was short but adult in content: the Italian Concerto by Bach, Beethoven's Sonata in A♭, Op. 26, Weber's *Perpetuum mobile* and Chopin's *Fantaisie-Impromptu*. The audience response was very positive. Marie Hicks Davidson, the critic of the *Call-Post*, wrote that Hephzibah 'enthralled men who were leading orchestras and writing sonatas before she was born'. This was presumably a reference to Louis Persinger and the composer Ernest Bloch, head of the San Francisco Conservatory, who had become a family friend during the previous summer. Music criticism in the 1920s was a rhapsodic business. Ms Davidson painted a picture of

grey-haired men and women who wept in recollection of the despair which possessed them in times agone [sic] when they attempted the Bach [Italian] Concerto, which Hephzibah played as fluently as even old Sebastian himself could have wished . . . And down in the front row, with her parents, was six-year-old Yaltah, who reads *Plutarch's Lives* in French.

'Yehudi had better look out,' was another reviewer's summing up. 'Verily San Francisco has another musical prodigy.' Hephzibah had done exceptionally well. Obliged to study with three different teachers within a year because of the family's travels, she acquitted herself with honour and could clearly look forward to a musical career – if Marutha would allow it. But the family was not without its local critics. The *Argonaut* (27 October 1928) criticized them for hypocrisy because in a press release the parents had claimed they were not striving to make their daughter a professional musician. The concert, they said, was 'primarily an educational and cultural experience'. 'But with seat prices ranging from $1:00 to $2:00 she *is* a professional musician.' Sensitive to this criticism, her parents did not allow Hephzibah to play in public again for five years.

The summer and autumn of 1928 proved to be the Menuhins' last seasons as residents of San Francisco. The pull of 'old Europe' was too strong; to 'reach the potential of their extraordinary gifts' as Moshe put it, the children needed to study there. Another Lake Tahoe vacation with the Ehrmans, by then more family friends than benefactors, gave them the opportunity to talk through their plans with Uncle Sidney. Yehudi had demonstrated an almost frightening earning power. His fee for his farewell concert in December would bring him another $10,000. At the Shrine auditorium in Los Angeles, one of the first stops on the projected American tour, Moshe boasted to a newspaper that the box office 'take' would be a mighty $18,500. (In the event the numbers were much smaller because of an influenza epidemic.) Every other concert he gave would earn him a minimum of $3,500 plus 20 per cent of the margin over the guarantee. So there would be ample funds for travel abroad as a family, to give concerts in Berlin and Leipzig (at Fritz Busch's invitation) and to take a house in Basel for the months when Yehudi would be studying with Adolf Busch.

Marutha and the girls would reside there all year round, but for Yehudi and his manager–father, the winters would henceforth be devoted to astonishingly lucrative American tours, which along with recording royalties were to be the basis of the Menuhins' economic well-being. The 1929 Wall Street Crash and the Depression of the 1930s had no impact whatsoever on their affluence, although the fate of the starving workers (some of whom he would have seen camping out in New York's Central Park) certainly aroused compassion in Yehudi's heart.

On 5 December he gave his 'farewell' concert to San Francisco before setting out on his second odyssey. He may well have been playing the 1740 Guadagnini violin restored and presented to him that summer by Sidney Ehrman. The audience was estimated by different newspapers to be between seven and a half and ten thousand. The *San Francisco Call-Post* reviewer was bursting with local pride:

California has loomed large in the world's news this year. We have sent a president [Stanford-educated Hoover], a great symphony [Bloch's prize-winning *America*] and great football teams to the East: comes now a great violinist . . . He has a greater virility than when last heard in public. Tone and quality [*sic*] have acquired grandeur and soulfulness . . . He achieves a *pianissimo* without diminution of tone.

The critic of the *News*, the improbably named Curran D. Swint, claimed to have heard every performance of Yehudi's

since he took a quarter-size violin in his chubby hands at the age of four [*sic*]. Gone is the child and in his place a master musician . . . His growth and development in the past year have been phenomenal . . . He probes far deeper into that unfathomable thing called soul than could be expected from anyone but a genius.

Swint admired Yehudi's relaxed stage manner: 'Entirely self-possessed, he gives a quick look around at his friends on the front row and smiles to his mother in the midst of them . . .' Then he launched into Sam Franko's transcription of the Vivaldi G minor Concerto. Alexander Fried commented that 'the finish of the youngster's style, his subtle, expressive imagination, were in every turn of phrase astounding'. In the great D minor Sonata of Brahms, perhaps the most demanding work, musically speaking, that Yehudi had attempted in a recital programme since the 'Kreutzer', Fried noted the 'gravity and repose' of his conception of the slow movement but suggested that 'his grasp of this monumental music will grow surer with time' – the nearest he dared come to criticism of San Francisco's favourite son.

After the intermission Yehudi played Bloch's *Nigun*, with the bearded composer sitting in the front row alongside Moshe and Marutha. After observing that Yehudi now tuned his violin himself instead of handing it to Persinger, Alexander Fried allowed himself to be carried away by the emotional atmosphere of what he described as 'an unforgettable evening'. *Nigun* was:

one of Bloch's full-throated Hebrew melodies, music soaring in ecstatic devotion, sad with racial sorrow, but hopeful. From the violin came singing eloquence that wove a spell. The aged cantor of the synagogue knows no fuller feeling of his creed than Yehudi showed them. He is well named. An eager gesture from the boy called Bloch to his feet, beaming. Applause did not cease until *Nigun* was repeated.

Bloch had recently visited the family at Steiner Street. A few days before Yehudi's concert he wrote somewhat fulsomely to Moshe describing his sense of empathy with the Menuhin children:

When they asked me to say good night in their little beds I could have cried. How Christ was right! Only children know the Truth! . . . Your children are extraordinary and yet so normal, healthy and so true! What a superb living example of eugenics and what a hope . . . I am preparing a surprise for Yehudi; don't tell him. Since years I wanted to arrange the beautiful 'Abodah' melody for violin but always waited. Now I know why . . . as it will be done for *him* and I hope to be ready before you leave.

Yehudi gave the first performance of *Abodah* ('God's Worship') in Los Angeles on 16 December. It was the first of many dozens of compositions for violin that he inspired over the next seven decades.

Before the Los Angeles concert they lived quietly, staying at a family hotel halfway out of town. Sightseeing and boating in the municipal park were the height of their social activity. But the concert itself was another electrifying occasion:

In years to come he will play differently but I doubt that he will ever play better . . . He knows the joy of life but not its grossness, its pity and pathos but not its bitterness . . .

Thus Patterson Greene in the *Los Angeles Examiner* (17 December 1928). A crowd of well-wishers came backstage at the Shrine Auditorium, among them no less a hero than Jascha Heifetz. But Yehudi probably remembered the evening best for the subsequent meeting with another world star who played the violin, if only as a sideline. His name was Charlie Chaplin. Yehudi, Moshe and Persinger were invited to spend a day with him at his film studio in Hollywood. 'Chaplin cancelled all his work that day,' Moshe recalled,

declared a holiday for his employees, and then, on our arrival, gave us a personal tour and a private performance, complete with the famous Chaplin moustache, cane, hat and walk. But he also showed us his serious, philosophical side . . . I began to get anxious that we might miss our train. Yehudi and Persinger thought it absurd to think of giving up a minute of Charlie Chaplin to wait in a railway station. Chaplin himself would not let us leave until the very last moment . . . Then his chauffeur whisked us and our baggage to the station at top speed. Twice we were stopped by the police. We barely made it to our train.

They were travelling light: 'a minimum of baggage' was how Moshe put it, 'but plenty of books and music scores, a large envelope of press clippings, a chess set and a chequerboard'. In New York they made their base with the Garbat family, friends of Moshe's since his earliest days in New York. They transferred to the Colonial Hotel only when Marutha, who treasured her independence and privacy, joined them with the girls for the last month before their departure for Europe. Dr Garbat was a prosperous music-loving doctor who lived on East Eighty-first Street between Park and Lexington Avenues. His wife Rachel was the daughter of a Russian-Jewish tea-importer who had been among the founders of the Zionist movement in America; her family had befriended the Menuhins even before her marriage. Moshe claimed later that she already had her eye on Yehudi with a view to marriage to her daughter. The Garbats had adjoining houses, Yehudi remembered with a certain awe, one serving as the family home (they had children of Hephzibah's and Yaltah's ages) and the other for the medical practice. He was particularly impressed by 'a quantity of books, files, machines and all manner of surgical paraphernalia'. Yehudi's lifelong interest in health, sickness and treatment, both alternative and traditional, dates from that stay. While carrying out a private experiment he cut his finger – a violinist's nightmare. He kept quiet about it until it began to turn septic.

Within days of arriving in New York Yehudi was thrown in the deep end and only just managed to struggle to the side of the musical pool. He was booked to play the Tchaikovsky Concerto at two concerts given by the newly merged New York Philharmonic Symphony Orchestra under its regular conductor, the redoubtable Willem Mengelberg. This was the tenth in the orchestra's first annual subscription series on 28 and 29 December 1928. What looked on paper to be a prestigious occasion proved to be a hideous mistake. For the first time in his life Yehudi collected a bunch of bad reviews.

Pitts Sandborn in the *New York Telegram* described his performance as being 'marred by harsh tone, false intonation and capricious rhythm . . . He has no real notion of what the music was all about.' Olin Downes of the *Times* said the playing was 'considerably less admirable than in 1927' and even attacked Yehudi's concert clothes.

'Why is it necessary to dress a child of twelve as if he were seven and in a way not particularly appropriate to a concert at night time in a metropolitan auditorium?' A good question. But Marutha wanted it that way: a velvet shirt and knickerbockers were still the order of the day.

Oscar Thompson of the *Post* wrote in similar vein: 'His real career should begin after he has donned his first pair of long pants.' The *Evening World* painted a pathetic picture of Yehudi's youthful limbs quivering with the strain. In his hands, wrote Richard Stokes, Tchaikovsky's melodies were 'shallow as puddles'. Lawrence Gilman in the *Herald Tribune* took a reproving, headmasterly line: 'The best thing that could happen to Master Yehudi would be an enforced absence from the concert stage for several years.'

What had gone wrong? Basically Yehudi was uncomfortable with the instrument on which he was playing, a borrowed Guarnerius. Writing in 1995, he said it was the so-called 'Bâle' Guarnerius, loaned to him by Wurlitzer. Moshe wrote equally confidently that it was the so-called 'Baron Vitta' Guarnerius, made in Cremona in 1730, and that Louis Persinger had arranged its loan from the firm of Lyon and Healy in Chicago. Oscar Thompson also thought it was the 'Baron Vitta', adding that it came from the Wurlitzer collection. The instrument was larger than Yehudi's familiar Grancino and the change necessitated 'constant stretching and adjusting, a continuous effort to get the right note'. The violin probably had a big sound appropriate for Carnegie Hall but it was rash of Moshe, an inexperienced tour manager, to have allowed Yehudi to use this borrowed instrument at such an important concert after a running-in period of only five days.

Another reason for the bad reviews was a disastrous lack of rehearsal time. The first half of the concert was taken up by the world première of a suite from a recent stage work by the thirty-year-old Alexander Tansman entitled *La Nuit Kurde*, described by the veteran critic W. J. Henderson as forty-five minutes long and 'excessively dull'. The performance was actually hissed by the audience. According to a report a few days later in the *New York Telegraph* (the story was probably supplied by Moshe since his own account, in his autobiography, is very similar), Mengelberg did not call Yehudi for rehearsal on the day before the concert, even though he had been booked, and spent most of the final rehearsal working on the Tansman, allowing only the last twenty-five minutes for the Tchaikovsky.

It then transpired that there were discrepancies between the orchestral parts and what Yehudi was expecting to play. (Poor management again, not to have checked in advance.) The article included a long-winded story about Yehudi having lent the orchestral parts three weeks previously to a San Francisco violinist who failed to restore the cuts he had inserted for his own performance. Mengelberg spent the rest of the rehearsal sorting out the muddle. Since going into overtime was unheard of, even for a child prodigy, the evening's performance was given without benefit of rehearsal. In the third movement, the newspaper report continued,

Mr Mengelberg took the tempo at a speed which was not what Yehudi used . . . [Yehudi] thought fast. Would he embarrass Mr Mengelberg and the orchestra [by asking them to start again] and appear an impudent boy? He decided to take a chance. He jumped into the breach, took Mengelberg's tempo, hurt his own performance and saved the other musicians.

There's something a little fishy about this attempt at damage limitation in the wake of Yehudi's bad press. It would have been standard practice for Mengelberg to hold a preliminary meeting with Yehudi in his dressing room (or at his hotel the previous day) in order to go through the tempi if nothing else. The orchestra does indeed begin the third movement, but the soloist enters after only a few bars with a brief unaccompanied cadenza and this would have permitted Yehudi to adjust the tempo to his own preference. In any case the critics were not complaining merely about a misunderstanding over tempi. Although the audience had applauded mightily at the concerto's conclusion and Mengelberg 'kissed and embraced Yehudi many times', it was, in the opinion of the reliable W. J. Henderson, 'a very crude and unfinished performance'. Yehudi made no mention of the Mengelberg episode in his memoirs. He could hardly be expected to discuss each and every concert of his entire childhood and he evidently preferred to repress memories of this particularly bad moment.

Ten days later, Yehudi gave a recital, again at Carnegie Hall. The dip in his fortunes continued. Tickets were at a premium and the police were present in force because 700 forgeries had been printed. Moshe let it be known to all the papers that he had been unable to get a seat himself and would be standing at the back – but even standing room cost $2. A 'prodigious mob' was said to have attended – 'richly per-fumed in furs and velvets and jewels with long lines of motorcars wait-ing outside' – but Olin Downes of the *Times* returned to the attack.

Yehudi's style, he wrote, 'is prevailingly more sensational and less distinguished than it was in his first season'. The critical finger was pointing at the man who had been coaching him for the past year, Louis Persinger. And poor Persinger was also attacked for his accompanying. Samuel Chotzinoff commented that Yehudi deserved 'a qualified assistant at the piano'. Downes was harsher: Persinger was 'inadequate'. The *Brooklyn Eagle* rammed it home: Persinger's playing 'throughout the evening was far from accurate'. He accompanied Yehudi in one more New York recital, at the end of February, but the boy's first American tour proved to be the end of Louis Persinger's working relationship with the Menuhins.

The immediate problem of playing on a borrowed and troublesome instrument was soon resolved. Indeed it was dispatched with such rapidity that one suspects it must have been under discussion for rather longer than previous biographers have allowed. Among Dr Garbat's wealthy patients was a music-loving banker named Henry Goldman, a scion of the New York banking firm Goldman Sachs. He had been interested in violins since the days of his youth when as a recent arrival from Germany he had earned a relatively honest buck as a door-to-door salesman peddling cheap violins stamped STRADIVARIUS FECIT. Dr Garbat had attended the concert at which Yehudi played the Beethoven Concerto and had afterwards asked Fritz Busch what instrument the boy played. To which Busch was said to have replied, 'Yehudi Menuhin could play the Beethoven Concerto on a broomstick!'

A year later Dr Garbat invited Henry Goldman to his Carnegie Hall box to hear Yehudi play the Tchaikovsky Concerto. Afterwards it was made known to Goldman – whether by Garbat, Persinger or Moshe himself is unclear – that Yehudi was playing on a borrowed instrument and desperately needed a violin appropriate to his skills. To judge from the reviews quoted above, this must have been obvious to any well-informed listener. Goldman had a substantial personal fortune to dispense on good causes. Yehudi and his father were invited to call on him and his wife Babette at their apartment on Fifth Avenue. On the walls were Old Master paintings to rival those in the Metropolitan Museum across the road. Sadly the banker had gone blind, but he still remembered the works in his collection and began by taking the Menuhins on a tour of inspection. Yehudi noted a Cellini bronze inkstand, a Van Dyck portrait, a sculpture by Donatello and a set of Holbein miniatures – an impressive power of recall for a boy of twelve.

He also remembered that Goldman adored chocolate and cigars: 'When you're blind I suppose they're a great satisfaction.'

After half an hour the conversation turned to the point of the visit. 'Uncle Henry', as he became known when, like 'Uncle Sidney' before him, the benefactor was transformed into a staunch family friend, made an astonishing offer which Yehudi quoted verbatim in his memoirs: 'Now you must choose any violin, no matter what the price. Choose it; it's yours.' Moshe's version is more elaborate:

It will be a privilege for me to give Yehudi a Stradivarius. I want you to feel completely free and independent. Look for a Stradivarius as if you were buying it yourself. When you've found what you want, just send me the bill.

Walking on air, as he puts it, and armed with this fantastic blank cheque, Yehudi visited all the *luthiers* in town, among them the celebrated New York and Berlin-based dealer Emil Herrman. In San Francisco the previous year Herrman had called on the Menuhins at Steiner Street to show them some of his best violins. Now Yehudi could indulge the fantasy from which he had previously had to turn away. Herrman's stock included the 'Maximilian' Strad, later bought by the Berlin Philharmonic; the 'Betts' Strad, now at the Library of Congress; and the 'Prince Khevenhüller', named after the Austrian prince who was its first owner. Yehudi had fallen in love at first sight when shown this violin in San Francisco. At $60,000 its price was not much more than half that of the 'Betts'.

After consultations with his teacher and with the great violinist and collector Efrem Zimbalist, who had been Louis Persinger's friend since Leipzig student days, Yehudi played on all three instruments and opted for the 'Khevenhüller'. (As a test piece he played 'The Prayer' from Handel's Dettingen *Te Deum*.) It was to be his principal instrument for over twenty years. He described it as 'ample and round, varnished in a deep, glowing red, its grand proportions . . . matched by a sound at once powerful, mellow and sweet.' Antonio Stradivarius had made the instrument in 1733, his ninetieth year, when despite his advancing years he was still at the peak of his powers. Heifetz's Strad was made in 1731; Ysaÿe's the year after and Kreisler's in 1734. Herrman had acquired the 'Prince Khevenhüller' in Moscow, probably for a song, after the Revolution.

When Herrman added an exceptionally valuable violin bow by the great Tourte as a bonus, Moshe must have uttered a silent prayer that his son would not meet any gypsies while it was in his possession. Ever realistic, and obviously concerned by the problems Yehudi had experienced with the borrowed Guarnerius, Moshe instructed Evans and Salter to postpone the concerts in Pittsburgh and Cincinnati planned for January so as to give Yehudi time to familiarize himself with his new instrument. The press was told that Yehudi wanted to attend New York concerts by Heifetz and the celebrated pianist Walter Gieseking.

On 22 January 1929, a photocall was arranged for Yehudi's 'official' twelfth birthday. In every New York newspaper the grinning boy was pictured holding his so-called birthday present, the 'Khevenhüller' Stradivarius, flanked by its generous donors, Mr and Mrs Goldman. Seeking to emphasize Goldman's generosity, Yehudi wrote in his memoirs that the gift was made a week after the Wall Street Crash of 1929. He was wrong by nine months: the Crash occurred on 24 October.

The only puzzle for the historian concerning Goldman's splendid gift is that on 10 January 1929 Moshe told a reporter in Washington that Yehudi 'didn't know that a $60,000 Stradivarius was waiting for him in San Francisco'. Either the reporter or Moshe must have got his cities confused and substituted San Francisco for New York. Moshe also spoke to a San Francisco newspaper about a new violin for Yehudi back in July 1928: 'Rumors have reached us concerning the gift of an $80,000 Strad'. Perhaps Dr Garbat had been talking to his patient Henry Goldman back in the summer.

The first highlight of Yehudi's winter tour was a VIP week in Washington, culminating in a meeting with the outgoing US President, Calvin Coolidge. Moshe the American patriot could hardly have failed to be moved, but the White House conversation, as he reported it, was not on the most exalted of levels.

The President and the First Lady seemed anxious about Yehudi's knees. Yehudi was wearing short trousers and long, woollen English stockings. The President said to me: 'Make sure the boy does not catch cold.'

When he talked to the press about his son's early career Moshe's imagination started to run wild:

His mother and I believed he wanted a violin, so we wrote to an uncle who sent us $15 for the purpose, probably believing we were crazy. [This would seem to be a reference to Moshe's chicken-farmer brother Louis in Hayward, California; the story was never repeated.] We rented a violin with that money and the boy began to play . . . when Yehudi was four we asked Persinger to come to the house to hear him. He came, accepted . . . within six months Yehudi gave his first recital.

Why could Moshe not tell the truth? It was just as good a story. He added a comment to his interviewer which hints at a feeling of unease: 'At least I hope I'm not a reincarnation of Mozart's father.'

But in some respects he was. Despite his claims to the contrary, the schedule he was imposing on Yehudi would strike modern parents and educators as exploitative: a week or two in each city, sightseeing and performing and then off to the next venue, with nobody for company but two middle-aged men, his father and his teacher. But Yehudi remembered his touring with affection:

Persinger accompanied me at recitals, was present at the concerts with orchestra, worked with me every morning and in between times played chess and went sightseeing with us. And I took it all for granted, living in my balloon.

At the end of the month, at Cleveland's Masonic Hall, Yehudi played the Beethoven Concerto for the first time on his new Strad. He returned to Cleveland in February for a recital. The city stuck in his memory because for once he made the acquaintance of a boy of his own age, Alan Geismer, who possessed a splendid electric train set laid out on the floor of the family attic. At the concert a woman seated behind Yehudi on the stage fainted and a first-aid group with a stretcher appeared. 'I will not go', she said firmly. 'I will not miss any of this programme. Not if I faint time after time!'

Of the major cities in the east only Boston was excluded, because of a city ordinance preventing public performance by minors under the age of sixteen. A second New York recital was hastily arranged at Carnegie Hall on 24 February. The *Musical Courier*'s review commented on the warmth of the new Strad: 'The beauty of the child's tone seems to grow at each hearing.' The *Brooklyn Eagle* singled out his playing in the Beethoven Romance in F: 'a tone of ethereal, chaste, sexless quality, unbelievably mature'. But the backlash continued in some quarters, among them the *New York World*:

Dutifully he fiddled his way through Bach's Concerto in E major, apparently unaware or not caring to know what it was about except long pages of notes . . . then there were flashes of his best form but mostly only the body was present.

Yehudi was trying out the Bach with only piano accompaniment in anticipation of his forthcoming 'Three Bs' (Bach, Beethoven and Brahms) concert in Berlin. In America no promoter would allow him to play more than one concerto in an evening.

When he visited Chicago, early in March, a patriotic local critic from the *Music News* was underwhelmed by the child prodigy:

His attainments stop short of the sensational for he lacks the magic touch which so immediately touches the heart . . . and his repertoire is a decidedly limited and restricted one . . . As another matter of fact he has not nearly the flair for the violin . . . which has been shown so often by the little Bustato girl at the Chicago Musical College, and several other prodigies who might be mentioned.

The American-born Guila Bustabo, three years younger than Yehudi, had a remarkable talent, later developed by both Persinger and Enesco.

Minneapolis on 8 March was Yehudi's final port of call, and the last important test in his preparations for the eagerly awaited 'Three Bs' orchestral concert in Berlin. He had played the Bach at his second New York recital and performed the Beethoven in Cleveland. Now he was to play the Brahms Concerto for the first time in public and the wily Moshe invited reporters to attend the rehearsal. To judge from the *Minneapolis Evening Tribune* (7 March 1929) the omens were very positive:

Sixty blasé musicians forgot their dignity and took part in a mad demonstration. Tears trickled down grizzled chins and splashed into the bass horns. Music stands were upset as musicians leaped to their feet and shook the rafters with a chorus of 'Bravos' – which is a few steps further than a dyed-in-the-wool musician usually allows himself to go. Yehudi grinned happily and boyishly and offered to try it again if they liked.

At the performance the audience applauded at the end of the first movement, no doubt responding to the cadenza composed by George Enesco the previous year especially for Yehudi. Their pleasure in the slow movement was interrupted when Yehudi faltered only a few bars into his solo and stopped playing. For the first time in his performing career he had lost the thread – despite the fact that Brahms's melody is of an exquisite purity and individuality. He turned to the conductor Henri Verbrugghen, a violinist himself, and whispered, 'We must not bluff Brahms!' Verbrugghen stopped the orchestra and told the audience 'in the kindliest manner', according to the *Minneapolis Journal*, 'that the little *lapsus* was caused by the fact he had never played it in public before'. He came off at the end of the Concerto deeply disturbed, exclaiming to the faithful Persinger, 'This will never happen to me again!' And indeed it did not, although he once fell asleep on his feet in Boston during the second orchestral *tutti* of the first movement of the Beethoven, emerging from his reverie just in time to respond to Dr Koussevitzky's agitated cue.

The *Minneapolis Tribune*'s critic gave a favourable spin to the Brahms episode: 'Greatly to the youngster's credit was his calm ability to think his way through the crisis and bring the movement to a splendid conclusion.' But it was a crisis all the same, a black mark to add to the miserable Tchaikovsky experience in New York and the implied rebuke from President Coolidge about his inappropriate dress code. Despite his happy exterior, 'living in my balloon' as he described it, Yehudi's mishap in Minneapolis was the result of quite severe stress: 'I was keyed up to the performance,' he said later, 'seeking to recapture the overpowering vitality of Brahms.' His happiest memory of the visit was of an invitation from the genial Verbrugghen to play chamber music together at his home. Perhaps they talked about Ysaÿe, with whom the conductor had studied in his youth.

There seems to have been some doubt as to whether Marutha and the girls would travel to Berlin for Yehudi's concert. The *San Francisco Examiner* reported in February that

Mrs Menuhin, *contrary to previous plans* [my italics], will travel with the family to Europe. She offered her home at 1043 Steiner Street for permanent leasing. 'The house no longer meets our needs – but we cannot bear to give it up. We are thinking of building at Burlingame soon.'

Nothing came of that idea – a lucky escape, some might say, since Burlingame is adjacent to San Francisco's international airport.

Before setting off for Europe she gave a farewell dinner. The guests included the impresario Selby Oppenheimer and two of Yehudi's most supportive critics, Redfern Mason and Curran Swint. Mason obviously adored Yehudi and got to know him quite well. He had been a guest at his going-away party the previous December: 'Yehudi is a born arguer,' he wrote. 'If he went into trade he would get the better of a Greek pedlar.'

The resumption of family life in New York in March 1929 marked Marutha's return to her customary position of central influence and authority. Magidoff's biography states (on what authority is unclear) that there had been considerable tension between the parents. Marutha was said to have been suspicious of the motives behind Henry Goldman's gift of the violin. She was also critical (with some justification) of what she thought was Moshe's undignified and boastful handling of the press. When, together, they accepted a luncheon invitation to the Goldmans, there was a colourful incident involving Yehudi. Sent to the library for a rest after the meal, he amused himself by making a rough suit of armour out of the many silver and pewter ashtrays lying around the room. He tied the objects together with some of the string he always carried in his pocket, along with a penknife and other schoolboy paraphernalia. Hosts and parents found him strutting round the library pretending to be a medieval knight.

Seeing the anger in his mother's eyes, Yehudi hastily began taking off his shining armour but Mrs Goldman exclaimed, 'Don Quixote!' and she led her blind husband to the boy to feel the ingenious knots Yehudi had devised to keep the ashtrays together. The two immediately got involved in a discussion of medieval armour and sailor's knots, both displaying a surprising knowledge in two odd and unrelated fields.

It makes a touching tale, but Marutha was not amused. Before their departure for Europe she declined an invitation to take tea with Mrs Goldman. She also fell out with her old friend Mrs Garbat after Fifi, the Garbat daughter, presented Hephzibah and Yaltah with one of her dolls. It had to be returned: playing with dolls, Marutha ruled, was a waste of time. Later, when they dined with the Garbats, she sent Yehudi out of the room for what she considered an ill-judged remark. She justified her action by asserting that it was important for a child's development to maintain discipline. Relations soured when Marutha was herself gently criticized by Dr Garbat for imposing rather too much of it. Sealed off in his 'balloon', Yehudi seemed oblivious to the humiliation. When a sympathetic grown-up raised an eyebrow at his mother's insistence that he always wear heavy woollen underwear, even when the weather was warm, he responded that one day he would be making his own decisions – after he was twenty-one.

As for Marutha's criticism of her husband's new skills as a publicist, it is true that he had taken to banging the drum with a relentlessness that would not have been out of place in the employment of Barnum and Bailey. But he had every right to be proud of his son and, to give him his due, he sometimes expressed himself in language that matched that pride: 'Once in every century, God in a burst of joyousness sends down a "new soul", pure, gifted, endowed with heavenly power.' And how did he account for the great depth of feeling in his son's playing?

It is racial. It is taken from generations of Jewish life. Yehudi has simply inherited an intense feeling and instructive understanding of life from the experiences of thousands of years of his people's history.

It was pouring with rain in New York on 23 March 1929 when the family boarded the SS *Deutschland* destined for Cuxhaven in Germany, where they would take the train to Berlin. The press in attendance noted that Yehudi wanted to play with other children making the Atlantic voyage but he was restrained by his father. Yehudi said, 'If other kids get their feet wet, why can't I?' Moshe relented. 'OK, but don't get them *too* wet.'

Recommended Recordings

Dinicu, arr. Heifetz: *Hora staccato*
with Hendrick Endt (piano)
from the CD *Yehudi Menuhin Plays Virtuoso Violin Music*
BID LAB 126: track 18
Recorded 14 March 1939
Menuhin gives an authentic gypsy-style performance, doubtless inspired by his teacher, Dinicu's Romanian compatriot, George Enesco.

Tartini, arr. Kreisler: Sonata in G minor ('Devil's Trill')
with Artur Balsam (piano)
from the CD *The Young Yehudi Menuhin*
BID LAB 046: tracks 1–4
Recorded 20 May 1932
The work Yehudi played to the gypsies in Sinaia, Romania, when he was ten.

Franck: Sonata in A minor
with Hephzibah Menuhin (piano)
from the CD *The Young Yehudi Menuhin*
BID LAB 058
Recorded 6 and 7 January 1936
A work Yehudi first studied with Enesco in Paris in the summer of 1927. His first recording of it was made with his sister Hephzibah in 1936.

Beethoven: Violin Concerto in D, Op. 61
Lucerne Festival Orchestra, conducted by Wilhelm Furtwängler
EMI7 69799 2
Recorded 1953
The work with which Yehudi made his concerto début in New York in November 1927. When he played it in Berlin, eighteen months later, it prompted Einstein's exclamation concerning the proof of God. The Beethoven remained one of YM's finest interpretations. This mono recording dates from 1953.

4 Swiss Family Menuhin

Reading congratulatory telegrams after his concerto début in New York

1929: April: Bach, Beethoven and Brahms concertos in Berlin; summer: studies in Basel with Adolf Busch; November: début in London and first recordings for HMV; 1930: January: New York and US tour; May: return to Europe and second summer with Adolf Busch at Basel; autumn: tour of Europe and UK; 1931: early months: US winter tour; driving test in San Francisco; May: return to Europe and move to new home at Ville d'Avray outside Paris.

THE MENUHINS sailed to Europe on a German ship, the SS *Deutschland*, so they could practise the language they had been so assiduously studying in preparation for their second great family adventure. Father and son visited the ship's engine room. Yehudi was fascinated both by the machines themselves and also by working conditions for the toiling stokers. His questions, Moshe remembered, were as much concerned with pay and hours as with turbine engines and Plimsoll lines. From their Cuxhaven landfall they went by rail to Berlin. It was the first time Yehudi encountered a train equipped with a telephone – he always loved making telephone calls.

For professional American musicians, Berlin in the 1920s was the capital city of the musical world. Earlier in the decade, when Serge Koussevitzky was still in residence, Paris had a rival claim. So too had Vienna, where for two wonderful years Richard Strauss was in charge of the opera. But no other city could rival Berlin's wealth of musical activity in the late 1920s. It boasted three opera houses and four symphony orchestras, including one run by a radio station (not that Moshe would countenance selling the broadcast rights of his son's performances). They were all supported by a substantial music-loving public, a substantial proportion of them Jewish. Furtwängler, Kleiber, Klemperer and Walter and were regular conductors of opera and symphony concerts. Yehudi's unofficial sponsor, Fritz Busch, was a frequent guest conductor of the Berlin Philharmonic.

Musical life in the United States was largely dominated by German musicians and German attitudes. The Menuhins knew about Berlin at first hand from Yehudi's teacher Louis Persinger, who had been concertmaster of the Berlin Philharmonic before the war, and from their German conductor friend Alfred Hertz, who had recorded excerpts from *Parsifal* with the Berlin Philharmonic. (Back in 1903 Hertz had defied Wagner's stated wishes and conducted a staging of the 'holy' *Parsifal* at the Metropolitan, New York: he had consequently been banned in Bayreuth and other major German opera houses.) There was no higher goal, whether measured in terms of prestige or of market value – a factor that Moshe must have taken into account – than success in Berlin.

Yehudi had his own ideas of what would constitute success: he called it 'fun'. He had made his New York début with the Beethoven Concerto, the most sublime work in the repertoire. For his Berlin venture he had the decidedly unconventional 'fun' notion of a concert devoted entirely to three of the greatest violin concertos. To Berlin's conservative music-lovers the programme smacked of gimmickry but the three works – Bach's E major (BWV 1042), the Beethoven and the Brahms – were strongly contrasted musical masterpieces, not flashy visiting cards, and for all his *naïveté* the young Yehudi knew he had both the insight and the stamina to carry them off. Busch's participation guaranteed Yehudi's artistic integrity. Busch, who had originally mocked the idea of Yehudi playing the Beethoven Concerto in New York, had become a willing ally. His letter of recommendation to the concert promoter Luise Wolff, a leading figure in Berlin's musical life, was widely publicized and helped to attract a full house.

Menuhin took to calling this his '*Mayflower* concert', a reference to the ship that transported to New England the original Puritan settlers, whom half the population of America apparently claimed as ancestors. During the next half-century he met many thousands of German-born concertgoers who claimed to have been present that day in Berlin's old Philharmonie Hall, whose capacity was no more than two thousand.

Just before the concert Fritz Busch's father died suddenly, and the conductor was obliged to withdraw. To save the day, Bruno Walter agreed to take over, cancelling an opera performance in order to do so. Moshe wrote that the first of the planned two rehearsals had to be cancelled because of the bereavement but Walter referred in his autobiography to 'rehearsals' rather than a single run-through, so despite Busch's withdrawal the concert appears to have been thoroughly prepared, and indeed the *Hauptprobe* (dress rehearsal) was attended by a full house of students. The substitution was in fact advantageous: Walter was a conductor of even greater renown than Busch. Berlin-born and with worldwide experience, he was Chief Conductor of Berlin's Municipal Opera and later that year succeeded Furtwängler at the Leipzig Gewandhaus.

Walter praised Yehudi's spiritual mastery:

He was a child and yet he was a man and a great artist . . . I felt as one with him. I could have made a suggestion here and there during the rehearsals but it was not necessary: the mutual understanding was complete. Yehudi's musicianship was particularly striking in the slow movement of the Bach; it is sublime music, which requires complete technical authority and cannot be played without the deepest insight.

For his part Yehudi revelled in the partnership:

I marvelled to find such support, such adaptability; it seemed to me that whatever I did, he was always there, perfectly with me, an accompanist such as I had never known.

Among the conducting partners of Yehudi's youth, only Enesco and Toscanini received an equally positive assessment.

The concert on 12 April was the triumph the Menuhins had hoped for. 'One among millions,' was how the Berliner *Zeitung am Mittags* described Yehudi, adding – with Prussian pride – that he 'will still grow under the tutelage of Adolf Busch'. The *New York Times* reported that 'the most severe critics were full of praise for the sturdy little chap'. Applause again broke out after the cadenza of the first movement of the Beethoven and, at the end of the evening, 'Police had to escort out persistent crowds that threatened to rush the platform.'

Albert Einstein, celebrated for his formulation of the General Theory of Relativity, published in 1916, and a keen amateur violinist, had been seated in the front row of the audience. Bruno Walter (presumably able to take note of his surroundings while Yehudi was playing the cadenza) remembers the expression of amazement and joy on Einstein's face. An American journalist reported that, at the end of the concert, Einstein was imprisoned for thirty minutes by the rush of people towards the stage, 'his hands high above his head, where he had placed them to clap his approval'. Meanwhile Yehudi took more than a dozen bows. Eventually Einstein was able to congratulate him in person. The crush overflowed around the dressing room and Yehudi received his admirers on stage. He was standing there surrounded by well-wishers – among them the impresario Max Reinhardt, the conductor and pianist Ossip Gabrilowitch, the violinists Fritz Kreisler and Carl Flesch, and his American benefactors Sidney Ehrman and Henry Goldman – when Einstein emerged from a door at the side of the stage. Quivering with emotion, the great scientist is reported to have said, 'My dear Yehudi, tonight you have taught me my first new lesson in many years . . . I have made a new discovery. I see that the day of miracles is not over . . . Our dear old Jehovah is still on the job.'

As the remark was flashed round the world and became the most frequently quoted appreciation of Yehudi's youthful genius, it would be satisfying for a biographer to be able to confirm the text of Einstein's glowing testimony from a less partial source than Yehudi's father. Unfortunately all the variants seem to have emanated from the creative memory of Moshe Menuhin. A slightly tamer translation has Einstein's exclaiming, 'Yehudi's playing proved that our Jehovah is still alive.' Another version (adjusted, one suspects, for non-Jewish readers) has Einstein asserting that Yehudi's playing was 'proof of the existence of God'. If Einstein spoke in German (this detail is nowhere recorded) the phrase might be a different translation of the line quoted by Yehudi in his memoirs: 'Now I know there is a God in heaven!'

The American reporter B. H. Knickerbocker slipped backstage to ascertain Yehudi's own response to the ovations and overheard this conversation between conductor and soloist:

Bruno Walter: 'Now what, Yehudi?'
  'Oh now,' said Yehudi, 'I will have some ice-cream.'
  'Strawberry ice-cream with whipped cream on top?' asked Walter.
  And Yehudi's face beamed assent.

The Berlin *Morgenpost* commented that Yehudi was 'almost grotesquely fat'.

A few days later, on 22 April, Yehudi reached his true thirteenth birthday, customarily the age when Jewish boys go through the bar mitzvah ceremony and are formally acknowledged as adults. There was no synagogue ceremony for Yehudi, such was not the Menuhins' way, but elements of the rite of passage were nevertheless enacted. Almost seventy years later he recalled being asked formal questions and given salt radishes to nibble.

Moshe presented his son with a most splendid birthday gift, sixty volumes of the Bach Gesellschaft *Urtext* edition of the complete works of J. S. Bach – the same series he had admired in Paris on George Enesco's shelves. Moshe located a set that had previously belonged to Max Bruch. The composer had been dead for thirteen years: his will instructed his executors that the scores should be sold only to a worthy scholar–musician. Who better than Yehudi? Moshe bought them on credit, claiming to be too short of funds to purchase them outright. Since Yehudi had earned $200,000 the previous season, Moshe must have been referring to cash in hand, which he probably kept low bearing in mind the uncertainties of the world's banking system in the year that Britain came off the gold standard. The debt was paid from Yehudi's German tour earnings later that year and Bach's music was to take pride of place in the Menuhins' new home in Basel. The original texts became his constant inspiration in the systematic study of Bach's violin works which he began under Adolf Busch.

The German triumphs continued. In Dresden, where Fritz Busch was head of the opera, Yehudi repeated his three-concerto marathon, this time with Busch conducting, as originally planned. It was the first time the opera house had been used for a symphony concert. Three concertos in one evening was too much, commented one reviewer. Too much, that is, for the audience, but not for performer: the critic of the *Dresdner Nachrichten* commented that Yehudi looked fresh enough to have played the entire Mendelssohn Concerto as an encore. A veteran who had heard Mischa Elman's début said Yehudi's was the more auspicious. The only mildly dissenting voice came from the *Vossiche Zeitung* complaining that the cadenzas (by Enesco, Kreisler and Joachim respectively) revealed some 'virtuoso vanities'.

While in Dresden Yehudi struck up a friendship with Fritz Busch's son Hans. It was probably more fun than the eight-course dinner he had to sit through after his concert. Moshe remembered that they 'played with electric trains, ran along the banks of the Elbe and talked their heads off about cars, machinery, America and Germany'. But not for long. Back in Berlin for a recital, Yehudi was photographed laying a wreath at the statue of Beethoven in the Tiergarten.

He attended a concert at which Mischa Elman played the Mendelssohn Concerto and confessed in his memoirs that he wished he might be able 'to jump in and play it in his stead: not that [Elman] didn't play it beautifully but in my youthful eagerness – or ignorance – I felt I could play it more beautifully yet'. He also heard Fritz Kreisler in the flesh for the first time. And he finally met Adolf Busch, after a Busch Quartet concert that included music by Beethoven and Reger. He was far too diplomatic to say so, but the teenager Yehudi was obviously mystified by Busch's devotion to Max Reger, a composer who was, he wrote, 'easier to admire than to love; it was like being shown into a library heavy with the works of Kant and Hegel and realizing with failing heart that not until all these volumes had been read and a thesis written could one be considered truly civilized'. Nevertheless an Aria for the G string by Reger was dutifully included in his Carnegie Hall recital the next season.

Adolf Busch himself made a strong and sympathetic impression on his future pupil. He was 'youthful, blond and boyish', Yehudi wrote – at thirty-seven, he was in fact only eighteen months younger than his conductor brother – 'and his face was of such open goodness that it would have melted any prejudice'. After the briefest of auditions it was confirmed that Yehudi would study with Busch that summer. After such a huge success in Berlin (for which he prepared himself without the help of teacher or coach) it could have been argued that he was ready to launch his concert career then and there. All credit to his parents, therefore, and to Yehudi himself, for sticking to the study plan outlined for him by Enesco.

Adolf Busch was such an assiduous concert-giver that he would not be able to start teaching Yehudi at his Basel home until June, so the family had time to take a holiday in Baden-Baden as guests of their new benefactor, the German-born Henry Goldman. He offered them a suite in his hotel but Marutha insisted on sticking to the relatively simple life and they stayed instead in a *pension*. Yehudi's social conscience was too acutely developed for him fully to enjoy the German version of the good life. The spa town was, he wrote, 'excessively coherent' and he took against

the quantities of efficient cheerful maidservants, the eiderdowns in snowy linen covers . . . the ample, delicious fattening foods . . . the evening concerts at the Kursaal and Elena Gerhardt singing Schubert songs . . . I found it all too charming to be quite real . . . the fact that Baden-Baden attracted the retired and the elderly reinforced the impression.

His compensation was a pair of high-powered Zeiss binoculars with which he could observe Baden-Baden's exotically tranquil goings-on.

Paris in May was more familiar territory, although a new concert venue for Yehudi, the Opéra, was both intriguing and lucrative. He played the 'Three Bs' concert a third time, with Philippe Gaubert conducting the Conservatoire Orchestra. Even on short visits, routines still had to be followed. There were ball games in the Bois de Boulogne with his father followed by tea and cakes back home with his sisters and mother.

Moshe had earlier informed the press that Yehudi would be taking ten months out for study after his April concerts in Germany but in mid-May there was a recital in Paris and Moshe announced that Yehudi would make his London début on 10 November, so the ten months had swiftly been whittled down to six. The discrepancy would not be worth noting were it not for Moshe's frequent references to his desire to shield his son from undue exploitation.

The sojourn in Basel that followed made a welcome change from the life of constant travel that had been Yehudi's lot since leaving San Francisco the previous November. For his sisters, now aged only nine and seven and without the goal of concert-giving as a spur, the disruption their brother's professional engagements occasioned must have been a cause for concern. Aware of the danger, Marutha once again took control. Adolf Busch had wanted Yehudi to live *en famille* with his wife and daughter and the pianist Rudolf Serkin, then twenty-six, who was Busch's occasional accompanist. Yehudi would have become another such disciple: the entire day at the Busch home was devoted to music, with informal chamber music in the evenings and the singing of Bach chorales around the table as a nightcap.

Instead the Menuhins opted for family life of their own. They leased a house close to the Busch's, at 12 Gartenstrasse, the middle residence in a block of three covered by a single roof whose eaves sloped down almost to street level. The walls were decorated with flower boxes at every level of the stuccoed façade but the architectural feature Yehudi most enjoyed was a balcony where afternoon tea was taken. On Thursday afternoons they would watch the weekly Graf Zeppelin flight from Buenos Aires heading for its landfall a hundred miles east at Friedrichshafen on the Bodensee – 'an almost silent, vast, silvery cigar shining in the sunlight'. Earlier Yehudi's idol had been the aviator Colonel Lindbergh. By 1930 he had switched allegiance to Admiral Byrd, the balloon-flying explorer of polar landscapes.

Basel was to be the nearest thing to home for the next two years. Yehudi treasured it for its calm. Marutha bought congenial furniture and oriental wall hangings while other precious belongings were sent over in crates from San Francisco. German was now the daily language of the household. It was taught, Yehudi remembered, by an elderly man named Justin Gehrig-Geisst, with whom he read the plays of Schiller and Lessing. He was thirteen. Marutha showed the children how to write German in the old-fashioned Gothic script she herself had learned as a girl. Soon an Italian coach was added, Signorina Anna Contro from Milan, 'a dear good Italian schoolmistress who was in every way voluminous, in size of heart as in garb'. It was from their Italian studies that the family settled on 'Mammina' as the regular name for their mother, no matter which language they were speaking. The children had previously used the Hebrew word 'Imma'. Moshe was still addressed by everybody as 'Aba'.

There were three pianos in the house, and for exercise there was the nearby garden which gave the street its name. As they grew older the children were permitted slight relaxations in their daily routine – 'dissipations', Yehudi calls them, with no hint of irony – but the diversions seem very Swiss in their placidity: 'On Saturdays we would go to the casino to sit at outside tables, hear the band play and watch the dancers.' Closer to Yehudi's heart, perhaps, were the long country walks and the weekend explorations of the neighbouring cantons, undertaken in a big second-hand Packard.

The point of being in Basel was to study with Adolf Busch, and this Yehudi did with total dedication. Indeed his parents had difficulty in stopping him practising. One warm summer's day they pleaded with him to take a break but found him fiddling away in his underpants, determined to master a Bach sonata. Enesco had recommended Busch for discipline. 'You come to each lesson with a different fingering,' Enesco had told his pupil. 'That's very wonderful but if you are going to become an artist you have to settle for something.' Much as he treasured what he called the 'gypsy' element in his playing, Yehudi knew he needed a firm hand. Busch instilled in him the great German violin tradition, of which he had been an exponent since he began teaching at the Berlin Hochschule in 1918.

According to *New Grove* Busch commanded a superb technique but 'disliked showmanship and superficial charm, and concentrated on showing the true qualities of the music with honesty, clarity and intensity'. Among the characteristics of his playing 'were a careful control of vibrato, sparing use of *portamento* and subtle variation in shades of *staccato* and *legato*'. Yehudi said that Enesco left the details of bowing and fingering to his own inclinations and moods. 'Busch, on the other hand, tended to emphasize and supervise the execution of the minutest details, although he did not neglect general characteristics, the spirit and inspiration of a piece.' Enesco never used a metronome during practice; Busch was rarely without it. Writing the following autumn, while on tour in Germany, Yehudi told his mother that from a spiritual standpoint nobody in the world came up to the level of Adolf Busch. 'And as the years go by he can do more and more for me. NOW particularly!' Busch's sensibility, he wrote elsewhere, 'combined scholarship and passion, and was never dry . . . He presented me with German culture . . . without Busch I would not have entered into that spirit which later took me to the depths of the great German composers.'

A review of Yehudi's first New York performance of the Beethoven Concerto had referred to 'overstressed vibrato' and 'over-sentimentalized phrasing when the music becomes strongly emotional'. One can assume that Busch insisted on a more austere approach to whatever was being studied. Yehudi knew this treatment was what he needed and so he persevered for two summers before returning to Enesco's more congenial regime in Paris for the final four years of his youth. One cannot call them his 'apprentice' years, despite the fact that he was still being coached by Busch and Enesco, because the achievement was too substantial. It has even been argued that Yehudi never recaptured the combination of technical flawlessness and spiritual depth that characterized his youthful playing, but close study of his later recordings and concert reviews does not support this simplistic proposition.

Life was not all sweetness and light in Basel. Relations with Mrs Frieda Busch were not entirely friendly. Her husband Adolf was putty in her hands, according to Moshe, and she got off on the wrong foot by telling Moshe that Yehudi and his advisers had been misguided to allow him to play the 'Three Bs' concert before he had received coaching from her Adolf. Then she urged him again to allow Yehudi to live *en famille* while the rest of the Menuhins returned to America: 'Yehudi will learn true *Kultur* and will not develop into a Kreisler or a Heifetz, who have sold their souls to the devil for money. One cannot be a great musician and a great money-maker.' Since the Menuhins were committed to the alternative proposition that you could have your cake and eat it – so long as you did so with due decorum – there was bound to be friction. Frau Busch was a pianist and had been her husband's accompanist until family duties took over. She must have resented the fact that Yehudi already earned at least five times the fee her husband could command. But the Buschs were proud and would accept no payment for the tuition. 'Adolf regards Yehudi as his friend and loves him as a son,' wrote Mrs Busch to Moshe. 'One cannot take money from a friend or a son . . . Herr [Rudolf] Serkin [who was giving piano lessons to Hephzibah] asks me to tell you that he feels the same.' But a few weeks later she suggested that the Menuhins might contribute to a $500 scholarship for a student from London who was studying with Busch. Grumbling privately, Moshe duly coughed up.

The family's expenses had been increased by the need to hire a professional accompanist for Yehudi's lessons as well as the forthcoming tour. At Busch's recommendation Moshe engaged a young pianist from Stuttgart named Hubert Giesen. He lived with the Menuhins and slept up in the attic, next to the maids and the Italian coach. Giesen toured with them for two seasons in Europe and America as well as making several recordings with Yehudi, including the Beethoven D major

Sonata. This was Yehudi's most ambitious recording to date and a work whose pianistic demands would have sorely taxed Louis Persinger, Yehudi's accompanist at both his earlier recording sessions. Giesen was an enthusiastic performer, imbued with such a sense of the dramatic (clearly evident in the Beethoven Sonata), that the sly young Yehudi had occasionally to plead with him to play more softly, 'so that I can accompany you more effectively'.

Moshe felt that 'Hupsie', as they called Giesen, was far from ideal, being 'too romantic and undisciplined and lacking in refinement'. Yehudi was also somewhat equivocal about Giesen, describing him as 'absolutely reliable and firmly within the German tradition, if somewhat inelastic'. He trusted Hupsie's playing, he adds, 'and on the whole enjoyed his company'. But Marutha disliked him so much that she refused to return to America for Yehudi's 1929–30 tour and came with them the following year only after being assured that Giesen would depart as soon as the tour was over. At Sam Franko's suggestion, the young Polish pianist Artur Balsam, who had attended the 'Mayflower concert' was then engaged as the official accompanist. Ten years older than Yehudi, Balsam lived with the family for several years.

After a summer of solid study spent polishing the new repertoire, which included a Bach sonata and the rarely played Dvořák Concerto, Yehudi set off on a new six-month tour. In Hamburg he took time out to visit the zoological gardens, where he was shown a sea-elephant from the South Pole region, weighing 5,500 pounds. 'I watched him eat his lunch', Yehudi noted in a letter published back home in San Francisco.

It consisted of 200 pounds of fish. Then two fat German keepers rode on him to make him take his daily exercise. Oh how I laughed to see the flop made by the massive animal at every step he tried to take!

In Berlin they lived modestly at the Steinplatz *pension*. The lodger in the room next to the Menuhin's was 'invaded twice a day by friends who wanted to listen through the wall to Yehudi practising' – from 8 a.m. till noon and again from 4 to 6 p.m. The report added that he was

a still greater virtuoso with his erector set [presumably Meccano or an equivalent] than on his violin. There he was, building Jewish colonies in Palestine and surrounding the little houses with little lead figures he called *chalutzim* [pioneer settlers].

The most significant German recital was in Munich. In that notoriously anti-Semitic city Yehudi had scheduled Bloch's *Nigun*. He was bombarded by phone messages and telegrams from the local concert promoter urging him to drop such an inflammatory work, but Yehudi stuck to his plans. 'If we give in to this sort of hysteria,' he told his father, 'the next thing we know, they'll be asking me to change my name. I *shall* play *Nigun* and I dare them to throw anything at me.' Moshe reported that his son performed 'with special *élan*, pouring out his heart so powerfully that the entire audience gave him a standing ovation and demanded an encore.'

On 4 November 1929, Yehudi made his London début, playing the Brahms Concerto under the managerial auspices of Lionel Powell, London's most important impresario. His office was divided, Yehudi remembered, into spheres of influence, with each room assigned to a different continent.

As a minor Yehudi had to apply for a London County Council permit to perform in public. He and Moshe stood in line with a crowd of children registering for Christmas pantomime. The venue was the Queen's Hall, the orchestra the London Symphony and the conductor Fritz Busch – the Menuhins had insisted on his being brought over from Dresden after he expressed a great desire to work in England. Little did he dream that less than five years later he would decide to leave Germany and become the Music Director of a new opera house in – of all places – Glyndebourne in Sussex. Instead of repeating the 'Three Bs' programme, Yehudi ceded half the concert to Busch, who conducted the *Egmont* Overture before Yehudi played the Brahms Concerto. The second half comprised Haydn's 'Clock' Symphony and the Prelude to *Die Meistersinger*. A charming photograph shows the diminutive Yehudi, now thirteen and a half, dressed in short trousers and an equally short overcoat, walking arm in arm with a fur-coated Busch past a sentry posted outside Buckingham Palace. Reviewing the concert in *The Sunday Times,* Ernest Newman commented drolly that Yehudi was 'evidently an organism sent into the world for the express purpose of playing the violin as Walter Lindrum was put together for the sole purpose of playing billiards'.

A recital at the Royal Albert Hall the following Sunday, 10 November, attracted an audience of six thousand. The English pianist and accompanist Ivor Newton, another musician who had attended the '*Mayflower* concert' in Berlin the previous April, remembered being press-ganged into turning the pages for Hubert Giesen in the César Franck Sonata, after the man designated for the job lost his nerve in the face of Hupsie's exuberance and the momentousness of the occasion. Afterwards Yehudi presented him with a photograph signed 'To Ivor Newton, page turner to His Majesty Yehudi'. 'What a horrid little boy I must have been!' he commented to Newton many years later.

The recital concluded with an 'astounding' performance of Wieniawski's *Scherzo-tarantelle*, after which the vast crowd in the body of the hall and the several hundred who had been seated on the stage simultaneously made 'a mad surge to get closer to Yehudi. For a space', the *Musical Courier*'s report continued (under the heading 'Menuhin "mobbed" in London'),

it looked as if Yehudi would be engulfed by his ecstatic public. An SOS call brought a squad of firemen. Linking hands they formed a circle about the boy while he smiled and played on. Still insatiable, the crowd kept yelling for more until the lights were put out. A heavy guard about Yehudi had to fight a way for him to the waiting automobile where he boyishly waved goodbye.

Yehudi's sister Yaltah still remembers the panic engendered by such surging crowds: she and her sister would feel a horrifying claustrophobia. Their father seems to have revelled in it, however, and probably provided the copy on which the *Musical Courier* based its eye-witness report.

On the morning after the recital Yehudi and his family were out walking in Hyde Park when a rider dismounted from his horse on Rotten Row and introduced himself as Alexander Howard, a wood merchant. His knowledge of his subject, as Yehudi put it, 'went beyond the demands of commerce into delight in the thing itself'. He showed them round London's monuments and at his home invited them to admire his collection of woods from every part of the globe. 'He was my first example of that amateurism, an elevated interest and pleasure in life, which I count among Britain's most admirable qualities.'

Two days later Yehudi made his first recordings with His Master's Voice, HMV, the English gramophone company with which he was to remain in close association for well over half a century. In America, RCA Victor had opted to concentrate on the production of radio receivers and it transferred its classical music contracts to its English 'sister' company. (Yehudi thought this was a result of the Wall Street Crash, but the policy shift had occurred earlier in the year.) In a single day he recorded Bach's unaccompanied Sonata in C (BWV 1005), the Beethoven Sonata in D, Op. 12 No. 1, and the F major slow movement from Mozart's C major Sonata (K. 296), more than forty-five minutes in all. The Bach was the first work assigned to him by Busch:

It seemed to be the grandest thing for violin imaginable, and I felt I was playing the organ rather than the violin. The *Fugue* is especially immense, and over-whelming in its vast range of expression.

After a transatlantic crossing on the *Minnetonka*, Yehudi began his second American tour on 3 January at a Carnegie Hall 'packed and choked with humanity', as Olin Downes put it in *The Times*. He found Yehudi's development 'impressive but uneven', declaring his Beethoven Sonata to be conventional and ordinary. But Samuel Chotzinoff, writing in the *New York World*, said Yehudi's technique had become 'a smoother machine in the service of a more conscious individuality': he called the Beethoven 'a poetic achievement' and waxed lyrical about the Bach. 'Fugues by Bach are like cathedrals,' he wrote,

sometimes of fearful and mystical complexity. Such a fugue Menuhin intrepidly reconstructed for us last night, with no hint of difficulties overcome, this true *Wunderkind* evoked the ecstasy of the greater Bach and traced for us the long orderly rhapsody, separating the chief argument from its massive ornamentation with the neatness and skill of one who has seen the original plan.

The boy's concert attire was also under review. 'The former Menuhin middy blouse and panties [*sic*] have now given way to a dark coat and trim knickerbockers but the bearing of the sturdy little player remains as childish as ever.' At thirteen he was still not permitted long trousers: that sartorial development was not to come until November 1931.

The tour took in twelve cities and lasted almost four months. (Moshe wrote ten weeks but the last concert, in Portland, was on 19 April.) The itinerary included Cincinnati, Cleveland, Detroit, Chicago, Baltimore, Pittsburgh, Kansas City, Minneapolis, Los Angeles and San Francisco, with a return visit to New York for a 22 February recital attended by Toscanini, who was said to have bought his own ticket. Yehudi had a sore throat and Moshe had been all set to postpone the event until they heard that Toscanini planned to attend. After the concert Yehudi was rewarded with a backstage visit by the Italian maestro, then Principal Conductor of the New York Philharmonic and world renowned for his terrible temper. 'Bravissimo! Yehudi caro!' he shouted in the high-pitched voice that famously made his musicians tremble. 'Bravissimo!' Yehudi said he would like to perform the Brahms or the Beethoven with him. 'That will be a pleasure,' replied the maestro. 'We must arrange it.' And so a long friendship began, although it was another four years before Yehudi got his wish.

Toscanini was exceptionally well paid. In the darkest years of the Depression he still took home $100,000 for his ten weeks in Carnegie Hall. But over a full year Yehudi probably topped him, earning double that amount from his concerts in Europe and the United States. Photograph captions and newspaper headlines built up Yehudi's name in a relentless flow of hyperbole: he was 'The Miracle Boy', 'Uncle Sam's King David of the Violin', 'The Violinist of the Century', even 'The Einstein of the World's Virtuoso Violinists'. He was said to have objected to a banner calling him 'the world's most famous prodigy'. 'A person is either an artist or he is not,' he argued, with all the gravity a thirteen-year-old could muster. 'Age has little to do with it! There is only one standard by which music must be judged – it is either good or bad.'

The tour involved an endless round of publicity interviews and a plethora of 'human interest' stories as they criss-crossed their way across the continent. The accompanist Hubert Giesen garnered good reviews for himself but was miserably homesick and spoke not a word of English. 'Yehudi translates all conversation within earshot into his native German,' Moshe reported. 'He will never leave his friend to mope in his hotel.' Yehudi confided that he loved 'the afternoon hour, when Hupsie and I make chamber music for our own pleasure'. He added tactfully that although he had been learning German in Europe for the past year he was 'after all an American boy, very, very proud of our great country, the wonderful United States of America'.

In Minneapolis he kept people cheerful with his mechanical mouse. 'When everybody is talking at dinner you just wind up the mouse and let it run across the table,' he said gleefully. 'Then you ought to see people jump.' Another newspaper story is tinged with sadness: 'He watched scores of boys sailing iceboats across Lake Harriet. He cannot take part in any of the ordinary sports of boys because of the danger of injuring his hands, which are his fortune.' In Cleveland Yehudi the practical joker reappeared. He saw the conductor Nikolai Sokoloff take a cigarette from a case. 'May I offer you a light?' Yehudi enquired, handing over a trick matchbox he had brought back from Germany. It duly snapped and clattered, reported the *Cleveland News*, 'and Sokoloff jumped. And the Menuhin kid laughed for ten minutes.' In Cincinnati a Jewish publication, *Every Friday*, took note of the name 'Yehudi':

'Every Golus [Diaspora] Jew is attracted subconsciously by the name. It arouses a feeling of hero worship.' Moshe told the paper that he was a direct descendant of the great Hasidic dynasty of Tzemach Tzedek and the Schneersons, adding that the present Lubawitcher Rebbe ('who has recently come to this country from the Soviet Union') was his uncle. Moshe noted proudly that Bloch's *Nigun* 'brings out the Hasidic in Yehudi'. In Detroit a reviewer put it more poetically: 'To hear Yehudi play is to capture forgotten faiths; to remember that there are unseen and mysterious forces operating on the sons of man.'

In March he was greeted like a returning hero by the municipal band at San Francisco's Southern Pacific station. He'd been away fourteen months. He stayed with his father at the Fairmont Hotel, took swimming lessons and attended a marshmallow party in Oakland honouring a rabbi friend of Moshe. Yehudi offered him a round tin box labelled 'Imported Marshmallow'. When the unsuspecting rabbi removed the tin cover

there leaped out on me a three-foot green papier-mâché serpent coiled on springs inside. My sudden start drew from Yehudi a shout of laughter (even though I must have been the hundredth victim).

The Ehrmans were away in England, keeping vigil at the bedside of their mortally sick son. While studying at Cambridge he had been involved in a riding accident from which he never recovered. But Barney, the family chauffeur, was at home and he drove Yehudi, Hupsie and Moshe in the Rolls-Royce to the Yosemite National Park. Yehudi sat in the front, Moshe remembered, talking with Barney about 'driving, traffic, mechanical problems and, undoubtedly, Yehudi's secret inventions'. Unbeknown to his parents he was in correspondence with the US Patents Office about various ideas. 'I like machinery,' he told a reporter on the *Portland Oregonian*. 'I can drive a car real well . . . In California I can drive when I'm fourteen so I want that time to come quickly.' In fact his fourteenth birthday occurred only days later, but he was still trapped in his father's fatuous fiction that he wouldn't be fourteen until January 1931.

He attended a performance of *Das Rheingold* at the San Francisco Opera but the gossip columns suggest that Yehudi enjoyed the more obvious pleasures of being a teenager. At the Oakland marshmallow party a journalist had watched him chatting up a girl who had been a childhood playmate. 'Aren't you going to kiss me?' he asked. 'Not now,' came the reply. 'I will after the concert if you play well on Monday night.' The concert brought nearly seven thousand people to the Civic Auditorium. Two weeks later his presence ensured a sold-out house of eleven thousand when the San Francisco Symphony Orchestra bade farewell to their maestro Alfred Hertz. Yehudi played the Brahms Concerto and followed it up with encores, the concertmaster Michael Piastro turning the pages for Giesen. This time Yehudi did not donate his services to help the cash-strapped musicians. The orchestra made a substantial $2000 dollar profit, nevertheless – even though outgoings were twice as high as for any other concert in the season. The programme booklet reproduced a handwritten farewell tribute from Yehudi:

Dear friend Mr Hertz:
    I feel heartbroken to see you go! You who have done so much for music in San Francisco in general and for me in my early childhood in particular!
    Your loving,
    Yehudi Menuhin.

By May 1930, Yehudi and his father were back in Europe. Marutha and the girls came to Paris from Basel to greet them after a separation of over four months. Still he went on working. His 8 May appearance at the Salle Pleyel drew three and a half thousand listeners. He had been on the road continuously for nearly eight months. In later life he claimed he did not think of it as exploitation: he loved touring and so did his father. 'I looked forward to the open road,' Yehudi wrote in his autobiography. 'The smell of autumn and of steam engines blended in my nostrils into the very breath of the nomadic life.' His concert engagements were widely enough spaced for him to see the sights in each of the great cities he visited – and to meet young people of his own age. 'Every voyage was a voyage of discovery.' That was the way he chose to look at it and he continued to do so for a lifetime.

The second summer of study with Adolf Busch was as fruitful as the first. In July Moshe sent Salter and Evans a news bulletin about his son for distribution to the newspapers and the American promoters whose concerts formed the basis of the family fortune.

With his French master he reads and discusses Montesquieu, Voltaire and Rousseau. With his father he reads English works, general history and likes to solve puzzles in mathematics . . . With Yehudi it's not a matter of poring over things but instantly absorbing them by reading and debating. He scans clippings culled by his father from newspapers, the *Geographic* and the *Scientific American*.

He romps with his dog, plays handball with his little sisters and hikes in the out-doors to his heart's content.

According to Herr Busch, the report added,

Yehudi has grown tremendously . . . His intonation is faultless, his interpretations heavenly. He is self-sustaining and needs no teachers or collaborators. He is his own most rigid teacher and critic.

The family Packard was brought out of storage and used for week-end expeditions, not only around the cantons but further afield, to France, Germany and Italy. One journey, undertaken with the Ehrmans, almost ended in disaster and the story was published in the *San Francisco Examiner*. The car stalled at a level crossing – apparently they had been sold petrol adulterated with water. A lorry pulled them to safety just in time. 'It was not a bootlegger's truck but a cheese-legger's that saved us,' wrote Yehudi. The car stalled again right out-side their Basel house. 'Thanks', said Yehudi to Moshe, after they'd pushed the car into the garage, 'for driving us forty miles in five hours on water and bringing us home on our own power.'

There was a visit to the Bach Festival in Leipzig, and then the sum-mer holidays were to be spent walking in the High Alps. Yehudi was enthusiastic about his new walking boots, which were equipped with spikes in the soles. Moshe had talked earlier of a break until November but on 29 September Yehudi was back in Paris for his first concert of the new season. He told an American reporter that he had had a car race with a train from Basel to Paris. 'We beat the train by half an hour, and I drove more than half the way. And over the Alps, too,' he added with a grin. In October he gave two recitals in Berlin where, according to the *American Hebrew* newspaper (faithfully clipped by Moshe), 'This youthful David apparently dispelled anti-Semitic frenzy with his magical bow.' Thibaud, Elman and the American violinist Albert Spalding were in the audience to hear Yehudi's new programme, which included Mozart's B♭ Sonata (KV. 378), Schubert's *Rondo brillant* in B minor and Viotti's A minor Concerto. The applause went on for forty-five minutes.

For this second big European tour Moshe added Budapest, Geneva and Vienna to the itinerary 'to broaden Yehudi's experience and popularity and to lay the foundations for a worldwide career'. In another new venue, Rome, Yehudi told a reporter that he loved play-ing with great orchestras (he performed the Brahms Concerto with the

Augusteo Orchestra) but 'even more I love to play with other boys'. Moshe claimed that Mussolini himself (a keen amateur violinist) had issued the invitation. He did not attend the concert but he had arranged, Moshe boasted, for the entire family to travel free on the state railway and for them to be exempted from income tax. In Vienna Yehudi's talent was said to be 'overpowering' and one critic cautiously hailed him as 'not merely a discreetly advertised wonder but . . . a rising star'. With his father he visited the workers' handsome new apartments built by the socialist city council. When Karl-Marx Stadt was later bombarded by the Austrian Nazis, 'The memory of the hours we had spent there', Moshe wrote, 'brought Yehudi to personal "spontaneous combustion".'

In Leipzig Yehudi was initiated by no less a colleague than Bruno Walter into the ritual of the rub-down: 'Curiously enough, it had not been my practice to change my shirt after performing until . . . Bruno Walter taught me better, giving me a bottle of his own pine-scented liniment and advising a change of clothes and a rub-down every time.'

The Menuhins then ran into musical prejudice that had nothing to do with the Nazis. When an enthusiastic Gewandhaus audience demanded encores he played music by Debussy and Moszkowski. 'Afterwards,' Moshe reported, 'the old president of that famous hall said, "Herr Menuhin, there is no room in the Gewandhaus for this sort of stuff."' In Budapest the manager wanted Yehudi to drop the Brahms sonata he'd announced, allegedly because of the 'fake' Hungarian dance in its finale. Moshe was also told the public would stone his son if he inflicted on them one of Bach's interminable solo sonatas. All or nothing was Yehudi's reply: the programme went ahead as announced.

In London persecution took a more insidious form. Moshe was served with an income tax demand for £84 8s., arising out of Yehudi's appearances the previous season. The *Daily News* headline read, 'Violin genius has a fiddling lesson'. Yehudi's appearances were received with only qualified rapture. Richard Capell in the *Telegraph* said the Mendelssohn Concerto was 'too fast' and Yehudi 'seemed tired'. At the second concert he was described as 'pale with fatigue after an exhausting day'. Between the concerts he had done more recording for HMV, laying down another twenty minutes of music, most of it in lighter vein than the Bach and Beethoven of the previous year's session. Corelli's *La folia*, arranged by Enesco, and Paganini's *La campanella* were the best-known works, plus shorter pieces by

Monsigny and Rimsky-Korsakov (arranged by his friend Sam Franko) and one of the violin virtuoso's 'stocks-in-trade', as Yehudi described it, the *Perpetuum mobile* by Nováček.

The Menuhin family returned to the United States for Yehudi's 1931 winter tour. They took up residence in New York, occupying a suite on one of the upper floors of the Hotel Ansonia, and between her son's out-of-town trips Marutha again created some sort of family life. She and Moshe were still firmly opposed to Hephzibah and Yaltah following in their brother's footsteps. 'The girls will not prepare for careers,' Moshe had told journalists the previous spring. 'We have concluded that a career is a man's job and one in the family is enough.' Yehudi's new concert venues included Seattle and Pasadena in the west and Boston, Columbus and Rochester in the east. Jewish communities fêted him wherever he went. He was made an honorary member of the Boy Scouts of Troop 63 of Rochester's Temple Beth 'El. In Chicago, where he happened to be playing on his 'official' fourteenth birthday, a rabbi celebrated *bar mitzvah*.

But after his concert a Chicago critic, Herman Devries, expressed stern disappointment. Yehudi's playing had deteriorated, he thought, since his appearance in 1929. He should never have stopped studying with Persinger: 'I feel no longer the thrill he awakened at his first recital.' In New York there had also been critical voices. Oscar Thompson thought Adolf Busch had not helped him to master the Brahms G major Sonata, summing it up as 'small and somewhat unimaginative and monotonous as to treatment'. (The review did not affect Busch's reputation as a performer. Thanks to the Menuhins' recommendation, Toscanini offered him a concerto engagement with the New York Philharmonic, a fact about which Moshe boasted in several interviews.) The critic W. J. Henderson admired Yehudi's tone, referring to beautiful texture and sensuous enchantment, but felt the interpretation of the Brahms lacked depth or solidity. He poured scorn on Kreisler's arrangement of the *Largo* from the 'New World' Symphony, which the programme erroneously labelled a 'Negro Spiritual Melody'.

In San Francisco there was important extra-musical business to be done. On 16 April 1931, just a week short of his fifteenth birthday, Yehudi took his driving test in his own sedan and passed it without dropping a mark. Under a report headed 'Symphony in eight cylinders', the *San Francisco Chronicle* reported that 'Thomas A. Maloney Jr of the State Motor Vehicles Department had examined the boy and no error had occurred while he drove in traffic on Market Street and Van Ness Avenue.' He was asked what he would do if a red-headed girl riding a white horse attempted to take his right of way. (Yehudi's answer was not recorded but he would certainly have yielded to a pretty girl.) He had been driving every day since his return to California. In Los Angeles he and his father had rented a car. They had been presented with a set of automobile maps but preferred to take pot luck: 'Twice a day the gas tank is filled up and off we go, wherever our noses point, in good vagabond fashion.' The newspapers couldn't get enough of this feel-good material. A Hollywood photo opportunity was created: Jackie Coogan and Yehudi were photographed smiling together, the richest boys in the world. Moshe had been boasting to reporters all winter that his son had contracts guaranteeing a mini-mum of $300,000. Yehudi was growing up; the *Los Angeles Times* noted, 'He has added three inches to his stature and in his eyes there is a quest for freedom.' His dress, the inevitable flat cap and an immac-ulate three-piece knickerbocker suit, was still a matter for raised eye-brows. Talking to the press Yehudi tactfully dropped his highbrow allusions to Montesquieu and Rousseau in favour of Mark Twain and Bret Harte. He thought *A Connecticut Yankee at King Arthur's Court* was particularly good:

I never laughed before so hard as I did at that story. I enjoyed *Tom Sawyer* and *Huck Finn* but not as much as I did the *Yankee*. I've read a number of Bret Harte stories. There's a wilderness in life there that we do not see any more. I would like to have known some Bret Harte characters.

Surprisingly, he didn't mention his admiration for the novelist Willa Cather, with whom he developed an unlikely relationship that spring, first in New York and later on the West Coast where she travelled to receive an honorary degree from the University of California. 'Aunt Willa' had become especially close to Marutha. 'She was the most wholesome person I've ever known,' wrote Yehudi, 'crystal-pure and simple, and with a sharp intelligence . . . She had the strength of the American soil which she loved so much and understood so well.'

Yehudi told another press conference that he had travelled fifty thousand miles in the season now coming to an end. The following year, he said, his family would buy a ranch and settle in California. Moshe expanded on the dream, announcing a grandiose three-year plan. Yehudi would return to Europe in May for studies with Enesco and Busch. (They still had their rented house in Basel.) Then he would give a series of three-concerto concerts with twelve of the world's greatest orchestras. Six venues and conductors had already been announced: Hamburg (under Karl Muck, then in his seventies); Berlin (Busch); Leipzig (Walter); Budapest (Dohnányi); Paris (Enesco) and Vienna (Schalk). His summers would henceforth be spent in California, and in 1934 he would undertake a world tour, with India, China and Japan among the destinations.

They returned to Europe on the liner *France*, and made Paris their first destination. At a grand banquet in June, Yehudi was named an honorary member of the association of winners of the coveted Premier Prix du Conservatoire. More importantly he sat next to Nadia Boulanger and a lifetime friendship began, based on their shared love of Bach. In July Moshe announced a complete change of plan, following what he called 'due reflection over our parental duty'. The 'world tour' was postponed (until 1935) and never did include India or the Far East. By then, Hitler had come to power and the grandiose twelve-city concerto festival was scrapped. Yehudi's parents had decided they must sacrifice their own wishes and comforts (as Moshe put it) to the necessities of their growing children, and

whether they want it or not, Yehudi and his sisters are just now at the right age to get out of Europe the utmost of culture, and more and more of the great store-house of treasures in art and music which the Old World offers.

The idea of returning to live in California was shelved. Instead the Menuhins leased a villa outside Paris as their family home. August would be spent on the Italian Riviera, September and October in Basel and then Yehudi's next European tour would begin while the girls stayed with Marutha in Paris.

Neither Yehudi's memoirs nor those of his father offer a clue as what prompted the change of heart but one can assume that an ultimatum from Yehudi was at the bottom of it. He wanted to spend more time with Enesco and less with Busch. In the event, he did return to Basel but only to have his appendix removed by good Swiss surgeons. He seems never to have met Busch again. The village of Ville d'Avray, between Paris and Versailles, became his home for the next three years. It was to prove the most idyllic and arguably the most fruitful period of his entire life.

Recommended Recordings

Beethoven: Sonata No. 1 in D for violin and piano, Op. 12 No. 1
with Hubert Giesen (piano)
BID LAB 032 *The Young Yehudi Menuhin*
Recorded: November 1929
The first record Yehudi made with HMV in London. He had been coached by
Adolf Busch.

Bach: Sonata No. 3 in C for violin solo
BID LAB 032 *The Young Yehudi Menuhin*
Yehudi called this 'one of the seminal works in my musical development'. It was
the first Bach he studied with Busch.

PART TWO
Youth
1931–1941

—Post-Gazette Photo.

Fined by a Finleyville constable for driving through a "stop" sign he could not see, Yehudi Menuhin, 15-year-old concert violinist, who played here Friday, opined yesterday that the business of a constable had possibilities of profit almost as great as that of a concert artist.

Yehudi, who drives on a California license, was at the wheel of an automobile, owned by Mrs. Enoch Rauh, city director of welfare, when he was stopped and fined. He is shown above in the driver's seat, with Miss Helen Rauh, daughter of the welfare director, and his hostess during his visit to Pittsburgh, beside him.

In the driver's seat, 1932

5 Jeunesse dorée

A mid-ocean masterclass with Arturo Toscanini

1931: summer: Residence at Ville d'Avray; appendix operation in Basel; autumn: tour of Europe; YM's first tuxedo; records Bruch G minor Concerto with London Symphony Orchestra; 1932: coaching with Toscanini on board the SS France; records Bach Double Concerto with Enesco; July: records the Elgar Concerto in London; November: plays Elgar Concerto at public concert; November– December: major UK tour; 1933: Elgar visits Paris.

SINCE HIS FIRST APPEARANCE there four years earlier, Yehudi had always loved Paris. 'As a family we were more at ease in French than in German,' he noted in his memoirs, adding that it was his mother who took the snap decision to rent the house found for them by their violinist friend Jan Hambourg: 'She never hesitated about important decisions – she knew what she wanted and recognized it when she found it.' Yehudi described Villa Les Fauvettes, 32 rue Pradier, in the village of Ville d'Avray, as a suburban Petit Trianon, slightly dilapidated but 'a real home', spacious and elegantly proportioned. Behind the house, separated only by a pathway and a wall, was the Parc St Cloud. The villa's main gates were lined with metal sheets to prevent passers-by from peeping in.

The three-storey house was set back from the road amid spacious lawns. The handsome flight of stone steps leading up to the front door was frequently used over the next few years as the backdrop for photocalls with distinguished visitors such as Pierre Monteux, Jacques Thibaud and George Enesco, who came to pay their respects to the family and to make music with the by now world-famous Menuhin children. The music room was on the raised ground floor, as was the dining room. From his wistaria-lined study window on the first floor Yehudi looked out over sloping lawns and mature trees. A higher floor housed his mother's sitting room and the quarters of the Italian staff found for them by the Hambourgs: the cook Bigina was as amply proportioned as her name might suggest while Ferrucio, her slim-built handyman husband – a former jockey according to biographer Magidoff and a professional athlete in Yehudi's memoirs – was a merry fellow who joined his wife in mellifluous operatic arias as they churned the home-made ice-cream, nicknamed 'La-la-la', that was Yehudi's especial delight.

Moshe bought a handsome four-door Delage motor car (right-hand drive, Yehudi remembered) which was used for weekly trips to the market at Les Halles. Money being in plentiful supply, Moshe had five individual valises custom made for 'Mo-Ma-Ye-He-Ya', as the family signed themselves in collective correspondence. The cases fitted snugly on the Delage, Yaltah recalls; two on the roof and three at the back for continental touring. For Yehudi, driving in pre-war Paris was 'a superb game, especially at some great roundabout like the Arc de Triomphe'. After being thwarted in hilly San Francisco, the children finally learned to ride bicycles in the Parc St Cloud, clandestinely borrowing the machines of the family next door until they could prove to their nervous parents that there was no risk to their precious hands. Yehudi presented his parents with a *fait accompli* by cycling up the gravel drive when the whole family was sitting outside preparing for a picnic lunch.

(The neighbours, who owned the Menuhin house, were the Vians, one of whose sons, Boris, rose to post-war fame as a poet and night-club entertainer.) 'We carved out an empire in the neighbouring woods,' Yehudi wrote of their halcyon bicycling days, 'sending our mechanical steeds up mounds and across ditches, learning every crooked bridle path, sailing down broad tracks through the awesomely beautiful cathedrals of the trees'. The tennis star Suzanne Lenglen lived near by. When he was next touring in the US he claimed to like playing tennis with her, though there's no photograph to confirm it. Another neighbour was Edmond Rostand jun., son of the author of *Cyrano de Bergerac*. Yehudi said he felt sorry for the twelve-year-old grandson: 'He's got five tutors; I've only got one, so you see I don't study so hard.'

In fact several part-time tutors were engaged for the Menuhin children. Giuliana del Pelopardi taught Italian, and a refugee from the Bolsheviks, Lozinsky by name, taught Russian, in preparation for a tour of the USSR which was often mooted by Moshe – he told journalists that Moscow was offering $6000 a concert – but which did not materialize until after the war, in 1945. Undoubtedly the most influential instructors were Félix Bertaux and his son Pierre, from nearby Sèvres. They were both Sorbonne professors, German-language scholars and experts in French literature. Hephzibah, eleven, developed a crush on Pierre, who by Yehudi's account was a positive paragon, 'exciting, cultivated, romantic, fiery and witty'. He fought with the Resistance during the war and later became a distinguished civil servant. Moshe Menuhin summed up the somewhat spartan spirit of the months passed at Ville d'Avray:

In the Menuhin family a day's time had to amount to a day's work: progress through lessons, reading, music-making and music practice. One always had to square one's joy of living with growing. It was not a rush to achieve things. Far from it! It was to do interesting things, to learn new things thirstily.

Inevitably music remained the centre of Yehudi's life, even in these more relaxed summer months. Every week he had a long study session with Enesco and on Saturday evenings there was chamber music at home, often running on to past midnight. At one marathon session they were said to have played all fifteen of Beethoven's string quartets, but this report may be an example of Moshe's hyperbole. The violin parts were generally shared between Enesco, Yehudi and another new friend, Jacqueline Salomons, a fellow pupil of Enesco for whom Yehudi confessed to hold 'silently cherished sentimental feelings'. She later married one of Yehudi's accompanists, Marcel Gazelle – according to Yaltah she was forced into the marriage by Marutha's matchmaking activities. Enesco usually played the viola, unless Pierre Monteux was there, and the cellist was Maurice Eisenberg. Hephzibah sometimes joined the group for chamber music involving the piano. She was being taught once again by Marcel Ciampi while Yaltah had lessons from Joaquin Nin-Culmel, son of the Cuban composer Joaquin Nin, brother of the libidinous Anaïs Nin and a pupil of Alfred Cortot. The conductor Nikolai Sokoloff told an American newspaper about an unforgettable musical occasion when he heard the renowned trio of Cortot, Jacques Thibaud and Pablo Casals playing at the Menuhin house in the summer of 1931. On the same evening Hephzibah played a movement from the Schumann Piano Concerto with Cortot accompanying her at the second piano. Marutha once again remarked that she didn't want Hephzibah to become a professional musician. Then, as if to challenge her, Yaltah (only nine at the time) joined in with some Mozart. These evenings of chamber music were very important for Yehudi: 'I have never had enough of it since and visualize an ideal retirement as a member of a string quartet endlessly playing to, for and with each other.' That particular dream did not materialize because he never stopped working. But chamber music figured more largely in his adult professional life than it does for many violin virtuosi, notably in a series of recordings with Casals and others made in Prades in the 1950s, in the nineteenth-century trios he later recorded with his sister Hephzibah and the cellist Maurice Gendron, and in the baroque trio sonatas he recorded with Ambrose Gauntlett and George Malcolm.

In September Yehudi had his appendix removed. He fell ill while in Basel preparing for his autumn recital tour. There was no end to the boy's precociousness, it seemed: 'On the way to the hospital,' reported the *New York Herald*, 'Yehudi asked his father to be sure that his German teacher would bring his favourite book, *Nathan the Wise*'. The *San Francisco Call Bulletin* took a more parochial line: 'YEHUDI UNDER KNIFE ABROAD' was its headline and a lot of fun was had by its columnist following an earlier press report that the surgeon carrying out the operation had compared Yehudi's hands with those of Michelangelo: 'We have written to enquire whether the physician is the same one who treated Michelangelo in his final illness and if so to arrange an interview.' On the operating table Yehudi had been told to think of something beautiful before inhaling the ether used as an anaesthetic.

'Oh,' answered Yehudi, 'I have been thinking all evening of the *Urtext* of Bach I have at home. Bach unedited is so perfect, so satisfying, so . . .' And he fell asleep with happiness while the surgeons removed his appendix.

Engagements for October 1931 had to be cancelled but by November he was back on course in London. On 23 November he played the Beethoven Concerto at the Queen's Hall, accompanied – 'with most reverent care', according to *The Times* – by the London Symphony Orchestra under Sir Thomas Beecham:

It is hard to know what to praise most in his playing: the dead accuracy of intonation, which yet does not restrict in coldness of tone, the virile rhythms, the flexibility of phrasing and the evident musical understanding . . . The cadenza to the first movement was the most astonishing moment of all, for Master Menuhin justified, to an extent we have rarely experienced, the display of virtuosity.

The *Daily Sketch* reported he took forty bows after the performance. Sartorially speaking, this was a landmark concert; it was the first time Yehudi performed in long trousers. Aged fifteen, he wore a tuxedo with a soft shirt collar and a small black tie.

Three days later Yehudi made his first recording of a violin concerto. Not the Beethoven, unfortunately, which he didn't record until 1947 (with Wilhelm Furtwängler) but Max Bruch's Concerto No. 1 in G minor, a work he had studied with Persinger in 1928 and played in recital in San Francisco but had never performed with an orchestra. Sir Landon Ronald, then in his late fifties, was the conductor. Ronald had been HMV's adviser since its inception thirty-one years earlier and was an excellent accompanist. With the London Symphony Orchestra in fine form the recording is a splendid example of what might be dubbed 'First Period' Menuhin.

Marutha wanted to keep an eye on Yehudi during his convalescence so the entire family was travelling once again. The popular newspapers were encouraged to emphasize the human angle. The children spent a morning looking for a fox terrier to present to Yehudi's idol Fritz Kreisler and it can have been no coincidence that the animal with which they were eventually photographed looked exactly like Nipper, the dog in the famous Barraud painting who listens in fascination to his master's voice emanating from a gramophone horn. To the London gossip writers Moshe trotted out his customary economies with the truth:

I allow him to play in public for five months only in the year and I try to make each concert a big event for him. In this way I am doing my best to preserve his genius.

And also, it has to be said, to make a lot of money.

Yehudi's 'farewell' concert, for which Moshe had negotiated the huge fee of £2,500, was at the Royal Albert Hall. A London 'pea-souper' fog didn't deter nearly seven thousand people from attending, packed so tightly on the platform itself that only a thin strip remained at the front for the performers. The Menuhin family looked on from one of the boxes. Afterwards

the two small fair-haired sisters clung happily to him as they made their way to the waiting car. The boy himself seemed the freshest of the party. He was posing and smiling, satisfied scores of autograph hunters and shook hands all round.

The reviews, however, were sceptical in tone: his recent illness may well have contributed to a less than compelling performance. Ferruccio Bonavia in the *Daily Telegraph* was scathing: 'The "Kreutzer" Sonata appeared to mean no more to him than the *Ronde des lutins*'; the slow movement of the Bruch Concerto 'lacked quiet charm and intimacy'. (But what did Bonavia expect in the cavernous Albert Hall?) 'More of an exhibition than an interpretation,' grumbled the *Evening News*. But Yehudi's powers of recovery were astonishing. Only three days later he was enjoying new triumphs in Europe. With Bruno Walter conducting, he played the Beethoven and Mendelssohn Concertos at the Leipzig Gewandhaus. Two of Mendelssohn's grandchildren were in the audience, along with the Director of J. S. Bach's Thomaskirche. After the performance, Moshe related, Bruno Walter stood in the wings as Yehudi took twenty curtain calls, exclaiming with his hand on his heart: 'Miracle! Godly! Genius!'

A few days later, in Brussels, Queen Elisabeth of the Belgians sent word during the interval that she would like Yehudi to visit her in her *loge*. Well trained by Marutha, Moshe declined. Yehudi had a cold and he would not interrupt the alcohol rub *à la* Bruno Walter that he was about to administer. 'As I was taking Yehudi's shirt off . . . [the Queen] came in, apologized for her request and insisted on helping me to rub down Yehudi.' Toscanini was to claim a similar *droit de seigneur* when he attended Yehudi's début recital in Milan.

At the Salle Pleyel in Paris Yehudi played the Bach Double Concerto for the first time, with Enesco as his partner and their friend Monteux conducting, as part of a concerto triple-bill that included the Beethoven Concerto and what at the time seems to have been Yehudi's favourite Mozart concerto, K.271A – despite its unreliable provenance. Moshe boasted that no fewer than seven Paris concertmasters were playing in the string section of the orchestra. The Bach was particularly well received and Fred Gaisberg of HMV nominated it immediately for a recording in Paris the following June. His company had recently merged with its leading rival, Columbia, and as the self-effacing but all-powerful Artistic Director for EMI (Electrical and Musical Industries) Gaisberg had an almost infallible instinct for what would sell well and have a long shelf life. 'At one moment' – the observation is that of his successor, David Bicknell – 'Yehudi was unknown, and a moment later Fred was producing a steady stream of records which matched and sustained Yehudi's rapidly expanding career.'

The last two concerts of the European tour were given in Rome and on 7 January Yehudi and his father departed from Naples on the *Conte Biancomano*, bound for New York and a fourteen-city tour of the United States. Moshe did the unforgivable and forgot his wife's birthday on the day of his departure. According to Yehudi, Moshe attributed her stony mood to their imminent separation rather than to his forgetfulness – but the fact that Yehudi did not give his father a nudge at the time suggests that he, too, had been forgetful, perhaps because the family had played fast and loose for so long with the date of his own birthday.

New York in January 1932 was in the throes of the Depression. Naturally Yehudi made a sightseeing trip to the top of the newly completed Empire State Building. But he also worried about the poverty he witnessed and sent a $500 cheque to the Musicians' Emergency Aid Committee. 'It breaks my heart', he wrote,

to see the horrible misery and helplessness of legitimate musicians who find themselves out of work and unprotected in this sorry world. During the short time since we arrived from Europe, we hear and see more misery here than we have observed during our entire tour of two months in the big capitals of Europe. What is wrong with our great and rich country? Oh I wish there was more justice in this inhuman or rather stupid world.

The Carnegie Hall recital on 23 January was Yehudi's first US appearance in long trousers, something the *Times* critic Olin Downes had campaigned for in earlier seasons. 'Menuhin has graduated', Downes wrote, 'from the ranks of *Wunderkinder*. He can make a commonplace phrase golden. His technic is much more dazzling than before. Yesterday he set at rest those who were sceptical about his lasting qualities of growth.' The programme was a good one: Schumann's

Violin Sonata in D minor, Bach's Sonata in A minor (BWV 1003), and Ravel's *Tzigane*. Moshe noted that Yehudi had given more than a dozen recitals in New York and never repeated himself – adding mysteriously that his son had recently been offered a six-figure sum for unspecified work that was 'not in keeping with his best development'. The American press always brought out the worst in Moshe: 'Would I sell my daughter for prostitition? No! Then would I sell my son's art for prostitution? No!' One wonders what type of night-club proposition prompted this outburst of self-righteousness.

Touring in America in deepest winter can't have been any easier for Yehudi as a fifteen-year-old than in previous years. The distances were as gruelling as ever. The venues included Akron, Boston, Houston, Montreal, New Orleans and Richmond, Virginia, where he played his Stradivarius in Thomas Jefferson's study (at nearby Monticello) using the President's own music stand. In Atlanta the auditorium proved an embarrassment to the *Atlanta Journal*: 'Great music was spoiled by clanking steam radiators, soft-drink vendors, inadequate and poorly controlled lights and extreme cold because of an inefficient heating system.' Through a thin partition wall came the noise of seven hundred part-time national guardsmen doing their drill exercises. It was not, one imagines, a happy evening for Yehudi: 'The boy's eyes blazed and his face grew red.'

In Minneapolis the critic John K. Sherman analysed the elements of Menuhin's technique: his tone had fibre, his bow mercurial agility and his left hand suppleness and accuracy. It added up to 'nothing short of true genius'. Another perceptive reviewer, Thomas B. Sherman of St Louis, noted that 'in one upstroke of his bow things would happen – subtle expansion of volume and differentiation of character – that in a second adumbrated his vision of the whole composition'. Toronto's *Daily Star* summed up Yehudi's charisma succinctly: 'crowd huge, enthusiasm enormous, program titanic'. The *Pittsburgh Press* called him 'the transcendent genius of the century'.

More mundanely, it was in Pittsburgh that Yehudi collected his first motoring ticket – $8.50 – for driving through a stop sign which he inevitably claimed was 'almost invisible'. Prevented by his parents' caution from travelling by aeroplane, he discovered a new speed sensation on a long-distance train journey from St Louis. A friendly engineer invited him to take over in the driver's cab.

Grasping the throttle, Yehudi experienced the elation of driving a monster engine at the rate of 40 [*sic*] miles an hour. Wind rushed in his face; cinders rained. 'Can't we go faster?' demanded the boy. The engineer burst out laughing. Here was a kid after his own heart. The train leaped forward at a rate of 50 miles an hour. For two and a half hours Yehudi ran the train and rang the engine bell, the latter perhaps oftener than was absolutely necessary.

At fifteen Yehudi was a little old for such escapades but his publicists were still clearly capitalizing on his youth as most of the photographs used to illustrate such agency stories were of a significantly younger Yehudi.

In truth, puberty had finally caught up with him. He still did not need to shave but in San Francisco it was noticed that his voice had broken. It was now – a week short of his sixteenth birthday – 'a slightly crackly baritone'. Moshe grumbled that none of Yehudi's clothes fitted, adding that his son had grown four inches in a year and he couldn't find stockings for him. For normal outdoor wear he still dressed in what were described as golf knickers with a cap and a short tan over-coat. Conventional long trousers were mostly reserved for the concert platform. Yehudi was interviewed by a fanciful reporter in San Francisco who described Moshe as an 'elderly satyr instructing his precocious son in the wiles of forest and brook'. There were mocking references to the father's constant supervision. 'Who selects your reading?' Yehudi was asked. (That spring it included *Crime and Punishment*.) 'My father,' came the reply.

Musically the highlight of the 1932 winter tour was a performance of the Brahms Concerto with the New York Philharmonic conducted by Bruno Walter. Four days before the concert a recital at the same venue, Carnegie Hall, had clearly been a disappointment. The *Herald Tribune* found Yehudi's playing to be in a 'transitional' state and its critic Francis Perkins noted 'some loss in the consistent clarity and polish of tone which had marked [his work] two or three seasons ago'. But by the end of the first movement of the concerto performance, on 18 February, all reservations had been swept away. 'There was a roar from the whole assembly', wrote W. J. Henderson in the *New York Sun*. 'All perceived that something above the extraordinary had occurred . . . the boy has arrived', revealing 'a breadth, depth and feeling which he had not shown before. It was no longer external but from within.'

The marked improvement in his playing from one event to the next, four days later, can surely be put down to the renewed partnership with Bruno Walter. The previous year, Walter had had the same influence in Leipzig after Yehudi's disappointing recital in London. Olin Downes was in no doubt:

Menuhin seemed to gain added authority and power from Walter's mastery . . . from the moment Menuhin's bow gripped the strings he played with a conquering authority and inspiration. The second entrance of the solo instrument was just as impressive as the first, in a wholly different vein of dark and rich colour. The soloist had not merely his own part but the whole score as thoroughly in his consciousness as the conductor [had].

But there was another factor at work in New York. Yehudi's father added an explanatory gloss to Downes's glowing account. George Enesco was in New York and naturally he attended his pupil's morning rehearsal.

He followed Yehudi and me to our hotel and put it plainly: 'That was not the way to play the Brahms Concerto, my dear Yehudi! You cannot play it like that tonight! We must go over the whole work.'

When Yehudi reminded him that they were all expected at a reception he got a brusque rejoinder: 'I don't care whether we eat lunch or not.' And they worked on the Concerto all afternoon.

Yehudi remembered the episode rather differently. After the rehearsal he was due to have lunch with Esther, the daughter of his benefactor Sidney Ehrman, the girl he had worshipped when he was a boy in San Francisco.

She was by then married to the dashing young Claude Lazard and expecting their first child – yet none the less [she was] my Dulcinea – and distracted by this appointment, fearing I would be late for it, I took the last movement far too quickly, losing all vigour and tension. There could be no question of leaving matters in this unsatisfactory state, Enesco admonished me; the movement must be put right for the evening. I recall telling him that the lady with whom I was to lunch was pregnant; his chivalry perfectly comprehended my concern. 'Ah! That is the most sacred condition of woman,' he said. Nevertheless my duty to Brahms came first.

Enesco's link with Brahms went back to Vienna where he played the First Symphony in a student orchestra conducted by the composer.

On 30 April, Yehudi and and his father sailed for Europe on the SS *Ile de France*. Moshe had negotiated an exclusivity deal, similar to those that prominent musicians arrange with the manufacturers of grand pianos, whereby the Menuhins would always cross the Atlantic on a vessel of the French Line (Compagnie Générale Transatlantique). Among their fellow passengers was Arturo Toscanini. 'We are having an ideal crossing', Moshe cabled excitedly to a London friend,

exhilarated spiritually even more than physically, for Yehudi's life dream has come true. Daily he and I spend hours with Toscanini making music and discussing the classics in a friendly, intimate atmosphere . . . They have decided to make music daily from 11 a.m. to 1 or 2 o'clock. From the beginning the boy insisted, 'Please, maestro, criticize me right and left without hesitation; these will be my most precious lessons', to which Toscanini reportedly replied, 'You don't know how to make a mistake! Just go on playing!'

With Arthur Balsam on hand for the accompaniments, Yehudi gave him Bach, Mozart, Beethoven and Brahms. 'Oh, how little good music I hear in my life!' the maestro was said to have exclaimed. He was subsequently introduced to Mozart's K. 271A and according to Moshe got more and more excited as he turned the pages for Balsam: 'Wonderful, it's true Mozart! Mozart at his best!' Moshe said later that it was 'an atmosphere of activity, feverish work and intense enthusiasm'.

On the last evening of the voyage Yehudi and Balsam gave a benefit concert for the ship's crew. Moshe was so impressed by this episode that he stuck more than seventy different press cuttings about it into his giant scrapbook, all recounting that Yehudi had made only one stipulation: the recital must be open to all classes on the ship. Toscanini was in charge of the box office and a sufficient number of well-heeled passengers attended for the 'take' to be over 40,000 francs (about $1,500). Moshe developed his own friendship with the maestro. 'They walked the deck together,' Yehudi recalled, 'and my father learned how Toscanini devised his season in New York so as not to earn too much within a single tax year.'

Yehudi's 1932 Paris spring saw a remarkable burst of studio activity. He admired Fred Gaisberg and his HMV engineers, who thought nothing of taking the car ferry across from England and setting up their bulky equipment in the Salle Pleyel. Over three dates in late May they recorded Tartini's 'Devil's Trill' Sonata, the Schubert *Ave Maria* and Ravel's *Tzigane,* as well as popular encores by Wieniawski, Moszkowski, Rimsky-Korsakov, Kreisler, Falla and Debussy. June 4 saw an exceptionally productive day's work for both recording team and musicians during which the Bach Double Concerto was performed by Menuhin and Enesco with Monteux conducting, as well as the *Andante* from Bach's unaccompanied A minor Sonata. For the session

Yehudi borrowed the Guarnerius violin that had belonged to Ysaÿe, reportedly because the 'Prince Khevenhüller' was 'sick' and needed some minor repairs. Ysaÿe died in May 1931. Yehudi loved the instrument: 'There was no effort on my part. I had just to hold the violin and it seemed to perform by itself.' (It is possible that Yehudi also used the Guarnerius for his famous recording of the Bach 'Double'.) Three days later Enesco conducted Yehudi in Mozart's K.271A. (The contract with HMV stipulated Enesco as conductor whenever he was available.)

When the record came out later in the year the English critic A. H. Fox-Strangways lauded Yehudi's smooth trills, 'his unforced G string, his minimum of vibrato, his un-dragged up-bow, his middle-of-the-note everywhere'. The Concerto's provenance continued to worry the experts. Sir Thomas Beecham thought Michael Haydn had a hand in its composition. But Neville Cardus in the *Manchester Guardian* had no reservations. It is, he wrote, 'a bonny work, proud of carriage, and full of harmonies that go to the heart and stay there'. Yehudi's performance was 'pure in line but vital and spontaneous in rhythm'.

Gaisberg had even bigger fish to fry. Since 1925 he had been trying without success to persuade Fritz Kreisler, its dedicatee, to record Elgar's Violin Concerto. This was the last major work of Elgar's still not recorded by HMV. The company's new Abbey Road Studio 1 had been inaugurated the previous November with Elgar's symphonic poem *Falstaff*. Gaisberg decided to take a gamble on young Yehudi – who had never played the work but was evidently an intuitive stylist with tremendous sales appeal. Publicly, Gaisberg could not place the emphasis on such a commercial consideration. In his memoirs he wrote that

as a youthful and pliant performer without prejudice who would respond best to Elgar's instructions, I selected Yehudi Menuhin as the most promising soloist. I posted him the music with a letter asking him to prepare it for recording, and promised him that Sir Edward would coach him and conduct the records in person. Also I suggested that he should include the Concerto in an Albert Hall Sunday concert programme with Sir Edward in charge of the orchestra.

Yehudi had never heard a note of Elgar's, let alone the Concerto, which is one of the longest and the most taxing in the repertoire. Moshe reported that Yehudi was beside himself with excitement when he received the score and claimed to remember his son's exact words:

'Father, this Concerto belongs to the masterpieces; it is great stuff, I love it. I am just crazy about its many lovely melodies. They haunt me.'

The themes filled the air around our forest walks and all the members of the family, even our Italian valet and his wife, were whistling bits from it while washing dishes and cleaning furniture; the gardener always gave us the slow movement.

Despite its mighty proportions the Concerto was quickly learned and submitted to George Enesco for comment. He didn't know the work either but he had an instinctive feel for the music: Yehudi remembered in particular his response to the broad second subject in the first movement (the melody over which Elgar was later to pencil in the score the syllables 'YE-HU-DI ME-NU-HIN'). 'You're not playing it the right way,' Enesco said to his pupil. 'It's so very English.' By which he meant, according to Yehudi, a combination of innocence and ecstasy.

Despite the rich orchestration – trombones and tuba are called for, where Beethoven and Brahms use only trumpets [in their violin concertos] – it mustn't be heavy or sentimental. The climaxes must never be hard. No other composer writes *fortissimo dolce*.

On Friday, 8 July, Yehudi and his father were met at Dover by their English manager Harold Holt, who had taken over the concert agency after Lionel Powell's sudden death the previous autumn. Holt drove them up to London in an ancient Rolls-Royce, much admired by Yehudi, and installed them in what had become their favourite hotel, the Grosvenor House in Mayfair. (Yehudi was barred from entering its dining room because, even though he was sixteen, he still sported short trousers.) Three days had been set aside for coaching. The celebrated accompanist Ivor Newton was hired to go through the Concerto the next morning in preparation for the first rehearsal with Sir Edward. For anybody else this would have been a daunting assignment: the recording of a major contemporary work (composed twenty-one years previously, in 1911) under the guidance of its creator, a work that was uncharted territory for Yehudi. He came through the ordeal triumphantly.

The great man had celebrated his seventy-fifth birthday the month before. When he arrived at 2 o'clock – Yehudi was very specific about the hour – he seemed far more venerable than the prophet-like Bloch or the chivalrous Enesco, the two composers Yehudi already knew. Yehudi and his pianist began to play the first movement through. But before Yehudi had even reached the second subject, the 'English' theme on which he and Enesco had worked so hard, the composer stopped him. In a frequently quoted passage in his memoirs, Yehudi wrote of his astonishment at Elgar's reaction. 'He was sure, he said, that the recording would go beautifully and meanwhile if we would excuse him, he was off to the races!' If the audition did indeed begin at 2 p.m., one is permitted to wonder which race meeting Sir Edward had it in mind to attend. He might conceivably have reached Kempton Park in time for the three thirty.

Moshe can be relied on, as always, to recall verbatim a more substantial conversation. In his account, Elgar

arose with great excitement, embraced Yehudi, and exclaimed, 'It is better than I ever heard it. Play no more. I know the recording will be wonderful. Just play it as you have prepared it. Now, let's go out on the town, to the races, anything.'

According to Fred Gaisberg's memoirs, which must be hearsay, Elgar said:

I can add nothing . . . You need not work on it any longer, and let's go to the races instead. It's a fine day and I shall show you something of London.

The details may vary in the telling but this is surely one of the best-known anecdotes in musical history. Yet the accompanist Ivor Newton gave a radically different version in his autobiography, lacing it with sufficient circumstantial detail to make his account the authoritative one:

We played right through the Concerto except for the *tutti*s, [then] Menuhin and Elgar discussed the music like equals, but with great courtesy and lack of self-consciousness on the boy's part . . . There is a point at the beginning of the finale where a passage of rushing semi-quavers from the soloist goes into octaves which are extremely hard to manage neatly.
   'Can I make a slight *rallentando* where I go into the octaves?' the soloist asked.
   'No,' replied the composer. 'No *rallentando*; the music must rush on.'
   'If you want it to rush on, why did you put it into octaves?' asked Yehudi.

Eventually, Newton reports, Moshe invited everybody to lunch. (So the rehearsal took place in the morning, not at 2 p.m.)

Elgar, whose secret vice was a love of racing, claimed an important appointment at Newmarket and departed.

Moshe, too, had other engagements after lunch so Newton was left to entertain Yehudi

as if he were a young prince.
   'He must not be left alone,' his father declared, obviously fearing goodness knows what injury to the boy's hands or the even worse scrapes that a high-spirited youngster might find tempting.

'Perhaps you'd like to go through the Concerto again?' I suggested.
'Oh no,' said Yehudi with great decision. 'There's no need for that.'

So they walked across Hyde Park with the intention of visiting the Science Museum in Kensington. But the sight of the boats on the Serpentine was too tempting and Newton spent an athletic afternoon paddling his precious protégé round the lake while Yehudi steered, 'often into a passing rowing boat from which he would look innocently away when we knew that impact was inevitable'.

Yehudi's friendship with Elgar was cemented a few days later with the recording sessions at Abbey Road. They lasted only a day and a half (14–15 July) – good going for a work of that length – and Sir Edward, an experienced studio man, couldn't have been kinder. 'All was ease and equanimity,' wrote Yehudi, 'almost as if his presence and movements were superfluous [of course they were not]. He was a figure of great dignity but without a shred of self-importance.'

A session photograph conveys the atmosphere well: Elgar stands on a high rostrum like the captain on the bridge of an ocean liner. Yehudi appears very chic in white flannels and a short V-necked pullover with a kerchief at his neck. Despite the fact that the music had to be recorded in short sections the studio was crowded with visitors. What a sense of privilege they must have felt to be allowed to sit in on what proved to be one of the greatest recordings of the century.

Later that summer – the last before the Nazis' accession to power in 1933 – Moshe and Yehudi drove to Salzburg to attend the annual Mozart Festival. Enesco had taught his pupil that Mozart's music was

essentially a music of syllable and gesture; when I saw it presented dramatically and could visualize the situation behind each phrase, I would understand that even his orchestral and chamber works were built on human drama and would play (or mime) it very much better . . . We had a marvellous time [in Salzburg] with sung Masses in the morning, operas in the evening and between times picnics in the mountains.

In later life he was to conduct most of Mozart's operas. Moshe remembered the trip for a less idyllic reason. Fritz Kreisler's wife criticized his choice of car: 'My husband has a long career behind him,' she told him, 'but he cannot afford to drive in a big Packard as you do. We drive only in a Ford.'

Summer holidays were Marutha's domain. At Ospedaletti, on the Italian Riviera close to San Remo, they spent their time swimming, sunbathing, reading, competing as to who could eat the most figs, walking in the hills or driving on the *corniches*. On the beach, Moshe tells us, ever anxious to underline his educational endeavours, the children read Dante's *Divine Comedy*, in the original Italian. At the end of the holiday they drove up to Sils Maria in the Swiss Engadine for ten days of mountain air and alpine hikes: it was a recipe for good health.

In September 1932 Moshe filed a report to his English agent Harold Holt: 'Yehudi has progressed musically in the course of the past year tenfold! How has his art ripened? . . . Through our regular principled procedure.' He singled out the sea crossing with Toscanini as a vital episode. It lasted only six days but 'He couldn't have learned the same from anybody else in two months.'

In November 1932, the second stage of Gaisberg's Elgar project proved a tremendous success when the Violin Concerto was given a public performance on the 20th at the Royal Albert Hall, again with the London Symphony Orchestra under the composer. It was the climax of a concert in which Yehudi played concertos by Bach and Mozart in the first half, conducted by Sir Thomas Beecham and described as 'sheer perfection'. With Ramsay MacDonald, the Prime Minister, in the audience, the occasion was like a state tribute – not only to old Elgar, but to young Yehudi as well. 'English music for once really rose to the occasion,' wrote Francis Toye in the *Morning Post*.

We offered him as collaborators our best orchestra, our most famous conductor, our leading composer. Indeed there was something touching in the spectacle of the veteran Elgar conducting his lovely concerto [sitting down, on a red velvet stool] with this boy of genius by his side.

At the end, the *New York Times* reported, the two men stood clasping hands: 'Each thought the cheers were intended for the other. Finally Menuhin pushed Sir Edward on to the stage ahead of him.'

Among the reviewers, only Ernest Newman chose to carp, suggesting perversely that Yehudi played too beautifully and sounded too rich and sensuous, to such a degree that the Concerto was 'robbed of its English reserve and austerity'. Elgar told his friend Neville Cardus that he didn't agree:

This is how I heard the slow movement when I was composing it. Why does Ernest Newman object that Menuhin makes the second subject of the first movement lovely and luscious – it is a lovely and luscious theme, isn't it? Austerity be damned! I am not an austere man, am I?

The composer also despatched a letter of gratitude to Fred Gaisberg:

I shd. be an ungrateful person if I did not at once send hearty thanks to you, who are really the cause of it all, for bringing about the wonderful performance. Yehudi was marvellous & I am sure would never have heard of the Concerto if you had not set the thing in motion.

To Moshe, Elgar confided that he was

overcome by the 'majesty' of Yehudi's playing. His tender and affectionate candour to me (this I prize perhaps more than anything) . . . are very happy memories.

In December, after Yehudi had given a recital in Birmingham as part of a two-month tour of the United Kingdom, the Menuhins went to dinner with Sir Edward at his home in nearby Worcester. 'We sat down,' Moshe remembered, 'with Marco and Mina, Sir Edward's beloved dogs. Each had a chair on either side of their master and they ate out of his hand.'

A plan was devised to repeat the performance of Elgar's Concerto in Paris the following spring. In a letter to Moshe, the old man was sceptical:

I fear my appearance in Paris might do more harm to you than good. The attitude of the press I feel sure would be that dear Yehudi was making a mistake in appearing with a musician of very inferior calibre (me).

The Menuhins refused to let him back out. Enesco had already been invited to conduct the concert but Yehudi persuaded him to stand down in the second half so Elgar could be in charge of his own work.

According to both Moshe and Fred Gaisberg the event proved to be a highlight of the Paris spring season in 1933, with politicians and diplomats thronging the Salle Pleyel. But first, during the winter, Yehudi had to earn the family's bread and butter playing concerts in the United Kingdom and Europe as well as undertaking his annual tour of North America.

In October 1932, before his London concert with Elgar, he had appeared in Berlin, in what proved to be his last visit to Germany for thirteen years. Herbert Klein, an American journalist working in Berlin, went walking with him in the Tiergarten. Yehudi told him he was not impressed by musical taste in Leipzig, where the audience had encored fripperies. He was probably referring to the contretemps Moshe had had with the manager of the Gewandhaus (see page 112). German audiences were in general too 'set' in their tastes, he added, while Italians were 'noisy and indiscriminate'. Amsterdam's was 'the only really intelligent audience in Europe' – but this was before the tumultuous applause he received for the Elgar Concerto in the Royal Albert Hall.

After London, came the British 'provinces': the Birmingham concert mentioned above prompted a prophetic review, signed 'CFM', in the *Birmingham Mail*: 'His human frailty seemed only to be shown in his bow arm, for his left hand seemed impeccable.' A weak bowing arm – allowing the bow to bounce out of control on the strings – is what let Menuhin down increasingly in his sixties and seventies.

Among the other cities visited were Dundee, Glasgow, Edinburgh, Bristol, Manchester, Sheffield and Liverpool. According to his British press release, the hyperbole of which suggests it was dictated by Moshe, Yehudi had forty-eight concertos in his repertoire, as well as 'twelve Bach sonatas, all of Beethoven, Brahms, Schubert, Schumann, Mozart and a host of others'. But apart from the Elgar Concerto, which he subsequently included in recitals, there was as yet very little twentieth-century music: a Pizzetti sonata, short works by Szymanowski and Bloch, Ravel's 1924 *Tzigane* and one of Enesco's sonatas. He was to make up for this neglect in the decades to come, most notably by championing the violin works of Béla Bartók, among them the Sonata for unaccompanied violin which he commissioned in 1943.

As the distances involved were much shorter than in the US, Moshe's much vaunted policy of allowing Yehudi to give only one concert a week was tacitly shelved for the busy British tour. Three days after appearing in Liverpool, where a local critic described him as having 'the head of a man on boy's shoulders, a powerful intellectual head, with beautifully formed features of great sensitiveness', Yehudi was playing in Paris with a once and future prime minister, Edouard Herriot, in his audience. He played in Milan three days after that; in the interval of his recital, Toscanini performed the ritual of the alcoholic rub-down. According to Moshe, the maestro had cut short a stay in Berlin in order to welcome Yehudi and his father and show them round the boulevards of his adopted city. The maestro stayed backstage throughout the evening, sending Yehudi out and receiving him back, applauding and cheering as loudly as his Italian blood dictated, wiping Yehudi's forehead, holding his fiddle, urging him on stage again and again for extra curtain calls, completely replacing Yehudi's father, and indeed muttering to himself in a stage whisper, 'Tonight I am Papa!'

Toscanini also hosted a banquet to honour Yehudi, and before parting whispered to Yehudi, 'We simply must play together next season in New York.' And so it came to pass, thirteen months later, on Yehudi's 'official' birthday, 22 January 1934.

In Florence on Christmas Day, Vittorio Gui conducted his recently formed Maggio Musicale orchestra with Yehudi playing concertos by Mozart and Beethoven. Then it was off to the New World by boat from Genoa. The family cook, Ferruccio, travelled with them to prepare special food for Moshe, who had been suffering increasingly acute gall-bladder pain. Yaltah recalls that he kept a collection of kidney stones in a glass jar at home. At the end of January he took to his bed at the Hotel Ansonia in New York and Marutha and the girls accompanied Yehudi to Philadelphia, ordering a Steinway into their hotel for piano practice and hiring a young lady to read Shakespeare to them. Described as 'slight, nervous and good-looking', Marutha took over her husband's publicist role in her own inimitable style. She told the *Philadelphia Record* that she wanted Yehudi 'to be a fine man, good in health and character. Then, if he wants, he can be a musician.'

Yehudi's touring continued through February, overshadowed by his father's illness. Gall-bladder operations were dangerous affairs and Moshe had been putting off his for years. He recovered sufficiently to resume his tour-managing duties as far as Louisville, Kentucky, but when they returned to New York, Yehudi spent a sleepless night writing out a memorandum on the Ansonia's notepaper. It was headed IT MUST BE DONE!!! On the left-hand side he listed six solid reasons for an operation; on the right side, under the heading AGAINST, there were six zeros. Moshe hesitated no longer and booked his operation at the Lenox Hill hospital for 4 March, the very day that Franklin Delano Roosevelt was inaugurated as President and made his famous speech to a nation in crisis: 'The only thing we have to fear is fear itself.' The previous day Moshe had deposited $5000 dollars in the Fifth Avenue Bank for Marutha to draw on while he was in hospital. When he learned next morning that his bank had been forced to close because the nation was on the point of going bankrupt, he requested postponement of the operation until he could read the new President's inaugural statement. Then, reassured, he submitted to the surgeon's knife.

The operation was successful and he was back on the road three weeks later. A memorandum he prepared to cover his period of absence provides a useful insight into Yehudi's working conditions:

Your career is going to be 100 per cent in your hands . . . It will be an interesting experience for you during the next few weeks of not only taking care of yourself but also showing how serious, responsible and reliable you are in caring for your little, great mother and your younger sisters . . . Do not allow anything to slip! Thoughtful work; careful resting; healthy living; clean, worthy, serious thinking. You are a Man!

Polonius could not have said it better. Then came the practicalities:

Always check up on your portfolio to see that you have all the music for violin and piano. When you go to Washington, Baltimore, Cleveland and Richmond, be sure to take along the Lalo *Symphonie espagnole* orchestral parts and score . . . After the Boston concert, practise daily alone, and with Balsam, the full New York recital programme. Daily! Particularly the Bach, Elgar, Mozart and the several new pieces, as well as the encores on which you have decided. Daily! Daily! Don't rely too much on your great talents!

After more in the same vein, Moshe signed off

with Love and sincere blessings from your father, manager, valet, adviser and above all, friend.

In April the Menuhins reached home territory, San Francisco. Interviewed by the press, they pronounced themselves deeply shocked by Hitler's recent victory in the German elections. 'They are going to substitute Wotan for Jehovah,' Marutha told her music-critic friend Redfern Mason. Moshe deplored the burning of Heine's poems by the Nazis. 'But they'll still remember them,' added Yehudi optimistically. 'I played in Germany a lot last October,' he told another journalist, 'and I know that present conditions – in regard to music at least – cannot prevail too long. The Germans love their music too much.' He was soon to be disillusioned on that score.

As President Roosevelt developed America's New Deal in his first hundred days in office, Yehudi hastened to add his own naïve (but characteristically idealistic) observations about the new Machine Age, a world, he wrote, where

everyone has a job and the potential wherewithal for a Ford and an electric refrigerator . . . We must learn to use [the machine] so that it won't lick mankind. Why don't we pass legislation cutting the working day to a few hours, raising wages so that even the lowliest workers make a good living wage and can live comfortably? Then we would have accomplished a sort of painless revolution. We're so way ahead of Europe with its history of decadence.

In 1933 he told the *Jewish Times* that his current reading included

J. M. Barrie, Cervantes (*Don Quixote*) and Daudet (*Lettres de mon moulin*), the *National Geographic* and *Scientific American* magazines and the marine explorer Dr William Beebe's *Beneath Tropical Seas*. Moshe reported that Yehudi had put on 15 pounds over the previous year and now weighed in at 10 stone. That was in February 1933. Only two months later, in Portland, Oregon, his weight was said to have risen to 159 pounds (11st. 5lbs). Nineteen pounds in two months must surely be an exaggeration, no doubt occasioned by Moshe's love of high figures as much as by Yehudi's unflagging penchant for ice-cream. At 5 feet 8 inches in height he was as tall as he was ever to be, but as the *San Francisco Call* put it, 'The young virtuoso's face is still innocent of a razor.' He was said to be patiently nursing a moustache, but it was so slight that the camera failed to register it in the photographs accompanying his latest paean of praise for his home town. The city was bathed in a golden, translucent mist.

'It's an unusual fog, isn't it?' he laughed, a semibaritone laugh that somewhat embarrassed him. 'But I like it this way. I love the sound of the fog horns and the clank of the cable cars coming up the hills.'

In the same newspaper feature Yehudi was shy about his musical tastes but admitted to loathing jazz:

We stopped in Denver. Father and I went to a hotel for lunch and there was a jazz orchestra playing. It almost ruined my appetite, but not quite.

Yehudi played three concertos on his first appearance at the new War Memorial Opera House on 5 May. This was a benefit concert for the local symphony orchestra, which was named in the programme as 'Complete Symphony Orchestra conducted by Alfred Hertz'. There were legal problems preventing the appearance of the official San Francisco Symphony for a fund-raiser: it was close to extinction. A few days later he gave a recital promoted by the enterprising Associated Students of Stanford University, with Lev Shorr at the piano.

Yehudi was probably more intrigued by the social engagements in his diary. On 11 May the city's Mayor, Angelo J. Rossi, presented him with a golden plaque and he was sworn in by the Police Commissioner as an Honorary Member of the city's Police Force. On the reverse of his badge of office (which allowed him, he later boasted, to park with impunity opposite a fire hydrant) was inscribed the message, 'San Francisco is extremely proud of the achievements of its favourite son.'

Not to be outdone, the Fire Chief made him an honorary *pompier*, after which Yehudi reportedly took the wheel of a fire engine and drove through the downtown streets at 60 m.p.h., with Hephzibah sitting next to him and Yaltah banging furiously on the alarm bell. They ended up in the docks, where a French warship was conveniently anchored. According to this surrealistic publicity blurb (reproduced in the programme book of a subsequent Paris recital) the Mayor then presented Yehudi to the ship's captain, who knew all about Yehudi: 'The proof is that we have his recording of the Bach Double Concerto on board.' It emerged that every vessel in the French navy had been issued with 78s of the Bach, presumably to provide some moral uplift at sea.

The family sailed for France on the SS *Paris* on 19 May. Within hours of resuming residence at Ville d'Avray Yehudi plunged into preparations for Elgar's visit to Paris. Enesco rehearsed the orchestra in advance of the composer's arrival. At the month's end, Elgar flew with Fred Gaisberg from Croydon to Le Bourget, his first flight and a great adventure for the old man. After running through the Concerto next morning (without a single interruption, so well had Enesco done his job) he and Gaisberg lunched with the Menuhins at Ville d'Avray. Moshe remembered Elgar as fresh and boyish, regaling the family with funny stories, holding hands with Yehudi, Hephzibah and Yaltah as they danced round the table out on the lawn. After a nap he then (at Gaisberg's suggestion) drove over to Grez-sur-Loing to call on Frederick Delius, whom he'd not met for over twenty years. Yehudi always regretted turning down the invitation to join that expedition. He had never heard of Delius and it was not until the 1970s that he was to perform Delius's music for the violin.

'The way that boy plays my Concerto is amazing,' Elgar told Delius. They drank a bottle of champagne together and talked for over three hours before Elgar drove back to Paris. It was a long and demanding day for an old man who, Yehudi remembered, was suffering from a stomach disorder: Marutha fed him a diet of nothing except onion soup, even for breakfast next morning. He stayed with the Menuhins overnight. After the concert he flew home to England in time to attend the Derby and receive news, on the eve of his seventy-sixth birthday, that he had been awarded the GCVO.

Despite the ovations on the 31 May gala evening, the concert was only a *succès d'estime* for Elgar. 'One felt', wrote Gaisberg prophetically, 'that it had not made the impression that was its due. I fear Elgar's music will never receive real appreciation from Frenchmen, at least in our generation.' The *Daily Mail* said Menuhin was to be congratulated 'for imposing superior values' on the French. Plans for Serge Koussevitzky to include the Violin Concerto in an Elgar festival to be mounted by the Boston Symphony foundered with the English composer's death nine months later. Elgar himself had once again been overwhelmed by Yehudi's interpretation of the Concerto. 'You have made it your own,' he wrote from England, 'and your playing last week was, in some way, grander than last year, although last year I did not think it was possible to improve on your reading.'

Recommended Recordings

Bruch: Violin Concerto No. 1 in G minor
London Symphony Orchestra, conducted by Sir Landon Ronald
BID LAB 031
Recorded: 1931
The first of at least five recordings of the Bruch made by YM over the space of forty years. The most recent, with Boult and the LSO, was recorded in stereo in 1971 (EMI 7 62519 2); see chapter 17.

Ravel: *Tzigane*
with Artur Balsam (piano)
BID LAB 046
Recorded: May 1932
This is on the same CD as the recording of Lalo's *Symphonie espagnole* under Enesco.

Bach: Concerto in D minor (BWV 1043) for two violins
with George Enesco (violin) and the Paris Symphony Orchestra
EMI 7 61018 2
Recorded: 1932
A recording that sustained many listeners on active service during the Second World War. On the BBC *Brains Trust* Professor C. E. M. Joad memorably likened the slow movement to a duet of angels.

Elgar: Violin Concerto
London Symphony Orchestra, conducted by the composer
EMI 5 55221 2
Recorded: July 1932
This famous HMV recording has been issued and reissued many times, most recently by Naxos. If a more recent recording in stereo is preferred, the Elgar Concerto was performed by YM with Boult conducting the New Philharmonia in 1966 on EMI 7 64725 2.

6 The World Tour

In Australia in 1935, aged nineteen

1933: summer: head-shaving of the Menuhin children; September: recording duo début with Hephzibah; 1934: concert in New York with Toscanini; US network radio début; chooses place to live at Los Gatos; weighs 12 st. 10 lbs at eighteen; Hephzibah's public duo début in Paris; 1935: 'world tour' begins, including US, Australia, New Zealand, South Africa and Europe; 1936: March: 'farewell' concert at Carnegie Hall before retiring to new Californian home for an extended sabbatical year.

J UNE 1933 WAS HARDLY the 'vacation period' indicated to the press by Moshe. On the 20th HMV started an intense spell of recording activity with Yehudi. It included his first recordings of Chausson's *Poème* and the *Symphonie espagnole* by Lalo, with George Enesco conducting an *ad hoc* band rather grandly described as the Orchestre

Symphonique de Paris. Back in 1926, when Yehudi first performed Lalo's attractive 'Spanish Symphony' for violin solo and orchestra – a concerto in all but name – he had played only three of its five movements, omitting the second and third as was the custom at the time. Encouraged by Enesco, he now recorded the complete work. This is an early example of his preference – long before the attractions of 'authenticity' were more generally acknowledged – for going back to original sources and restoring 'lost' or forgotten violin scores. Unfortunately he sometimes threw his weight behind dubious examples of 1930s musicology, among them a Mozart concerto (the 'Adelaide') that turned out to be a fake.

Yehudi wrote that Chausson's *Poème* was the only work for which he had had access to Enesco's complete bowings and fingerings. Enesco himself had made what Yehudi called a 'gorgeous' recording of it with piano accompaniment and it was 'a wonderful inspiration' to have him conduct the work with the orchestra. Yehudi was in the Salle Pleyel studio for four days out of five. On Midsummer's Eve came a solo Bach partita and next day more Bach, the E major Violin Concerto (BWV 1042) and the solo Sonata No. 1 in G minor (BWV 1001). Only then could the family's holiday get under way.

Idling at her mother's dressing table, the eleven-year-old Yaltah came across some hair clippers of the kind barbers use to tidy up the back of the neck. Marutha had been suffering from arthritis in her arms, which prevented her from lifting a brush to her hair. A doctor in Rome had told her the previous winter to shave her head and wear a wig; hence the clippers. Yaltah picked them up and started chopping aimlessly at her long curls, removing so many substantial tufts that her scalp was clearly visible. When she emerged for the family picnic lunch, Ferruccio was so shocked by her appearance that he dropped a plate of fresh asparagus. Harsh words ensued, with Marutha deciding there was only one solution: to shave off Yaltah's hair entirely. It would do the scalp good, she argued, to let it breathe. Yehudi restored peace with the radical proposal that he and Hephzibah would undergo the same drastic treatment. Crew cuts were not entirely inappropriate for a vacation in the hot Italian sunshine but fellow holiday-makers on the Mediterranean must have gasped to see the Menuhin children go bathing with heads completely shaven, like youthful Tibetan monks. Hephzibah said Yehudi was always the peacemaker in the family.

After the Italian seaside holiday at Ospedaletti came a spell in the

Swiss mountains. The Menuhins rented a peasant cottage, two hundred years old, in the lower Fex valley. Goats supplied all the milk, cheese, butter and cream. There were fifteen chickens to provide eggs. A lamb was slaughtered by a neighbour and fresh meat stored in the cellar, under which ran an ice-cold stream fed by the nearby glacier. Fruit was bought from a mountain pedlar. And to this rural idyll, prefiguring their dreams of Californian ranch life, was added music: two pianos were shipped in from Zurich for the girls and when Yehudi took out his fiddle – 'just to try out his fingers', it was reported at the time, though in truth he was busy studying a new, *Urtext* edition of the Paganini D major Concerto – a crowd of vacationers was soon standing outside, 'rapt in their enjoyment'. It sounds more like a circus than a summer vacation.

The pianist Vladimir Horowitz, then twenty-nine, was vacationing near by with his fiancée, Wanda Toscanini, the maestro's daughter. He was chauffeur-driven everywhere in what Yehudi remembered enviously as a particularly beautiful Rolls-Royce convertible, 'small but so elegant'. The cellist Gregor Piatigorsky and the conductor Bruno Walter were also part of the holiday crowd. A photograph shows a large group of hikers lined up at the start of an expedition to the glacier. During the climb Horowitz consulted Moshe about business affairs. Moshe was, after all, the personal manager of the highest-paid artist of his time. But the pianist left the party early, his life dominated by an obsession with practice. While the others were enjoying their Alpine picnic Horowitz spent the rest of the day working on Chopin's 'Revolutionary' Etude. That night, Yehudi recalled, 'He couldn't wait to play it for us because he knew he had mastered it and it was really hair-raising.'

Moshe and Marutha organized musical evenings for this distinguished company and took care to inform the media of what they were doing. The London *Daily Telegraph* sent a special correspondent who saw no need to hold back on the schmaltz:

The moon was full and the wind was gently sighing through the pine-clad Alps, and a silvery waterfall was dropping thousands of feet into the running stream below. On the Alpine fastnesses, tawny cattle wandered and you heard the mellow, tinkling bells as they moved – but all else was still. Our host and hostess . . . had given us one of those 'alfresco' suppers which only seem possible in a foreign land. Here were no Paris gowns, no glittering jewels, starched shirts or evening dress, no great concert hall with the hum and excitement of gathering expectant crowds –

but just a little country house-party of fifteen who were admitted 'free', who took what seats they could . . . within the unpainted, pine-panelled room which served the purpose of a music salon.

A pile of music was introduced, music stands set out, a troublesome light over the piano adjusted and then the concert began: trios by Schubert and Brahms, sonatas by Mozart and Beethoven. The report is worth quoting if only because it prefigures the atmosphere of the modest chamber-music festival in the Swiss resort town of Gstaad that Yehudi was to inaugurate twenty-four years later.

Yehudi remembered Horowitz listening 'with great admiration' while Hephzibah took part in the Brahms C major Trio. It was no longer possible for her mother to deny that Hephzibah's extraordinary musicianship deserved to be heard by a wider audience than the family circle. She was only thirteen years old but Enesco had already urged her reluctant parents to accept the idea and the time had come to launch her professional career, not yet as a soloist but sharing the lime-light with her brother. The first engagement, in September 1933, was in HMV's studio rather than at a public concert. The work chosen was Mozart's A major Sonata (K. 526), and the recording later won the Candide prize (10,000 francs) for the best new chamber-music discs of the year in France. (When the Menuhin–Enesco recording of the Bach Double Concerto had won a similar award the previous year Moshe had given away the cash to unemployed Parisian musicians.)

Meanwhile politics and the rise of the Nazis must have dominated the conversation at the Menuhins' musical evenings in August 1933. Only a few months had elapsed since their friend Bruno Walter had arrived for a rehearsal at the Leipzig Gewandhaus – where he had suc-ceeded Furtwängler four years previously – to find the door to his own hall locked and a notice pinned up announcing the cancellation of his concert on the spurious grounds of a threat to public safety. He left Germany immediately. In the summer of 1933 another friend of the Menuhins, Arturo Toscanini, cancelled his conducting engagements at the Bayreuth Festival in order to protest against the Nazis' treatment of Jewish musicians.

In an attempt to demonstrate that art was above politics Wilhelm Furtwängler sent letters inviting a number of internationally renowned Jewish soloists to appear with the Berlin Philharmonic in the following season, among them the great pianist Artur Schnabel and three violinists:

Bronisław Huberman, Fritz Kreisler and Yehudi Menuhin. 'Someone must make a beginning to break down the walls that keep us apart,' the German conductor wrote to Yehudi, with what in hindsight seems like pathetic *naïveté*,

Accept this invitation and you fulfil not only one of my most ardent wishes, but you will also register with the world that the threads that tie musical Germany to the outside world are not completely broken! We artists must keep ourselves free from politics even when the politicians make it difficult for us!

Yehudi's cabled refusal was the first to reach Berlin. Other celebrated musicians in the Menuhin circle who were not Jewish, such as the cellist Gregor Piatigorsky and the violinist Jacques Thibaud, also rejected Furtwängler's approach. Indeed the only musician of note to accept (after first declining) was yet another friend, the pianist Alfred Cortot, who was later to become a Vichy collaborator after Germany's defeat of France. Yehudi's Jewish manager in Berlin, Erich Sachs, had been forced out of business by the Nazis' new anti-Semitic laws. His Catholic partner, Luise Wolff, fought hard to maintain her concert agency against the encroachments of the Nazis as Bertha Geissmar's *The Baton and the Jackboot* makes clear. Wolff pleaded with the Menuhins to accept Furtwängler's invitation:

All Germany will greet Yehudi's return as a great historical moment. We can reassure you that the government, too, will welcome this step. A Yehudi Menuhin concert in Germany at this stage would start a new chapter in international relations . . . You will perform a priceless service.

And the engagement would of course have been a feather in Frau Wolff's hat.

The Menuhins' response to the much respected but seriously flawed Wilhelm Furtwängler was admirably direct:

Dear and beloved Maestro and friend [neither father nor son had ever met him]
We cannot see our way clear to allow YM to benefit by the particular exception conferred upon him. With infinite regrets but ardent hopes for a happier opportunity in the very near future.

In a follow-up letter Moshe expanded on their position. Double standards such as Furtwängler was proposing could not be tolerated: 'Art must be served on a human and socially equal plane.' Furtwängler's reply attempted to shift the blame for the subsequent deterioration of German musical life on to the shoulders of Menuhin and his fellow artists:

You do not seem to understand that my invitation to artists like Yehudi Menuhin and Huberman is not an exception but was to be the beginning of the normalization in our musical life which the government hopes to settle. If this normalization goes now at a slower pace than I had hoped, the responsibility falls to a great part on those who have refused me help in my endeavour.

The details of Yehudi's stand, placing principle above opportunism, were not revealed to the public until the Menuhins returned to the United States at the end of the year. In her letter Frau Wolff had reminded Yehudi of the great popularity and prestige he had accumulated in Germany in the four years since his Berlin début in 1929: 'We know how much you love Germany. Do not forget, please, the fact that Germany and the Germans have Yehudi locked in their hearts!' Yehudi did not forget. He never played in Nazi Germany but he made a point of returning at the earliest opportunity, giving concerts in Belsen and elsewhere in July and August 1945, less than three months after the war in Europe ended.

The abrupt closure of the German market (to put it in commercial terms) meant a later start to Yehudi's autumn touring. He played his first recital at the Salle Pleyel on 1 December, the same day that the new recording of the Mozart sonata with Hephzibah was released. The programme included the Paganini Concerto he had been studying in the summer: it was in the repertoire when the Menuhins moved on to London. In a hotel interview for the *Daily Express* Moshe spoke of the work's insuperable difficulties. 'You've been looping the loop on that violin,' murmured the journalist when Yehudi joined them from his practising in the next room. '"I'm glad it sounds like that," replied the boy simply. "It's really quite easy."' The *Express* man noticed that for all his nonchalance one of Yehudi's fingers was bleeding 'from quick work on the strings'.

The D major Concerto became a new cause for Yehudi to uphold. For many years it had been performed in an arrangement by August Wilhelmj, a nineteenth-century German violinist of great renown. Wilhelmj had been the leader of Wagner's orchestra for the first *Ring* cycle in Bayreuth and later taught at the Guildhall in London, but he was not the most tasteful of editors. 'I refused to play Wilhelmj's Hollywood heebe-jeebies vulgarization,' Yehudi told another reporter. 'I wanted the entire work as Paganini did it.' The *Express* columnist didn't miss the fact that Yehudi was still under Moshe's thumb:

'Go to bed, my boy: tomorrow you must finish all that fruit [on the sideboard] because we leave the next day.'

'Yes, father.'

The London recital was sold out, with many turned away, but Elgar's absence cast a pall. 'Dearest Yehudi', he wrote from his sick bed in Worcester,

it is very gloomy here after the brilliant days of twelve months ago. You and your dear father must forgive my absence from your triumphs as I am quite laid by in a nursing home. Dear love from your friend.

London was at its most wintry and inhospitable. 'Many of the audience will have caught chill,' reported the *Express*. 'The Royal Albert Hall is the most difficult place from which to obtain homeward locomotion.'

Concerts followed in The Hague and Amsterdam, then it was across the Alps to Rome. While Yehudi was playing a fugue from a Bach solo sonata at his Augusteum recital a voice was clearly heard from an upstairs box: '*Che noioso!*' ('How boring!') Moshe thought it was no less a critic than Mussolini's Minister of Culture. At all events there was much shushing in the auditorium and the conclusion brought a double-barrelled demonstration, *for* Yehudi and *against* the Fascist government. (That, at least, was Moshe's story.)

The family embarked from Genoa for the voyage to New York. Toscanini was again a fellow passenger and although the crossing was extremely rough the two men made music together – of a somewhat macabre nature:

Toscanini sang and whistled in his unlit suite every night of the passage from Italy while the Italian liner *Rex* breasted heavy head seas. Yehudi played an accompaniment to the erratic whistling and headnote falsetto of Maestro Toscanini.

The on-board repertoire consisted of the newly discovered concerto known as the 'Adelaide', said to have been composed by the boy Mozart when he was in Paris, and the Beethoven Concerto, which they were shortly to perform together in New York. 'It's his spirit', commented Yehudi gamely of Toscanini, 'that made this rare music. He needed no orchestra.' And they had very few witnesses on the voyage: Moshe, Marutha and the girls were all below the *Rex*'s rearing decks, 'clinging to their beds'.

In New York the Menuhins again set up base in the Ansonia Hotel, which was to be their home for three months while Yehudi undertook his fifth annual continental tour. And his first as a man, if the need to shave is taken as the ultimate proof of manhood.

On 22 January, which was still being observed publicly as his 'official' birthday, his mother presented him with a gold razor (of British make) and according to Moshe it took his son 'a half-hour to shave off the two and one half hairs on his face'. It reads as if he was trying to humiliate Yehudi, but perhaps he was merely attempting a lighter touch:

My boy was excited about it until he cut himself the first time. After that he began to take it more seriously and by the time he was through he said he was glad he only had to do it once a week.

At his concert in Cincinnati a reporter noted that he 'looked more than the seventeen years which are claimed for him' – an astute observation since he was in fact only three months off his eighteenth birthday. 'The illusion of extreme youth', the newspaper continued,

is still maintained for this violinistic genius by his careful managers – he wears neither dinner-jacket nor 'tails' for his stage appearance, but sports an extremely smart double-breasted buttoned coat and trousers to match.

Yehudi was much more open with the American press than he had been in London. He told one journalist about his teenage passions, which included

aeronautics, girls – if they're good sports and swimmers – the study of languages, spinach [Popeye was all the rage], wine but not cigarettes, the Californian climate but not carrots, and discussions on governmental policies.

The report added that he admitted to membership of the left wing. 'Every intelligent person should be concerned in everything that has to do with the happiness of the people,' he told the *Washington Post*'s readers, adding that his ideal in life was 'sympathy and understanding between man and man'. His father must have briefed him to provide reporters with an example of his latest intellectual exploit:

I am starting to learn Russian. It is a wonderfully compact language: sometimes a few of its compound adjectives and its verb-aspects [*sic*] contain so much that it requires a long sentence in English to translate them. I have just finished Pushkin's *The Bronze Horseman*, which I liked immensely.

Moshe said they had no desire to capitalize on the plight of Germany's Jews and he requested (rather uncharacteristically) that no sensation be made of the Menuhins' rejection of the invitation to play in Nazi Germany. But the authentic voice of the mature Yehudi is already discernible in his ringing statement to the *New York Times* that 'we musicians . . . should think of upholding the tradition of liberty and freedom. The more we see of Europe the more we should be proud of the fact that in America we can speak freely.' Later on the tour he was outraged when he learned of the Austrian Heimwehr's bombardment of the workers' model city-buildings in Vienna. Austria was still free but evidently under threat: he urged Washington reporters to record that he was 'unilaterally opposed to Hitler and his merciless form of government'.

Yehudi made his network radio début on the same tour. The commercial stations took classical music seriously in the 1930s and when Yehudi was engaged for his first broadcast on 7 January he was to be accompanied by the 'Cadillac Symphony Orchestra' (mostly members of the New York Philharmonic) under Walter Damrosch. Lalo's *Symphonie espagnole* was the main work on the show, supplemented by Mendelssohn's 'Fingal's Cave' Overture, a couple of movements from Tchaikovsky's Fifth Symphony and Wagner's *The Ride of the Valkyries*. It was an attractive engagement and exceptionally lucrative.

Imagine the family drama, therefore, when Yehudi was taken ill! He was photographed at the Ansonia, appearing 'in blue-striped pyjamas and a deep-red plaid dressing-gown, with a light tan muffler about his throat'. A heavy cold had engendered talk of an enforced postponement. Then the ailing Yehudi reminded his mother that Toscanini had promised to attend. The show had to go on. So Marutha prepared one of her famous hot mustard plasters (famous within the Menuhin circle, that is) and with the unorthodox medication strapped to his chest Yehudi gave what his father inevitably described as a 'thrilling' performance. But the radio show was under-running. Now it was Moshe's turn to come to the rescue:

In response to an urgent plea from the broadcast's programme director, I dug the score of the Sarasate *Zapateado* from the collection of encore pieces I always carried and Yehudi completed that in time for the closing commercial to be given.

It's a nice story, but the advance publicity for the concert actually specified that Yehudi would play not one but two of Sarasate's salon pieces to round off the commercial hour.

Whether Toscanini attended the studio performance to witness Yehudi's heroic mustard-plaster performance has not been recorded for posterity but two weeks later rehearsals began for Yehudi's performances with him of the Beethoven Violin Concerto. It was their first and – despite declarations of mutual artistic sympathy – their only collaboration. Yehudi and his father called on the maestro at his suite in the Hotel Astor. During the run-through, at which Toscanini himself played the orchestral part on the piano, the telephone rang. 'The conductor excused himself,' Moshe relates,

and went to his wife's room to ask her to see to it that the phone didn't ring until after Yehudi and he had finished making music. The telephone rang again after a few minutes, just as Yehudi began to play the heavenly slow movement. Toscanini stopped and, looking furious, went to see his wife again. Ten minutes later the phone rang yet again. That was too much for Toscanini.

Yehudi takes up the tale:

We had reached the middle of the slow movement where, after a second *tutti*, the sound marked *perdendosi* hangs by a thread. [I was] tensely aware that the pressure in the room was boiling up to a reaction. At the third ring Toscanini stopped, rose from the piano stool, and with light quick determined steps walked not to the telephone but to the installation in the wall and jerked the whole thing bodily out, wooden fitting, plaster, dust, severed dangling wires; then without a word uttered, he came back to take up where we had stopped, in total serenity. When the third movement ended there was a timid knock on the door. Relaxed, unembarrassed, amiable, Toscanini gently called, '*Avanti*!' – his first word since the incident – and the door opened on an abject trio: Mrs Toscanini, the hotel proprietor and an electrician, all promising to do better another time.

In Moshe's account Toscanini *does* speak. '*Caro*,' he says, 'let us start again from the beginning of the second movement.'

This unseemly demonstration did not impress Marutha. She never hid her dislike of Toscanini's lack of self-control (she labelled him 'Tosca-ninny') and criticized his arrogance. Her genius of a son was, she felt, unnecessarily subservient to him. At the Carnegie Hall concert Yehudi showed his reverence for the maestro by bowing to him at the end of the performance before turning to acknowledge the applause of the audience. Marutha called the gesture an exaggerated display of humility. 'But this is Toscanini,' protested Yehudi. 'But you are Yehudi Menuhin,' she is said to have angrily replied. The following summer she blocked an invitation from Toscanini when the Menuhins were holidaying at Ospedaletti: 'If the maestro wants to see you and play with you, he will be welcome here.' Yehudi himself was mightily impressed by the telephone incident:

Taught from childhood to keep my emotion under rigid control, I early learned to sublimate into music-making everything that was in me of the dark free world of impulse. But here, before my own eyes, a person obeyed his impulse, and the others thought it natural. *They* apologized . . . The closest I ever came to a similar indulgence happened some two years later, when, in a fit of irritation, I slammed the door of our automobile, breaking the glass. I was so shocked at myself that I never again allowed my emotions to run out of control.

Yehudi's interpretation of the Beethoven Concerto, with Toscanini conducting the New York Philharmonic, was heard on 18 and 19 January 1934. 'Violin playing of the first order,' summed up the critic W. J. Henderson. 'The boy projected his spiritual immersion in the music with an art that defied analysis.' Henderson had heard Yehudi's performance of the Beethoven in November 1927 under Fritz Busch, describing it as 'sheer rapture of a gifted nature'. Seven years on, 'The youth played with a passionate adoration born of a new vision and manly emotion.' The new interpretation, no doubt achieved under Toscanini's influence, combined 'depth, tenderness and the eager service of the artist soul'. Toscanini conducted the 'Eroica' Symphony in the second part of the programme, which according to Olin Downes was 'a great concert'. Unfortunately it was neither recorded nor broadcast.

Similar acclaim greeted Yehudi on his tour. Washington hailed 'the greatest violin and orchestra programme ever given here'; Los Angeles, where he made his concerto début with Otto Klemperer conducting, called him 'the violin of the century'; his broadcast with the Philadelphia Orchestra was 'an electrifying and exceptional occasion'. This last performance was in breach of the exclusive contract Moshe had signed with the *Cadillac Hour* radio show. Philadelphia had jumped the gun by offering Yehudi's concert, with Stokowski conducting, for a national broadcast. After tortuous negotiations Yehudi donated his concert fee of $3000 to the Philadelphia Orchestra's benevolent fund. But he still received a massive $4,500 from CBS Radio. Moshe's memoirs do not relate how the *Cadillac Hour* was recompensed for its loss of exclusivity. He did, however, include a fan letter to his son from a certain physics professor in Princeton:

My beloved and adored Yehudi Menuhin! The day before yesterday I listened to you through the radio in your performance of the Beethoven and Bach Concertos. It was a glorious life-event for me, for no other violinist can ever play as you know how.
Lovingly and respectfully yours,
A. Einstein.

A performance of the slow movement of a Bach concerto was played at the concert as a tribute to Elgar, who had died the previous week, on 23 February.

In his 1955 biography Robert Magidoff wrote extensively about Yehudi's gloomy moods during the winter months of touring from the family's New York base at the Ansonia, his 'adolescent urges', his 'listlessness, silent moods and cheerlessness', and there is the occasional hint in the press confirming that such mood swings were affecting his performances. Thus a Toronto critic suggested that he was no longer flawless because he had become a teenager. To add to the disagreement over Toscanini, Yehudi and his mother were said to have had a clash of wills over a request from Yehudi's benefactor Henry Goldman, who was now totally blind and no longer able to attend concerts. Goldman asked if Yehudi would play for him at home. According to Magidoff, who gave no source, Yehudi was willing but Marutha was adamantly opposed: there were no exceptions to the rule of no private performances. Yehudi was said to have been humiliated by the slight to Goldman.

When the biography appeared, Moshe angrily denied the entire story. However Magidoff also recounted an incident which he personally observed twenty years later in Amsterdam when he was with Yehudi researching his biography. Yehudi received a letter from a total stranger pleading with him to play at the bedside of his eighteen-year-old daughter, who was dying of leukaemia. With Magidoff in attendance, Yehudi visited her sickbed and played her a Bach chaconne.

'This *is* Bach. I feel I've touched him,' the girl said in a hardly audible voice.

On the way back to the hotel, [Magidoff] asked: 'Will you ever forget Mr Goldman, Yehudi?'

'No, I cannot, and I fear I never will!'

The girl died a few weeks later. She bequeathed her bracelet to Yehudi's daughter.

Magidoff added that even George Enesco, 'the very soul of gentleness and discretion', chastised Marutha to her face concerning the treatment of Henry Goldman when he visited the Menuhins, whom he dubbed the 'Biblical Family Menuhin'. Yehudi expected an angry reaction from his mother and was getting ready to side with his teacher but, according to the biographer, Marutha sensed the danger and laughed off the criticism, declaring that thank God Yehudi would soon be old enough to make his own decisions. 'His first independent act, she hoped, would be to choose a girl and get married.'

The only candidates for the role of Yehudi's official girlfriend were Rosalie Leventritt, the daughter of Moshe's lawyer (and later a noted musical philanthropist) and her friend Lydia Perera, daughter of an Italian banker in New York. At the time, Yehudi's teenage timidity astonished them. 'All we could say', Rosalie remembered, 'was "Oh, no, it cannot be!" and left it at that. We somehow could not get through to him even when his parents weren't around.' There was another row with Marutha when on an impulse after a pleasant lunch Yehudi took Rosalie to the theatre one afternoon without consulting his parents in advance. As a general rule he wasn't permitted even to cross the road without Moshe to see him safely to the other side.

To judge from the warmth of his tribute in *Unfinished Journey*, Yehudi's best friend in New York was the writer Willa Cather, who wrote grand novels about country people in the days of the pioneers. With their mother's blessing the children went for long walks with 'Aunt Willa' around the Central Park reservoir. She 'revealed a face of America to us youngsters who were growing up amongst adults largely born abroad'. Yehudi wrote his first magazine article during the winter and its patriotic tone (decrying the lack of esteem in which most Americans held their culture) owes something to Cather's inspiration as well as his father's. 'I am always up in arms', he declared,

against that American inferiority complex, that self-effacement, self-belittlement, that Americans manifest almost to a pathological point whenever we speak of European versus American! . . . The *Baedeker* is one thing for sightseeing, but quite another thing when your soul craves for spiritual and artistic inner development. There, it is the individual alone, as well as the contact with other individuals, that counts. It is only the atmosphere of your own soul, your own home, your own life's philosophy, outlook and ideals, that counts. And so far as the outside atmosphere counts, in our youthful, healthy, socially minded, peaceful country, with a people that is anxious to learn, to improve the general material and spiritual life of everybody; in our country where there is still to be found a spirit of pioneeering, we have a healthier atmosphere in which to develop our art, if we have the talent.

Perhaps it was also Willa Cather who nudged Yehudi's family towards the idea of coming home, of living once again in America. By April 1934 the decision had been taken to buy a substantial plot of land in California and build on it a permanent home – the concept of a ranch, which would also be an informal music centre, was a dream to which Yehudi often referred in his conversations with journalists. Willa Cather was concerned by the Menuhin family's linguistic rootlessness. So many foreign tongues had been acquired that they were in danger of neglecting what in the girls' case at least was their native tongue. Yehudi had first talked in his parents' modern Hebrew, but English was effectively his mother tongue, too. Cather's antidote was Shakespeare: *Richard II, Macbeth* and *Hamlet*. At the Menuhin's suite in the Ansonia, a spare room, 'small enough to be cosy', Yehudi remembered, was furnished with a table

around which Aunt Willa, Hephzibah, Yaltah, myself and often Aunt Willa's companion Edith Lewis, gathered for Shakespearean readings, each taking several parts, and Aunt Willa commenting on the language and situations in such a way as to draw us into her own pleasure and excitement.

Not that Cather was oblivious to the merits of foreign literature: Yehudi omitted to mention that two years earlier, on his sixteenth birthday, she had presented him with a book of poems by Heinrich Heine.

The North American tour pressed on relentlessly: he played to 'the ladies of the Boston Morning Musicale' on 14 March, and then gave a Carnegie Hall recital on the 18th, at which he performed the controversial 'Adelaide' Concerto, complete with cadenzas by no less a figure than the composer Paul Hindemith. *En route* for San Francisco there were recitals in far-flung Winnipeg and Denver and it was April by the time he reached his home town. The purpose of the visit was to honour a promise and play a fund-raising concert in aid of the San Francisco Symphony, which was still experiencing financially hard times. The headlines said he raised $9,200. The accountant eventually brought that down to a still very useful $5,687.73, enough for one enthusiastic caption writer to describe him as 'the man who saved the San Francisco Symphony'. (Alas, it went bankrupt later in the year.) On 8 April a vast Sunday afternoon audience at the Civic Auditorium saw him presented with a laurel wreath and hailed as the city's greatest citizen – after they'd heard him play three concertos, none of which (according to the always reliable and readable Redfern Mason of the *San Francisco Examiner*) had ever previously been heard in the city in its entirety: the five-movement *Symphonie espagnole* by Lalo, the Mozart 'Adelaide' (which eventually turned out to be a fake) and the *Urtext* edition of the Paganini No. 1 in D. Yehudi's playing, wrote Mason, went some way to answering two questions that had apparently been posed by the late Sir Edward Elgar:

'What still remains to be achieved by Yehudi?' and 'What will happen if and when he breaks loose from parental authority?' The answer to the first question is that Yehudi has achieved classic calm and authority. His reading of the Mozart . . . had the touch of inevitability which reveals the mature artist. It sang with delicious sweetness, yet never slipped over the fine dividing line which parts sincere feeling from sentimentality. The Lalo is . . . Spain with a strong tinge of Hebraic sentiment. Here Yehudi proved that he could indulge in the luxury of romanticism. But it does not seem possible that he could have played that *Kol nidrei*-ish chant as he did if he had not been steeped in the grand old melodies of the synagogue. The Paganini was a *tour de force* in which the wonders of transcendental technique were played with an assurance and a seeming effortlessness that brought to mind Emerson's saying about Plato: 'He is never calmer than when his miracles are flashing in the air.'

As to Elgar's second question, Mason was in no doubt that

without any uncomfortable break, without any overt act of revolt, the lad has emancipated himself from the parental apron strings. In a hundred phrases you felt that he was thinking the music in his own way . . . Like Toscanini he looks beneath the notes for the mystery which inspired them.

The emancipation was from Enesco and Busch rather than from Moshe and Marutha, but it is clear from the photographs of the period that Yehudi was in every respect becoming his own man. Apart from musical considerations, there was his sheer bulk to contend with, now up to 12st. 10lbs. 'I shall lose a few pounds', he confided to the press, 'when I hike over the Santa Cruz mountains looking for my future home.'

Father and son finally went in search of a property where they might put down roots. They lodged with their artist friends George Dennison and Frank Ingerson and eventually bought a 100-acre plot off the Soda Springs Road in Cathedral Oaks, Alma, high in the hills overlooking Los Gatos. According to a report in the *New York Times* – anything involving Yehudi was news – it was 'a redwood estate formerly owned by playwright Richard Walter Tully'. Tully was the author of *Rose of the Rancho*. A better-remembered writer, John Steinbeck, also lived near by in Salinas Valley. 'An old country home [*sic*] duplicating the European birthplace of Mrs Menuhin will be erected,' the *Times* continued. 'They intend to use it as a rural Music Center.'

A copy of a Crimean house of the 1890s seems a little far-fetched as a design concept, even by Moshe's standards. A Los Angeles architect, Paul Williams, was hired to design the main house (to be called 'Villa Cherkess' – after Marutha's supposed ancestry) as well as a smaller guest cottage in the grounds. A dream seemed on the way to reality:

the summer of 1934 proved to be the Menuhins' last at Ville d'Avray. When Yehudi undertook his final spell of study with Enesco, in the winter of 1935–6, the family lodged at the Hôtel Majestic in Paris.

They returned to France on the SS *Champlain* and Yehudi was soon recording concertos for HMV. Pierre Monteux was the conductor for both the Paganini No. 1 and Mozart's 'Adelaide'. Moshe must have taken the opportunity to discuss the vacant post of chief conductor of the San Francisco Symphony since he claimed he was instrumental in bringing about Monteux's appointment for the following season. Yehudi's fund-raising potential enabled Moshe to put pressure on the Symphony Association, which in turn persuaded the city to levy an extra tax in order to underwrite the hiring of Monteux.

Later in the summer Yehudi made another recording with Hephzibah, choosing Schumann's Violin Sonata No. 2 in D minor, Op. 121. Yehudi described it as 'a grand work . . . rarely performed today . . . a rich and passionate score which captures the sombre quality beneath the exuberant surface of Schumann's music'. The recording lives up to that promise. After the summer holiday (once again spent in Ospedaletti and Sils Maria) Hephzibah made her concert début as Yehudi's partner at the Salle Pleyel in Paris. ('Don't describe her as my accompanist,' he pleaded with an American reporter.) In addition to the Schumann and the Mozart A major Sonata, learned the previous year, they played Beethoven's 'Kreutzer'. They played together again later in the season in London (28 October) and New York (6 December) but nowhere else. Moshe said he turned down a hundred invitations.

As Hephzibah recalled, she and her brother developed a unique sense of rapport: 'We were really one person. We would be playing back to back yet each would know exactly the other's feelings and intentions.' Moshe told a reporter they actually practised together in the dark, a striking way of developing instinctive rapport. At the concerts Yehudi wore a short dinner-jacket and his sister was dressed in a long pink frock: 'A demure little tow-haired maiden . . . She simply would not take a bow,' reported the *Jewish Tribune* in New York.

Never even glancing at the keyboard between the movements, she rose at the end of each number, grasped the hand of Yehudi and looked into his eyes. Yehudi's gentle coaxing had no effect.

Musically speaking, the critical response was not all positive. The *Minneapolis Register* reported that Hephzibah 'sometimes pounded egregiously . . . leaving her gentler brother fading at times into a sort of desperate inaudibility'. An English reviewer had described this imbalance as being beneficial: 'In accompanying his sister, Yehudi had revealed a new virtue, rare among virtuosi: the ability to subordinate personality.' Olin Downes of the *New York Times* described the duo as 'two young people . . . making music excellently, beautifully, intelligently, with joy in their task and bringing to it equal enthusiasm and seriousness'. Inevitably they were compared to the young Mozart and his sister. But Marutha was still insistent that Hephzibah and Yaltah 'shall not enter music commercially'. Hephzibah could have a quality musical career, her father added, 'but not a quantity one. We are modern and radical. The world is not radical enough for us. The first urge of a woman is to have a home.'

At the time Hephzibah seems to have taken the restriction without complaint, choosing to hide her feelings: 'I was very ashamed of expressing emotions,' she admitted twenty years later. It was left to Yaltah, only twelve, to kick over the traces. Moshe described her to journalists as 'the devil in the family'. In August she insisted on going to see *Little Women* in a Paris cinema. It was the second film they had seen in eighteen months, Hephzibah told a journalist with some pride. So the other-worldly Yehudi at least knew the name of Katharine Hepburn, one of *Little Women*'s stars, when in December she attended his recital in Hartford, Connecticut. Celebrities were two a penny in the Menuhins' lives: Count John McCormack, the Irish tenor, was among the audience at Yehudi's and Hephzibah's London recital.

According to Moshe's press releases, Yehudi's much trumpeted world tour would be initiated with the family's departure by ship from Los Angeles. In fact the odyssey had been under way since the previous autumn. It was to last over a year and take the entire family first through Western Europe, then some of the major cities of the United States, across the Pacific via Hawaii to Australia and New Zealand, onwards to South Africa and finally back to Europe. There were to be 110 concerts in 72 cities, Moshe boasted, and all except the American engagements were personally negotiated and administered by him in what proved to be the climactic period of his career as his son's manager.

Yehudi's regular European tour in the autumn of 1934 took him among other cities to Aberdeen, where he bought a splendid Royal Stuart tartan dressing-gown, and to Liège, in Belgium, where his recital was divided into four sections and lasted nearly four hours. It transpired that the local printer had inadvertently run together two of Yehudi's regular programmes. The customers had bought their tickets in good faith and were not to be disappointed.

A couple of months later, in Pittsburgh, he invited the local press to attend a preview performance of Enesco's Third Violin Sonata (composed in 1926 in Romanian folk style). He played it twice through at the Schenley Hotel, despite Moshe urging him to rest. 'It will offer better acquaintance to those listening and besides, it will do me good.' He was to repeat this initiative many times when introducing new music.

At the end of February he was in Texas, where a *Houston Press* writer described him entertainingly as 'a man with the hands of a girl, a profile that might have found its way on to a Greek coin, and a pair of dark eyes that are fastened on distant objects, including, I'm afraid, the door'. The same article commented that the parents were 'modestly conscious of their fading importance'. Other journalists kept the world abreast of Yehudi's high-flown reading, which included *Techniques of Civilisation* by Lewis Mumford and *Freedom versus Civilisation* by Bertrand Russell. He was ready to pass on what he was learning: to an interviewer in Buffalo (where he visited the Niagara Falls) he announced that

mechanical civilization can destroy all our good qualities . . . our disregard of politeness in this country has built our railroads and made us great. But it seems to me it's time we got back to courtesy.

Yehudi also took to dispatching letters without informing his father. To Albert Einstein he wrote asking how the professor could reconcile his pacifism with his support for the democracies currently undertaking rearmament and conscription. To the Soviet Union's Ambassador in the US he protested against Russia's lack of response to the recent destruction of the workers' apartments in Vienna. Moshe reported that the Ambassador wrote back to compliment Yehudi on the performance he had given with the Philadelphia Orchestra under Stokowski and inviting him to dinner in Washington.

Yehudi let go with a barrage of questions that had been bothering him for a long time . . . including one about the horrible executions taking place in Russia . . . To that Mr Troyanowsky anwered: 'You in America have an expression, "You cannot make an omelette without breaking eggs."'

This was far from being the last passage of arms Yehudi experienced with Russian officialdom.

In California in March 1935 the family visited Los Gatos, where (an agency report announced) they 'laid the cornerstone of Villa Cherkess, their new home and ranch in the Santa Cruz mountains'. Yehudi recalled the family spending three weeks with their artist friends Frank Ingerson and George Dennison, 'talking, thinking, dreaming, eating and drinking house design'. At this juncture Moshe appeared to have no qualms about the financial implications of building a large home. Yehudi's earnings were prodigious and an additional source of funds was now on offer from Hollywood.

Moshe received emissaries from the Vitaphone Company, inviting Yehudi to take part in a movie ('a new version of *Humoresque* or some such sob story') offering a fee of $100,000 and all expenses. When he turned the offer down, Moshe was reminded by the film people that 'decent parents do not deprive their children of financial security when fortune knocks on the door'. He gave a different account of the offer to the *Boston Sunday Globe*: the deal was said to be worth $250,000 and when it was declined the Hollywood man is alleged to have said, 'You fellows, you reds – you think the revolution is coming tomorrow so you won't need money.' To which Moshe responded, 'Yehudi doesn't want to be rich. All he want is to be a violinist, not a millionaire.'

To another Hollywood approach, this time from Paramount, with a story outline entitled 'The Way of All Flesh', Moshe replied with unconcealed disdain (and an arrogance that could have come only from total ignorance of the quality that Hollywood could achieve) that, 'Between Yehudi's art, his mission, his interests in music, and your field of entertainment there is an abyss that no clever, talented, scenario writer can bridge!' The fact remains that had Yehudi been permitted to accept a film engagement there would have been adequate funding for Villa Cherkess, and the débâcle of cancelled contracts could easily have been avoided.

Moshe planned Yehudi's tour to coincide with the autumn concert season in Australia and New Zealand. With the family and a mountain of luggage occupying five cabins on the SS *Malolo*, the first port of call out of California was Honolulu, where Yehudi responded to the traditional gift of a *lei* – a garland of flowers hung around his neck – with a characteristic reply: 'It's charming but the flowers will die.' A decade later he was to play to mutilated US marines in Honolulu hospital wards – the survivors of bloody Pacific battles with the Japanese.

The nature of Yehudi's subsequent box-office success in the

Antipodes is encapsulated up by the headline in the show-business weekly *Variety*: 'Down under Yehudi did *smash biz* . . . Kid is the biggest b.o. ever imported.' In Brisbane the audience was the largest for five years and many members of the audience had their names printed in the newspapers. Thirty thousand people attended his eleven concerts in Sydney. His conductor was the remarkable Portuguese-Jewish musician Maurice de Abravanel, then in his early thirties and brought over by the *Sydney Herald* to supervise the training of a respectable symphony orchestra in both Sydney and Melbourne. Yehudi found himself caught up in the traditional rivalry between Australia's two largest cities, neither of which would have been able to sustain a full-time orchestra without the help of ABC, the Australian public radio service.

Early in Yehudi's tour the composer Percy Grainger published a breathtaking attack on what he called Continental (i.e. European) music: 'The symphony orchestra is the worst musical institution ever thought of . . . The arrant stupidity of the Continentals comes out in their lousy music and filthy musicians.' Grainger was paying a rare visit to his home town Melbourne, apparently, according to the *New Grove*, to establish an ethno-musicological museum there. There is no reason to suppose that the ebullient composer had Yehudi in his sights as one of the 'filthy musicians' but our hero was swift to respond. Originally intending to play a single Bach movement as an encore in a recital given the day after Grainger's inflammatory article appeared, he decided to perform the complete solo sonata; it was his response to the jibe concerning 'lousy' European music.

When Yehudi's concerto concert in Melbourne was broadcast internationally by short-wave radio – something Moshe agreed to only because of the enormous distances in Australia – a Sydney critic wrote that, 'The melancholy thinness of the orchestral support reduced the concertos to violin solos with an inadequate orchestral accompaniment . . . It was little better than a student band.' Moshe sprang to the Melbourne orchestra's defence:

But this is monstrous. Not since Yehudi played with the Boston Symphony Orchestra under the great Serge Koussevitzky, a year ago, has Yehudi been so well supported by an orchestra as he was last night under Professor [Bernard] Heinze's baton.

He went on to praise the Melbourne public's 'educated appreciation' and called the Sydney attack 'gutter tactics'. He might have added that it was unwise to judge the quality of an orchestral balance from a short-wave broadcast.

Yehudi also played ten concerts in New Zealand. His favourite city, he confided, was the 'intellectual and sympathetic' university town of Dunedin; it reminded him of Melbourne 'where I found most of dignity and culture'. The sentiment was mutual: a Melbourne enthusiast wrote that Yehudi had 'definitely lifted to a higher plane our standard of musical culture'.

Yehudi's sympathy for Australia in general – 'fresh and young and open and spacious' – and for Melbourne in particular had a profound sequel. In the audience at his first Sydney concert was a music-loving youngster named Lindsay Nicholas and his sixteen-year-old sister, Nola. Next day she wrote enthusiastically to her father in Melbourne about the 'Magnificent Yehudi', whose face she had urged her brother to study during the recital. She even enclosed a copy of the article Yehudi had recently published in *Musical America*. Nola and Yehudi were not to meet until 1938, but when they did, backstage at the Royal Albert Hall in the company of Bernard Heinze, the result was explosive.

Moshe now fell foul of the New South Wales state tax requirements and was obliged to postpone the family's departure while he negotiated a deal with the authorities. If Yehudi was such a great violinist, the inspectors asked, why did he need an accompanist and a secretary? Why did he not live cheaply rather than taking suites in expensive hotels? Moshe felt humiliated by the philistine queries. Part of the problem must have arisen from the vagaries of Australian concert management. 'Subscribers to the first few concerts in Sydney and Melbourne', Moshe wrote,

had the prices of admission printed on the tickets but the major part of the tour [five extra concerts were arranged in Sydney alone] consisted of 'supply and demand' concerts. Most of the tickets were sold just two or three hours before the concerts began. The prices of the seats in the different sections were determined by the length of the lines at the box office and the mood of the people in the line – in other words by market forces.

At their joint press conference Yehudi expressed sympathy: 'You don't ever want to go back to school teaching, father . . . Say you'll stay with me always and continue to look after this dirty part of my career' – a request on which he was to renege only four years later.

It must have been Moshe's concern about the family's high outgoings that led him to take a gloomy view of the architectural blueprints for Villa Cherkess when they arrived from California. The cost was in the order of $60,000, not much higher than the original estimate, but to the dismay of his family Moshe prevaricated, eventually authorizing only the construction of a small guest cottage. 'We'll supervise the building of the main house ourselves' was his excuse, but the cancellation of the more substantial architectural work (for such it proved to be) led to a rift between Moshe and 'the boys', George Dennison and Frank Ingerson, that was never healed. At the time Yehudi must have believed it was only a postponement since he continued to wax lyrical about the project, telling an Adelaide journalist that the villa was intended as a thank-you present for his mother, 'for her devotion to him and as compensation for the ten years of vagabond life it has been necessary for him to live'. In March 1936 a Californian newspaper reported that a Los Gatos contractor was 'building a seven-room guest house in which the Menuhins will reside while their own house is being built. Plans for the main residence are complete.' But alas for the music-centre dreams and Yehudi's expressions of gratitude: Marutha was never to live in her Villa Cherkess.

On the long train journey across the continent to Western Australia the family travelled in the utmost luxury, ensconced in the special carriage that had been built for the Prince of Wales and served by a butler and cook (all, presumably, tax deductible). At a stop in the desert to take on water, the train was surrounded by Aborigines begging for food. 'Our children began to raid the kitchen,' Moshe remembered,

as well as our own private supplies which we had bought for the trip, and threw food out to the Aborigines until our cook began to warn us that we would have little left for the rest of the trip if this continued. I noticed that the obviously starving original Australians were eating the oranges and bananas we had given them with the peel still on!

Yehudi hated the treatment of the Aborigines:

I don't think they should be allowed to come down to the railway line. Contact with the people on trains does them no good at all. Awful! They were most depressing.

When they reached Adelaide, Hephzibah fell sick and stayed at home with her mother and sister while Yehudi gave his concert at the Town Hall. She told a journalist that she and Marutha followed the concert *mentally*. 'And when we got home,' Yehudi interjected, 'we found that mother had been two bars behind all evening.'

On the fortnight's voyage from Perth to South Africa on the *Nestor*, a small but comfortable ocean liner of the Blue Funnel Line's fleet, Yehudi underwent the equivalent of Saul's conversion on the road to Damascus, an experience concerning music that marked a watershed in his development. 'Midway through our travels,' he wrote, 'I first analysed a piece of music to my satisfaction.' In his autobiography he devoted a paltry four lines to his 'very wonderful' world cruise and seven pages to his discovery of musical form. The work he studied was the Sonata in G by the Belgian composer Guillaume Lekeu. His was not a conventional sonata-form analysis, identifying exposition, development, recapitulation and coda, which he dismissed as 'unilluminating', but an understanding of the

inevitability of the notes chosen to carry the impulse of the music from start to finish . . . Like a biochemist discovering that every human cell bears the imprint of the body which it belongs to, I had to establish why these notes and no others belonged to this sonata . . . I would track Lekeu's inspiration from the first note . . . to the second, then to the third, and eventually to the last, explaining each in terms of what preceded it; and thus (I hoped) basing the shape I gave his phrases, the speed, the volume and the relation between these factors, on certainty.

It is surprising that he had not been encouraged by Enesco or Busch to undertake any close textual study earlier in his teens. Even odder is the fact that in the next analysis he made in his memoirs – of the opening bars of the solo violin's first entry in the Beethoven Violin Concerto – he presented as a personal discovery the very obvious point that the violin's dominant seventh arpeggio, rising through the octaves, is a mirror reflection of the downward arpeggios heard in the previous two bars in the orchestra. After six pages of basic thematic dissection of the Beethoven he observed rather opaquely that stating the obvious made him feel 'less contingent': 'Discerning a form glassed in its smallest constituent part, I saw myself though a mirror and thus made a first conscious step towards adulthood.' Talking to a Johannesburg journalist soon after his arrival in South Africa, he was more specific about his new approach to music and the loss of innocence that it implied.

The Beethoven Violin Concerto now appears in a different light. I understand it much better than I did . . . I have gained more than I have lost but there was something about my playing then [Berlin, 1929] – something that one cannot keep. The Beethoven is much clearer than before, but that very clarity takes away a sort of – he hesitates – a sort of mystery about it. But I am not sorry.

South Africa embraced Yehudi as overwhelmingly as Australia had done. He gave five recitals in Johannesburg, two in Cape Town and one each in Pretoria, Pietermaritzburg and Durban. Another concert scheduled for Port Elizabeth had to be cancelled because Yehudi caught cold after descending 4000 feet to inspect a gold mine. He expressed sympathy for the toiling miners, whose working conditions he declared intolerable. Above ground he declined a ride in a Durban rickshaw operated by a Zulu boy: 'I would not like to be pulled by a human being.' His abiding South African memory was of the singing of the Zulu tribes. He loved them, and their music thrilled him. He told an American journalist that he preferred his Zulu recordings to jazz (whose attractions were to pass him by, despite the educational efforts of his first wife, until he met Stéphane Grappelli thirty-six years later).

Within a few weeks of discovering the nuts and bolts of musical composition, and embarking on a voyage of self-discovery, Yehudi decided to call a halt to the incessant touring of the previous decade. In Australia he had talked about his concert-giving routine in a high-flown way as if it were a sacred trust bestowed on him from on high. But his undoubted love of making music was coupled with commercial considerations that had been enthusiastically pursued by Moshe and his professional associates. The music agency run by Jack Salter and Laurence Evans had recently been incorporated as a division of Columbia Artists. Yehudi was big business: Moshe had just told South African journalists that Yehudi could not return there before 1941 because he was fully booked for the next five years. There was a degree of exaggeration in the claim, no doubt, but around this time their agent Jack Salter told the *Hollywood Reporter* that 'Yehudi has asked to be allowed to play in Russia for no fee – since he's already made huge amounts for everybody.'

Yehudi dropped his bombshell in a late-night discussion with his parents. Forty years after the event Moshe was able to reproduce his son's line of argument *verbatim*: 'The tour has been marvellous,' Yehudi began.

It's been fascinating to meet people of different nations and races, men of universal culture [Abravanel and Heinze?] and men of a primitive state of life [the Aborigines? or perhaps the New Zealanders?]. But now I have a new dream: two years of study, contemplation and research work; the broadening and deepening of my music! Ovations and so-called triumphs are not enough for me. There's so much to learn, to do . . . I want to delve into the literature of music . . . The time has come for me to start swimming on my own, even though I'll work with our dear Enesco. Two years on our ranch in California and a part of the time in Paris with Enesco. Do you think we can afford it?

The question was frankly grotesque. Here was the family bread-winner, not yet twenty and earning hundreds of thousands of dollars a year, obliged to plead for what amounted to the 'gap' year taken by many nineteen-year-olds before they go up to university. But retire-ment, even of a temporary nature, had not been on Moshe's agenda, let alone that of the industrious Evans and Salter. They accepted Yehudi's admirable decision with good grace after initial wails of woe. The sabbatical period was eventually whittled down to eighteen months, beginning in April 1936, so that extra concerts could be inserted into the New York schedule in March. The trip to study with Enesco in Paris did not materialize but in February 1937 they played together at a studio concert in New York, one of a pair of lucrative radio broadcasts which helped to cushion the loss of touring income. Yehudi's ambition to carry out musical research was eventually satis-fied by the rehabilitation of Robert Schumann's 'lost' Violin Concerto.

The Menuhins sailed for Southampton from Cape Town at the end of October and two weeks later, somewhere between the Canary Islands and Madeira, the siblings celebrated Moshe's forty-second birthday with a surprise party. Yehudi made a fine speech, in French, honouring his parents. Moshe translated sections of it for his memoirs:

My very dear father! This great day is for us like Bastille Day or the Fourth of July . . . Our beautiful and happy union is the fruit of your souls and it is an imper-ishable fruit which we enjoy always. This fruit represents our debt to you and this debt is our good fortune . . . It is you, you and mother, only the two of you, who have earned this good fortune . . . We owe it all to you. It is you who have pro-cured it for us with your sacrifices.

The World Tour continued with concerts in London, where one of his first actions was to present £20 to the Elgar Birthplace Fund. At his London press conference he spoke in a very modern way of his plans 'to develop my inner self'. He told journalists that he felt 'far greater things still to be dormant within him'; the forthcoming sabbatical had the purpose of 'broadening and deepening his musical powers'. It was noted that he had grown a pencil-thin moustache, Ronald Colman style, 'to celebrate his eighteen years'. (He was actually nineteen and a half.) After the interviews he 'retired to his dressing room to take the two cod-liver oil capsules which his mother requires him to take daily'.

His concert was not well received. 'One detected the inevitable change in his mentality', wrote *The Sunday Times*, whose critic disliked the 'anachronistic' cadenza composed by Sam Franko for the Mozart G major Concerto and attacked Yehudi for performing concertos at the Royal Albert Hall with only a piano accompaniment. The second London recital, with Hephzibah, was considered a more important event: the critic and violinist Ferrucio Bonavia likened their partnership to that of Ysaÿe and Busoni. But Yehudi, Bonavia wrote perceptively, had entered a period of transition:

Neither child nor man, he has lost the divine simplicity of the former without having laid the foundations of the individual style that is necessary in the grown man. The innocence has passed to his sister.

But a few months later, when they played the same sonata recital in New York – the Enesco No. 3, the Brahms D minor and the César Franck – the American critic Pitts Sandborn had no such reservations concerning Yehudi's playing, noting that his tone

had taken on a new transparent beauty . . . its capacity for color and shading was apparently boundless. The unfailingly beautiful purity of the tone, too, even in the most rapid passage work, was something to marvel at. Then the lordly ease and security of his execution supplied another marvel.

The European leg of Yehudi's world tour took in Madrid for the first time, just before the Civil War broke out. Germany was of course excluded and several concerts in Italy were cancelled after Fascist thugs had attacked some visiting American musicians. Moshe had once boasted that they travelled free on Italian State Railways at the invitation of Mussolini himself but now the dictator was hotly criticized by Yehudi. He had already told journalists in Australia that he was suffering deeply because Italy, a country he loved, was threatening to invade Abyssinia.

'Europe is like a volcano,' Moshe said. 'Nobody knows when it will erupt.' So he was exceptionally anxious to get his family back to America. But first there was a great deal of work to be done in Paris for HMV, both making up for the time lost during Yehudi's thirteen-month tour and also stock-piling material for the forthcoming two-season sabbatical. For three months Yehudi did little else but make recordings. On 19 December he played Mozart's G major Concerto (K.216), with Enesco conducting, and two works by Bach for solo violin – the B minor Partita (BWV 1002) and the G minor Sonata (BWV 1001). Two days later Yehudi returned with one of his favourite accompanists, Marcel Gazelle, to dispatch no fewer than eleven popular favourites, among them the *Tambourin chinois* and *Schön Rosmarin* by Fritz Kreisler. (In *Unfinished Journey* Yehudi described this as a 1936 disc but the recording date of December 1935 is correct.) To pin down Kreisler's elusive brand of worldly sophistication was a challenge he had long deferred. Eventually he bought the Austrian violinist's own recording and shut himself up in his room at the Majestic Hotel where he 'listened to it, played in the intervals of listening to it, played with it, and after a solid week's work I knew I had it'.

In January 1936 Hephzibah joined her brother to record Enesco's Third Sonata, Op. 25, and – as a 'filler' for the sixth side – the spirited finale of Beethoven's G major Sonata Op. 30 No. 3; unfortunately they never recorded the complete sonata. A fortnight later came a second batch of 'pops' including the famous *Praeludium and Allegro* which Kreisler had originally ascribed to Pugnani but later confessed to be his own inspired baroque pastiche. Two weeks later, on 3 February, came another pair of solo works by Bach, the Partita No. 3 in E (BWV 1006) and the Sonata No. 2 in A minor (BWV 1003). On the same day he recorded, as an extreme contrast, two Paganini caprices. A third caprice followed on 21 February, with Enesco at the piano, before Yehudi reverted to Bach for a recording of the A minor Concerto (BWV 1041), accompanied by a 'session' orchestra under Enesco's baton. Next day Maurice Gazelle took over at the keyboard for a clutch of 'pops', among them Slavonic Dances by Dvořák, a Hungarian Dance by Brahms and the *Caprice viennois* by Kreisler.

Only a week later Yehudi recorded the Dvořák Violin Concerto. This time the accompaniment was provided by a named orchestra, that of the Société des Concerts du Conservatoire, once again with Enesco in command. Excellent photographs were taken of the two men at rehearsal: Enesco is at his most serene, Yehudi sports his little moustache and Hephzibah looks on adoringly. On the final studio dates of this HMV marathon, 4 and 5 March, fine chamber-music recordings were made of Tchaikovsky's Trio, Op. 50, and Beethoven's 'Ghost' Trio, Op. 70. Hephzibah was joined by the German-born cellist, Maurice Eisenberg, who was a professor at the Paris Conservatoire.

On Yehudi's 'official' nineteenth birthday, 22 January 1936 (incredibly, the fiction was still preserved), his violin-maker friend Emile

Français made an emotional presentation ('tears rolled down his cheeks') of the perfect replica he had made of Yehudi's 'Prince Khevenhüller' Stradivarius. It is not clear whether it was used for any of the recordings mentioned above, but he did occasionally play it in concerts (without informing the critics in advance), claiming that it had the same qualities as the original. Français had spared no effort in its construction, giving it eighteen separate coats of varnish and even arranging for the instrument to be left out in the Italian sunshine at a violin workshop in Cremona, Stradivarius's home town.

The three-month sojourn in Paris was probably the longest period Yehudi ever spent in one location in his entire life. He delayed his departure to attend the dress rehearsal of Enesco's opera Œdipe, which had a libretto by Edmond Fleg. Fleg's two sons were among Yehudi's few teenage friends. Daniel was invited to join them in California later in the year and Hephzibah had a crush on the older, Maurice, who was killed soon after the outbreak of the war. Daniel later committed suicide in Occupied France.

The world tour concluded in New York in March 1936 with two musical occasions: the concert with Hephzibah, already described, and a nationwide broadcast from Radio City. Toscanini attended the Carnegie Hall recital and sent down a request that Yehudi and Hephzibah should add some Mozart to their programme. They obliged with two encores, the slow movement from the E flat Sonata (K. 302) and the *Allegro* from the A major (K. 526). Moshe's self-delusion about his children continued, despite the frantic period of recording activity just concluded in France: 'We do not intend to exploit Hephzibah. Yehudi has not been exploited. For every period of concert playing Yehudi has had a corresponding period of rest.'

After attending his New York recital his friend Lydia Perera did not agree. In her diary she noted, 'Yehudi looks tired and weak. Mobs rushing through the centre aisle, shouting their acclaim.' The entry is headed by the correct date, 22 March, but gives the wrong venue, 'Town Hall'. And there is no centre aisle at Carnegie Hall. The mystery deepens in Lydia's next entry:

29 March 1936. Last concert [no venue given] before Yehudi's retirement. Russian music. Yehudi looks tired, indifferent and sad. The music fits his looks and mood. I had to grit my teeth as I left the Hall.

Lydia Perera died long ago: the mood she depicts in her diary may be accurate but not the facts.

On 29 March Yehudi was taking part in a 'farewell' broadcast from 10 to 11 p.m. with the General Motors Symphony Orchestra at New York's Radio City, under the baton of the Hungarian Erno Rapee, whose weekly series was hugely popular in the 1930s. Far from playing Russian music, Yehudi's contribution to the programme consisted of the *Adagio* from the Mozart G major Concerto and shorter pieces by Nováček, Kreisler and Brahms. *Variety* gave the broadcast a rave review: 'Menuhin whipped his magic horsehair across those pulsating strings and made the music gush forth . . . Menuhin and Rapee together make music that the average radioite will appreciate.' Another report mentioned the producer's injunction to Yehudi before the broadcast began: 'Get the violin four inches closer to the mike. Don't even glance at the conductor.'

The new guest house in Alma would not be ready until 1 May so the family spent a few more weeks in New York. To while away the time Yehudi and his sisters studied ballroom dancing. Yehudi learned the tango to the tune of 'Jealousy'. Witnesses suggested he was withdrawn and unhappy and there was the incident in Central Park to which allusion has already been made when, in a sudden fit of pique, he slammed the door of his new Cadillac so hard that the glass shattered. Twenty years after the event his biographer Robert Magidoff wrote confidently that 'whatever freedom he might have wrested he had no idea how to use' but the suggestion that he was a prisoner, supervised to the point of suffocation by his parents, seems far-fetched, and publicly there was universal approval for his decision to withdraw from the music scene for eighteen months. To speed him on his way, General Motors had given him a new Cadillac loaded with extras. It was freighted out to California along with their 'monstrosity of an old Delage' which Moshe had imported from France: 'When we drive down Fifth Avenue everybody jeers!'

Accompanied by twenty-three trunks and suitcases (a separate trunkful of scores had been sent on ahead) the family took the Overland Express to Oakland, the very same destination to which young Moshe Mnuchin had booked his wife and baby's passage from Grand Central station close on two decades earlier. They turned their back on Europe because of what Moshe called 'its nightly scare that the sky will rain bombs'. Ironically their first experience in California was an explosion of sorts: their car had a blow-out while they were driving at speed. But soon they were off again, heading for their new home in the Santa Clara hills. 'I'll raise fruit and vegetables and chickens,' Yehudi told reporters. 'I'm going back to the good earth. I have no set programme. Life in the country imposes none.'

Recommended Recordings

Chausson: *Poème* for violin and orchestra
Orchestre symphonique de Paris, conducted by George Enesco
EMI 5 65960 2
Recorded: June 1933
YM received intense personal coaching from Enesco for this recording.

Mozart: Sonata in A (K. 526) for violin and piano
with Hephzibah Menuhin (piano)
EMI 7 63834 2
Recorded: September 1933
The first Yehudi–Hephzibah duo recording.

Paganini: Concerto No. 1 in D
Paris Symphony Orchestra, conducted by Pierre Monteux
EMI 5 65959 2
Recorded: June 1934
The virtuosity of the eighteen-year-old is heard at full flood. In the slow movement his generous flow of lyrical tone reminds us that he said he felt like an opera singer when performing this work.

Beethoven: Trio in D, Op. 70 No. 1 ('Ghost')
with Maurice Eisenberg (cello) and Hephzibah Menuhin (piano)
BID LAB 127
Recorded: March 1936
YM's first recording of chamber music; the Tchaikovsky Trio, Op. 50, is on the same CD. The recording was made just before YM's 'sabbatical'.

Enesco: Sonata No. 3 in A minor, Op. 25, 'in the popular Romanian style'
with Hephzibah Menuhin (piano)
Recorded: May 1938
The Menuhin duo's tribute to its mentor and friend.

Kreisler: *Schön Rosmarin; Praeludium e Allegro in the style of Pugnani*
with Marcel Gazelle (piano)
BID LAB 126 – *Menuhin Plays Virtuoso Violin Music*
Recorded: 1935–36
Two of YM's favourite Kreisler works. Their popularity helped to lift his record sales above those of Kreisler himself (and Heifetz).

7 Escape from Paradise

The Menuhins wrapping up well for an ocean voyage

1936: May: establishment of family home at Los Gatos; the 'sabbatical' routine; 1937: February: Radio concerts in New York; November: American première of Schumann's 'lost' Violin Concerto; 1938: March: meeting with Lindsay and Nola Nicholas in London; May: marriage of Yehudi and Nola.

MOSHE SHOULD HAVE REALIZED that the guest house would never be big enough for a family residence. Not, at any rate, for the Menuhin family, with its violinist son who intended to play quartets once a week while he was on holiday, its two pianist daughters pounding away at their practice on separate pianos every day, its resident cook and handyman (Chinese), its long list of teenager friends invited for different months of the summer to share the vacation. The panoramic view from the new house was breathtaking but with memories still relatively fresh of the undulating green lawns and the wistaria around the windows of their former home at Ville d'Avray, how cruelly bare the clearing bulldozed out of the Californian forest must have seemed. Yehudi reported graphically that there were 'no trees or flowers to soften its crude nudity'. So the brave talk of the family intending to spend an entire year on their Californian 'ranch' was something of a fraud. Moshe and Yehudi had spoken so glowingly and so often about their plans for the so-called retirement period that the reality was a terrible let-down.

Not only was the guest house too small; its isolated position also posed a real danger. Ever since March 1932, when Charles Lindbergh's son had been kidnapped and then murdered, the fear of an abduction and ransom threat had haunted Yehudi's parents. A few weeks earlier, when they were still in New York, reports of a 'snatch-proof electric fence' for the new Menuhin estate had been circulating in Californian newspapers; it was said to be equipped with 'an intricate system of electric eyes and electric alarms . . . the last word in protection against gangsters'. It was intended 'to out-Alcatraz Alcatraz'. Moshe was reported to carry a loaded revolver; he said his family had been 'living in a glass house' and their new home would therefore be 'shutter-proof to prying eyes'.

When he got back to California Moshe claimed this outbreak of sensationalism must have been put about either by an idiotic prankster or as a vengeful act by 'a disgruntled or disappointed person'. (He was thinking, perhaps, of 'the boys', Dennison and Ingerson, with whom he was no longer on speaking terms since cancelling the Villa Cherkess project, over which the two men had laboured hard on the absent Menuhins' behalf. Or could it have been the Los Angeles architect who had been deprived of his commission for the unbuilt big house?) Unable to resist making an issue out of anything associated with his son, Moshe sent the press cuttings to J. Edgar Hoover, Director of the FBI, requesting advice. He was presumably unaware that Mr Hoover would have been highly suspicious of Moshe's own radical attitudes, had he known them, let alone of Yehudi's. Fortunately Mr Hoover was familiar only with Yehudi's fame. 'I want you to feel', he wrote to Moshe, 'that I personally stand ready to assist you in any way possible if any occasion arises which necessitates the use of the facilities of this bureau.' But no case of attempted kidnapping was ever detected.

'It is too lonely and too dangerous.' Marutha's chilling verdict on the new Menuhin property broke Moshe's heart but he knew she was right. His fantasy was shattered: 'I buried on that hill all my personal, innocent, fateful dreams, my poetry, my romance, my attachment to the soil and nature.' With her husband self-confessedly 'defeated, bereaved', and her children in shock, Marutha took charge. The family drove back to the Hotel Lyndon in Los Gatos and stayed there a month while Marutha went house-hunting, just as she had done in Paris after the sudden abandonment of Adolf Busch and their Basel home. Yehudi's sabbatical had been planned as 'her' year with her son before he went out into the world as a man (another fantasy: Yehudi was already twenty) and she was not going to allow it to be spoilt by her husband's shilly-shallying incompetence, first in shying away from building Villa Cherkess and more recently by deluding himself that they could all squeeze in to what Yehudi described as 'a little, hot, dusty, flimsy cottage'.

She discovered a lovely yellow clapboard family house standing in a large garden on a hill above the town. It rambled in every direction, Yehudi recalled, 'with flower beds and greensward framing an ancient oak, and a guest house in whose main room we could perform plays among ourselves, as the previous owner had built a stage there'. From its terrace on a clear day you could see down the Santa Clara valley as far as the Pacific. The property was next to the large estate of the Sacred Heart Novitiate, a Jesuit college whose substantial fruit orchards and vineyards ran up the hillside behind the house. The Menuhins were invited by the Rector, the hospitable Father Dunn, to use the novitiate's trails and the tennis courts whenever they felt so inclined. 'A foothold in paradise' is how Yehudi described the new family home, which was later named Rancho Yaltah. Neither Yehudi nor his father mentioned the price in their books but Yaltah's son Lionel Rolfe says the place was bought (in the aftermath of the Depression) for as little as $30,000, half the projected cost of building Villa Cherkess. So perhaps Moshe's caution was well advised after all.

Back on course after a stormy overture, the summer of 1936 proved as 'happy and carefree as had been intended'. The violin remained untouched for months, temporarily displaced in Yehudi's affections by the Cadillac, which had been re-equipped after the blow-out with elegant white-walled tyres. 'I had a sense of style in motor cars,' he wrote proudly, adding that in those days one could lose oneself for hours on the country roads without meeting another soul.

I would make expeditions to the sea at Monterey, to the observatory on Mount Hamilton across the valley or just up into the hills . . . few motor cars can have backed up more one-way tracks or fought their way over more impassable trails than I did in my Cadillac.

It's not clear whether he ever drove alone. According to Daniel Fleg, the friend from Paris who joined them later in the summer, Moshe was nervous about letting Yehudi take the wheel so Fleg was placed in charge when he and the young Menuhins drove down to the coast resort of Carmel to pick up their friends Victor and Rosalie Leventritt. But Yehudi took over the driving as soon as they left Los Gatos, prepared to risk Moshe's displeasure when they returned. 'Today,' Fleg noted in his diary, 'Yehudi has made, symbolically speaking, a great step towards the independent and normal life of the adolescent of our times!'

At twenty Yehudi was technically no longer an adolescent, although Fleg was doubtless among those who thought his friend was still nineteen, since his 'official' twentieth birthday was not until 22 January 1937. There were other signs that Yehudi was rather young for his age in non-musical matters; indeed Marutha seems positively to have encouraged a regression to childhood. Thus the family adopted several pets or, as Yehudi romantically expands it, 'a whole menagerie', among them two stray cats, Jamilla and Pasha, and a former police dog named Alupka (after a town in the Crimea). Yehudi gave his mother a goat named Feodosya after 'a centre of Karaitic culture' – yet another of Marutha's references to her Crimean homeland, unvisited since she was a little girl. All her oriental rugs and wall hangings were shipped back from Ville d'Avray so she was once again able to establish her very personal ambience. She had just turned forty. Rosalie Leventritt described her as

very beautiful with those wonderfully blue eyes of hers and the dusty-blond hair one can see from under the big straw hats she wears. She rules the household with an iron hand but pretends not to . . . you are always aware of the steel claws you cannot see. Anything she says she needs to say only once.

Daniel Fleg also felt Yehudi was under constant surveillance, commenting in his diary that there was 'something excessive, almost offensive' in the way he was supervised. Another visitor noted that Marutha always found a place to sit that was quite high, 'so she can keep an eye on everything'. This nightmare vision of a permanently patrolled house party is softened by Fleg's account of merry charades and play-acting. Yehudi played the lead in *Cyrano de Bergerac*, mounted in honour of his parents' twenty-second wedding anniversary; Hephzibah was Roxane and Yaltah did all the other parts. Yehudi wrote nostalgically of nocturnal rambles in the Jesuits' estate when 'the cool air was balmy with the scent of vegetation'. Moon and stars provided illumination most nights, 'but without any light at all I could find my way surefooted, so well had I come to know the different fragrances of copse and trail'. Sometimes they would pick the shrivelled but extra-sweet grapes forgotten in the harvest or they would climb to the top of the hill, which was

crowned by four or five immense rustling eucalyptus trees, the folded landscape beneath us dimly sensed in the night's faint glow; and so home again in a state of exaltation to make ourselves omelettes at dissolute hours.

Moshe made sure the holidays were structured: 'There were hours for walking, hours for resting, reading, swimming and sunbathing.' The pool had been installed as soon as they moved in. Daniel Fleg, ailing when he arrived and in need of sunshine and building up, was 'hired' for three hours a day to help with its construction. Moshe listed other young people invited to share the Californian fun:

Many were the boys and girls who came for short or long stays: Beveridge and Ferguson Webster from Pittsburgh, both fine pianists; Mary-Louise Bine and her sister Barbara from San Francisco; Max Kahn and his niece Ida Fertig; Bernard Kaufman and his sister Joyce; Shirley Kay, the sweet daughter of our dearest friends Joseph and Ann Kay from Berkeley.

Moshe doesn't mention it but there was surely an element of the marriage market in this constant coming and going. Marutha made no secret of it. Interviewed about Yehudi in October 1936 she was widely reported as saying, 'I hope he will marry early and have a home and children of his own.' On his next trip to New York Yehudi impulsively invited his friend Shirley Kay to join the train: 'We'll take good care of you. Come on, I dare you!' Shirley declined the challenge. For Moshe this was one of the great might-have-beens in his son's life. Moshe's other favourite among Yehudi's teenage feminine friends, Lydia Perera, did not make the trip to Los Gatos.

Another guest was William Stix, a young lawyer from St Louis who took a shine to Hephzibah, who had temporarily lost her heart to Maurice Fleg, Daniel's older brother. Meanwhile Yaltah, then fourteen, was quick to develop crushes on the visiting young men. She wrote poems for her adored ones – in a selection of three languages. For her fifteenth birthday in October the family mounted a masquerade at which Yehudi distinguished himself in front of a hundred guests by dancing the tango to the tune of 'Jealousy'. He said it was 'twice as hard as a sonata recital'. When Yehudi began his popular series of jazz duets with Stéphane Grappelli in 1971, 'Jealousy' turned out to be the only piece of popular music he knew.

In his memoirs Yehudi didn't even mention Shirley Kay. His own declared favourite was Rosalie Leventritt, the future musical philanthropist. His description of her is hardly the stuff of romance, however – 'a very vital, interesting, pretty girl' – and as a house guest she had a serious drawback, 'an ungovernable horror of cats'. She had certain privileges none the less, being the first to dive into the newly completed pool. Yehudi played Mozart sonatas with her and danced with her more than with anybody else. Moshe said she departed 'with a tear in her eye' but when Yehudi drove her to catch the train that would take her back to her parents, who were vacationing at Carmel, he apparently couldn't bring himself even to kiss her goodbye. After she had gone Yehudi confided in Willa Cather, whose response cannot have been much comfort: 'A little heartache is a good companion for a young man on his holiday.' Given the friendship between Marutha and Cather it comes as no surprise to learn that the American novelist, writing to Yehudi, was not in favour of frivolous, modern American women: 'I rather think you will need a girl with a more disciplined nature than our girls are likely to have . . . Fortune has always been good to you, my boy, and I rather suspect her crowning favor will be a girl like that: slight, heroic, delicate, unconquerable (sounds as if I were describing Marutha, doesn't it?). Well, like enough you will marry someone much your mother's type.' How wrong she was!

In fact his closest emotional tie at this period was with his own sister Hephzibah. Yaltah remembers being an awkward third – as she so often was in her childhood – while her elder brother and sister 'would take long walks . . . hand-in-hand reciting poems about nature and man, picking flowers along the way'. Years later, after they had both got married, they were still describing themselves as 'the incestuous sonata players'.

The Menuhins fell out of the public gaze in the summer of 1936. It was news of only local interest when Yehudi became a sponsor of the San José Opera Association, which was rehearsing *The Gondoliers* at the time, or took out a liquor licence in order to release from bond the crates of champagne sent over by European well-wishers. Apart from a few trips into San Francisco to attend the opera and to hear Fritz Kreisler in concert, it was a full nine months before Yehudi's 'retirement' was interrupted. Then, at the end of January 1937, travelling in their own railroad car, the entire family went to New York to watch Yehudi taking part in another of Erno Rapee's regular Sunday night broadcasts, this time from Carnegie Hall.

Middle-brow, popular culture was at its zenith in America. George Enesco was in town, serving as guest conductor of the New York Philharmonic in its first season since Toscanini's departure, and he was invited to play the Bach Double Concerto with his former pupil and also to conduct the radio orchestra for Yehudi's performance of Sarasate's *Gypsy Airs*. As a further compliment to Enesco, Erno Rapee conducted his First Rhapsody. Mozart's *Figaro* Overture and Debussy's *Fêtes* topped and tailed another attractive broadcast: 'The apotheosis of radio programs . . . we were hearing ethereal music – the ambrosia of the gods. The singing tones [of the violins] resembled seraphic voices.' After the broadcast Enesco declared that Yehudi 'has nothing to learn from me now'.

Moshe had only a few days to get his personal publicity machine up and running, but he achieved an impressive photograph of Marutha giving her daughters a cooking lesson in their New York hotel suite. 'My first wish for my daughters', she was quoted as saying, 'is a happy home life. I have enjoyed motherhood and I'd hate for my girls to miss it.' Her position on her daughters pursuing a musical career, hitherto adamantly hostile, had softened significantly: 'However, if they have an overpowering urge for a career in music at the sacrifice of these things, I would not stop them although I would be disappointed.' She had been forced to modify her stance because of the broadcast Hephzibah was about to make with her brother on CBS's Ford Sunday Evening Hour. For a fee of $10,000, which (inevitably) Moshe claimed to be the highest ever paid, the American radio public would at last have a chance to enjoy 'these famous musical partners'. A few weeks later Hephzibah dutifully told another journalist that she was 'proud of the fact that she can bake bread and cooks the entire dinner for the family on cook's night out'. But her heart was surely in her music. For her broadcast début she played solo Chopin and, with her brother, movements from violin and piano sonatas by Mozart and Franck. Accompanied by the Detroit Symphony under Eugene Ormandy, Yehudi concluded the show with Ravel's *Tzigane*.

When Yehudi was approached to play on the Ford Hour, Moshe stipulated that the programme should be of violin and piano sonatas only, with no 'popular' pieces. Words were then put into his mouth by the *New York Post*:

Mr Henry Ford and Mr Edsel Ford frankly confessed that they did not know what sonatas were. So we explained, and you might say that they got a quick musical education. But I must say the Ford people took a sensible businesslike view of the matter. They said that, since Yehudi receives a greater fee than any other concert artist in the world, he must be good, and they'd be glad to have him, sonatas and all.

Moshe was furious about the *Post*'s story. It was a fabrication: he had never met the Fords and all the negotiations had been in the hands of Yehudi's agent. All Moshe knew of the automobile magnates' musical expertise was that Henry Ford was a collector of precious old Italian violins. When all three generations of the Ford family called on the Menuhins at their Detroit hotel, Moshe added, 'We were absolutely charmed by them.' The radio concert was given in Detroit's Masonic Hall, before a live audience of five thousand. Just before it began, Yehudi discovered that during his sabbatical he had grown out of his concert tails. Marutha had to cut them off and pin them back with safety pins.

B. H. Haggin, the *Brooklyn Eagle*'s somewhat curmudgeonly critic, did not enjoy the broadcast. It had originally been announced as a recital but then modified, he grumbled, so it ended up as three fast sonata movements in succession. He objected to the slanted interval talk promoting the Ford management view in an industrial dispute. Worse, Hephzibah played her solos badly.

The Los Gatos retreat resumed at the beginning of March 1937. In July, two months before Yehudi's return to the concert platform, the family gave a joint interview to the *San Francisco News* (5 July 1937). 'We are self-sustaining,' said Moshe, 'spiritually, socially and humanly.' Marutha's satisfaction with the holiday routine suggested she had had enough of the travelling life. Los Gatos for her was 'heaven, just perfect! I wish we never had to set foot off this place again.' Moshe agreed, 'Our children are having the time of their lives with the groups of boys and girls coming each month from such places as Australia, South Africa, France, New Zealand and other eastern cities [of the US].' The image was of an international cultural youth camp. Mrs Menuhin repeated her mantra. She 'wants the children to marry and is very frank about it'. Moshe toed the party line. He, too, hoped Yehudi would marry young and when he did (ominously), 'His wife will have to become part of his family.' He 'wants a little colony of Menuhins on the Los Gatos hills.'

The children sang a different song in the interview. The Californian retreat was 'all right, but I get sort of restless' (Yehudi); 'very pleasant but I miss my friends in Paris' (Yaltah); 'I can be happy any place. What I miss is Europe' (Hephzibah). Marutha was scathing about Hephzibah: 'She yearns for Paris and solo recitals and a career of her own. I say that it is better that she should be happy than famous.' God knows what rebellious thoughts passed through Hephzibah's mind but outwardly the picture of a contented family was maintained.

The last family entertainment of the summer took place on the parents' twenty-third wedding anniversary, 7 August. Following family tradition, it was a theatrical performance: Chekhov's one-act play *The Proposal*, acted by the youngsters in Russian. There was a certain irony in the title: within twelve months all three Menuhin children would have made or received proposals and be married. Moshe reported that his son had drunk an entire bottle of champagne at the party after the play with no after-effects: 'We call ourselves the mad Menuhins,' he added. The candid press interview was part of the campaign to let the world know about Yehudi's return to the international concert circuit. New repertoire was promised, including the Lalo Violin Concerto, Op. 20, and Pizzetti's Third Sonata, both of which Yehudi had studied with Enesco in the final spurt before his sabbatical. His engagement book was said to be 'booked solid', even though a projected tour of Scandinavia had been abandoned 'owing to the terrible state of affairs in Europe'. A second tour of Australia was booked for 1940.

Yehudi seems to have been quite happy to recommence the arduous touring life that his agents Evans and Salter had mapped out on familiar lines and which Moshe had enthusiastically endorsed, even though the efforts of a new press aide, Salter's wife Grace, were a private cause for complaint: she planted sentimental stories about animals singing outside his window while he practised. But the new Yehudi, twenty-one when he re-emerged from the sabbatical, was looking for an extra dimension to his career, for musical experiences well beyond the standard repertoire. Under Adolf Busch's influence he had already become something of a scholar, studying his Bach from the original manuscripts, reverting to Paganini's original orchestration for his D major Concerto, performing the complete *Symphonie espagnole* by Lalo rather than a truncated version, and championing little-known concertos by Mozart. In 1937 he embraced a cause that was to bring him into direct confrontation with the Nazis, that of the so-called 'lost' Violin Concerto by Robert Schumann.

Schumann took only a fortnight to compose the Concerto in 1853, a few months before the onset of his mental illness. Like the *Phantasie* for violin and orchestra which he had composed a few weeks earlier, and which by a happy coincidence Yehudi was studying privately at Los Gatos in the spring of 1937, it was written for the twenty-two-year-old violin virtuoso Joseph Joachim. For the remainder of Schumann's brief life Joachim had loyally professed enthusiasm for the work but he never performed it in public and at his death in 1907 he bequeathed the manuscript to the Prussian State Library in Berlin, with the instruction that it was not to be released for a hundred years. And there it lay in decent obscurity, presumed unworthy of inclusion in the master's published *oeuvre*, until in 1933 the violinist Jelly d'Arányi, a great-niece of Joachim, claimed to have received a spirit message from the composer urging her to have the work exhumed, as it were, and then performed. Despite opposition from Schumann's family, the German music publisher Schott began the preparation of a performing edition and in April 1937 Yehudi was sent a photostat with a request for his opinion.

Moshe said his son's eyes were glowing and his enthusiasm knew no bounds when he had finished studying the score. It was, he pronounced, 'great Schumann music – sorrowful, romantic, mature and lyrical', and he requested international performing rights for the following season. Schotts negotiated with the curator of the library, obtained the consent of Joachim's son to publish the score (thus breaking the terms of the bequest) and reached an agreement with Schumann's only surviving child, an eighty-six-year-old daughter living in Switzerland. Classical music was suddenly headline news. 'I feel as if I have a holy trust,' Yehudi told the *San Francisco Chronicle* (11 August 1937). 'The work is great and so beautiful.' The *New York Times* carried a long feature by Olin Downes. The *March of Time* newsreel series promised a screen dramatization of the story of the Concerto's composition. A Californian paper said Yehudi would introduce the concerto at his 30 September San Francisco Opera House recital. Next day the *Pensacola News* – Moshe's cutting service was very thorough – said the first performance anywhere would be on 12 November in St Louis. But a Cleveland paper reported the unlikely news that Yehudi was going to Leipzig to give the première at the Gewandhaus on 6 October. Meanwhile Jelly d'Arányi announced that as the person who had, so to speak, discovered the Concerto *she* would be giving the world première with the BBC Symphony Orchestra – on 20 October in London.

Neither violinist had reckoned with the Nazis. It was unthinkable that they would permit the world première of a work by one of the fatherland's greatest composers to be given anywhere but in Germany, and certainly not by a Jew. Early in September Yehudi received what Moshe called 'a thunderbolt of an enigmatic short cablegram'. No performance could be given in America, it said, until after the première by the German violinist Georg Kulenkampff in Leipzig on 12 October. Moshe immediately announced that Yehudi would include the Concerto in his Los Angeles recital on 17 October. The Germans then delayed the première until 13 November, at the Reichskulturkammer in Berlin, thus putting paid to Yehudi's St Louis dates. 'Reich forces violinist to change plans' was the headline. There was no way Yehudi could steal a march on the Germans since Schotts had all the orchestral material in Europe and would not release it for shipment until the German date was in place. But at least Yehudi managed to dissuade them from publishing an edited, 'performing' version of the concerto: he insisted on working from the *Urtext*.

When the première eventually took place at a morning concert on 26 November, with Kulenkampff and the Berlin Philharmonic under Karl Böhm, the performance was broadcast worldwide from Berlin. Yehudi heard it at six in the morning in Richmond, Virginia, where he was touring. Kulenkampff, he said, was a violinist of 'the first brand', but the edition he played was not the original. 'He deliberately streamlined the last movement – it lacked the virility it needed.' At the same so-called celebration concert Dr Goebbels boasted that three thousand Jews had been ousted from the ranks of German musicians since 1933.

In the early days of the controversy Yehudi had taken a relaxed view: 'I ask no special rights, no monopolies', he told *Time* magazine

(23 August 1937). 'Let anyone play it who realizes the greatness of the work.' A month later his patience was fraying and he branded the Germans' insistence on postponement as a 'shocking decision' which 'interfered with serious contractual obligations'. Although the voice of Moshe can be heard huffing and puffing in the background here, a week later Yehudi's natural, bridge-building warmth had returned:

Because I am a non-Aryan is no reason why I cannot be pleasant about the matter. I feel no rancour towards Germany. Music-lovers of Germany want to hear the Concerto first. Can I blame them for that?

By now it was clear that this was a battle he could not win, a battle he had been ill advised to undertake in the first place. The fracas with the Nazis helped to create publicity for the forthcoming tour, but his artistic judgement was called into question. Not for the first time he threw his reputation behind a work that for all its incidental beauties is flawed and to this day survives only on the margin of the violin concerto repertoire. Olin Downes dismissed it as 'a very weak composition: Joachim was right in consigning this work to the archives'. In his autobiography Yehudi made no reference whatsoever to the Schumann episode. But at the time he was very keen to present the world with his *Urtext* reading as soon after the German première as possible. A performance with orchestra had to be deferred to a swiftly rearranged concert under his old friend Vladimir Golschmann on 23 December in St Louis. That was preceded by a performance with piano accompaniment in Carnegie Hall on 5 December and while on tour he played the Concerto privately to the music critics of several cities. On 30 November he visited the Boston home of Dr Serge Koussevitzky, who immediately scheduled it for performance the following February, commenting that it was so similar to the Brahms Concerto that 'Joachim was protecting his friend Brahms's reputation from possible criticism of plagiarism.' Brahms never heard the Concerto but it is possible that he may have seen the manuscript as he first visited Schumann on the very day the work was completed.

Yehudi's tussle with the German authorities, coupled with a photo feature about him in the widely read *Life* magazine (a portrait of his hands was on the cover), put him back into the public eye just as he began his seventy-concert autumn and winter tour. The eighteen-month holiday régime of hiking and swimming (press photos reveal him to have been a nifty diver) had eliminated any trace of pudginess and transformed him into 'a tall, straight and very slender young man'. A cartoon showed his former shorts and blouse on a hanger with the caption 'Yehudi's Mr Menuhin now'. There were countless photo reports of Moshe helping his son to don his first white tie and tails for the opening of the concert season. Characteristically Yehudi forgot his waistcoat after the interval and had to be reminded by his valet, the ubiquitous Moshe, who 'changes every stitch of Yehudi's clothing at intermission from the skin out'.

Yehudi contributed his own programme notes for his San Francisco recital, where the 'largest audience ever jammed in to the Memorial Opera House' (4,540) heard him play a new programme that included Lalo's unknown Concerto in F, sonatas by Mozart and Pizzetti and bravura music by Paganini. A second San Francisco recital featured the Mendelssohn Concerto (with his friend Ferguson Webster again at the piano) together with sonatas by Bach and Beethoven and more Paganini fireworks. 'A breath-taking splash' by 'the world's supreme violinist' summed up the general verdict on his performance. Returning after his long lay-off he was 'perhaps a finer craftsman than ever. Infinite refinement and subtlety of detail distinguished his every phrase and shading'; 'Grown-up Yehudi, same rare spirit'. A solitary hostile note was struck in Washington the following January. The critic of the *Herald*, one Glenn Dillard Gunn, feared that Adolf Busch's teaching had been detrimental. 'Yehudi returned to the US trying to play like a German and doing it badly enough. Freedom had departed from his brow and luster from his tone.' That Yehudi had not received a lesson from Busch for over six years seems to have escaped Mr Gunn.

The West Coast tour took Yehudi north to Seattle and south to Los Angeles, where Hollywood film moguls were again on the prowl, this time for an MGM project tentatively entitled 'Symphony of Six Million'. Half a million dollars were on offer to Yehudi but a 'shocked' Moshe once again spoke snobbishly of the abyss between Hollywood and the Menuhins. Yaltah thinks Marutha was behind these constant refusals: the cinema was simply not part of her culture. For his part Moshe had a vision: 'The time will come when there will be film theatres for music,' he told the *Los Angeles Times*. 'Concert halls for thousands in which regular concerts of great music will be seen and heard from sound film.' Yehudi was to help the concept become reality a decade later, only for it to be overtaken by the advent of television.

During the winter, he was joined by Hephzibah for another CBS

Music Hour radio concert, relayed from the Masonic Temple in Detroit. She played the César Franck *Symphonic Variations* and he the last two movements of the Mendelssohn Concerto; together they performed part of a Mozart sonata. After a public duo concert a few weeks later, the *New York Times* noted that the brother and sister had 'a hypnotic effect upon their audiences, not based exclusively on their music making. Their bearing and demeanour have the quality of unspoiled directness.' Yet Marutha remained bewitched by her son and as determined as ever to denigrate Hephzibah. In an interview she stated that Yehudi was by far the most remarkable member of the family.

Yehudi certainly stayed in the limelight that winter. A critic commented sarcastically that the Schumann Concerto was given as much press attention as a presidential fishing trip or a Hollywood divorce. Yehudi performed it with orchestra for the first time in St Louis over Christmas, then in New York under Enesco in January and in Boston in February under Koussevitzky (who vetoed a proposal to do the Brahms in the second half, preferring the Mendelssohn). A flurry of recitals followed, including a duo evening at the Metropolitan Opera House which Olin Downes likened to a performance heard through the wrong end of opera glasses. Yehudi and Hephzibah played in front of a cloth which *The New Yorker* said looked like a happily discarded setting for the bridal scene in *Lucia di Lammermoor*. Time was also found to make a recording of the Schumann Concerto with the New York Philharmonic under its new chief conductor, John Barbirolli.

Journalists seemed ready to give Yehudi a platform on any subject he chose. 'Compulsory education should be abolished,' he announced in Cincinnati.

We are a literate nation so why should we have a school system whose purpose is mainly to encourage literacy? Literacy would survive without schools. It would be handed down from parents to children. And that's what we should have. Such a system would make for individuality instead of the mass thinking which comes from mass education. It would strengthen the family unit and that would be a bulwark against Fascism. The governments of dictators live by absorbing the family unit in the state.

He naïvely added that Italy and Germany will bluff 'but will not fight the democratic nations'. Sometimes the reporters made him sound like a budding Oscar Wilde. 'Marriage is not always fatal,' he told the *Philadephia Evening Public Ledger*. 'I would like nothing better than to get married. Of course I haven't met the girl yet.'

Moshe was overheard grumbling about the backstage crush of young women who came to greet his son: 'Really we can't be too careful these days.' He owned up to an inadequacy:

I can't read a note of music. I could hardly be a page-turner. I appreciate good music but I have no talent for it. I have the dignity of a father but the duties of a valet.

After he let it be known that during his sabbatical Yehudi had turned down fees worth $2 million, the number of girls who came seeking autographs (and who knows what else beside) did not diminish. 'I have plenty of young boy and girl friends,' Yehudi told a Rochester reporter.

We have great fun together. But I do not go to night clubs or travel with country-club sets. I think my social life is broader than most boys', but in a different way. After all I have friends all over the world. I have crossed the Atlantic eighteen times.

But he had never seen a baseball game.

On 12 February 1938, he was off to Europe again, one of the 311 passengers who sailed on the SS *Ile de France*. He was to give eighteen concerts in Ireland, England and Scotland, where a picture of Yehudi playing the bagpipes was headlined: 'Hoots Mon, 'Tis MacMenuhin!' To readers of the *Aberdonian* he piped an increasingly familiar air:

I have never written a love letter and when I do it will be my first and last . . . My parents want me to marry as early as they did. I am afraid my great passion will always be my violin playing but I have a place for an ideal girl, too.

It was not long before she made her appearance – less than a month after he spoke those prophetic words.

But first, on Sunday, 6 March, there was the unveiling of the Schumann Concerto in London, with the London Philharmonic under the aegis of Sir Henry Wood, a conductor new to Yehudi on the rostrum although they had met five years previously at a London lunch party organized by his socially assiduous father. In addition to the Schumann, Yehudi played both the Brahms and the Mendelssohn, so it was another marathon event. 'Technical difficulties do not exist for him,' wrote Ferruccio Bonavia in the *Daily Telegraph*. Yehudi's tone and intonation were flawless; 'Something has gone, however.' He evoked Yehudi's performances of Mozart earlier in the decade,

which combined in a miraculous way a naturalness as charming as the voice of a child with absolute mastery of exposition. That simplicity has now given place to a sweetness that charms and gives warmth and a certain character to any phrase that does not call for virile attack. Such playing is extremely attractive and supremely finished.

Reading between the lines, Bonavia seems to be saying that Yehudi's interpretations were a little lacking in energy.

Two Sundays later Yehudi was back in London for an afternoon recital that almost failed to materialize. The hapless accompanist Ferguson Webster arrived at the Menuhins' hotel an hour before the concert to confess that after lunching near Piccadilly Circus he had left his music behind on an omnibus. Next morning, *The Times* reported gravely that

Scotland Yard detectives with officials of the Albert Hall and London Transport co-operated in the hunt for the missing music. Buses on the 73 route were stopped and searched but to no avail.

The Menuhins got to the hall ten minutes after the advertised starting time. The capacity audience was stamping its feet with impatience when the impresario Harold Holt finally went out to explain the cause of the delay. He offered five pounds for a taxi to anybody who could produce the necessary scores and a student promptly threw down his copy of the 'Devil's Trill' Sonata from the gallery so the concert could at last get under way. The second work on the programme was unac-companied Bach, which Yehudi knew by heart. An interval was then announced, during which Yehudi, calmly sipping orange juice, observed that he would be happy if the rest of the concert could be devoted to a recital of unaccompanied Bach. But in rushed the violin-ist Albert Sammons, who had hurried home to get his copy of the Lalo Concerto. Others brought in some of the shorter pieces announced in the programme and so Yehudi's dream – and the promoter's nightmare – of an hour of solo Bach was avoided. To add to Yehudi's woes a tiny piece of his Stradivarius broke off while he was playing. Naturally it was beneath the dignity of the critics to comment on the disruptions: Ernest Newman noted merely that Yehudi's tone was 'ineffably sweet' throughout the concert, 'if fine rather than robust in volume'.

For Yehudi the real disruption came *after* the recital. Among the queue of well-wishers (the longest ever, according to Moshe) was the conductor of his Melbourne concerts two and a half years previously, Dr Bernard Heinze. Heinze had brought along two young Australian friends to introduce to him. Lindsay Nicholas, then twenty-two, was a tall, red-haired, handsome music-lover who for a hobby collected records and scores. Nola, his equally good-looking sister, was nineteen. Yehudi took an instant liking to them and so did Hephzibah. (She had attended her brother's recital and had no doubt been tempted – with the music lost – to step up on stage and play some of their joint repertoire from memory.) It transpired that both families were staying at the same hotel, the Grosvenor House, and the Nicholases invited the Menuhins to join them in their suite later that evening when they would be viewing home movies of the sheep station that Lindsay managed back in Australia. (He had 30,000 sheep under his care on an estate of 23,000 acres.)

The family was wealthy. George Nicholas, their father, had made a fortune in the First World War by inventing Aspro, a substitute for the German-manufactured drug known as Aspirin. They resided in one of the best parts of Melbourne but in other respects life had been hard: George's wife had died when Nola was only five. Envious glances must have been cast by the Nicholases at the close-knit Menuhin clan, all travelling together on Yehudi's winter tour. Nola had grown up to become a beautiful and vivacious redhead, one of the leaders of the 'younger set' in Melbourne society. She'd been staying in London with her elder sister and was presented at the Court of St James during the Coronation season.

While Moshe gave interviews to the press, Marutha and Yaltah joined the others at the screening. The visual interest of sheep farming might be limited but the young people had other subjects on their minds. Moshe recalled that it was after midnight when they returned:

I instantly sensed a spirit of elation in Yehudi and Hephzibah. Their eyes were glowing. When Yaltah casually mentioned that Nola had asked Marutha's permission to call her *Mammina* my heart began to beat.

Nola was surely being a little forward in affecting such intimacies on the very day they were introduced, but she was after all an up-front Australian and the Menuhins had loved Australians ever since Yehudi's grand tour in 1935: they were the nearest people in spirit to native Californians, 'fresh and young and open'. Sixty years later, Yehudi remembered Nola's red hair and a manner that was 'a little, shall we say "obvious" . . . not as refined as [other girls] I had known but for that very reason offering the potential, the opportunity, of total abandon'.

Over the next two weeks in London the friendships were cemented while Yehudi and Hephzibah prepared for a joint recital at the Queen's Hall, and took part in two mammoth recording sessions producing no fewer than eight double-sided discs. At the studio Lindsay turned the pages for Hephzibah. Nola had a white Jaguar sports car, which impressed Yehudi mightily. The brothers and sisters would set off for drives around London whenever there was a spare moment – and there was no space in the car for Marutha.

I knew and my sister knew that this was the only natural, authorized way to establish a new life . . . to leave the family without the justification or the pretext or the excuse of marriage would have been almost impossible.

Marriage was already on Yehudi's mind when the Menuhin caravan moved on to Holland, for a concert at the Concertgebouw under Willem Mengelberg, their first collaboration since the disastrous Tchaikovsky Concerto performance in New York in 1930. Tucked up for the night in his hotel bedroom Yehudi got under the bedclothes in order not to be overheard by his parents in the adjoining suite and started telephoning Nola in London. Each night he asked her to marry him. She played for time; after all, they hardly knew each other. Oblivious to the implication that Nola was an object, like a violin, Yehudi said he trusted his instinct; he had hardly known his 'Prince Khevenhüller' Stradivarius when he opted for it ten years earlier. At the end of their stay, Moshe was querying the $200 telephone bill with the hotel reception when a flustered Yehudi arrived to explain. He had been talking every night with Nola and she had agreed to marry him. But the union would need her father's blessing since she was under age. No mention was made of the fact that among her many admirers back home a young Australian named Ron was particularly assiduous in his attentions: he appears to have been hastily dumped.

After concerts in Liège and Paris and a batch of Paris recordings, among them the Pizzetti Sonata with Hephzibah and the Mendelssohn Concerto with Enesco conducting, the Menuhins returned to London for a joyful reunion. Nola's father had meanwhile arrived from Melbourne accompanied by his own new bride. Yehudi made a formal request for the hand of his daughter and on 10 May the great engagement was announced. 'Nola is my ideal girl,' Yehudi told the *Daily Sketch*, 'the girl I have always dreamed about, the girl I have despaired of ever finding. A few months ago I said I was married to my violin but now I have changed my mind.'

A blushing Nola interrupted, 'I'm so thrilled, though I'm not at all the sort of girl a violinist should marry. I have never touched a violin, or any musical instrument. I'm a sports girl: surf-riding, golf, tennis, that's my life.'

'But she loves listening to my playing, which is all that matters,' Yehudi broke in, oblivious to the common sense his fiancée was talking.

But Nola had already accepted her post-marital lot: 'We shall go to America and settle down on Yehudi's ranch.'

Another reporter found them at Victoria Station, departing for the Continent. 'Does Nola play at all?' he asked.

'No,' she replied.

Yehudi broke in: 'But she does!'

Nola, 'charming in a luxurious fur coat and a saucy blue hat, tilted her head to her fiancé in bewilderment'.

'Yes,' said Yehudi gravely. 'She plays tennis, she plays golf, she plays bridge.'

Nola was being unduly modest about her musical accomplishments; she had studied both violin and piano as a child, playing second violin in her school orchestra, and in a letter to her future step-mother she wrote of having just passed a piano examination with honours. Her mother had played the violin in a Melbourne symphony orchestra.

In private Yehudi was naturally much more serious than when joking with journalists. From Zurich, where he had journeyed for a recital, he wrote to his future father-in-law at Claridges in London. 'Dear Dad,' the letter begins, in unbuttoned Australian style.

My heart is so full that although my pen is poor these words must tell you what I feel.

Already God knows I always believed that each thing living is the product of all others and so I look with gratitude upon every tree and flower, animal, human being, for having contributed to fashion, in however small a way, that adorable girl and heavenly soul that is my Nola.

But it is to you in particular that I write these words, to you in your role of Nola's Father and Mother. The most important and powerful factor in a human life, that which places its existence beyond the reach of events as well as beyond our own reach, is the conscious feeling that we belong not wholly to ourselves in the narrowest sense, but rather to all the past and all the future.

We live by the grace of God and the most beautiful religion is the memory of a Mother. In your family you have been the High Priest of this cult.

The reward is the perpetuation of the best we have in us, by way of children like Nola and Lindsay. Thus only can there be nothing lost.

Our happiness is your handiwork. As it develops in intensity and as I reach the bounds of human felicity, it is with an ever-deepening sense of the religious devotion that I think of my own parents and of you.

They were fine sentiments from a very serious young man. But Yehudi's engagement triggered the sudden disintegration – no gentler word will do – of the Menuhin family. Within days, Hephzibah had decided to marry Lindsay Nicholas. Nicholas family tradition had it that she put the question to Lindsay, not the other way round. Just eighteen, Hephzibah had had other romances in her life, most seriously with their Ville d'Avray neighbour Maurice Fleg, who is said (by Yaltah's son Lionel) to have journeyed to London that very month to make an unsuccessful bid for her hand. The prospect of losing her brother and musical partner seems to have prompted Hephzibah to take the symmetrical, romantic but hopelessly unrealistic decision to marry Nola's brother. In doing so she escaped from her parents but abandoned her brother and sister, and her musical career. The previous summer she had been complaining that she missed her friends in Europe. Yet here she was, condemning herself to life on a remote sheep station 125 miles from Melbourne. Yes, there would be short-wave music broadcasts and 78 rpm recordings to listen to, and a grand piano on which to make music and play duets with her husband. But she would be abandoning her promising partnership with Yehudi and the solo career she had longed for. She even had to cancel her concerto début the following season with the New York Philharmonic under her great champion George Enesco.

Why was she taking this step? Was she determined to get away from her domineering mother, no matter what the cost? Could she not bear to share her brother with another woman, however sympathetic? Or, taking her cue as usual from her brother, was she simply in love with the idea of being in love? That she and Yehudi did experience romantic love for Lindsay and Nola is not in doubt. What seems strange is their parents' complaisance in this headlong rush to wedlock. Marutha had always maintained that her daughters' place was at the side of their husbands, bringing up a family, but her vision had been of a settlement of Menuhins in California, all in close proximity to Los Gatos. The schism represented by Hephzibah's sudden departure for Australia cannot have been part of her plans. But if she had misgivings about the geographical separation now being organized, she concealed them. Yehudi, her favourite, would still be close to her.

Marutha also encouraged Yaltah, then only sixteen, to accept an offer of marriage from the St Louis lawyer William Stix who had paid court to Hephzibah at Los Gatos the previous year. Stix apparently wrote to Hephzibah in the spring of 1938 proposing marriage. Hephzibah replied to the effect that she was not herself free because – to adopt the language of romantic protocol – she had accepted Lindsay Nicholas's proposal, but she happened to know that Yaltah entertained tender feelings towards him. In fact Yaltah had only recently been dissuaded from rushing off to Gretna Green to marry Keith Pulver-macher, the son of the senior journalist on the *Daily Telegraph*. Marutha had apparently been ready to countenance that match on one condition, that the young man change his name. The boy's father testily declined, pointing out that the name had been good enough to get the family into Buckingham Palace when he was given a knighthood.

On 17 May, only a week after his son's engagement was announced, Moshe was telling the world that both his daughters were also to wed before the summer was out, Yaltah in June and Hephzibah in July, after she and Yehudi had played a duo recital in San Francisco. Two of the family's chroniclers, Tony Palmer and Lionel Rolfe, have hinted darkly that Marutha somehow engineered her daughters' marriages. She is said to have dictated the message about Yaltah's availability to William Stix and to have intercepted and concealed a love letter (pre-sumably from Maurice Fleg) to Hephzibah so that she might concen-trate on Lindsay Nicholas. But if Marutha is to be criticized it would be for rushing her children into the frame of mind in which marriage seemed the obvious – indeed the only – option. On the face of it the highly musical Rosalie Leventritt would have been a better match for Yehudi, but she was not approved because she came from a conven-tional Jewish background. To Marutha's non-conformist eyes, Nola was a suitable marriage partner for Yehudi precisely because she was a non-Jewish Australian girl and therefore exotic – as well as being sturdily built for child-bearing. Religious differences were a source of satisfaction rather than a bar, as Harold Holt, the Menuhins' London agent, was quick to point out: 'Yehudi has never been Orthodox and has never been inside a synagogue. If he had loved a Chinese or an Eskimo it would have been "all right" with his father.' For Moshe, as Yehudi rather unkindly observed in his memoirs, Nola's principal attraction was that she was rich. Nobody could say she was marrying Yehudi for his money.

The Nicholas fortune was much in evidence over the next few days. The London *Daily Sketch* carried a photograph of a workshop crowded with seamstresses, identified in the caption as some of the '200 girls who for two weeks have beeen working night and day in Mme Hermine's London workrooms to complete the wonderful 500-piece trousseau'. The *Daily Mail* had a photo of the trousseau's containers, ten pieces of custom-built luggage. There were three wardrobe trunks, one 'special long trunk', three full-size steamer trunks, one shoe case (holding 27 pairs of shoes) one hat case (holding scores of hats) and a gramophone and book case. A gossip columnist had already revealed Nola's fondness for recorded music: she had recently been observed travelling on a train from Milan to Marseilles, on which she 'produced a portable gramophone and played a record she had just bought of *La Tosca*'.

While Mme Hermine's sweatshop seamstresses were beavering away on the wedding dress, the Nicholas and Menuhin clans took a brief holiday on the Bay of Naples, staying near the Jan Hambourgs in Sorrento and visiting the island of Capri. Hephzibah characterized it later as 'a week of insuperable happiness'. 'There is no more romantic background for lovers,' wrote Moshe, who described an excursion to the summit of Mount Vesuvius – 'making our way carefully between crevices that were streaming with burning liquid lava' – and a rooftop dinner accompanied by sentimental music, 'the youngsters whispering intimacies to each other'. The young people spent much of their time alone, Moshe added, noting rather primly that 'everything seemed wholesome and romantic. Except during that holiday, our children never travelled anywhere alone with Nola and Lindsay before they were married.'

Walking hand in hand in the moonlight, Nola 'marvelled at the shy youth she was about to marry. Indeed the whole family seemed odd to this modernly brought-up girl.' Not merely odd but ignorant of ordinary life; they seemed to think music was the only thing that mattered and when they played charades for relaxation they displayed 'an infantile kind of self-forgetfulness'. Not having a mother of her own, Nola was said to have taken a novel pleasure in abiding by Marutha's wishes, 'such as to tone down a bit the gaiety of her clothes and to learn languages'. At a party Nola impulsively bent over to hug her fiancé, but he 'disengaged himself and whispered, "Not now – after we get married . . ."'

Yehudi provided no details of his courtship in his autobiography. It is tempting to compare his situation – he was writing in 1976 – with that of Richard Wagner, who when dictating his life story to his second wife skated over the details of his first marriage. Yehudi mentioned only that his mother showed no sign of emotion at the departure of her two daughters for Australia and St Louis, preferring to think of Nola as the new daughter who would replace them. 'One of the prettiest débutantes of the year' must already have begun to wonder what she had let herself in for.

The wedding took place in London on 26 May at the Caxton Hall Register Office. No explanation has ever been offered as to why it went forward in such a rush, scarcely two months after Yehudi and Nola had first met. On the face of it, a double wedding back home in California would have been more appropriate. Perhaps Moshe was affected by the feverish atmosphere in Europe that spring. Hitler had annexed Austria back in March, forcing the Menuhins' friend Bruno Walter to cancel all engagements with the Vienna Philharmonic and the Salzburg Festival. Rearmament had been adopted as government policy in France and Great Britain. Air-raid shelters were being hastily constructed after observers noted the horrendous damage inflicted by Luftwaffe planes supporting General Franco during the Spanish Civil War.

Musical rather than political reasons prompted the actual date of the wedding. Yehudi discovered that Toscanini was conducting the Verdi *Requiem* in London on 27 May, the original date selected. There was to be a repeat of the Verdi on the 29th, however, and the Menuhins were still in town on the 30th; on that day Yehudi recorded a solo Bach partita movement and made his only recording with Yaltah as his accompanist, the slow movement from Mozart's B♭ Sonata (K. 378). Yaltah remembers that Hephzibah was busy with Lindsay, which is why she got her chance – at very short notice. But on a tight schedule the wedding was brought forward to Saturday, 26 May, so they could attend the *Requiem* the next day.

Perhaps Yehudi selected a Saturday with a certain sense of devilment, in order to emphasize that he was a liberated Jew for whom observance of the sabbath laws was of no significance. When he was criticized for it later (in an Orthodox Jewish publication which described the marriage as *Hillul Lashem*, a profanation of God) Moshe returned the fire with both barrels blazing:

a Jew who brands a fellow Jew for daring to marry an individual, sympathetic Gentile is not a bit less medieval and detestable than the beastly gangsters now ruling poor Germany, who preach through ostracism, the whip and the concentration camp, the mad theories of racial superiority.

Yehudi produced the ring too early but otherwise the ceremony passed without a hitch, though it was accompanied by the disagreeable clatter of building work in the basement where a shelter was under construction. It's perhaps odd that the family did not insist on music for such a solemn occasion, if only a solo violin, but register-office weddings are usually brisk and soulless affairs. The newsreel footage shows Nola looking beautiful and glamorous, wearing 'an ice-blue two-piece ensemble with an upturned straw hat to match and a spray of orchids pinned to her coat'. Yehudi was equally elegant in striped trousers and black coat under a heavy black overcoat, with a blue and white silk muffler at his throat. A news report said the crowd in the street dispersed when they heard it was not a film star's wedding 'but only a violinist'. Both families were there in some strength, among them Yehudi's Aunt Edie Miller from Richmond (who would also witness Yehudi's second London wedding less than ten years later). There was no honeymoon. Yehudi had his recording session the following Wednesday and then the Menuhins were off to Plymouth to board the *Ile de France* for New York and a new life.

Recommended Recordings

Schumann: Violin Concerto in D minor
New York Philharmonic Orchestra, conducted by John Barbirolli
BID LAB 047
Recorded: 9 February 1938
The second movement is particularly powerful in this, the première recording of the Concerto.

Mendelssohn: Violin Concerto in E minor
Colonne Orchestra, conducted by George Enesco
EMI 7 63822 2
Recorded: 2 May 1938
Recorded in Paris, a week before the engagement to Nola was announced.

Mozart: Sonata in B♭ (K. 378) – slow movement
with Yaltah Menuhin (piano)
BID LAB 129

Recorded: 30 May 1938 (NB some sources prefer 7 May)
Yehudi's younger pianist sister here makes her only appearance in the Menuhin discography.

Lekeu: Sonata in G (1892)
with Hephzibah Menuhin (piano)
BID LAB 058
Recorded: 29 March 1938
The Sonata was recorded soon after the first meeting with Lindsay and Nola Nicholas. YM used the Lekeu Sonata for his first attempt at musical analysis, while sailing between Australia and South Africa on the *Nestor* (see p. 164).

Beethoven: Sonata No. 7 in C minor, Op. 30 No. 2
with Hephzibah Menuhin (piano)
BID LAB 124
Recorded: 30 March 1938
One of Yehudi's favourite Beethoven sonatas. The recording was made soon after the Menuhins met the Nicholases. At the session Lindsay turned the pages for his future bride.

8 Midsummer Marriages

Yehudi and Nola soon after their marriage

1938: summer: marriages of Yaltah in New York and Hephzibah at Los Gatos; deferred honeymoon and establishment of Nola's and Yehudi's home at Alma; dispute with the AGMA musicians' union; 1939: summer: Nola's gift of Guarnerius violin; September: birth of Zamira; 1940: June: reunion with Hephzibah in Australia; August: birth of son Krov; 1941: military draft deferred; friction with Marutha; first tour of South America; 7 December: US enters Second World War.

MARUTHA HAD RUSHED her son into marriage but now seemed loath to let him go. On the *Ile de France* the Menuhins ate all their meals privately as usual. Nola's natural high spirits were dampened by Marutha's insistence that there be no departure from the family's customary isolation. When a steward asked about the delivery to their state cabins of Nola's trunks, Marutha said they should be stored in the hold. After Nola protested that they contained her evening dresses, she was brusquely told, 'You'll have no occasion to wear them on this trip.' Since Nola had a great many suitcases Marutha might have had a point, but this was not transatlantic travel the way Nola knew it, with a regular place at the captain's table guaranteed by her good looks and her father's wealth. She took to her bed with a cold, only to be forced by Marutha to endure exceptionally hot baths as a cure. 'The scorching water certainly killed the cold,' she commented ruefully, 'but at the time I thought I'd go with it.'

Yehudi watched passively as his mother inflicted any number of little humiliations on his bride. She insisted on a French waiter for room service so that Nola would have to order breakfast in a language she didn't speak. She instructed Yehudi to read through a Pirandello play with his bride so she could also get started on her Italian. Poor Nola was teased about her hand-embroidered lingerie and even criticized by her mother-in-law for eating double-decker sandwiches, Australian style: 'How plebeian of you!'

As the *Ile de France* approached New York harbour, young William Stix, 'dark, handsome and soft spoken', talked his way on to the quarantine boat and went aboard to greet his child bride Yaltah and slip a platinum ring on to her engagement finger. A lawyer with liberal views, Stix worked in Washington for the Counsel for Senate Civil Liberties Committee and since he had quickly to return to his duties, red tape was cut and the couple were married by special licence the very next day, 7 June, in New York City. Supreme Court Justice Perora performed the ceremony in his chambers and not a single photograph of it has survived. Yaltah was sixteen. She left immediately with Stix to set up home of a sort in Washington.

The marriage lasted less than a year and was dissolved on grounds of non-consummation. Retrospectively, Moshe claimed to have had doubts from the beginning about the match with Stix, describing his younger daughter as 'completely immature', but on the day of Yaltah's marriage he sang a different song to the press concerning the marriages of his three children. 'Why should we be excited?' he asked. 'My wife was only seventeen when we married.' (She had actually been nineteen, but Moshe was always rather casual with ages and birthdays.) 'We Menuhins know how to enjoy life,' he went on, expressing a confidence about his children's feelings to which, with hindsight, exception might be taken:

Only one thing I want the public to understand. This is not a case of wholesale marriage. These are just individual love affairs which just happened to burst out in full bloom in one season.

It was not Moshe's finest hour.

Or Marutha's either. Life at Los Gatos over the next few months was far from smooth. Moshe wrote that he gave Yehudi the Villa Cherkess estate as a wedding present, though it was hardly his to give since Yehudi's earnings had paid for it in the first place. The house was unfinished and the location was still considered too isolated for a permanent home. Yehudi accepted without demur his mother's proposal that he and Nola should live at the family's main house in Los Gatos, while Marutha and Moshe moved in to the guest house where the little theatre was situated. So Yehudi and his bride began married life *en famille*, with Nola feeling that Marutha was watching her every move. 'Only I was to blame,' Yehudi wrote, 'for the failure to grasp independence . . . In this half-and-half condition I knew I wasn't making Nola happy.'

Lindsay Nicholas had returned to Australia with his father, leaving Hephzibah to live at home with her family and her new sister-in-law. A month before the wedding she and Yehudi gave a duo recital in San Francisco. There were those who thought Yehudi was sacrificing his individuality to the partnership: 'The girl is lovely,' a member of the public observed, 'but I wish Yehudi were playing alone. He's so solicitous about his sister that he hasn't his usual freedom.' The San Francisco critic John Barry agreed:

Yehudi's problem is 'temperamental inhibition'. It was exquisite playing [at the duo concert] but it never suggested the emotional resourcefulness that made the playing of Fritz Kreisler so notable. Yehudi is not yet capable of expressing tremendous passion.

The applause was thunderous, nevertheless. One eye-witness described Hephzibah in a white silk dress and Yehudi 'clasping each other's hands as if for support against the demands of the audience' – but it would not be far-fetched to imagine that they were also bidding each other a musical farewell. They must have felt a private foreboding as the reality sank in of what they were soon to lose after nearly five years of wonderful musical partnership. The recordings they made a few months earlier, notably of the Beethoven Sonatas in C minor and G major, give an indication of what they were already achieving. On the very morning of her marriage Hephzibah wrote to Bruno Zirato, assistant manager of the New York Philharmonic Orchestra, withdrawing from her concerto engagement the following February:

As a good wife I will sacrifice everything I have loved up to now, to go with my husband . . . to cheer his solitude, to play the piano for him, to teach him the Italian language and animate the plateaux of his immense property with winged vision, with thoughts gathered from other countries, other people, other times. This is the career I have chosen.

With the Nicholas clan due to arrive for Hephzibah's wedding, the guest house up at Villa Cherkess was made habitable in order to accommodate the overflow of guests streaming in from Australia. Lindsay was accompanied by his father, who brought with him his new wife, Shirley. She was the sister of Dr Edward Alcock, who was married to Nola's elder sister, Betty. (Shirley was therefore both Nola's stepmother and the sister of Nola's brother-in-law, a tortuous relationship reminiscent of Brünnhilde's and Sieglinde's in Wagner's *Ring*.) Edward and Betty Alcock came to Los Gatos, too, complete with baby and nurse, as did Lindsay's younger brother and his tutor. On the Menuhin side only Yaltah, the child bride, was missing from the assembly: she says her mother banned her from attending. Hephzibah's marriage to Lindsay was celebrated on a Saturday afternoon, 16 July, under an oak tree in the garden at Los Gatos, with the mayor officiating, Hephzibah wearing a string of pearls given to her by Lindsay and Marutha crying softly into a handkerchief – a rare demonstration of emotion confirmed by a local reporter. The thirty guests then ate supper in the music room.

After the ceremony the newly-weds lingered for a further six weeks in the Californian sunshine. At Moshe's and Marutha's annual wedding-anniversary party everybody acted in a J. M. Barrie play, *The Old Lady Shows Her Medals*. Hephzibah was able to play more duets with Yehudi before she and Lindsay embarked in mid-September for the voyage to Australia. The home movie of their departure reveals Hephzibah to have been a radiant and exceptionally pretty young woman, the very image of her mother at the same age. What it did not capture was the symbolic moment when Hephzibah left her husband's side on the SS *Mariposa* to rush down to her cabin, where she gathered up her heavy-boned corsets and returned on deck in time to hurl the offending articles into San Francisco Bay, in full view of her mother standing on the pier.

Yehudi and Nola then set off on a deferred honeymoon to the Yosemite National Park. The trip was decided on at the last moment after Yehudi had hurt Nola's feelings by not making time to hear her recite in German a poem by Heinrich Heine which she had memorized especially to please him. (She used the book given to Yehudi by Willa Cather.) The young couple took their ciné camera with them and half a century later the film-maker Tony Palmer was given access to the 'rushes'. 'The home movies show a young couple brimming with love', Palmer reports,

she constantly petting and kissing him; he, chubby and still a boy in some ways, giggling inanely at the pleasure of it all; she, 'larking about' in her nightclothes, fondling a dog, an irrepressible bundle of energy and happiness; he, paddling in a stream, a little embarrassed by the relentless attention, trying to give as good as he's getting.

Yehudi said that when he set off he was 'plagued' by a sense of guilt towards his parents for having gone on holiday without them. But when he was truly alone with Nola for the first time, the guilt feelings 'completely disappeared, never to come back again . . . I realized that my life had become divorced from my previous existence.' After watching a sublime sunset near Glacier Point Yehudi decided it was time to face up to Marutha and make a show of independence. He had already been chastised by Nola's father, characterized rather frighteningly by Yehudi in his autobiography as 'a remarkable person, upright with Protestant principle, shrewd and successful in business, strong with the confidence of a self-made man'. George Nicholas had scolded his son-in-law about his daughter's unhappiness with the living arrangements at Los Gatos. Now Yehudi announced to his parents by letter that at the end of their holiday they would go directly to Villa Cherkess. He waited 'with some apprehension' for their reaction. 'How little I understood them after all!' he wrote, and there seems to be no irony intended in the sentence that follows: 'They accepted the development serenely, as though it were perfectly natural for a married man to leave his parents. From this moment I began to grow into independence.'

Once they were in residence at Alma (nobody called it Villa Cherkess after that) the young couple installed a swimming pool, went riding and took dancing lessons. Nola wrote Yehudi's letters for him. They were looked after by Marutha's 'temperamental but marvellous' Chinese couple but Nola had hardly learned to bake bread and do grills for her husband at 'the little ranch house', as she called Alma, before they were off on their concert travels. Moshe and Jack Salter (who had attended the Los Gatos wedding) evidently intended Yehudi's professional life to proceed much as it had before his marriage; Nola joined the back-up group consisting of the accompanist – the Dutchman Hendrick Endt – and the manager – Moshe – as Yehudi undertook his regular autumn tour in the US.

He was due to follow that with a visit to Western Europe and then visit new territory for him, the Scandinavian countries. There were to be special fund-raising concerts in support of Jewish refugees, in London, Paris and Amsterdam. (The London event, held at the Royal Albert Hall on 16 April 1939, was in aid of the Women's Appeal Committee for the relief of German and Austrian Jewish refugee women and children who were being helped to resettle in Palestine. Yehudi's efforts earned $4000 for the cause.) The difference from this tour and previous seasons was that Yehudi planned to travel for only six months before taking six months off for rest and research. He was then booked to go on another world tour, fourteen months in duration, which would be followed by a sabbatical of the same length.

Events both political and personal were to scupper the new plan before it was properly under way. Even the first leg of the American tour was rocked by crisis. Early in November Yehudi was booked to play concertos with the Los Angeles Philharmonic under Otto Klemperer. Only days before the concert date he received a letter from the orchestra's administrator, Mrs Leland Atherton Irish, informing him that he would not be permitted to perform unless he joined AGMA, the American Guild of Music Artists. Such an ultimatum was like a red rag to Moshe: 'Yehudi cannot be persuaded to do something by threats of coercion or concentration camp methods as is the case of Germany or Russia.' When he signed his contract the previous year, there had been no mention of union membership. Yehudi's response was less intemperate but he too was up in arms:

I feel that the right of an individual in a democratic country is involved in this demand and that my freedom as an artist is at stake. If this continues we will have only one kind of art – the kind which conforms to union regulations. Art and artists must be free or there will be a general levelling of art standards. It is not a question of money – it costs only $70 or $75 to join. No, it is the principle of labor organization involved. I have always sympathized with union labor but I have no interests requiring collective bargaining.

AGMA had been founded only two years earlier in response to claims of corruption in the older union, the American Federation of Musicians. *Time* magazine characterized AGMA as 'a dress-collar union formed by Laurence Tibbett and 114 other highly paid opera and concert artists'. Charter members included Serge Koussevitzky, Mischa Elman and Kirsten Flagstad. Toscanini and Klemperer were not members, however; neither, among the violinists, was Fritz Kreisler. AGMA's Vice President was Jascha Heifetz, whom Moshe had already rebuffed when first approached by him in 1936. The union's statement about the Los Angeles dispute was issued under Heifetz's name. He was obviously gunning for both father and son:

Young Mr Menuhin may be remote from the struggles besetting . . . poor artists who work less frequently and for smaller fees, but we cannot believe that any of us can close his eyes to existing conditions purely on personal grounds. We are afraid that Mr Menuhin has let himself be influenced by bad advice.

But the Menuhins' position was legally strong since they had a binding contract, signed before the Los Angeles Philharmonic joined AGMA. They also knew that Yehudi's two performances were already sold out, so cancellation would be a financial disaster for the orchestra. Yehudi conferred with union representatives as soon as he arrived in Los Angeles and emerged to say 'They're just bluffing.' Accompanying a photograph of his rehearsal with Klemperer was a quotation from Yehudi of which Margaret Thatcher would have been proud: 'I will give up my career rather than sacrifice my art to a closed shop.'

The *Los Angeles Evening News* lined up behind its orchestra. Throughout his teens, Yehudi had been described as a golden boy. Suddenly he was 'a pimply faced youth whose sandy red hair is perpetually in need of comb and clippers'. Moshe, depicted as 'tiny, bald and very polite' was said to have brought Yehudi up

like a hothouse flower and even went on honeymoon with him . . . [The] only person who seemed not to care was red-headed Nola Nicholas Menuhin, the Austrian [*sic*] girl who became Yehudi's bride five months ago.

Overnight the orchestra backed down. A clause was invoked permitting 10 per cent of its hirings to be non-union and the concert went ahead as planned, 'without the threatened heckling and hissing'. When AGMA's local chairman, Frank Chapman, said the proposed strike of orchestral players would have been 'breaking faith with the public', Moshe commented tartly that Chapman 'was the only gentleman among the AGMA crowd'. At the concert, press photographers made such a disturbance with their flashbulbs when Yehudi played his opening solo in the Mozart D major Concerto that Klemperer stopped the orchestra and gruffly commanded them to begin again.

Time characterized the episode as newly wed Yehudi's 'first conflict with life's brutalities and aggressive impositions'. But he was seen to be 'standing on his own feet as a free and proud citizen of a free America'. In Washington, however, a journalist described him as the unwitting tool of the artists' agents, who, the paper alleged, had created a cartel: 'They know that their commissions are arbitrarily high and have been mutually agreed upon so that they no longer have to compete with each other.'

A concert a fortnight later in nearby Pasadena was far from full. It was 'the first time the famous young violinist did not attract a capacity public in this city'. A new concerto in Yehudi's programme, by the mid-nineteenth century virtuoso Heinrich Wilhelm Ernst, was dismissed by a reviewer as 'sickeningly trashy' and 'unspeakably banal'. His Bach and Brahms interpretations 'revealed spell-binding profundity', but according to the *Pasadena Star News* he did not seem to be 'the same inwardly fully-balanced young artist of a year or two ago. The AGMA controversy and life in general may be making disturbing demands on him.' In Chicago a week later he was still working through a rough patch in his playing; reviews praised his warmth and intensity and confirmed his position as 'a member of the little band of really great violinists', but added that his playing lacking 'tonal impeccability' – a polite way of saying he was out of tune. Later in the tour Olin Downes was another critic who called Yehudi's artistic judgement into question. His playing of Bach was 'flawless' but Lalo's Violin Concerto was rudely dismissed as 'second-class inspiration'. Yehudi took the criticisms in his stride. 'I'm a million miles away from perfection,' he told the *Milwaukee Journal*.

The tour included many of the Menuhins' regular staging posts and Moshe continued to call press conferences wherever they went. In Philadelphia he spoke out against the actions of Nazi vandals who had just smashed a statue of Mendelssohn at the Leipzig Gewandhaus. Ever the optimist, Yehudi disagreed with his father's conclusion that the Spirit of Germany had been quenched:

Barbarism may engulf the whole country, true. But although it may close in on a temple of music from all sides, it cannot touch that spirit. The Gewandhaus, I think, is an inviolable oasis in Nazi Germany.

A few weeks earlier he put his weight behind another anti-Fascist cause, signing a public letter asking President Roosevelt to lift the arms embargo on Loyalist Spain.

Meanwhile, in Columbus, Ohio, Moshe finally owned up to having misrepresented Yehudi's date of birth for nearly twenty years: 'It was the only criminal thing I ever did,' he told a journalist on 2 January 1939. Presumably he had been asked how Yehudi would celebrate his 'forthcoming' twenty-second birthday. Or perhaps Nola insisted on his telling the truth.

Moshe faced more embarrassment after it was reported that there had been a rift between William Stix and his wife. They had been photographed together at Yehudi's Carnegie Hall concert in December but the following month Mrs Stix returned to Los Gatos with her mother. 'Yaltah married the wrong man,' Moshe coolly told the *Daily Mail*. 'She was only sixteen but she made a mistake.' He didn't add that he and Marutha could easily have withheld permission for the marriage to go ahead in the first place. Yaltah believes it to be evidence of the poor esteem in which her mother held her.

When the Menuhins (accompanied by eight trunks and fifteen valises) travelled to England on the *Queen Mary*, Moshe kept himself to himself. 'I did not once eat with them on the voyage,' he told the man from the *Manchester Evening News*. The recital in Manchester was a triumph. Neville Cardus wrote that Yehudi's art had grown 'wiser and sadder; he is . . . the most poetic and sensitive of contemporary violinists'.

Nola was finding it difficult to adjust to the life of travelling companion to a virtuoso. She was a fun-loving girl and on the American part of the tour she made post-concert reservations at supper clubs for them both. But Yehudi vetoed them, disliking their atmosphere of soft music and hard drink. At his concerts she sometimes chose to sit in the $2 seats, in the hope that she could persuade him literally to play to the gallery – a democratic gesture but one that would have upset Moshe, since she could not be in the gods and at the same time stand in the wings to greet her husband when he came off stage needing a change of dress clothes and a rub-down. Moshe says he encouraged her to assume more of his duties and at one point delivered a passionate lecture on her responsibilities:

Do not for one single moment, not for one single day, forget that Yehudi is away on a strenuous concert which demands peace of mind, relaxation, rest, sleep and work . . . He cannot dissipate his time and energy on social 'obligations' and satisfy everybody you knew or know. There is a higher noble obligation Yehudi has to his destiny, to his art, his world of music, to which he has to dedicate himself! To this purpose we must all help serve him, spare him, guard him. Do not permit the telephone, the doorbells, society, the curious, to take a minute of Yehudi's time, an ounce of his energy. When you two go (or Yehudi alone) to rest, please do not forget to order the telephone disconnected and place a DO NOT DISTURB sign outside Yehudi's door. The nervous system requires that.

Moshe wrote that when they reached New York with its theatres and night life, Nola was in her element. They stayed first at the Savoy Plaza and then moved into an apartment at the Hampshire House. But Nola fell ill with appendicitis on Christmas Eve and later kept to her room suffering from a heavy cold. When they reached England in early March she was reported to be 'tired' and she stayed in London for Yehudi's lengthy tour, which took him from Bournemouth to Newcastle. From Bristol he wrote to his father-in-law, evidently responding to another ticking off:

As regards Nola, I am very grateful for the information and advice you gave me. I will certainly shield her from all unpleasantness to the full extent of my powers. Dear Dad, it is quite impossible for me to tell you how much I love Nola . . . blessed above most other women with a sensible thoughtful nature. It is a treasure that cannot be too highly prized.

Nobody knew it, but Nola was pregnant. She herself might not yet have been completely certain but since her child was born at the end of September it must have been conceived around the turn of the year. She surely had mixed feelings about the news. It was what Marutha expected of her, and doubtless Yehudi too, but what a blow to be deprived so soon of the outdoor life she adored! She revealed the extent of her depression to a sympathetic London interviewer:

I have had to give up my tennis and golf because I never have time now. Sometimes I get very tired of packing and unpacking. We always seem to be travelling. But then I look at my husband and think that he has twice as much to do as I have and I am ashamed. He swims to relax . . . I tried to give him dancing lessons, as I am very fond of dancing myself, but he always looks so bored . . . He says he enjoys dancing with me, but he has never done much of it. He doesn't object to jazz in small doses [sic – jazz was like medicine] in fact he rather likes it. Once I was locked in his practice room and thought that I would get into mischief. I took one of his violins and started to play. I was very soon let out!

Late in the 1990s Yehudi could still recall his shock when Nola told him (while they were on a winter vacation in New England) that they had so little in common she feared their marriage would not work out. Yehudi would not allow either of them to accept such a pessimistic appraisal. In March he told the *Manchester Guardian* that he wanted to retire soon 'for further research and study', which suggests that he already perceived, if somewhat dimly, that he would have to re-order his life if he wanted to retain Nola's affection. Returning home to California after his brief European tour, he informed the local newspaper that 'he believed his happy marriage had much to do with his sense of really belonging in the Santa Clara valley and the Los Gatos hills'. His autumn tour was not scheduled to begin until 1 October 1939, and he stayed with Nola for the remainder of her pregnancy.

Some time in the summer she gave him a fine 1742 Guarnerius violin. He had tried it out during a visit to Emil Herrman's workshop the previous winter in New York and reluctantly decided it was too expensive. Nola had since consulted Moshe and arranged for its purchase, presumably with her own funds since it was described as a present to mark the birth of their first child. He was enthusiastic about his new acquisition, calling it the perfect 'mate' for the 'Prince Khevenhüller'. The instrument had 'exactly the same dimensions as my Strad (the Strad has a little higher arch, that's all)'. He played it in concerts that autumn but it does not seem to have retained a permanent place in his affections. He was always a Stradivarius man. He compared his flirtations with violins made by Guarnerius – he had already borrowed Ysaÿe's, it will be remembered – to that of a husband who occasionally has affairs but always returns to his wife.

Surprisingly, there is no reference to Nola's gift in the sub-chapter about his violins included in his book *The Violin*, published in 1996. Yehudi refers there to his 'second Guarnerius' without mentioning the first. At a late stage in the preparation of the book he must have been advised to omit any discussion of Nola's 'Guarnerius' because of the potentially embarrassing discovery that the instrument was not, as had always been supposed, by Joseph Guarnerius del Gesù. In 1939 Yehudi told journalists that the instrument had been constructed in the same years as the one owned by Paganini and that its dimensions were identical. There is no suggestion that the dealer Emil Herrman had knowingly sold a fake, but in the light of modern research it could no longer be guaranteed as a Guarnerius. It was eventually sold to a Japanese collector for half a million dollars.

As well as a new violin, Yehudi also took delivery of a perambulator, importing it all the way from England. It was, he wrote, 'a tall elegant baby carriage, such as used to throng Kensington Gardens in a more gracious age'. He considered prams more healthy than the modern, low-slung pushchairs which expose the infant to exhaust fumes from passing motor cars. He admitted that an element of wish fulfilment was also involved: 'Suspecting that I should never own a Rolls-Royce, I made sure of the baby-carriage equivalent.' It had a further merit: it was large enough for two babies.

'Mrs Menuhin arrested again' was a local paper's headline on 27 July 1939. Even though she was six months pregnant, Nola was finding it hard to curb her love of fast cars. (Yehudi was at her side, no doubt urging her on.) She was subsequently fined for driving at 60 m.p.h. in a 45 m.p.h. zone. In August news came from Australia that Hephzibah was expecting her first child in February. Prompted by Moshe's press release, many newspapers ran stories referring to the 'Double Cousins'. Yehudi wrote a touching letter to his father-in-law about the ante-natal sessions he was attending with Nola in San Francisco:

Our Nola is very well, radiating happiness and physical well-being. At 'our' weekly examinations the doctor and I nod our heads in understanding approval, analysing X-ray pictures and straining at the stethoscope:– for I am never out of the picture! I do not understand why this should be extraordinary or astonishing; nevertheless I feel very privileged to be thus continually beside my darling. It seems to me only natural that the husband should be present at these investigations and desirable from all points of view. It is reassuring for the wife, satisfying as well as instructive for the husband, correct for the doctor and creates a beautiful warm feeling between these three people striving for the same goal. On one occasion I succeeded in making out the heart beats of our 'little fellow'; at first I could hardly believe that what sounded like the putt-putt of a motor-boat was really the thumping of a person-to-be. It was certainly a vigorous 'tuning up' and I felt certain that the little heart would go quite far.

The letter then drifts into mystical realms in which Yehudi struggles to square the circle, claiming that while he and Nola are very different personalities they inhabit through marriage 'a single cell':

We of course share the tribulations of our world, and very painful they are to us as our lives are so infinitely bound up with different places, contrasting people and divergent opinions. However, our existence seems to rest so closely upon the less complicated, less complex forms and structures of the universe that we partake of the blessed feeling of unity, nearer to the indivisible, to the inviolable – like the single cell, for instance. Nola and I form a single cell, for we have taken root in each other's nature and share the same prerequisites for our existence.

Descent from the metaphysical plane is swift:

We are now sun-bathing on our new sleeping porch – or rather room. It is a glorious location exposed to the four winds, so we are in that enviable position of believing to the utmost that saying 'Whichever way the wind doth blow, some heart is glad to have it so!'

Yehudi had evidently created sleeping arrangements similar to those at Steiner Street fifteen years earlier.

A week before Yehudi wrote that letter, Ribbentrop and Molotov signed the Nazi-Soviet non-aggression pact and on 1 September Germany invaded Poland; World War II had begun. Yehudi's 1940 European tour was first cancelled but then merely 'suspended' because it was widely thought that the war would be over by Christmas. Yehudi's mind was on other things that month. On 29 September, at 1 p.m., his wife was delivered of a baby girl weighing 6 lbs 11 oz. The father donned a surgical mask and observed the birth at the University of California hospital. Then he rushed off for a rehearsal, or so the papers said; perhaps it was just a convenient excuse for leaving when he got a little bored. Moshe recycled a story (based on the fact that Yehudi had once played with forceps and scalpels at the home of their friend Dr Garbat) that as a youngster Yehudi had wanted to be a surgeon. But the press was probably more interested in the name chosen for the new arrival: Zamira, meaning – approximately – 'for Peace': *Za Mir*, in Russian, and Russia was, after all, the mother country of her grandparents. Moshe pointed out later that Zamira also meant, very prettily, 'song bird' in Hebrew. Yehudi told his father how he had settled the obstetrician's fee:

I asked the doctor what I owed him.
    'Oh, I'll leave that to you, Mr Menuhin.'
    Well, I thought, my lowest concert fee is $2000, so I made out a cheque for that amount.

Moshe pointed out that a doctor can deliver five babies in a day, whereas not even Yehudi could perform five concerts.

Only two days after Zamira's birth, Yehudi departed to give concerts in Portland, Vancouver, Seattle and other north-western cities. Father and daughter were not to see each other for over a month. They were reunited in Chicago, in the week that the State Department announced the invalidation of many US passports because of the war in Europe. Yehudi's plans were seriously affected: he would conclude his American tour on 19 January and then retire to Los Gatos. This was reportedly good news for the Menuhin family, if not for his admirers in Europe: 'Heavy-set, tousle-haired Yehudi was all aglow contemplating the pleasure he'll get from his long enforced holiday.' Meanwhile *Life* magazine arranged an elaborate photo-shoot for its Christmas issue. Its readers, many millions of them, were regaled with page after page of tenderly intimate family photographs, including the first picture (and so far as can be ascertained the last) of Yehudi engaged in the father's time-honoured routine of nappy-changing.

Beneath the surface, relations between Yehudi and his father were strained to breaking point. At issue was the question of who would accompany Yehudi on his winter tour. Originally Yehudi told Moshe that he liked his company as he travelled across the continent and that it was better for Nola and the baby to go direct to New York to await his arrival. But, according to Moshe, Nola had come under the influence of Grace Aaronson, the second Mrs Jack Salter, whom he described as 'an overbearing publicity woman' foisted on Yehudi at Nola's insistence. (She it was who invented the banner headline on the season's publicity material to which the Menuhins took violent exception: 'The Prodigy of Yesterday. The Genius of To-day. The Immortal of To-morrow.') Moshe insisted that Yehudi choose between himself and Mrs Salter and she was reluctantly paid off with a $750 cheque.

Soon afterwards Nola must have intervened to question Moshe's role since in Toledo, Ohio, just before playing a concert, Yehudi made a U-turn and asked his father to quit the travelling and manage his affairs only at long distance. According to this hostile passage in Robert Magidoff's 1955 biography:

Moshe failed to sense the inevitable, despite all the signs, and was unable to spare Yehudi the embarrassment of having to tell his father that he need no longer accompany him on concert tours.

Moshe took great offence when he read that account and dashed off a furious letter to his son:

What an ugly and coarse and false picture your author describes of a dramatic, historical moment . . . we were dreaming of the approaching day of 'managing your affairs from a distance' but had it only been done *before* the season started,

1 Moshe Mnuchin and his bride Marutha. On his mother's side Moshe was a Schneerson, distantly related to Isaiah Berlin. Both spent their early teens in Palestine.

2 Yaltah, Hephzibah and Yehudi – beauty in the buff – 1922.

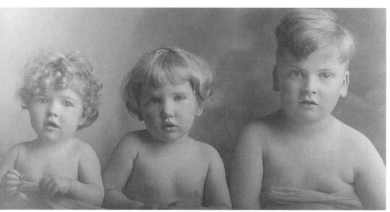

e apartment block in Buchanan Street e Bronx; Yehudi's first home was on hird floor. Before he was one year old amily moved to Elisabeth, New Jersey, in January 1918 to California.

4 Moshe let garage space in the basement of 1043, Steiner Street, San Francisco, to pay their monthly mortgage. Yehudi moved into the turret room when his earnings allowed the family to stop taking lodgers.

5 Yehudi with his teacher and friend Louis Persinger about the time of his first San Francisco appearance, in 1924. Persinger was concert-master of the San Francisco Symphony Orchestra for a decade; his concerto performances were Yehudi's first inspiration. Persinger became his first accompanist on recordings and US tours.

I really pride myself on looking nicer but you will understand that. Réve your friend Yehudi Menuhin Dec 18 1928 L.J.

Early days as a maestro. The twelve-year-old Yehudi, his hair askew, coaches Hephzibah soon after her recital début in 1928. 'I really pride myself on looking nicer . . .'

British Capital Acclaims Menuhin at Début Concert in Queen's Hall

Yehudi Menuhin and Fritz Busch Snapped in Front of Buckingham Palace, London

The first visit to London. Yehudi, then thirteen, played the Brahms concerto with the LSO, conducted by his fellow tourist Fritz Busch.

8 A concert at San Francisco's Civic Auditorium, Alfred Hertz conducting, with a reco
11,000 in the audience. Yehudi first played a concerto here in 1926, when he was only

10 George Enesco playing for Yehudi (
sports a hint of a moustache), Hephzib
and her teacher Marcel Ciampi. The d
recorded Enesco's Third Sonata in Janu
1936.

9 Portrait of the Artist as a Young Man.
The photographer was the Swiss-American
composer Ernest Bloch, who wrote *Avodah*
especially for him in 1928 as well as two
Suites for solo violin at the end of his life.

11 'Les Fauvettes' in the village of Ville d'Avray, the family home in the early 1930s.

13 *Very* short back and sides: posing with scouting acquaintances soon after Yaltah chopped all her hair off. Note the family car - a Delage.

12 At the foot of the Fex Glacier near Sils Maria in the Engadine – the beginning of a lifelong love of the Swiss Alps.

14 Outside HMV's Abbey Road studio with Sir Edward Elgar and the veteran produce Fred Gaisberg, after Yehudi's most famous recording session.

15 A month before his twentieth birthday, Yehudi and his sister gave a duo concert in New York.
16 Summer excursion in Ville d'Avray
17 'A violinist goes sledding in Central Park: Yehudi Menuhin and his sisters'.

left: 18 June, 1934. Sweetnesss and light: the last family summer in Europe.
19 Wedding day, May 1938: Nola and a somewhat apprehensive Yehudi outside Caxton Hall, London. They had met two months earlier.

ressing room routine, winter tour
: Moshe provides the interval back-
vhile Nola contemplates her future.

21 The quietly happy couple await the birth of their first child at their home in California. Their nicknames for one another were 'Nittles' (Nola) and 'Noots' (YM). The dog was called Laska.

22 Christmas, 1939: a serenade for Zamira.

23 'You can't imagine a bird saying I a tired today, I am not going to fly . . .'

24 'Alma' – Nola and Yehudi's home outside Los Gatos.

25 Proud parents. When Nola gave bir their son in August 1940, Yehudi cable his parents from Australia: 'The dear g triumphantly, gratefully and smilingly our lusty healthy seven and half pound Krov Nicholas Menuhin ideal labour u three hours feel blessed immeasurably'.

or after, or independently of Grace Salter, who by that time was the shadow ruling your life via her victim Nola – it was an ukase that came from Grace in revenge of my eliminating her with her $7\frac{1}{2}$ per cent for her disgusting publicity . . .

These are the murky waters: one senses the swirling emotions of battles fought and lost many decades before.

The centenary of Paganini's death fell in 1940 and Yehudi included the Second Concerto in B minor in his first concert of the new year, on 4 January, with the Philadelphia Orchestra under Eugene Ormandy. Nola accompanied him to his recital at Asheville, North Carolina, and on to nearby Chattanooga; they were home at Alma by 24 January. 'They will stay there until the late fall,' Moshe announced very firmly in a press release, perhaps because he knew that Nola was pregnant again; her second child was expected in August.

With the European war showing no sign of a resolution, Yehudi's international career was close to standstill. Even in America there were signs of recession in the public's appetite for Yehudi Menuhin concerts. Smaller cities were included on the tour itineraries for the first time, while some larger venues were now visited once every three years rather than two. The only concerts on the horizon were his annual autumn tour of the US and his first visit to South America, scheduled to begin in April 1941. As if to show that he still valued his father's involvement, he was to take Moshe with him on that trip rather than his agent Jack Salter.

Moshe never referred in his memoirs and interviews to any investments he might have made on Yehudi's behalf but it seems safe to assume that enough money had been put aside to see Yehudi and his family through a long period of inactivity. The retreat to Alma did at least provide time for the 'further research and study' that Yehudi had promised himself. He initiated chamber-music sessions, reminiscent of the regular Monday evenings he had enjoyed with Enesco and the others at Ville d'Avray. His partners drove down once a week from San Francisco and sometimes stayed the night. The viola player, Nathan Firestone, had been a member of Louis Persinger's quartet. When he died, in 1944, he bequeathed Yehudi his Testori viola. Yehudi played Brahms on it at Firestone's funeral and, many years later, the solo part in Bach's Sixth Brandenburg Concerto. The instrument was subsequently loaned to Yehudi's school.

Yehudi was continually improving the Alma estate. When he got married the novitiates of the Jesuit college next door had dug up twenty pine trees and planted them round the new house. Now he erected a small guest cottage, complete with studio, bedroom, kitchen and dining room, intended for use by his accompanist. Moshe thought this was an unnecessary expense but his son overruled him. The *Dallas News* reported that 'Yehudi's own study, where he grinds and polishes his repertoire, is a lofty room overlooking 100 miles of valley. Wild deer are looked after with a water tub and salt slab.' The woods were full of hunters, but killing animals was never one of Yehudi's country pastimes.

'We are back in our lovely home,' he wrote to his Australian father-in-law on 20 February,

where we dream of welcoming you . . . Few things would fill me with more joy than to bring our darling Nola to you and all the dear ones she left so long ago. My great compensation however is that Nola is exuberantly happy, her head and soul so completely planted in our life, that those wasting feelings of longing find little haven in her.

He wrote rather sweetly about 'great and glorious' Zamira, who is

developing with every day. Even though my pride and tenderness have suffered some rude blows at her hand such as when I endeavour to feed or pacify her only to find Nola or Louise [the nanny] more suited to the attempt.

Yehudi felt close to his Australian family. Dismayed by events in Europe and sceptical of the quality of American culture, he was beginning to think of Australia as an amalgam of the best of Europe and California:

What a thrill I will feel when the time will be ripe to be there again – this time as one of the country. It is indeed a priviledge [*sic*] to have been able to taste so deeply of the cultures [*sic*] of Europe when it was yet time and to have finally grafted one-self to the sturdy and forward-looking roots of Australia.

At the beginning of March came news of the birth of Hephzibah's first child, a son named Kronrod – allegedly after a Crimean relative of Marutha. The new arrival must have prompted intense family discussions and frantic business calls on both sides of the Pacific, since three weeks later Yehudi sailed for Australia. The trip had been decided on only five days earlier, the press was told. It was primarily a vacation, a twenty-first birthday present for Nola, but Yehudi would pick up the pieces of his cancelled Australian tour. He would give recitals in Sydney and Melbourne and, partnered by Hephzibah, also make recordings for HMV (who had been unable to record new repertoire with him in London because of the war).

Brother and sister were thus to be reunited after only eighteen months' separation, while Nola would be able to see her father again and inspect his new son Michael, her half-brother, to whom his second wife Shirley had given birth a few months before Zamira's arrival. Zamira was to be looked after by her nanny Louise Blochman and the Menuhin party was completed by accompanist Hendrik Endt and sister Yaltah, who came much against her parents' wishes. Yehudi helped her to get a passport and more or less smuggled her out of Los Gatos, bringing down Moshe's fury on his head. Yaltah was reported to be thinking of settling in Australia with her sister. Australian newspapers were to hint unkindly that she was on the look out for a new husband. When the party sailed from San Francisco on 26 March they were accompanied by a grand piano, thirty pieces of luggage and a large perambulator.

Vacation it might be, but Yehudi took advantage of the SS *Mariposa*'s brief stop in Honolulu to give a late-afternoon recital. The ship docked at 2 p.m. and departed at 8. 'Had wonderful concert at Honolulu,' he cabled his father. 'Feel radiantly well. *Yehnolira Yalta*.' The signature derived from '*Yeh*udi, *No*la, Zam*Ira*' – an awkward variant on the original family cluster *MoMaYeHeYa*, which itself was none too elegant but at least saved on per-word cable charges.

The Menuhin and Nicholas families enjoyed a happy reunion at George Nicholas's home in Melbourne, where they arrived on Yehudi's twenty-fourth birthday. A home movie shows the three mothers, Nola, Hephzibah and step-mama Shirley, proudly wheeling their babies in well-sprung prams. A few weeks later Yehudi started his recital series in Sydney; it was five years since he had made his début there. On 15 May the English critic Neville Cardus was in the audience to hear him. 'A blind man', he wrote, 'might with excuse have imagined that not one but at least three master fiddlers were playing the Bach unaccompanied sonata.'

The news from Europe was desperate; 'a great mass worry' Yehudi called it. Holland had just surrendered. The rump of the British army was about to escape from Dunkirk. Yehudi's beloved Paris was soon to be occupied by the Germans. In June Yehudi announced an immediate return to America because of the emergency but changed his mind just before the boat sailed and instead returned to the Nicholas sheep farm for a real vacation.

With Nola by now seven months pregnant it was prudent to avoid the interminable and possibly stormy ocean crossing. Before going out to the ranch he played the Beethoven Concerto at a concert in Melbourne, on 19 June, for the benefit of the French Red Cross. Other charity recitals raised funds for the Australian Red Cross and for Lord Rothschild's Jewish Appeal for war victims and refugee children in Britain. Later in the year, when Yehudi was facing call-up under the US's new draft law, Moshe claimed he had raised $70,000 for war charities – the implication being that he would not be able to continue such work if he was forced to join the army.

The home movies reveal Yehudi to have been in ebullient mood during his Australian stay. He had never looked happier than when he was on the Nicholas sheep farm at Terinallum. Hephzibah, just twenty, confided in her diary that there was a 'liaison spirituel' between herself and her brother. The film shows them clambering on to the roof of a barn, he handsome and slim in jodphurs and riding boots, she petite and pretty in chic new clothes, not a bit like the embarrassing garments her mother used to run up for her. Here were two young people bursting with good health and boundless love of life. (By then eight months pregnant, Nola kept herself out of the picture.) Hephzibah told her brother she was no longer haunted by fears of displeasing anybody. Indeed she seemed totally wedded to her new existence as a farmer's wife – but perhaps she was acting up a little too enthusiastically for the benefit of the camera. We see her on horseback, rounding up the sheep, revelling in the outdoor life. Her husband Lindsay was totally dedicated to her and she to him, accepting what she described in a letter as his 'totally inadequate education'. Unlike Yehudi, Hephzibah did not invite her spouse to learn Heine poems in the original German.

On 7 August the grown-up children gave an informal concert for Australian friends to mark the twenty-sixth wedding anniversary of their parents, who were comfortably distant in California (whither the restless Yaltah had returned). Soon afterwards Nola moved into a Melbourne maternity hospital run by nuns to await her confinement. Yehudi remembered that the Sisters of Mercy, who brought him breakfast every morning, 'made no objection to my practice and altogether treated me with the greatest consideration'. The hours before the birth remained, he said, vivid in his memory:

A wealthy Melbourne merchant had lent me his collection of violins, and I remember trying them out in the hospital and then walking to the Town Hall for a rehearsal of the Brahms Concerto, not knowing which would arrive the sooner, the baby or Brahms.

It has proved difficult to confirm the chronology of this anecdote. The birth was on 17 August. Information concerning a performance of the Brahms Concerto on 16 or 17 August have not come to light. Yehudi did, however, give a joint recital with Hephzibah at the end of the month and later made a recording for HMV of the Brahms G major Sonata – on 18 September, just before he returned to California. Perhaps he confused concerto and sonata in his memory.

Nola's second baby was a boy whom they named Krov Nicholas. Nicholas was to honour his grandfather but 'Krov' was made up by Yehudi, who said he inherited from his mother a dislike of 'generationally conservative' names such as Tom, Dick and Harry. In his autobiography he explained that he simply wanted a short word with an 'r' in it. If you pull the pronunciation around you can make *krov* sound like the Russian word for 'roof' or 'shelter'. If you soften the ending, as in *kroyveh*, it resembles the Russian word for 'blood'. In Hebrew *krov* signifies 'war' or 'battle', and since the Battle of Britain entered a crucial phase on 15 August there is circumstantial evidence to favour this theory, which he offered to a Texan journalist when he visited Houston two months later. But in his memoirs the war isn't mentioned. 'Krov has come to mean Krov,' he wrote conclusively.

Back home in California Yehudi was required to register for the draft. 'I've got three dependents now,' he told reporters as he left Los Gatos City Hall. His case became a *cause célèbre*. Would his fame save him from military service? The theory was that a man with a wife and two children could be deferred if he was the sole source of income in the family. Nola was rumoured to have a private fortune but Moshe argued that her funds were blocked because of the war between the British Empire and Germany. The five-man draft tribunal was split on the issue. One member said Yehudi should be treated like any other American; another, presumably anti-Semitic, 'didn't like the name'. Yehudi's number (2648) was way down the list, said the first, and probably wouldn't be called soon anyway. There was no war yet and it was not the government's intention to break up families. 'Besides he's too fat and probably unfit for Army life.' On a 3–2 vote he was graded Class A (fit for service) but was granted a ninety-day deferment while his financial circumstances were assessed. A second deferment in February 1941 enabled him to proceed with the planned tour of South America.

Yehudi's public position was impeccable:

My intentions are to do my bit in the capacity most serviceable to my country without jeopardizing the security of my wife and children. If my country needs me I shall be glad to serve.

Meanwhile he could resume his life as a concert artist. When Heifetz fell ill, he stood in for him at twenty-four hours' notice in Chicago. He caught the midnight express from New York after a Town Hall performance and played the Beethoven Concerto without rehearsal. Other recital engagements took him to Havana, Miami and Fort Wayne, where he played for serving troops and spoke about the Nazis' victories in Europe.

At this darkest moment for Western democracy there was powerful support for isolationism in the US but Yehudi expressed himself resolutely anti-Hitler:

I don't see how he can ever coalesce the peoples of Europe into a homogeneous unit. He is trying to do so under compulsion, but he is dealing with nations and groups that are totally different. They have been under many conquerors. Even the best of [the dictators], Bonaparte and Caesar, could not last. Europe can only achieve its ideas as a happy union of totally free countries.

He gave a 'farewell' concert in San Francisco on the eve of his departure for Argentina. The *Chronicle*'s new critic, Alfred Frankenstein, said his performance 'lacked much of the fire and bite' required in the Brahms Concerto but the public seemed well enough pleased: after the first movement his old friend Pierre Monteux led the applause – from the rostrum. In Argentina and Brazil he enjoyed even greater success: 'Ten consecutive sold-out concerts in Buenos Aires alone,' reported Moshe, who was in his element serving one last time as the tour manager. After Yehudi's first concert in Rio de Janeiro the audience stayed on in the hall for an hour. 'People went wild about him,' Nola wrote to her father. 'Never has anyone had such a success there before.' But by 1996 Yehudi remembered precious little of the trip except a colourful exchange with a Jewish stevedore: 'Moi aussi, je suis piqué,' the man shouted to Yehudi as his ship docked in Rio de Janeiro. The expression of racial brotherhood stuck in his mind. The tour was supposed to be part of Washington's 'good neighbors' policy towards Latin America, but when he returned to the US, Yehudi spoke out against condescension from Uncle Sam in artistic matters: 'South Americans resent artificial attempts to establish cultural relations.

Many feel they are being patronized and dealt with dishonourably. I felt instinctively that was not what was wanted.'

In the summer of 1941 he accepted bookings on the lucrative summer circuit for the first time, playing at the Hollywood Bowl, the Robin Hood Dell (outside Philadelphia) and the Lewisohn Stadium in New York (which was pulled down in the 1960s), where his appearance attracted a huge audience of twenty-three thousand. Nola wrote enthusiastically to her stepmother:

They have symphony concerts every night, with performances of the Ballet Russe and occasional solo artists. Then we go on to Chicago on the *20th Century*. Have two concerts at Ravinia Park, a beautiful place 20 miles out of Chicago, where people who have no seats *lie* on the beautiful lawns and even sit in the trees. We hope to take the plane out of Chicago on Saturday night after the concert, arriving in early Sunday morning to be back with our pets, I get ill for them.

Nola had been away from her babies for three months, leaving the faithful nanny Louise in charge.

When she returned to Los Gatos the simmering animosity between Nola and her mother-in-law burst into flames. Nola gave a vivid account of Marutha's brand of vitriol in a letter to her father which began by thanking him for a set of photos of Hephzibah.

I gave them to Aba [Moshe] first, as this is the only way to hear his honest opinion – he reacted just as we did, 'Isn't she beautiful, oh how lovely these are', etc. He then handed them to Mammina [Marutha], whose face, on seeing Hephzibah's beauty and her sophisticated appearance, clouded more than ever with jalousie and bitterness. She hated her hair, saying she looks like any 'Tom, Dick or Harry', then 'her eyes are unhealthy', and in the smiling [photo] 'her mouth isn't the same, she has acquired a typical Australian smile'; every Australian she has ever met has the same smile, a lot of teeth, similar to our Hollywood girls, very very artificial. When I said, 'Australians are flattered, Mammina, besides they have every reason to laugh openly being such a happy carefree people', to which M. answered in such a common tone of voice and wave of the hand, 'Oh, nonsense, child; living with all those pettinesses, you mean you were not happy to return [to the US] when you did?' I said, 'If not for Yehudi's tours we would still be there, and we will certainly return as soon as is possible for us.'

Looking again at the photo of her daughter smiling, Marutha returned to the attack:

'Oh she may be smiling but there is such sadness behind the eyes.' God! That woman. I said, 'Give them [the photos] to me, Mammina, you can see all this if you want to see it but they really are *two* excellent photos, of an extremely attractive person.' So she is not going to frame one of the photos, not one! (To use her own words.) I may add all this took place in front of a dozen people there.

Nola said that Yehudi shared her shock:

Aba, to we two, seems to have had his eyes opened at last to what his mate really is, and how she has failed him; and she is just full of bitterness and hatred for all the world, so much so it affects her looks and her whole being. 'Noots' [Nola's pet name for Yehudi] just sits there apart, and looks most unhappy and far away; we dislike going there intensely, but just now, Nanny having returned yesterday, and the house not being liveable as yet, we have to go there to sleep, which throws us into a deep depression and hatred for the place but this state is soon dispelled when we enter our property and are reunited with our family here.

This morning Noots did not come down to breakfast. He had an egg flip in our room and continued practising, which left me alone with the heads of the family A. and M. Oh my! what a session. 'Noots is not looking well, is far too thin.' M. hates summer concerts, always feels very sorry for the artist who has to give up his summers to concertize just for funds. I told her Noots would laugh at her if he knew she pitied him, as he is so well and happy and also loves to experience playing at these summer concerts. To which she flew up saying Noots would not laugh at any *grown* woman and certainly not her etc etc *etc* !!! . . . I'm full to the top hair with it all and wish to forget it and them.

Yehudi had evidently been troubled for some time about the way his life was developing. In a guarded but still surprisingly frank interview with the music journalist Ross Parmenter, published in the *New York Times* at the time of his Lewisohn Stadium appearance and reprinted in Los Angeles on the very day of the scene Nola recounts above, Yehudi discussed the transition from prodigy to artist and came close to denouncing the education his parents had provided for him:

The realization of a need for change came gradually. He feels that his awakening to an awareness of life was later than most young people's and that it would have come earlier if he had gone to school or taken part in a common enterprise like other young children. Then he would have developed a feeling for his place in the undertaking and the bit he had to contribute. It was not until he was past twenty that he began to understand the ways of life, the processes of change and the extent of man's independence and subjection in the world. Then he realized that he had to be responsible to himself, that he had to be his own voice and therefore he had to have a voice . . . a complete understanding of what he was about . . . 'Up to that point I was quite instinctive as to what I did. But there comes a time when the instinct falters . . .' The process of readjustment has made it necessary to restudy his whole repertoire.

His younger sister also felt a need to find her own voice. In October 1941 Yaltah eloped to Reno to marry Benjamin Rolfe, a Minneapolis lawyer who had been called up under the draft laws and was doing military training at a nearby army camp. When Yaltah met him at a party he confided that he was engaged to a woman he did not love (the same fate as Moshe's sister). Soon he fell for Yaltah and they made their secret way to Reno. She continued to live at home, however, where one of her daily tasks was to take her mother breakfast and read to her from the morning paper. Because of her family name, news of the secret marriage leaked out and she took a rebel's delight in reading out loud to her mother the story of her own escapade – a moment to treasure in the long-running battle between mother and daughter.

Yaltah then became a soldier's wife, living in military camps for the next four years and giving birth to two sons. Her second marriage lasted considerably longer than the first but also ended in divorce. Only with her third marriage, to the American pianist and psychiatrist Joel Ryce, was she to find lasting happiness.

America was on tenterhooks after Germany's invasion of Russia in June 1941 and Japan's increasing hostile position in the Pacific. Yehudi gave very few concerts in the autumn. Instead he worked at home with his new accompanist, Adolph Baller, a Polish Jew who had studied when only a boy with Leschetizky in Vienna, where the Nazis had tortured him and damaged his hands. He had escaped to the US, and first met Yehudi in New York. The property at Alma was further developed. Baller and his wife lived in the guest cottage. The children now had 'a glassed-in playroom where they could make all the noise they want to'. Thirty-five years later Yehudi wrote that what he called his 'interventions in their upbringing may well have seemed sporadic and theoretical. I would give them raw brains to eat, milk from a neighbouring cow to drink, and take them pickaback on long arduous walks in the hills.' He was being unduly hard on himself. The few letters that survive from Nola to her father contain no hint of criticism.

Early in December he took his children to their first concert, down the road from Alma at Santa Cruz. It was quite an eventful week, one way and another. On the 5th, returning from a concert in San Francisco, he was involved in a serious car crash from which he and Moshe escaped unharmed. The next day he set off for Mexico City where he was to give a series of four concerts. On 7 December he had reached the frontier town of El Paso when the news broke that the Japanese had bombed Pearl Harbor. US passports were declared null and void. Other fathers and husbands might have felt it appropriate to return home at such a critical moment but Yehudi merely telephoned

Nola (as he did every day when he was away) and waited for clearance from Washington: he then proceeded to Mexico City to honour his musical engagements.

Yehudi never fired a shot in anger but the war was to be the making of him as a man.

———

Recommended Recordings

Beethoven: Sonata in C minor, for violin and piano, Op. 30 No. 2
with Hephzibah Menuhin (piano)
BID LAB 124
Recorded: 30 March 1938
A good example of the youthful Menuhin duo.

Brahms: Sonata for violin and piano, No. 1 in G, Op. 78
with Hephzibah Menuhin (piano)
BID LAB 125
Recorded: 18 September 1940
YM's recording contract was with a British company, HMV/EMI, and when the Second World War broke out in 1939 his recording career came to a virtual standstill. But the Australian branch of the company recorded this Brahms sonata in Sydney with Hephzibah (Mrs Lindsay Nicholas) shortly after the birth of YM's son Krov.

PART THREE

Coming of Age
1941–1956

On holiday in Switzerland with Nola, Zamira and Krov, 1946

9 Menuhin at War –
'I have come to know my American brother'

Playing for the wounded, Hawaii, 1944

1942: wartime tours for troops, a new awareness of general public;
1943: February: visits Latin America and Caribbean; March: first
wartime visit to UK; November: meets Bartók and commissions solo
Sonata; 1944: March: troop concerts in Alaska and Aleutians; June:
plays for US troops in Hawaii; September: second wartime visit to UK,
meets Diana Gould; October: concerts in recently liberated Antwerp,
Brussels and Paris; November: gives première in New York of Bartók's
solo Sonata.

YEHUDI'S FOUR CONCERTS in Mexico City (on 11, 13, 15 and 17
December 1941) were all sold out. In the audience was the exiled
Carol II of Romania, who in the late 1920s (at the time of Yehudi's
boyhood escapade in the throne room of the royal summer palace at
Sinaia) had ceded power to his son Michael. He had then taken the

throne back in 1930, only to be forced to abdicate a second time after bowing to Nazi pressure and allowing a sizeable chunk of Transylvania to be transferred to Hungary. (In post-war years Yehudi would become close to several ex-kings and a friend of Princess Margherita, Michael's daughter.) In Mexico he met the members of the Léner Quartet, a distinguished Hungarian ensemble with whom he and Adolph Baller were to play chamber music (Chausson's Concert for piano, violin and string quartet) in New York after the war. He also gave a 'free-for-all' broadcast for students and schoolchildren.

He was soon back at Alma for what, five years later, he described cryptically as 'a dreary Christmas although I was at home'. Troops had just moved into the Los Gatos area, he later explained to a journalist:

The war, just beginning, seemed as if it would burst into flame in our midst: somebody thought we should do something for all those boys and I gave a concert for them, the first of many hundreds that I gave for the 'armed forces'.

A thousand people, 850 of them servicemen, heard him play in the auditorium of the local high school on 30 December. There was no printed programme; the audience called out what they wanted to hear. In some of his later troop concerts he would announce only the first movement of a concerto and after the applause at its conclusion ask if the concertgoers would like to hear more. His ability to generate an emotional response from even the least educated of his listeners had to do with the warmth of his personality. Bruno Walter noted perceptively that music is a good conductor of personality just as metal is a good conductor of heat: 'Through music, man himself speaks. The audience sense the man and that which they sense in Yehudi they love.'

Nola and the children travelled with him to New York, which as in pre-war days was to be his winter base. They stayed at Hampshire House on Central Park South, a more fashionable (and expensive) address than the hotels chosen by Moshe in the previous decade. (Later in the war they rented an apartment in Manhattan. Nola and her friend Klari Dorati were to train as nurses in New York.) Yehudi took the ailing Fritz Kreisler's place for a winter tour and gave additional charity concerts for the Red Cross. He played at military camps near the big cities and by May, when he returned to California, he had given eighteen such recitals, organized by Camp Shows Inc. for the United Services Organisation (USO). He appeared at Fort Snelling and Fort Devens, at the Akron Armory and the Camp Grant Service Club.

He played for the American Women's Voluntary Services, for Russian War Relief and for the Red Cross – this last concert was a sold-out event at Carnegie Hall conducted by Barbirolli. A Miami journalist commented that Yehudi was 'giving so many war benefit concerts you wonder how he'll manage to get in one that will really bring him in a few shekels'. In fact he made five appearances that winter in New York City alone, among them a rare performance of the Dvořák Concerto with the New York Philharmonic under Eugene Goossens's baton and a recital that included a solo sonata by Hindemith (Op. 31 No. 4) – perhaps the inspiration for the commission he was to offer Béla Bartók two years later.

Playing for ordinary men in uniform had an immediate impact on Menuhin. As early as January 1942, after only a handful of visits to the troops, he described his new public as 'the most cultivated and extraordinary audience I have ever had. I experimented with different types of music and they were responsive to everything.' Such democratic and socially correct observations were only to be expected in a press interview but Yehudi expanded on this reaction in a private letter to his father-in-law in Australia, written a few months later when he was at Alma:

The war has brought many fine things along with the bad. A great fluidity has come upon this country, set free by the merging of personal interests into the one all-embracing necessity; this has come at a time when our country is most threatened by opposing groups. The Union Jack and the Hammer and Sickle wave in brotherhood, men of every condition join in the work, rewarded by merit alone and (for the time being at least) thoughts, aspirations, ambitions are all above board.

I have come to know my American brother, I have come to know my own generation, something which I particularly, in my life, have been somewhat denied. Playing to these men places music as well as the musician entirely at the mercy of the moment – no tradition, concert-like ceremonial stand in the way of direct contact . . . This activity will probably remain my 'sole' war activity. You may laugh, but judging from a few letters I have received, music *can* boost that 'fighting spirit'. By no manner of means can you interpret this to mean I leave an audience raving mad, only that our men as well as your men [i.e. the Australian troops] need only remember the beauty and the priviledges [*sic*] of their homelands to give them purpose and stamina on the battlefields.

Summer was at hand, Yehudi noted in the same letter, reporting that the Alma landscape had been transformed from 'the barren restricted ground' the Nicholas family had known when they had stayed there four years previously on the occasion of Hephzibah's wedding to Lindsay. 'Our beautiful home', he wrote,

is being quietly assimilated into our being and no longer do we stand in awe of the dish-washing machine, the significance of our green living-room carpet or the indirect lighting of our music room. The outside work, swimming pool, lawn, paths and stone work should be completed by the end of next week.

Yehudi always wrote to Australia in optimistic mood. He also reported that Nola – 'sweetest, most adorable being' – was now doing the cooking. Cooks, indeed any kind of servant, were hard to come by in wartime California. Adolph Baller and his wife had moved in to the guest cottage, Nola wrote to her father. Yehudi played in so many army camps (he was off the following day to Sacramento) that it was good to have Mr Baller close to hand.

In August Yehudi gave an interview that showed the way his thoughts were running, even at that dark period before the tide started to turn in the Allies' favour:

When the war is over, the intense hatred generated by it will smoulder on. It will be at that moment that the values humanity has created through artistic appreciation and aesthetic values will become weapons to fight the inroads [that] savagery has made upon the millions exposed to it.

Three years later he was the first classical musician to perform for the survivors of the Belsen concentration camp and the first foreigner to play for Germans in the British Zone – over the radio.

In June 1942 Yehudi conceded defeat in a long-running battle with Cesar J. Petrillo, the flamboyant boss of the American Federation of Musicians. He described the union's campaign against him at some length in his autobiography. With a real war being fought elsewhere – Yehudi's 6 June letter of compliance spoke of not wanting to make a fuss – he joined the AFM's Santa Clara County 'Local' or branch. Membership ensured his availability for lucrative outdoor engagements later in the summer at the Lewisohn Stadium in New York and Grant Field in Chicago, where, as Nola wrote with pride to her father, he had an audience of two hundred thousand. From Chicago he brought back a toy violin for his son Krov's second birthday.

By the autumn, Yehudi's frequent absences were beginning to take their toll on his wife's sanguine nature. He was off next day, Nola wrote from her isolated hillside home, to give three concerts in Los Angeles and after only four more days at home he would be away for three weeks: 'I do not like seeing him go, I feel so alone here.' She added that she would not be going east that winter: Yehudi's engagements were better than those of other artists but they were still short of money. The letter was dated 10 November. Three days earlier the Americans had invaded French Northern Africa in Operation Torch, the first stage of America's fight back against the Axis powers. Inadvertently it thwarted one of Yehudi's cherished plans. He had earlier written to his London agent asking him to arrange some concerts in war-time England and in the autumn a formal invitation had been issued. His arrival was announced for 25 October but, Nola reported to her father:

After spending a week of nervous anticipation in New York awaiting orders to go to England, they found it at the last minute impossible to obtain air passage so as to have him back by the time his American tour began. The English people were so broken-hearted that Harold Holt simply postponed the concerts instead of cancelling them.

The official story was that every inch of cargo space had been commandeered in order to transport vital war material needed for the imminent invasion of North Africa. Yehudi's disappointment was mollified when the day after his own flight was cancelled he saw the headline: 'Mrs Eleanor Roosevelt flies to London.' In later years he would never suffer the indignity of being bumped off a flight.

The authorities had accepted his proposition that a concert artist might be dispatched across the Atlantic with more general supplies: 'a truffle', as he put it, 'in the next cargo of Spam'. His expedition to Britain was rearranged for March 1943. It meant cancelling prior engagements but the war gave Yehudi a new sense of freedom and control over his life. Before the UK trip he undertook a second tour of Latin America which included Mexico, Costa Rica, Panama, Chile, Peru, Argentina, Brazil and (on the way home) the Caribbean, where he arranged to play at as many US camps and naval bases as possible. Yehudi told the press (as musicians will) that music was the most effective way of promoting international good feeling, but one can only guess at Nola's personal emotions when she contemplated her husband's long and sometimes dangerous absences – a fate she shared with millions of service wives.

It was while flying in the Caribbean that Yehudi was involved in his only air crash, which he brushed aside engagingly as 'a minor affair *de rien du tout*'. Attempting to take off in Puerto Rico his army bi-plane was caught by a gust of wind and ended up in a sugar plantation. Happily it did not catch fire: to have been immolated in a blaze of burnt sugar would have been an incongruous death for one who was later to speak out so strongly against that substance in the daily diet. The accident occurred after he had been taking part in a jam session with a group of army musicians stationed in Puerto Rico. A publicity photo shows a somewhat mournful quartet – bass, banjo and electric guitar – performing the 'St Louis Blues', a melody Yehudi had probably never heard before in his life.

He found the Caribbean tour tough going:

Every day I played at least one concert in a camp and I must say at the end of those two weeks, getting up in the morning at five o'clock, taking the plane to a new camp before lunch and possibly afterwards, getting ready for the evening concert, afterwards a little supper . . . It was the only time in my life when the sight of a human being was more than I could bear. Any bi-ped was beyond my patience.

Further proof of the way war changed his life came with Yehudi's participation in a feature film. Moshe's high-flown objections to pre-war Hollywood proposals were hardly relevant to this modest project, a film version of the popular *Stage Door Canteen*. A regular New York attraction during the war, this music-hall pot-pourri was intended for troops on leave in the city. Films were distributed to US military bases around the world and the February 1943 edition included a segment in which Yehudi and Adolph Baller gave a wonderfully intense reading of Schubert's *Ave Maria* to a raptly attentive audience of servicemen.

In March 1943 Yehudi finally got to fly to England – with the Royal Air Force. He took off from Montreal in what Moshe's press release described as a 'special bomber'. The transatlantic flight was said to have been 'hazardous'. He arrived 'half frozen after hours spent cramped in the nose of an American bomber'. He stayed six weeks, playing in munitions factories as well as in US Army and RAF camps. 'Everything gloriously wonderful,' he cabled to his father. The climax of the visit came on 5 April when he gave a fine performance of the Brahms Violin Concerto, broadcast nationally from the BBC's Maida Vale studio – the BBC Symphony Orchestra made a special trip to London for the event from its wartime base in Bedford. At the end of the performance the applause was led by the conductor, Sir Adrian Boult. (On the archive recording his 'Bravo' comes over loud and clear.) An unsigned article next day in the *Daily Telegraph* wondered whether Yehudi realized

the joy he gives us during the war and how grateful we are to him for coming over here . . . As I listened entranced to his superb rendering of the Brahms I thought of the joy he was giving those other listeners, musical men and women in the Forces, and perhaps many who are suffering in Europe were also able to hear the unearthly beauty of the playing. He must surely have strengthened their faith in the survival of civilization and all it can give the world!

Yehudi derived equal satisfaction from a concert given at the Royal Albert Hall in aid of the Free French. General Charles de Gaulle subsequently decorated him with the Croix de Lorraine and invited him to lunch at the Savoy with the French 'cabinet' in exile. And after a break of four years Yehudi was at last able to resume work for HMV. His only recordings in the intervening years had been made in Australia: the Brahms Op. 78 Sonata, with Hephzibah. A Wieniawski concerto with the ABC Symphony of Sydney (under Dr Heinze) was never released, presumably because the orchestra did not come up to HMV's standard. On 31 March 1943, he recorded the Mozart Concerto in D (K.218) in Liverpool, with Malcom Sargent conducting the Liverpool Philharmonic. With Marcel Gazelle reinstated as his pianist he performed a handful of popular single-sided 78s especially appropriate for wartime listening, among them Bach's Air on the G string and Schubert's *Ave Maria*. (Gazelle had escaped from Belgium during the 1940 Dunkirk evacuation.)

When Yehudi was delayed on his flight back to America, the ground staff at the aerodrome were reported to have

fitted up a warm jacket to keep his precious Stradivarius in an equable temperature while the plane was in the upper ice regions . . . Menuhin gave them an impromptu recital . . . accompanied at the piano by an RAF embarkation officer who despite 'nerves' got through not too badly and was patted on the back by the maestro. It is said that his fiddle was insured for a larger amount than the value of the wonderful bomber in which he flew!

Presumably Yehudi did not want to spoil a good story by revealing that he had left his real Strad at home. He was probably playing the Emile Français replica.

Menuhin's championing of the music of Béla Bartók dates from later this year, 1943. He had already decided he should be playing more contemporary music and he spent part of the summer reading through new scores with Adolph Baller. He came to Bartók through the enthusiasm of another Hungarian, the conductor Antal Dorati. He and Nola had met Dorati and his wife Klari in 1940 on the Pacific voyage to Australia, where Dorati was to conduct ballet performances. Their daughters, Zamira and Tonina, were similar in age and the wives became particularly close friends. In New York Dorati was Music Director of Ballet Theater and of the modest New Opera Company. He invited Menuhin to an evening of chamber music at his home at which Bartók's music was performed – provoking an angry reaction from neighbours in the Dorati's apartment block. The conductor related in his memoirs that 'an enormous policeman appeared in the doorway, shouting at us in a furious voice: "Shut that radio!!!"' The musicians were Yehudi, William Primrose, Gregor Piatigorsky and Dorati himself: they were playing Brahms when the cop arrived.

Dorati's advocacy was reinforced by that of another conductor, Dimitri Mitropoulos, who – perhaps not by coincidence – had invited Yehudi to perform Bartók's Second Violin Concerto with the Minneapolis Orchestra in November 1943. Yehudi was attracted to it immediately, describing it as 'a powerful work that suited my temperament', and he was deeply impressed by Mitropoulos who conducted not only the performance but the rehearsals from memory. Bartók's music exercised a peculiar spell: 'No other composer has drawn me as irresistibly as Bartók,' he later told BBC listeners.

I felt at one with his implacable and complex rhythms, at one with the abstract yet intensely expressive construction of his melodic lines, at one with his incredibly rich range of harmonies – sometimes simple, sometimes clashing or ironical – and, above all, at one with that streamlined cleanness of design and execution, always without a trace of irrelevance or sentimentality.

Yehudi had scheduled Bartók's First Violin Sonata for a Carnegie Hall recital later in his 1943 season, a few weeks after the concerto performance. The Hungarian composer was then living in New York in conditions of economic hardship and physical weakness; he was to die two years later of leukaemia. Yehudi wrote asking if he and Baller might play the Sonata through for him. Bartók had recently completed his Concerto for Orchestra, arguably the most genial and approachable work of his late period, but his reputation was one of highly strung aloofness.

The audition was held one wintry afternoon at the Park Avenue home of one of Yehudi's childhood 'aunts', Kitty Perera, mother of his friend Lydia. The meeting was etched on Yehudi's memory. Fifty years later he could describe it with precise detail. Bartók was there when the performers arrived.

He had already drawn up an armchair, music on his lap, pencil in his hand, the real Hungarian strict professor. No warmth, no 'How are you to-day?'; not a word. There was nothing to do except unpack the violin and begin playing. Fortunately we played it as I really wanted to play it and his very first words [after the run-through of the first movement] were 'I did not think works could be played that beautifully until long after the composer was dead' – in the most perfect English. It was the heavens opening! To be able to please the composer . . . gave me an incredible sense of deep satisfaction. I felt that I knew him, knew his heart and his temperament and his integrity.

On the spot Yehudi commissioned a solo sonata:

I thought, well, here's my chance. And not only because he needed money, though little did I anticipate that he wouldn't cash my cheque until after he'd finished the work, such was his integrity. I'm sure he would have written a concerto for me because at that moment he would have done anything I asked, but I limited myself to a modest request . . . I wanted to impose the least possible burden on him so that he could spend as little time as he wanted. He gave me the great Sonata in four movements, without a doubt the greatest work for solo violin since Bach.

Bartók composed the Sonata at the winter retreat provided for him by the American composers' organization ASCAP in Asheville, North Carolina. At the composer's request Yehudi then added 'the necessary changes in bowing and' – as Bartók put it – 'the absolutely necessary fingering and other suggestions'. Antal Dorati was present when Yehudi played the Sonata through for him privately. 'It is a fiendishly difficult work,' he wrote in his memoirs. Knowing this, Bartók accommodated Menuhin's request for minor changes wherever he could – 'but was quite firm in refusing them when he felt the need'. When the revision work was concluded Bartók sent his thanks, adding drily, 'I am very glad to hear that the work is playable.'

Yehudi gave the first performance on 26 November 1944 with Nola and Zamira in the audience at a Carnegie Hall concert which prompted Bartók (like Elgar before him) to express unbounded admiration:

He played . . . Bach's C major Sonata in a grand, classical style. My Sonata, too, was exceedingly well done. When there is a real great artist, then the composer's advice and help is not necessary, the performer finds his way quite well, alone. It is altogether a happy thing that a young artist [Yehudi was then twenty-seven] is interested in contemporary works which draw no public and likes them, and performs them *comme il faut.*

Yet Yehudi himself was dissatisfied:

I regret that I was not able to let him hear it in a truly finished interpretation, for over the years the music has come to speak to me, and I believe all of us, in the deepest spiritual terms.

He added that the Sonata's fugue movement was 'perhaps the most aggressive, brutal music I was ever to play'. The press reception was cool. Perhaps Yehudi should have revived his pre-war practice of inviting the critics to attend previews of unfamiliar music. Olin Downes said the Sonata was 'a test for ears, the intelligence, the receptiveness of the most learned listener . . . on initial acquaintance we take none too kindly to the piece'. A younger critic, Arthur Berger, writing in the *Sun*, described Bartók as an undeniably important composer of our time; the new work was well written, he added, but 'lacked profile'. Forty years later Paul Griffiths, a distinguished Bartók biographer, labelled the solo Sonata – one might almost say libelled it – as Bartók's most awkward work, as 'awkward to hear as it is to play'.

Menuhin never had such reservations. He took the Sonata into his repertoire, played it to the troops and recorded it in London in 1947. He spoke of an intimate bond between himself and the composer, a friendship that might well be deeper than many relationships of longer standing because, as he put it, 'the thrill of knowing Bartók was the realization that through his music and without any words, his heart had been revealed to me'. The composer reserves the core of his personality, the essence of his self, for his works, and with that Bartókian essence Menuhin became very familiar: he played the Second Violin Concerto all over the world, gave its British première on BBC Radio in 1944 and recorded it no fewer than three times with Dorati (not to mention a fine version with Furtwängler). He included Bartók's seven Romanian Folk Dances in many of his wartime recitals. Later, in 1958, he gave the première (outside Switzerland) of the earlier, previously unpublished First Violin Concerto. He recorded the Viola Concerto in 1966, and made several recordings of the First Sonata for violin and piano. From the 1960s onwards, Bartók's *Divertimento* was one of the orchestral works he most enjoyed conducting.

The year 1944 was the *annus mirabilis* of Menuhin's early adult life.

Before the Bartók première in November 1944 he undertook three extended tours for the armed forces that ought to have brought him more than they did in the way of honours to add to the decoration he had already received from General de Gaulle. The military expeditions began in February with a four-week tour of Alaska and the Aleutian Islands, for the most part flying in unheated planes with metal-frame seats that left him and Baller shaken up and wobbly on their feet. Yehudi described the islands as bare rocks jutting out of the North Pacific like stepping stones between America and Russia. The enemy had been driven out of the islands nearest Japan so there was no immediate danger, but the area was inhospitable, remote and damp. Morale was low and the men were bored, but they were prepared to listen to music, Yehudi found. In one hospital the piano had collapsed and was being used as a dustbin for empty beer bottles, so Yehudi boldly played a programme of unaccompanied Bach and had the conscripts cheering for more. On the island of Adak, where an airstrip was being built with a view to bombing mainland Japan, Yehudi was lodged with the station commander, whose rank conferred on him the right to an indoor toilet. Yehudi's accompanist, Adolph Baller, was less fortunate. He was seated on an outside convenience when the fragile hut in which it was installed was blown away by an unfriendly Arctic wind. Much jollity ensued.

The intense cold and fog often caused problems. The musicians' island-hopping plane would skim the ocean and then rear up with stomach-wrenching suddenness when land came into view through the mist. On the airstrip of the island of Shemya huge oil flares burned around the clock. On one occasion the plane wandered so far off course that it strayed into enemy territory:

Hastening back from the Japanese side of the ocean we were relieved to see them [the flares] glowing through the fog, but I was equally relieved to quit a station so isolated and tense.'

A family in San José, the nearest town to the Menuhins' home at Los Gatos, received a letter from an army captain serving in the Aleutians concerning their local hero:

It was quite an interesting thing seeing Yehudi playing in a sweater to only a mess hall full of men who wore muddy work clothing and who have been separated from all civilization for three-quarters of a year. I could not help contrasting that scene with an auditorium appearance of that great Yehudi – where gentlemen were dressed and women were undressed to the dictates of the latest fashion. Yet, the applause for the playing was just as long and loud and probably much more sincere than that in the great musical halls of the world. And I believe Yehudi appreciated it as much. He seemed to doubt the warmth of his reception until the applause told him otherwise. We were all impressed by his attitude, acting not like an untouchable prodigy but as a plain 'guy' like the rest of us!

The prevailing chill of the North Pacific made it exceptionally difficult for Yehudi to play and he would wrap up in thick pullovers with mittens on his precious fingers until the last possible moment. There is no mention of it in contemporary accounts but it seems probable that he did not risk his 'Prince Khevenhüller' Strad for such an expedition, preferring to employ Emile Français's facsimile – as he certainly did when he went on active service later in the year. As for coping with the cold, a Navy lieutenant from Altadena provided an eye-witness account of one solution, which was seized on by Moshe for recycling in a press release headed 'Servicemen prefer Menuhin to Movies':

I was in the steam room – stark naked of course – when who should walk in but Yehudi Menuhin! He was in the raw, too . . . We sat on the wooden bleachers in the steam room and sweated and chatted for about ten minutes. He's quite a swell guy. He had come over to play for the boys in our new auditorium later that evening and was obviously concerned how they would like his type of art . . . His accompaniment was by a Sea-bee [a member of one of the US Navy construction battalions building naval shore facilities in combat zones] who had been a concert pianist. He played on an old tin-panny upright – some of the keys worked, and many did not. But I am pretty sure Yehudi will always remember this concert. He was obviously delighted and could have played there all night if they had let him. The audience booed the picture when it finally started – they wanted more of Yehudi! . . . Funny world, isn't it? At home these same guys probably wouldn't cross the street to hear a concert.

Moshe drafted another press release at the end of June. It was emotively headed 'Yehudi Menuhin in Pearl Harbor, Hawaii'. Six weeks after Yehudi's extended tour of the Aleutians and Alaska, the military in Hawaii invited him to undertake a similar tour for US marines on active service in the central Pacific, much closer to the real war. In his press release, the proud father seems to be making a virtue of his son's neglect of family duties:

Yehudi Menuhin promptly accepted the request, and in spite of having promised his wife and children that this time he will have a little vacation with them at home (after eighteen months of giving constantly war concerts) . . . he flew overnight

Saturday [i.e. 23 June] in an army bomber and is now already touring various camps and bases in the islands.

Moshe's bland account of his son's activities (which included two professional concerts for civilians to cover the cost of his accompanist and hotels) concealed a period of high emotion for Yehudi:

The most terrifying audience I had during the war was in Hawaii, playing for soldiers who were going to be airlifted to the battlefield. They were kept out of contact for four or five days so they were prisoners in a compound, being trained night and day for what they were going to face, possibly the last days of their lives.

Menuhin noted that although the men were physically prepared to fighting pitch, spiritually they had been given no preparation to help them face near-certain death or maiming. He played music from the serious side of his repertoire, including the ever popular *Ave Maria*, but his audience was unresponsive: 'I really don't know what could have given them relief.'

Yehudi's sense of inadequacy was intensified by contact with recently wounded soldiers: planes and ships were streaming back with them to Hawaii from the war zone. In June 1944, bloody battles were being fought to retake Guam, Saipan and the strategically vital Marianas Islands. Twenty-five thousand Americans were killed or maimed during the brief campaign. Yehudi remembered ambulances lining the roads from the airport and the harbour, nose to tail for miles on end, all crammed with wounded men happy to know they had survived. Violin in hand, he walked through the hospital wards, pausing in each one to play a twenty-minute recital. The palpable relief and high spirits provided, he remembered, a 'wonderful contrast to the tension and misery of the marines on their way to war'.

The Shakespearean actor Maurice Evans was the US Army captain in charge of entertainments on the islands. Yehudi remembered him with affection: 'Often I would take part in jam sessions lasting past midnight, punctuated by singing, juggling, playing, or, best of all, Evans's recitations from Shakespeare.' Willa Cather would have been pleased that he was keeping up his interest in the Bard.

Yehudi was lodged in a beach cottage. Before starting work in the morning he would take a swim in the ocean, and there he came across a group of Japanese women, Hawaiian residents, gathering seaweed – a substitute for the fish their husbands had been forbidden by wartime regulations to catch. In the midst of so much emotional buffeting, the ever curious Yehudi found time to talk to the women. After he had waded out to join them he was given seaweed in souvenir bottles which he took home to Alma. (What a film sequence could be developed from such an incident, intercutting between the women gathering seaweed, the marines fearful of the future, the Japanese suicide pilots dive-bombing the American invasion flotilla, the ambulance lines, the hospital beds filled with grinning survivors, and over it all the *Ave Maria* . . .)

Yehudi returned to California in time to open the season at the Hollywood Bowl on 12 July. His new friend Dimitri Mitropoulos conducted the Los Angeles Philharmonic and inspired a flight of Greek fancy in the *Herald Express* reviewer, Carl Bronson, who compared the venue to a Delphic shrine. Yehudi, he wrote, played the Brahms Concerto with 'an entirely Orphic impressiveness . . . [he] made the very trees to dance, and could easily have persuaded Persephone to release her adored Eurydice'. Meanwhile Moshe seemed to take a perverse pleasure in chronicling the increasing isolation of his daughter-in-law. 'The months of September and October,' he wrote in a press release, 'which were also [like June and July] set aside for home life and preparation for the coming season, will in all probability go to another bomber flight to Great Britain.'

Yehudi's second tour of Britain was arranged with the British authorities rather than the Americans, who were, he remembered, too bureaucratic and insistent on exclusivity: 'They would not allow me to give my own concerts for any charity . . . so I made my own arrangements.' (This attitude may have been a reason for the absence of American honours to match de Gaulle's.) He crossed the Atlantic from Baltimore in a flying boat and his first assignment was a week with the British Navy in Scapa Flow. 'I am very fond of British things,' he told a reporter from the *Orkney Blast*, a navy paper, 'and there is nothing more British than the Home Fleet.'

The usual round of concerts in mess halls and aircraft hangars concluded with a performance of the Bach Double Concerto, in which he was joined by the leader of the Home Fleet Naval Orchestra. A photograph captioned 'Big Guns' shows a slim and windswept Yehudi on the deck of the *Duke of York*, the Fleet's flagship, flanked by admirals sporting a great many gold rings on their sleeves and dwarfed by four enormous guns. From the British equivalent of the Aleutian Islands (though rather less cold) he travelled down to Bedford, where the BBC had invited him to give the British première of Bartók's Second Violin Concerto. The enlightened programme planners thought it such an important work that two separate live broadcasts were scheduled, the first on 20 September at 7.15 p.m., when he played the Bach E major Concerto in the first half of the concert, and the second at 2.30 p.m. on a Sunday afternoon, 8 October.

The intervening fortnight was one of the most momentous periods in Yehudi's life. It began conventionally enough with concerts in Oxford and Salisbury Cathedral, where the two thousand servicemen in the audience were requested not to clap after his performance of unaccompanied Bach. He visited military hospitals in Cheltenham. He played for Mrs Churchill's Aid to Russia, for the Airborne Troops Comfort Fund and for Lady Cripps's Aid to China. He entertained a thousand people at the Marson Excelsior works in Wolverhampton and hundreds more at the Pilkington glass factory at St Helen's in Lancashire. Interviewed by the *Evening Standard* he confessed that he had come to Britain without his Strad – he borrowed a Guarnerius from Hills, the London violin-dealers. The reporter noted approvingly that he was dressed in loose and comfortable clothes, a pale-blue Russian-style tunic over darker-blue flannel trousers. On 1 October came the climax of the British visit, a fund-raising concert of concertos at the Royal Albert Hall which raised £4000 for a long list of charities, including the Airborne Forces Security fund which had been created only days before, expressly for the dependants of servicemen who had lost their lives in the failed airborne landing at Arnhem.

The following day, 2 October, Yehudi set out over the English Channel for the front line of the war in Western Europe. London had been thrust into gloom by the failure of the Airborne Division to capture the Rhine bridge at Arnhem. Until the bitter fighting in Holland, the war in Europe had been going well for the Allies. Paris had been liberated on 25 August and on 30 September troops reached Brussels and Antwerp. Accompanied by Marcel Gazelle, who was elated at the thought of returning to his homeland, Yehudi gave concerts in the two Belgian cities on 2 and 3 October. In Brussels he appeared at the Palais des Beaux Arts, where once his mother had made him decline an invitation to pay a courtesy visit to Queen Elisabeth in her box.

The thirty-mile drive from Brussels to Antwerp was, Yehudi reported, a frightening business:

Between danger zones, mined roads and blown-up bridges, travel across the devastated landscape was an ingenious sequence of contrivances in borrowed cars and trucks, over army pontoon bridges and by private-enterprise ferry.

Those who criticize his parents for mollycoddling their teenage son would be hard put to explain Yehudi's enterprise and canniness – not to mention bravery – when it came to organizing his wartime travel. Menuhin and Gazelle were repeatedly challenged *en route* by Americans, Canadians, Belgians returning from exile and the local Maquis. Fortunately their documents satisfied all interrogators and they reached Antwerp safely, but the Germans were still in the suburbs, a mere four kilometres to the north, and they had shelled the city the previous night.

The musicians gave their concert none the less, early in the evening to escape the German shelling, and after his recital Yehudi was invited to an official reception given by the municipality in the house next door to what until a few days earlier had been the headquarters of the Gestapo. It was, he said, 'the most eerie festivity of my life'. The Antwerpians brought out of hiding their finest crystal and silver and a handsome supply of fine wines. But as if still under the shadow of the Occupation, everybody spoke in a whisper. Toasts were murmured. A change of vintage was announced as if in a conspiracy. Horrors and hardships were recalled on verbal tiptoe. It was, Yehudi recalled, like the meeting of a secret society.

Before the sun had set Menuhin and Gazelle were on their way back to Brussels and yet another recital. At the airport next morning, Wednesday 4 October, they hitched a ride on an American Dakota to Paris. Yehudi implied that this was an impromptu excursion but back in the summer a press release by Moshe had reported his intention to be the first musician to play in Paris after the Liberation, 'thus to carry out a promise he made to General Charles de Gaulle in London, when the latter pinned on him the Cross of Lorraine'. Yehudi didn't mention this promise in his memoirs and a contemporary report suggested that it was the General who made the promise to Yehudi rather than the other way round, after they had drunk a toast (at the Savoy, in April 1943) to the city's eventual liberation. It may be assumed either way that the French authorities had some inkling of Yehudi's plans and that the Americans were also in the picture. In return for the promise of a concert for the US troops stationed at Villacoublay, Yehudi was provided with a chauffeured car in Paris and a flight back to England on

Saturday evening, 7 October, so that he could fulfil his BBC broadcast engagement the next day.

Yehudi took a room at the Ritz, where the food was skimpy and the heating and hot water non-existent, and – to quote an interview given a week later to the *New York Times* – he fell in love with Paris all over again. He contacted his faithful concert manager Maurice Dandelot and gave him three days to organize a concert. Public theatres had been closed following an assassination attempt on General de Gaulle soon after his arrival and Yehudi's concert would be the first to be mounted at the Opéra since the Liberation.

Meanwhile he drove out to Ville d'Avray to find the former Menuhin home stripped of all its furnishings. But the Vian family, the next-door neighbours, were safe, and so were Bigina the cook and her husband Ferruccio, who were still running a restaurant in the village. The Menuhins' old friend Jacques Thibaud was well, too, and he not only gave Yehudi the news that Enesco was alive in Romania but also lent him his Stradivarius for the concert at the Opéra. However, another old friend, Alfred Cortot, had collaborated with the Nazis and was, Yehudi suggested, 'done for'. He had heard good reports, on the other hand, concerning Wilhelm Furtwängler who (he told the *New York Times*) had helped Jewish members of his Berlin orchestra and 'won the respect of the Parisian populace by refusing to conduct Nazi-sponsored concerts on several occasions'. Clemens Krauss and Herbert von Karajan had no such scruples about appearing in Paris.

For the American forces Yehudi gave two recitals in the beautiful rococo theatre built for Marie Antoinette in the Palace of Versailles and on Saturday 7 October came the great concert at the Opéra, with Charles Munch conducting the orchestra of the Société des Concerts du Conservatoire. Tickets had been put on sale only that morning but the house was packed and tears flowed copiously when the orchestra launched into 'La Marseillaise'. It was being played at the Opéra for the first time since 1940. Yehudi played it with the orchestra and thereafter dominated the afternoon, performing the Beethoven Concerto after the interval and Lalo's *Symphonie espagnole* before it, preceded by another work that had been banned for four years, the E minor Violin Concerto by Mendelssohn. Munch was so excited before it began that he shouted the composer's opening tempo instruction to the players: 'Allegro molto appassionato!'

The demand for encores was insatiable. Yehudi's American pilot was standing in the wings, urging him to depart while the sun was still up; his plane was not equipped for night flying. Yehudi must by then have returned Thibaud's Strad to its owner because he borrowed the concertmaster's instrument to play one last offering and then they were off in an American jeep, racing north to Le Bourget airfield. It was just the sort of adventure Yehudi loved – reminiscent of the escapade on the fire engine in San Francisco all those years previously. To add to the drama, the plane's electrical system failed over the English Channel and the pilot had to make a forced landing in a field somewhere in Kent. The story ends incongruously with Menuhin and Gazelle carrying their bags to a road and catching first a country bus and then a local train to London. In his half-empty violin case – there was space for two instruments and Yehudi was travelling with only the Emile Français replica – he found room for a bottle of champagne, some French perfume and a Reblochon cheese.

That evening he sent a long cable to his father which began:

BRUSSELS ANTWERP PARIS DEEPLY MOVING AUDIENCE SATURDAY AFTERNOON OPERA HOUSE SHOUTED THEIR LUNGS OUT IN UNBRIDLED ENTHUSIASM WORDS FAIL ME TO DESCRIBE STIRRING EMOTIONAL CONTENT LAST FIVE DAYS STOP

The next morning he travelled to Bedford to repeat his BBC broadcast of the Bartók concerto. Adrian Boult was his conductor. 'We had a refresher rehearsal,' Boult remembered,

and I arranged for lunch and transport so we could get back in good time.

'No thanks, I think I must just stay right here and sleep,' [Yehudi responded].

We were at Bedford School where there was nowhere to sleep and nothing to sleep on. However, a little Red Cross room was open just by the hall (most rooms were locked) and I suggested putting two or three chairs together for him.

'No thanks, this will do nicely – please wake me at two.'

He curled up on quite a small table and was asleep almost before I had left the room. He had not moved when I went in to wake him. Had he done so, he would have been on the floor.

The next day Yehudi flew to New York. The *annus mirabilis* was not yet over, for in November he gave the première of the Bartók solo Sonata and in December he joined forces with the harpsichord player Wanda Landowska, the era's greatest interpreter of Bach's keyboard music, to play a concert of Bach violin sonatas at Town Hall. These were milestones in his musical career but they were surpassed in emotional impact by the tremors he experienced at the end of September when he met the woman who became his second wife.

He'd arrived in London furnished by his Los Gatos friends Frank and George with the name of a musical friend of theirs, a certain Mrs Evelyn Harcourt. He phoned her, invited himself to lunch and there met Mrs Harcourt's daughter Diana, with whom he fell in love at first sight. The story, recounted in all Menuhin memoirs and biographies, contains minor mysteries. The Menuhins had known Frank Ingerson and George Dennison since 1927, and they had been coming to London since 1929, so why did it take fifteen years for an introduction to be effected? And since Mrs Harcourt maintained a musical *salon* of some distinction before the war – Furtwängler was a regular visitor when he was conducting in London – why had she never invited the Menuhins, nor even gone backstage to salute Yehudi after one of the recitals she and her daughters had attended in the 1930s? Diana said it was because her mother was a proud woman, too proud to make the first move when she knew that the Menuhins had been given a letter of introduction from 'the boys', Frank and George. With her dislike of kowtowing, Marutha had probably vetoed using it to make contact.

But at last, on 29 September 1944, Mrs Harcourt finally held a luncheon party in Yehudi's honour at her flat in Belgravia. As Evelyn Suart, she had trained as a concert pianist; indeed her photograph used to hang on the wall of the artists' room at the Wigmore Hall. Her first husband, an Irish career diplomat named Gerard Gould, had died when she was only thirty, leaving her with three young children to bring up on her own. Later she married a naval officer, Cecil Harcourt, who was knighted in 1946 and rose to be Commander of the Nore. (The rank of Commander is only one grade below that of First Sea Lord, as Yehudi would take endless pains to explain in later years.) Mrs Harcourt had summoned her two daughters to be with her for Yehudi's visit. Diana was then thirty-one, and her sister Griselda two years younger. Both were sharp-tongued, clever and discriminating, which may explain why, despite their considerable beauty, they were neither of them married. The other male guests were family friends, the actor Michael Redgrave, with whom Diana was working on the translation of a French play, and the celebrated film director Anthony Asquith. It made quite a distinguished table, and a refreshing change from the military people with whom Yehudi had spent so much of his time over the previous three years. Redgrave expressed himself nervous about meeting a genius and Diana told him not to use such a horrible word: 'I don't know him but I'm sure he'd hate it.'

Diana enjoyed telling the story of her first meeting with her future husband:

We all turned up at Mummy's flat looking rather grey and faded as a result of five years of living on Ryvita and fingernails, and into the room came this radiant vision, rather as if somebody had turned a light on. [Yehudi was] a little bit over-weight, with a beautiful pink and white complexion, lots of golden hair . . . modest at the same time, not pushy, not talking very much, but his presence was extraordinary even then.

For Yehudi, Diana was 'the most beautiful woman I had ever seen' . . . a 'tall, dark, slender girl' of 'grace, intelligence, ardour, vitality and depth of feeling'. He compared the lunch-table conversational volleys of the two sisters to razor-sharp blades bolted together: 'They scissored language with incredible rapidity, throwing upon our heads a confetti of fanciful cut-outs and profiles in epigram.'

After lunch Yehudi wanted to take Diana off for a drive but she had a dentist's appointment, so instead he dropped her and Redgrave at Piccadilly Circus. At some point, when Diana had been alone with him, he impulsively announced he was going to marry her. 'When he told me that,' Diana remembered, 'I said, "Nonsense, today is your daughter Zamira's fifth birthday and there's no question of your ever marrying me." He said, "None the less I decided."' 'That reveals Yehudi's character,' Diana added. 'If he wants something he goes for it. He's rather like a sea anemone – he opens when he sees something he wants, and grabs it.' This might seem a harsh judgement were it not for the haste with which Yehudi had chosen his first bride – and earlier, his first Stradivarius.

A *coup de foudre* it most certainly was, and two days later Yehudi invited Diana and Michael Redgrave to his concert at the Royal Albert Hall. But when he flew back from his Paris triumph a week later, he was perhaps mindful of Diana's reproach that he was a married man, and he did not seek to see her again – or if he did, then they had both forgotten by the time they independently wrote their memoirs. She heard his broadcast, however. Her diary entry for 8 October notes: 'Listened to Menuhin 2:30 Bartók 4:15 Mendelssohn on the radio.' She was listening with the Redgrave family, including their young children Vanessa and Corin. The orchestra gave two separate broadcasts that afternoon, one for home listeners and the other for the forces. Hence the long gap between the concertos.

After another exhausting Atlantic flight, which in those days would have involved three or four stops for refuelling, Yehudi woke up Nola in their New York apartment at 2.30 in the morning. His normal life – the gypsy mode – was about to resume. 'He will spend one day with his wife and babes,' a newspaper reported, because he was late for his autumn tour and his European adventures had already obliged him to postpone some engagements. His son's return to the US prompted Moshe to issue another press release:

Last year, because he stayed in London a few weeks longer than he planned originally, Menuhin paid out many thousands of dollars to local managers who have lost money because he could not deliver his concerts on the appointed time . . . This time General Eisenhower cabled from the Supreme Headquarters directly appealing to Menuhin's American managers to make it possible for Menuhin to help the Boys on the fighting lines.

Then came the text of the Eisenhower cable:

We request that you definitely cancel all arrangements for Menuhin concerts up to and including 13 October. His presence in Europe with fighting troops at this critical juncture of the war is essential in its effect upon their morale and most important.

Eisenhower's endorsement makes it seem doubly strange that Menuhin received no national honour from his country after the war to mark his contribution to final victory. It could be argued that he was doing no more than his duty. But he had taken risks and worn himself out in the Allied cause; there ought to have been a way for Washington to say thank you even if Yehudi regularly declined to allow American authorities to control his activities. He did at least receive a handsome citation from the Admiral of the Pacific Central fleet following his visit to Hawaii.

At some point during the winter of 1944–5 Yehudi and Nola faced up to their marital difficulties. Writing a decade later, the biographer Robert Magidoff dubbed it the 'final rupture' but this is incorrect since in 1946 the couple tried to patch up their differences for the sake of their children. In 1996 Yehudi remembered Nola as being the first to broach the subject, and dates the confrontation not to October, when he flew home to New York, but to January 1945, when he returned to California to record Bruch's First Violin Concerto with Pierre Monteux:

I'd come back from Europe very much in love with Diana and met my then wife in San Francisco and the first word she told me was that she was in love with someone else. I shouldn't have taken it that badly: after all, it should have been good news for me, but I was torn.

Torn, that is, between what his heart told him and what was right according to the Jewish tradition of monogamy. He added that initially he had misread Nola's response:

When I first told her about Diana, which was immediately when I returned, she had said, 'Well, I'm in love with somebody else so it should be all right.' I had the impression that she was ready to give me my freedom as I would give her hers. But then she rather wanted to remain my wife . . .

It seems clear that like millions of couples before and since, Nola was in two minds and so was Yehudi. She had met a young RAF pilot while working as a nurse in a New York hospital. He had met an attractive actress while serving the war effort in Europe. Their indecision was to make the next three years very uncomfortable for all concerned. It may also have contributed to the malaise Yehudi sometimes experienced in his public appearances.

The received opinion is that his playing was effectively ruined by his wartime lifestyle of constant travel and lack of practice. Study of the evidence provided by contemporary recordings and reviews suggests a different story. No true artist plays supremely well at every concert, but when he was on form – for example the BBC broadcast of the Brahms Concerto in 1943, or the Bach sonatas he recorded with Wanda Landowska in 1944 – Yehudi's playing was every bit as good as it had been before the war. We shall return to this subject when considering Diana Menuhin's claim that after her marriage her prime task was 'to put Humpty Dumpty together again'. For the moment it is enough to note that Yehudi's wartime *annus mirabilis* was followed not only by the darkest years of his personal life but also by some of the most stirring of his musical and human experiences.

Recommended Recordings

Mozart: Concerto No. 4 in D (K.218) for violin and orchestra
Liverpool Philharmonic Orchestra, conducted by Malcolm Sargent
EMI 7 638342
Recorded: 31 March 1943
An opportunity to assess YM's wartime playing. This is one of the rare recordings for which he composed his own cadenzas.

Brahms: Violin Concerto in D
BBC Symphony Orchestra, conductor Sir Adrian Boult

Issued to accompany the *BBC Music Magazine*, vol. VI, no. 1 (September 1997)
Recorded: 5 April 1943
A superb live broadcast performance delivered in the Maida Vale studio on YM's same wartime visit to the UK.

Schubert (arr. Wilhelmj): *Ave Maria*
with Marcel Gazelle (piano)
BID LAB 128
Recorded: 6 April 1943
Recorded in London with Marcel Gazelle, who escaped from Belgium at the time of Dunkirk. The Schubert piece was played at all YM's troop concerts.

Debussy (arr. Hartmann): *La fille aux cheveux de lin*
with Adolph Baller (piano)
BID LAB 128 or RCA 61395-2
Recorded: 28 December 1944
Another popular wartime *bonne-bouche* available on the same Biddulph CD as the Schubert.

Bach: Sonata No. 3 in E (BWV 1016) for violin and keyboard
with Wanda Landowska (harpsichord)
BID LHW 031
Recorded: December 1944
The complete New York Town Hall recital with Landowska has recently been released on CD: A Classical Record (made in Canada), ACR 45. This invigorating partnership was never repeated; it makes a fascinating contrast to YM's later harpsichord Bach recordings with George Malcolm, and with the pianists Glenn Gould (Sonata No. 4), Louis Kentner and Hephzibah Menuhin.

10 The Uneasy Peace

With Benjamin Britten before visiting Belsen, 1945

1945: April: plays for delegates to first United Nations conference, San Francisco; June: visits London to record soundtrack for The Magic Bow *and renews friendship with Diana Gould; July: plays at Belsen with Britten; November: visits Moscow; 1946: April: tense reunion with Nola and children in London; May: visits Romania with his family; September: plays in Salzburg and Budapest; autumn: sees Diana in New York and California; 1947: January: début as orchestral conductor in Dallas; March: US and European tour with Hephzibah; June: holidays in France and Switzerland with Diana and children; August: plays for first time with Furtwängler; October: plays in Berlin with Furtwängler and confrontation with Jewish DPs; divorced from Nola; 19 October: marries Diana Gould in London.*

WHEN DELEGATES ARRIVED in San Francisco in April 1945 to attend the assembly that was to give birth to the United Nations Organization, the Russians were fighting their way into Yehudi's beloved Berlin. Hitler was dead (and President Roosevelt, too) and the war in Europe would be over in a few days. The sight of the massive

US Pacific Fleet anchored in the bay near the Golden Gate on the day of the inaugural concert, 28 April, gave Yehudi a tremendous thrill – 'not specifically American, just a sense of human achievement, the triumph of matter and courage'. He likened his emotion – 'primitive yet exalted' – to that kindled by the return of the big tune at the end of Tchaikovsky's Fifth, the symphony that shared the San Francisco Symphony's programme with the Beethoven Violin Concerto. A spectacular setting had been devised for the Civic Auditorium, and it was colourfully described in Yehudi's home newspaper, the *San José Mercury Herald*:

Against the huge silken drop which screened the mighty municipal organ, the forty-six flags of the United Nations stood bravely . . . blood-red rhododendrons banked the stage for the orchestra – as if music were the only thing left amid a sea of blood . . . the central floor of the huge auditorium was laid out in boxes for the honoured delegates . . . As they all streamed in, some in sable and some in dress of the utmost simplicity, the mighty diapason of a cosmic refrain permeated all the air: 'God of Love, Give Us Peace and Justice'.

On 10 May another local paper, the *Los Gatos Times*, reported that Yehudi was leaving for England to record the music for a romantic feature film about Paganini. The report added that Nola was taking Zamira and Krov to Australia to visit her family. Although that visit was deferred until the end of the war in the Pacific, a *de facto* separation had begun. Yehudi had accepted an offer from the J. Arthur Rank film-making organization, thus reversing his father's pre-war policy of having nothing to do with commercial cinema. Britain had just celebrated VE Day – Victory in Europe. London, where Yehudi was heading, was exhausted after six years of war, and the war against the Japanese in Asia was still to be won. The London concert season was virtually over, but that did not deter Yehudi: the filming assignment would provide him with a reason to spend several weeks in London and the opportunity to seek out the company of Diana Gould.

He was hired to act as a consultant on Paganini's life as well as to make soundtrack recordings of substantial excerpts from his compositions. To help establish an authentic period flavour he brought with him copies of Paganini's correspondence, recently published by the museum in Genoa, the composer's birthplace. But this was the heyday of romantic tosh in the cinema, when films such as *The Wicked Lady* were all the rage, and biographical exactitude was evidently not required. The Rank Organization had engaged Britain's No. 1 heart throb, Stewart Granger, to play Paganini, with Phyllis Calvert as the principal love interest. Tongue in cheek, Yehudi suggested he should be tested for the on-screen role of Paganini as well as recording his music. Surprisingly, the film's director, Stephen Knowles, agreed. Yehudi perhaps let slip that he had acted in many plays at home (usually in French or Russian to please his mother) so Knowles might genuinely have believed that Yehudi had the makings of a film star, but it seems more likely that this idea was a gimmick, aided and abetted by a studio publicist. Stewart Granger was said to have been 'a trifle put out' by the very notion of a musician challenging him for top billing.

Diana Gould was rehearsing for a West End play when Yehudi telephoned her. Surprisingly, he had not been in touch with Diana since their first meeting nine months earlier although he had told Nola about her the previous winter. But now he was on the look-out for emotional adventure: would she come over to Claridge's and help him study his lines? It was a novel approach and it worked. Their friendship was renewed and Diana accompanied him to the studio for his screen test. Mighty elegant he was, too, in his shoulder-length brown wig, green frockcoat, buckled shoes and knee breeches that revealed a shapely calf. But the real Niccolò Paganini had a truly saturnine presence and was said to have been in league with the Devil. Yehudi looked merely affable.

Despite Diana's coaching, Yehudi did not displace Stewart Granger but the publicity stills amused his children. So as to take advantage of a new sound-recording technique, the bulk of the shooting was postponed until the autumn but Yehudi proceeded to record all the sequences where his hands would be seen in the final film. His accompanist Gerald Moore noted tartly that the tedium of the filming sessions at the Gainsborough Studios – 'when the *Moses* Variations and other bravura pieces were repeated time after time *ad nauseam*' – was as nothing compared to the boredom of watching the completed picture. Yehudi was too diplomatic ever to offer an opinion on *The Magic Bow*.

The acetates of the soundtrack recordings still exist and at least one number was developed as the 'title song': the American composer Johnny Green, later well known as Head of Music for the MGM Studios in Hollywood, wrote an exceptionally soupy treatment of the big tune from the first movement of the D major Concerto and had the temerity to evoke the shades of Rakhmaninov by entitling it *Romance on a Theme of Paganini*. Had they heard Yehudi swooning away, both composers would have turned in their graves. Moshe's worst fears about the corruption of Yehudi's art if exposed on celluloid were on the point of being realized. Luckily the film did not have much success but, as Yehudi himself later admitted, it was 'perhaps my one compromise in pandering to popular taste'.

Meanwhile an off-screen romance had been well and truly launched. Over the next few weeks Yehudi saw a great deal of Diana Gould. She describes their ripening friendship rather touchingly in the second of her two books of memoirs. (To the first she gave the anti-romantic title *Fiddler's Moll*; its successor, devoted to her dancing years before she married Menuhin, was entitled *A Glimpse of Olympus*.) On their second evening she recalls walking on the Embankment and watching the tugs chugging up the River Thames. Yehudi stole a kiss and told her he was in love. She was much more guarded: 'I chose not to tell him that I loved him deeply and decided to grant him whatever he wanted, free of any obligation.'

Yehudi became something of a stage-door johnny, calling for Diana every night at the Piccadilly Theatre after she had finished her cameo role as the mistress in Franz Werfel's *Jacobowsky and the Colonel*, a play starring Michael Redgrave. They would go to the Berkeley Hotel for supper, where he must have revelled in the company of somebody who spoke French as fluently as he did, and whose knowledge of world literature and poetry was certainly greater, even though, like Yehudi, she had missed out on a secondary or university education. (Lawrence Durrell had been one of her many admirers while she was working with a theatre company in Cairo the previous year.) Yehudi never saw Diana dance. She had abandoned that career before the war in favour of acting, finally driven to give up ballet, she wrote, by the undisguised hostility of her old teacher Marie Rambert. She was too tall for the major classical roles but as a girl of nineteen she had understudied Diana Cooper in Max Reinhardt's *The Miracle* and later danced the hostess in Nijinska's production for the Markova–Dolin Company of *Les Biches*. The year before she met Yehudi, in the winter of 1943–4, she played the minor role of Frou-Frou in a touring production of *The Merry Widow* with considerable success, appearing in Brussels a few months after Yehudi had performed there. But the very fact that she had been a ballerina and worked with choreographers as distinguished as Nijinska, Massine and Ashton, revived in Yehudi his boyhood memory of Anna Pavlova, witnessed at the Curran Theater in San

Francisco. When Diana told him that she had auditioned for Pavlova, and had actually been invited to join her company, only for the great lady to die of pneumonia before the engagement could begin, he must have felt that their friendship had been ordained in heaven. Gradually, between trips abroad – he played in Amsterdam in June, on the very day Queen Wilhelmina returned from exile – he began to reveal his insecurities. The bright light he had given off when he first walked into her mother's drawing room was, Diana said, 'dimming visibly'. With her tough training as a dancer, she could sympathize with the physical problems Yehudi was experiencing after his many months of touring for the troops and the lack of time to practise. But what was blowing him furthest off course was, as she put it, the fragmentation of his marriage. She must have known that there was no point in trying to force his hand. Her strength lay in her understanding of his imaginative world. With her he found it possible to talk, very diffidently, of his conception of music. Since childhood, he told her, he felt he had been given a voice 'to bring bliss and to heal all the troubles in the world'. Within days he was to put that belief into practice in the most practical way possible, by playing to the survivors of Belsen.

First he sat for the sculptor Jacob Epstein, who was then at the height of his fame. After two sittings the plaster cast was accidentally broken, knocked over by a cat in the night. Diana accompanied Yehudi to the sitting when Epstein started again. At the end of the session the sculptor said, 'Come again tomorrow, my dear; he looks different when you are there.' But the portrait head was unfinished when Menuhin had to leave, this time for Germany.

Yehudi had successfully approached the British Army of Occupation with a request that he might be allowed to fulfil his dream of playing for Jewish survivors and German civilians. The extent of the degradation inflicted by the Germans on fellow human beings was revealed to the world in an appalling documentary film shot at Belsen within days of its liberation. Yehudi argued that music must be used as a weapon in the fight to counteract the inroads of Nazi savagery. Gerald Moore had already been invited to serve as his accompanist when Yehudi met Benjamin Britten at a party given by the publishers Boosey and Hawkes a few days after a performance, which he attended at Sadler's Wells, of the composer's new opera, *Peter Grimes*.

Britten had registered as a conscientious objector after his return from the US in 1942. He had successfully appealed against being forced to serve in a non-combative part of the armed forces such as the Royal Army Medical Corps and instead had been permitted to work unfettered as a composer and pianist. Britten was so impressed by Menuhin's attitude that he persuaded Gerald Moore to let him take his place. Britten was very much the composer of the moment after his success with *Peter Grimes*, and there was no problem with obtaining permissions; the two musicians set off for Germany at the end of July.

It has been suggested by the film-maker Tony Palmer that the experience of visiting Belsen was a trauma from which neither Britten nor Menuhin ever recovered. But Belsen had been liberated in April and the camp itself had been razed to the ground many weeks before their visit. Menuhin told Palmer that they were shown where the gas chambers had been and 'the actual remains of . . . people', but this hardly seems likely after three months of clearing up. Teeth, perhaps, and hair, and that would be distressing enough, but 'remains'? Writing to Peter Pears, Britten avoided the subject: 'We stayed the night in Belsen, & saw over the hospital – & I needn't describe that to you.' Menuhin spoke to Palmer of 'the sounds and cries of agony in the German hospitals we visited' but he had been hardened to the sight of suffering after his tour of duty in the Pacific the previous year, playing to wounded Marines.

In fact the concert tour was a surrealistic mixture of horror and normalcy: 'We travelled in a small car over bad roads,' Britten wrote in his letter to Pears,

& got hopelessly lost often. But we saw heavenly little German villages, with sweetest people in them . . . And then on the other side there were the millions of D.P.s (displaced persons) in, some of them, appalling states, who could scarcely sit still & listen, & yet were thrilled to be played to.

A survivor of Belsen, the cellist Anita Lasker, wrote an eye-witness account to a relative:

On Friday [27 July 1945] Menuhin was really here . . . It was a beautiful evening. Both soloist and accompanist [at the second of two concerts at Belsen] were of a simplicity regarding their attire which almost bordered on the slovenly, which fitted the local atmosphere perfectly.

Fifty-four years later Anita Lasker explained that Menuhin and Britten both played in shorts and that the waistband of Yehudi's underpants was showing.

No need to mention that Menuhin played violinistically to perfection. After all he is Yehudi Menuhin, but I must say . . . I was a little disappointed. Soulful (like I imagine Casals's playing), it was not . . . It may well be that the prevailing atmosphere did not exactly inspire him. It was impossible to achieve silence in the hall, and I felt really ashamed of the audience. A miracle that he did not just break up in the middle.

Lasker praised the pianist, whose name was not given; at another concert on the brief tour it appeared in the programme as Mr Button. She concluded:

Yes, who would have believed that Belsen Camp would ever hear Menuhin? By the way, they played Prelude and Fugue Bach/Kreisler, the 'Kreutzer' Sonata, Mendelssohn Concerto, something by Debussy [*La fille aux cheveux de lin*] and several other unknown things.

An English nurse working in the camp spoke of the glorious melody the two musicians created as they moved among the people 'who were difficult to rouse with the deadly mental lethargy which was the result of the horrors and privations they had suffered'.

A German-language newspaper, the *Hanover Courier* (3 August), reported on a concert given for eight hundred Polish refugees in the camp of Bardowiek. The bare wooden stage was lit by a single bulb hanging from the ceiling. When the artists made their entrance the piano was being tuned – at least Germany could still find piano technicians (unlike the Americans in the Aleutians), even in its darkest days. There was no dressing room. Yehudi was in short sleeves and Britten wore a woollen waistcoat. According to a letter published in the London *Jewish Chronicle* some five years later (after Yehudi had been assailed in Israel for bringing succour to the Germans) this casual garb may inadvertently have given offence to their listeners. The same correspondent suggested that the classical music performed might also have been upsetting to an audience that was in 'a highly wrought emotional mood'. The DPs, it was said,

resented and rejected the unaccompanied Bach he played. They expected and wanted to listen to such melodies as 'Eili, Eili' and 'Kol nidrei' and popular tunes of their native Poland. It is because of this incident that Menuhin was labelled as cold and unsympathetic and his subsequent efforts on their behalf were looked on with disfavour.

Yehudi remembered that members of his Belsen audience wore shapeless garments hastily run up by two Jewish tailors from sacking provided by the military. The inhabitants had made a great effort to make Britten and Menuhin welcome: the bells of the camp chapel had been rung on their arrival; they were showered (*überschüttet*) with flowers and taken back to their lodgings in a horse-drawn carriage. Britten summed up the four-day tour to Pears: 'Yehudi was nice, & under the circumstances the music was as good as it could be – with all that travelling all over the country & two, & sometimes three con- certs a day.' Astonishingly, they made no attempt to rehearse. They had looked at potential repertoire for a few minutes in London before deciding that their mutual understanding was such that there was no need to practise in advance.

This brief but gruelling tour was the beginning of a lifelong friend- ship that saw Menuhin make frequent appearances in Britten's music festival at Aldeburgh. Britten reciprocated by appearing with his partner Peter Pears in Menuhin's festivals at Gstaad and Bath. Yehudi took no fee for the concerts in Germany and donated part of the fees earned earlier in England to charities connected with the camps. He submitted a report urging their swift dissolution. Two years later, after playing to DPs in Berlin he wrote again:

Too long has our government allowed conditions to drift. We should have liqui- dated the DP camps two years ago, quite independently of any other problems or their solutions. This is a human problem, and these victims should have been offered a choice of nationalities in various countries after the war.

On his last day in Germany Yehudi was entertained at an officers' mess in Hamburg. His host, Major Jack Bornoff of the British Army of Occupation, was in charge of music for the radio station Nord- deutscher Rundfunk. He had recently toured the DP camps himself, in the company of the German conductor Hans Schmidt-Isserstedt, recruiting players for NDR's newly re-formed symphony orchestra. Their inaugural concert was to be broadcast the following day. The concertmaster was down to play the Mendelssohn Violin Concerto. On the spur of the moment Bornoff asked Yehudi whether he would take over as soloist. He jumped at the chance (as he had in Paris the previous October) and his German radio audience had its first oppor- tunity to hear the Concerto since the Nazis had banned Mendelssohn's music in 1933.

Yehudi returned to London just long enough for Epstein to complete the maquette of his bronze portrait, which exaggerated to freakish proportions the wide setting of his eyes. Diana's presence may have brought out some special quality in the sitter in Epstein's mind but it has to be said that the end result is still ineffably kitsch. When, in November, Yehudi was photographed next to the finished bronze his expression was one of boredom verging on distaste. (David Wynne's bronze portrait, made in 1963, gets closer to Yehudi's spiritual world.)

Yehudi was back in California by the second week of August, just as the war with Japan was being brought to an abrupt close by the dropping of atom bombs on Hiroshima and Nagasaki. Final victory had not been in doubt for over a year but an invasion of Japan from the sea would have been a hugely bloody business. Having played for the troops for almost four years, Yehudi was finally served his draft notice only days before the first bomb exploded. He was able to evade the order while keeping his honour intact:

I received a phone call from the local board saying, 'Don't go; once you are in, it may take a year or two to get you out and the war may be over soon.' So that's how I never joined the army.

With peace achieved he would be able to resume his pre-war pattern of a lucrative American concert tour in the winter months, although for a time he entertained an alternative plan to make a third concert tour of Australia. However, when Nola finally decided to sail home with their children – she had not departed in May as originally planned – he changed his mind abruptly. Or perhaps Nola asked him to stay away. At all events, Moshe reported that his son's American season was suddenly reinstated. The first engagement was on 4 December in Brooklyn and on 9 December he gave a performance of the Beethoven Concerto under Artur Rodzinski which was broadcast from Carnegie Hall, his first live radio relay with the New York Philharmonic.

But first he returned to Europe. He had been invited to visit Moscow. As the war ended his reputation was at its apogee and his application to play in the Soviet Union was given an unexpected green light. When the BBC's proverbially parsimonious planners learned that he would be passing through London *en route* for the Soviet Union they issued an invitation to perform Bartók's Second Violin Concerto – for the third time. The composer had died in September 1945 and Yehudi recorded a fine obituary tribute when he reached London: 'For several years already', he said,

Bartók's body had seemed but a thinly taut parchment stretched over a resonant cavity, hollowing itself out with every fatal reverberating pulse . . . Symbolically speaking, it was a drum, primitive and barbaric, whereon Destiny beat its merciless tune.

As his plans took shape it became clear that Yehudi was driven by two considerations that autumn: an ambition to assert his position on the international stage as the world's leading ambassador for music and a pressing desire to see as much as possible of Diana Gould. She wrote to him every day. They could keep in contact easily because Nola was far away in Australia. (She had taken her RAF lover, Tony Williams, with her.) In her memoirs Diana writes that less than a month after he left London Yehudi phoned her from California to say he was coming back soon and would she wait for him. He again asked her if she would consider marrying him. 'I told him never to use that phrase again until he was free to do so, but my unguarded heart leapt.' Following his star, he returned to London in October. 'Again we found each other,' wrote Diana, 'sharing like experiences of aspiration and struggle.' (When they became lovers is a subject on which she maintained a discreet silence – as did Yehudi.)

He played the Brahms Concerto with the London Symphony Orchestra under George Weldon at the Royal Albert Hall on the 28th and made plans to spend time with Diana in Paris after his forthcoming visit to Moscow. She had been to Paris just before the war to hear Furtwängler conduct; she knew the City of Light almost as well as he did and from a more sophisticated social viewpoint. Her father had been a diplomat, after all, and what with her parents' circle and that of her naval stepfather (who was placed in charge of Hong Kong after its liberation and knighted in December 1945) she was rather well connected.

Before the trip to Moscow, Yehudi embarked on another diplomatic adventure. On 31 October, he flew to Czechoslovakia in a British plane whose principal passengers (so he stated in his memoirs) were VIPs, members of the Czech government-in-exile returning from London. They were led by either Jan Masaryk or Eduard Beneš – he couldn't remember which. (In fact the Czechs in exile had returned to Prague from London six months earlier, after the collapse of Nazi Germany.) Menuhin wangled a seat on the plane because he had agreed to play a benefit concert in Prague. When the Dakota took off from Croydon the weather forecast was good but conditions worsened rapidly over the Czech–German border and the plane was forced to descend through cloud and land at the airstrip of Karlovy Vary (Karlsbad), where it was immediately surrounded by Russian soldiers who spoke neither Czech nor English. They ordered everybody out, but the captain was insistent that his orders were to remain with his plane and guard its precious cargo of secret state documents. He refused to budge and the Russians became rather menacing until Yehudi intervened. He had learned Russian as a child, in anticipation of a pre-war visit to Moscow that had never materialized, and in pidgin Russian he mounted a passionate defence of the pilot, Captain Speller. Phone calls were made summoning road vehicles from Prague and during the long wait the Russians led the party to their officers' mess, whose tables were laden, Yehudi remembered, 'with at least seven or eight different glasses for wines, beers, vodkas, etc.' There was only an unsavoury stew to eat but many toasts were drunk and a great deal of liquor consumed before a fleet of black cars arrived to take the stranded travellers to their destination. It was five in the morning when they reached Prague.

A few hours later Yehudi went with the Czech President, Dr Beneš, to take part in what he understood to be the latter's first official duty since his return, laying a wreath in tribute to the people of Lidice who had been murdered by the Nazis. When he later played the Dvořák Concerto in Prague his performance was not enhanced, he wrote, by his alcoholic stopover in Karlsbad.

It's a charming anecdote, but a search of Czech Philharmonic archive shows that Yehudi's only Prague appearance in 1945 was not until three days later, on 4 November, by which time the effects of the Russians' alcohol would surely have worn off. He played both the Dvořák and the Mendelssohn Concertos at a charity event in aid of the village of Lidice. Dr Beneš had been back in Prague since May but in October his position as President was reconfirmed, which might account for the special security surrounding the British plane on which Yehudi flew from London. The Lidice archive has no record of Dr Beneš speaking there after June 1945 so perhaps Yehudi's vodka-infused memory was playing tricks on him.

Yehudi's wartime travels had given him a penchant for hitching rides on military planes and he travelled around Europe that autumn like an airborne gypsy. The Russians sent a plane to Prague specifically, so he was told, to collect him and fly directly to Moscow, but Yehudi was in love and he wanted to spend more time with Diana, so he coolly informed the Russians that he had changed his plans and instead flew back to London. The detour gave him a few more days of courting but when he eventually reached Berlin to transfer to his Moscow flight, bad weather made it impossible to continue the journey. He could not arrange to give a concert because he had no idea how long his plane would be grounded. He spent two days wandering among the ruins of the city he had loved as a boy, before the Russians sent word that his plane could take off.

The Americans drove him to Adlershof airport early in the morning.

The Russian soldiers were shaving, walking around with mugs of warm water, their faces covered in shaving soap – using old-fashioned razors, of course. I was interrogated by the head of the airfield. As usual, in the important positions, where authority is really required, the Russians put women in charge, *formidable* women; this one even had a bit of a moustache. She looks me up and down and says, 'Have you ever won any medals for war work?'

I said, 'No, I'm sorry.'

'Well, Oistrakh has,' she said. 'He is a Hero of the Soviet Union.'

Mildly impressed by the information that Yehudi was that very day expecting to meet David Oistrakh in Moscow, she allowed him on to the plane, a DC–3 that had been voluptuously customized by the Russians with velvet settees and pretty little tassles on the window blinds – a far cry from his acutely uncomfortable transport in the Aleutians the previous year.

True to his word, Oistrakh was on the tarmac to meet him in Moscow, accompanied by two old ladies who were related to Marutha, and by a man named Schneerson (Moshe's Hasidic family connection) who worked for the national concert agency. Yehudi was the first musician from the West to visit Moscow since the end of the war and all the stops were pulled out in his honour. His five-day visit ended, after another postponed flight, with a farewell party that broke up at five in the morning. 'Feel thrilled beyond words following volcanic ovation at first Moscow concert,' he cabled to his parents,

EIGHT ENCORES TO RIOTOUS PUBLIC STOP PLAY TONIGHT ANOTHER RECITAL AND WITH ORCHESTRA ON SUNDAY STOP STAGE AND ROOMS BOWER OF FLOWERS . . . AM PAINTING RED MOSCOW MORE RED I LOVE EVERY MINUTE OF IT HERE STOP

He took no fees but lived as handsomely as anybody could in post-war Moscow, staying in an apartment at the famous Hotel Metropole overlooking Red Square. Food, they told him, was in short supply.

I said I don't want white bread. I don't want skyscrapers. I want to know you and work with you and play for audiences . . . My favourite food is black bread and sour milk. And of course if you have any caviare I wouldn't refuse it. And that was my diet; I recommend it!

The American ambassador Averell Harriman gave a formal lunch. Yehudi met Shostakovich, 'unassertive and shy', who later coaxed him 'to say a few laborious words in Russian' on the children's radio programme he hosted each week. He saw the dazzling Ulanova dance in *Cinderella* at the Bolshoi. A visit to the Soviet Union's Central School of Music, an organization 'shining like a lone good deed in war-drained Moscow', sowed the seed that was to flower eighteen years later with his own school for gifted young musicians. To the *New York Times*'s special correspondent Brooks Atkinson he spoke warmly not only about the Russian education system, which he felt gave youthful talent a wider opportunity to develop than in the US, but also about Moscow audiences, who liked tense, passionate music and responded warmly to his interpretation of Bartók's Romanian Dances. But he confessed to Atkinson that he had been obliged to leave his Stradivarius behind in London for running repairs and had not played as well as he would have wished.

The Russian pianist Dmitry Paperno, then a sixteen-year-old student, concluded that Menuhin was very good but not a demi-god. He wrote that, 'for those expecting technical perfection', his recital in the Great Hall of the Conservatoire was a slight disappointment: 'Some of us, with the cruelty of youth, even demanded as encores the virtuoso miniatures we had recently heard on his recordings.' But a friend of Paperno heard Menuhin playing the Beethoven Concerto at the Tchaikovsky Hall and said he would remember the slow movement until the end of his days. Igor Oistrakh, David's son, then fourteen, was ecstatic: 'It was not just fantastic playing; it had poetry, an aesthetic dimension, almost a spiritual visualization of the music that made us feel we had been taken up to heaven.' The young Mstislav Rostropovich, later a firm friend, was similarly enthralled. The Soviet Union had its own great violinists but Yehudi was accorded his due: Moscow's Overseas News Agency wrote that 'Menuhin can compel you to follow him with bated breath through every bar of the gigantic *Chaconne* of Bach.'

To judge from the recordings made at the concerts Yehudi's performances were occasionally rough at the edges but their passion shines

through, notably in the 'Kreutzer' Sonata, in which Menuhin was part-
nered – reportedly with no rehearsal – by the pianist Lev Oborin.
Yehudi was particularly excited about his meeting with David
Oistrakh. Eight years his senior, Oistrakh was born and trained in
Odessa, not far from the Crimea – where Marutha had been born.
Yehudi felt they were brothers in spirit, both Russian-Jewish violinists.
Had his parents not emigrated, this would have been his homeland,
too. *Newsweek* reported that they played the Bach Double Concerto
together at one of Yehudi's two Moscow symphony concerts. Other
articles say he played three concertos in each of two symphony concerts, mentioning works by Bach, Beethoven, Brahms and Dvořák.

The only crack in the sheen of good will was a strained meeting with
the father of his friend Gregor Piatigorsky. The cellist had sent him
innumerable messages and food parcels from the US but none had got
through and his father was uncomfortably and noisily bitter at what
he saw as his son's defection to America; the conversation made a
sharp contrast with the idyllic day Yehudi had spent hiking in the Alps
with the young Piatigorsky a decade earlier.

On his return to the West his gifts included wine from the Crimea
for his mother, embroidery and linen for Nola, and for Diana a handsome book about ballet history unearthed in a Moscow junk shop.
Several large tins of caviare were later repackaged into smaller containers and distributed by Diana to her London friends. The DC–3 was
crowded with Russian families *en route* for Berlin to visit their loved
ones in the Army of Occupation. Yehudi remembered their packages
of greasy brown paper containing 'tid-bits' of goose and sausage. As a
reward for entertaining them on his violin during the flight he was
offered cheese, boiled eggs and vodka. It was, he said, a merry and
heartwarming journey as his fellow passengers recited poems by
Pushkin and Lermontov and sang – above the drone of the engines –
songs and choruses, often with Yehudi's violin accompaniment. His
first (and only) aerial concert was, he reported, 'grand fun'. To Brooks
Atkinson he had expressed disapproval of the Soviet ideology, but of
Russian traditional culture he had become a tremendous admirer.

His high spirits were dampened by more fog in Berlin: all planes
were grounded and he was forced to cancel his and Diana's dream of
a meeting in Paris. The only way to get back to her in London was by
rail and road. With characteristic chutzpah he talked his way into being
allowed to join a delegation of London-bound Russian diplomats

headed by the future foreign minister Andrei Gromyko. With Yehudi tagging on at the back of the convoy in a grey US Army car, a fleet of Soviet saloons set off from Berlin for the British Sector, from whence a train took them all the way to Calais. He could not afford to be marooned in Berlin because he was due to play the very next evening at a special Thanksgiving Day concert at the Royal Albert Hall to be attended by the wartime generals Eisenhower and Montgomery. For the BBC he then repeated his performance of the Bartók Violin Concerto, described by the critic Edward Lockspeiser as 'one of the most important works broadcast during the war', even though cautious BBC chiefs were expressing concern at the disturbing amount of Bartók's music currently being broadcast.

At the beginning of December Yehudi flew back to New York to begin a five-month tour. Diana described a gloomy farewell at Hurn airport in Hampshire. Her mood was of black despair. Her sister Griselda was seriously ill with tuberculosis and her lover was leaving her with no firm plans to return and without giving any indication that he was prepared to break with Nola. He did, however, manage to call her nearly every day over the next few months while touring America, establishing a pattern of telephone contact that was not to vary over half a century. To help Diana's ailing sister he approached the inventor of penicillin, Sir Alexander Fleming, and since he was unhindered by Britain's strict currency regulations he was able to advance the funds needed to pay for Griselda Gould's eventual hospitalization in Davos and for a supply of penicillin to help effect a cure.

As soon as he reached New York, Yehudi started a campaign in support of Wilhelm Furtwängler. They had never met but Diana knew him well from his visits to her mother's soirées before the war. (She suggested in *A Glimpse of Olympus* that Furtwängler was infatuated with her sister Griselda.) Furtwängler had stayed in Berlin throughout the aerial bombardments but early in 1945 Albert Speer warned him that Himmler was on his track and he had fled to Switzerland. He was not allowed to forget his long collaboration with the Nazis and in December he was back in the news when concerts he was to conduct in Zurich had to be cancelled, while in nearby Winterthur four thousand normally peaceful Swiss citizens demonstrated against him.

In *Time* magazine, under the headline 'Menuhin to the defense', Yehudi was quoted along similar lines to the argument he had already deployed in 1944: 'If there is one musician who deserves to be reinstated it is Furtwängler . . . He would be welcomed in Paris . . . if the French can take a German I'm sure we should have no qualms about it.' But Jewish militants in New York were up in arms at what they took to be a naïve piece of whitewashing. The Nuremberg trial of the Nazi war criminals was under way:

At the very moment when the employers of Mr Furtwängler are facing international trial for mass butchery, that anyone should attempt to give a clear bill of health to one of their conspirators seems incredible,

wrote Ira A. Hirschmann in a letter to the *New York Times*. Hirschmann had been actively anti-Furtwängler since 1936 when he had successfully led public protest at the New York Philharmonic's attempt to appoint the German as Toscanini's successor.

In 1945 Furtwängler's position was extraordinarily delicate. He was never a conspirator and he certainly helped Jewish musicians. But if we accept the testimony of Richard Wolff, a violinist with the Berlin Philharmonic, cited in John Ardoin's book *The Furtwängler Record*, it was only half-Jews and the partners of Jews who were allowed to stay in the Berlin Philharmonic. Furtwängler could not prevent full Jews from being dismissed. He did help Jews to leave the country without undue harassment, however, as in the case of the great violin teacher Carl Flesch. It is also true that the conductor had many brushes with leading Nazis in the early days of the regime, among them Goebbels and Hitler himself, who when visiting Bayreuth in 1934 had gone so far as to threaten him with a spell in a concentration camp if he failed to collaborate with the Nazis.

Of proud Prussian stock, Furtwängler thought he could take on the Nazis and win – through the power of German art. To his credit, he continued to include Mendelssohn in his programmes. He would not conduct the 'Horst Wessel Lied', the Nazis' national hymn, or give the Nazi salute at concerts. But in order to guarantee the orchestra's continuation when it was threatened with bankruptcy – because of the loss of the substantial Jewish audience – he was obliged to do a deal with Goebbels. Many observers, particularly those abroad, felt he had sold his soul to the Devil. He could have left the country, like Fritz Busch and Erich Kleiber, but he chose to stay. In purely musical authority he was still the most important artist of his age, but morally he was compromised.

The Menuhins, father and son, took Furtwängler's part with almost embarrassing enthusiasm. Moshe was always ready to detect a conspiracy. The German conductor was, he wrote, 'a victim of envious and jealous rivals who had to resort to publicity, to smear, to calumny in order to keep him out of America'. For several weeks the New York newspapers reverberated with the controversy, and in February 1946, although he had not yet gone before a de-Nazification tribunal and so was in effect being condemned without trial, Furtwängler was banned by the Americans from conducting in West Germany on the grounds that he had 'lent an aura of respectability' to the Nazi Party. Yehudi immediately fired off a cable attacking the decision:

[I] do not believe that the fact of remaining in one's own country, particularly when fulfilling a job of this nature [conducting] . . . is alone sufficient to condemn a man . . . He saved, and for that we are his debtors, the best part and the only salvageable part of his own German culture.

Yehudi blamed the pre-war Western powers for making morally indefensible pacts and treaties with the Nazis. Now, he argued, 'it would be patently unjust and most cowardly for us to make of Furtwängler a scapegoat for our own crimes'.

Three months later, in May 1946, Yehudi met Furtwängler for the first time when both men were witnesses at the marriage in Zurich of Griselda Gould, Diana's sister, to Louis Kentner. The Hungarian pianist had lived in London since the 1930s and was to become one of Yehudi's most frequent recital partners. It must have been gratifying for Yehudi to be able to show his love for Diana by supporting somebody she and her sister admired so much. (Perhaps his support for Furtwängler as early as his return from Paris in autumn 1944 was sparked off by Diana's evident affection.)

Furtwängler was prevented from conducting anywhere in the West for many months until, at the end of 1946, he was finally taken to Berlin to appear before the all-German De-Nazification Court of Creative Artists. The four charges included serving the Nazi regime and performing at Nazi Party functions. He was acquitted on all counts and survived further attacks in the press. His first conducting engagement for over two years was in Rome, in April 1947. He conducted the Berlin Philharmonic in May and in August made his first post-war appearance at the Salzburg Festival. Menuhin was with him on that occasion, playing the Beethoven Violin Concerto: his eloquent and unwavering support had been of great importance in the rehabilitation but it triggered a wave of hostility from his fellow Jews, as Yehudi was to discover when he visited Berlin in September 1947. The two musicians shared a mistaken belief that music transcends politics.

Yehudi's American concerts in the early months of 1946 were the first opportunity for several years that many regional critics had had to assess his playing. These were the months when his thoughts were wrapped up in contemplation of Diana (and a substantial proportion of his fees was spent on telephone calls to her in London). Quite a few critics were unflattering. In Minneapolis one reviewer described him as 'a rather flaccid violinist with too much vibrato. He has a dull streak in his make-up.' Another Minneapolis reviewer said there was 'something essentially cold and smug about his playing; cold Brahms is no treat'. A different performance of the Brahms Concerto, in St Paul, was described as being of 'silken smoothness', but there was 'a touch of unevenness which interrupted the flow of the music and gave it a jerkiness'. A Chicago critic, Charles Buckley, was of the same mind as the Moscow observer who wrote that Menuhin was no demi-god: 'He is not a great violinist but a very good one. His vibrato seems changed and his tone is warm and vital without the purple passion of former years.' On the eve of that Chicago concert Diana recorded in her diary a phone call from Yehudi wishing her good luck with the first flight of her life. She was accompanying her sister to Zurich *en route* to the Swiss sanatorium that was to save her life. Perhaps Yehudi's preoccupation caused a few glitches, duly noted by Buckley, in his performance of the Elgar Concerto: 'He is not a great technician and intonation falls below perfection.' At least Yehudi could rely on the Chicago, one of America's 'Big Five' orchestras, to do justice to the accompaniment. He had taken the score and orchestral parts of the Elgar to Moscow but did not dare perform it in view of the lack of rehearsal time.

In San Francisco he was praised for his choice of repertoire. He was doing more contemporary music than ever before: Szymanowski's *The Fountain of Arethusa*, Enesco's Second Sonata, a bagatelle by Poulenc. Presumably he thought San Francisco was not yet ready for unaccompanied Bartók. The received view – already mentioned – that his technique had deteriorated during the war through lack of practice and over-exertion is difficult to sustain when faced with the enthusiasm of Marjorie Fisher, critic of the *San Francisco Commercial News*. 'Other violinists', wrote Miss Fisher, 'have a bigger and more sensuous tone . . . but Menuhin has an innate something, call it purity of concept, that places him in a class of his own.' Alfred Wallenstein in the *Chronicle* disagreed: Yehudi was 'not at his best'; 'not up to snuff'. The Enesco work was, he grumbled, 'false rhetoric, soggy César Franck, hollow heroics'. Yehudi should have played something 'genuinely modern'. At the recital he was presented with a citation from the Music War Council by the commander of the Western Sea Frontier, Admiral R. S. Edwards, thanking him 'for his extraordinary work [in the Aleutian Islands and Honolulu] on behalf of the armed forces of this country'. No doubt mindful of the day the outside latrine had been blown away in an Aleutian gale, Yehudi shared the honour with his accompanist Adolph Baller.

Even in New York opinions about Yehudi's playing were divided. The new, advertisement-free *PM* newspaper had a gossipy unsigned piece about Yehudi's supposed waywardness: 'Sometimes he is masterly in a cold, calculating way but very often lately he is like a once beautiful woman desperately in need of recapturing her youth.' But the reliable Louis Biancolli, writing in the *World-Telegram* after a recital, refuted dire predictions that Yehudi's talent was slipping: 'I heard none of that last night. I heard what I thought was a new warmth.' Whenever Yehudi took time off, Biancolli added, 'he came back freshened by new study'. In the autumn of 1946 Yehudi returned to New York for more concerts and again there was no unanimity in the reviews. John Briggs in the *Post* said he was still 'the wonder child whose playing is as remarkable – and as artless – as the song of a bird. He appears to have no profound convictions about the music he performs.' Yet of the same concert, Olin Downes wrote that it was 'the most authoritative and matured interpretation he has given.'

While he no longer commanded unreserved admiration, Menuhin was still one of the three most formidable violinists on the international circuit. The others were Heifetz and Szigeti but Menuhin's concert fee was considerably higher. He was occasionally the victim of momentary lapses of concentration and he could not always maintain a steady pressure of the bow on the strings. But even on his 'off' days he never lost the 'innate something' that made him so popular with audiences and it would be wrong to accept the proposition advanced in many quarters that by the late 1940s and 1950s his playing had passed its peak. The evidence of the reviews, the broadcasts and the recordings of the period suggests that his playing was less affected than has previously been suggested. He was a man who could not help enjoying his life as a musician, no matter what his personal worries.

In the winter of 1946 he gave a helping hand to his friend Antal Dorati. The Hungarian conductor had recently been named the first Director of the newly formed Dallas Symphony Orchestra. (Before the war the Texan city had supported a more modest 35-piece band.) In the autumn of 1945 Dorati recruited and drilled his players for three months and in January Menuhin joined them to give several performances of Bartók's Second Violin Concerto. There were separate recording sessions of the Concerto for RCA Victor, a bold venture, artistically as well as commercially, given Bartók's reputation as a 'difficult' composer, but their inspired reading – the first of three recordings of the work Dorati and Menuhin made together – put the Dallas orchestra on the national map.

During the rehearsals, Yehudi appeared in the local gossip pages: the orchestra's assistant concertmaster had just got married and when his fellow musicians saluted him with a performance of Mendelssohn's Wedding March, Yehudi moved into his seat – the only recorded sighting in America of Menuhin as an orchestral player. A few days later *Variety* reported that Yehudi was taking conducting lessons from Dorati and in April he returned to Texas to make his first appearance on the rostrum. At 4 p.m. on Saturday, 6 April, the Dallas Symphony Orchestra made its début on the ABC network, broadcasting from the Fair Park Auditorium to 192 stations, with Antal Dorati conducting. At the end of the rehearsal for the broadcast Dorati welcomed the audience and then announced – as a surprise bonus – that as well as witnessing the launch of their new orchestra's radio career, the audience would also, before the transmission began, be present at another significant 'first': that of Maestro Menuhin as a conductor. (In *Unfinished Journey*, 397, Menuhin gives the date wrongly as 1942.)

The *Dallas News* reported 'a well-prepared reading' of the Prelude to *Die Meistersinger* by Wagner:

His beat was clear and rhythmically firm. He had given considerable attention to balancing the complicated polyphonies of the piece. The fugue itself was neatly co-ordinated. The Prelude, moreover, was not a timid affair but a robust, full-throated proclamation . . . Menuhin had committed the music to memory and conducted without a score.

Yehudi remembered that Dorati gave him an enormous baton and virtually pushed him on to the platform. He began very timidly. Conducting had reminded him, he joked, of his first experience on horseback, when he had felt equally timid and his riding partner Adolph Baller – a town boy from Vienna – had innocently asked the whereabouts of the self-starter. Yehudi was innocent of conducting technique, too:

I knew you had to begin by raising the baton. I'd seen conductors doing that. And I had barely lifted my arms when this huge C major chord appeared, as if from nowhere, so that gave me the courage to go on.

Dorati was sufficiently sure of his pupil's potential to ask him back the following season to direct an hour-long concert broadcast.

In March 1946, when Yehudi was approaching the end of his American concert season, a San Francisco gossip columnist named Herb Caen – an old friend of Marutha and Moshe – reported that Nola had gone to Australia with their children the previous October and did not intend to return. At one point, the columnist continued, Yehudi had been on the point of flying there himself to plead with her to end their separation. Nola was now, it seemed, expected back in Alma in April. She changed her plans quite abruptly. Her father disliked Tony Williams, who had a brush with the law for passing himself off as an RAF squadron leader. George Nicholas urged Nola to patch things up with Yehudi. Obediently she flew all the way from Australia to England with Zamira and Krov (then respectively six and five years old) in order to be reunited with her husband in London. Diana, meanwhile, was nursing her sister in a Davos sanatorium. On 15 April, when Nola was in mid-flight, Yehudi cabled Diana from California to say that he was on his way to Europe. After nineteen weeks of separation they were soon to be reunited. He did not mention his wife's imminent arrival in London. Even if he knew of her plans then he must have believed that he could negotiate some kind of arrangement with her which would eventually give him the freedom to marry Diana. This was not unreasonable: Nola had told him she loved somebody else and he had spoken of his love for Diana.

It took a mere twenty-four hours for such hopes to be dashed. When he arrived in London Yehudi rang Diana in Switzerland. Their meeting would have to be delayed just one more day, he told her over the phone, because 'by a cruel stroke of fortune' (Diana's phrase) Nola and their children were about to fly in from Australia. He would be obliged to greet them and 'settle them in' before he flew out to join her. It was an impossible dream. The reality was that the Menuhin family's reunion was reported in the gossip columns of London's popular press. Yehudi was photographed romping with his children on the hotel carpet and Diana was, to put it bluntly, ditched.

Writing from her standpoint as the other woman, Diana believed that Nola, with her 'astute knowledge' of Yehudi, persuaded him to return to the marital fold by 'mercilessly' playing on his inherent good nature and his 'readiness for self-sacrifice' – a characteristic hitherto not much in evidence, it must be admitted. But it is clear from a long letter she sent her stepmother Shirley Nicholas the day after she arrived in London that Nola was making sacrifices, too, and that she was determined, for the sake of her children, to resume married life. The letter provides a rare glimpse of Nola's spirited personality and suggests that her motives were less calculating and more honourable than Diana imagined.

Nola's gruelling flight in a BOAC flying boat from Australia had involved overnight stops in Singapore, Rangoon, Karachi and Cairo, where she had gone out with a group of travellers to dinner at Shepherds Hotel and then had 'a complete blow-out' at a night-club – it had been very good for her, she wrote, after being cooped up in a small cabin for five days with a couple of boisterous children. There were more high-spirited revels lasting until dawn at Fort Augusta in Sicily, the last port of call before the aircraft reached Poole, on the English south coast. Already in London, Yehudi borrowed a Packard from a friend and drove down to meet his travel-stained family.

'The meeting was cordial but cold', Nola wrote.

As soon as we arrived [in a London hotel] after I asked which was our room, etc. – he said, 'I thought Krov could sleep with me and Miras [Zamira] with you – is that all right?' Being so desperately tired I said, 'Oh yes, that will be fine if you want it.' So that *is*!! After the children went to bed we ordered supper and talked about current problems – I told him I wanted to carry on, that my married life, even tho' it wasn't ideal, because of the kids had to come first always and I wanted to try it that way. It appears he really is in love with Diana and I gathered was rather disappointed I don't want a divorce right away – however I stuck to my point and put myself out to be loving, etc. – I don't know how it will end. *Today*, I feel he is very disappointed and wants nothing or no one but Diana but is controlling himself after what I put forth about the children, etc. He is going to Switzerland where she [Diana] is at present with her sister Griselda – the latter being engaged to Kentner the pianist, whom he is taking with him!! Marcel Gazelle is playing for him elsewhere. However this doesn't worry me – but according to his behaviour so far he seems to love Diana very much – which after all is all right by me. We really do speak a different language. We are too different, Shirl – here I am after a tiring trip, full of life and fun, and he just yawns and says he's tired and has to sleep. Oh my God, even in one morning I contain myself but it's not me, darling, not my life and I already wonder whether I can manage to get by with him. However, patience! we may settle down to something worth while!

He is downstairs lunching with Kentner now. I'm here minding the children – I'm sure Kentner is in the know – but what a sissy! – Gawd! I can't bear men like this! I'm too forceful for them, Shirl, they are too womanly for me.

Louis Kentner had actually taken a room in the same hotel, Claridge's, to try to persuade Yehudi to leave Nola and do the right thing by Diana. His daily letters to his fiancée Griselda Gould give a ringside view of the battle being played out. Ten years older and with a failed marriage behind him, Kentner was fond of Menuhin, who was then on the eve of his thirtieth birthday but lacked the maturity of outlook that might be expected to accompany such a staging post in his life. 'Yehudi may not be a great intellectual illuminary,' Kentner observed affectionately in one of his reports, 'but I don't think he is a weakling.' When they lunched together Yehudi confessed, 'with tears in his eyes, that he couldn't love anybody in the world more than he does Diana'. But his defection to her was far from certain. Once faced with his children he had 'a sentimental idea of duty and, certainly, remnants of his old affection for Nola'. Kentner's worldly wise bulletins from Claridge's go so far as to make the surprising suggestion that Diana was not in love with Yehudi. The Hungarian counsels Griselda to warn her sister, tactfully, against 'too much optimism and staking all on this one card'. Yehudi, he thinks, 'will never leave his children. His responsibilities are of eight years' standing as compared with the three days' romance with Diana.' Kentner thought Diana's undoubted dramatic talent made her overplay her reaction to the news of Nola's return. Besides, he noted cynically, 'she played her cards badly: she should never have gone to bed so quickly with a boy like that!' Now instead of letting events take their course, which would have favoured her in the end, she was pressing Yehudi too hard to leave his wife immediately, 'seeking to satisfy her worldly ambition. It was not even a sexual attachment; she should not have set her heart on a marriage which would be based on a falsehood, which could not have given her happiness, only worldly gratification.'

Yehudi's vacillations continued. In the course of another conversation he confided to Kentner that he had 'never had a mistress before and assumed that such a thing must lead to a divorce and another marriage . . . He thought one thing one day and another the next,' he told Kentner. The decision not to part was 'only temporary . . . He intends to spend the whole summer in Switzerland . . . Nola was ready for divorce but Yehudi was dragging his feet because of his feelings about the children.' Kentner's assessment proved wrong in the long run, and surely underestimated the strength of Diana's feelings. But her immediate hopes would have been further dashed by a news item in the London *Star* a few days later. It was headlined 'The Menuhins in Close Harmony'. Accompanied by a photograph of Yehudi helping his children to construct a model aeroplane, with Nola fondly looking on, the story reported that the Menuhin family was

getting to know each other again after six months' parting . . . They are a delightful bunch, full of fun and high spirits . . . Both parents believe it wrong to teach music to an unwilling child. 'It spoils them for life,' said Mrs Menuhin.

The months that followed were hell for all concerned as Yehudi and Nola tried, in the modern parlance, to work things out. Late in May, Yehudi joined Diana in Zurich, as Nola had forecast, but only to serve as best man at the wedding of Louis Kentner to Griselda, happily recovered from her TB. Zamira remembers that Nola and Diana came face to face at the Dolder Hotel in Zurich, where the Kentners were spending their honeymoon. When she learned that they were to meet, Diana changed into a self-effacing black dress. It must have been a tumultuous time for Yehudi with wife, mistress and the revered master Wilhelm Furtwängler (a former admirer of Griselda and now Kentner's other best man) all under one roof. Thereafter Diana was thrust into the background of Yehudi's life, although he still telephoned her from the Continent whenever he could, using a priority telephone code the Americans gave him that was supposed to be reserved for top-secret military conversations.

Earlier in May Yehudi had flown with Nola and the children to Romania to be reunited with his old master George Enesco. He was then sixty-five and suffering from a progressive disease of the spine which left his back bent and his head twisted to one side as if he was perpetually playing his violin. But their reunion after seven years was a fruitful one – and it allowed Yehudi to escape into music. The two men gave concerts every evening and held public rehearsals every morning. 'It was an Enesco festival,' Yehudi later wrote, 'an Enesco orgy, an Enesco delirium.' Yehudi came to Bucharest as a conquering hero, the American Jew who was Enesco's most famous disciple. The American Embassy lent him a car so he could revisit Enesco's summer home in Sinaia. Later he lunched with King Michael, at whose carriage he had thrown a stone when they were both small boys. Romania was crowded with Jewish refugees hoping to get passages to Palestine. There were two hundred thousand in the capital alone, gathered from many parts of Eastern Europe. When a service was held in Yehudi's honour – in itself an unusual occurrence, given his complete lack of interest in formal worship – the streets around the synagogue were, he wrote, 'dense with Jews, moved to exaltation at thus affirming their existence'. Such a demonstration was gratifying after the wave of hostility from the New York Jewish community that had greeted him six months earlier when he spoke up in favour of Furtwängler. Menuhin played for nothing in Bucharest, as he had in Moscow the previous autumn. Instead he donated his fees, 20 million lei, worth precisely $1,273, to provide scholarships for young Romanian musicians. He felt rather let down when the cost of providing his private plane was subtracted from the fund.

Later that summer the Menuhin and Dorati families rented an idyllic house on Lake Geneva between Montreux and Vevey. One weekend Nola took her husband off for a hiking trip near Arolla. 'Yehudi is nervous and overworking,' she wrote to her stepmother, enclosing a photograph of herself taken by Yehudi beneath a snow-capped mountain.

We walked sixteen miles in one day and climbed three thousand metres in two and a half hours hours – my calves are still suffering! We had to ride five miles on mules to reach this isolated spot. No mules coming down – so walked the five miles in pouring rain. My God what I wouldn't do for a friend!

Nola was level-headed about their attempted reconciliation: 'These past months have been devilish hard . . . We've both come to the conclusion we don't belong, however don't get excited – we're working it out the best way we can.'

The plan involved making their base in New York for the following winter, since in December Nola wrote from there to Shirley Nicholas reporting that her children were loving their first serious year of school. Tonina, Antal Dorati's daughter, remembers Zamira and Krov leading her into all sorts of mischief. The previous summer in Switzerland Zamira had pulled out the plug of an artificial pond at the hotel. Tonina also recalls that the fathers were mostly absent from the Swiss holiday. Dorati and Menuhin flew first to the Salzburg Festival, where Yehudi made his début in a recital on 2 September. They then travelled on via Vienna to Budapest, giving concerts in Dorati's home city on 5 and 6 September. Yehudi played the Bartók Violin Concerto, which had become a sort of European visiting card, nowhere more appropriate than in the Hungarian capital.

But it was the actual journey that Yehudi remembered best from this tour. Once again the American Occupation forces gave the musicians a helping hand. At the US base at Friedrichshafen in Southern Germany, on the banks of Lake Constance – where before the war the Zeppelin airships had taken off for their weekly crossing to South America – three light aircraft were placed at their disposal: one for Menuhin, one for Dorati and a third for their luggage and orchestral scores. They were open twin-seater planes, with the pilot sitting in front and his passenger behind. Menuhin legend has it that a section of Vienna's Ringstrasse, the tree-lined boulevard that encircles the old city, was cleared so that the planes could land with the minimum of delay: the big hotels in the American and British zones were only a few yards away. Returning from Budapest Menuhin left Dorati and flew back alone. After taking off at five in the evening the American pilot learned that Lake Constance was shrouded in fog so he put down instead in Salzburg. That evening Yehudi spoke to Diana for about an hour until, as he recalled,

a very sweet, very gentle Englishman's voice came through and said, 'This is not a military conversation.' He gave us about five minutes to wind up and as it was the last time I needed it [he was flying to America the next day], I had made full use of that military number.

The next day Yehudi returned to the Salzburg airport:

I love the early morning at airports; it has a sense of adventure about it and especially getting into this tiny, windy, noisy plane. We took off and about an hour later we were circling over Lake Constance, absolutely covered in clouds – no question of landing. I didn't want to go to Friederichshafen anyway; I told the pilot I needed to get to Zurich but the American military were reluctant to force-land on Swiss soil because they ran the risk of internment. I said I'd make sure he was all right with the authorities and he turned round and shouted, 'Do you speak the Swiss language?'

The engine was too loud for Yehudi to attempt to explain the linguistic basis of the Helvetic Federation. He nodded his assent but Zurich was also fog-bound and the plane eventually put down in a field. Carrying fiddle and valise, Yehudi knocked on a nearby farmhouse door to be greeted by a Swiss farmer still in his nightshirt. Belonging to a rural folk that keeps its feelings hidden, the man showed no emotion at the sight of an itinerant violinist on his doorstep at six in the morning. A taxi was summoned by telephone. *En route* for Zurich a Swiss border policeman stopped Yehudi's car:

'Have you heard the sound of an aeroplane?' he asked.
I said, 'No, never', and off we went.
That was the only time I entered a country as a spy.

Yehudi told the story three decades later at the ceremony when he was given honorary Swiss citizenship.

Such escapades provided a release from Yehudi's continuing emotional crisis. But Diana passed a miserable summer. Much of the previous year had been spent battling with various authorities to get her ailing sister into a Swiss sanatorium, and now that Griselda was cured and married to Louis Kentner she had nothing to distract her from the love affair that had gone miserably wrong.

She fell into a profound depression. A visit to Paris in search of work as a dancer was unsuccessful and she wrote that she became 'very ill'. She gives no details as to the nature of the illness, which forced her to check in to a clinic, but it would undoubtedly have added to her misery – and to Yehudi's sense of guilt. She added that she was living in limbo: the London flat she and her sister had formerly shared in Belgravia had become hateful to her. Griselda had taken her things away to furnish her new home so the place was depressingly bare. Diana hated 'wandering in my mind', as she put it, 'through the rooms where Yehudi and I had grown to love each other'. There were further meetings in Switzerland, possibly clandestine since Zamira remembers being taken for a walk by her father during their summer holiday and meeting Diana on the lakeside.

Diana resolved not to let the love of her life slip away from her without a fight and late in September 1946 she flew to New York, ostensibly to look for work: she hoped that friends from her ballet life then working in the US, such as Anton Dolin and Alicia Markova, might be able to help her. She writes somewhat elusively that many months earlier – 'in a another world and time' – she had bought a ticket and arranged a visa for the United States, so perhaps she and Yehudi had earlier discussed spending time together in New York. But by the autumn he needed 'space' for reflection and he warned her he could not afford to keep her there. Diana appears to have accepted this: 'I had not even got Yehudi's address as I had no intention of seeing him again nor getting in the way of the marriage.' Nevertheless they did meet several times in New York, thanks to Dorati's wife Klari, who put them in touch. Diana remembers them as bleak encounters: 'He knew there was nothing he could say, nor could anything have brought me to unburden myself of all the shock and anguish that might only seem like condemnation.' She described her three months in Manhattan as a nightmare period and confessed that she had entertained thoughts of suicide. At an earlier, happier moment in their affair she had given Yehudi an anthology of verse inscribed with the opening lines of a Shakespeare sonnet: 'Let me not to the marriage of true minds admit impediment.' She now felt closer to the sentiment of the poem by Andrew Marvell that begins 'My love is of a birth as rare . . .' and ends 'As lines . . . Though parallel can never meet.'

Yehudi was engaged in his regular autumn season, based in New York but appearing in cities as far afield as Denver and Louisville. In October he played the Brahms Concerto three times with the New York Philharmonic under Rodzinski. It may be surmised that he was under considerable pressure, since his interpretation, according to the *New York Journal American*, 'left a good deal to be desired in imagination and technical fluency . . . There was a lack of ease in the more exacting passages and because of a pressure of bowing some of the exacting double-stoppings were rough and ready.' And yet we should not read too much into this bad review since this was the very same concert that prompted the exceptionally positive comment by the *Times* critic Olin Downes quoted earlier in this chapter (see p. 264).

Emotionally, however, Yehudi was undeniably in deep trouble, with the two women in his life both in the same city. He felt trapped, unable to make a move. 'How helpless music proved to be in this personal defeat!' he wrote. 'Many mistakes – today I am tempted to call them crimes – lay heavily on my heart and I was powerless to do anything about them.' Then Diana was invited by her mother's friends Frank Ingerson and George Dennison to spend Christmas with them in California. Their home, Cathedral Oaks, was down the hill from Alma, where Yehudi had lived with Nola since 1938. Diana arrived there on 13 December. A week earlier Nola wrote to her stepmother Shirley from New York that she was 'sick of holding out and seeing who is going to give in first'. The letter did not mention Diana's presence in New York nor her plan to take up residence on Yehudi's doorstep before he came home to spend the festive season with his parents; presumably she was being kept in the dark. 'Y wants me to become an American citizen,' was all Nola added, from which it might be deduced that he still intended the marriage to continue. But Yehudi had reintroduced his daughter to Diana in New York and thereafter Zamira (then seven years old) would telephone every morning, begging to see her. 'We would go for walks,' Diana remembered, 'or to the ballet or I would cook dinner.' Even had Yehudi wanted to remain silent about Diana's presence in America, Nola would surely have found out later in December from her brother Lindsay. He flew in from Australia with Hephzibah and their two children to spend Christmas in Alma with Yehudi and his parents. (With something of her brother's panache when it came to flying, Hephzibah persuaded the airline pilot to make an unscheduled stop in San Francisco.)

Nola did not travel west for a Christmas family reunion. She stayed in New York with Zamira and Krov. Zamira remembers her mother telling Klari Dorati in their kitchen that she was 'sick of the hassle'. Not long previously Yehudi had spoken very cautiously about the future in a newspaper interview, saying he planned to devote much of 1947 to study: 'I will spend some time in Europe and some time with my family, of whom I don't see very much.' To a Californian reporter he confided that Christmas 1946 would be his best yet because he and his two sisters Hephzibah and Yaltah were to be reunited. Nola was not mentioned in the interview but the inevitable crisis was drawing nearer. Diana relates in her memoirs that only a few days into her stay with Frank and George, 'it appeared that Yehudi had arrived at his house above and one morning he came down the valley and asked me to come and meet his parents'. Evidently it was easier for him to resume their former relationship with Nola three thousand miles away.

On Christmas Eve Moshe and Marutha gave their customary party at Los Gatos. Their old friend Ezra Shapeero dressed up as Father Christmas and arrived with a sack of presents for Hephzibah's boys. 'To that party', Moshe recalled, 'Yehudi brought Diana Gould . . . we found her to be charming, smart and determined.' That was Yaltah's impression, too. She remembers her mother greeting the guests around the table (among them Diana) with the chilling phrase 'And now we are complete.' Yaltah's husband was absent, banned by Marutha, and so was Nola. Yehudi found it impossible to confide in his parents but inevitably they sensed (as Moshe noted) that 'something was going on'. When his son played the Mendelssohn Concerto in San Francisco just after Christmas, Moshe felt that his interpretation of the slow movement contained something alien to his usual 'purely philosophical form of expression'. It 'seemed to contain a personal cry'. The unhappy Yehudi was trapped by his own temperament:

I couldn't bring myself to divorce or accuse a woman who had been my wife and with whom I'd been in love. I couldn't make a turnabout and suddenly say we're to negate [the marriage]; it had to be from her.

Meanwhile Diana's presence was accepted with warmth by Lindsay and Hephzibah Nicholas, who were staying in Los Gatos with Moshe and Marutha. To judge from a letter Nola wrote to her stepmother at the end of January 1947, her brother had more of a problem coping with his in-laws than with Diana: 'Lindsay says he is feeling twenty years older after the gruelling weeks spent vacationing in Alma and the subsequent crazy phone calls which followed them wherever they go.' Nola had no qualms about indicting her parents-in-law:

Maybe finally someone sane will realize the unnatural and poisonous atmosphere which has surrounded me these past eight years. However I pray all the good and happier aspects will live in my heart and not be 'interred with his bones', as Shakespeare put it.

More than six years had gone by since Yehudi had seen his beloved sister. The reunion must have been overshadowed by the break-up of his marriage, about which there could no longer be much doubt, given Diana's presence in their midst. On the musical level, however, there was a great deal to celebrate as brother and sister laid plans and studied repertoire for an ambitious tour of the US and Europe. Rather to Diana's surprise, Lindsay took her under his wing and even pleaded her cause by flying to New York to talk to Nola about what was now seen to be the inevitable divorce. Nola had hired a tough lawyer and negotiations proved long and difficult. Yet, from the tone of her letter to her stepmother, Nola seemed determined to take a positive attitude:

I hope now to settle down to build and live a good and constructive life – thereby I may in some way make up for twenty-seven years of disappointments to Dad and myself. The start was bad but I have regained strength and courage and the conviction I can and will do some good.

On 16 January 1947, Yehudi made his public début as a conductor: an hour-long local broadcast in the regular *Dallas Symphony Hour* series. The programme consisted of Weber's *Oberon* Overture, the 'Unfinished' Symphony by Schubert and four Slavonic Dances by Dvořák. No reviews have survived. A preview article reported that Yehudi had to rehearse without help from Antal Dorati because the Dallas orchestra's regular maestro was conducting in New York until the day of his friend's concert. The publicity blurb noted three other instrumental virtuosi who had also become conductors. The pianist José Iturbi was the best known of them but the other two would have given Yehudi a sense of belonging to a tradition: they were the violinists George Enesco and EugèneYsaÿe, who had been in charge of the Cincinnati Symphony Orchestra in the 1920s.

In February Yehudi made a bizarre move: he rented a seaside house in St Petersburg, Florida, to which he invited his brother-in-law, his sisters, their children and Diana. In his memoirs he described it as a gathering of the clan. Moshe was told it was a 'secret retreat' where his son and daughter could work up their duo sonata programme for their forthcoming concert at the Metropolitan Opera House in New York, but there was a more prosaic reason for choosing Florida. Yehudi had learned of a trail-blazing doctor named Page who resided in St Petersburg and was a disciple of Walter Price, the author of an early healthy-diet book entitled *Nutrition and Physical Degeneration*. White flour and sugar were the enemies and for a month the Menuhins were placed on a strict diet, their meals cooked for them by none other than Diana Gould, who was fast making herself indispensable to Yehudi. What neither he nor his future wife mentioned in their separate memoirs, although Yaltah remembers it well, was that the sojourn gave Diana the opportunity to fix her teeth, which had been ravaged by six years of wartime malnutrition.

The duo concert at the Metropolitan Opera on 17 March was the first time brother and sister had played together in New York for more than a decade. In the publicity stills Yehudi sported an orange-red beard he had grown in Florida – Zamira burst into tears when she saw it. A gossip columnist said, 'His whiskers were a bit ragged and do not improve his appearance.' When Zamira persuaded him to shave it off he complied, but in instalments, half the moustache one day, the opposite half of the beard the next, and so on until he was clean-shaven for the concert. Afterwards Yehudi and Hephzibah visited Willa Cather with their four children. The apartment was filled once again with children's laughter as it had been when the Menuhins were young but

Cather's partner, Edith Lewis, wrote that 'under the gaiety and happiness that morning there was somehow a sense of heartbreak'.

A week later Yehudi and Hephzibah boarded the *Queen Elizabeth*. Lindsay was travelling with them to Europe. Earlier Nola had suggested joining the family party and (according to Yaltah) Yehudi had raised no objection save to point out rather helplessly that Diana would also be travelling with the group. Nola thought better of the idea. Diana noted in her memoirs that she shared a cabin with Hephzibah's son Marston and his governess – as if this would stave off any suggestion of impropriety in the press. Yehudi and Hephzibah were scheduled to give sonata recitals in Paris, Prague and Budapest, and in Amsterdam Yehudi was to play the Bartók Second Concerto with the Concertgebouw Orchestra under Eduard van Beinum.

Before their departure for the Continent Lindsay asked Diana to join what she dubbed the 'Menuhin/Nicholas caravan' on their forthcoming tour. He would do all in his power to persuade her, he said, because Yehudi needed her help and companionship. But Diana turned down Lindsay's request. She said it was not simply a matter of *amour propre*: 'You are asking me to risk rekindling in myself something it has taken months of struggle and anguish to bury.' Diana wrote in her memoirs that she found herself torn to shreds, 'no longer clear of head or heart . . . caught in a thornbush in which every move only brought self-condemnation'. Yet it is difficult to avoid the conclusion that had she really wanted to bury her friendship with Yehudi – and why should she? – she would never have gone to New York, or to California, or to Florida. She had been sustained during that winter of considerable humiliation, during which Yehudi made no move to divorce Nola, by the certainty of their mutual love. At the last moment Yehudi's London cousin, 'Aunt' Edie, provided her with a veneer of respectability by asking her to act as chaperone for her daughter Sonia, and she decided it would after all be acceptable for her to travel with Yehudi.

It proved to be a very enjoyable expedition. In Prague Yehudi and Hephzibah took part in the exhilarating 1947 Spring Festival which brought Dimitri Shostakovich from the Soviet Union, Leonard Bernstein from America and William Walton from Britain. Yehudi played the Bach Double Concerto with his soulmate David Oistrakh and indulged in carefree chamber-music playing until late at night in the home of the conductor and Festival Director Rafael Kubelik. The effect on Diana may be imagined. She had heard many great artists in her mother's pre-war salon and had worked with distinguished choreographers in her earlier ballet career, but the war years had been spent dancing for the troops in insalubrious locations. Since meeting Yehudi her life had been fraught with disappointments and had offered nothing in the way of solid work in the theatre as compensation. At last, after many months of what can best be described as hanging on, here she was beside the man she loved at the glamorous heart of the international music world. And she was seeing Yehudi at his most endearing, talking politics with Jan Masaryk in Prague, giving a controversial press conference in Budapest, dining at Pruniers in Paris – and not having the cash to pay the bill. He signed it, she tells us, with a pen inscribed with his name that had recently been given to him by a new television station in New York.

In June Yehudi presented Diana with what proved to be the final trial of her loyalty. Before Lindsay returned to Australia with Hephzibah and their children, he spoke again to his sister about a divorce. Terms for a settlement more favourable to Nola had been discussed. (Ironically, Lindsay was soon to find himself cuckolded by a Polish immigrant with whom Hephzibah fell in love when they returned to Australia.) In a separate development, Moshe remonstrated with Yehudi about Nola's reckless use of their joint cheque account. Nola continued to hold up a legal dissolution, refusing to make a move because, according to Diana,

She could not leave the children for the six weeks necessary to obtain a divorce in Florida . . . Yehudi had promptly suggested sending them both over to him in the summer and quite extraordinarily she had accepted.

Yehudi made the offer without consulting Diana but it was clear he expected her to take on the job of looking after his children: Zamira and Krov were due to arrive in Paris on 13 June. She says she argued to herself that if she refused it would look like pettiness or retaliation.

Nola's side of the story is rather different. 'Zamira and Krov are already in Paris,' she wrote to her father in mid-June.

We won't go into that because it was too hard for me. Hephzibah [who had by then returned to Australia after her European tour with Yehudi] knows infinitely more than I do. Trying to work out a settlement at long distance is, to say the least, difficult; I begged Yehudi to come back and get the thing settled but he did not want to put himself out so I just have to struggle alone. I hated to send the children over to Europe this summer and I do think Yehudi should have come back and taken them to Alma. So much better for them and also for him but there it is.

I think Yehudi was afraid to spend the summer so near the family [i.e. Moshe and Marutha] and I don't blame him; I don't relish being there myself. The Doratis are driving out to Alma. It will be wonderful to have them near me.

In the event Nola sued for divorce in Reno, not Florida. At her lawyer's insistence she resided there incognito, avoiding publicity and successfully filing for mental cruelty. Meanwhile Diana took command of what proved to be a three-month holiday with Yehudi's and Nola's two children. It had been wished on her by their father and she was determined to prove that she could cope with anything the Fates threw at her, most notably – as she relates at some length in her memoirs – the vagaries of a handsome but capricious car of pre-war construction, a white-roofed convertible found for Yehudi by his Paris manager Maurice Dandelot. It was given the nickname 'Dégé' – Diana's initials, D.G., in French – and it broke down with monotonous regularity.

The vacation began with a long drive to St Tropez, where Yehudi had rented a farmhouse recommended by his former tutor Pierre Bertaux. A Resistance fighter during the war, Bertaux had recently been named Préfet of Lyon. Leaving Diana and Bertaux's wife to cope with their families, the two men drove across country to Prades so that Yehudi, restless as always, might pay his respects to another old family friend, the exiled Pablo Casals.

The previous year the cellist had announced his decision not to play in public as a protest against General Franco. Yehudi's mission was to persuade him to make a recording with him of the Brahms Double Concerto, with Furtwängler conducting. Casals agreed in principle but after several years of prevarication admitted that although he greatly admired the German conductor, his own anti-Fascist position would be compromised if he collaborated with somebody who had had a *modus vivendi* with the Nazis and had stayed in Berlin until the last few months of the war. Casals's position was very different from his own but Yehudi's admiration for the Spanish musician knew no bounds, and he became a regular visitor to Casals's Prades Festival in the 1950s. (He eventually recorded the Brahms Double with Paul Tortelier.)

The rented holiday farmhouse at Gassin, a few miles from St Tropez, had no hot water but it proved an ideal base for a seaside holiday on what Diana remembers to have been wellnigh empty beaches, still encumbered with barbed wire laid by the Germans in a fruitless attempt to prevent the Allied invasion two summers earlier. At the end of July Yehudi packed Zamira, Krov and Diana into the big convertible and they drove up the Rhône valley, following Hannibal's route into Switzerland, to spend a month in the mountains – just as the original Menuhin family had done, with Moshe at the wheel, in the 1930s, after their Mediterranean holidays at Ospedaletti.

Once again Yehudi left Diana in charge of his children while he departed on musical business, this time to play the Beethoven Concerto at the Salzburg Festival. Wilhelm Furtwängler was making his first appearance there since the war, a historic occasion. A week later Diana joined Yehudi when he and Furtwängler performed the Beethoven again at the Lucerne Festival. HMV made a recording, which John Ardoin, the noted historian of Furtwängler's discography, prefers on artistic merit to the 1953 version the two artists made on a mono LP with the Philharmonia Orchestra in London. He describes the interpretation as 'majestic in scope and remarkably free in stride . . . There is passion here but it is tempered with grave dignity and a rare depth of expression.' Yehudi himself was thrilled to be working at last with the German conductor for whom he had fought so hard, and he rashly announced that he never wanted to play the work with any other conductor. (Furtwängler died in 1954; Yehudi's income would otherwise have suffered substantially.) He described their artistic collaboration as 'a quite wonderful communion of inspiration . . . He wasn't predictable. He believed in living and enjoying the moment of making music.'

The visit to the Lucerne Festival, at which Yehudi also played the Bartók Second Violin Concerto under Ernest Ansermet, resulted in one of Menuhin's most important commissions. From a chance meeting on a Swiss train, Diana learned that the composer William Walton was desperate to acquire some hard currency to pay for medical treatment for his friend Lady Alice Wimborne. While *en route* for Capri with Walton she had been taken ill and obliged to enter a Swiss clinic suffering from cancer of the bronchus. She was rich – indeed she had been supporting Walton for fifteen years – but in 1947 British citizens were forbidden to take more than £10 out of the country. In Lucerne Diana introduced Walton to Menuhin (they seem not to have met in Prague the previous year) and she remembers that a deal was struck on the spot:

Yehudi said, 'Of course I'll give you money [2000 Swiss francs] but on one condition, that you write me a piece. For instance, what about a sonata that Lou [Kentner] and I can play together?' In his rather vague way (he wrote fairly slowly) Willie said that he would – so Yehudi decided to buy the manuscript paper and pencils there and then, and off they went to a big music store. I waited outside and in the shop window I saw a chair with a portrait of Benjamin Britten and the music of *Lucretia* and *Albert Herring* [which were being performed at the Lucerne Festival]. Wicked Willie had a marvellous sense of humour . . . suddenly I saw a panel open and into the window he stepped. He bent down, picked up the picture of Ben and turned it face downwards on the chair, wiped his hands and walked back into the shop.

The commission was an echo of another long-standing rivalry, that between Menuhin and Jascha Heifetz, who a decade earlier had commissioned Walton to compose a concerto. Sadly, Alice Wimborne's medical treatment was unsuccessful and she died the following year. When Walton eventually completed the Sonata, in 1949, it was dedicated to Diana and her sister Griselda, with whom Walton shared an affectionate and racy correspondence both before and after her marriage. To Griselda he observed tartly, 'If Yehudi doesn't marry Diana, nobody will.'

Menuhin's children saw more of their father in those three summer months than ever before (or afterwards in Krov's case), and Diana wrote that she ended up feeling emotionally bound to them as well as to their father. Zamira and Krov also cherish the memory of a happy holiday, with Diana at her sunniest. Apart from Yehudi's absences at the music festivals, they spent August and much of September together in their rented Swiss chalet (looked after, as always, by devoted servants) before Zamira and Krov finally flew back to their mother in time to resume school in New York. Nola had meanwhile completed the obligatory six weeks of residence in Reno and obtained a divorce. Her lawyer described the case as one of 'simple incompatibility'. Newspapers reported that the court was handed a 'sealed property settlement' which must have favoured Nola since in an unguarded moment fifty years later Yehudi confided that he was so anxious to be free that he made over to her what he described as the major part of his earnings for years to come: 'I wasn't even making $100,000 a year and I was committed to $40,000 to her, and the children's education. I had nothing in the bank except the property [the ranch at Alma].'

Degrees of financial hardship are relative for somebody who since childhood had always had whatever he wanted – a month after the settlement Yehudi was able to purchase a Jaguar motor car in London. Nola was the daughter of a rich man with her own trust fund but she had clearly been advised by lawyers to hold out for favourable terms. She was on the point of marrying her former RAF flying officer,

Anthony Williams. Eight days before the wedding, on 9 October, Nola wrote to her stepmother:

Zamira has already asked Tony if he would please marry Mummy as she would be so happy – it is comforting to know they love him as much as he does them. They also seem to love Diana, too. Miras [Zamira] wants Daddy to marry her!

So Diana had done her job well. She still felt she was living on the edge of a precipice but the battle was won and it was only a matter of weeks now, dependent on the delivery of the divorce papers, before Yehudi would be free to marry again.

At the end of September Diana accompanied him to Berlin on a six-day concert tour organized by the US Office of Military Government for Germany. Berlin, divided into four Zones of Occupation, was an ideological battlefield where, by 1947, the Americans were reaching the conclusion that confrontation with the Russians was inevitable. The wartime alliance was dead and it seemed impossible that the warmth of Yehudi's reception in Moscow two autumns previously could be repeated. But events were to illustrate his extraordinary power to overcome prejudice and stimulate a positive atmosphere. At the end of his visit Yehudi was invited by the Russians to give a concert in their Zone at the Staatsoper, the only cultural building to have escaped the Allied bombs. As the official account by the American Music Officer, Walter Hinrichsen, reported:

There were ovations for half an hour for Mr Menuhin, and Russian officers and many concertgoers agreed that the Staatsoper had never before witnessed such an outburst of enthusiasm for any artist.

The box-office receipts for this benefit were 75,400 Marks, a record tally, and proceeds were donated to the small Jewish community that had been re-established in Berlin. After the concert the Russians hosted a dinner at an artists' club in the Eastern Zone, where several speakers hailed Yehudi as the world's greatest violinist.

But an accommodation with the Russians was not the prime purpose of the visit. 'There could have been no better representative of American top-ranking artists to initiate the programme of appearances before German audiences,' wrote Hinrichsen. The Americans wanted to get the Germans on their side and Yehudi was their secret weapon. Arriving on 27 September, Menuhin gave six performances during five crowded days which also included 'reorientation meetings' with countless German music critics and cultural commentators, from the highly respected H. H. Stuckenschmidt downwards. From the reviews in German newspapers, Hinrichsen added, 'It also can be learned that Menuhin's unselfish attitude in wishing to donate all proceeds of his concerts . . . crowned his masterly artistic achievement.' Yehudi had proved his ability as a fund-raiser during the war. In Berlin his concerts raised $3000 for charity. The city was in the grip of a polio epidemic and $1000 was donated to purchase orthopaedic instruments. A further $2000 was divided between the five (!) Berlin orchestras, to buy new instruments, bows, reeds and strings. From the concert he gave specifically for the German public Menuhin ear-marked 15,000 Marks for scholarships to Berlin music schools.

Yehudi tackled the whole assignment with the energy of a campaigning politician. Within minutes of his arrival at Tempelhof airport – on the first regular KLM flight to land in Berlin – he was giving an interview on the American-licensed radio station RIAS. Then he talked to reporters from twenty German newspapers. His message was summed up by his father: 'Help, give, serve, inspire, heal the wounds of hatred.' Then he and Diana drove through the ruined streets of Berlin. Diana recalls that

The rubble of demolished buildings had been cleared on either side, making a grim causeway through canyons edged with the jagged profiles of those few houses that still retained one or two storeys.

Eighty minutes after touch-down Yehudi was at the Titania Palast cinema, in the relatively unscathed suburb of Dahlem, to rehearse the Beethoven Concerto with Furtwängler and the Berlin Philharmonic. This was to be a benefit concert attended only by American and British personnel; it raised the $3000 mentioned above. An armed US soldier walked in from the street and tried to stop the rehearsal in order to make way for the next booking, an army event, in the hall. Furtwängler ignored him and Yehudi hissed at him to go away, which he did; a press photo shows him scratching his head in bewilderment. This was probably the occasion when Yehudi heard Furtwängler sigh: 'Wo ist mein Deutschland?' ['Where is my Germany?'] The concert was an especially moving occasion for Yehudi because of the presence in the orchestra of veteran musicians who had played the Beethoven Concerto with him when he made his Berlin début in 1929. And then there was Furtwängler: 'To play the greatest of German music', he wrote, 'with this greatest of German conductors was an experience of almost religious intensity.'

The second symphony concert, for Berliners only, was given two days later. The third, organized by the Russians at the Staatsoper, was open to anybody. Yehudi and Diana also attended two rehearsals of *Tristan und Isolde* which Furtwängler was conducting at the Opera, and – to turn from the sublime to the relatively ridiculous – Yehudi was the guest of honour at a film gala launching his Paganini film *The Magic Bow*. Before the screening began, he made a 'live' appearance before the white-tie audience to play his favourite Bach *Chaconne*. History does not record whether he and Diana stayed until the end of a film they must already have seen in London.

Hinrichsen's ecstatic report noted that 'the enthusiastic and grateful reception given to him by the various audiences . . . proved that Menuhin fulfilled his mission in every sense of the word'. This is not entirely true: a terse entry in official diary of the visit notes that at 5 p.m. on 1 October, his fifth day in Berlin, Yehudi played 'for the benefit of DP audience (Bach recital)'. In fact this recital was something of a disaster. As Yehudi himself put it, 'I came down from the clouds to find myself a traitor.' Yehudi had not forgotten the emotion generated by his visit to the Displaced Persons camps two years earlier, and the recital had been scheduled at his request. The Americans organized the event at another Berlin cinema, the thousand-seat Tivoli, and they laid on fleets of buses to transport the refugees from the Deuppel Centre at Schlachtensee.

When Yehudi arrived to perform, the camp commander, an American-Jewish army captain, met him with the unwelcome news that the hall was virtually empty. According to Diana there were only fourteen people in the audience; Yehudi's estimate was 'fewer than fifty'; contemporary press reports suggested at most a few hundred. Backstage he was shown an editorial in that morning's issue of the camp's newspaper. Its readers had been advised to boycott Yehudi's concert, because he had played the previous evening for Germans, the murderers of the Jewish people. Menuhin was also attacked by the leader writer, who signed himself 'Jonas of Lemberg', for giving money to German children suffering from polio:

When I read of your 'human deeds' towards 'distressed German youth' and of how your new worshippers applauded you, I knew that in your audience there must have sat those two passionate lovers of music, Eppel and Kempke – SS men from the Kurewitz camp near Lemberg, who liked to have us sing while they shot our brothers down . . . Wherever you travel, our newspaper will follow you like a curse until your conscience awakens.

The camp residents had answered this call by staying away in their hundreds. Undeterred, Yehudi went ahead with his planned Bach recital and there the matter might have rested had Diana not prompted him to ask for an opportunity to speak directly to the DPs. Diana quoted Captain Fishbein's gratitude in her memoirs:

D'ya know what you're letting yourself in for? These poor wretches are brutalized by years of appalling treatment and hardship and are hardly human any more, and this fellow [Jonas of Lemberg] has brought out the worst in them. I'll have to get the Military Police to handle it.

The next morning Yehudi and Diana drove into the lions' den of the Deuppel Centre. Their car was surrounded by an angry crowd of refugees. Diana was the first to emerge. In the midst of what she described as 'a hedge of hating faces' stood the man who had written the boycott editorial. 'Herr Jonas, guten Tag,' she remembers saying, firmly holding out her hand – she was, after all, the stepdaughter of an admiral – and insisting that he shook it. Yehudi followed suit and then they were pushed through the hostile crowd and into the meeting hall by two burly white-helmeted MPs. 'Boos, hisses and imprecations followed us all the way,' Yehudi reported, adding that the DPs were

sallow-face men and women in threadbare suits, and babushkas who felt themselves outlawed among outlaws . . . condemned who had not quite died . . . Packed shoulder to shoulder, crouched on shelves and windowsills, hanging on to pillars, they waited for my defence.

Ironically he was obliged to speak in the language of the former oppressor, German, but his childhood years in German-speaking Basel stood him in good stead: 'I've come to speak to you as a Jew, and to tell you that what I've done I've done as a Jew.' A voice from the back of the hall interjected: 'You have played for the murderers.' Yehudi pressed on doggedly.

I have behaved in the only way I could. When the Germans allowed Hitler to come to power, I refused to play for them. When they were defeated, my first thoughts were of my own people and I went to the death camps with my violin. We cannot and we must not forget the past, but a time has come to face the future and to begin building it. To behave towards the Germans the way the Nazis behaved towards us is to admit that we have grown to be like the Nazis; our only way of proving the birthright and the greatness of our race is by asserting its strength and virtues and not by imitating evil. We cannot build our future on hatred. We cannot put an end to war and persecution by acts of revenge.

When the heckler repeated his mantra, 'Go on, play for the murderers!', other DPs silenced him and Yehudi continued:

I cannot blame anyone for his bitterness. You have suffered too much, you have lost parents, children, brothers and sisters. I have been spared this torture. And still, I do say that you simply cannot rebuild your life on your suffering . . . We Jews don't beg, we work! We are the best cobblers, the best tailors, the best doctors, the best musicians! I have come to Germany to restore that image, to show how false was Hitler's caricature . . . Your future is in hard honest work, just as is mine and that of all living people. I cannot change myself. I am what my music, my country and my race have made me, and can only act as I feel and think is right. You may not agree with me but you must believe in me and not think of me as a traitor to my people.

Such sustained eloquence carried the day. When the DPs began shouting, 'Our Yehudi! Our Yehudi!', he privately compared them (in his memoirs) to the Underworld shades who at first did not recognize Orpheus when he came to Hell in search of Eurydice. The DPs begged him to play again for them but he had cautiously left his violin at the hotel and his diary was crowded with meetings and concerts until the moment of his departure. To make his moral victory complete, the previously hostile Jonas of Lemberg called on him before his departure to make his peace. Later Jonas told American reporters – the incident was widely reported in the US press, including *Time* magazine – that 'If Menuhin offered us a concert today we would all go.' But he added a postscript that critics of Menuhin's philosophy were still echoing fifty years later: 'Perhaps it is too much to expect that those who have not experienced persecutions and camps should understand our feelings.'

When Yehudi flew out of Berlin on 3 October, Diana was by his side. Both wore parachutes and were belted to the open steel struts that lined the US plane's fuselage. In Frankfurt they were taken to the Reichsbank and shown gruesome relics of the Holocaust: buckets filled to the brim with gold teeth. 'Lying hideously among them,' Diana noticed, 'was a handful of little brooches, pins and rings, the detritus culled from thousands of humans who had known the misfortune of being born into the wrong race.' The week spent facing up to recent German history must have been every bit as emotional as Yehudi's visit to Belsen with Britten. But now it was over and Yehudi could resume the life of a conventional concert violinist. He did so with a flourish, playing in Stockholm, Oslo and Copenhagen, where a Danish critic described him, presumably unaware of the testing time he had just been through in Berlin, as 'a young Teuton, Siegfried in a well-fitting evening dress'.

Six and a half thousand people filled Copenhagen's rebuilt Forum, which was being used as a concert hall for the first time since the Nazi Occupation. For another Danish critic it was 'the most important event in the capital's musical life for many years'. For Diana and Yehudi the visit had quite other connotations: it was here that Yehudi asked Diana to marry him. He had received news of his 'freedom' – the decree absolute – a week earlier in Stockholm but there had been no celebration. His reserved nature, as Diana put it, and her wariness after so many disappointments stifled what might have been a joyous occasion. She perceived that the news had to work its way slowly through her lover's mental system, 'cleaning away goodness knows what clogging in his psychological arteries'. That process completed, he asked her if she would consider marrying him. She asked him whether he was certain of his feelings. He acknowledged that he had failed her back in April 1946 when Nola's insistence on his duty and his abiding affection for Nola and love of his children had combined to throw him off his declared course. He had since been plagued by a feeling that what he longed for most was beyond his reach and his rights. This was Diana's recollection, not Yehudi's. He gave the reader of his memoirs no insight into his state of mind but recalled that at the marriage ceremony a few days later in London (an attempt to marry next day in Copenhagen had been foiled by a stuffy British diplomat's refusal to waive the formalities) he was teased, if not rebuked, by his new wife for his mournful looks. 'I had not the smallest doubt of her,' he was to write,

but doubts about my own maturity I had in abundance. I had proved myself a pretty quarter-baked husband, unpossessive, uncommanding, possibly unprotective . . . My uncertainty that I deserved Diana was reason enough for a worried face; it seemed a defiance of fate to celebrate a victory not yet earned.

Back in London Diana evaded the waiting photographers and lodged with her sister while Yehudi checked in to Claridge's. Diana went incognito to arrange the special marriage licence (price £2 13s 4d) at the Chelsea Register Office, whose officials rejoiced in the names of Mr Marsh and Mr Stream. They kindly agreed to keep the Sunday morning appointment secret from reporters, to whom Diana's mother had been hinting that wedding bells were in the offing. Yehudi spent a stag night playing Beethoven violin sonatas with his future brother-in-law Louis Kentner and on the eve of the wedding the Kentners joined Yehudi and Diana for a cheerful evening at Britten's new operatic comedy *Albert Herring*, before enjoying a bumper supper at Boulestin's restaurant.

At 9.15 a.m. on Sunday, 19 October 1947, Diana and Yehudi were married. (With an extraordinary sense of symmetry, Nola had remarried two days earlier.) Her ring had been bought at Cartier's. There were only six witnesses: Diana's mother ('the relieved female parent'); her sister Griselda ('making witty copy in her head') and her step-grandmother ('in her best black, looking pure Galsworthy'). Louis Kentner and Yehudi's agent Harold Holt were the only men. Yehudi's solitary relative, who had also attended the wedding to Nola nine years previously, was his 'Aunt Edie'. After a 'dismal', 'scurried' ceremony (the comments are all Diana's) the group adjourned to the Kentners' house close by on the King's Road, Chelsea, where Griselda cracked open a magnum of Mumm. Diana described the occasion in her sharpest manner:

Glasses were raised, dispelling the last wisps of fog from the gloomy morning, and just as I was beginning to smell a faint whiff of orange blossom, Y. put down his untouched glass, took me soberly by the elbow, kissed everyone a hasty farewell, propelled me into the car and off we went, hell-bent for the Albert Hall just in time for the rehearsal of the Paganini B minor Violin Concerto. And so it has been ever since.

As Diana put it herself, she had chained herself to a firefly.

Recommended Recordings

Bartók: Sonata for solo violin
EMI 7 69804 2
Recorded: 2 and 3 June 1947
Recorded three years after YM gave the première. Menuhin felt that such intense music needed many performances to penetrate to its deepest core. His recording on 78s was replaced but not superseded by an LP in 1974.

Bartók: Violin Concerto No. 2
Dallas Symphony Orchestra, conducted by Antal Dorati
RCA 61395–2
Recorded: 15 and 16 January 1946
YM recorded the big Bartók Concerto on at least three other occasions, including

an HMV mono LP with Furtwängler, but the energy and intensity of this first recording (which was also the inaugural recording of the Dallas–Dorati team) is unsurpassable.

Beethoven: Violin Concerto in D
Lucerne Festival Orchestra, conducted by Wilhelm Furtwängler
Testament SBT 1109
Recorded: 28 and 29 August 1947
John Ardoin's glowing appreciation, quoted in this chapter, needs no endorsement.

11 Life with Diana

Diana Gould on holiday with Yehudi and his children in Switzerland, 1947

1947: December: filming Concert Magic; *1948: July: birth of son, Gerard; August: first appearance at Edinburgh Festival; October: visit to Philippines; 1949: unsuccessful support for Furtwängler's engagement in Chicago; 1950: February: London première of Walton's Violin Sonata, first post-war tour of South Africa; April: first visit to Israel; June: conducts the Vienna Philharmonic in Bach; July: South American tour with flying grasshoppers; 1951: May: inaugural recital with Hephzibah at London's Royal Festival Hall; June: visit to Australia and New Zealand, discovery of yoga; October: first visit to Japan; November: birth of son Jeremy.*

At half a century's distance it is hard to find any rational explanation for the absurdly pressured life that Yehudi imposed on his new wife from the first day of their marriage. The wedding breakfast was followed by the mad dash to the rehearsal at the Royal Albert Hall, from which the second Mrs Menuhin was later photographed emerging in an elegant fur. The newspaper caption next morning named her as 'Miss Diana Gould' – the marriage vows having been taken in secret. The afternoon concert involved two concertos and the additional tension of a BBC broadcast. Then came a single night's 'honeymoon' in the Kent countryside, at the cottage of Diana's actor–director friend Cyril Ritchard, after which Yehudi was off, new bride at his side, on his routine annual tour of the British provinces. It had no doubt been planned the previous year and in Yehudi's eyes was not to be cancelled for anything as worldly as a honeymoon.

News of the marriage was soon made public and at Leicester, to which they travelled by train, the romantic couple was greeted by the station master, resplendent in top hat and morning suit – a perfect photo opportunity for a British press starved of glamour in Britain's post-war age of austerity. William Walton was in the audience that night, having motored over from Ashby, the country seat of his ailing mistress, Alice Wimborne. According to Diana he hissed,

in his most Sitwellian manner, 'Oh God, not the D minor Partita? Let's skip this one and come back at the interval.'

'Willie, I must stay,' the new bride hissed back, and with a grin he did so.

Diana had effectively become Yehudi's partner six months earlier at the time of his European tour with Hephzibah and Lindsay. But her rush to be married at the first opportunity was understandable. Although she thought of herself as something of a Bohemian, and had a fifteen-year career behind her in theatre and ballet, Diana came from an upper-crust background and deep down the respectability (and certainty) conferred by a wedding ring was important to her – as it would have been to Yehudi, once his mind had been made up for him about the advisability of marrying again. At thirty-five, Diana must also have been aware that motherhood could not be postponed with equanimity for much longer. As a young dancer she had avoided sex as a consequence of seeing so many of her colleagues obliged to make traumatic visits to Parisian back-street abortionists. So long as there were doubts about Yehudi's will to leave Nola her anxieties must have continued, but at last there was no need for caution: her first child was born nine months and three days after the wedding.

On 8 November they flew to America. Diana told a journalist they had managed to buy a British-made car – a Jaguar – and she was looking forward to driving in California with a GB plate. She had been in the Los Gatos area the previous winter, staying with Frank and George, but now she was to become the chatelaine of Alma, the house higher up the mountain where Yehudi and Nola had lived off and on for close on a decade. It had been shut for many months. The rock garden was 'as bare as a set of dentures', Diana noted with characteristic sharpness when they arrived (the state of her own teeth had been something of a problem), and she thought the two flowerbeds, one at the front and the other at the back, had been 'laid down like parlour carpets to impress casual callers'.

Even in defeat Nola was allowed no quarter. Diana attacked her predecessor's bedroom like a person possessed:

Every drawer was stuffed full, every hanger dripping with clothes such as I had not seen in a decade, to say nothing of eighty pairs of shoes and a bathroom closet bursting, as were the dressing-table shelves, with quarts and pints of scent, eau-de-Cologne, lavender water and other more practical and less savoury adjuncts to the art of living as a luxurious female.

To the loser rather than the winner went the spoils. Diana discovered the fourteen trunks and valises purchased by Nola's father as part of her 1938 wedding trousseau.

Folding these lovely clothes with envious care and masses of tissue paper . . . [I] despatched the lot to New York. In their place I hung my two coats, three dresses and one pair of trousers, filled about half a row of shelves with my spare jerseys and shirts and lingerie and shamefacedly hooked four pairs of battered shoes on the racks . . . they spoke of the war and the Blitz and of an extraordinary epoch.

Yehudi himself made no mention of the marital takeover in his memoirs. Meeting his parents the day after their arrival, Diana realized that with Marutha she was back at ballet school dealing with the larger-than-life type of Russian martinet who had dominated her own childhood. Moshe she found 'alive with nervous energy' and 'thoroughly delighted' to see his son after many months of absence. What none of the three chronicled in their memoirs was Moshe's extreme displeasure when he learned of a partnership deal Yehudi had just struck with a film producer named Paul Gordon. Yehudi had already made a brief appearance in a film called *Duffy's Landing*, produced by Paramount, for which he received a massive cheque for $15,000 early in 1947. But it must have been galling for Moshe to find his son involved in a major project with a producer working in Hollywood, whose values he had always maintained were irreconcilable with those of an artist such as

Yehudi. Even worse news for Moshe was the fact that Yehudi's post-war bankability had dropped like a stone: the current deal would bring in nothing like the $½m fee that had been mentioned several times in the 1930s.

Paul Gordon, a Hungarian-Jewish refugee, born Stefan Keleman, persuaded Yehudi to perform a substantial recital in a film studio with the admirable intention of distributing the product to cinemas around the world. He was neither the first producer nor the last to believe – for the most part erroneously – that there was money to be made out of providing culture for the masses. In the film's portentous opening sequence, spoken over an orchestral version of Bach's Air on the G string, Gordon's voice is heard dedicating the film to those millions of music-lovers for whom 'live' performance is inaccessible because of where they live. This is, he proudly states,

the first motion picture in concert form to present itself before audiences without the contrivance of a story, without make-up, without pretence or embellishment; it brings the best of the concert halls of the great metropolitan centres to the most remote communities of every nation.

Doubtless Yehudi was attracted by this democratic concept and doubtless (to judge by Moshe's wrath, which was expressed in his correspondence) he waived his fee, or most of it, in return for a share of future profits. What he had not realized was that television was soon to sweep away the educational element in the film business.

Filming at Charlie Chaplin's old studio on North La Brea took several days at the end of 1947. The repertoire was undemanding, consisting for the most part of works Yehudi had been playing for twenty-five years, among them a movement from Beethoven's Sonata in D, Op. 12 No. 1, the *Scherzo-tarantelle* by Wieniawski, *Malaguena* and *Gypsy Airs* by Sarasate, *Labyrinth* by Locatelli and a Hungarian Dance by Brahms. To round out the programme, the pianist Jakob Gimpel was filmed playing solos by Mendelssohn, Chopin and Liszt; the American contralto Eula Beal sang songs by Schubert, Gounod and Tchaikovsky and 'Erbarme dich' from the *St Matthew Passion*, in which Yehudi played the violin obbligato and Antal Dorati conducted the 'Hollywood Symphony Orchestra'.

The film was unveiled the following October at the Stagedoor Theatre in San Francisco under the title *Concert Magic* – with the top ticket price a modest $1.20. The *Variety* review was succinct but kind:

'Picture was made for art-lovers and should draw strong coin in art houses.' The cameraman, Paul Ivano, was given credit for

a magnificent job in lensing what could be described as inanimate objects. [One wonders how anybody could describe Yehudi Menuhin as an inanimate object!] Camera angles and lighting perpetuate interest to the eye where ordinarily the only sustained interest would be to the ear.

It is a fair assessment of a dignified but achingly stiff piece of filming in which invisible hands turn programme pages between the musical offerings. Television at that period was only in its infancy and electronic cameras at a concert location could not have provided the revealing close-ups of Yehudi's left hand or given us the overhead shot which combined images of the violin in the foreground, at the bottom of the frame, and above it the piano keyboard – further from the lens but still clearly defined. (A tight budget prevented the use of a crane camera. This is a blessing. The simplicity of the set-ups allows one to concentrate on the music.) The dress is formal, white tie and tails, even though the settings for the performances are rooms, not halls, and there is no audience.

Yehudi looks deeply uncomfortable, indeed positively sulky. His hair is slicked down, his eyes remain closed and he hardly moves his body; the cameraman had probably begged him to keep still so that the image would not go out of focus. *Concert Magic* is therefore a useful but somewhat misleading and disappointing record of how Menuhin played in his early thirties. Fortunately Paul Gordon's film sessions covered more ground than was released in the seventy-minute *Concert Magic*. An additional project was to create a small library of individual 'shorts' of five to ten minutes in duration; these could be rented by cinema distributors for use as high-class fillers between the double features that were standard fare in cinemas in the 1940s. Paganini's Twenty-fourth Caprice was one of the additional works filmed for later release, performed in Kreisler's enjoyable if hopelessly unauthentic arrangement with piano accompaniment. Fifty years later, in 1998, Menuhin made an analysis of his performance, variation by variation, for an as yet unpublished documentary film. He declared himself well pleased (for the most part) with his younger self's technical prowess. Another film 'short' was a Hungarian Dance by Brahms in which Antal Dorati takes over at the keyboard, improvising a cimbalom-type piano accompaniment that is far fresher than Adolph Baller's rather wooden contributions. There's also a movement from a Bach solo partita, but the most important work to be filmed was a complete performance of the Mendelssohn Violin Concerto under Dorati. This seems never to have received a cinema release, probably because there was an unholy row about fees and the ownership of rights. Moshe prepared a memorandum concerning Paul Gordon for the lawyers: 'Yehudi will keep on repeating that Paul Gordon meant well but that the cruel interests of Monopoly intervened.' The grumbling Moshe is presumably referring to monopolistic film distributors rather than the famous family game. Nobody passed Go or collected £200 on this venture.

Moshe ended his note with a lively complaint concerning the undiscriminating generosity of his son, whose income and tax affairs he still monitored every year:

He has not yet learned to turn over all free benefit concert solicitations on the part of Ladies and Lords and Shnorrers to his good managers in London, Paris, New York, etc. Hence his constant giving benefit concerts and paying all fares, pianists, hotels, and other necessary and unnecessary costs . . . which make his professional expenses infinitely higher than any other living artist in the world and MAKES THINGS FOR ME ALMOST UNBEARABLE EACH YEAR TO WORK OUT HIS TAX BILLS AND HIS NETS [i.e. net income].

This was a sphere of activity in which Diana might have been expected to assume greater authority – Yehudi took to introducing her to the press as his secretary and sock-darner – but she failed miserably: her memoirs are strewn with anecdotes concerning her husband's inability to say no. One of the more humorous ones refers to the delivery of a Heath Robinson-type gadget designed to turn the pages of a musical score automatically. Looking like a cross between a deck chair and a crucifix, it came with a pedal

upon which the standing player pressed at the requisite moment, thus releasing a ghostly hand which . . . grabbed the page and with great if jerky deliberation turned it over and patted it into place . . . The miracle eventually died a natural death when the hand developed a nasty habit of turning three pages at once.

Other tales, mentioned by more than one observer, confirm her husband's gullibility. In October 1948, after Yehudi had made two visits via the Air-Lift to what had become blockaded Berlin, an American officer (Betty McCluskey) serving in Germany noted in a memo:

All of us who love him would like to see him take better care of himself and be a little more critical of the people who he is ready to help instead of pouring his love indiscriminately on the worthy and unworthy alike.

It was to be a refrain echoed by his nearest and dearest for half a century.

Yehudi's annual American tour had resumed in January 1948, after the Hollywood filming. It included several appearances in New York, where he gave the first performance in that city of Prokofiev's Violin Sonata, Op. 80, written before the war but only recently available in the West – David Oistrakh had presented him with a copy in Prague the previous spring. (Joseph Szigeti beat him to the American première by a fortnight.) The choice of repertoire was timely since in Moscow the Russians were in the process of denigrating their leading composer (together with the younger Shostakovich) for his alleged formalist, bourgeois tendencies. Yehudi leapt to his defence, calling a press conference on 12 February at which he blasted the Soviet authorities for their 'infantile policy' – fighting talk from an artist who had been fêted in Moscow only a couple of years previously. The subsequent recording, with Marcel Gazelle, was described in the *Gramophone* as masterly – 'not only in technique (one scarcely need mention that) – but in its authority and, indeed, its irresistible persuasiveness'.

Diana's introduction to Yehudi's America was every bit as relentless as the touring schedule Nola had endured (and to which she eventually succumbed) nine years earlier: wintry weather, tedious journeys, interminable practice in hotel suites in Chicago, Milwaukee and Baltimore. Then they travelled down south to Memphis and on to Miami, where Yehudi gave two performances of the Beethoven Concerto in one afternoon, under Pierre Monteux. That was followed by a flight over the Straits of Florida to Havana, where Yehudi contracted measles (Diana said he looked as red as a Spanish pimento and felt as hot as a Russian stove) and instead of enjoying the deferred honeymoon he had promised her, they had to beat a temporary retreat to observe quarantine in California. Not for long, however. Vancouver, Seattle, Spokane, San Diego and Los Angeles were on the West Coast itinerary, and on 2 April 1948 Yehudi appeared on television in what was billed as 'the first telecast of classical music west of Philadelphia'. This was before *Concert Magic* was unveiled and the threat to the cinema from television was a mere smudge on the horizon; there were said to be only seventeen thousand set-owners in the entire greater Los Angeles area. (The transmitting station was Don Lee's W6XAO.) Yehudi played the Tchaikovsky Concerto with the Los Angeles Philharmonic under Alfred Wallenstein. *Time* magazine noted the experimental relay but dismissed the images as 'dull and fuzzy'. Yehudi's playing seems to have suffered, too: 'His bowing was often rough and his tone rather thin,' reported *Daily Variety*, but later in the performance he played 'warmly and with great beauty'. The pessimistic verdict was: 'strictly for longhairs . . . not enough [camera] movement to excite the senses'.

Yehudi's illness had revived all Marutha's maternal instincts. She was convinced, Diana said, that adult measles led to 'gangrene, pyorrhoea and creeping paralysis of the nervous system'. The new wife's response was to keep on the road with Yehudi. Her Christian Scientist upbringing had taught her to eschew medicine and eat healthily – though not crankily; she was forever mocking Yehudi's food fads, instilled by *his* mother – and her wartime touring had given her a thicker skin than Nola ever acquired. Naturally she was less than enchanted by the fact that Yehudi was always greeted by adoring committee ladies 'all agog to see him' while she was left to fend for herself, nostalgically treading the boards backstage during his recitals and thinking of her own abandoned (and never very successful) theatrical career. From April 1948 onwards the world was invited to share her all-too-visible secret: she was five months pregnant. She was determined not to give up the way Nola had done: she accompanied Yehudi to Berlin for more concerts under the auspices of the US occupying forces, to Paris, where he was made a member of the Légion d'honneur, and to London, where he played to a record audience of ten thousand at the Harringay Arena.

Yehudi had been invited to appear at the Edinburgh International Festival, then in its second year, and they decided that their first child should be born in Scotland. Being away from home might have been considered an additional stress for Diana but she had spent very little time at Alma and probably felt safer in the care of Britain's newly established National Health Service. They rented an entire wing of a Lutyens-designed house named Greywalls. Plenty of space was required because Yehudi had invited Zamira (eight) and Krov (almost seven) to spend the summer with them. Louis Kentner would also be there, working with Yehudi on the Beethoven violin and piano sonatas they were to present as a cycle at the Festival. Yehudi had also hired a housekeeper: being a stickler for tradition he had traced the lady who had coached his family in Italian when they were living in Basel eighteen years previously. Thus Signorina Anna was with the group awaiting Yehudi's return from Eastern Europe.

Diana had arranged that they would all take the night train up to Edinburgh but Yehudi failed to turn up. Several hours after he was due in London, his accompanist Marcel Gazelle, who had been with him in Budapest, telephoned in some agitation from Brussels to report that Russian and Czech military policemen had taken Yehudi off his plane at Prague airport, where he was making a connection on his way home. No reason had been given and Yehudi claimed to have no idea, given his previous popularity with the Soviets, why he should have been treated so cavalierly. He had perhaps forgotten his fierce attack on Soviet music policy just half a year earlier. The Russians have long memories but on this occasion it seems their intention was only to scare him: he was lodged in a Prague hotel overnight and sent on his way to London next day. Meanwhile Diana, already installed in her Scottish mansion, was gripped by images of her husband being banished to Siberia. (There were genuine grounds for anxiety: the USSR was gripped by anti-Western hysteria and Prokofiev's estranged wife Lina had recently been sentenced to twenty years in a Siberian labour camp for maintaining contacts with Western diplomats.) However, Yehudi drove up to Scotland with his pianist brother-in-law only two days late, having been through nothing worse than a brush with a lorry on the Great North Road in Kentner's Triumph motor car.

A boy was born to the Menuhins on 23 July 1948. He was named Gerard after his Irish grandfather and Anthony after his godfather, Anthony Asquith. The child's nickname, Diana told everybody, would be even more ordinary: Smith, or Smithy. It was later corrupted from Smith to 'Mita', as 'Smith' tended to be pronounced by foreign nannies. Diana had made sure she was thousands of miles from Marutha's influence and she was having no truck with outlandish names such as Krov (Yehudi's eldest son) or Kronrod and Marston (Hephzibah's boys). A Scottish nurse named Craigie was engaged for Mita, and a month later Yehudi resumed his concert life, making a host of appearances at the Edinburgh Festival. He and Kentner played their Beethoven cycle from memory, a considerable feat. Menuhin also performed the Brahms Double Concerto for the first time, working with his friend from an Alpine hiking holiday half a lifetime earlier, Gregor Piatigorsky.

After two months in Scotland the Menuhin caravan rolled on. Krov and Zamira were sent back to New York and the Menuhins went to Paris, where, as well as making the customary round of recitals and recordings, Yehudi developed his taste in art under Diana's guidance. They visited the studio of Marie Laurencin, from whom the hard-up couple bought a painting. (Later, when they were living in Switzerland, the painters Balthus and Kokoschka were to become neighbours and friends.)

Still breast-feeding her son, Diana took him home to California with his nurse while Yehudi resumed his globe-trotting with a concert tour of the Philippines, reached by way of concert stop-overs in Lisbon and Panama. A local newspaper claimed that Manila was the only city in the Orient that could muster a substantial audience for classical music so soon after the war. When Yehudi bravely agreed to appear with the Manila Symphony Orchestra at an open-air event conducted by a local musician, the event attracted 'the largest crowd of music-lovers ever gathered in a concert hall in the Philippines'. The *Manila Bulletin* added that as an encore he 'played a difficult piece without accompaniment'. Yehudi revelled in his role as a world ambassador for classical music and entered cheerfully into the spirit of the place. (A photograph shows him surrounded by a bevy of beautiful girls.) He toured the southern islands, he included a work by a local composer among his encores (*Tulog na Bunso*, a lullaby by Professor Ramon Tapales) and happily donned a 'barong tagalog' (a ceremonial, hand-embroidered tunic) to show his identification with the indigenous clothing industry.

He was less well advised with the Chinese tailor he chose in Manila to run up overnight a Western-style grey pinstripe suit for him. When he arrived in Honolulu – two days late – his wife, who had flown out from California to join him, *sans* baby Smithy, failed to recognize him as he left the plane. She had been made understandably nervous by this latest example of his inability to turn up at the allotted hour. 'Did you have to add to the agony', she asked, 'by coming disguised as an Asian trader in his bigger brother's clothes?' Her memoirs pile on the discomfiture. He had bought her a shirt made of pineapple fibre ('only slightly stained down the front with banana pulp') but the gift failed to mollify her and on the first night of their deferred honeymoon she fell asleep: 'The memory of failing him', she wrote, 'is forever burnt into my persecution maniac's masochistic mind.' But the week that followed in a seaside bungalow, with fresh coconut milk supplied every morning by a native boy, was a genuinely 'magic idyll', a rare break in a travel routine which became so taxing for Diana that 'it scraped the skin off my nerves; I felt like an over-age Girl Guide married to a commercial traveller with a nice line in Beethoven and Bartók.'

In January 1949 Yehudi was once again at loggerheads with his Jewish colleagues over Wilhelm Furtwängler. The Chicago Symphony Orchestra had long been on the look-out for a world-class conductor to revive its fortunes, which had been flagging under the Belgian, Desiré Defauw. In a move that caught the musical world unawares, Chicago negotiated a contract with Furtwängler which provoked a hornets' nest of criticism. Gregor Piatigorsky was among the protesters, although back in the 1920s he had played first cello in the Berlin Philharmonic under Furtwängler. Another was the pianist Vladimir Horowitz, the son-in-law of Toscanini. (Back in 1936, Toscanini had offered Furtwängler the succession to the New York Philharmonic Orchestra, reportedly in order to give the Prussian an honourable opportunity for leaving Nazi Germany.) Nathan Milstein and Isaac Stern were among the violinists who threatened a boycott. The pianist Artur Rubinstein sent a telegram to the orchestra's trustees that began: 'I will not collaborate, musically or otherwise, with anyone who has collaborated with Hitler, Goering and Goebbels.'

Yehudi was up in arms immediately:

I have never encountered a more brazen attitude than that of the three or four ringleaders in their frantic and obvious efforts to exclude an illustrious colleague from their happy hunting grounds. I consider their behaviour beneath contempt.

On 12 January he announced from Rome that he would not play with the Chicago Symphony if Furtwängler was forced out. But a week later his friend did resign, claiming that:

The protest of American artists against my coming to Chicago is based on the news which the official propaganda in Nazi Germany chose to publish about me and not on the truth. It is inconceivable that artists should perpetrate hatred indefinitely while all the world is longing for peace. In order to spare the Chicago Symphony Orchestra further difficulties I withdraw herewith from the already concluded contract.

Furtwängler particularly resented the double standards of Stern and Piatigorsky, who had recently appeared at the Lucerne Festival despite its known connection with him. In his notebook he added:

and there is also Artur Rubinstein, whom I do not know, but who plainly does not know me – for he should know that I was the one artist who remained in Germany and emphatically intervened on behalf of the Jews until the very end.

Furtwängler had no luck where America was concerned: Rudolf Bing's attempt to engage him as Music Director at the Metropolitan Opera was scotched by his board, which was still smarting over Mr Bing's insistence on re-hiring the Norwegian soprano Kirsten Flagstad, whose husband had collaborated with the Nazis during the war. In 1954 Furtwängler was preparing to lead the Berlin Philharmonic on an extended tour of the US but he died before he could face that ultimate test of American hostility.

Yehudi's self-imposed ban was short lived. In December 1949 Rafael Kubelik was appointed to Chicago's vacant post of Music Director and Yehudi played the Beethoven Violin Concerto under his direction in November 1950. Doubtless the close friendship they had struck up in Prague helped to heal the wound between Yehudi and the orchestra. In passing it may be noted that Yehudi had already performed the Beethoven Concerto in Chicago in five different seasons: 1948, 1944, 1941 (February and July) and 1938.

Meanwhile his dogged loyalty to the German conductor led to further examples of hostility from extremist Jewish organizations. When Carnegie Hall was only half full for one of his recitals, it was rumoured (although no proof was ever offered) that his enemies had bought tickets and thrown them away in order to underline his isolation. In South America, which he toured in the summer of 1949, he was threatened with a boycott. It failed, he wrote, 'to the extent of provoking counter-demonstrations. In Buenos Aires the Jewish community put on a special service and invited me, to assure me of my welcome among them.'

Later on the South American tour he and Diana escaped from musical politics to make a visit to the lost Inca city of Machu Picchu. It was a strenuous episode. Yehudi noted that from the Spanish town of Cuzco,

the route led steeply downhill for perhaps a hundred miles, across a valley, and then steeply uphill for mile or two. We accomplished the first downhill stage in a car whose tyres had been removed, substituting iron rims to run on rails; a method of progress which risked breaking every bone in one's body and inhibited speech lest one bite one's tongue in two. One circumstance saved us from being bounced bodily out of our unlikely chariot: with six passengers . . . we were wedged in too tightly to move . . . A string of mules should have been waiting in the village to carry us up to Machu Picchu but the arrangements had broken down, and from this point we were on our own.

The travellers decided to follow the course of a river, climbing towards the lost city. At first they sang and chattered but later they were 'silent and puffing and exhausted. It was, I believe, the severest test I have ever undergone.' Eventually they reached a modest guest house, to be rewarded next morning by a vision of the ruins of the city, 'a beautiful, enigmatic witness to a vanished civilization'.

There was inevitably a downside to this adventure, as Diana chronicled: 'At eleven thousand feet one could without exaggerated optimism hope that no one would know Yehudi from a mango.' But when they returned to Cuzco 'a deputation had assembled demanding that Y gave a concert'. In the local school hall there was a battered upright piano for Yehudi's Dutch accompanist, Theodore Saidenberg. The performance was

vintage Laurel and Hardy. Even Y succumbed to an occasional giggle . . . Beethoven, however manfully Y strove to drown the piano, sounded more like Schoenberg than I have ever heard him before or since; as for Brahms (D mi, I suspect) that well-worn sonata wandered from key to key until it was finally brought to a merciful if premature end by the sudden disembowelment of the piano caused by van Nederland's furious poundings. As the strings poured out of their threadbare casing in a cascade of relief (very amusing, this) the merry evening grew to a close. Y gave them a pennyworth of unaccompanied Bach and, to the sound of rousing cheers (more than earned, I would say) we returned to a banquet at the little hotel.

From Peru the Menuhins journeyed to Ecuador, where a recital in Guayaquil was enlivened by the presence of what they took to be locusts. The insects were later revealed as flying grasshoppers, four inches in length (according to Diana) and with a wing-span half as long again; they boasted speed and manoeuvrability to match the latest military aircraft. Their only inconvenience, Yehudi observed mildly, was

their mindless habit of flying into obstacles at high speed without looking where they were going . . . The recital was enlivened by their darting hither and thither and crashing into people and furniture.

Yehudi claimed to have played on unperturbed but Diana told a different story:

A particularly musical-minded insect perched dreamily on the bridge of his Stradivarius and remained there while poor Y, squinting like a clown, drew his bow with dynamic force, souped up his vibrato with heedless disregard for taste yet utterly failed in this desperate attempt to dislodge the beast.

Memories of the South American tour prompted one of Diana's more entertaining sallies against the working habits of her husband.

I was rapidly becoming expert in the ordained concert duties of a chief performer's wife. I was learning fast . . . not to panic over a missing vest, but to search calmly, finding it perhaps stuffed between a copy of the Beethoven sonata and *La fille aux cheveux de lin* in Y's music case. Next I would check on the handkerchief in the right-hand pocket and the comb before every concert, and concoct the 'picnic bag' for sustenance during intervals (for the Kosher rites of his ancestors had been transmuted by him [and Marutha!] into far fiercer laws of pure organic food), the necessary provision being difficult enough to find, for plastic junk had already begun to spread its rubbery claws into all nutrition. [Then] there was the thermos to fill with various herb teas smelling strongly to my tightening nostrils of the Augean stables before Hercules got at them, and honey to provide, honey that spreads as only it can over everything bar the violin. And beside this I had to remember a jarful of nuts and raisins of curious provenance and several small bottles of magic tablets of hideous hue and worse taste ranging from seaweed (good for the elbows, no doubt) to vitamins starting with the first letter and ending on the last of some alphabet much longer than that of the Romans . . . I learned to look on that bag with its incurable periods of clotted disorder as a kind of microcosm of my life.

The Menuhins returned to Californian civilization in time for Yehudi to open the Hollywood Bowl season on 12 July 1949. He then spent a month at Alma with baby Smithy, who was now almost a year old, before his summer vacation had to be cut short (as his press release put it – presumably he could have said no) for a reunion with Furtwängler in Lucerne, where the Brahms Violin Concerto was recorded at the end of August. John Ardoin places it at the summit of their collaborations, calling it 'spacious, uncomplicated and even-tempered'. Yehudi's crusade on behalf of Furtwängler had run its course, and it was only in America that he was still ostracized. Their collaborations continued for another fruitful half-decade: Yehudi recorded with him the Mendelssohn (in 1952, with the Berlin Philharmonic), the Bartók Second Concerto and a second version of the Beethoven (both in 1953 with the Philharmonia). He and Furt-wängler appeared together in London early in October 1949 when the Vienna Philharmonic played a series of concerts in London to mark Goethe's bicentenary.

Yehudi might well have been reflecting on his need to identify a new extra-musical cause when, a few days earlier, in Berlin, he gave a fund-raising concert in aid of the city's new Free University. In a speech to the students he declared he was opposed to all manifestations of racism, an unexceptionable position which he was soon to back up with positive action in South Africa. He also organized a concert with Berlin's Staatskapelle Orchestra in the Russian Zone, as if to emphasize that he was not going to toe the political line of the West. But after his five-day visit, which involved a recording of the Tchaikovsky Concerto with the rising conducting star Ferenc Fricsay, he was warmly thanked by the US High Commissioner James McCloy. He wrote expressing gratitude for all Yehudi had done 'over the past three years as a cultural representative of your country'.

The autumn days were lived at exceptionally high pressure. Between Berlin and his London concert with Furtwängler he squeezed in a recital in Zurich, on 30 September, at which he and Louis Kentner gave the world première of the Sonata he had commissioned from William Walton. The composer took it away for revisions before the first London performance the following year. That second première, on 5 February 1949, was somewhat marred by a bizarre choice of location, the Theatre Royal, Drury Lane, a splendid setting during the week for the musical *Oklahoma!* but much too large for Sunday evening chamber music. The two-movement Sonata was later said by the composer to have been a 'dead flop' at its London première (which he had not attended) but this was characteristic of Walton's self-deprecating humour. Two days later he wrote from Ischia to one of the Sonata's dedicatees, Griselda Kentner:

We are delighted and rapturous that the Sonata went so well and too sorry we weren't there to hear the marvellous performance, (we've had eye-witness accounts of that from others not only yourselves) of the wonderful work – it was those three extra bars in the coda that worked it!

Why a third movement, a five-minute *Scherzetto*, was dropped from the Sonata has never been satisfactorily explained, although the canny Walton is said to have decided that two movements was all Yehudi should get for his 2000 Swiss francs. According to another note from Walton to Griselda Kentner the fee was £1000, which surely warranted a middle movement.

The critics' response to the Sonata was one of qualified rapture. Both musicians played from the music – a contrast to their 1948 Edinburgh Festival Beethoven cycle for which they had memorized all ten sonatas. Yehudi's playing was at times 'strained and rough' according to Mosco Carner in *Time and Tide*, while Desmond Shawe-Taylor in the *New Statesman* said he played 'with firm mastery but a curiously puzzled air'. Nevertheless the musical world can be grateful to Menuhin for having commissioned the Sonata. Walton's biographer, Michael Kennedy, described it as 'one of its creator's greatest works by virtue of its sustained invention and mastery of the violin's expressive capacity'. Any disappointment at its première – and the present writer, then a teenager, remembers only the excitement occasioned by the broadcast of a brand new work by Walton – could perhaps be explained by a nightmare Atlantic flight Yehudi had endured a week earlier on his journey to London. He had been engaged by the *Daily Telegraph* – the newspaper that had published Yehudi's correspondence with Elgar fifteen years previously – to play the Elgar Concerto (and the Mendelssohn) at an Albert Hall charity concert to raise funds to build a lecture room at the composer's birthplace.

The flight turned into one of the nightmare journeys that punctuate Diana's memoirs. The Menuhins had boarded a plane in New York two and a half days earlier, only to be disembarked and told to return next morning by which time a fault would have been rectified. The extra evening in Manhattan gave them the opportunity of hearing a Heifetz concert, so the day was far from wasted. Next morning the plane was three hours out over the Atlantic when an engine failed ('through our porthole we saw the impotent blades of one engine hanging like a disused windmill') and they returned to La Guardia. Another plane – a Boeing Stratocruiser, nicknamed by Diana the 'Pregnant Cow' – was wheeled out and after refuelling in 'one of those wild and lonely Canadian airports with ornithological names' (Goose Bay or Gander), they touched down next morning at Shannon. Yehudi was due to perform that evening at 8 p.m. but London, they learned, was shrouded in fog. Unperturbed, he practised for several hours in the airport manager's office while a smaller Aer Lingus plane was chartered from Dublin. It never arrived but at 3.15 the London weather had improved sufficiently for the Stratocruiser to depart, only for it to come to a dead stop at the end of the runway: its radio had broken down. Another attempt at 4.15 was more successful and news of Menuhin's delayed flight, at last on its way, was carried in the Stop Press column of London's evening papers. But once airborne the captain announced that London was again closed because of fog and the plane would be obliged to divert to Manston, a former RAF base in

East Kent. The plane touched down at 5.56 – reportedly the first commercial airliner ever to land there.

Yehudi and Diana made a rapid exit down the emergency escape chute; customs formalities were waived and the 8 p.m. concert deadline still seemed possible to achieve. But fog descended on the road and it was so chilly that Diana took off her fur coat and wrapped it around Yehudi's violin. The chauffeured car was obliged to creep up to London, finally arriving outside the hall at 8.50. Photographers were waiting to snap Yehudi leaping out, an airline luggage label attached to the lapel of his jacket. A few minutes later, still in his lounge suit but minus the label, he was on the platform playing the Mendelssohn Concerto, to be followed by the Elgar. The concert was being broadcast, so in order to keep the audience cheerful its conductor, Sir Adrian Boult, had switched the programme order and conducted the *Enigma Variations*. 'As we are without our Hamlet,' Boult had told his anxious listeners, 'we shall have the Symphony first.' Yehudi loved such adventures.

The year 1950 proved to be yet another whirlwind for the Menuhins: 5 continents visited in 5 months; 75 separate flights; 147 concerts – and very little time spent in Alma with young Gerard, who inevitably grew closer to his new nurse, Schwester Marie from Switzerland, than to his own parents.

The nature of his Jewishness was looming large in his mind. The independent state of Israel, declared in May 1948, had been fighting for its life ever since. Jews everywhere, but particularly in America, felt obliged to take a position concerning the Zionist movement. Yehudi's father was among the small minority who had vehemently opposed the creation of a national state, preferring the alternative of assimilation which since his student days had seemed a genuinely realizable dream. Had Moshe maintained close relations with his fellow students at the Herzlia Gymnasium, many of whom became leaders of the new Israeli state, he might well have been invited to serve that country in a political role, even (if we are to accept the optimistic assertion of his grandson, Lionel Rolfe) as an ambassador. Instead Moshe, an American citizen since 1919, retreated to his six-acre estate, cultivated his garden of fruit and vegetables, and for over thirty years poured scorn on the way Israel was developing.

Something of his extreme hostility towards Zionism undoubtedly brushed off on to Yehudi, who despite his mild manner always liked to provoke a storm. Had he not married outside his faith for a second time? And had he not contracted to play a concert in Manchester on the first evening of Yom Kippur? When apprised of his mistake he hastily rescheduled his performance to take place before sundown on that day (2 October 1949), accepting a sharply reduced fee, but the damage was done: the charity that had engaged him (of all unlikely beneficiaries the Motor and Cycle Trades Benevolent Fund) lost half its expected revenue.

Despite his name, which meant 'the Jew', Yehudi was simply not Jewish enough in the eyes of his critics. He had made the mistake of adopting an untenable position on the Furtwängler affair: in Jewish law it was for the victim alone to forgive a crime, and neither Yehudi nor members of his family had personally been victims of the Nazis. Yehudi must have felt that he needed to embrace once again his Jewish inheritance, as he had already done so eloquently in Berlin in 1947. To that end he accepted a proposal to visit Israel. He had already given several benefit concerts in the US in aid of the new state and had been invited to perform there with the Israel Philharmonic, the orchestra founded in 1936 as the Palestine Symphony and conducted in its inaugural season by Arturo Toscanini. But after the Furtwängler fracas in 1949 the orchestra's management withdrew its invitation – somewhat timorously, one might think, since Yehudi and his Israeli manager Baruch Gillon were given no opportunity to argue their case. Yehudi was obliged to make do with an extended recital tour, but this at least enabled him to renew his commitment to the people of his own faith.

But he must also have felt growing within him a contradictory message, a sense of being above the divisions of religion as well as of nationalism, of wishing to speak through his music-making to the entire world. Within the space of less than three years he visited the intensely Catholic South America, the brash melting-pot of Australia, humiliated Japan (predominantly Buddhist) and mysterious India (both Hindu and Muslim). What he saw of the world reinforced his instinctive belief in tolerance. He began to see himself as some sort of spiritual ambassador, with a duty to speak out against injustice wherever he found it.

It would have come as no surprise to his friends, therefore, when Yehudi turned a visit to South Africa in February 1950 (his first for fifteen years, undertaken two months before the Israel tour) into a stand against the evil of apartheid, a topic that had recently been brought to the world's attention by Alan Paton in his powerful novel of two families, *Cry the Beloved Country*. As soon as he arrived, Yehudi looked up the phone number in the Johannesburg telephone directory to invite himself to play for the black boys who were inmates of Diepkloof Reformatory, the school of which Paton had been Director for thirteen years. Paton himself was away in Europe preparing the film version of his book, but no less a figure than the reforming Anglican priest Father Trevor Huddleston drove Diana and Yehudi out to Diepkloof next day. Soon after the Boer War Mahatma Gandhi had been kept prisoner in Diepkloof's grim surroundings but Paton had had the barbed wire pulled down and replaced by geraniums.

Yehudi's short concert was held outdoors in the compound. An old upright piano was perched on the narrow veranda for Marcel Gazelle's accompaniments and the reform school boys – five hundred of them, lined up in rows – squatted on their haunches in the sunshine while Yehudi played some of the most popular music in his repertoire. Showpieces by Sarasate and Kreisler are fun to hear no matter what the listener's cultural background, but how – as a reporter asked – do you translate *Caprice viennois* into Xosa, or Zulu, or Sotho?

Another journalist waxed lyrical as he described what must have been a magical hour for Yehudi:

Across the path in the trees the doves, coming home under the setting sun, cooed in bewilderment and then settled down to sleep to a strange new lullaby. A hawk, silhouetted in the sunset, hovered.

Then Menuhin and his listeners exchanged roles and the Zulu children sang a Xos hymn to the white visitors, 'We are on the Way': 'They stood and chanted in that deep resonant way they have . . . very moving and very impressive.' 'That convinced me there is music in these people,' commented Yehudi, before he and Diana looked over the boys' quarters and heard for themselves how apartheid affected blacks and Zulus in the townships. Yehudi likened conditions to those in his own country, in the Deep South.

It was a private visit but somebody had told the press, and photographs appeared next morning in the leading newspapers. The South African tour manager was furious. By adding an extra concert Yehudi was breaking his contract. 'I suggested', wrote Yehudi,

that he must be talking nonsense, for black Africans, certainly black African boys, could not attend my concerts. 'Or can they?' I added innocently.

'Of course not!' he said indignantly, neatly falling into the trap.

'Well then,' I said, 'I'll arrange to give duplicate concerts for the Africans on the mornings of my regular concerts.'

The City Hall was the chosen venue: blacks and whites could still use the same premises, if at different times, and Johannesburg's Jewish mayor gave Yehudi enthusiastic support. He also supplied the municipal orchestra for a concert in a shanty settlement when Yehudi returned to Johannesburg a month later. 'As we drove out to the church,' wrote Trevor Huddleston, 'he turned and said, "Remember, Father, it was the Negro jazz band which first broke the colour bar in America."' Four years later Huddleston formed his own jazz band – after Yehudi's words had come back to him 'with strange and persistent force . . . I had caught from Menuhin the vision of African jazz bands as a way to freedom.'

Yehudi arrived in the township of Sophiatown at the height of a storm that had turned the streets into a swamp. The Church of Christ the King, with its beautiful paintings, was, wrote the *Johannesburg Star*, 'an island of warmth and happy expectation in a grey world'. Yehudi's short programme for an audience of schoolchildren and parishioners of the Anglican mission was much the same as he had given on scores of occasions for British factory workers and the US army during the war. He opened with Handel's *Prayer* and closed with Schubert's *Ave Maria*. 'The audience's "thank you" for each piece drowned the thunder,' noted the *Star*'s reporter.

In the evening came a concerto concert which Yehudi was to describe in his autobiography as 'one of the most affecting of my life'. He remembered it as taking place in Sophiatown but the actual venue was a community centre in the nearby township of Orlando. 'This was the happiest, most informal public occasion of the violinist's visit,' wrote the *Star*. 'The evening was one of sheer delight.' Yehudi, dubbed 'The Maestro', sat in the audience and cheered a local school choir of some eighty voices and their dynamic choirmaster Mr Malanda, who tuned up his choir beforehand as if it were an orchestra. 'Then with each section a perfect instrument the children sang enchanting sere-nades. The orchestra [the Johannesburg City Orchestra] was so moved that the players gave a present to the choir.' Then came the concertos, Bach and Mendelssohn. Yehudi played them 'joyously and superbly'. The reporter noted that the unrehearsed speeches that followed also had a musical quality. Yehudi remembered that they were delivered by black Africans who spoke in flawless English. 'It was from nobility of heart that Mr Menuhin came to us,' said the school supervisor. 'It is because of the immense humanity in him – a humanity you felt in his playing.' The compère, Mr K. V. Mngoma, chairman of the local music society, added his thanks: 'It is best that we should say, "Umgadinwa nangomso", which means "Do not be tired of us; come again" . . . and now we will all sing 'Nkosi Sikelele' as we have never sung it before.' After this song, which was the equivalent of 'God Bless Africa' and is now one of the South African National Anthems, they sang the less often heard Sesuto anthem, 'Morena Boloka Sechaba Sa Heso' ('God Save Our Race'). The singing had an electrifying effect, Yehudi recalled; it was as if the French had sung 'La Marseillaise' in Nazi-occupied Paris. The African spokesmen said that if they had been in charge of their own affairs, they would have made the occasion one for the giving of gifts of gold and silver to mark its importance. Instead they hoped the visitors would accept the traditional African greeting – at which point they hung the bead necklace of a chief around Yehudi's neck and went out into the audience to give his wife a circlet of beads that is the prerogative of a chief's wife.

'I get a greater intensity of feeling in my playing when I play for African natives,' he told the American columnist Leonard Lyons. He encouraged the local professional musicians to return to the townships to give lessons to young Africans – a pre-echo, as it were, of the educational activity for the underprivileged that he was to inaugurate in Britain in 1977 with the Live Music Now! organization. Yehudi's concert management remained implacably opposed to his extra-mural activities and soon there was a face-to-face confrontation. 'We shall have to sue you,' said the boss.

You have given all these concerts without any permission from us. You are in clear breach of contract. We find this situation quite unacceptable and must ask you to forfeit your fees.

There was no moral justification whatever for such an action, Yehudi retorted: he would make sure the world knew the whole story. And according to Diana he threatened to forward any writ they issued by express mail to the London *Daily Mirror*. He then marched out, slamming the door behind him. He was proud of this rare outburst of rage, likening it in his memoirs to the time when Toscanini tore the telephone out of its wall-mounting after the ringing bell had thrice interrupted their rehearsal. Moreover the display of anger made his South African management think again. He was a big earner, after all, and when the Menuhins reached Cape Town a representative was waiting to apologize. Yehudi was paid his earnings, a sizeable sum, which he promptly deposited in a local bank prior to transfer to his San Francisco account.

He then attended a parliamentary debate on the controversial Population Registration Bill in the company of William Blumberg, a Jewish opposition member and former mayor of Cape Town, who translated the Afrikaans to Yehudi as they sat in the public gallery. The extreme views of the supporters of apartheid appalled him. 'He got so excited', a report in the London *Observer* noted, 'that he had to be warned by a parliamentary messenger that if he leaned too far through the rail he might fall out.' When an opposition speaker attacked the bill, 'Yehudi Menuhin startled the House with a burst of clapping and a cry of "Bravo".' Fearing an incident, Diana called out, 'Come on quick', and dragged her husband up the gallery stairs to a long corridor where they came face to face with a furious warden demanding they leave the place forthwith.

'I can't wait,' said Yehudi, and he walked with great dignity down the red-carpeted corridor, the only drawback to his splendid exit being that he was clad in carpet slippers.

He was suffering from blisters caused by an over-long walk the previous day. When he returned to his hotel he was informed by his bank that the transfer of his funds to the US had been suspended.

No doubt because of the friendship he and Diana struck up with the veteran statesman General Smuts, the money eventually came through. (Yehudi was allowed back into South Africa six years later.) At the time of their meeting, J. C. Smuts was in his eightieth year. He had retired from his country's premiership two years previously and was an enormously respected figure in world politics. Despite his country's determination to push through the doctrine of apartheid, Smuts went out of his way to praise Yehudi for having played in the townships earlier in his tour. He died before the year was out.

Increasingly Yehudi saw himself in this ambassadorial role and wherever he went he sought out the company of the truly great (and the outstandingly good) such as General de Gaulle in wartime London, Mrs Eleanor Roosevelt in New York and the high commissioners of the four occupying powers in post-war Berlin. He had been dining at life's high table since his boyhood and Diana was no stranger to this world either. Within the year the Menuhins were to strike up enduring friendships with the President of Israel, Chaim Weizmann (and his wife Vera) and with the Prime Minister of India, Pandit Nehru.

On his way to Israel from South Africa, Yehudi made a stop-over in Italy. On 9 April 1950 he inaugurated (with unaccompanied Bach) a so-called 'temple of music' in the sixteenth-century Church of San Lorenzo, just outside Assisi. It had been restored by an eccentric Bostonian, Mary Lowell, the widow of the rich British Lord Berkeley. Then he travelled down to Rome, where he gave another recital before heading out to Fiumicino airport to catch his plane for Tel Aviv.

The concert had been sold out and among those unable to get tickets was the airport's chief customs officer. As Yehudi was passing through emigration formalities this gentleman, who was unknown to Yehudi, detained him for what he said were routine questions. 'What have you got in that case?' he demanded. Yehudi explained that it contained his Stradivarius. He was invited to open up and sure enough a violin was revealed. (In wartime years the case, designed to carry two violins, might also have contained caviare from Moscow, smoked salmon from Goose Bay or nylons from New York.)

'Who are you?' the inspector asked sternly.

'I am Yehudi Menuhin.'

'Oh, yes!' the inspector retorted. 'All violin smugglers say they are Yehudi Menuhin.'

Yehudi produced his passport but the inspector said coolly. 'They all have forged documents. If you really are Yehudi Menuhin, prove it.'

Yehudi took out his Stradivarius and played the ever popular *Caprice Viennoise*, appropriately lightweight stuff, he thought, for an audience that by now consisted of all the other customs officers on duty plus several hundred rapt bystanders. The customs inspector still appeared unconvinced.

'Signore, you play well,' he said, 'but not well enough for Yehudi Menuhin. I happen to know that Menuhin plays Bach sonatas for solo violin. Let us hear you play Bach.'

Yehudi felt he had no choice but to comply. When he had finished there were wild shouts of 'Bravo' from all sides. The inspector apologized profusely for his mistake, thanked Yehudi, and, as he accompanied him to the plane, whispered,

Caro Signore Menuhin, it was a set-up – for a bet. There are hundreds of music students in Rome who could not get tickets for your concert last night. Neither could some of us in the customs office. So, knowing that you were flying out tonight, we staged a little drama! We're so happy that we succeeded! God bless you! And please forgive us.

The story appears in Moshe's family memoirs and no doubt contains a grain or two of truth.

Yehudi's first visit to Israel was genuinely dangerous. Menachem Begin, the terrorist leader (who many years later became Israel's prime minister) had reportedly sent a threatening cable the previous year to Baruch Gillon: 'If the traitor Menuhin comes to Israel we will kill him as we killed Bernadotte last year.' (Folke Bernadotte, the UN's Swedish mediator during the Israeli war of independence, was assassinated in September 1948.) Yehudi wired back:

Precisely because I played in Berlin I wish to play in Israel. As to threats, they cannot put me off. If there are people who wish to hear me, I'll come and play.

The Furtwängler scandal, as Jews who took a hard line on the issue saw it, was on everybody's lips when Yehudi and Diana touched down at Lod airport near Tel Aviv early one April morning in 1950, to be greeted as they descended from the plane by a crowd in which Hephzibah Nicholas's seemed the only friendly face. Hephzibah had flown from Australia to partner Yehudi on the tour – their first collaboration for three years. The hostility came from Israeli journalists and demonstrators who were primed with the attitudes of the Berlin DP camp leader Jonas of Lemberg. They wanted to interrogate Yehudi there and then in the aircraft hangar but were 'conjured away' by the promise of a press conference the following day.

First there was a reunion to be held with family relatives, among them Moshe's sister Mussia, a half-sister, Vera, and a nephew, Paul. Moshe and Marutha had not so much lost touch as refused to recognize them. 'It was the first time we realized we weren't Adam and Eve,' Yehudi told his biographer nephew, Lionel Rolfe. 'We had relatives, just like other people. That was a tremendous relief.' Yehudi admitted he had been fed by his mother on a diet of 'semi-mystical forebears'; the real flesh-and-blood cousins he encountered were musical instrument makers or worked on farms and in the tourist industry. The Menuhins were also given news of Marutha's father, Nachum, who had returned from the US in his old age to live in Jerusalem.

Moshe made no mention of the renewal of family ties in his own account of Yehudi's visit to Israel. In particular he hated his sister Mussia (Mooshkeh) because of her treatment of their younger sister Shandel who had committed suicide. Moshe had cut loose from his family when he emigrated in 1913. But Yehudi and Hephzibah were setting foot for the first time on the soil of their parents' youth. The Promised Land, Yehudi wrote, had been 'part of the landscape of my imagination . . . looming in the family pre-history'. To a journalist in the Hebrew-language newspaper *Haaretz*, he described the visit as 'a meeting of heritage . . . a realization of a dream, confirmation of his roots and identity'.

First impressions of Israel were of a land of tension. Food was in short supply; life for the newly arrived settlers was hard, and the visit began in the floodlight of controversy with armed guards keeping vigil outside the Menuhins' bedrooms in the 'cramped little old Palestinian hotel . . . a remnant of the British "Raj"' (Diana's description) where they lodged in Tel Aviv. Questions had already been asked in the Knesset about the propriety of selling concert tickets in aid of somebody who had recently played for the Germans. More angry questions were posed at the press conference but under Diana's influence – she had talked things through with him at the hotel the previous evening – Yehudi went out of his way to offer olive branches to the Jews of Israel: 'I was born a Jew and have remained a Jew,' he told the United Press agency. 'If I had not wanted to remain one I could have changed my name. I come over to Israel to identify myself with the Jew again.'

I may have inadvertently reopened old wounds and caused pain. This I regret most deeply, and I offer my apologies to all those whom I may have hurt. But [and here the familiar, obstinate Yehudi reasserts himself] I cannot renounce the principles by which I live.

For the Menuhins' opening recital, cars were banned from the vicinity of the Ohel Shem concert hall for fear of bomb outrages; the audience was searched for guns and grenades, and soldiers patrolled inside as the brother and sister played. Fifteen hundred people, paying the equivalent of $14 a ticket, crowded into the hall. Once the Menuhins' music-making had been heard in the flesh, doubts and recriminations melted away and what Yehudi called 'a climate of unambiguous good will' soon prevailed. The armed guards were withdrawn from subsequent events. The duo was scheduled to give fourteen concerts and

ended up playing twenty-five, several of them in hospitals and collective farms. At the Ein Gev kibbutz, on the eastern shore of Lake
Tiberias, ten thousand people were said to have turned out. Later
Yehudi stood on a hillside and watched the lights of the trucks taking
his listeners, whom he identified as 'peasants', back to their communities. The starry night inspired him to new heights of romanticism
concerning the nature of work:

After a hard day in the fields, in the workshops, or on guard, they had come from
as far as Upper Samaria and Galilee to attend our concert . . . I stood there realizing that I was watching an entirely new type of peasant folk . . . If the peasant
[elsewhere in the world] could combine a scientific treatment of his tasks with a
powerful attachment to the soil and a strong urge for art and intellectual pursuits,
then he may achieve what is happening in Israel.

Like so many other visitors, the Menuhins admired the pioneer spirit
of the new state, its dynamism and energy. It prompted brother and
sister to reassert their Jewishness and to remind their critics of how
they had both raised substantial sums for Jewish charities. References
in the Western press to a boycott of his concerts by concentration
camp survivors were hotly denied. Yehudi pointed out that the mayors
of the towns where he played had already accepted invitations to
attend before he left Europe. 'Israel is the most tolerant country I
have ever visited,' he informed the *Jewish Chronicle* in London.
Accustomed to fame as a musician, he found himself approached 'by
rabbis with fur coats and side locks whose appraisal of me was one of
deep respect – not for me personally but for the fact that I am descended
from a famous line of distinguished rabbis'. He enjoyed the mix of
people among the pioneers, their 'range of background, temperament,
intelligence and opinions'. He loved the absence of cynicism:

The people everywhere are working, building . . . No one talks of money, of taxes,
only of plans for improvement in their towns, their settlements. No one complains
about rations. This completely different approach to life is so refreshing to the
spirit that it gives one a fresh impetus and faith in life.

At the end of his tour he was diplomacy personified: 'I am leaving my
sister Hephzibah here for another fourteen days,' he told journalists,
'and my heart for ever.'

The clearest sign of official approval was a visit to Israel's White
House at Rehovot, the home of President Chaim Weizmann and his
Russian-born wife Vera. Weizmann was a former British citizen who

had taught biochemistry at Manchester University before the First World War. An ardent Zionist, and one of the architects of the state of Israel, he was seventy-six and soon to suffer a debilitating heart attack. As his failing health meant he was too frail to attend public concerts, the Menuhins played for him informally. They also attended several private lunches where they met the scholar–general Moshe Dayan, a hero of the liberation war and famous for his black eye-patch.

Yehudi found Weizmann closer to his own liberal way of thinking than he had anticipated. His wife, too, being a member of a rich emancipated Russian-Jewish family, was entirely without the extremist, proselytizing attitude towards Zionism that so antagonized Moshe Menuhin. (Ironically, a fellow luncheon guest was Moshe Sharrett, the Foreign Minister, who had been at school with Yehudi's father.) The President's besetting fear, Diana reported, was not of the Arab enemies who surrounded the infant state. It was that the Jew, at last in possession of his national home and thrust into such active tasks as building, farming and fighting,

would lose his essential characteristics . . . his awareness, his intellect, his drive and passionate need to rise above danger and endemic persecution . . . his determination to reach the highest possible position in whatever task, whatever profession he uses his brain.

Forever the optimist, Yehudi wrote in the 1996 revised edition of his memoirs that on balance Weizmann was wrong to have entertained the fear

that the opportunities for action offered by the new state . . . might sap the strength of Jewish excellence in scholarship, philosophy, music, the abstract accomplishments of the Diaspora . . . The founding of the state not only opened up new paths but fuelled a tremendous upsurge in artistic activity and other traditional modes of Jewish expression.

As a practical endorsement of the new state's artistic enterprise, the Menuhins purchased several paintings by the Israeli artist Moshe Castel. Before Yehudi departed he was invited to return the following season to play with the Israel Philharmonic, but conflicting engagements delayed his début with the orchestra until 1955. His second visit, in April 1951, lasted eighteen days. With Robert Levin as his accompanist he played twenty-three recitals, eleven of them for charitable causes.

The month of June 1950 found Yehudi in Vienna. As a renowned performer of Bach's violin works he was invited to appear at a major festival marking the bicentenary of Bach's death. He gave two recitals with Louis Kentner, and at the opening symphony concert played the Double Concerto with Wolfgang Schneiderhan. Herbert von Karajan directed from the harpsichord. The idea of conducting while playing an instrument must have lodged in Yehudi's mind as a more appropriate activity for himself than the 'maestro' type of conducting he had undertaken three years earlier in Dallas. Only days later he had the opportunity to try it out for himself when the conductor Hans Knappertsbusch cancelled at short notice and Yehudi, violin under his chin, led the Vienna Philharmonic in performances of the First Brandenburg Concerto and the E major Violin Concerto. The Concerto's *Adagio* movement was reportedly the emotional highpoint of the evening and Menuhin was universally praised for his sympathetic artistry.

A newspaper article pictures Kentner, Menuhin and their wives grouped around an upright piano with Diana holding Gerard in her arms for the benefit of the photographer, although at almost two he was clearly a hefty bundle. Diana had seen very little of her son over the previous six months, what with the concerts in England in late January and then the tours of South Africa and Israel. The reunion was sweet. She wrote that 'no one who has not been separated again and again from a very small child can know the yearning and the excitement'. The boy had a double adjustment to make over the next few weeks: getting to know his parents again and adjusting to a new nurse. (Schwester Marie had resigned but reclaimed her post a year later after she attended a recital in Berne and learned from Yehudi that Diana was pregnant again. She stayed with the family for another decade.) The Menuhins took over the annexe of a big hotel in Bad Gastein. Zamira (eleven) and Krov (ten) joined them for their annual summer holiday and although Yehudi still practised and studied new works, the holiday, Diana remembered, offered

picnics in the woods, long walks up the forested hills, glorious Austrian food, lots of reading in French and German, excursions to Salzburg for heavenly music and that ravishing countryside that is Austria's blessing.

But the respite was brief: in September Yehudi travelled yet again to Berlin before launching his North Atlantic autumn season in Montreal.

The sudden death, in late October, of Diana's mother prompted only a brief pause in what she described as her 'breathless, non-analysing pursuit' of her husband's artistic aspirations. Elsewhere she joked that she began to feel 'like some buckle-kneed Rosinante wearily carrying her Don Quixote forward to the next windmill'. Nothing, it seemed, could dissuade him from undertaking the annual visit to the Hollywood Bowl, the arduous but lucrative American tours, the recordings in London and everywhere the conquest of new audiences. Contemplating the loss of her mother, Diana said she felt dislocated, 'wobbling precariously' between her past heritage, which she craved for desperately, and her current nomadic life. At least they could spend Christmas *en famille* at Los Gatos. Yehudi played Bartók's Second Concerto in San Francisco one day and Father Christmas at Alma the next: his son burst out crying when he saw Yehudi dressed up in red and disguised behind a mass of cottonwool. But all too soon it was time to fly away again.

Yehudi was off to North Africa and inevitably Diana went with him. There were concerts in Casablanca, Marrakesh, Oran and Tangier and then an all-but-disastrous drive south back for a final recital in Casablanca. *En route* their hired station wagon got stuck after a flash flood obliterated the road. Marooned on the running board a desperate Yehudi was recognized – his fame had carried, it seemed, even to Spanish Morocco. Recounting the adventure to a friend Diana explained that

a bright little Jewish boy among the Arabs had first picked him out. Within a few minutes the entire Jewish population of the Arab village was surrounding Yehudi and asking for autographs. The local head of the Alliance Israélite Universel (the society to which Yehudi donated the proceeds of his only Paris concert last autumn and which serves Oriental Jews in North African countries) escorted Yehudi to the police station where, thanks to the chief of police, the only truck in the village was sent to load our car – with the back wheels hanging precariously over the edge. Fortifying us with loaves of bread and salami the entire village escorted us to the flood. Amid whoops and hurrahs and blown kisses we plunged and splashed through the water, hanging on to the truck, for it was thought too dangerous to stay inside the station wagon, whose back wheels were fastened by tattered rags to the extreme flap of the truck. We finally arrived at the French Moroccan border dirty and dishevelled and arousing tremendous envy in the frustrated breasts of some dozen carloads of stranded tourists. Yehudi played a grand concert immediately after our arrival.

In the spring of 1951, after his triumphant return to Israel, Yehudi and Hephzibah gave the very first recital, on 6 May, in the new Royal Festival Hall in London. It was an immensely popular event. Hephzibah's husband's home movie (shot from the wings) reveals that additional seating brought members of the overflow audience on to the platform only a few feet from the performers. But Yehudi was not impressed. The hall's acoustic was too dry for his taste (and nearly everybody else's) and he pointed out a serious design fault for soloists: the concert platform was only a foot higher than the public exit it adjoined, which meant that 'the performer coming back onstage to make his bow was screened from half the house by people streaming out to catch their last bus home'. The stage was later raised but Yehudi remained critical. He never liked entering a hall from the side: it meant he could not look at the public as he made his way to centre stage. He preferred venues like Carnegie Hall where the artist walks in from the back. Writing in 1996 he dismissed the Royal Festival Hall as 'still calculated to reduce a concert to a street incident'.

In June 1951 the Menuhins travelled to Australia for symphony concerts and more duo recitals with Hephzibah. Diana was five months pregnant but clearly reluctant to take a back seat when it came to newspaper interviews; she probably felt obliged to make a strong showing as the woman who had displaced a Melbourne girl as Yehudi's wife. Within days of arriving she was castigating the Australians (at a press reception) for their horrible accents. It was Yehudi's turn to quieten things down – by taking up with journalists the anodyne subject of violin maintenance. 'He uses dry rice to clean his Strad' was a typical, sleep-inducing headline.

Twice a week he puts a handful of dry rice into the inside of his Strad, shakes it around and pours it out again through the F-holes. 'It brings out a tremendous amount of dirt,' he said. 'The vibrations of playing shake a lot of dust and resin into the violin.'

This was hardly the sort of stuff to set Sydney harbour on fire. In another interview Diana, who had been a dancer for fifteen years before she married, announced provocatively that most ballet bored her. And she ticked her husband off in public for being too generous.

'Always he gives his money away,' she said. 'A young violinist must go to Europe? Yehudi wants to pay. Special lessons for a young lady who fiddles? Yehudi must pay. Always Yehudi must pay. He is the most generous man in the world – and the most lovable.'

While Diana rested with Gerard at Lindsay Nicholas's ranch, where a breeding herd of Angus cattle had been added to the vast flock of sheep, Hephzibah and Yehudi visited New Zealand. 'It has been the most tremendous thrill to be together again after so many years and we are loving every moment of it,' she told the radio station 3ZB in Christchurch.

We've laughed so much we couldn't have been sensible before lunch . . . Last Sunday we spent the day tramping the Tinakori Hills. Wellington looked lovely from the heights . . . But I love Christchurch, too [she was quick to add]. It's such a restful place.

For Yehudi the most important event in New Zealand had nothing to do with either tramping or music. Sitting in an Auckland osteopath's reception room waiting for his sister to complete a massage, he came across a book about yoga. He knew nothing about the subject but was instantly struck, 'with the force of a revelation', as he put it, that a study of yoga could point a way to further comprehension of violin playing. After working on his *asanas* – the name given to the various bodily postures of hatha yoga – he thought he might also be able to fulfil a childhood longing to walk on his hands. He borrowed the book and spent the rest of the week practising in hotel bedrooms,

finding much pleasure in exercises which demanded no strain but on the contrary inner quietness, which were neither aggressive nor competitive but [were] to be done in solitude, which required no equipment but a few feet of floor space.

Yehudi's forthcoming visit to India, already being planned, proved most serendipitous because it enabled him to meet yoga practitioners of the highest quality. Once learned, the exercises were practised for the rest of his life.

After less than two weeks at home in California (and even those few days were interrupted by concerts in Philadelphia and the Hollywood Bowl, where he donated his fee to help save the Bowl from property developers) Yehudi set off on his first tour of Japan. In her eighth month of pregnancy, Diana drew the line at travelling with him. On the long Pacific flight with Japan Airlines he unpacked a kimono and passed the hours alternately sleeping and learning to use chopsticks, leaving his wife, as she wrote, in an 'agony of loneliness and fear'.

Yehudi was the most famous Western classical musician to visit the country since 1941 and Pearl Harbor. The Far East region was still no easy option for travellers: the Americans and their allies were waging war in nearby Korea and it was feared that Communist China might soon be drawn into the fray. Only a year earlier Yehudi had been commended by an American general in Berlin as an ideal ambassador and, according to Diana, he went to Japan at the personal invitation of General MacArthur. But by the time of Yehudi's arrival that bellicose warrior had been removed by President Truman and replaced by General Ridgway, who duly attended Yehudi's first recital in Tokyo on 18 September.

Japan could hardly be expected to awake in Yehudi the same sense of mission that had led him to visit Belsen within two months of its liberation. This was his first visit to Japan, a projected tour in 1940 having been cancelled after the European war broke out, and he had no inkling of the language. Despite his ambassadorial inclinations this was essentially a commercial affair. There was a pressing need for cash to pay Nola's alimony as well as to finance his family commitments and his support for good causes in other parts of the world. His box-office appeal was not in doubt: all tickets for his five Tokyo recitals were sold within four hours of going on sale at the end of July. During a five-week tour he and Adolph Baller visited the four major islands and gave twenty recitals, five each in Tokyo and Osaka, and others in Nagoya, Kyoto, Okayama, Ube, Sasebo and Fukuoka. He also appeared in five symphony concerts, playing two concertos in each. To this crowded schedule must be added a two-day marathon for the Japanese Victor record company, fixed up at short notice, during which over 140 minutes of music were recorded. According to the expert Eric Wen, 'there is no trace of unsteadiness or fatigue in the violinist's technical powers and the records display his expressive musicianship to full measure' – proof that Yehudi could still deliver the goods when the mood was upon him, although the results were never issued in the West during his lifetime.

His public utterances in Japan were cautious, apolitical and frankly banal, showing nothing of the desire to shock and run against the grain that had become part of his charm elsewhere. Japanese audiences, he told a *Chicago News* reporter, were the best in the world: 'They don't cough, sneeze, scrape their feet or rustle their programmes.' A message on the back of the concert tickets formally enjoined the public to avoid such behaviour, but Yehudi probably didn't know that. He said he found the Japanese lack of assertiveness most pleasing: 'It gives the artist a feeling of aloneness which is very helpful.' But he added that no artist wants to feel alone when he has finished his performance and for that reason he was glad when listeners in Osaka 'did everything to show their approval but whistle and stamp their feet'. He was polite about Japanese music, but unenthusiastic: 'Nothing is done without purpose in this country, where nothing is wasted and every atom of soil is cultivated . . . [but nevertheless Japanese classical music] gives me the impression of being accidental.' How different from his response to Indian music a few months later, and how different, too, from the reaction of his friend Benjamin Britten, whose Japanese visit in 1956 eventually inspired the opera *Curlew River*. Menuhin did not have time to attend a performance of the Nō theatre, as Britten was to do.

He flew back to California accompanied by a mountain of excess-baggage crates and packing cases. When he arrived a domestic crisis was in full flood: Diana was dissatisfied with the servants she had only recently hired and Yehudi was given the task of sacking them. With Yehudi scarcely pausing for breath (according to Diana) the cases were then unpacked and out fell

bolts of exquisite ancient brocade, roll after roll of silks and satins, an antique Japanese ceremonial robe in red, blue and green, complete with crêpe silk kimono to be worn underneath, obi, and satin slippers; vases, an ancient Chinese terracotta bull hauling a cart with enormous wheels, lacquer bowls and trays, bundles of ivory chopsticks, thick satin kerchiefs – the bedroom looked like a glorious bazaar.

Somehow Yehudi had found time in the midst of the music-making to carry out a shopping expedition on the grand scale and with it he won back his wife's sorely tested affections.

He had returned in the nick of time. Jeremy Menuhin was born at San Francisco's Stanford Hospital in the early hours of 2 November 1951. Diana was just ten days short of her thirty-ninth birthday.

Recommended Recordings

Walton: Sonata for violin and piano
with Louis Kentner (piano)
EMI 5 66122 2
Recorded: 8 May 1950, three months after the London première

Menuhin in Japan
BID LAB 162/163
Recorded: October 1951
The two CDs contain all the recordings YM made with Adoph Baller at the end of his Japanese tour (1: Bach: Sonata No. 1 in G minor and Partita No. 3 in E; Beethoven: 'Spring' Sonata; Tartini: 'The Devil's Trill'; 2: Beethoven: 'Kreutzer' Sonata; Bartók: Romanian Folk Dances, and many favourite encore pieces).

12 Discovery of India

The first yoga lesson with Mr B. K. S. Iyengar, Bombay, 1952

1952: first visit to India and subsequent support for cause of Indian music; 1953: revival of US reputation; decision to stop flying; 1954: first teaching sessions, at Fontainebleau; 1955: August: birth of Alexis, who died within an hour; October: rift with parents over publication of Robert Magidoff's biography; decision to leave Alma.

THERE WAS NO QUESTION of Yehudi suspending his concert tours in order to take extended paternity leave. Less than two months after the birth of his third son, Jeremy, he was on the road again – and with another of his discoveries. On 4 February 1952, he introduced his Carnegie Hall audience to a 'lost' concerto, for solo violin and strings in D minor, written by Mendelssohn when he was a boy of thirteen. Yehudi had been shown the manuscript in London the previous year by the rare-books dealer Albi Rosenthal, an amateur violinist who as a boy had heard Yehudi give his first concert in Munich, the anti-Semitic city where the Jewish child prodigy had insisted on playing Bloch's *Nigun*. Rosenthal was so thrilled, he remembers, that he persuaded his mother to take him next day to the kosher restaurant – in 1929 such a thing still existed in Munich – where his idol was eating with his parents. He had been too shy to approach Yehudi then, but in London a bond was established and they were to remain friends for life. Yehudi was enchanted by the manuscript and promptly bought it. Despite the burden of maintenance payments to Nola, his finances had been sufficiently restored by his Japanese tour to enable him to make another major purchase: his second Stradivarius, a legendary instrument known as the 'Soil'.

Mendelssohn's D minor Concerto was dedicated to the violinist Eduard Rietz, who was to lead the orchestra in Mendelssohn's historic performance of Bach's *St Matthew Passion*. (Other members of the Rietz family, the former owners of the manuscript, had been distinguished musical contemporaries of the composer.) Yehudi edited the Concerto for performance, had it published by Peters Edition and included it in his recitals for the following season. In a preface he professed to find significant parallels with Mendelssohn's great E minor Concerto:

Both are in the minor in a somewhat tumultuous mood. Both have written-out cadenzas for the second and third movements. A long passage of short notes in the finale resembles the passage before the recapitulation of the first movement in the E minor Concerto.

Yehudi noted admiringly the Schubertian modulations of the finale and the noble song of the slow movement, claiming that overall the concerto was full of invention and 'not in any way inhibited by too conventional concepts'.

A string band of fifteen musicians was recruited for the Carnegie Hall performance, the first occasion on which Yehudi directed an orchestra in his native city. (The players also accompanied Yehudi in an orchestral arrangement, by Hugo Kander, of Tartini's 'Devil's Trill' Sonata, a version violinists might find rewarding to revive.) In the *New York Times* Olin Downes admired the new Concerto's 'lively jesting finale in the gypsy style' while Louis Biancolli, in the *New York Sun*, found the whole work

utterly delightful. Its three movements are well made, crisp in form and variety of rhythm. They fairly burst with the sweet melodies that Mendelssohn seemed to shake from his coat sleeves even in his teens . . . Mr Menuhin deserves everybody's thanks for bringing the manuscript to the attention of the music world. Fellow violinists owe him a round of thanks for thus broadening a rather lean repertory.

This was Yehudi's most important act of restitution since his pre-war championship of the 'lost' Schumann Concerto, but fellow violinists cannot be said to have endorsed his discovery. Mendelssohn's D minor Concerto, composed soon after a visit to Goethe, does not quite qualify as a neglected masterpiece and it has not established a regular place in the repertoire. Yehudi loved it greatly and undertook three recordings. In the first, made in New York immediately after the première, he also conducted the RCA Victor string orchestra (his début on disk as a conductor). The second, made the following year, was with Sir Adrian Boult and the Philharmonia. The most recent, in 1971, was conducted by Rafael Frühbeck de Burgos. Menuhin still owned the manuscript at the time of his death.

At the end of February 1952 the Menuhins embarked on a tour of India which was to provide the extra-musical focus Yehudi had probably been seeking since the cooling down of the Furtwängler debate. The state of India had come into being in 1947. With remarkable prescience, the wife of the first British High Commissioner, Sir Archibald Nye, had suggested Yehudi's name to Pandit Nehru, India's Prime Minister, as the sort of artist who might help to build a bridge between Eastern and Western cultures. 'I have fulfilled a long cherished desire,' Yehudi told journalists waiting for him at New Delhi's airport. What attracted him to India, he added, with his customary diplomacy, was the gentle spirit and peace-loving nature of its people. At his first formal press conference he launched into a paean of praise for his new discovery – not Mendelssohn but yoga. He called it India's greatest gift to world culture. 'I have practised standing on my head for several years. I can control my breath for two minutes.' Yoga, he claimed, at once increased and indexed one's mental and physical potential:

It helps me to attain poise and balance. Lack of sleep, fatigue or bad thoughts are as effectively reflected during my performances of yogic exercises as in the nuances of my music.

Nehru took a personal interest in Yehudi's tour, and also in Diana; she must have seemed like a younger version of Edwina Mountbatten, with whom he had forged a close and still continuing friendship during the last Viceroy's tumultuous term of office. After Delhi, Yehudi was to give recitals in Bombay, Bangalore, Madras and Calcutta, before taking a holiday in Kashmir. He had offered in advance to donate his fees to Nehru's national famine relief fund and his hosts were determined to reciprocate his generosity by treating the Menuhins like visiting royalty. They found themselves on an itinerary similar to that arranged during the same period for Eleanor Roosevelt.

The ambitious plans for Yehudi's musical engagements had been made by Mehli Mehta, a Parsee from Bombay who before the war, as a young violinist and rare exponent of Western music, had put together an orchestra to accompany Anna Pavlova (Yehudi's idol) on her Indian tour of 1935. After the war a scholarship from Bombay's wealthy Parsee community had enabled Mehta to study the violin for four years at New York's Juilliard School with Ivan Galamian, and since his return home to his family he had run the modest Bombay Symphony Orchestra. Mehta agreed to organize Menuhin's entire tour in return for the chance to put on some benefit concerts in Bombay with Yehudi as soloist with his orchestra. At the preliminary rehearsal in Bombay before either Yehudi or the conductor arrived, Mehta played the violin solos and his son Zubin, then fifteen, took over the baton – the boy's very first experience as a conductor.

A state banquet in Delhi soon gave Diana an opportunity to make her mark on the social scene. Observing a bust of the Prime Minister, lit rather dramatically and decked out with fresh flowers, she asked, tongue in cheek, whether it was a shrine. Before their return the following day it had been removed. At the reception Nehru, who was born in Kashmir, talked with some bitterness about the departed British Raj. Diana bridled. 'I thought I was going to meet my first Kashmiri Brahmin,' she exclaimed in mock horror, 'and what do I find? An irascible British lawyer.' Nehru remained imperturbable. He had read Yehudi's boast in the newspapers that he could stand on his head and reminded his guests that the practice of yoga had been a great solace during his many imprisonments under the British. In his clipped Harrow and Cambridge accent, already the delight of mimics on All-India Radio, he peremptorily invited Yehudi to demonstrate his skill in the *shishasana*.

Although it was quite the wrong time of day for exercises, Yehudi promptly removed his shoes and socks and eagerly hoisted himself into position – in full evening dress. Nehru expressed himself mildly impressed but assured his guest that he still had a long way to go. Whereupon, as Diana recalled,

He took off his Gandhi cap, clasped his hands on the floor, cupped his head in them and slowly and gracefully unfurled his legs till he stood, a perfect column inverted.

Watched by Nehru's sister Lakshmi, his daughter Indira Gandhi (who had earlier greeted the Menuhins at the airport) and by several venerable leaders of the Congress Party, the world's most famous musician and one of its most powerful politicians were busy showing off their *shishasanas* in friendly rivalry when a turbaned major-domo, magnificent in his blue and gold uniform, came to the door of the long drawing room, whose Bournemouth armchairs, sofas and bridge tables suggested to Diana 'ghosts of long-gone English colonels'. Without batting an eyelid he gravely announced, 'Mr Prime Minister, dinner is served', as if his master's physical exertions, and those of his guest, were perfectly normal at New Delhi welcoming parties.

An excursion to Agra followed, in Nehru's personal plane. The Menuhins saw the Taj Mahal, of course, but also, at the Prime Minister's personal recommendation, the exquisite small temple of Itmud-ud-Dowlah. Then Yehudi gave his first concert, with Marcel Gazelle, in the auditorium of the National Physical Laboratory. Hosted by Saeed Jaffrey, then a young radio announcer and later a film and stage actor of international reputation, the recital was simultaneously broadcast all over India. It was well reviewed in the English-language press, as was every concert on the tour.

Apart from European and US diplomats and businessmen, it was only well-educated Indians, those who maintained their pre-war links with Western culture and society despite the nation's newly granted independence, who understood and enjoyed Western music. It was an art form in which India's teeming millions were – as Yehudi put it at the time – 'in a virginal state'. Before he left he dreamed up an ambitious plan in which his new friend Mehli Mehta would head a national conservatoire and a national orchestra. But in the event Nehru had more pressing national priorities. Mehta was soon to move to England, where he played for some years in the Hallé Orchestra. He then settled in Los Angeles, where he ran the American Youth Orchestra. However a National Academy for the Performing Arts was eventually established in Bombay – so Yehudi's efforts were not entirely in vain. And thanks to his enthusiasm, many millions of Westerners were to have their ears opened to the beauties of Indian music a full decade before the Beatles discovered the sitar, so Nehru's invitation proved to have been an astute one.

While still in New Delhi, Yehudi was introduced to an influential administrator with All-India Radio, Dr Naryana Menon. He was an accomplished veena player and the holder of a doctorate from Edinburgh University – his thesis was on the poetry of W. B. Yeats. *New Grove* states that Menon attended Sir Donald Tovey's Edinburgh University concerts in 1939 and that he was Head of Staff Training with All-India Radio, 1948–63, and subsequently Director-General. Saeed Jaffrey, who worked for him, describes Menon as a 'friend, philosopher and guide'. Menon eventually became Director of the National Academy mentioned in the previous paragraph and was later voted President of the International Music Council after Yehudi had held the post.

Menon was the ideal person to initiate Yehudi into the intricacies of Indian music: as a broadcaster in the BBC's Eastern Service during the war he had hosted a regular programme called *Music of the East and West*. Now he supervised the broadcasts of Yehudi's recitals and introduced him to the country's leading performer, Ravi Shankar. It transpired that Shankar had heard Yehudi play in 1934, when he was living in Paris as a member of his brother Uday's dance troupe. The younger by four years, Shankar was, like Yehudi, a child prodigy who later developed a second career – in his case as a composer, not a conductor. He was as well known in India as Menuhin was in the Western world and Yehudi was immediately enchanted by both his playing and his personality. 'He seemed to be so overwhelmed,' Shankar recalled. 'He embraced me and asked me so many questions, and we became such good friends from that moment.' Diana also remembers the impact Shankar's beauty had on them both, and 'the gentleness of his manner . . . as he explained the multiple sophistications of his exquisite sitar'.

The sitar is a long-necked lute. Its seven bronze and steel strings are backed up by eleven or more 'sympathetic' under-strings which increase the instrument's resonance. The sitar's base, a hollow gourd, serves as a sounding board and is reinforced by an extra gourd mounted high up on the neck of the instrument. The basic musical form of Shankar's music is the raga, halfway between a scale and a melody. There are many hundreds of ragas, linked to the months of the year and the hours of the day. According to a Sanskrit saying, 'That which colours the mind is a raga.' Shankar himself wrote that

The raga reflects the spiritual hope of the people, the constant struggle for life. It is drawn out of the moods of the seasons and the prayers in our temples, for our music is not written down; it is passed from heart to heart.

Diana was as enthusiastic as her husband:

Ravi played magically together with Chatur Lal his tabla player (a tabla being the pair of small Indian drums that support and accompany the improvisations of the sitar), another virtuoso whose inner ear and mind seemed to anticipate every change in pitch, tempo or mood till the two of them took flight in an interlocking web of sound that was part dialogue, part song, wholly communication.

Nothing had moved Yehudi so much since he had heard the improvisations of the gypsy fiddlers in Romania back in 1927. He loved the gypsies' wild approach to music-making and if he found himself in a Hungarian restaurant would happily do a turn in the gypsy fiddler's style, which is relatively easy to imitate. In his memoirs the conductor Antal Dorati paints an engaging picture of a birthday party in New York in the 1940s for which he had hired a genuine gypsy band from an uptown Hungarian café:

In the course of that merry evening Yehudi played an improvised solo. This was too much for the double-bass player. He leapt with his instrument into the centre of the room and played a virtuoso solo . . . to be rewarded by Menuhin with a bearhug.

Yet the joy of true improvisation – and the self-abandon it encourages – was something Yehudi had never personally experienced and as he listened to Shankar he might well have resolved that one day he would himself attempt to play Indian music. Meanwhile it became, like yoga, an abiding passion, something whose virtues and joys he would preach for the next twenty years. 'It is like a river', he told viewers of his television history *The Music of Man*:

ever-fluid and subtly changing, whereas European music is like a building, carefully structured upon constant principles. The Indian experiences his music as part of his sense of the eternal continuity of life. We see ours as distinctly man-made, a separate artefact . . . Their music does not favour sharp contrasts of mood as ours does; it is meant to create a sense of being, not put the listener through an emotional wringer.

Yehudi's commitment was substantial and immediate. In 1953 he was elected President of the influential Asian Music Circle in London. In 1955, he presented Indian musicians and dancers in a concert at the Museum of Modern Art in New York, repeating the show on American television's experimental arts programme *Omnibus*. In Britain, both BBC Radio and Television hosted many more such broadcasts, in which he attempted to explain the intricacies of the raga and the tala. (If the raga is the warp, then the woof of Indian music is the tala, the measure of its complex rhythms.) In London the British Council subsidized educational long-playing records of Indian music, narrated most persuasively by Yehudi. In 1959 he introduced Indian music at the first Bath Festival planned under his auspices and thus established a continuing tradition. Ravi Shankar played at Bath on several occasions and Yehudi also invited him to give demonstrations at his new school for gifted child musicians.

Eventually Yehudi commissioned Shankar to compose music in which he could participate himself. *West Meets East*, a sort of double concerto for sitar and violin, was heard for the first time at the Bath Festival in 1966 and a year later performed at a special concert at the General Assembly of the United Nations with what Shankar described as 'thunderous success'. That same year, 1967, Shankar was taken up by the world of pop music. Once the Beatle guitarist George Harrison had chosen him as a musical guru, he performed as much in California as in New Delhi; eventually he settled there. Their friendship endured but Yehudi's passion for Indian music subsided. In the early 1970s he found another great musician with whom he could indulge his love of improvisation, the French jazz violinist Stéphane Grappelli.

Yehudi's 1952 Indian expedition made a profound impression on him. Nothing he experienced on his exceptionally pressurized tour of Japan could compare with the magic wand of Nehru's personal blessing. That he immediately felt so at home in India was, however, largely because of his fascination with yoga. Lunching with India's President, he was delighted to learn that a visit had been arranged to the class of India's oldest practising yogi.

I was taken at four o'clock in the morning to witness . . . a bearded sage of perhaps eighty, naked but for a band about his loins, go through his exercises on a leopard

skin in a forest clearing surrounded by disciples. The reverence of this little ceremony compelled recognition of an acceptance of life in all its conditions that we
in the West have lost . . . Indian wisdom – with erotic sculpture as with yoga –
offers grateful tribute to the body.

Diana's memoirs provide an entertaining coda to such solemnity:

I asked Y how he had enjoyed his dawn diversion and was horrified to hear him
say that it was so enthralling he had found it irresistible not to comply with their
demands and had divested himself of his outer clothing and joined in.

Photographs of the event forwarded to Diana revealed

a large circle of venerable old dhoti-clad gentlemen in the centre of which, standing on his head, his loose underpants dropping dangerously around his buttocks,
was the recognizable and otherwise naked figure of Yehudi Menuhin, the violinist.

Once he had made his interest in yoga known in the Indian newspapers he was besieged with offers to teach him; indeed he spent his
first morning in Bombay interviewing applicants. The successful can-
didate, the *Times of India* reported, 'should be prepared to go with
him to his native California and initiate his little children into the
occult sciences'. The man selected was Mr B. K. S. Iyengar from
Poona. The names behind the initials cannot have meant much to
Yehudi since in his memoirs he always omitted them. He characterized
Mr Iyengar as 'no bearded ascetic but a good young man with a wife
and children'. The future guru turned up unannounced one morning at
Government House, where Yehudi was residing in the Prime Minister's
favourite Point Bungalow at the edge of the Indian Ocean. Mr Iyengar
had never heard of Mr Menuhin until asked to call on him by a mutual
friend. 'If I was a name to be reckoned with,' wrote Yehudi, 'whose
favour he could imagine rebounding upon him, I was for all my
celebrity another Western body knotted through and through.' Yehudi
told him he had only five minutes to spare. 'He bade me lie still, touching me here and there. One hour later, I awoke, feeling more refreshed
than I had felt for ages.' Yehudi said the experience was akin to the
spell he had fallen under when Louis Persinger first played Bach to
him. Next morning at dawn, to an accompaniment of scoffing mynah
birds (if Diana's account is to be believed), he began practising yoga
under his guru's supervision in the gardens of Government House.
Thanks to Yehudi, Mr Iyengar became an international yoga authority.
He travelled regularly to Europe in the summer to hold an intensive
course with the Menuhins (and many others), and whenever Yehudi

returned to India Mr Iyengar would put him through his paces every day.

In New Delhi the concert-going public had clapped between the movements during one of Yehudi's recitals, much to the displeasure of 'Lancet', a local columnist who noted that the intrusion had been tactfully edited out in the All-India Radio recorded broadcast. He had been at the concert and was particularly riled when the audience forgot such age-old courtesies as 'to rise from their seats to do honour to the Governor's lady, and to the Governor himself and to a great American lady [Mrs Eleanor Roosevelt] who is a guest in our land'. In Bombay Yehudi's four concerts sold out in an hour; people were said to have slept out on the pavements in order to be first in the queue (although people sleeping on the street is an all too common sight in many Indian cities). Western musical celebrities who had visited the city were rare indeed: Heifetz, Kubelik, Galli-Curci. The excitement Yehudi generated was intense and so, too, was the atmosphere – on one occasion, literally so: the ventilation fans at Bombay's Excelsior Theatre were so noisy they had to be turned off but with 1,100 people crammed into a location officially seating only 840, the heat was unbearable. The *Sunday Standard* reported that when Yehudi left the stage after playing Tartini's 'Devil's Trill' Sonata,

there was a small pool of sweat where he had stood . . . It was not only the heat that worried M. Marcel Gazelle. The action of the grand piano was not working evenly. A group of five notes reacted sluggishly every time it was depressed; M. Gazelle had to use a free hand every so often to pull this key up again.

At the two orchestral concerts Yehudi played the Mendelssohn and Beethoven Concertos. The trumpeters in the band, Diana remembered, had been 'wrenched from the navy, timpani from the army, violinists from all over. Mehli Mehta had coached them all lovingly, section by section.' The baton for the concert was in the hands of a Goanese-born conductor from Calcutta, Francesco Casanovas, described by the *Evening News of India* as 'the most energetic musician east of Suez'. The paper reported that the enchantingly named conductor 'spent a strenuous long weekend coaxing and instructing a new ensemble through the incredible task of perfecting its technique . . . The results have been nothing short of brilliant.'

'They weren't at all bad', Diana informed Moshe, 'and made up in devotion and endeavour for any musical shortcomings there may have been!' She was delighted with Bombay: for the first time since her marriage she did not have to wash or iron a thing: 'We are so comfortable and so beautifully looked after.' Their Indian organizers never let them down:

Cars, planes, entertainments turn up as if by magic . . . taking us on wonderful excursions by private plane and car to see fantastic caves and temples, putting on dancing and musical shows and finally presenting Yehudi with an invaluable fifth-century Buddha's head and me with a lovely amethyst charm . . . an enamel scent bottle and a handsome pink and gold sari, to say nothing of masses of fruit and flowers all the time . . . Mrs Roosevelt was at the concert last night and was as sweet and friendly as she always is.

Thousands of miles away in Los Gatos, Moshe was also kept in touch by Mrs Daruvala, secretary of the Bombay concert promoter:

The wonderful gesture your son made towards helping Bombay to have a permanent orchestra is deeply appreciated . . . It was so good of him to have lent Mr Mehli [Mehta] his wonderful violin to play on. It is no wonder that people feel that he has the true quality of yoga in him, which is essential goodness for the sake of goodness . . . It would be wonderful if you could come out to India next time with your son . . . We always feel that a person's greatness is a reflection of his parents' goodness and care, and we know that your son does appreciate you very much.

The tour took them to Trivandrum in the deep south, where Yehudi had been invited to play for a maharani who had given 10,000 rupees to the Prime Minister's Relief Fund. Then it was on to Bangalore, where concert-giving took second place to sight-seeing. After they had climbed 630 steps to admire the impressive Jain statue at Sravana-belagola, Yehudi expressed awe at its 'serene contemplation'; Diana's reaction after struggling to the top was more caustic: 'Its vast size was only matched by its utter hideousness.' Undeterred, Yehudi recalled advancing to the rock edge 'where the overhang measured some thousands of feet to the plain below'. There he watched an eagle flying in to be given food at the foot of the Buddha. Like countless generations of eagles before it, he was told, the bird arrives promptly at 12 noon. Yehudi meditated on this daily spectacle:

It is the Indian's sense of time which lies behind the doctrine of reincarnation, the belief in a continuity so unbreakable that what is present belongs to the past and future, to earth and heaven; and it is this sense which until now has given India its stability.

Nobody would wish to challenge the validity of Yehudi's thoughts on the continuity of Indian history but facts are a different matter. In

Diana's account, published eight years after her husband's and thirty years after their visit, there were two eagles, not one, and the feeding ritual occurred at a different temple site, Thirukkalikundram, near Madras. (A recent guidebook states that the birds sighted there are not eagles but vultures.)

In Madras, Yehudi included the solo Sonata by Bartók in his second programme. 'Those Hungarian dissonances approach the Indian idiom so closely they will love it,' he had explained to Diana. But at the recital she had to hold the British Governor's hand while he wriggled wretchedly, whispering, 'Oi, oi, what terrible noises.' The Bartók has at least the merit of brevity. Diana herself declined an invitation to a long evening at the Central College of Carnatica Music, where Yehudi listened admiringly to what others, less enthusiastic, might have thought to be interminable recitals on both flute and violin. He expressed himself amazed at the local violinist's virtuosity on an instrument that appeared structurally as weak as a matchbox. Together the Menuhins visited a theosophist arts centre at Kalakshetra, where he wrote in the guest book that he was 'charmed by the music and the dance; I felt I was among kindred spirits who are being potently assisted in finding themselves'.

Soon afterwards he was invested for the first time with the status of a seer. A newspaper report from Kalakshetra ended:

An Indian old lady said of him, 'He is a Ghandarva'; may he and every messenger of beauty bring the world together into a brotherhood of beauty – a brotherhood of all kingdoms, of nature, of man and the Gods!

Another devout Hindu placed a photograph on his private altar; Yehudi had become a holy person to whom one dedicated offerings and prayers. In Bombay a Parsee artist friend had told Diana that her husband could not possibly be of Jewish or Middle Eastern extraction.

He comes from here. He has the perfect Indo-Hellenic head of the Ghandara period, when Alexander the Great tramped through Northern India and left much Greek influence behind.

Trailing clouds of goodwill, our Indo-Hellenic hero gave more concerts in Calcutta, where Nehru took an hour off from an assembly of state governors to show the Menuhins an extraordinary park:

Its clearings and pathways, in sun and shade, covered many acres and all this wide extent was in fact one single banyan tree! Here was a work which only time could accomplish . . . confirmation of my belief that patience is all, that whether one considers a banyan tree or a marriage or a culture, one must wait to reap the fruits.

Yehudi praised the dignity and peace of mind of the Indian people and immediately set his mind to solving the problem of poverty, dispatching an earnest note to the US Ambassador to India, Chester Bowles:

Until India has sufficient electrical power and the other basic means of industrialization (they are working on it but this takes time), we can help them develop more efficient methods for their own time-honoured cottage industries. There is for instance the brick which they bake in mud flats in the south of India; it is brittle and disintegrates too quickly. We can easily show them how to produce a brick more like the adobe we use in California, mixed with oil and various other ingredients which make for a highly resistant, attractive, and insulating material. There is the thatching of houses. We might develop some way of making their thatching fireproof.

His advice went unheeded. After a final week savouring the beauties of Kashmir, the Menuhins – world citizens before the concept had been invented – left the subcontinent in a state of euphoria. 'Your visit', Nehru wrote,

was an event which none who saw or heard you is likely to forget . . . it was a delight to meet you and Diana and to find so much kinship of mind and spirit. Such a discovery lightens the gloom and makes one think a little more hopefully and generously of this world of ours.

According to Yehudi, 'yoga promised release from physical impediments' and his playing seems to have taken on a new bloom in the months that followed what one might describe as his mystical conversion. In May 1952 he was in England, playing at the Bath Festival with Kentner: 'If this concert had consisted simply of the movement from the 'Kreutzer' Sonata which was given as the third encore, the audience would still have had their money's worth,' wrote the *Bath Critic*. Two days earlier, in London, he recorded the E minor Mendelssohn Concerto with Furtwängler. John Ardoin's appreciation is worth quoting at length since it contradicts so comprehensively the received view that Menuhin's star was on the wane. 'Wonderfully alive', he begins,

Menuhin, supported by Furtwängler's passionate collaboration, takes hold of the music and our imagination from his first entrance. His sound is eager, vaulting, and brims with warmth and vitality. The few orchestral *tuttis* in the first movement are vivid and pulsating, and Furtwängler takes the slow movement at a breathing, walking pace that is a bit quicker than the norm and that results in a true reverie of sentiment rather than sentimentality. Though the finale is as fleet as one might want, it, too, has a backbone and intensity that show there is more to the music than simplistic prettiness.

Yehudi conducted the same concerto (as well as playing it) at a public concert with the London Symphony Orchestra at the Royal Albert Hall, but at the interval he prudently handed over the baton to Joseph Krips; he might well have remembered coming to grief when he performed the Tchaikovsky Concerto in New York with Mengelberg back in 1930. The work needs a more experienced controlling hand than Yehudi could muster at the time.

He gathered exceptional reviews on his next annual American tour, the twenty-fifth anniversary of his New York début. In January 1953 the *New York Times* critic Howard Taubman wrote that

the Yehudi Menuhin who played in Carnegie Hall last night performed like an important new violinist. The importance lay in the thrust and personality Mr Menuhin revealed as an interpreter. It was as though he had moved up to a higher level of accomplishment, a level one had expected him to achieve sooner. But maturity as an artist is not won easily . . . In recent years there has been evidence of a struggle going on within him. Whatever private difficulties he has had with his art, he seemed to have conquered them.

A few days later a profile appeared in the influential *Newsweek* magazine. The headline read, a little oddly, 'Menuhin comes of age'. He was already thirty-six; such a summing up would have been more appropriate in 1938 when, aged twenty-one, he played the Schumann Concerto in New York. But as Taubman's review confirmed, *Newsweek* was not alone in suggesting that Yehudi had lived through a protracted adolescence, brought about by the excessive supervision of his parents during his childhood. But now he was undoubtedly his own man, and according to the magazine, 'easily the best-known American virtuoso . . . It annoys him when people assume he is a European.' The article applauded his recent recital, in which he introduced another 'rediscovered' work by Mendelssohn, this time an early sonata for violin and piano in F. Yehudi's performance of a Bartók sonata was said to have

stunned both audience and critics. It was technical wizardry, coupled with interpretive powers of the highest order. The fair-haired boy with gold in his fiddle had outlived his growing pains. The promise of tone and technique had been fulfilled and, at thirty-six, a master musician had come of age.

Working overtime, Yehudi's press agent also arranged a photo interview with the even bigger-circulation weekly magazine, *Life*. The idea
was that he should demonstrate different yoga exercises and discuss
their benefits. Diana attended the session and kept a beady eye on the
proceedings. Convinced that all was going well, she slipped out to buy
rehearsal shirts for Yehudi's next Carnegie Hall concert. When the
magazine was published the main photograph was of her nearly nude
husband on his knees, his tongue stuck out and his eyes bulging like a
dervish. The caption read, 'Violent virtuosity is displayed by Menuhin
as he does a *Simhāsana* (lion pose) with his Indian yoga instructor. The
exercise helps eyes and throat.' Zamira stayed away from school for
two days out of embarrassment but Yehudi was perfectly happy with
the article, which does indeed provide a fascinating introduction to
physical yoga and its various *asanas*. One bird's-eye-view showed
Yehudi literally in knots, unwinding from a headstand. A single such
exercise, he said, was equivalent to ten miles of walking. In the
Bhastrika exercise he was working on breath control: he explained
that holding his breath as long as possible gave him 'a light-headed,
floating feeling'. When he twisted his spine in the *Ardha-
Matshendrāsana*, he made his back more supple. And by pulling a
piece of string through his nose and out of his mouth – the *Neti Kriya* –
he claimed he was 'helping his sense of smell and making eyes burn
bright'. The graphic photographs proved his point.

The *Newsweek* profile had been illustrated by a more conventional
photograph of Yehudi, Diana and all four Menuhin children, perched
on a fallen tree trunk at Alma and giving every appearance of an
extended and happy family. Jeremy was not yet four months old when
they'd set off for India the previous February, leaving Schwester Marie
in charge. In her memoirs Diana did not shirk from discussing her
responsibilities as a mother. How, she asked rhetorically, could she
create the family life that Yehudi 'in his undefining way desired so
deeply' and yet continue by her husband's side in his career, 'supporting, encouraging, sharing'? But what hope did she have of creating a
family nucleus and a sense of nest for her young children when, as she
put it herself, 'the parent birds, singly or together, were constantly flying away from it'? In fact she almost always put her husband first; she
knew from her own experience in wartime London how his eye could
wander when he was travelling alone. The irony was that ever since the
summer holiday in 1947 she had proved to be good at creating and

rebuilding family relationships. At Alma there were always plenty of walks, swims in the pool, visits to Moshe and Marutha, picnics, readings, music on the radiogram and an evening story for the older children which continued in instalments over supper.

Nola's second marriage had proved less successful than Yehudi's and she married a third time, to William Hawthorne. In 1953, she proposed to take her children out of school for a term so they could travel to Australia. Krov hated their upstate New York boarding school and was ready to go along with the plan, but his sister was concerned that she would never catch up. Krov remembers thinking that Zamira admired Diana's lifestyle and was frightened by the violence that occasionally erupted between their mother and her partners.

By the end of the summer holiday Zamira, thirteen in July, had decided to transfer her allegiance full-time from Nola to Yehudi. She told Diana 'she wanted to be a child before it was too late'. In fact Yehudi had already expressed concern at his daughter's lifestyle: Nola apparently allowed her to roam the New York streets without supervision. When he went to collect her it was without prior warning. Nola was in Australia and only the new husband was at the apartment. It was early and he was still in his bathrobe. Zamira remembers being embarrassed but her father was perfectly at ease: '"Go and collect your things," he said, and I did, not that there was much to collect.' The transfer was not without pain. Krov, a year younger, remained close to his mother and hardly ever saw his father or his sister during his teenage years. Diana gives a supremely optimistic account of the struggle for the control of her stepdaughter: 'After a few tussles all was happily settled and we sent her to stay with English friends in New York where she subsequently attended the excellent Dalton School.' But the Menuhins were soon looking for a suitable school for Zamira in Switzerland. She found she had exchanged life in New York with an unhappy mother for a succession of boarding schools in different countries, interspersed with glamorous holidays in the company of her father and stepmother, but no home.

As her own elder son Gerard approached school age, Diana expressed herself increasingly unhappy with the Californian lifestyle:

You think you can bring up children in the glories of the Santa Cruz mountains but of course you can't. There you are with two hundred acres, the sun's shining nine months in the year, absolutely ravishing, but you don't grow any mental muscle.

he Aleutian Islands, March 1944. Yehudi with his pianist Adolph Baller and Air
ɔs Major Stanley A. Paterson.

27 On the back of this publicity still, taken at a recording session for *The Magic Bow*, Yehudi wrote: 'To Diana with love and thanks for retouching this "rough-proof" – for indelible scars are life's retouching. Yehudi July 29, 1945 London'. (He left next day to play to survivors of Belsen).

29 Nola and Yehudi visit George Enescu Romania, May 1946.

28 Yehudi in Switzerland with Zamira Krov after the reconciliation with Nola 1946.

urich, May 1946: wedding party for Griselda Gould (third from right) and the pianist Kentner (left). Diana Gould is on the right; Yehudi (second left) stands next to his witness Wilhelm Furtwängler, whose wife Elisabeth is between the Gould sisters.

reen test as Paganini at ainsborough Film os, 1945.

32 In March 1947 Hephzibah and Yehudi (bearded for a few days) gave a duo recital at the Metropolitan Opera House, their first joint appearance in New York since before the war.

33 Wedding Day No. 2, also in London. The Registry Office ceremony was at 9:15 an the afternoon Yehudi played a Paganini concerto at the Royal Albert Hall; he and Dia were snapped emerging from Claridges, where he took 'a little nap' after his morning rehearsal. The honeymoon lasted a single night before his autumn tour began.

34 The extended family at Alma, September 1952. Gerard (b. 1948), Jeremy (b. 1951 Diana, Zamira, Krov and Yehudi.

This St Trinian's couple won first prize fancy dress competition on board the *Victoria*, bound for Bombay: Zamira her father in 1954.

36 Their first sonata: Jeremy, aged six, with his father at I Tatti, Bernard Berenson's home outside Florence.

Party time at the Menuhins' Gstaad chalet with a family friend, Benjamin Britten.

38 Bath Festival: the artistic director with thermos flask and muse.

39 With a fellow conductor, Rudolf Barshai, and admiring members of the Moscow Chamber Orchestra.

40 September 1963: opening day of the Menuhin School. Yehudi is flanked by Ronan Magill (pianist) and Rosemary Furniss (violinist, now Mrs Christopher Warren Greene). At the left, one step behind, is his son Jeremy. The teachers include (left of Yehudi, in ascending order) Marcel Gazelle, Maurice Gendron, Lionel Tertis, Barbara Hubicki and George Malcolm. Behind him (right) are Frederick Grinke and Robert Masters, Christopher Bunting and (top right) Alberto Lysy.

41 With Mstislav Rostropovich, now President of the Menuhin School.

When Yehudi became a British citizen in 1985 he could finally take delivery of the knighthood awarded twenty years earlier. He was accompanied to Buckingham Palace by daughter 'Miras' and his second wife 'Diny'.

After the summer concert at Castel Gandolfo, 1983.

At Oxford Gardens School, London: Yehudi, aged 79, practising what he preached.

44 The new member of the Académie des Beaux-Arts, 1988.

46 Stadthalle, Wuppertal, 6 March 1999: on tour in Germany with the Sinfonia Varso
Yehudi had just conducted the 'Scottish' Symphony by Mendelssohn. He died suddenly
only six days later.

She expressed her fear for her sons in her memoirs: 'In all the luxury and lavishness they would develop no anti-bodies against physical or psychological germs.' She was determined to move but it took years to persuade Yehudi: 'He was afraid, like the good Jewish boy that he was, that his parents would be furious if they left.' Diana reminded him that Moshe and Marutha had had no qualms about settling in Paris for five years during his own childhood, but Yehudi was a creature of habit and it took many factors to shift him. One was the unavoidable reality that the peace and quiet of Alma was under threat from the construction of a new dam: 'We have been kept awake nights', Yehudi wrote to the *Los Gatos Times* in March 1953, 'by the sound of the earth-moving equipment . . . we hear the minutest sounds right across the valley.' The prospect of speedboats on the dam's narrow, man-made lake appalled him: the area, he thundered, 'should be (and remain) a place of pilgimage'. Another determining factor was his increasing disenchantment with air travel. He told *Newsweek* that he had recently reduced his schedule from 350–400 appearances a year – a preposterously exaggerated figure that should not have been published without checking – down to 150, but his engagements around this time do not suggest that he had made a serious effort to rationalize his travelling.

He was still on the move incessantly and did not take a long break in the summer. Recordings were another factor: he made a lightning visit to Copenhagen in September 1952 to record Carl Nielsen's little-known Violin Concerto; his was the first recording by an international soloist. In April 1953 he was in London for a busy week with EMI for the HMV label: new to the catalogue were the A minor Concerto (No. 22) by Viotti, to mark that composer's bicentenary, the 'Il Piacere' Concerto by Vivaldi (another work he had 'discovered') and the Mendelssohn D minor. He also made his first LP of the Beethoven Concerto, with Furtwängler conducting the Philharmonia. More EMI recording sessions followed in July, August and September. The advent of long-playing records, first in mono and by the end of the decade in stereo, provided Yehudi with the opportunity to re-record most of his repertoire – apart from the salon pieces which had been a charming element in his pre-war output but no longer figured substantially in his recitals. He rarely listened to his recordings but they were a vital source of income and enabled him to explore new works such as the Nielsen Concerto and, later in the decade, the Sibelius.

In May 1953 he appeared with Furtwängler in Munich and with his old friend Paul Paray in Paris, where he also took part in a tribute to his revered teacher Enesco. He was shocked by the lowly state to which his master had been reduced by illness and the imperious ways of his wife, the increasingly eccentric Princess Cantacuzène. Hard times had forced the Enescos to give up the spacious third-floor apartment at 26 rue de Clichy, where Yehudi had presented himself for his pre-dawn audition back in January 1927, and move down to two tiny, ill-lit rooms in the basement courtyard. 'Yehudi talked to him of music,' Diana noted,

and at one point Enesco ran his sadly twisted hands [over the piano] as if it were an extension of his own being . . . I noticed the frayed tie, the shabby jacket, the waxen face with its clean beautiful bones and serene eyes . . . 'Eh bien, chers enfants,' he said, with a heart-rending mixture of defensive pride and hidden shame. 'Me voilà!'

At the Belgian Embassy in Paris the Menuhins met another of Enesco's pupils, Elisabeth, the Queen Mother. Together they worked out a scheme whereby Yehudi would pay Enesco a monthly stipend as an advance against the anticipated royalty income from the reissue of his compositions by the publishers Salabert. But Enesco was too proud to accept the proposal. By the time of their last visit, in 1954, Enesco had become semi-paralysed after a stroke. He knew he could never play the violin again and he gave Yehudi his Guarnerius for safe-keeping in America. 'He is the only person whom I completely trust,' he wrote. But his wife claimed that Yehudi had stolen the violin and insisted it be returned so that she could dispose of it (as her husband had feared she would) in order to meet their daily expenses. Enesco had already made a gift to Yehudi of another of his violins, a less prestigious Santo Serafino which Yehudi kept until his own death. When Enesco died, in May 1955, Yehudi was in New York. He sent a wreath of three hundred roses in homage, inscribed 'To my master'. On the hearse, his floral tribute hung next to that sent by Romania's Communist government. There was a riot when exiled Romanians tore it down.

In June 1953 Yehudi was back in London for a Royal Festival Hall concert with Rafael Kubelik and the Philharmonia. The *Daily Herald*'s critic echoed the 'coming of age' theme that had surfaced in the US earlier in the year: he played Bach, it reported, with searching beauty and radiance. 'This was a greater Menuhin, who had criticized himself, approached the score afresh, and grown closer to the master'. In the same month he visited Dublin, showing his customary sympathy for the underdog when he observed that the down-trodden Irish had much in common with the Hebrew race. And he made his first appearance on BBC Television, playing concertos by Vivaldi and Mendelssohn with the London Philharmonic conducted by Boult. 'Superb close-ups showed us the expression on his face and his eloquent fingers,' said one review, headed 'Genius at work', but others were less kind. One complained about 'fancy shots of such irrelevances as the back of Mr Menuhin's head' and another said 'the constant switching about of cameras almost ruined the performance'.

The stress of being the 'fiddler's moll', as Diana took to calling herself, forced her into a Swiss clinic for two months in the spring of 1953. She was still recovering from an appendectomy when Yehudi came to collect her for the journey to a villa near Lerici, on the Gulf of La Spezia, at the other end of the Ligurian Sea from his childhood favourite, Ospedaletti. Schwester Marie was already settled in with Zamira and the young boys. When she awoke on her first morning at the seaside, Diana revelled in the sunshine on her bedroom wall and the comforting smells of coffee and fresh rolls wafting up from the kitchen. She evoked the scene when Yehudi arrived with her breakfast tray:

'There, darling,' says he with that fanatical gleam with which I was becoming more and more familiar. 'There is a breakfast that will really strengthen you and do you good!'

She remembers glaring at the Spartan jug of hot water and lemon, beside it a plate of dry rusks and honey. She had endured Yehudi's wilder dietetic experiments for six years, his interest in bonemeal, in seaweed patties, even in horse serum. At the clinic she had existed, she claimed, on little more than cabbage and ether. Something snapped: 'Suddenly I saw red and with a yell, picked up the whole tray and threw it through the open window.' The crestfallen Yehudi ordered a hearty calorific breakfast to be sent up with strong coffee and retreated to the garden to rescue the broken crockery and defenestrated health food.

In September 1953 Yehudi returned to the Edinburgh Festival. With Gioconda da Vito and Isaac Stern he played the Vivaldi Triple Concerto, drawing lots to decide who would play which part. Stern felt a little excluded, Diana remembers, by the merry Italian banter of his fellow soloists. In recitals Yehudi performed the complete solo works of Bach, music he never tired of. And to mark the death of the French violinist Jacques Thibaud in an air crash (on 1 September) he dedicated a performance of the Beethoven Concerto to the memory of this elegant Mozartian, his sparring partner and friend from his Ville d'Avray childhood. Afterwards the audience stood, motionless, before leaving the hall in respectful silence.

Only weeks later, at the end of October, another fine musician died in an air crash and this time the accident was virtually on the Menuhins' doorstep. William Kapell, one of the best young American pianists of his generation, was a passenger in a plane that slammed into the mountains not far from Los Gatos. Only thirty-one, he was on a flight returning from Australia – the very journey Hephzibah had made a few years previously. Yehudi was in Indianapolis on his annual American tour. He did not know Kapell personally, but the tragedy, coming so soon after the loss of Thibaud, and the death in another air crash four years earlier of the violinist Ginette Neveu (Enesco's most distinguished French pupil) drove him to take a decision. He telephoned Diana to announce that he would stop flying until radar was installed in all civilian aircraft. He had already written a letter on the subject to the London *Times* in May, and had been publicly supported by Ecko, the British radar manufacturers. Diana cried with relief at his resolve.

For the next seven years they resumed the more leisurely transportation of Yehudi's pre-war days: by luxury liners such as the *Queen Mary* and long-distance express trains like the Orient Express. He was criticized as a consequence in the British press for turning his back on progress: a journalist went so far as to imply that he was acting out of cowardice. Given his wartime transatlantic flights and his adventures in the Aleutians, Yehudi could hardly be described as lily-livered and a letter from a Wiltshire colonel put the subject into perspective: 'Damn me, Menuhin, travel by camel if you wish to.'

The following year, 1954, was literally much slower for the Menuhins as a result of the self-imposed flying ban. A second tour of India had already been planned and the journey east was now undertaken by sea. Zamira, then fourteen, was taken out of her Swiss boarding school to be given her first taste of the Orient. She remembers winning first prize with her father in a fancy-dress competition organized on board the MV *Victoria* sailing from Aden to Bombay.

Hephzibah was due to travel from Australia to be Yehudi's pianist partner. When she suddenly cancelled, a request was cabled to Louis Kentner to take her place, with the injunction that he should book his passage as soon as possible – by air, despite Yehudi's much publicized doubts concerning the safety of that mode of transport.

Hephzibah had to withdraw because her marriage was in turmoil. Life in Australia was no longer the sheep-farming idyll in which she had revelled in the early 1940s. She took a leading part in her new country's professional musical life and concerned herself with social issues, among them women's rights and fair play for the Jewish immigrants who crowded into Australia from Europe at the end of the war. She fell in love with one of former DPs, a Pole named Paul Morawetz. Their two-year affair ended in 1950 but by the time of the proposed Indian tour with her brother she was deeply involved with another European, Richard Hauser. They first met when Hauser talked his way into a brief meeting with Yehudi during his 1951 Australian tour. A highly opinionated Austrian-born sociologist with a British passport, Hauser had been hired to advise on Sydney's municipal transport system. After sixteen years of marriage to somebody else Hephzibah seems to have looked on Hauser as her predestined life partner. The rebel genes that occasionally flared in Yehudi were deeply embedded in his sister.

She had loved Lindsay – indeed she had proposed to him rather than he to her – but she found him too buttoned up emotionally and poorly educated, despite his love of music. (His favourite pastime was conducting gramophone records – with a baton.) She resolved to break away. Lindsay had by then sold his estate at Terinallum and moved closer to Melbourne. One morning she abruptly said goodbye to him and her boys, Kronrod and Marston, and with tears in her eyes but resolution in her soul departed to set up home with Hauser in Sydney. The day she chose to leave was Marston's first at a new school. Three years of scandal and pain were to follow before she saw either boy again, but she was determined to follow her new husband's star as a social reformer. In 1955 she gave birth to a daughter, Clara, and in due course the Hauser family moved to London. They established an Institute of Group Studies which was involved in the 1959 race riots in Notting Hill. Later they moved south of the Thames and worked with sick and homeless people at a Centre for Human Rights near Clapham Common.

The Menuhins' second visit to India was less of a royal tour than the first but its eleven concerts raised a lakh (approximately $20,000) for famine relief. Only a modest income of about 7000 rupees (close to $1,500) remained for Yehudi after travelling expenses had been deducted. Criss-crossing India by train, Yehudi appeared in Bombay, Calcutta, Madras and New Delhi, where his Guarnerius violin was adversely affected by the heat. (Just what prompted him to choose one particular violin for a tour rather than another could form the subject of a doctoral thesis.) This Guarnerius must have been the instrument given to him by Nola and later loaned to his first pupil, Alberto Lysy. After it had been diagnosed as 'unfit for playing', a Bombay violin collector, Parshos Ratnagar, stepped into the breach. He owned a fine Stradivarius and was prepared to fly with it to Delhi and save the day. A relieved Yehudi was happy to foot the bill. (Once again he had been obliged to put aside his reservations concerning air transport, this time for kith rather than kin.) A Bombay newspaper carried a quote from Isaac Stern, who had performed in the city a few months previously. He flew 50,000 miles every year, he said scornfully. 'Air travel is no more dangerous than crossing the street.'

It soon became clear when Yehudi played in Bombay that the city's orchestral standards had not improved in his absence. Mehli Mehta had arranged three concerts. The *Sunday Standard*'s Cecil Mendoza wrote that in the finale of the Brahms Concerto the conductor (Mehta) and his orchestra 'failed completely to grasp the Hungarian gist so adequately announced by Mr Menuhin in the opening bars', while in the second concert the playing of the orchestral sections in a Bach concerto were said to be 'appalling'. Another reviewer complained that the woodwinds were 'often erratic in tempo and frequently in pitch'. Apart from the flautists, all the brass and woodwind players were members of the band of the Indian Navy, accustomed to playing outdoors and, no doubt, at a slightly different pitch. Yehudi's almost saintly tolerance must have been sorely tested. At the third and farewell concert Mehli Mehta joined the imperturbable Yehudi to play the Bach Double Concerto with Louis Kentner conducting. Kentner was then the soloist in Beethoven's Third Piano Concerto before departing at the interval to catch his plane home to London. In the second half Yehudi played the Bruch G minor Concerto, which made, said the fulsome report, 'an exquisitely suitable finale'.

*

In May 1954 Yehudi made musical history when he became the first performer ever to give a solo recital at the war-damaged St Paul's Cathedral in London. It was in aid of the restoration fund and a charity for sufferers from cerebral palsy. The *Jewish Chronicle* gave the event a different spin: Yehudi, the newspaper claimed, was the first *Jewish* soloist to play there. Wren's glorious architecture provided a magnificent setting but, as Diana noted in her diary, the Cathedral has an echo of eight seconds: 'It seemed a sacrilege that the music should ruin the occasion.' Playing more slowly did not help, she added. A Bach fugue would still sound 'like "Jabberwocky" translated into Chinese'. Yehudi stood on a platform in front of the choir stalls, on which was perched a temporary wooden construction not unlike a sentry box. This cut down the overtones (Diana's phrase) and pushed the violin sound out towards the audience of three thousand.

The splendour of that great drawing room of a church, the packed pews, the Queen Mother sitting on a throne-like chair at the front of the nave, all made one harmonious whole, but . . . the sentry box into which Yehudi stepped did somewhat blight the grandeur, and I was afraid that there might be a dreadful undertone (to replace the overtones) of 'They're changing guard at Buckingham Palace'. I need not have worried. As soon as the first notes of the heavenly *Praeludium* from the Bach E major Partita welled out under that great dome, travelled down the nave and reached round the great pillars into every corner of that most beautiful of baroque churches, I knew it would be all right. Y looked very small in his black suit, half enclosed in his sentry box. He seemed to dissolve until there was nothing but sound, pure and clear, belling out in a kind of benediction.

At the end of May the Menuhins returned to America on the *Queen Mary*. They had not seen their sons for four months, nor Yehudi's parents, who had meanwhile moved into a new, more modest home on Kimble Avenue in Los Gatos. Moshe had suffered a heart attack and when not challenging the very concept of an Israeli state – at his own expense he was to publish *The Decadence of Judaism in our Time* in 1965 – he contented himself with looking after his wife and planting fruit trees on his acre of land. As usual in the summer, Yehudi earned big money by appearing at the outdoor venues such as the Robin Hood Dell in Philadelphia but it was while raising money for a good cause in Santa Barbara, California, that he was caught up in a Tati-esque comedy: a sudden breeze blew all the performers' music off the stands and into the swimming pool around which a charity concert had been scheduled. When the sodden pages had been retrieved and the concert was eventually resumed, the sound of Mozart was immediately drowned by a nearby flotilla of speedboats heading for the open sea; They sported in the waves like a school of dolphins, their riders oblivious to the rival charms of classical music. Yehudi, seen but not heard for most of the evening, professed himself happy simply to have had the chance to make music once again with the conductor Antal Dorati. The comments of the black-tie $200-per-ticket audience were not recorded but the repeat concert the next day was moved indoors.

By the end of July the Menuhins were sailing back to Europe. Gerard's sixth birthday was celebrated in mid-Atlantic with a cake that literally fell flat – to general consternation – because Yehudi had instructed the liner's chef to use wholemeal flour – another anecdote ridiculing her husband's obsessions in Diana's frequently waspish memoirs. Coming ashore Gerard was photographed carrying his own violin case, no doubt a birthday present, but he did not persevere with violin studies, preferring words to music from an early age. In France Yehudi taught a violin class at the American Academy in Fontainebleau run by his old friend Nadia Boulanger, thus taking the first step towards the creation of his own school nine years later. In Germany he appeared at the Ansbach Festival. While he was practising in his hotel room a heavy chandelier crashed down from the ceiling, narrowly missing both the maestro and his wife, who was writing a letter in bed.

August saw the Menuhins installed in a rented chalet in Gstaad, a fashionable resort in the Bernese Alps. According to Diana the place was tastelessly furnished and its view was restricted to the Mercedes saloons parked at the back of Gstaad's famous Palace Hotel. She was further displeased when on their first morning she looked out of the window from the breakfast table and saw through the rain the improbable spectacle of Mr B. K. S. Iyengar striding up the drive, a soaking dhoti clinging to his muscular legs. Yehudi ran to the door to welcome his guru. 'Didn't I tell you?' he asked his wife in all innocence. 'Mr Iyengar is spending the summer with us.' There was a yoga session every morning at seven and Yehudi's womenfolk hated it; Diana confessed she was 'black with ill-will and red with suppressed rage'. The former ballerina had made her views on yoga known when *Life* magazine had produced its profile the previous year: 'I've been putting my leg behind my ear for years but I always got paid for it.' But there were other activities that summer to which nobody raised objections. Yehudi's regular delight, informal chamber music, was revived at the chalet. Piano trios were the order of the day; Louis Kentner came out from London, to be joined by the ebullient Spanish cellist Gaspar Cassado.

The Menuhins liked Gstaad well enough to rent a more congenial chalet the following summer and then to put down permanent roots. On a sloping meadow overlooking the mountains, a site found for them by Schwester Marie, they built a handsome and capacious new chalet, to which Diana, prompted by T. S. Eliot, gave the name 'Chankly Bore', derived from Edward Lear's 'The Jumblies' – 'For they've been to the Lakes, and the Torrible Zone, / And the hills of the Chankly Bore'. Many a Swiss postman's head must have been scratched in total incomprehension.

Back in London again in November and December 1954 Yehudi celebrated the twenty-fifth anniversary of his 1929 début by playing the complete sonatas of Beethoven with his brother-in-law. He then succumbed ignominiously to chickenpox, caught from Gerard. It was an inauspicious beginning to a year whose most significant musical activity was to be a substantial participation in the Bath Festival. Having created the first so-called Bath Assembly in 1948, the eternally optimistic impresario Ian Hunter was back in charge, and for 1955 he had cunningly named Sir Thomas Beecham as the Artistic Director, devising with him a stylish and ambitious programme. Hunter was Yehudi's British manager, a role he had taken over from the late Harold Holt, and he played his Menuhin cards astutely: a sold-out duo recital with Gioconda da Vito, who was the wife of EMI's classical music chief, David Bicknell; a Viotti concerto conducted by Beecham at the Guildhall – the performance ran late and to the fury of many listeners the last few minutes of the broadcast were faded by the BBC to make room for the scheduled sports relay – and an evening of solo Bach in Bath Abbey. This last occasion inspired Marcus Pooley, the local music critic, to match the purple prose that Redfern Mason in San Francisco used to produce when Yehudi was a boy:

A solitary figure, clutching a violin, stood in front of the choir stalls . . . and paused while the huge crowd who had flocked to hear him settled quietly in their seats. Behind him the newly restored east window stood out in bold relief like a beacon of faith; before him a sea of upturned faces waited expectantly. And as he drew his bow across the strings, magic seemed to fill the air. For ninety minutes he played almost continuously . . .

Bath's local council decided against a festival in 1956 (because of

Hunter's overspend in 1955) and plans for the following year were scuppered when petrol rationing had to be introduced in the aftermath of the Suez débâcle. But in 1958 Ian Hunter was back in charge and Yehudi made further appearances, playing the Beethoven Concerto (with the gifted young Colin Davis as his conductor) and violin and piano duos with his sister Hephzibah. In the light of his tremendous popularity with the public and his evident willingness to become more closely involved, he was then invited to take artistic responsibility for the entire fortnight in 1959. 'A festival arranged with Yehudi Menuhin' was the formula adopted by Hunter, who remained in command behind the scenes. It was not until 1966 that Yehudi was described as Artistic Director.

The year 1955 marked the ninetieth birthday of Jean Sibelius. Invited to participate in the inevitable festivities Yehudi had to confess that he did not know Sibelius's Violin Concerto. He was always a quick learner, however, and in June he recorded the work in London's Kingsway Hall studio, with Sir Adrian Boult conducting. He later travelled to Helsinki to perform the Concerto as part of the celebrations. The old man was too frail to attend but he listened to the broadcast and afterwards, Yehudi reported, 'telephoned to express his satisfaction'. To judge from the recording, Sibelius was not a composer for whom Yehudi felt an especial sympathy, but he nevertheless made the pilgrimage to what he described as the composer's 'cosy wooden house . . . standing in its own stretch of the forest' where Sibelius had lived in retirement, his muse silent, for almost thirty years.

Whom, he soon asked me, did I consider the greatest composer of the twentieth century? Thus challenged by one who had himself some claim to the title, I was at a stand [sic] between honesty and civility, but while I hesitated he rescued me. 'Bartók is our greatest composer,' he pronounced . . . I could have hugged him – for casting me a lifeline but more for his generosity and clear-sightedness.

From the near sublime to the somewhat ridiculous: two days after Sibelius's birthday, the Menuhins were on the Orient Express, heading for Israel by way of a concert engagement in Athens. Diana's diary entry reads:

Y discovered to his fury that there was no communicating door between our two cabins. Undeterred he smashed through the thin panel above the washbasins so that at least we could poke our heads through and maintain some kind of contact – the splintered remnants of the Orient Express's best and most ancient marquetry he hid under the bed.

Yehudi's surprisingly violent reaction recalls Enesco's remark comparing his pupil's temperament to that of the music of Mozart: a vineyard
on the slopes of Mount Vesuvius.

Farce ensued when the Menuhins arrived in Greece. Their luggage,
supposedly loaded on the train in London by the staff of Claridge's,
failed to materialize. Yehudi was due to give a charity recital that
evening in the presence of King Paul and Queen Frederica; his partner
was to be the distinguished German pianist Wilhelm Kempff. An artist
of the old school, Kempff was far too conventional to consider playing in anything but formal attire, so a sartorially acceptable solution
had to be found and hiring tails from the Athenian equivalent of Moss
Bros was apparently not an option. The Menuhins were staying at the
British Embassy. (Despite Yehudi's American nationality, this was their
preferred accommodation when travelling abroad; Diana claimed that
most of Her Majesty's ambassadors had been boyfriends of hers in
their youth, and owed her a favour for having turned down their
marriage proposals.) Sir Charles Peake, our man in Athens, was six
foot four and unable to help the five foot eight Menuhin but Catherine
Peake lent Diana a velvet dress and while Yehudi rehearsed with
Kempff – it was their first joint recital – household staff were
despatched to other embassies with pleas for help. It proved a difficult
assignment. Yehudi normally had all his clothes tailored especially for
him because, as Diana once explained, he had a big thorax but
dwindled away to very narrow hips and legs.

When he eventually went on the concert platform he resembled
Charlie Chaplin in his guise as a tramp. Diana says she had to stifle her
giggles behind her bouquet. The dress trousers had been borrowed from
the French Ambassador and were much too long; the Athenian maid had
taken them up with a needle and thread and pressed them sideways so
there were creases down the outside of his legs. Yehudi's feet were very
small and narrow, but he shuffled in wearing a pair of large, shiny-
black lace-up boots. His tailcoat reached almost to the ground at the back
and, instead of his customary soft piqué shirt, he sported an enormous
boiled garment whose starched cuffs dwarfed his hands and were so long
and stiff that he had to keep on hitching up his sleeves while playing to
prevent them from striking the violin strings along with his bow. The
performance went off well, all things considered, but at the reception
after the concert the Italian Ambassador took Diana on one side to suggest that her husband ought to consider going to a better tailor.

The story of the lost luggage is narrated in Diana's log-book (published in *Fiddler's Moll*) in a forced, almost hysterical tone which becomes understandable in the light of the crisis she and Yehudi had recently been through. A few months earlier, in August 1955, Diana had given birth to her third son, whom they named Alexis. During her pregnancy she had a 'horrid foreboding' that all was not well but she kept her fears to herself and at her final consultation her San Francisco gynaecologist had expressed himself totally satisfied. She records what happened next: 'At 6 a.m. I went into Stanford University Hospital. At 4.35 in the afternoon a perfect boy weighing 7lb 3oz was born. He died twenty minutes later.' Diana was forty-two. She discussed how driven she had become at this period in an interview in 1996:

I was becoming almost masochistic, too proud. I thought I'm *inébranlable* [steadfast, unshakeable]. I took on Yehudi's life: if he wanted a thing it could be done. Of course I should have said, 'I'm not going to do it; I'm not going to be in Fontainebleau at a temperature of 108 degrees in the shade or travel on a broken-down boat.'

In her 1984 memoirs she had written that the doctors 'never fathomed the reason why' her child had died but in 1996 she gave an explanation. She had caught dysentery on the boat returning to California from Europe. She had spent the earlier summer in Gstaad and it might have been more prudent to stay there.

A low-grade infection killed the child. The child was perfect, but it had pneumonia in both its lungs. It was my fault, utterly my fault. I should have taken over and said, 'No, Yehudi dear, I'm sorry but I'm not going.'

She was being a little hard on herself. With Yehudi's blessing she had lain low for 'five or six weeks' of her pregnancy at the Bircher clinic in Switzerland. As she recuperated, comforted by her weeping husband, they faced up to their loss. 'One cannot help always returning to the great question "why?",' wrote Yehudi in response to a consolatory note from Sir Adrian Boult. But he could offer no coherent answer, as this excerpt from his letter indicates:

There is nothing more depressing than innocence wronged. However, for my part, this is additional proof that we cannot really consider ourselves as isolated units in creation, for being held accountable for debts beyond our immediate control should prove that we cannot really consider ourselves innocent of guilt so long as we are part and parcel of a larger ignorance or a larger intelligence.

It had been a bad twelve months: Furtwängler had died in October

1954, and in May 1955 Enesco finally succumbed to his wasting illness. Two months after the death of baby Alexis Yehudi's woes increased when a biography of the first forty years of his life was published in America, with the subtitle 'The Story of the Man and the Musician'. Its 300-page narrative is enlivened by dozens of interviews and concert reviews; it features fanciful chapter headings such as *The Submerged Part of the Iceberg* and pseudo-philosophical passages concerning Yehudi's crisis of confidence as a violinist in his early manhood.

The author, Robert Magidoff, was an American journalist and poet who had first met Yehudi in Russia in November 1945. (With sadly characteristic inaccuracy he stated that it was a wartime visit.) When they met again five years later Magidoff made his first informal proposal for a biography and in 1952 Yehudi gave his approval. He was only thirty-six at the time, absurdly young for an 'official' biography. The biographer then received a great deal of co-operation from virtually everybody in the family except Marutha. Yehudi drew up a long list of names and contacts to be followed up with interviews; Moshe provided files and press cuttings; later Diana went through the page proofs; she wrote to Zamira that she was having two editing sessions a day with the author.

When the book came out in October 1955, entitled *Yehudi Menuhin*, it was received very positively. The *New York Times* called it 'fascinating and penetrating . . . a frank account of a prodigy's life, the bitter mingled with the sweet'. The *Boston Globe* said it was a painful story, 'a skilfully organized psychological study'. But Moshe and Marutha, respectively sixty-two and fifty-nine years old, were deeply hurt by what the book said about them, wounded to an extent that can be fully appreciated only by reading Moshe's twelve-page, single-spaced typed memorandum. 'To my sorrow and heartache,' he wrote, 'there are many terrible lies, inventions, fantasies, about your parents which assume the form of a DEFAMATION of them.' Moshe's anger was to some extent justified: Magidoff meant well but many of his facts were wrong and there is a discernible bias against Marutha in the early chapters, which might well have been prompted by her refusal to help with his researches. Moshe's fury was partly directed against Diana:

When she returned home while you were still on the road last April I offered to

351

read the proofs . . . if only to save you from the regret of printing falsehoods about your parents. She refused me point blank.

Yet Moshe had heard that there were six copies of the proofs at Alma; they were intentionally keeping him in the dark. He felt stabbed in the back by Yehudi:

We were chums, and free, equal partners, who talked freely even as we debated the issues in the Manchester *Guardian* and the *Nation*.

He was also hurt by the inclusion in the book of a long, undated letter from Hephzibah to her brother which did not beat about the bush in its criticism of their parents. Writing just after her divorce and her subsequent marriage to Richard Hauser, Hephzibah looks back on the mistakes in the siblings' broken lives:

Perhaps the worst was that lack of contact with life as it is generally lived amongst those who are not absolutely sheltered from everyday's troubles, as we were. It made awful fools of us when we faced our first life situations.

Reading page after page of his elder daughter's recriminations, Moshe is reduced to tears.

What happened to you, my darling sweet butter, Hephzibah??? Almost up to the day of your sudden abduction by your new husband, you always raved about your wonderful, easy and kind and accommodating Lindsay . . . Of course you had some domestic problems of some human sort. Who has not, and overcomes it? . . . You the happy-go-lucky, beautiful, serene, satisfied, healthy charming woman, now going on thirty-six – with a Past that is the envy of any girl on earth . . . why do you translate your tragedy or transgression into a tirade against your innocent, loving, self-sacrificing parents? WHY??

Yehudi is criticized, too, along with Richard Hauser, whom Moshe must have met when he visited Australia the previous year:

If only you had not, at this tragic moment in Hephzibah's life, contributed to her delinquency, and [instead] let her stew for a while in the mess she suddenly, unexpectedly, brewed up to the downfall of her husband and her wonderful two sons, who need her so much more than the mentally and morally degenerate [drop-outs] for whom she aids her new husband in his business.

One may judge that Moshe's reproof was intended for all three of his children:

You turn your insides into a glass house for all to watch the emergence and slow evolution – some day you will fully grow up but I fear we shall be dead, of age and sorrow . . . and when new editions of the biography of you, Yehudi, will be rewritten, by some more honest and less materialistic, boot-licking Magidoff, you will be . . . ashamed of this slap and punishment you gave . . . your father and mother.

Alexander Fried, the critic of the *San Francisco Examiner*, was on Moshe's side. 'Bitterly unjust,' he called the book. Magidoff was trying to inject a phoney conflict into the story.

Some of us 'were there', as the saying goes. We have been in an intimate position for the whole of Yehudi's career to see one basic fact: far from having borne a burden in his parents, Yehudi and his biographer can thank them infinitely for the artist and person they made of him.

Magidoff's book came out in the same month as a generally favourable two-part *New Yorker* profile entitled 'Prodigy's Progress' written by the respected music journalist Winthrop Sargeant. The peppery Moshe fired off letters of complaint about that biographical study too. But the unbiased observer must surely sympathize with his diatribe concerning Yehudi's personal crisis, labelled by Magidoff as the 'battle of the violin'. The biography is 'full of this absurd battle', Moshe complained, as were the profiles in the *New Yorker*.

Why not call it the 'battle of the wives'??? You know that you have had under Persinger and Enesco all the technical studies that any living student of the violin ever had. Great surgeons and great engineers take up always REFRESHER COURSES to learn the new researches discovered in their fields, apply the new ideas and thus learn as they grow, on and on, to their last days, without writing about the 'Battle of the Scalpel' or the 'Battle of the Sliding rule'. For several years you were humanly torn between two battling wives for the possession of your person. It was a miracle that you surmounted and recovered your position on the peak of your profession without many noticing the tribulations and strain you lived through.

Such uncomfortable home truths can only have strengthened Diana's resolve to remove her family from California and give up the fiction that Alma, with its 'hollow beauty and its false sense of security', was in any real sense home. She decided that her boys should be educated at boarding schools in England. (Zamira had already moved on to a finishing school in Paris.) The getaway was prepared slowly and even surreptitiously. Her farewell to Moshe and Marutha was 'loving but vague'. The actual 'Hegira', as she dubbed their flight from Alma, was almost indecently precipitate since the only home they had in Europe at the time was a rented chalet in Gstaad. But over the next three years all that was to change. Their own chalet was soon to be built in

Gstaad. In 1958 the art historian Bernard Berenson lent them a small villa on his estate outside Florence; it became an alternative European 'nest' for a couple of years. And, as the decade turned, Diana finally got what she had no doubt wanted all along, a lovely home in London. As Yehudi put it, she had been 'too shy to suggest settling directly in London' which is why their first choice was Switzerland, 'for its sanity, schools, healthy living and central location'. Before he left Alma in the spring of 1956, Yehudi allayed his still guilty conscience by presenting his parents with open-dated return air tickets to Europe so they could come and visit whenever they wanted. The irony of offering them a potentially dangerous mode of transport which he had personally forsworn seems to have escaped him. In any case Marutha turned them down.

Recommended Recordings

Mendelssohn: Violin Concerto in E minor
Berlin Philharmonic Orchestra, conducted by Wilhelm Furtwängler
EMI 7 69799 2
Recorded: 25 and 26 May 1952
The only LP YM made with his idol in Berlin. John Ardoin commends it thus: 'strong in line and intent, and wonderfully alive . . . His sound is eager, vaulting and brims with warmth.' (See pages 335–6.)

Nielsen: Violin Concerto in D
Danish State Radio Symphony Orchestra, conducted by Mogens Wöldike
EMI 7 63987 2
Recorded: 28 September 1952
A good example of the speed and confidence with which YM could assimilate an unfamiliar work.

PART FOUR
The Sage of Highgate
1956–1968

Hiking in the mountains near Gstaad

13 Moving to Europe

Zamira, Jeremy, Yehudi, Diana and Gerard; the first summer in Gstaad, 1954

1956: third visit to South Africa; introduces Shostakovich Concerto at Johannesburg Festival; back operation in Cape Town; 1957: first Gstaad Festival; introduces Bloch Concerto in New York, dispute with New York Philharmonic Orchestra over encores; 1958: family takes up residence at Florence estate of B.B. (Bernard Berenson); they take up residence at 2 The Grove in London and also move into the Chankly Bore chalet in Gstaad.

YEHUDI MENUHIN WAS EXACTLY FORTY when he abandoned his home in California. He had spent so much time abroad in the previous decade that he had been obliged to remind a *Newsweek* interviewer that he actually was an American – on which fact the success of his profitable US recital tours must to some extent have depended.

Since taking up residence with Nola in 1938 he had rarely lived for more than a few weeks at a time at Alma, but his departure had a symbolic importance none the less: Europe had become the centre of his artistic world; he had rejected his parents' American Dream. A decade later he tried to play down the defection: two Swiss cantons made him an honorary citizen and as a consequence the US State Department (the consulate in Frankfurt, to be specific) refused his application to renew his passport. This was tantamount to depriving him of his American citizenship, but after he pointed out that Sir Winston Churchill had been granted honorary American citizenship without anybody questioning his loyalty to the British crown, the Secretary of State, William P. Rogers, wrote to apologize for the misunderstanding, as Yehudi reported, 'hoping I would always be an American, congratulating me on Switzerland's gesture'.

In 1985 Menuhin became a British citizen, at last entitled to call himself 'Sir Yehudi' – he had been made an honorary KBE (Knight of the Order of the British Empire) as early as 1965. He never lost an American burr in his speaking voice and he never renounced his American citizenship but he did, to quote his manager, writing in 1999, 'voluntarily and very quietly give it up a few years ago . . . he felt strongly he was so closely identified with Europe'.

For two years after leaving America the Menuhins lived in their normal manner, out of suitcases, returning from their various cultural safaris to see their boys in Gstaad; Schwester Marie was happily ensconced at their rented chalet, which rejoiced in the Swiss-German name of 'Wasserngrat'. Gerard was eight and going to school locally, at the Chalet Flora; Jeremy was five. The idea of leaving one's children in the care of a trained and trusted woman was perfectly acceptable in the upper-class circle from which Diana herself had emerged. Recalling her own childhood she wrote that 'for most of the time we were left in the company of nurses and governesses'. Marie Blaser, 'Schwester Marie', was simply a person to whom she could entrust her children with complete confidence. She had the additional merit, in Diana's eyes, of greatly preferring 'dull old Switzerland to pink balloon California'.

In the autumn of 1956, having paid his last respects to the eighty-nine-year-old Toscanini, who was living in unwilling retirement at his island home on Lake Como, Yehudi sailed to South Africa to take part in the Johannesburg Festival. Toscanini's protégé Guido Cantelli was among the conductors at this epoch-making assembly of international musicians. Andrés Segovia was another renowned soloist and Margot Fonteyn led the dancers. The music and drama at the Festival were in the hands of Ernest Fleischmann, a dynamic young German-born South African who was to become an influential administrator as manager of the London Symphony Orchestra, inviting Yehudi to do Brahms, Schubert and Enesco with the LSO in the 1960s. He was one of the first to encourage Yehudi's symphonic conducting ambitions.

Yehudi gave nine concerts in all, introducing Shostakovich's new Violin Concerto in A minor, Op. 99 – perhaps the most challenging contemporary work he ever championed. His friend David Oistrakh had introduced it to the world a year earlier. Yehudi had not seen Shostakovich since his visit to Moscow in 1945 but he felt close to him through his warm friendship with Oistrakh. He had recently persuaded the US State Department to grant Oistrakh a visa, despite the chilly relations between the two superpowers, and was at Idlewild airport to greet the Russian at the beginning of his American tour in the autumn of 1955. From Johannesburg Yehudi sent a cable to Shostakovich informing him rather grandly of 'the southern hemisphere première' of the Concerto and promising an unscheduled repeat performance the following week. In October 1961 Yehudi was to give the Concerto's first performance by an American violinist in America. Louis Biancolli in the *World-Telegram and Sun* ranked it with Alban Berg's as one of the two greatest violin concertos of the previous fifty years.

Most of us were becoming convinced that the Concerto was reserved for Soviet astronauts of the bow like Oistrakh and Kagan. Mr Menuhin seems to be the first American to match them at their game. While by no means a virtuoso of faultless power, his performance rang with compelling strength and rhythmic élan.

When Yehudi left Johannesburg after an intensive fortnight of recitals and concerto performances, the *Star*'s reviewer singled out among his contributions to the Festival his 'fineness as a person'. This was probably a reference to the fact that Yehudi had donated the proceeds of his final concert (over £1000) to a relief fund for Hungarian refugees. While the British and French were preoccupied by their ignoble invasion of Suez and the humiliating withdrawal under American pressure, the Russians put down a popular uprising in Budapest and thousands of Hungarians fled to the West in search of a freer life. Yehudi was to be closely connected with the orchestra of refugee Hungarian musicians set up in Germany soon afterwards under Antal

Dorati's leadership. With the Shostakovich Concerto in mind, the *Star*'s man also cited Yehudi's 'great executant powers and his eagerness to adventure among the newer masterpieces'. The article began with a reference to Yehudi's continuing fight against apartheid, thanking him 'for his generous willingness to give extra concerts for non-Europeans'. Yehudi had also accepted the presidency of the Arts Federation of South Africa, whose aim was 'to encourage opportunities for non-Whites to experience and enjoy all the arts'; among his co-officials was Father Trevor Huddleston. So he did what he could, but he left South Africa resolved not to play there again until the evil of apartheid had been removed.

True to his word he stayed away for almost forty years – until the peaceful revolution that brought President Mandela to power. In the spring of 1995 Yehudi conducted Handel's *Messiah* in a township outside Johannesburg with, as he wrote,

an excellent black choir and a wonderful black South African mezzo-soprano Sibongile Khamalo . . . Before the audience would let us leave, the choir broke quite spontaneously into some of their own traditional songs and dances.

Yehudi normally never missed a concert but a bad back forced him to cancel much of his 1956 South African tour. He played the last of his nine Johannesburg concerts leaning against a high stool for support. In Cape Town he managed to play the Beethoven and Mendelssohn Concertos (with Hugo Rignold conducting) but he was in considerable pain and on 16 November underwent an operation for a slipped disc. He then spent several weeks recuperating under Diana's watchful eye at the seaside resort of Hermanus, forbidden to touch his violin but joined by his family and Schwester Marie for Christmas. He returned to England on the *Winchester Castle*, practising so assiduously that only two days after docking at Southampton he was back in action. It had been his longest involuntary lay-off in thirty years of concert-giving. 'I was obliged to wear a corset for three months', he remembered. 'I looked very much like the most elegant of Prussian officers . . . I played the Tchaikovsky Concerto at the Albert Hall and enjoyed it greatly.'

The summers at Gstaad, where there had been no regular music-making since the end of the war, took on an important new dimension after Yehudi was asked by the local director of tourism, Paul Valentin, whether he would 'come to their rescue' by kindly arranging a few concerts to entertain summer visitors to the Bernese Oberland. Grace Kelly and her husband Prince Rainier were among the holiday-makers, along with the usual crowd of celebrities. Monsieur Valentin wrote an article in the local paper reporting that Yehudi had recently purchased an Alphorn and could be heard practising it with his sons.

In his memoirs Menuhin stated that the first Gstaad Festival was held in August 1956. This is incorrect. He met Benjamin Britten and Peter Pears that month and Diana's diary confirms that they discussed the idea of summer music in the mountains but the first Festival, consisting of just two concerts, was held on 4 and 6 August 1957. The chosen location was in the neighbouring village of Saanen, where Antal Dorati had tipped the Menuhins off that a church dating from the early 1600s possessed a fine acoustic. The cellist Maurice Gendron joined Pears, Britten and Menuhin for some rare musical treats. The programme included music by Bach and Telemann for the unusual combination of tenor, violin, cello and harpsichord, as well as songs by Purcell and Schubert and the Schubert *Fantaisie* (D.934), a work that Britten and Menuhin had played together at Belsen twelve years earlier. It was a modest but distinctive beginning to a most agreeable festival with which the Menuhins were to be intimately connected for forty years. The following year, 1958, saw an expansion to five concerts. It was then that Vivaldi's *Seasons* were performed (with Pears narrating the poetic texts and Britten conducting from the harpsichord) – not 1956 as *Unfinished Journey* would have it.

Yehudi's commitment to new music, which endured to the end of his life, is an element in his musical philosophy that has been insufficiently recognized. After the Shostakovich Concerto, he tackled another big contemporary work, the Violin Concerto by his friend Ernest Bloch, whom he had known since childhood days in San Francisco. Completed in 1938, it had never been performed at a New York Philharmonic concert until Yehudi introduced it in December 1957, when the composer was in his late seventies and already seriously ill. The Concerto is of course a more complex work than Bloch's overtly Jewish music such as *Abodah* and *Nigun* which Yehudi had played when a boy. With his infallible ability swiftly to grasp a work's structure and its emotional core he delivered what was evidently a fine interpretation. 'His identity with the concerto was complete,' wrote Jay Harrison in the *Herald Tribune*.

Every facet of its eclectic style, every phrase and every measure, was delivered with the assurance of a musician whose interpretation is going just the way he wants it to.

Howard Taubman in the *New York Times* regretted that

a bit of the sparkle and security has gone from his playing, but it was easy to forgive him in view of his communication of Bloch's essential thought. In the hushed, mysterious slow movement Mr Menuhin was at his best; here his playing had purity of tone and feeling.

The applause was generous and unrestrained. Yehudi was called back three times. Then, with the conductor's blessing, he decided to play an encore. Had there been an appropriate Bloch work he would surely have chosen it as a further gesture of affectionate sympathy (the composer was too frail to attend in person). Instead he played unaccompanied Bach (the *Praeludium* of the E major Partita) and although the public departed happy for the interval, a major row immediately broke out backstage. Bruno Zirato, the orchestra's manager and a friend ever since Yehudi's Carnegie Hall début with Fritz Busch in 1927, was, Diana noted in her diary,

yelling in Italian at Y as though he were the bad boy of the Lower Third. How dare he have the colossal impertinence to play an encore? Didn't he know perfectly well that such vulgarities were never permitted by the management in these sanctified walls?

Yehudi had it explained to him that encores by soloists could upset broadcast timings and break a mood; they were simply not done at the Philharmonic. (That encores might run the management into overtime payments for the players was not mentioned but was certainly the underlying reason for the ban.) The following afternoon Yehudi gave a second performance of the Bloch Concerto. Again there was mighty applause, and again Yehudi gave an encore. The story became headline news: 'Encores by Menuhin draw fire – "rebel" Menuhin explains his stand.'

In the 1950s the Philharmonic gave four concerts on successive days; its weekend programmes were often lighter and for Saturday and Sunday Yehudi switched from the Bloch to Paganini's Concerto in D. According to the *New York Times* his playing was under par in the first movement:

The melancholy second movement is finer music and Mr Menuhin was at his best here, giving nobility and intensity to the songful solo part. In the brilliant finale he was in better technical form and was warmly applauded by the orchestra players as well as audience. He was recalled several times as speculation mounted in the audience as to the possibility of an encore. Finally Mr Menuhin gestured for silence. He smiled and said, 'I am not allowed.' There was more applause. Mr Menuhin added, 'I am not at all sure you are allowed to applaud either.'

Yehudi the rebel was on song. What he was sure about, he continued, was

that if Bach could realize what even two or three minutes of his music could do to the traditions and budget of this great orchestra, he would be very sorry.

And then he declared war:

In spite of the fact that this orchestra, unlike many others, seems to be run by non-musical, or extra-musical, forces, I would like to assure you for myself and my colleagues here on the stage that we love and are grateful for your enthusiasm and that you may applaud whenever, and as long as, you like.

This sally was greeted by laughter and more applause; he was even brought back to take another bow. The management, in the person of Bruno Zirato, kept below the parapet, making no public comment. This was the Christmas season, after all, as one columnist noted: 'Whatever one's personal convictions we can only applaud everybody concerned for being good-natured about this rather explosive situation.'

At his final concert the next afternoon Yehudi took seven bows from an audience that scented blood and hoped for further sensation, but he said nothing. 'Yehudi sore, but yields' was the headline in the *New York Mirror*. The management was sore, too. Yehudi was a huge box-office draw and by far the highest-paid violinist on their roster; he was receiving $5000 an engagement as far back as 1946. He had played with the orchestra for five seasons out of the previous seven but after this stand-off he was not invited back until 1964.

He argued his defence in a letter to *Saturday Review*, saying that his decision to play an encore was

an impulse, sparked off by the strange phenomenon that is the collective heart and spirit of a friendly crowd. In this mass-communications era people still go to concerts because they find in the concert hall the irreplaceable satisfaction of belonging to, and being an essential ingredient of the occasion.

Hence the applause, he claimed, and hence the call for an encore. It was a plausible explanation but it takes no account of the Philharmonic's 'no encore' tradition, something Yehudi must surely have known about since childhood. There was undoubtedly an impishness about his reaction, particularly the decision to give an encore after the second concert. A concert notice by Howard Taubman, the shrewd observer from the *New York Times*, was probably what had stung him to make a little more mischief. Writing after the first concert, Taubman accepted that Yehudi had responded spontaneously.

But the gesture reflected a lack of professional tact. It violated a tradition of an organization whose guest Mr Menuhin was. What was worse, it disturbed the balance of the programme and provided an unwarranted intrusion on the mood left by Bloch. And worst of all, Mr Menuhin played the encore badly . . . [taking] it at a vertiginous pace which he could not support technically.

A few weeks later, when the Menuhins were touring in California, Yehudi took advantage of a free day to make the long pilgrimage up the Pacific coast to visit Ernest Bloch at his cliffside home at Agate Beach, Oregon. He described his destination as 'a wild, forlorn stretch of coastline looking down upon waves coming all the way from Asia . . . a place which suited the grandeur and intensity of his character'. Soon after they set out, in a small car driven by Bloch's daughter, a storm of great intensity blew in from the ocean. As usual, Diana saw the funny side:

The prospect of a fascinating journey up that glorious coast was soon transformed into an adventure compared with which Wagner's *Ride of the Valkyries* would have seemed a children's gymkhana.

Yehudi was oblivious to the discomfort: he was on a mission similar to that which had prompted his approach to the ailing Bartók in 1943. When they struggled in from the rain and wind a welcome fire was burning in the Blochs' hearth.

Y and Ernest sat down talking happily, discussing the solo [suites] he had commissioned, mulling over the days of old while we slowly dried off and were given glorious coffee by his wife.

Before they left, Bloch filled Diana's pockets with rough agates gathered from the beach far below. Yehudi later described the two suites Bloch wrote for him as 'expressive, melodic, classical in a manner that calls to mind latter-day Bach'. He recorded them in the mid-1970s, after making a fine version of Bloch's Violin Concerto in 1963 with the Philharmonic under Paul Kletzki.

Yehudi admired Bloch but he loved Bartók. In 1959 he added the Hungarian composer's recently revealed First Violin Concerto to his repertoire. This strange and puzzling work, twenty minutes long, dates from 1907 and had lain unpublished in its original form in the collection of its dedicatee, Stefi Geyer, a Hungarian violinist with whom Bartók had been in love. (The opening movement was soon recycled as the first of the 1910 *Two Portraits*.) After Geyer's death the world première was reserved, as her will stipulated, for a Swiss colleague, Hansheinz Schneeberger, but Bartók's executor then gave Yehudi exclusivity on performances for a year. The Concerto duly took its place alongside those by Schumann and Mendelssohn (the D minor) whose cause had already been championed by Yehudi.

In the late 1950s, when the avant-garde was losing touch with the regular concertgoing public, Yehudi's commitment to new music was particularly important. In October 1958 he wrote an article on the subject for the London *Sunday Times*:

We – composers and performers – must have a sympathetic understanding of the great effort required on the part of the public today. In the past any given audience was immersed in a regional or period style and even the newest creations emerged from that style. It was therefore much easier to assimilate new works. For instance it has taken some years for the works of Bartók to command the respect and reverence they now receive. It was as recently as 1946 that my first performance of the Second Violin Sonata evoked from isolated quarters of a sold-out Salle Pleyel, shouts of 'Ridicule! Absurde!' and so forth. I played it there again last year, when such a manifestation would have been impossible . . . Little-known or unknown works have in my experience always acted as a stimulant to artist, audience and connoisseur alike. The contrast, the accelerated mental and physical activity, induced by the strange – if only at its lowest level of surprise – unfailingly heightens the enjoyment of the familiar.

The paper's editor noted approvingly that Yehudi had recently given the première of Ross Lee Finney's two-movement *Fantasy*, a serial work commissioned for the American pavilion at the Brussels 1958 World Fair. When he advertised the Finney work as part of his next London recital, the advance ticket sales were disappointingly poor for a Menuhin concert. With his manager's connivance he announced a change of programme: the twelve-tone Finney composition would be replaced by Beethoven's 'Kreutzer' Sonata. 'The tickets straight away sold out,' he recalled.

At the concert I gently admonished the audience. 'I hope you don't feel you're here under false pretences,' I said . . . 'We announced we would play the "Kreutzer" and so we will. But first you must listen to Ross Lee Finney.'

When he assessed his long career in his memoirs he claimed, rightly,

that he had done his best to modernize violin recitals: 'It's a rare programme today that only looks back to the past.'

In 1958 the Menuhins owned no property in Europe. Five years
later they had a fine London town house, a summer home in the Swiss
mountains and a modest cottage on the island of Mykonos. And yet
their first attempt to put down roots can only have sent their friends'
eyebrows rising in disbelief. A converted farmhouse on the estate of a
nonagenarian art historian must have seemed an unlikely headquarters
for an itinerant musician of Yehudi's stature, particularly when he had
already established a home of sorts in a rented chalet in an equally
inaccessible Swiss ski resort. But when he took a fancy to a house
nothing would stop him – a trait he inherited from his mother – and
in the autumn of 1958 the Menuhins moved into the *villino* at the
celebrated Tuscan home of Bernard Berenson.

Florence was then a backwater with an awkward train service and
no international airport. I Tatti, five miles north-east on the Settignano
road, had been Berenson's home for many years; he had made a handsome fortune from his expertise in Renaissance painting. Habitually
dressed in a dazzling white suit (pale grey in the winter), he lived like
a lord and entertained a constant stream of visitors. The Menuhins had
been introduced to him by their American writer friend Iris Origo four
years earlier, and in 1955 Diana had written from her Swiss clinic to
congratulate him on his ninetieth birthday. A lively correspondence
ensued and the Menuhins had taken the train from Switzerland a
couple of times for short stays at I Tatti before Yehudi noticed the
farmhouse on the estate (it was occupied at the time by the young art
historian William Mostyn Owen) and dropped the hint that he would
like to convert it into a home for his family. The snobbish 'B.B.' was
happy to oblige. He loved walking on the hills and taking drives
around Fiesole in Diana's company. Yehudi offered cash for rent but
seems to have paid only in kind, by doing up the *villino* and providing
Berenson with distinguished chamber music whenever he was in
residence.

Diana was in her element putting the place in order. Furnishings
brought over from Alma were supplemented by household essentials
(such as a decent stove and a coffee percolator) and second-hand
knick-knacks unearthed in Florence antique shops. Set among pines
and arbutus trees but within sight of the grandiose I Tatti, the *villino*
became a real home and family snaps exist to prove it: Zamira, Gerard

and Jeremy in fancy dress for Yehudi's forty-third birthday party; Diana picnicking in the woods with a frail B.B. sporting a straw hat; Yehudi and Jeremy playing a sonata together – the seven-year-old boy took piano lessons from a Signora Nardi and attended Miss Burbridge's little school for English and American children. (Gerard meanwhile had become a boarder at the highly reputed Hermanns-berg, a German preparatory school founded by Kurt Hahn of Gordon-stoun fame.)

Living in Italy proved an idyllic interlude: the Menuhins were probably happier together here than anywhere. Yehudi had inherited from his mother a fondness for all things Italian, including food, though he made Schwester Marie use organic substances for his choco-late birthday cake. Cocoa beans and sugar were banned – to be sub-stituted, according to Diana, by such patented health alternatives as 'Cocomerde' or 'Grottochoc'. The cake turned out

like a huge cowpat, reducing the children [and their nurse] to angry tears as they finally abandoned the attempt to make forty-three candles stay upright in the sticky mess.

Yehudi ignored such problems. He retreated into what in earlier days he had described as his 'glass box'. For him the entire Florentine episode was delightful. Despite her inability to resist scoring points off her husband when she came to write her memoirs, Diana was happier with Yehudi, too. She enjoyed spending Christmas with their friends the Origo family and setting up her own little home was 'like moving into the sun from the shade'. She writes enthusiastically of conversa-tions of interest and wit with Berenson, his life companion Nicky Mariano and their guests. Life was almost bearable for her:

Colour and warmth and beauty and liveliness to fill up the still rare gaps between work and duties, but all made lighter, illuminated by Latin incandescence and loving company.

The idyll was not to last a second summer: Berenson, ninety-five, was growing more frail by the month and increasingly deaf. He died soon after the Menuhins departed in March 1960, refusing to allow them in to say farewell.

While they were at the *villino* Diana joined Yehudi on an Italian recital tour. She had a sharp eye for the absurdities of her husband's interminable round of concertgiving. At the San Carlo opera house, plump Neapolitan ladies were chattering in their boxes throughout his recital. An outraged gentleman in the stalls kept shouting 'Silenzio!' but that only made them redouble their gossiping. When a grateful Diana went to thank the protester she discovered he was not a Neapolitan but a German tourist. He was rewarded by a backstage visit to Yehudi, who merely smiled and said he loved the Italians' volubility.

Diana noticed that a sinister figure carrying a large briefcase always arrived in the dressing room during the interval of the recitals. She also observed that Yehudi's pianist partner Marcel Gazelle, normally the slimmest of Belgians, seemed suddenly to put on weight around the buttocks and thighs in the second half of the concerts. By the time they reached Genoa, the penny had dropped: the briefcase contained the duo's fee, which was paid in cash by the wary concert agent only when it was clear that the artists would not renege on their contracts. The prudent Gazelle looked after such matters for his unworldly partner. Distrustful of security backstage, he secreted the fee about his person. The cash must have been delivered in notes of very small denomination, since the pianist appeared to be perched on at least two telephone directories.

Italy was fun but the Menuhins were being pulled irresistibly towards England. Yehudi claimed he had always felt at home in what he described as 'the most liveable country in the world'. He had strong ties with Paris, too, where he had spent much of his youth, but in England there was so much more for him to do, apart from giving concerts. For somebody as intellectually curious as Yehudi, England's attraction was what he called the horizontality of its society:

You happen to be a famous violinist; you happen to win recognition; and this, you find, wins you acquaintance with scientists, sociologists, painters, captains of industry, actors, statesmen.

He wrote articles for a London newspaper, lectured to the Royal Society, broadcast on the Third Programme and appeared on BBC Television's *The Brains Trust*. He had an 'organically controlled mind', said Diana. The vision of the happy, more settled family life that he had experienced in Florence must be re-created, transformed to London, where he could play the roles of sage and teacher in addition to impresario and conductor. London was his wife's home town, after all, and they had dozens of friends there. From one of them, Lady Crosfield, the Greek-born music-loving wife of a shipping magnate, they learned that a fine house was up for sale in Highgate, an unspoilt, leafy area in north London that retained the atmosphere of a village but was only five miles from the West End. It adjoined the Crosfields' estate, Witanhurst, on the edge of Hampstead Heath.

Number 2, The Grove, was part of a row of 'Grace and Favour' houses built in the 1660s by Charles II as a safe retreat for his mistresses at the time of the Plague. The poet Coleridge had died next door, at the home of his doctor. At the back was a large and lovely garden: standing on its lawn, in the shade of a giant ilex tree, you could imagine yourself in the country, far from the booming traffic's roar. And the Menuhin boys would be able to cycle on the Heath beyond, as Yehudi had done with his sisters when they lived outside Paris in the 1930s. The property was inspected by the Menuhins, declared by Diana 'exquisite but far too expensive' and promptly bought by Yehudi from its American owner Bill Whitney. Whitney was married to the actress Adrianne Allen: Daniel and Anna, her children by her earlier marriage to Raymond Massey, lived with her, and Anna Massey remembers the handover to the Menuhins: 'My mother had painted over some of the original oak panelling and I'm afraid Diana didn't approve.' She thinks the price paid was £27,000, a medium-sized fortune in 1959. Yehudi loved the panelling too. 'In my conception all wooden objects have a life of their own,' he said, 'and deserve to be acknowledged with tributes of wax and polish.'

As if reorganizing and refurnishing a large London house was insufficient challenge for his long-suffering, home-building spouse, Yehudi chose the same season, 1959–60, to construct the Chankly Bore chalet in Gstaad. This simultaneous advance on two fronts suggests that he wanted to avoid any repetition of the humiliating disaster of his father's cancelled house-building plan at Los Gatos twenty-five years earlier. Architects were hired and all year long, while Yehudi's regular touring life continued, plans were submitted for house and garden in Gstaad; builders were chivvied by Diana, trees planted, flowerbeds dug, furniture purchased in Berne and a handsome music room incorporated into the design, so that by July 1960 the chalet was ready for the family to move in, just in time for the annual Gstaad Festival – and for the regular summer visit of Mr Iyengar, who duly arrived at seven on their first morning in their new Swiss Alps home.

Recommended Recordings

Bloch: Violin Concerto
Philharmonia Orchestra, conducted by Paul Kletzki
EMI 7 63989 2
Recorded: 18 and 19 June 1963
Played with the same passionate commitment that must have informed Yehudi's première performance in New York. (The same CD includes the Alban Berg Violin Concerto discussed in chapter 16.)

Bartók: Violin Concerto No. 1
New Philharmonia Orchestra, conducted by Antal Dorati
EMI 7 63985 2
Recorded: 24 February 1965 and 3 October 1966
Essential listening for Bartók lovers.

Pablo Casals: Casals Festival at Prades, vol. 1
Mozart: Piano Quartet No. 2 in E♭ (K.493)
    with Ernst Wallfisch (viola), Pablo Casals (cello)
    and Mieczyslaw Horszowski (piano)
    Recorded: 1956
Beethoven: Trio in C, Op. 1 No. 3
    with Pablo Casals (cello) and Hephzibah Menuhin (piano)
    Recorded: 1959
Brahms: Trio No. 3 in C minor, Op. 101
    with Pablo Casals (cello) and Eugene Istomin (piano)
    Recorded: 1955
Music and Arts CD–688
An astonishing document – live performances, recorded at concerts in Prades.

Beethoven: Sonata in F, Op. 24 ('Spring')
with Hephzibah Menuhin (piano)
EMI 4 78108 2
Recorded: 4 October 1957 and 6 January 1959
YM recorded the Beethoven sonatas many times. Unfortunately his earlier 1950s cycle with Louis Kentner has not yet been transferred to CD. He first played Beethoven with Wilhelm Kempff in 1955 and recorded the cycle in 1970. He recorded most of the sonatas yet again with his son in the 1980s. But this 1958 recording with his sister, made in London, is perhaps the most enjoyable of them all.

14 The Impresario

With his sisters at a Bath Festival rehearsal, 1963

1959: begins regular conducting of chamber orchestra and records Bach's Brandenburg Concertos with EMI; 1960s: establishes a London secretariat; 1959–68: Bath Festival; 1969–72: Windsor Festival.

BY 1960 A PATTERN can be discerned in Yehudi's life: each year there was a lengthy and lucrative recital tour of the US and shorter tours in the UK and Europe. Once in a while he made an expedition further afield, to Australia, India or the Soviet Union. Appearances at international festivals (and his own more modest affairs in Gstaad and Bath) enlivened the summer months. In the 1960s there were to be new passions, among them the foundation of an international school for

371

young musicians and a campaign to release dissidents from the Soviet Union. A second career developed as an impresario, notably at the Bath Festival, and a third as a conductor. He continued to record chamber music and the major violin concertos: in the 1960s he returned to Bruch, Beethoven and Elgar and added, among others, Berg, Bloch and Walton to his catalogue. But as both solo violinist and conductor he greatly expanded his activities to include concerts and recordings devoted to eighteenth-century music, to twentieth-century masterpieces for small orchestra (mostly performed by the Bath Festival Orchestra, later renamed the Menuhin Festival Orchestra) and to new works for violin, which he commissioned.

Taking possession of his homes in London and Gstaad marked a watershed in Menuhin's life. He was not to know it at the time, of course, but 1960 proved to be the halfway mark: almost four decades had passed since he began to play the violin and he was to live almost four decades longer. The outline of his life will continue to unfold chronologically but the remaining chapters in this narrative will concentrate in turn on different concerns in the second half of his life, such as his School, his work for the International Music Council and his campaigns in support of cultural minorities. What follows now is an account of his fourteen years as an English impresario.

Permanent residence in London saw Yehudi slowly turning into an institution, with a cadre of loyal, long-serving staff to look after him and his family. A secretary who spoke three languages, Mrs Wiggington, was hired to look after the ever expanding correspondence. A separate office had to be rented to manage Yehudi's non-musical business. His personal chauffeur in England, known simply as Leach, had been in his service since his marriage in 1947. When he died he was succeeded by a redoubtable chauffeuse named Hope MacBride, 'Mrs McB' to the family. The Whitneys' housekeeper at The Grove, Millie, was invited to stay on temporarily to help run the place and was still there twenty-three years later when Diana finally persuaded Yehudi to quit Highgate, which had by then become the victim of so-called 'relief-road' planning that brought lorries thundering through its streets incessantly.

Disenchantment had set in when it became clear to her that for Yehudi the Highgate house was not, as she planned it to be, 'a graceful house occasionally filled with music and good talk, alive and loved for its warmth and beauty'. On special occasions that was indeed the impression conveyed to their friends, among them the Julian Huxleys, the Isaiah Berlins and the Kenneth Clarks. But in the daytime 2 The Grove was perpetually overrun by as motley a crowd of supplicants as ever assembled for the Marschallin's morning levée in *Der Rosenkavalier*. There were musicians waiting to rehearse or to audition (a very young Jacqueline du Pré among them); television crews preparing interviews (their power cables running out of the front door into the street); specialists in ergonomic chair design (Yehudi fought bad design tenaciously); whole-food practitioners (he helped fund a health-food shop, the first of its kind, in Baker Street), and campaigners for scores of good causes, from the banning of battery farming to the restoration of drinking troughs for carthorses on London's streets.

Music remained paramount, however, and from the moment Yehudi assumed artistic responsibility for the Bath Festival in 1959 he was also caught up in a stream of new recordings for EMI. The festivals were much more than test beds for recording projects, but from the very beginning there was a synergy between the two. The late 1950s was a time of feverish activity by the record companies as they restocked their catalogues to incorporate stereophonic recordings (issued on $33\frac{1}{3}$ r.p.m. long-playing records). EMI's Walter Legge, artistically the most influential producer of the 1950s and founder–director of the Philharmonia Orchestra, thought stereo was merely a gimmick and held out against it longer than his rivals. He was proved wrong in the long run but he had a point: the public's take-up of the new stereo technology was worryingly slow – record collectors were reluctant to re-equip so soon after switching to LP – and even Bach's six Brandenburg Concertos, which Yehudi conducted for EMI in July 1959, just after his first Bath Festival, were recorded in mono as well as stereo, using separate sets of microphones.

Yehudi performed the various solos for violin in the Concertos and in the Sixth made his first public appearance playing the viola, a larger, darker-toned instrument which requires substantial adjustment in fingering. Both at Bath and in the studio at Abbey Road, London, the Brandenburgs were played by a hand-picked orchestra drawn from the gifted freelance musicians who played regularly under the leadership of an outstanding Anglo-French violinist named Robert Masters; his colleagues included the violinists Rodney Friend, Jack Rothstein and Susanne Rosza and the cellists Ambrose Gauntlett, who also played the gamba, and Derek Simpson. Many of the musicians were also members of quartets and therefore accustomed to the democratic give and take of chamber-music rehearsal, which is how Yehudi liked to direct his performances. He later claimed that he was taught how to conduct by his orchestral colleagues: he was no longer an international celebrity who arrived at the studio to do a specific job; he had become a colleague. Earlier in 1959 he had attended an experimental session to explore questions of balance and microphone placing for the Brandenburgs. (The musicologist Denis Stevens advised them.) The recording offered new solutions to the perennial problem of instrumentation. Yehudi remembered that when George Enesco performed Concerto No. 1 in France he employed soprano saxophones for the awkwardly high and penetrative *corno da caccia* hunting-horn parts. But the producer, Peter Andry, persuaded him to opt for modern valve horns, with the young horn virtuoso Barry Tuckwell taking the lead. The oboists Janet Craxton and Michael Dobson were also distinguished soloists. Forty years later these recordings are still in the catalogue, a tribute to the engineering skills of Neville Boyling as well as to the musicians.

Over the next ten years the Bath Festival Orchestra (the qualifying 'chamber' was soon dropped) recorded no fewer than seventy-eight substantial compositions under Yehudi's baton and bow. Among the highlights, many of them since transferred to CD, are Bach's *Musical Offering*, the four Orchestral Suites and the Concerto for violin and oboe, with Leon Goossens as fellow soloist (the recording session was the subject of an early BBC Television music documentary); William Boyce's symphonies (another example of musical archaeology by Yehudi); Handel's organ concertos and string concerti grossi; Mozart's violin concertos and his concertos for one, two and three pianos.

From his first Festival Yehudi made it plain that his annual fortnight in Bath (eleven days, to be precise) was to be a family affair. For a performance of Mozart's Concerto for two pianos, Hephzibah, who was now living in England, was joined by her sister Yaltah. Yehudi was providing a touch of post-marital therapy: his younger sister had been divorced from her second husband the previous year. At the first rehearsal Yaltah was so excited to see her brother on the rostrum conducting that she forgot to come in with her trills at the beginning of the first movement. Her visit had a happy ending: while lodging in a musical boarding house in Kensington she met her third husband, the pianist Joel Ryce, with whom she remained happily married for nearly forty years. He later retrained as a Jungian psychotherapist. Other members of the family and close friends were frequent visitors to Bath: among them Fou Ts'ong (the Chinese pianist who married Zamira in 1960), Louis Kentner, Benjamin Britten and Peter Pears, Alberto Lysy (Yehudi's Argentinian pupil) and the cellists Gaspar Cassado and Maurice Gendron, both exceptionally lively characters with whom Yehudi and Hephzibah also recorded piano trios.

There has been a tendency to write off Menuhin's ten years at Bath as insufficiently ambitious. According to the arts administrator Amelia Freedman, herself in charge of the Festival in the 1980s,

It was a lovely, vivacious festival and he was a great man, but I think his Festival was very focused around the baroque repertoire, his Bath Festival Orchestra and his musical friends.

Sir Michael Tippett and Sir William Glock, Yehudi's immediate successors, both modernists, certainly broadened the Festival's thrust towards the contemporary but a closer look at the programmes from 1959 to 1968 reveals that Ian Hunter and Yehudi Menuhin did more to diversify the musical mix, and thus the overall flavour of the Festival, than received opinion allows.

As the 1959 Festival opened, the *Daily Telegraph* noted approvingly,

Not the least of Menuhin's gifts is his ability to create a special atmosphere of music-making . . . So wide and distinctive are his sympathies that a sense of unity is provided without the accompanying danger of personal whim.

In his first year Yehudi appeared in four guises: violinist, viola player, conductor and speaker, this last in a *Brains-Trust*-style discussion with Isaiah Berlin, William Glock and Nicholas Nabokov. He dropped the full-scale symphony concerts of previous Festivals in favour of chamber music, performing Bartók's *Contrasts* with Reginald Kell and his sister Hephzibah at the Guildhall. 'The choice of venues was so wonderful in Bath,' he remembered. 'So many beautiful buildings, and nothing too big.' Indian music was scheduled regularly from Yehudi's first year. At the Theatre Royal, a Georgian jewel, an operatic double-bill was imported from Ingestre Hall: Bizet's *Dr Miracle* coupled with Purcell's *Dido and Aeneas*, in which Dame Joan Hammond sang Dido; also in the cast as the Sorceress was the young Janet Baker, who became a regular visitor to Bath and subsequently made several recordings with Yehudi. Peter Pears and Benjamin Britten paid the first of many visits, bartering their recital fees here and in Gstaad in exchange for Yehudi's appearances at Aldeburgh. Also in 1959 the regional television company, Television West and Wales, paid for a violin competition, adjudicated by Yehudi himself and Manoug Parikian. (The winner was fourteen-year-old Peter Thomas, who went on to become the leader of the City of Birmingham Symphony Orchestra.) John Dankworth and Stéphane Grappelli were among the stars in a jazz festival that ran in tandem with the classical music.

The next year, 1960, Arnold Cooke's Concerto for small orchestra was premièred under Colin Davis's baton; Gina Bachauer gave a piano recital and the conductors included two more old friends, Sir Adrian Boult and Nadia Boulanger: Yehudi's circle of musical friendships was second to none. He was not responsible, however, for the fringe programming, which in 1960 included a festival ball, a carnival and an all-night jazz event; as dawn broke the erudite blues singer George Melly was heard singing "T'ain't no sin to take off your skin and dance around in your bones'. It is not recorded whether Yehudi was out dancing but at six in the morning he was more likely to have been standing on his head at the Lansdown Grove Hotel, his base for every Festival. Wherever he was, he was certainly having fun. He told an interviewer from *The Times* that he enjoyed directing the Festival as

an exercise in self-education. It gives me the chance to do things I haven't done before, and that's what I like best: just as, when I look at a menu in a foreign country I choose the dishes I don't know.

Preparing the Bach orchestral suites he found himself listening to recordings – for the first time in his life:

Usually anything new that I undertake hasn't yet been recorded, perhaps not even performed before. I found it fascinating to listen to so many contradictory interpretations and was particularly moved to hear an old recording of my former master Adolf Busch. None the less, much as I admired many aspects of these old recordings I did not find myself in agreement with all. I know that I like a certain amount of spice in Bach, by which I mean a nice application of rhythmic stress so that the bow follows the changing patterns as they vary from strong beats to weak beats and back again. This is what brings out the vitality and exhilaration in all music.

At the 1961 Festival there was worldwide press interest in a Roman Orgy at the Baths, where the public was not normally allowed to swim, let alone to hold a party. When revellers, some of them reportedly inebriated, declined to leave at four in the morning the plug was pulled out and the health-giving spa waters dribbled away. 'Some swam on down to the last puddle,' the local paper noted drily. Yehudi claimed later not to have been best pleased by such stunts. The fringe was certainly a vigorous affair: a dance festival named Jambeano circulated in different streets every night for communal dancing and the year's all-night jazz event, at Green Park station, featured Humphrey Lyttelton.

This 1961 Festival, Yehudi's third, was thought to have been the high-water mark, so to speak, in the first half of his directorate. But when he introduced Bath audiences to a fine new violin concerto by Lennox Berkeley, later to be recorded by EMI, performance conditions were, it seems, less than ideal. The programme was too long and Yehudi was involved in every work as either conductor or soloist. During the first movement of the concerto Yehudi's music fell off his stand and fluttered to the feet of the front row of the audience. Nobody returned it to him so he was obliged to call a halt and ask the composer, who was conducting, to start the movement again. In the same year Yehudi invited the enterprising early-music specialist Denis Stevens to arrange a baroque evening with his newly formed Accademia Monteverdiana, entitled 'Music from Mantua'; Yehudi played solos and became something of a convert. A few months later he recorded some Bach violin sonatas in authentic period style: 'I used the curved baroque bow; it doesn't suit modern music but within a narrow range of dynamics it gives more flexibility, more energy.' His partners were new friends, the viola da gamba player Ambrose Gauntlett and the harpsichordist George Malcolm, of whom he was particularly fond:

He was the only man who's ever induced me to smoke a cigarette (I only smoked four puffs in my life) because he brought a wonderful little Indian cigarette, which was made of a single leaf of tobacco with a mouthpiece. I thought if ever I smoke, this is it! No additives, no chemical preservatives!

The Festival was chronically underfunded by a local authority that despite the beauty of its city was not renowned for concern with culture. Ian Hunter often had to face the criticism that it was not getting through to the city's ordinary people. 'Bath is for the connoisseur of the arts,' he insisted, élitist to the core and proud of it, 'but [nevertheless] it can attract civic interest.' To prove the point Yehudi took a leading part in three sold-out concerts for Bath's young people arranged by the 'Youth and Music' organization for which tickets were available only through schools. Bath Abbey, the most spectacular of the city's concert venues (though outclassed by the grandeur of nearby

Wells Cathedral) was the setting for Fauré's Requiem conducted by Nadia Boulanger. Perhaps best of all in a rich year was a performance of Schubert's great C major Quintet with a sixteen-year-old girl playing the second cello. 'Young as she is', wrote the *Bath Chronicle*,

she at once showed the fine quality of her musicianship . . . [in the second movement passage] in which the violin is bowed and the cello plucked, she played with rare judgement and beautiful sensitivity. She matched, indeed, the perfection of Mr Menuhin himself.

Yehudi had heard the sixteen-year-old Jacqueline du Pré at a competition in London and invited her up to The Grove to play trios with himself and Hephzibah. The two Menuhins, then forty-two and thirty-nine respectively, quickly perceived that it was 'Jackie' and no longer they who represented the young generation. 'This passionate and gifted young sprig', Yehudi wrote,

probably felt, exactly as we had, that mixture of adventure and the unknown adding itself to the sheer joy of playing . . . We had a lovely time together, the rehearsals were minimal for we found we shared the same language.

The 1962 Festival maintained the standard: the guests included Rudolf Barshai and his brilliant Moscow Chamber Orchestra, described by the critic Henry Raynor as 'a group of the most sophisticated, disciplined and elegant musicians'. When the Russians and Yehudi's orchestra joined forces the combination provided 'some of the most superb playing to be heard anywhere'. (Raynor was referring in particular to a performance of Tippett's Concerto for Double String Orchestra given on the Russians' second visit in 1965.) The Royal Ballet presented a season in which Margot Fonteyn, partnered by David Blair, danced a *pas de deux* from *Swan Lake*. From a side box Yehudi provided the thrilling violin solo – he had recorded it with Efrem Kurtz and the Philharmonia three years previously. At a morning concert a young school teacher, Peter Maxwell Davies, conducted his own composition, *O Magnum Mysterium*, with his pupils from Cirencester School. Yehudi played a theme and variations for violin and harpsichord by Stephen Arnold, one of Maxwell Davies's sixteen-year-old pupils.

The Festival expanded that year to Bristol: Yehudi played in a Brahms sextet and the Schubert Octet at St Mary Redcliffe, a fine building, described by Queen Elizabeth I as 'the fairest, goodliest and most famous parish church in England', which became a regular Festival venue. Bristol is much larger than Bath and possessed in the

Colston Hall a venue that was acoustically and economically more appropriate for symphony concerts than either the Pavilion, the Guildhall or the Assembly Rooms in Bath. The Festival returned to Bristol in 1964 for Menotti's church opera *Martin's Lie* and for several symphony concerts, but Ian Hunter's attempt to yoke the two cities together culturally was not backed by substantial funding from either city.

Nor was Yehudi notably tactful when dealing with Bath City Council. In 1963 he spoke out fiercely against a plan not to use the distinctive local stone in a new police station; another year he led a campaign to restore the Bath and Newbury canal, taking a trip on a barge with Diana to make his point. In Bath itself Yehudi showed his commitment by conducting an orchestra of pupils from several local schools. A distinguished trio of younger conductors shared the programmes: David Lloyd Jones, Raymond Leppard and Roger Norrington.

The 1963 Festival was also noteworthy for Yehudi's first flirtation with jazz since performing the 'St Louis Blues' during the war with an army group in Puerto Rico. For the final concert he invited John Dankworth to follow in Gershwin's footsteps and bridge the gap between classical music and jazz. Dankworth and Raymond Leppard devised a framework for group improvisation, based on the folk song 'As I went out one May morning'. Three members of the Dankworth band shared the spotlight with Leppard, Menuhin and Maurice Gendron but this 'Music Encounter' did not impress the *Bath Chronicle*: overlong and too much jazz was its critic's verdict. Dankworth remembers Yehudi's nervousness about improvisation: at rehearsal he worked out a passage by himself and wrote it down. 'It was a bit mundane,' says Dankworth, 'but it was him all right.' Improvisation usually takes place over an a predetermined sequence of chords. Dankworth recalls suggesting a three-chord sequence, one of them the submediant. 'Let me see,' replied Yehudi, whose academic education consisted of a few weeks at the Juilliard when he was ten, 'which one is the submediant?' A classically trained clarinettist, Dankworth returned the following year to play Bartók's *Contrasts* with Yehudi and in 1965 he conducted his wife Cleo Laine in Weill's *Seven Deadly Sins* at Bristol's Colston Hall.

Was Bath really too much of a cosy family affair? In the early 1960s the strings of the Festival Orchestra performed and later recorded Bartók's *Divertimento*, Tippett's *Fantasia concertante on a Theme of*

Corelli and his Concerto for double string orchestra, Britten's *Variations on a Theme of Frank Bridge* and Stravinsky's Concerto in D. This is hardly the unvarying diet of baroque music deplored by Yehudi's critics. The collaboration with Tippett, who lived in nearby Corsham, was particularly fruitful even though Yehudi had difficulty at the rehearsals unravelling his sinuous contrapuntal lines.

Margot Fonteyn returned in 1964, this time with her glamorous new partner Rudolf Nureyev, to join the Western Theatre Ballet's evening of dance at the Theatre Royal. The first half of the programme was to climax with a new *pas de deux* choreographed by Kenneth MacMillan to the music of the Bartók solo Violin Sonata with Yehudi playing from the side of the stage. After the dress rehearsal, held on the evening before the first night, Fonteyn had to be told by a sympathetic Diana that her husband Tito Arias had been shot in Panama City and was critically ill. A flurry of overnight phone calls established that he was not in immediate danger and Fonteyn delivered a classic 'the-show-must-go-on' sound-bite: 'Naturally I want to go and see my husband but I don't like rushing off today and letting down the Festival.' She gamely stayed for the première. Yehudi remembered playing for her in a kind of sentry box: 'I loved it – just the feeling of seeing people dance to your music, whether in rhythm or inspired by the mood.' When she eventually reached Panama, Fonteyn found that the shooting had left her husband completely paralysed. The second performance four days later was danced by Lynn Seymour.

In April 1965 it was revealed that Yehudi had waived all his fees for the previous two Festivals. In effect he was subsidizing Bath but he always enjoyed himself there. In 1961 he had replied to a vote of thanks by asserting that he was working with the people he loved the most – the musicians: 'To make music with them – the music I love the best – is a dream that only comes to life in Bath.' The Bath fortnight was surely more fun than his 'day job' touring the concert halls of the US. The Festival Chairman, Sir Edwin Leather, lectured the city fathers: 'If you're going to have a genius like Menuhin you have got to provide him with proper facilities or you just don't have him at all.' Leather was bidding for a rise in the grant but it was not forthcoming. The City Council was not persuaded by the argument that the Festival brought extra trade into the city and again provided £2,500, only half the £5000 it had allocated in 1955 for Sir Thomas Beecham's Festival, when it had also coughed up £10,000 for an opera production.

Perhaps as a sop for wounded feelings, Bath offered Yehudi the Freedom of the Borough, an honour normally reserved for heads of state and army regiments. (For Yehudi it was a summer of official acclaim: in June he received a doctorate from Trinity College of Music in London and in August the Freedom of the City of Edinburgh; he was the first musician thus to be honoured in the Scottish Festival's nineteen-year history.)

Like three-star chefs forced to operate on wartime rations, Ian Hunter and his chief lieutenant Jack Phipps, the Festival's administrator, continued to work minor miracles on a modest subsidy. In 1965 the Festival included the first performance of a new concerto for violin and chamber orchestra commissioned by Yehudi from the Australian Malcolm Williamson. They played it through together at Highgate before the Festival began. A difficult passage in the cadenza defeated Yehudi and he asked for it to be changed. But before Williamson had even got home Yehudi had telephoned and left a message with the composer's young son, Peter. It was written out in chalk, Williamson remembers, on the kitchen blackboard: 'Mr Menuhin called apologizing. He cannot see how he can have been so stupid and he has found a way to finger it. Do not change anything.' Nevertheless Williamson later described the première as a 'disaster': he said the conductor, Yehudi's Israeli protégé Gary Bertini, was 'a dry biscuit, though not bad'. *Grove* praises the Concerto's 'authentic inner lyricism . . . and sustained rhapsodic form'; *The Times* admired the final *Adagio*:

A long, serenely expressive melodic line for violin, simply supported by orchestra, does convey feeling of a distinctive nature, a sort of numb aspiring melancholy that Mr Menuhin captured eloquently.

Yehudi edited the solo part for publication and his 1971 recording of the revised version for full orchestra, with Sir Adrian Boult conducting, is one of his most fruitful excursions into contemporary music.

Diana held informal court during every Festival but 1965 saw her elevated for the first time to the rank of performer. In her first appearance on stage for twenty years she narrated Saint-Saëns's *Carnival of the Animals*. Each movement is prefaced by a poem; she jettisoned the customary verses by the American humorist Ogden Nash and wrote her own neat and often witty substitutes, of which this is one:

The Turtles

There's naught as thoughtless as a tortoise
Who soporifically roams
So from his shell have we bethought
To wrought us objets d'art and combs.

The turtle, hurtling to his fate,
Poor paralytic nincompoop,
Will ever find he's just too late
To save himself from being soup.

In Yehudi's mind Camille Saint-Saëns's music was for ever associated with his boyhood memory of Anna Pavlova, whom he saw dancing *The Dying Swan* in San Francisco. Diana would have shocked her husband had she mocked such a noble bird and, besides, swans on the River Avon are an integral part of the Bath landscape. Diana's verse was rather touching:

The Swan

On the river lightly leaning,
Curved of neck and proudly preening
Image still and image flowing
Quiet above the tidal towing.
Floating bird of snowy feather
Swan and water joined together –
Mirrored rippling in the stream,
Lovely twice-enacted dream.

In April 1966 Yehudi celebrated his fiftieth birthday. A month later at Bath he took the title Artistic Director for the first time – in previous years the brochures announced 'a festival arranged with Yehudi Menuhin'. Interviewed about his plans, he declared that 'The Festival must develop from within.' He must have felt challenged to push himself into new activities, perhaps comparing himself to his Romanian master: 'Enesco's violin was too small to contain his powers,' he once wrote, and he expanded his own activities as Enesco had done before him, eventually going even further. His festival appearances took in the one-off Commonwealth Arts Festival in 1965 (in London) and – yet another creation of Ian Hunter – a new festival in Hong Kong.

Bath's 1966 programme had a genuinely festive ring to it, with pride of place going to Yehudi's first involvement with opera, *Così fan tutte*.

It was a production by Phoenix Opera given at the eighteenth-century Theatre Royal. When Sir Thomas Beecham conducted Grétry's *Zémire et Azor* there, a decade earlier, the reportedly splendid production had failed to sell out, prompting the tart observation from Ian Hunter that if he had announced it under the title *Beauty and the Beast* audiences would have come, 'thinking it was a pantomime'.

Phoenix Opera had been formed in 1964 by two formidable operatic *grandes dames*, Joan Cross and Anne Wood. They recruited a young group of singers and specialized in taking opera to small communities, often accompanied by no more than a piano. Hunter booked them for Bath, where Yehudi had his superb Festival Orchestra to conduct. Much of the musical preparation had been undertaken by David Lloyd Jones, who conducted one of the three performances – at drastically reduced prices – and the entire production had already been seen elsewhere. As one might expect, Yehudi's first venture in the pit was not an unqualified success. Jack Phipps remembers an early rehearsal at which he called out to his assistant Gary Bertini for help: 'I've stopped them and now I don't know how to get them started again.'

The *Daily Telegraph* review noted unkindly (and ponderously):

We learned hardly more about Mr Menuhin's ideas than we would have about Herbert von Karajan's if this conductor were to decide tomorrow to play the solo part in Beethoven's Violin Concerto.

In the influential *Opera* magazine, the experienced Arthur Jacobs hedged his bets. 'Menuhin's début as an opera director', he began, 'may fairly be called a gimmick designed to attract a public requiring a "guaranteed" name.' He then changed tack.

But for the first night, musically rewarding as it was, Menuhin can take due credit. His tempos were . . . sometimes too slow or not steady enough but there were many felicities in the playing of the Bath Festival Orchestra.

Among the singers Arthur Jacobs praised the stylish performance as Ferrando of a young tenor named Roger Norrington, adding that he would do well to concentrate on 'character' roles. It was one of the future Sir Roger's last appearances before giving his undivided attention to his burgeoning career as a conductor.

It had long been Yehudi's 'secret ambition' to conduct opera and when he wanted something he usually got it. But in taking charge of a three-hour opera, had he bitten off more than he could chew? Opera conducting needs inspiration and musicality, both of which he had in abundance, but he was short of experience in such practical matters of technique as giving cues to the singers, providing a clear beat for orchestral recitative and ensuring precision of ensemble. In his heart he must have known that he could not expect to master a Mozart score in a few days, as he did even the most difficult of solo concertos. But he enjoyed taking risks, relying on the collective professionalism of his colleagues to help him through and *Opera*'s verdict was cautiously positive: 'Menuhin's venture was artistically not unsuccessful.'

Yehudi was on equally risky ground in another of the 1966 Festival's innovations, a concert of Indian music in which he and Ravi Shankar performed a raga composed by Peter Feuchtwanger, a young Munich-born pianist. From the moment of their cheerful arrival at the railway station, the Indian musicians made an exhilarating impact on the city. They turned the Menuhins' hotel suite into – as Yehudi put it – a corner of Old Delhi. Furniture was pushed to one side, a colourful carpet spread on the floor and incense tapers lit in brass bowls so that rehearsals could get under way in the appropriate atmosphere. Food for their first meal break was personally delivered by Diana Menuhin. She knew that the hotel restaurant's luncheon 'special' (she guessed beef rissoles and raspberry blancmange) was unlikely to impress their guests and instead ordered an Indian takeaway from the city's most famous restaurant, the Hole in the Wall. Unable to find a taxi, she carried a large order of steaming curried vegetables up the hill in two heavy and very pungent baskets.

Banging the door of our room with my knee (the noise of the sitar, violin, tabla, drone and voices was overpowering), I succeeded in drawing attention to my arrival. The picture I presented must have held just the right amount of serio-comic. Ravi, Yehudi and Chatur Lal dropped their instruments and rushed towards me . . . they were overcome with joy at [the meal] which we all ate sitting on the floor to accompaniments of Ravi's better shady stories and jokes. The Indians have a marvellous gift for spontaneous humour which bubbles up from the cauldron that is their warmth of nature.

The concert was to conclude with the Indian music, the new piece being followed by two ragas for the Shankar players alone. The first half featured several Mozart works, among them two rarely heard sets of violin and piano variations for which Fou Ts'ong joined his father-in-law. Yehudi was dressed in conventional daytime concert garb of striped black trousers, double-breasted jacket, cream shirt, shiny black shoes and so on. At the interval he changed into his Indian 'costume':

a pair of navy-blue linen trousers and a fine embroidered white shirt presented to him by Ravi. Everything had been thoughtfully laid out by Diana but she had forgotten his footwear. He could hardly appear wearing black silk socks, particularly as he would be playing in the lotus position, cross-legged on the floor. 'Doesn't matter,' Ravi told Diana.

'He can go on barefoot.'

'Won't that look a bit odd, protruding from blue linen trousers? After all, *you*'ve got jodhpurs on.'

'Never mind – all will be splendid!'

In *West Meets East* Yehudi was required to perform Indian music as an equal partner with Ravi Shankar. They had worked hard over the previous days on what was to be the culminating point in their musical friendship, but genuine improvisation was still difficult for Yehudi and he performed initially from the manuscript composed by Feucht-wanger, who was a student of oriental music. As with his opera con-ducting, he was going out on a limb: he confessed later that he had never been more scared in his life and Diana said she had never seen him so green-faced. When he made his entrance on stage, looking as he put it, 'a trifle incongruous' in his blue trousers, there was a burst of laughter, which with his characteristic optimism he took to be not mockery but good will. For her part Diana revelled in the surrealistic scene:

The Guildhall mahogany, gilt, glass chandeliers, all the coldly graceful panoply of the eighteenth-century bureaucracy disturbed by an ugly platform covered in green cloth and barely redeemed by Ravi's beautiful carpets; the perfumed vapour rising quietly like scented grey plumes from the dais . . . and Yehudi, his pale skin look-ing like an ivory mask, his fair hair lending to the whole scene a weird touch of the mythopoeic.

She had a ringside seat at the performance:

At first Yehudi modestly played his melody [entitled *Raga Tilang*] and then, gath-ering spirit and speed from Ravi, let himself go until all three – Ravi, Chatur and Yehudi – were tearing through a conversational trio that carried the audience away until at the end they rose and called for more.

'You're making the greatest mistake of your life,' Yehudi told his lis-teners. 'I managed it once. I shan't be able to manage it again.' 'Go on', they cried. 'Risk it!' And risk it he did, performing Shankar's own com-positions at the UN General Assembly in New York in 1967 and, before the decade was out, in the Royal Albert Hall in London, when the recently invested Prince of Wales joined them on the platform, not, alas, to play his cello but to voice his admiration for Mahatma Gandhi.

Yehudi had yet another challenge to face at his 1966 Festival in the form of music by Alexander Goehr, one of Britain's leading avant-garde composers. The Festival commissioned Goehr to write a trio for piano, violin and cello for Hephzibah, Yehudi and Maurice Gendron. The commission had originally gone to Michael Tippett, who had already participated in several Festivals, but Tippett was too busy and suggested Goehr as his replacement. Menuhin already knew Goehr because they had both been involved earlier in the spring in the establishment of a new and more iconoclastic festival than Bath's in the gaudy seaside town of Brighton – another of Ian Hunter's brain-children. Veiled hints had even been dropped that Yehudi might take his festival away from Bath if the city was not more generous with its subsidy, which in 1966 was just ninepence in old currency (less than 4p) per head of the population. Yehudi's trio had never performed anything more contemporary than Ravel, but only the previous year he himself had performed Schoenberg's *Fantasy* with Glenn Gould in Toronto, and the encouragement of Goehr, a composer of the twelve-note persuasion, was presumably felt to be desirable for the image of the Festival. 'At first sight,' Yehudi wrote, 'passages in [the Trio] seemed to me unnecessarily complicated, and I asked Sandy why he didn't write more simply. His disconcerting answer was that he wanted to put me to the test!' Goehr remembers the episode differently. To talk about a test in connection with Yehudi would have been impertinent; what he actually said was: 'I wanted to make you sweat!' Goehr's Trio was one of the few works Yehudi introduced at Bath but did not then record. It was subsequently recorded by the Orion Trio.

In 1967 George Szell and Nadia Boulanger were among the guest conductors and there was a new commission for Yehudi to play, a concerto by the American Easley Blackwood. But the outstanding performance of the Festival was probably the concert in Colston Hall, Bristol, given by the BBC Symphony Orchestra under its Chief Conductor, Pierre Boulez, at which Yehudi played the Violin Concerto by Alban Berg for the first time in England. (He had already played it in Geneva with the Suisse Romande orchestra under Ansermet.) Before they worked together Boulez had an image of Menuhin as a legendary child wonder:

I remembered the famous recording of the Bach Double Concerto with Enesco; so to work with him on a piece which was not familiar to him was very important to me . . . It was not performed very often by the younger generation; I think for Yehudi it was a step forward; he wanted to take over the 'burden'. The quality of [his] sound was very emotional – his first goal was expression. First came the feeling, and second the virtuosity, and I think it was the right order . . . The second movement cadenza with its echoes of Bach and Bartók came naturally. [He gave] a very moving performance; he grasped very well the music's 'ironic nostalgia'.

If Boulez's presence added stature to the Festival, there was great disappointment when at the last moment Jacqueline du Pré cancelled her scheduled appearances. She had been booked to play the Boccherini Concerto with Yehudi's orchestra and to give a recital with his son-in-law, Fou Ts'ong, but at the end of May, a few days before the Festival opened, she flew to Israel with her fiancé, Daniel Barenboim. He was an Argentinian by birth but a citizen of Israel. The long-expected war in the Middle East finally erupted a week later and although it lasted only six days the romantic couple cancelled all their concert engagements in Europe, preferring to play for the victorious Israeli troops and generally celebrate the consolidation, indeed expansion, of the state. Their mood was so euphoric they decided to get married on the spot. Back home Emmy Tillett, Jacqueline du Pré's manager, called her a naughty girl for breaking her concert engagements. Yehudi, too, had always believed in the 'sanctity of the date' and for once did not disguise his displeasure: du Pré had to be replaced not only at the Festival but also for the subsequent North American tour with the Bath Festival Orchestra: it included concerts at Expo '67, the Montreal World Fair. (The rift was healed in due course. Yehudi visited her when she was struck down by multiple sclerosis in the 1970s; Daniel Barenboim conducted a fine tribute concert in Berlin after Menuhin's death in 1999.)

The 1967 Festival featured a boisterous production by Wendy Toye of Mozart's *The Abduction from the Seraglio*, sung in English. The Labour Government's Arts Minister, Jennie Lee, had attended the Festival in 1966 and been sufficiently impressed to persuade her friend Lord Goodman, Chairman of the Arts Council, to earmark £2000 for this new Mozart production – thus was subsidy sometimes arranged in those less accountable days. But to get *Seraglio* off the ground Yehudi was still obliged to dig into his own pocket to the tune of £3000. He got his money's worth, though; the production was much enjoyed. Even *Opera* magazine was less grudging in its praise:

Menuhin may not be an ideal opera conductor – ensemble sometimes falls apart and there were no vocal graces – but his account was loving and musical with the expected attention devoted to shaping the orchestral parts.

When EMI recorded the opera in the autumn David Hillman was replaced, some thought unfairly, by the Swedish tenor Nicolai Gedda, apparently as a sop to the American market. Reviewing the LP recording in *Opera*, the magazine's editor, Harold Rosenthal, confirmed Menuhin's care for Mozart's orchestral writing. 'Although this is only the second opera he has ever conducted,' he concluded, 'he seems to be a most sympathetic opera conductor: i.e. he carries his singers along with him, neither driving them nor merely following them.' The recording did not sell as well as Yehudi had hoped. Unaware of the original-language snobbery prevalent among opera-lovers, he mistakenly thought opera in English would sell in America and the British Commonwealth. Nevertheless it was, he declared, 'a great experience', which he likened to giving words to the violin concertos: 'Every note of Mozart's is a gesture.'

Yehudi appeared to be successfully launched on an operatic career: Bath might become a miniature Salzburg and he another von Karajan. But his enthusiasm for opera carried with it the seeds of destruction for 'his' festival. He had not taken into account the parsimonious attitude of the Bath Council nor the blinkered attitude of his own Festival Society. The 1967 accounts were less than £300 in the red, but for the philistines who were in the ascendancy in local affairs the Festival was becoming too esoteric. The Artistic Director and his manager, Ian Hunter, who rarely visited Bath outside the Festival, were soon to find themselves isolated. Jack Phipps was in the city almost every week to deal with administration: he says his warnings that trouble was brewing were ignored.

Tim Bullamore, the historian of the Bath Festival, confirms that a tide started to flow against Yehudi in 1967. An unsigned article in the *Bath Chronicle* complained of the Festival's 'rather anonymous pattern'. The writer, sheltering under his own anonymity, dared to speak the unspeakable: he called for a new director, one 'who can both rejuvenate the event artistically and permit a broader spread of interest'. A prominent member of the Festival Fringe defended Yehudi, arguing rather sweetly that he 'rated on a par with Beau Nash for the amount of good work he has done for Bath generally'. But even he supported the idea of change: 'Menuhin has become too large for Bath, or Bath too small for Menuhin.' Touring in America, ironically with the Bath Festival Orchestra, Yehudi responded by writing sharply to the Council: 'Don't count on my participation after 1968, my tenth Festival.'

That winter he proceeded to plan his next opera project, which was to conduct a new production of *The Magic Flute*. The casting had been completed before the Council of the Festival Society told him they could not afford it. Doubtless some members remembered that they had had their fingers burnt badly in 1955, when they put up £10,000 for Beecham's opera and lost most of it. Ian Hunter might well have gambled on negotiating a substantial rise in subsidy, essential if the Festival was to mount its own opera and not import a touring group such as Phoenix. If so, he miscalculated and this time Yehudi did not reach into his own pocket, as perhaps the Council was hoping he would. Instead he carried out his threat and a month before the Festival opened announced that it would be his last: the ten-year partnership was at an end.

Local criticism that Yehudi was an absentee landlord who left everything to his bailiff (Ian Hunter) cannot be sustained: the quality of the programmes speaks for itself. True, an iconoclastic mood gripped the entire Western world in the spring of 1968. Pierre Boulez wanted opera houses burnt down and arts festivals were a natural target for the students who rioted everywhere in Europe and occupied the Théâtre de l'Odéon in Paris. But there was nothing specifically political about the local opposition to Yehudi. Certain black-tie social occasions might have smacked of exclusivity but nobody could have described Mozart's sublime pantomime *The Magic Flute*, given in English, as an élitist entertainment. The regrettable truth seems to be that the Bath Festival Committee, under its Chairman Lord Strathcona (Sir Edwin Leather had retired in 1965) was mean, shortsighted and philistine. 'In the present economic situation,' droned their press release,

the society feels it is unable to keep pace with the financial requirements which Mr Menuhin considers necessary for the future rate of achievement and growth of a festival under his direction.

Yehudi summed up the situation more sharply in an article for the *Bristol Evening Post*:

I would say the trouble at Bath is a lack of vision. Bath is such a jewel of a city. It lulls people into a self-contentment. That does not at this moment rhyme with my own awareness of world news and problems, the terrifying situations that exist artistically, politically, financially and most importantly, humanly. A festival should bring these things to the fore and give expression to the ills of the century and the possible cures and solutions. I would not make it a political forum but I do want people to see art more as part of life. We fell apart on this matter. The financial angle was more a symptom than a cause.

Just what he had in mind that would reflect the century's ills is unclear but in an interview for the *Daily Telegraph* he elaborated his own vision: he had wanted, he said, 'to create something like Tanglewood in Massachusetts, with its own concert hall and providing something large for the region and especially its youth'.

Had he had a farsighted corporation behind him, like the elected officials in Birmingham who backed Simon Rattle in the early 1980s, Yehudi might have succeeded. But given the reality of civic funding, ten years was probably enough for one artistic team and privately both he and Ian Hunter thought it had been 'a good term'. As for the 1968 Festival, a surprisingly effective job was made of an unpromising situation. At the Theatre Royal, a low-budget music-theatre double-bill was swiftly devised to replace *The Magic Flute*. Mozart's farcical one-act opera, *The Impresario*, was coupled with *The Soldier's Tale* by Stravinsky, in which Yehudi played the important violin part and Gary Bertini conducted. Bertini was such a stickler for musical accuracy that Michael MacLiammoir lost his nerve and withdrew from the role of the narrator after the first day of musical rehearsal, to be replaced by Barry Foster. Publicly the Irish actor blamed cataract problems which were making it impossible to see the conductor but he confessed to the stage director, John Cox, that he had accepted the engagement only in order to boast he had been on the same stage as Yehudi Menuhin.

Yehudi himself found the angularities of Stravinsky's violin writing difficult to play in tune. At a rehearsal he innocently asked whether, since the soldier who had acquired the magic fiddle was an uncouth fellow with a rough style of playing, he shouldn't play a few notes out of tune – on purpose? Stifled laughter among the other players greeted the enquiry (John Cox remembers) and he was not encouraged to pursue this piece of 'method' performance. *The Soldier's Tale* was later transferred to television by the new company London Weekend, who thought it an ideal cultural calling card to inaugurate its prestigious *Saturday Special* series.

In Mozart's *Der Schauspieldirektor* – *The Impresario* – Yehudi took the part of 'Mr Baton, the conductor'. He dressed up in eighteenth-century breeches, stockings and ribboned hair for his first venture into period drama since playing Paganini's music in *The Magic Bow*. In the film, only close-ups of Menuhin's hands had been seen; for the long shots Stewart Granger had mimed to the pre-recorded soundtrack. But in Bath there was at last a professional sequel to all the play-acting Yehudi had done with his sisters on their parents' wedding anniversaries. Wendy Toye was the director. She and Diana had danced together in *The Miracle* back in 1932. And no less a figure than the portly actor–dramatist Robert Morley was engaged to dash off a new 'book', in which the action was moved from Vienna to a decrepit opera house in the provincial spa resort of Bad-himmel (heavenly Bath). And joy of joys for Yehudi, who was often reminded by his wife that she had sacrificed her career for his, Morley invented a non-singing role for Diana: adopting a heavy French accent modelled on the popular actress Yvonne Arnaud, she played Mademoiselle Douche, the pump-room attendant who is determined to make her mark with the impresario – as a ballerina. This was type-casting with a vengeance but the press loved it. The *Western Daily Press* rated it 'by far the most successful production yet staged at the Bath Festival'.

Other attractions in Yehudi's final year were the Batsheva Modern Dance Company from Israel, the pianists Clifford Curzon and Rafael Orozco, the violinist Igor Oistrakh, who played Bartók duets with Yehudi, and the soprano Elisabeth Schwarzkopf. The oratorio *A Child of Our Time* was performed in the Abbey; its composer, Michael Tippett, was to become Yehudi's successor as Festival Director. (For the first year Tippett worked in a triumvirate with the conductor Colin Davis and the administrator Jack Phipps, but the arrangement did not prosper and from 1970 Tippett ran the show alone, with local administrative support.)

The Festival's historian records that from 1959 to 1968 Yehudi appeared in 105 concerts and performed in 320 musical and theatrical items. According to an eyewitness, the arts administrator Luke Rittner, he left Bath

in a very dramatic way, making an extremely emotional speech on the last day of the Festival at the start of a recital. It was a very bitter speech and lots of the old faithful were very upset . . . cancelling their subscriptions.

Lord Goodman smoothed things over at the closing ceremony. Yehudi's generosity, he said diplomatically, was 'almost unequalled in musical history'. Honours meant very little to Mr Menuhin, Goodman continued, 'but I know this festival has a very special significance for him and means more than perhaps anything else he has created'. Yehudi was undoubtedly hurt by the manner of his going, but he put a brave face on it and went out in style, conducting his orchestra (thereafter known as the Menuhin Festival Orchestra) in a late-night evening of Strauss waltzes and polkas at a Festival Ball in the Assembly Rooms. He was again in costume, this time officiating as Johann Strauss II himself, with fiddle in hand. 'I've always wanted to be a bandmaster,' he told the *Guardian*'s reporter.

A survey of Yehudi's career as an English impresario must be rounded off with a brief mention of the Windsor Festival, of which he was joint Artistic Director for four years, from 1969 to 1972. The idea of another festival came from the ever optimistic Ian Hunter, who spotted Windsor Castle gleaming in the sunshine on the far side of the Thames while driving to London from his country cottage at Henley. The discreet bourgeois charm of the twin towns of Eton and Windsor, both boasting lovely medieval chapels, inspired him to create a second family-and-friends affair for Yehudi. He obtained the blessing of Windsor's Dean (who wanted help with a proposed American tour for his chapel choir) and successfully negotiated an added attraction, the outdoor pomp and circumstance that could be provided by the royal household regiments.

Windsor had a combination of architectural and historical associations that Yehudi relished: 'The atmosphere is so very English, and as I adore this country I could find no more perfect setting for a festival.' He enjoyed what he described as the area's 'tremendous gamut of population from the traditional aristocratic element [a thinly disguised reference to the Queen, who unfortunately would be in Balmoral at festival time] to the industrial towns of Hayes and Slough'. Yehudi already knew of Hayes because it was the manufacturing headquarters of his record company, EMI. Slough boasted a substantial cinema, the Adelphi, where Diana later performed *Carnival of the Animals* and a work specially composed for her by Edwin Roxburgh, *How Pleasant to Know Mr Lear*. Yehudi pronounced the Adelphi stage suitable for an opera production that he had in mind for that veritable Seville of the Home Counties: *Carmen*. It remained an unfulfilled dream.

Windsor's opening season featured Sir William Walton sharing the rostrum with Yehudi; the ceremonial music included Walton's *Crown Imperial* march and Handel's *Royal Fireworks Music*, for which a magnificent firework display was designed by John Piper. Indoor performances were given in the Waterloo Hall in the Castle itself, in the lovely St George's Chapel and in the newly built Farrar Theatre at Eton College, where the Menuhins' sons Gerard and Jeremy had both studied earlier in the decade. In the first year Yehudi conducted *Dido and Aeneas* with his friend Irmgard Seefried playing the doomed Queen of Carthage. William Mann, the *Times* critic, reported approvingly that 'Mr Menuhin caught the lilt of Purcell's music and the character of the string writing', but he added an admonitory footnote: 'The ensemble will surely gain precision before the end of the week.' In those days Eton College was a puritanical place: it offered neither drink nor food in the interval, so the first-nighters who paid full price for less than an hour of imprecise music-making might be said to have had a raw deal. Conventional opera did not reappear in subsequent Windsor Festivals. (Over a decade passed before Yehudi conducted opera again, first at the Cuvilliés-Theater in Munich, then in other German opera houses and the big tent at Gstaad.)

The following year, 1970, Britten's austere church parables replaced conventional opera; Yehudi's orchestral programmes included Bach's *St John Passion* and the world première of a new symphony, his second, by Britain's nineteen-year-old composing prodigy, Oliver Knussen. He remembers the Symphony as being 'experimental', featuring complex multi-layered textures and elaborate instrumental writing. He fell behind with its composition, and could supply only three of the projected four movements before meeting Yehudi:

I was expecting to get rapped on the knuckles for the tardy delivery of a problematical score. Not at all – he couldn't have been more welcoming, made us feel completely at home and simply asked me to show him how to beat the rapid and tricky changes of time-signature at the beginning of the score. (I suspect he hadn't been faced with this particular hurdle as a conductor at anything like the speed I wanted!) All very relaxed, very light-hearted and friendly – not a trace of grandeur or condescension. This marvellous attitude continued all through the rehearsals. He asked me to stay close to him in case I heard anything he didn't hear (how many conductors do that?) and encouraged me to intervene as much as necessary. Diana Menuhin was also wonderfully friendly and encouraging at the dress rehearsal in Windsor Castle. Although I must have caused more than a few frayed nerves to all and sundry (not least because I think the musical language was not quite what was anticipated in Windsor) I have nothing but warm memories of this brief encounter with a very great musician who was completely aware of his own technical limitations as a conductor and addressed them with total modesty . . . My Second Symphony is still played occasionally and I have often been asked, 'Did Menuhin really conduct the première of that?' – and I am always delighted to be able to recount this little tale.

West met East once more with the return of Ravi Shankar while America met Europe in the form of a concerto for two violins by the American violinist and musicologist Stanley Weiner. The local paper wrote sniffily that its finale displayed 'lingering connotations of Palm Court Hotel'. An old friend of the family, Princess Irene of Greece, played Mozart's two-piano Concerto in Eb (K.365) with her teacher, Gina Bachauer. Diana Menuhin had known the Princess since she was thirteen: by royal standards she was doubtless a gifted musician, but lukewarm critical reaction hinted that for once Yehudi had allowed his artistic standards to slip. In other concerts the pianist Yitkin Seow and the violinist Nigel Kennedy appeared in a programme given by young Menuhin School soloists and in another recital Yehudi presented Sylvia Marcovici, the prizewinner of a violin competition he had adjudicated the previous year in Romania. To honour Beethoven's bicentenary the cello sonatas were performed by Gendron and Kentner and Yehudi conducted the *Battle Symphony* with noisily enthusiastic participation by the military bands quartered in the district.

Yehudi remained at the helm for two more Windsor Festivals, both packed with good things that need not be chronicled in detail. In 1971 his son Jeremy, then not quite twenty, appeared in the K.449 Mozart Piano Concerto and in the following year, 1972, Yehudi conducted Haydn's *The Creation*. But the date of the Festival, at the end of September, was proving too close to his regular autumn tour in America and curtailed his precious Alpine summer, the period when he was briefly reunited with his family and could recharge his batteries and practise new repertoire.

He continued to direct the modestly proportioned Gstaad Festival every August. He was at home in Switzerland, making chamber music with friends, as he had done in the 1950s with Pablo Casals at Prades. Later, in the 1980s, when a large performance tent was acquired by the commune, the Gstaad Festival was to expand quite substantially, branching out into semi-staged opera and big symphony concerts. He was able to make up for what he had lost when he gave up Bath and then Windsor.

He had also felt himself obliged to give up his summer house on the Greek island of Mykonos when, in 1967, the Greek royal family was forced into exile: Yehudi, a devoted royalist, vowed not to return to Greece until democracy was restored. Once that happened, in 1974, the possibility of a leisurely late-summer holiday in the Aegean became too attractive to deny and Yehudi, by then almost sixty, put aside any thought of returning to a role as a festival director, although he never lost his flair for persuading fine artists to appear with him in memorable fund-raising gala performances. In the 1970s the greatest of his creations, his School, was a solid reality and he became deeply involved in international politics – inevitably of a musical nature.

Recommended Recordings

Bach: Brandenburg Concertos 1–6
various soloists with the Bath Festival Orchestra, conducted by YM
EMI 5 68345 2
Recorded: 6–11 July 1959
These are landmark recordings and are discussed in the text in some detail. Other Menuhin recordings of Bach from the fruitful days of the Bath Festival (and still available in the CD catalogues) include the concertos, the orchestral suites and *The Musical Offering*.

Mozart: *Sinfonia concertante* for violin and viola (K.364)
Igor Oistrakh (violin), David Oistrakh (viola)
Moscow Philharmonic Orchestra, conducted by YM
BBCL 4019–2
Recorded: 28 September 1963
Recorded by the BBC at a public concert. At the same Albert Hall concert, YM played the Beethoven Concerto with David Oistrakh conducting. On another CD version of the *Sinfonia concertante* (EMI 7 62710 2; recorded 2 July 1962), YM plays the viola with Rudolf Barshai (violin) and the Bath Festival Orchestra.

Berg: Violin Concerto
BBC Symphony Orchestra, conducted by Pierre Boulez
EMI 7 63989 2
Recorded: 8 and 9 February 1968
A deeply sympathetic recording of twentieth-century music to set beside the Bloch Concerto. The two works appear on the same CD.

Handel: Six Sonatas, Op. 1
with George Malcolm (harpsichord) and Ambrose Gauntlett (viola da gamba)
EMI CZS 573347 2

Recorded: 1967
The pleasure YM derived from working with first-class chamber players is communicated in full in these attractive performances.

Handel: Ten Organ Concertos
Simon Preston (organ), Menuhin Festival Orchestra, conducted by YM
Recorded: 1968, 1970
EMI 5 72676 2
A fascinating project employing a variety of period organs.

Mozart: Piano Concerto in E♭ (K.449)
Mozart: Piano Concerto in F (K.459)
Hephzibah Menuhin (piano), Bath Festival Orchestra, conducted by YM
EMI PCD 1944
YM hoped to conduct a cycle of Mozart piano concertos with his sister as soloist but sadly the project was not continued after 1965.

West Meets East No. 2: *Raga Piloo*
Ravi Shankar and YM
EMI 7 49070 2
Recorded in New York, at the UN General Assembly

15 Interlude – *by Diana Menuhin*
'A Day in the Life of Yehudi Moshevitch'

Rehearsal with Ravi Shankar (sitar), Alla Rakha (tabla) and Ali Akbar Khan (vina)

The programme book of the 1965 Bath Festival included this satirical offering by Diana Menuhin, later reproduced in Fiddler's Moll.

6 A.M. . . . LONELY UPON A PEAK in London N6, Yehudi Moshevitch begins his day. Upside-down.

6.30 a.m. Comes the first telephone call – from Moscow, and they have forgotten (or ignored) the time-lag. Repolarizing himself for better hearing, Y. Moshevitch lifts the receiver: David! Good morning! You can play at Bath next week? Bravo! The Double Bach together. Good and let's do the Mozart *Concertante* too. Do you want to play the viola or the violin part? Never mind, we can make up our minds on the day. Let's do a double Vivaldi too and the Spohr duos and the Bartók ones as well, as encores. Programme very long? In India concerts go on till dawn . . . very good for Western audiences . . . endurance test, love to Tamara, goodbye.

7 a.m. Telephone: Aloysius Crumpelstein from Agamemnon, NY. Did Y. Moshevitch recall his invitation for the Bathfest of 196x? To sing his exclusive song-cycle from the early Alleghenies settlers? Y.M. Oh! Ah! Of course! You say they are in dialect and mainly of a pornographic nature? Perfectly all right. Chance of the Lord Chamberlain's being conversant with seventeenth-century Hillbilly dialect very slender. Same goes for audience, incidentally. Fascinating programme. See you on the 15th. Goodbye, Mr Corkelberg.

7.30 a.m. Breakfast: Hagebutten tea; Birchermuesli; Echtesjungfrau-bienenhonig; Heiligesparkassebrot. (For translation refer Bircher Clinic, Zurich, Tel. 425262, 10 lines.)

7.32 a.m. Telephone call from Bathfest Administration, London. George? You feel forty-three soloists too many for the Festival? Nonsense. By the way you'll be glad to hear Oistrakh can come. He rang this morning, and Aloysius Canckelspiel too, so that makes forty-five. Quite all right. Besides, I'll play for nothing. Can't get them all into ten days? Tell you what: I won't appear at all and that'll leave twenty spaces. I'm sure Ian will agree. Goodbye.

7.40 a.m. Back to cold breakfast.

7.42 a.m. to 9.42 a.m. Telephone calls from Sydney, Hornsey, Monte-video, Asnières and Port Elizabeth.

10 a.m. Congealed breakfast abandoned for practising.

12 noon. Frantic secretary reinforced by wife put their heads round the door. Bathfest Admin. panic. Ian H. on the line from Borioboola-Gha (Independent East-West Africa): did Y.M. seriously mean to relinquish his performances of Beethoven, Bach, Bartók, Brahms and Berg in order to accommodate the Ulan Bator Collectives Quartet and the Borstal Boys' Drama Club rendering of *The Ballad of Reading Gaol*? Now look, Y., don't do anything till I'm back. I've one more place in the jungle to visit to hear a cannibal tribe playing a xylophone entirely made of missionary bones. Goodbye.

1 p.m. to 2.30 p.m. Lunch of a raw nature, prolonged by dictation of article to hungry secretary on 'The Ease of Running a Festival'.

3 p.m. to 5 p.m. Profound slumber on floor cleared for purpose of fan mail, love letters from Germany full of dried flowers, six types of experimental chin rests, the concert schedule till 1975 and part of a ten-tome treatise on *La musique, a-t-elle de l'avenir?* by Achille Andermatt, published in Bagnolles-sur-l'Orme, for which Y.M. has promised a 10,000 word preface for the English edition coming out next month.

5.02 p.m. Hears five-year-old violinist of Afro-Patagonian parents (sent by Hep [Hephzibah]).

6.02 p.m. Says good-bye to five-year-old violinist of Afro-Patagonian parents, having given it a lesson on how to hold the violin and advised it to take up the flute.

6.03 p.m. Finds six people waiting since 5.05 p.m. and sweeps them all into the library together to save time. After ten minutes' general conversation discovers they are severally: a man with a slipped disc wanting to know about yoga; the Gypsy King from Romford (sent by Hep); a man from ATV waiting to do a piece entitled *Whither Serialism?*; ditto from the BBC Third Programme to tape Gounod's *Ave Maria* and Tosti's *Goodbye*; the Minister for Groceries and the Arts to discuss Supermarket Music for Elysium New Town (sent by Hep), and the plumber who has been trying ineffectually to get into the kitchen for the last twenty minutes to mend the hot tap.

6.15 p.m. Fetches violin and gets the whole lot done by 6.30 p.m. and then stands on his head.

7.00 p.m. Descends from head full of new ideas and proceeds to jot down first ten pages of them while answering Ian H. on the telephone. No, really can't play for highest fee ever paid for Festival Brasilia, but what about nice charity concert for Sweat and Soil Association at Harringay Stadium instead? Money? Oh that always turns up. Ring you tomorrow. What, you're going into hospital for ulcers for next six weeks? Terribly sorry. Send you my earthworm cure – infallible. Dear George, can't imagine how you got them.

7.30 p.m. Meets secretary staggering home after ten-hour day. Beamingly signs fifty letters on stairs and dictates forty-four more.

9.00 p.m. Lets secretary out after advising her to do deep breathing while typing.

9.02 p.m. Eats dinner of groats and Ghanaian honey (sent by Hep), which has been waiting since 8 p.m.

9.05 p.m. Practises two Bach solo sonatas, a piece for violin and nose flute by a niece of Sukarno and a recently unearthed concerto of Paganini's entitled *Vesuvio! E vietato fumare*.

11.05 p.m. Recognizes wife on way to bedroom and decides to call it a day.

11.30 p.m. Gets into bed and prepares sketches of knee exercises for music-school children to strengthen their octave passages, which gets entangled with the galley proofs of a piece entitled 'Ornithological Brothels' (subtitled 'Battery Hens: A Protest'). Falls asleep, smiling.

1.05 a.m. Wife removes spectacles from Y.M.'s nose and turns out light.

16 The School –
Utopia in Stoke d'Abernon

With Nigel Kennedy, aged seven

1955–9: dissatisfaction with standards of violin teaching; 1962: visit to Central School for Young Musicians in Moscow; 1963: September: YM School opens in London; 1964: School transfers to Stoke d'Abernon; autumn: BBC2 masterclass includes lesson with Nigel Kennedy, aged seven; 1965: first orchestral concerts; 1969: publication of Menuhin's House of Music; *1970–2000: subsequent developments.*

YEHUDI HAD BEEN LIVING in London less than three years when in 1963 he launched what was to prove his most enduring contribution to musical life: the international school that bears his name. He had begun giving violin lessons at Nadia Boulanger's academy in Fontainebleau in 1954 but in none of his writings or press interviews in the 1940s and 1950s is there any mention of a project to create a permanent institution dedicated to the teaching of gifted children; the concept of founding such a school seems to have sprung into life as a direct result of a visit he made to Moscow in 1962. There had, it is true, been certain straws in the wind to suggest that teaching was to become a major preoccupation. He began to refer to falling educational standards after serving on the jury of the Queen Elisabeth of the Belgians international competition in 1955. (One of the finalists, Alberto Lysy from Agentina, persuaded Yehudi to take him as a pupil, his first.) Four years later, soon after presiding over a violin competition at the Bath Festival, he gave an interview to Jay Harrison in the *New York Herald Tribune*:

In the violin world of today the most heartening sign is to see people like Heifetz and myself go into teaching. [Heifetz had filmed an influential series of master-classses for American television.] It is terribly important, as a result of one's personal experience, to pass that on to youngsters, *especially since violin teaching at the moment is carried on at a very low level* [author's italics]. Fiddling is an art that requires constant contact and communication between pupil and master. It is rather in the nature of those eras where crafts were passed from the older to the younger generation, when the master impressed his style upon his followers. Now we no longer hope that a student will follow us exactly. We try as teachers to make each student express his own personality. That is what music needs . . . Teaching the violin requires extreme sensitivity. A careless teacher simply cannot communicate the essence of violin playing. I can understand why most youngsters want to study easier instruments than the fiddle, and why, therefore, there is a shortage of players. That is because the violin is so badly and so irresponsibly taught. It is up to us performers to propagate our knowledge, our discipline: if we have disciples, what we know can be properly disseminated. And most of us performers know a good deal.

Yehudi seems to be feeling his way towards a conclusion that became a guiding principle at his school, that the most important thing a gifted pupil can be taught is how to study:

Even though the teacher is important, most of what every violinist has to learn he discovers for himself. True, you can be taught a certain amount of technique, though not as much as on other instruments; but basically the fiddle is not a thing for which you can lay down a set of rules.

At this point in the interview Yehudi allowed himself a playful comparison which explained the sensational headline to the piece: 'Yehudi Menuhin declares the violin is a woman.' The violin, he explained, is an elusive mystery. 'The piano is a male instrument, it can be con-

quered, dominated like a man. But the fiddle needs patience, subtlety –
the things required to win a woman.' To play the violin well, he went on,

you must spend countless hours alone, for practising is solitary work . . . [you]
must go it alone, sometimes from kindergarten age. Then, too, I don't think you
can become a violinist unless the skill is born in you – and even then you need one
of the few right teachers to develop it. In my case I have never lost sight of my
growth from prodigy to artist. Progress, of course, is not in a straight line: it undu-
lates. My unhappiest days were those in which something I wanted to do escaped
me, in which I was not able to project what I thought. But then there are the
wonderful periods of discovery and consolation when the whole world suddenly
opens up and something you have been struggling with – perhaps only a tiny
phrase – instantaneously becomes clear. It is during these moments that it all seems
worthwhile, when all the immense labour of violin playing is forgotten. Suddenly
you realize that it is one of the most precious things one can give one's life to.

The poor state of contemporary violin teaching and his own experiences as a boy prodigy were clearly giving him food for thought. The
evidence of another interview, given three years later, suggests he had
found the inner strength needed to undertake the hugely ambitious
project of founding a new school. On tour in Australia in 1962,
Yehudi met a journalist, Alan Moyle, who had first interviewed him in
1935. Moyle noted that Yehudi, now forty-six, needed glasses for
reading:

I studied this boy who had become a great master . . . big-chested, in a short-
sleeved blue sweater, well-worn slacks, red socks and red hair on his slender but
muscular body, with strongly defined forehead bulge and prominent brows. A face
sensitive, relaxed, thoughtful, sympathetic. Essentially Yehudi had not changed
much over the years; and yet, he had – gone was the tentativeness that marked earlier days, and there were marks of struggle about his mouth which, however, had
not lost its humour, its frequent laughter. The years slipped by . . . I remembered
he had once told me about his theories of vibration – theories he had thrashed out
with his old friend Albert Einstein.

From his files Moyle produced an example of Yehudi's philosophizing
at the age of nineteen:

I have a theory about music and life . . . I see everywhere about me vibration,
vibration, vibration . . . in sound, of course; in music, inevitably; but also in everything that pulses and grows and draws life from the elements . . . Among people I
know intimately, those of more creative ability seem to function at a higher pitch
of vibration. They are more sensitive. An E string vibrates a thousand times more
highly than a G. I have rarely had a G string break. That is because the E string
must be strained so tensely to give the vibrations to reach the notes it alone can
produce.

Yehudi listened attentively to the words he had uttered a quarter of a century previously.

Of course I still think, after all this time, that life is built around vibration. Periodic vibration lies at the basis of all life, all thought, all communication, all music.

Moyle reminded him that in 1935 he admitted to losing up to a pound and a half in weight at every concert: 'I play in a bath of perspiration,' Yehudi had told him then. 'I must have at least two complete changes of clothing during a performance.' Pouring himself a glass of Vichy water, Yehudi said he now sweated much less during concerts than in former years:

I have more confidence, I still feel the music intensely, but the effort is easier. I am concerned less about technique, presentation. I can say more, because the mechanics of playing are more automatic. When I first talked about vibration to you it was at an interesting, restless, inquiring period of my life. A little later, in New Zealand, I tried to reduce the problem of human development to diagrammatic form. I made a diagram of the evolution of mankind – a sort of spiral of achievement; I began to understand the principle of design in all things.

And here we come face to face with the self-confident personality that Yehudi has become in his forties:

I think today [we] are evolving into a state of better understanding, in spite of all the international turmoil. There is more precision about living and life. There is certainly more precision in my life. I think I understand . . . something of the forces that are behind me and through me when I play. I was always a seeker and a searcher; I am still seeking and searching; but . . . with more order and scientific sense in my searching. I find much happiness now in life. I have found a better balance between theory and practice . . . And of course I have learned more of music. I have met other composers. Wider horizons of appreciation have opened up because I have been admitted more deeply into the minds of other men who make music. To me, as an interpreter, this has been invaluable as well as delightful.

Yehudi seems tacitly to acknowledge here that making music with the members of his Bath Festival Orchestra, notably Robert Masters, had been as important for his development as a musician as his wartime tours of military hospitals had been for his development as a man. In November 1962 his reputation was approaching its zenith in Britain. At a London concert that month the Royal Philharmonic Society presented him with its prestige-laden Gold Medal. He was only the fifth violinist to have received it in almost a century and the first for close on sixty years, the others being Joachim, Ysaÿe, Kubelik and most recently Kreisler – back in 1904. *The Times* noted that Menuhin

had won 'a very special place in the affection of British music-lovers'.
But its accompanying concert review began nevertheless with a hint of
criticism:

A flawless technique is not among the gifts for which Mr Menuhin is held in such
high esteem . . . but what no musical person can fail to respond to is the sheer generosity with which Mr Menuhin pours himself into the music he plays, identifying
himself with every phrase and stamping it with his unique warmth and intensity.

The next day he flew to Moscow, accompanied by Diana, Hephzibah and his manager Ian Hunter. (After eight years of interminable
ship and train journeys, flying had finally been reinstated as the preferred mode of transport, radar apparatus having long since been
installed on commercial airlines.) Hunter remembers taking supplies of
Cooper's Oxford marmalade to alleviate the ghastliness of the Russian
food. Yehudi's first concert tour there since the brief expedition of
1945 was a gruelling one, taking in Kiev, Lvov and Minsk as well as
the standard venues in Moscow and Leningrad. At one point they
passed through the town of Gomel, the birthplace of Yehudi's father.
A cable was duly dispatched to him. Odessa, the home town of Nathan
Milstein and David Oistrakh, was another port of call; when the audience crowded into Yehudi's dressing room after the concert they clam-
oured not for autographs but for details of bowings and fingerings.
Diana Menuhin's witty account of the tour is often scathing about the
incompetence of the Soviet concert agency Goskonzert but illuminating for its description of the Central School for Young Musicians in
Moscow, which Yehudi said later had inspired him to found his own
school. 'Aptly enough', wrote Diana, who saw everything in terms of
her own Russian Ballet training, the school

was established on exactly the same lines as had been the Tsar's Maryinsky Ballet
School, in which the pupils received scholastic and musical tuition under the same
roof, a system which Yehudi had long realized was the reason for which the
Russians reached the top of nearly all the international competitions. However the
morning we spent there held a current of anonymity and drill that was disturbing.
Dear little monsters aged four or five or six, their pigtails pinned to the crowns of
their heads, whipped their way through Chopin and Liszt and all the showy composers with a cool competence that was at once admirable though alarming. Later
we heard older boys and girls who had graduated to more serious but still
dramatic works, showing their paces with a skill and perfection of execution that
also left one baffled. Especially perplexing was the weird withholding of all names
either of the performer or – particularly – of the teacher. These were gifted and
well-tooled machines, part of the state's organization and property for home

consumption and export. Hephzibah remained silent; Yehudi was obviously more determined than ever to bring to the West his own version of such training.

The visit might have inspired Yehudi but it also helped to define what he did *not* want to do. He had been thinking of joining forces in London with the formidable figure of Dr Ruth Railton, who single-handedly had made a tremendous success since 1948 of the National Youth Orchestra of Great Britain. The previous year, 1961, he had sat in on a day of the NYO's rehearsals and then established a planning committee. 'We had many meetings in his house in Highgate,' wrote Ruth Railton in her memoirs.

The intricacies of the English educational system, especially regarding residential schools, were a complete mystery to him. All he wanted was a building full of eight-year-old violinists. In 1962 he asked our Council for two members for a joint committee.

The talks were ineffectual. At the end of the year the *Daily Telegraph* carried a report about 'the new London Junior Music School being planned by Yehudi Menuhin and Ruth Railton', but there was no real compatibility between the aims of two such powerful personalities. The NYO, whose members were aged between twelve and eighteen, met only three times a year and already had a sophisticated teaching structure in place; Yehudi wanted an all-year-round school, with a permanent academic and music staff and a much younger intake. He resembled the Jesuits: he wanted to catch them young. Relations soured when Dr Railton was not informed that young children from the new school would be sharing the accommodation that the NYO's handful of boarding students enjoyed at Princes Court, the Arts Educational Trust hostel in South Kensington. In the summer of 1963 she returned from an exhausting NYO tour of Poland to discover a shiny brass plate affixed to the front door: THE YEHUDI MENUHIN SCHOOL. Yehudi had taken the plunge.

He was far from ready, but backed by a group of affluent and influential friends, he had decided to go it alone. He nailed his colours to the mast in an article for the *Sunday Telegraph*. String players, he declared, were an endangered species:

Just as Sir Julian Huxley is so deeply concerned with the preservation of wild life . . . so do I feel that strong encouragement of string playing is required to preserve our species from extinction, as has already nearly overtaken our predecessors and inspiring violinistic colleagues, the gypsies of Eastern Europe.

Ever optimistic, he claimed that England was

the most likely of all countries to furnish the world with great violinists. Stylistically, no one can match her best chamber groups, such as the London Mozart Players or my own little Bath orchestra. The only disadvantage lies in that the teacher, however good he may be, is handicapped because he receives his pupils already too old, both mentally and physically, for the teaching of an instrument whose enormous complexity, almost as much as in the ballet, requires an early start.

Despite Diana's hostile evidence concerning its deadening regimentation, he claimed to have been inspired by the example of the Central Music School in Moscow. When he had first visited it, just after the war, there had been only twenty students;

now it is vast, with two buildings; one where the children get classes, the other where they live – about a hundred of them are boarders. It is the brightest, gayest place I have seen in Russia. The atmosphere is entirely happy; yet when the children play their poise is amazing. If only they wouldn't play such old-fashioned pieces! – but this is part of the Victorian world of primness in which so much of Russia is locked; perhaps we may help to free their fantasy. We in turn must learn their techniques of group teaching, and their extraordinary power of application.

Such flattering references would have rung a bell in the public's imagination: the Soviet Union was at the height of its power and prestige in the early 1960s. The Russians were beating the Americans in the space race and had recently threatened them with missile attacks from bases in Cuba, less than a hundred miles from the American mainland. Their performing musicians, too, were outstanding, notably Emil Gilels and Sviatoslav Richter among the pianists, David Oistrakh the violinist and Mstislav Rostropovich the cellist. In April 1963 Yehudi's pupil Alberto Lysy and his old friend Marcel Gazelle, who was professor of piano at the Ghent Conservatoire in his native Belgium, were dispatched to Moscow to see what more could be learned from the Russians.

In proposing a segregated educational establishment for talented youngsters Yehudi was happy to imply that he was following in Moscow's footsteps, but he had no desire to create a machine for turning out virtuosos. His instinct – and Diana affirms that he was always ruled by his gut feelings – was for a much smaller and gentler community, with the majority of the pupils to be prospective string players, preferably starting at the age of eight so that they could be properly taught from the outset of their musical lives. Everybody would also study the piano as part of their musical education. *The*

Times published a letter in which he invited nominations of gifted seven-year-olds. He later telephoned the distinguished violinist Frederick Grinke, a professor at the Royal Academy of Music, asking for recommendations. Everything was in place for the new establishment, Yehudi told him jokingly, but he had omitted to recruit any pupils. Grinke not only helped out but joined the teaching staff.

Yehudi's proposal captured the imagination of a far-sighted pedagogue named Grace Cone and she offered him a temporary share of the premises she had acquired for her Arts Educational Trust, which was already providing specialist education for gifted youngsters in ballet and drama. 'We had a womb to develop in,' wrote Yehudi. Among the music-loving great and good on his Music Academy Committee were the Marchioness of Cholmondeley, Lady Fermoy, Sir Miki Sekers, the Countess of Strafford, Lord Mottistone, Mr Paul Paget and many more friends; cash and good advice came rolling in, and in September the School opened its doors.

A photograph taken on the first day shows Yehudi on the front step surrounded by just fifteen pupils and almost as many staff. Just behind him in the group is Marcel Gazelle, piano professor and the school's first Director of Music. The impressive phalanx of teachers included the cellists Maurice Gendron and Christopher Bunting; Lionel Tertis, England's greatest viola player; George Malcolm the harpsichordist, who was Yehudi's favourite jazz-playing keyboard player; and the violinists Robert Masters and Alberto Lysy. Yehudi's son Jeremy, then twelve, was among the children. (Jeremy left before the year was over to study at Eton College – but only for a few terms before he was off again to study with Nadia Boulanger in Paris.) Academic lessons were held at the Trust's classrooms near Piccadilly. Music lessons were given in rented rooms at the old Prince of Wales Hotel (since destroyed) where some of the pupils also had their bedrooms. The pianist Ronan Magill, one of Marcel Gazelle's first piano students, remembers spending many happy hours shuttling between the centres in a school minibus. From the outset Yehudi insisted on health foods and exercise for his pupils. Magill, then a pre-pubescent nine-year-old, recalls one of the older girls, Mary Eade, putting on dance-class leggings before attending her yoga lesson. The School's first newsletter noted that in July 1964, 'Mr Iyengar the distinguished teacher of yoga from India paid the School three visits and gave classes to the children.' (Many years later Yehudi also encouraged the practice of t'ai chi.)

Sharing premises and facilities with another organization could never be a satisfactory arrangement in the long term and after a year the School moved to its present quarters, a large, gabled Victorian mansion with outhouses set in fifteen rolling acres of wooded parkland about twenty-five miles south-west of London, near the village of Stoke d'Abernon. Yehudi was taken to view it by one of his assistants who learned that the place was on the market – it had formerly served as a management training centre. The instinct he had inherited from his mother for making swift decisions about property did not let him down: he acquired a fine piece of real estate whose value can only have increased when, twenty-one years later, a concrete swathe of the M25 London orbital road was completed at the northern edge of the estate. The perpetual roar of motorway traffic is aggravating to this day, especially when the wind comes from the north, but communication with the capital and its airports has undoubtedly improved as a result. A mortgage was arranged with the Swiss-Israel Bank and the freehold was purchased a few years later for £50,000 with funds raised partly by individual gifts and charitable trust donations, and partly from the proceeds of an auction of works contributed by such friends as Jacob Epstein, Elisabeth Frink, Oskar Kokoschka and Henry Moore; the balance of the mortgage was reportedly 'almost paid off' seven years later.

Yehudi found a kindred spirit of his own generation to be the School's first Headmaster. Anthony Brackenbury was born a couple of years after him, in 1918. During the Second World War he had been a conscientious objector. He then taught classics at Bryanston for a time and served as head of sixth form studies for two years at a London comprehensive before Yehudi chose him, attracted (as he wrote later) by 'a quality of creative warmth'. Brackenbury passed this on to the School for a decade before heart problems forced early retirement. According to a fellow teacher, Peter Norris, Tony Brackenbury was the ideal person for the task of moulding an international school:

With his vision and strength of personality he was able to hold and draw together all the disparate elements of different nationalities, temperaments, age and outlooks. From the beginning he firmly refused to let it become the hothouse it so easily could have been.

'He believed in being in touch with everyone,' wrote another teacher,

and so before breakfast he greeted each pupil separately at his front door. At Morning Meetings he selected readings with spiritual and philosophical ideas, to be followed by a few minutes of silence for reflection . . . He taught all age groups, lunched daily with everyone and on Sunday evenings held an informal meeting with staff and pupils.

One has the right to expect such commitment from any caring head-master but Brackenbury had other characteristics that must have especially endeared him to Yehudi. He created his own compost heap, reared chickens which roamed around the grounds, encouraged the keeping of small pets and provided small plots of land for children and staff to cultivate individually. He also introduced and cared for a donkey named Patience, who provided fun for the younger children for fifteen years. The School's brochure spelled out its Headmaster's attitude: 'The image by which we are guided is that of an enlarged family, so that the day-to-day life and work of the place is shared between young and old.' There were no prefects and no school uniforms: the only uniformity that was encouraged concerned the care of musical instruments.

The Menuhin School was an instant success with the media. Special treatment for clever children made for a good story at a time when national policy under the new Labour government, which came to power soon after the School opened, was moving in the opposite direc-tion, towards comprehensive education. And Yehudi was always good for a poetic sound-bite. He spoke engagingly, if a little vaguely, of 'the precious sense of mystery, curiosity and delight [that is] dormant in every child'. But as he waxed lyrical about the merits of early special-ization for musically gifted youngsters his tongue sometimes ran away with him alarmingly. 'Music is a way of life', he declared in the preface to a book about the School;

often unconventional, nonconformist, it is the expression of what the creature is at heart, and his music reveals to the listener what this listener is to himself at heart. Music is the naked heart, the naked soul, the naked intellect, even – as some X-ray which transpierces all outer layers, skins and shells. Perhaps that phenomenon so dear to my heart – the untutored gypsy fiddler – comes nearest to expressing in the wild this way of life.

Happily there was good sense embedded in most of Yehudi's impromptu utterances.

Members of the Royal Family expressed keen interest in his work. Princess Marina was followed by the Queen Mother and then Prince Charles, who dropped in by helicopter one morning. Before long the music-loving Duchess of Kent became the School's Patron. Teachers, theorists, journalists and documentary-makers were all frequent visitors and during its very first term in the new premises, in the autumn of 1964, pupils from the school were featured on the BBC's new television channel, BBC2: in one of its first televised *Master Classes* Yehudi coached a shy little seven-year-old named Nigel Kennedy. And in 1969 came a portrait of the School in the form of a copiously illustrated book, *Menuhin's House of Music*, written by the composer Eric Fenby. He was something of a celebrity himself because his account of working for Delius in the 1930s had just been made into a splendid BBC film by Ken Russell. Fenby spent several days observing the School's activities. Thirty-six children were then in residence, their ages ranging from seven to a few sixteen-year-olds who were preparing for GCEs in English and French. Fenby came away deeply impressed: 'Four timetables were running concurrently to serve their various stages of advancement. The general impression is of extraordinary freedom within a discipline accepted reciprocally by all.' The youngest pupils, classed as Cs and Ds, did lessons while the older students practised their instruments, generally under the supervision of an adult. There would be a break at mid-morning, when Mr Brackenbury would lead the As and Bs in 'physical jerks', stretching their arms heavenward and taking in 'deep breaths of Surrey air'. Then the classes would switch; a similar pattern operated in the afternoons so that each day there would be at least four hours of practice and individual musical tuition, alternating with five forty-minute periods for scholastic studies.

The range of subjects on offer was limited until the School's expansion in the 1970s enabled more teaching staff to be employed. Chamber-music groups were created from among the children and soon an orchestra was formed; in the early years it tended to be a little top-heavy with violins. Choral practices were held twice a week and regular recitals given by staff and distinguished visitors such as the Allegri Quartet, Vlado Perlemuter and Ravi Shankar. The feeling of an international community was reinforced by the presence among the cooking and cleaning staff of half a dozen *au pair* helpers from abroad. After lunch ('plenty of salads and brown bread, fresh fruit and cheese . . . it is felt that processed and preserved foods are unsuitable') a twenty-minute rest on beds was compulsory for everybody. The painter Mary Fedden taught art, to be succeeded in 1970 by Jane Hoare. Supervised hobbies pursued in the early years included dress-making, chess and Scottish dancing. It is not entirely fanciful to imagine the spirits of Moshe and

Marutha Menuhin hovering over the fields of Stoke d'Abernon.

'This is no soft-option school,' wrote Eric Fenby. Group activities began at seven o'clock each morning, sometimes even earlier for the As and Bs, when the brains of the young were thought to be especially receptive. The pre-breakfast classes were on general musicianship and included ear tests, musical dictation, learning to recognize the sounds of chords, identifying key modulations and so on, all designed to make the children musically literate at an early age. Fenby approved whole-heartedly of Menuhin's insistence that all pupils should learn the system of note identification known as *solfège*. Nadia Boulanger would not have taught without it. Her regular visits, usually for several days, made a deep impression. 'Her lessons are quite original,' students told Fenby:

different and full of surprises. She quotes Valéry and draws on painting and philosophy. But most of all she shows one how to concentrate one's *deepest attention* on music; and how to awake in others a similar response to what one is playing oneself.

Another presence recalled from Yehudi's Parisian adolescence was the veteran pianist Marcel Ciampi, who had taught Hephzibah and Yaltah in Paris in the 1930s and recommended his young pupil Marcel Gazelle as Yehudi's regular accompanist; he was installed as the School's head of piano studies. Gazelle married the violinist Jacqueline Salomons, with whom Yehudi had regularly played quartets at Ville d'Avray thirty years previously. She, too, joined the staff and remained at the School for another decade after her husband died of cancer in 1969. Another Enesco pupil, Helen Dowling, also taught there. In surrounding himself with personalities from his musical childhood, Yehudi was re-creating the atmosphere of the happiest days of his life. Even the family tradition of putting on plays was revived: early school productions, usually mounted at the end of the summer term, included *The Caucasian Chalk Circle*, *The Importance of Being Earnest* and *Alice in Wonderland*.

The School had been designed to function without Yehudi. He was a member of its governing body but was otherwise listed simply as a visiting teacher. There was no mistaking his influence, however; he was never simply a figurehead. The normal timetable would be suspended for his visits once or twice a term (as it was for Nadia Boulanger) so that he could spend time with every pupil and give what was described as the 'Founder's Master Class'. In 1965 a *Times* reporter was gently rebuked for expressing surprise that he concerned himself with the training of complete novices. 'It is at this stage that the important teaching is done,' he said, not mentioning Sigmund Anker by name but surely remembering his own unhappiness at the age of six. The *Times* man noted that Yehudi listened to everything on offer, 'from the robust vigour of a Bach concerto to finger-stretching exercises of a beginner, with the same totally absorbed attention'.

The nub of his teaching was to make the pupils aware of what they were doing – the one thing he had not picked up from Enesco or Persinger. Fenby noted that his method of violin playing (in so far as it was a 'method' at all: Yehudi distrusted the word and preferred teaching from specifics) was based 'partly on a general physical condition of flexibility, resilience and balance and on good breathing, which requires a certain amount of preparation (or practice) away from the instrument'. Exercises were devised to exert control of the correct muscles and to strengthen the fingers. Yehudi gave his pupils a system he had originally worked out for himself, which aimed to reduce tension to the absolute minimum: 'It's done me so much good,' one of the girls told Fenby, 'I've studied it with my mother and it's helped her so much – and her pupils – that I feel, apart from anything else, it's my duty to hand it on to the next generation.' That sentiment would have pleased Yehudi. 'The aim is to produce fully educated musicians,' he told *The Times*, whose feature was headed 'Music school's homely atmosphere'. He would be happy, he added, if the present pupils provide the world with thirty good teachers rather than a handful of virtuosi.

In close on four decades the School has produced a broad range of musicians, some of whom did indeed become teachers, a few even returning to the School in that capacity. No statistical analysis is available but the number of teachers, leaders and section leaders, chamber-music players and musical administrators that the School has produced far outnumbers the virtuosi, of whom Nigel Kennedy and Tasmin Little are probably the best known among the violinists. Other distinguished alumni include the cellists Colin Carr and Paul Watkins and the pianists Paul Coker, Kathryn Stott and Melvyn Tan. Yehudi's favourite pastime, quartet playing, was encouraged from the beginning: Andrew Wilkinson, later the leader of the Endellion Quartet, was one of the earliest pupils and Corina Belcea studied there in the 1990s;

two other founder members of her fine Belcea Quartet were near contemporaries at the School.

A boarder from the tender age of seven, Nigel Kennedy felt 'really dreadful' in his early years. One of Mr Brackenbury's end-of-term reports said he was everybody's favourite, being the 'Benjamin' of the household, but added that he was shy and something of a dormouse. Kennedy revealed in his autobiography that soft toys, two koala bears and a stuffed platypus, kept in his bed, were some consolation for having been sent away from home so young. (His mother remarried soon after his departure.) Kennedy described the education as 'brilliant' but said he ignored 80 per cent of what he was taught. Left alone to practise for hours on end, he was a prey to doubts and dreams:

The rather unreal nature of the Menuhin School placed me initially in a void – which as I filled it with my own visions, heightened the strength of my emerging convictions.

But over a decade the School instilled in him a passion for European musical traditions which he waved, he wrote, 'like some cultural battle flag' when he moved on to the Juilliard in New York. Yehudi's admiration for the jazz violin of Stéphane Grappelli (discussed in the next chapter) came at exactly the right time for Kennedy as a teenager; when Grappelli came to play to the students he was asked on to the platform to join in a jam session. 'Standing up there with him was 100 per cent excitement.'

Nigel was grateful to Yehudi for giving him his basic education (the assistance was also financial: a scholarship personally provided in honour of Marutha and Moshe) but when he studied the Elgar Concerto with him he felt Yehudi was pushing him too hard to follow his own interpretations. Yehudi's playing was too passive for rebellious young Nigel's taste: 'He never really expresses his aggression in his playing.' In contrast, Tasmin Little, who came to the School in 1973 and stayed a decade, remembers Yehudi with unalloyed affection:

When I was seventeen I had the good fortune to play chamber music with him – I literally played 'second fiddle' to his first, in the Mendelssohn Octet. During an initial rehearsal it became apparent that he had skipped a bar and was out of time with the rest of the group. He stopped, turned to me and asked, 'Tasmin, am I ahead of you all?' Stumbling for the appropriate way to reply in the affirmative, I said hesitantly, 'Well, only one bar . . .' His face broke into an enormous smile and he gave the lovely gentle chuckle that I knew so well. It did not worry him at all that he had made a mistake. In fact he almost seemed to take delight in having been the one who was out of time! From that moment I learned that one should not be ashamed or frightened of making mistakes, as long as one learns from them, and that it is important to remember that we can never be 'perfect' musicians but can only strive to make the best music we can.

As the number of pupils rose and their average age grew higher – Nigel Kennedy, for instance, was a pupil for ten years before going on to win a scholarship to the Juilliard School in New York in 1974 – it became possible to create a string orchestra of concert-giving standard, often conducted by Yehudi. Its début concert was at nearby Esher, as early as 23 November 1965, and it made its first London appearance at the Wigmore Hall in 1968. Soon there were annual London concerts featuring soloists and chamber ensembles from the School as well as the orchestra. Mr Brackenbury proudly reported in 1970 that they had been described as the 'best young string players in Britain' after an appearance at the Windsor Festival. Yehudi remembered how much he had enjoyed travelling as a boy and organized many spectacular expeditions for the School. Trips abroad became regular occurrences, the first being in 1971 to play for a Nadia Boulanger gala at the Hôtel Singer-Polignac in Paris. In 1974 he led the students on a two-week tour of the United States and in 1976 they returned to the US and went to Switzerland to help celebrate the twentieth anniversary of the Gstaad Festival. In 1982 they visited China, joining forces with older, postgraduate players from the Academy Yehudi founded with Alberto Lysy in Gstaad. (Afterwards, Chinese music students were helped to attend the School by scholarships from British Petroleum.) In 1986 came a two-week tour of Israel followed by Italy in 1987 and France in 1988. Yehudi often engaged soloists from the School when conducting the Royal Philharmonic Orchestra both at home and abroad; Nigel Kennedy played the Elgar Concerto with him in 1979.

From 1978 onwards the School's profile with the general public increased substantially as its pupils regularly reached the final round of BBC TV's 'Young Musician of the Year' competition, although not until 1996 did it produce an outright winner in the eighteen-year-old violinist Rafal Payne. When the competition was expanded to include young composers, the school did well in that category, too. Yehudi took a positive view of competitions. In 1983 he founded one of his own to cater for gifted youngsters who tend to be outshone by older, more experienced players at the major international competitions in Brussels and Moscow (see page 465). Another competition he supported, specifically for light music, was named after Pablo Sarasate, the Spanish violinist from Pamplona whose *Gypsy Airs* Yehudi used to adore playing when he was young. He also presided over an international string quartet competition which began life in Portsmouth and later (in 1988) transferred to London. But he disliked the cut-throat atmosphere that sometimes contaminates the big international competitions and when he served as chairman of the televised 'Eurovision Young Musician' competition he disconcerted the organizers, who needed a clear-cut result, by informing the viewers that he had marked all seven finalists as equal first prize-winners. Competitions are tolerated at the School but pupils are given equal encouragement to take part in public concerts, often for audiences in small communities and hospices. Faced with criticism that the pupils' lives were too sheltered, Yehudi supported the annual visits made by senior children to a colliery village in South Yorkshire; they were organized by Peter Renshaw and his wife and fellow teacher.

In the 1970s, Yehudi's inspiration and persuasiveness brought substantial injections of cash from the Calouste Gulbenkian Foundation, the Wolfson Trust, the Rayne Foundation and countless other charitable donors, enabling the School to be enlarged and rebuilt. The local Friends organization helped with smaller but significant gifts. Headmaster Brackenbury dropped hints to them in his 1972 *Newsletter*:

Taking a leaf out of Plato's book, I believe in an environment of beauty as well as utility. Besides fine musical instruments and recording equipment – the school has no hi-fi system yet for listening to broadcast concerts – we need furniture and fabrics and books and pictures indoors, just as we need trees and shrubs in the gardens that will enhance the setting of our daily life and not allow it to be an unconsidered makeshift background. Let us emulate Thucydides' words about the Athenians, 'We are lovers of beauty without extravagance.'

Inevitably there was criticism that the school was élitist. But enlightened County Education Departments had offered grants for talented youngsters since the School's beginning. A visit by the Labour Arts Minister Jennie Lee resulted in an Arts Council subsidy. When the Tories regained power under the music-loving Edward Heath, the Secretary of State for Education, Margaret Thatcher, decided in 1972 to grant special status to the School, along with the Royal Ballet School in Richmond Park. It was a remarkable vote of confidence in an establishment not yet ten years old. Fees for United Kingdom students have been subsidized ever since, although private donations have always been needed to help pupils from overseas; Yehudi always aimed at a proportion of approximately two-thirds British to one-third foreigners. Annual boarding currently costs about £12,000.

As the facilities and accommodation continued to be improved and expanded, the numbers crept up. Nowadays over fifty pupils, speaking a dozen different first languages, enjoy sound-proofed music rooms in which to practise, custom-built teaching rooms, composition centres equipped with computers (including Sibelius software for the preparation of music manuscripts), a library and an orchestral rehearsal hall. The hall is not large enough for concerts with a substantial audience and plans are afoot to construct and endow a proper hall in Menuhin's memory: it could also serve as a professional recording studio. The personal accommodation has always been congenial by English boarding-school standards; as early as 1965 Yehudi was able to boast to *The Times* that his children were possibly the only boarders in Britain to have individual bedrooms, with washbasins and carpets on the floor.

The School's critics were initially sceptical as to whether the gains conferred by early specialization outweigh such disadvantages as tiny peer groups, no rough-and-tumble team sports and inadequate academic teaching. But the range of subjects offered has steadily expanded. In terms of intellectual stimulus it is certain that nobody could match what Nadia Boulanger provided in the School's first fifteen years. (She died in 1979, aged ninety-one.) Only Hans Keller, who taught in the 1980s, came near: he was only sixty-six when he died of motor neurone disease in 1985. 'Nobody who witnessed him coaching a young string quartet at my School', wrote Yehudi,

could fail to realize that a miracle was taking place. This was as evident to the four players as it was to those who observed their frail and ailing teacher committed and courageous beyond belief, who with utter devotion and with profound respect for the music, for the children and for their efforts to transform notes into a unique, living experience, gave his all . . . determined to fulfil the elusive task which is the musician's – that of bringing to life the notes of the page, and the hearts and minds of the young players.

There can never be another Keller but the School continues to invite musicians of the highest calibre to stimulate the children. Mstislav Rostropovich has succeeded Yehudi Menuhin as its Life President, a guarantee that the excitement and excellence will be maintained. (Yehudi raised the subject with 'Slava' at the time of his eightieth birthday.) Day-to-day control of the school is still shared between the Headmaster and the Director of Music. Tony Brackenbury was succeeded in the former post by a musician, Peter Renshaw (1975–83) and in 1988 by Nicolas Chisholm, a former singer who has now run a steady ship for longer than any of his predecessors. Music Directors have included Robert Masters, Peter Norris and Stephen Potts; the post is currently held by Malcolm Singer, who first joined the staff to teach composition in 1977.

Chisholm says that he and Singer are developing Menuhin's notion of giving something back to the community. 'Yehudi said to me one day that he would very much like to have children at the School aged five'; as a result there are now Children's Music Classes for local children aged between one and five. There is also a popular Young Strings project at the School which teaches the violin to beginners between the ages of five and six. A development of his project, involving young people from a school in north Guildford, was shown on BBC2 at Easter 2000.

Because it was never intended to create 'finished' musicians, the Menuhin School should not be compared with great teaching institutions such as the Paris Conservatoire or the Juilliard School in New York. But it has provided many hundreds of musically gifted children with a sympathetic atmosphere in which to develop their musical skills and artistry and the world is indisputably a better place because of it. Apart from his recordings Yehudi left no more significant legacy than this thriving community dedicated to the pursuit of musical excellence. On 19 March 1999, Yehudi was buried in the grounds of his School, under a tree that he had planted himself almost three years previously, on his eightieth birthday.

Recommended Recordings

Yehudi Menuhin's Young Virtuosi
Classic FM (CD and cassette): CFM CD8
Published: 1996
The CD includes:
Elgar: *Serenade for Strings*, conducted by YM
Verdi: String Quartet in E minor (first movement)
Popular solos by individual members of the Yehudi Menuhin School.

PART FIVE

'I was born old, and have been growing younger ever since'

1969–1999

Installation at the House of Lords with Lord Armstrong and Lord Jakobovits,
January 1994

17 Confrontations and Collaborations

With Stéphane Grappelli, 1986

1966: fiftieth birthday in London; 1969–75: President, International Music Council; 1971: speech upsets Russian hosts in Moscow; 1972: first jazz duets recorded with Stéphane Grappelli; 1973: conducts television show featuring Diana in speaker's role; 1976: sixtieth birthday and sabbatical year; 1977: establishment of International Yehudi Menuhin Academy in Gstaad and of Live Music Now! in UK; 1977–9: CBC TV series The Music of Man.

IN APRIL 1966 Yehudi celebrated his fiftieth birthday in fine style with the London Philharmonic at the Royal Festival Hall. His two sisters were joined by his youngest son, Jeremy (then thirteen, and making his London début), for a sparkling performance of the Concerto in F (K.242) for three pianos by Mozart. It was conducted by Yehudi and televised by the BBC. Leaders of orchestras from Paris, Vienna, London and Bath played one of Vivaldi's concertos for four violins, and Yehudi himself offered his favourite miniatures, Beethoven's two lovely Romances, with Sir Adrian Boult at the rostrum. The *New York Times* reported that

ambassadors, politicians, distinguished conductors, soloists and other musicians were in the audience, testifying to the high regard in which Mr Menuhin is held . . . as one of the rare spirits of this age. Born in New York, he is now a world citizen, the ex-*Wunderkind* who survived infant genius to become the realized artist and man.

Afterwards Sir Adrian presented Yehudi with the proceeds of the concert, a cheque for £10,000 destined for the Menuhin School.

There was to be no drawing in of horns at this strategic juncture, which proved to be the halfway mark in his adult life: as he moved into his sixth decade Yehudi was on a high plateau of musical achievement. His new international school was settling down well – its string orchestra gave its first public concert in November 1965 – while at the Bath Festival he'd proved that conducting was no flash in the pan but a viable additional career. And his violin playing was in peak condition at EMI's Abbey Road studio, where in the winter of 1965–6 he recorded the Elgar Concerto for the second time, with another great Elgarian conducting in the person of Sir Adrian Boult. It was the first recording of the Concerto to be made in stereo and inevitably there is a marked gain in technical quality. The 1932 version on 78s, which has since been transferred to CD, is an undisputed classic, forever associated with Yehudi's youthful ardour and Elgar's own generous spirit at the rostrum, but the 1965 version is equally eloquent: the *Penguin CD Guide* of 1996 described it as 'indispensable for its documentary value as well as its musical insights' and the *Gramophone* noted at the time that the very few weak moments in the old recording (the accompanied cadenza in the third movement was described as 'a real failure') had been corrected this time round.

In February 1966 Menuhin moved on from Elgar to make a new version of the Beethoven Concerto, with the great Otto Klemperer conducting. He had also devoted time to the viola, playing the solo in Colin Davis's recording of Berlioz's *Harold in Italy*, and in 1966 he recorded the Bartók Viola Concerto, with Antal Dorati as conductor. Two years later he resolved to record his friend William Walton's Viola Concerto; he told the composer's wife Susana that he had given up the fiddle for a month so that he could get the larger instrument firmly under his fingers. (He borrowed the viola belonging to Peter Schidlof of the Amadeus Quartet.) Walton's seventieth birthday was on the horizon and in 1969 Yehudi used his 'Prince Khevenhüller' Stradivarius, a magnificent instrument, to record Walton's much more virtuosic Violin Concerto. Its Gershwinesque opening melody has never sounded more beautiful. The work had been commissioned (and premièred in 1939) by Jascha Heifetz and had never previously been tackled by Yehudi, perhaps because he was reluctant to indulge in what might be seen as confrontational programming. But Heifetz was now living in semi-retirement, and was no longer a rival. Writing up the record in the *Gramophone* (October 1969) the critic Edward Greenfield commented that Menuhin was on top form,

firmly in the centre of the note for Walton's dreamily romantic melodies and apparently undaunted by the passages of double- and triple-stopped scraping . . . it was good to see him showing off with such enthusiasm.

In December 1966 Glenn Gould contributed an entertaining tribute to Yehudi in the magazine *Musical America*. 'The first thing to be said about him', Gould wrote, 'is that he is an astonishingly *au courant* musician, as ready to discuss the latest breakthrough at Baden-Baden . . . as the possibility of an alternate bowing for the Bach *Chaconne*.' Gould and Menuhin had recently recorded a recital of Bach and Beethoven sonatas for Canadian television which concluded with Schoenberg's *Fantasy*, Op. 47. 'The frequency and audacity of [his] insights', Gould wrote, 'make Menuhin wellnigh unique as a chamber music collaborator.' In fact Yehudi learned the Schoenberg overnight and he soon departed from the TV script Gould had prepared for him, making no secret in their conversation on camera that he found the violin writing 'curiously clumsy'. (Gould explained away Yehudi's unscheduled remarks by telling the studio technicians that the violinist had reading difficulties.) In the television programme the two men, both former child prodigies, are seen making music together joyously. But in print, a few months later, Glenn Gould was not averse to poking a little fun at his partner:

It is, of course, from his activity as a solo artist that Menuhin's chief fame derives. And here, forsaking all his other interests and promotions, from the recently founded shelter for insufferable prodigies outside London [i.e. the School] to his West End health-food shop, he devotes a major portion of each year . . . to checking the trap lines of the international concert circuit.

(Gould himself detested the touring life and had renounced playing in public four years earlier.)

And yet by some alchemy which I plan never to understand, Menuhin is able to minimize its incalculable emotional demands, to ignore the petty sniping of thwarted colleagues, to deny the banal drudgery of its routine, to accept the adrenaline-sapping crises that in this life are routine as well, and surmount all with an equanimity of disposition and a generosity of spirit which are legendary.

Menuhin, Gould concluded, is 'surfeited with an almost universal regard'; it marked him out as 'one of those rare individuals who could in time succeed to that unique place in the affections of mankind left vacant by the death of Albert Schweitzer'.

In the same year, 1966, Gould made his controversial forecast that public concerts would soon disappear in favour of recordings. He was ludicrously wide of the mark on that subject but remarkably prescient where Yehudi was concerned. George Steiner later described Yehudi as the world's most beloved musician.

Glenn Gould and Diana (née Gould but no relation of the pianist) enjoyed a bantering correspondence in which on one occasion she described her husband as 'the old fiddler'. In 1965, when the Queen bestowed an honorary knighthood on Yehudi – a title that as an American he could not use – Gould wrote to Mrs Menuhin:

My dear, I am at one with you in your embarrassment [over Yehudi's honorary knighthood; although Diana must in truth have been deeply gratified by her husband's award] . . . But what comfort it must be for you to know that men of goodwill rally around in this your hour of adversity . . . One thing more, dear Lady Diana: I have chosen not to comment directly upon Sir Yehudi's elevation to the Knighthood because, frankly, my nose is out of joint.

As the British Commonwealth's best-known performing artist Gould might well have expected some form of recognition from Buckingham Palace but here I suspect he was merely being facetious.

When Yehudi visited the pianist at his Toronto home he was appalled to find the apartment in total disarray. He murmured something to the effect that Glenn would benefit from having a woman in his life. 'But I do,' he responded cheerfully. 'She comes every Saturday afternoon.' Yehudi persevered: not a cleaning lady, but a wife. 'Ah, but there is only one Diana,' Gould responded gallantly, and the subject was closed.

Viewed in the foreshortening lens of history, the late 1960s can be seen as a transition period for Yehudi, preparatory to the assumption of a conspicuous international role. In 1967 his joint concert with Ravi Shankar at the United Nations General Assembly caused something of a stir in diplomatic circles. He was subsequently wooed by officials of the UN's cultural arm, UNESCO, whose founding President, in 1949, was his friend Sir Julian Huxley. In 1968 he was named President of the International Music Council, UNESCO's autonomous offshoot. There was little need for canvassing behind the scenes; in fact Yehudi did not even put in an appearance at the meeting in New York where he was unanimously elected. His candidature was very high profile by comparison with previous incumbents in the post, the most recent of whom was none other than his old friend Dr Narayana Menon from All-India Radio. Yehudi held the post for six years, from 1969 to 1975, being re-elected for the two additional two-year terms the statutes allowed.

The IMC was an organization after his polymathic heart. Its remit involved it in all types of music: traditional, folk, pop, jazz, contemporary and classical, and every type of musician from composers to publishers by way of scholars, performers and librarians. Representatives from sixty countries attended a congress every two years and in between looked after musicians' interests back home. Sceptical Anglo-Saxons tended to dismiss such talking shops as ineffectual. Yehudi confessed as much in a letter to the IMC's Secretary-General, Jack Bornoff.

I have been singularly ineffective in England and the United States, the two countries which lag so conspicuously behind . . . I also have given you a lot of trouble, viz. Russia, and despite it all I have shamefully enjoyed the tenure, my first (and perhaps last) post of so international a standing.

Despite his semi-official position, Yehudi had no qualms about criticizing the Soviet authorities. He told Bornoff that his

outspoken regret when the screws of censorship were tightened, when the Russians invaded Czechoslovakia and when Jews lost their jobs for applying to emigrate to Israel, incurred displeasure.

Relations worsened when he spoke up to deplore the lack of cultural freedom in the USSR. He offered support for Mstislav Rostropovich, who was sheltering in his dacha the disgraced novelist Alexander Solzhenitsyn, chronicler of the gulags in his *One Day in the Life of Ivan Denisovich*. The Russians responded by refusing to allow David Oistrakh to attend Yehudi's festival in Gstaad. Mrs Ekaterina Furtseva, the Iron Lady of Soviet culture, loftily informed the Swiss Ambassador in Moscow – Yehudi having just been granted Swiss citizenship – that no Russian artist would ever be allowed to play with Yehudi again. In that case, Yehudi responded, he would not attend the forthcoming congress of the International Music Council, which as luck would have it was due to be held in Moscow two months later. Anxious to avoid a diplomatic row, Mrs Furtseva relented to the extent that Oistrakh's son Igor was permitted to perform in Gstaad that summer.

Nevertheless Yehudi resolved to use his presidential platform to make a protest. A few weeks before the congress he told John Roberts, then Head of Music for CBC Radio and a fellow member of the IMC board, that he was working on a major speech that 'would expose the policies and tactics of the Soviets and sound a clarion call for change. At the very least he hoped that it would stop the Soviets from using the IMC events for propaganda purposes.' In order to make sure that his message was not watered down in the translation process Yehudi decided to deliver the speech in Russian, a language he had studied in his childhood. Before he left London he worked on it with a member of the BBC's Russian service. He also had the text translated into many languages including Japanese, Spanish, French, Italian and even Hebrew, for distribution to the foreign press. He marched through Moscow airport customs unchallenged with a suitcase full of photo-copies of the speech. Later, at his hotel, he continued to rehearse his Russian. While Diana talked loudly to throw eavesdroppers off the scent, he 'worked on it under the bedclothes in our room at the Metropole – because the room was wired as all rooms are'. When Tikhon Khrennikov, veteran Chairman of the Union of Soviet Composers, pressed for a copy of the speech, ostensibly for the inter-preters, he was told Yehudi was still revising it. Roberts remembers a cat-and-mouse game being played all day.

The first business of the congress was the election of officers. As the rules of the diplomatic game prescribed, the host delegation, the Russians, proposed Yehudi for a second term; the American seconded, and there was a unanimous vote in favour. Then came the formal opening ceremony in the historic Hall of Columns, for which the Russians had arranged an impressive show of music and dancing, all in traditional costume, from various parts of the Soviet empire. As predicted, it made excellent propaganda. Thus far, the proceedings of the IMC's seventh congress had been perfectly conventional. But then Yehudi delivered his address.

The opening words must have caused a stir in Moscow's prevailing anti-Semitic climate: 'I stand here not only as a musician, but as a Russian Jew, as one whose parents were born in this land for which they both retain a deep attachment.' His birthright permitted him, he continued, 'to express a little of what I feel might constitute the role of this vast and varied land in today's disruptive world'. He spoke of music's contribution to mankind, of Russia's contribution to music, of all nations' interdependence in today's shrunken world. After praising the Russian musical education system, from which – with perhaps more tact than truth – he claimed to have derived the inspiration to start his own school, he warned that music should not be used as propaganda. Next came an erudite allusion to the tritone, the augmented fourth or *diabolus in musica* forbidden by medieval music theoreticians. This was surely a coded reference to Tikhon Khrennikov, the Establishment man, who dictated the kind of music that Soviet composers should write: only the previous December Khrennikov had urged his colleagues to compose Leninist themes and avoid the formalism and cosmopolitanism that were, he claimed, 'a capitalist plot to divert people's attention from the political struggle and fill them with pessimism'. Yehudi warmed to his task:

The narrow motive composed of vanity and the will to dominate which would proclaim a superiority of one group, system or symbol over another has no place at the time when man has shed his last cloak of innocence and stands naked among the stars, fully aware of the consequences of every bad or wrong thought, i.e. of every thought either hateful or untrue, and of every false action wrongly motivated.

A draft of the speech in the Menuhin Archive reveals a complete rewrite in Diana's hand of the next paragraph. It is unclear whether these were her own thoughts or a crystallization of what Yehudi had sketched before completing the speech in London.

We know what such mistakes can cost in terms of astronauts' lives; we know what such mistakes can cost in terms of lively minds and independent spirits silenced or frozen into impotence by those whose vision is so short and imagination so limited that in the name of the present they can only dominate by isolating all enquiring or questioning; they jeopardize the future of their own country.

Then came the open reference to the dissidents which upset the Russians so much it reportedly cost Yehudi the highest Soviet decoration he was due to receive. As examples of the vision and the greatness of contemporary Russian artists he cited 'the size, power, depth and meaning of musical and poetic utterances such as those of a

Shostakovich, a Solzhenitsyn, a Yevtushenko and many others'. Among the delegates listening on headphones to the translation of Yehudi's speech was John Roberts.

I noticed that the interpreter sounded tense, as though she could hardly believe her ears. Obviously such open and direct criticism of Soviet attitudes, beliefs and policies was like a bombshell.

The speech concluded with a pointed reference to the absence from the hall of one of the IMC's individual members, Mstislav Rostropovich. (He had been detailed to accompany Mrs Furtseva on a courtesy visit to Vienna. Since his public support for Solzhenitsyn he had been banned from giving concerts abroad and was mostly restricted to engagements in the provinces.)

Yehudi had been told that a page of *Pravda* was reserved for coverage of his speech but in the event not a word was published or broadcast. Next day, samizdat (underground) copies of it began circulating.

People would come to me when I was walking in the streets of Moscow and shove a little piece of paper in my hand surreptitiously, just telling me how much they appreciated it.

John Roberts remembers that immediately after the session Khrennikov wanted to know why Yehudi had chosen to embarrass his hosts.

I noticed Yehudi responding without any compromise in a very quiet, typically calm manner . . . The attitude on the part of the Soviet and East European colleagues was that the congress had to be endured rather than enjoyed; they could not afford to make any mistakes. One of the delegates said to me quietly, 'I just want you to know that I hate my paper but it is what I am expected to present.' Everyone was . . . wondering whether the Soviets would come forward with some kind of response to Yehudi's comments. However, considering Yehudi's enormous international standing and the affection in which he was held by Russian audiences, Soviet officialdom held its silence.

The situations of two Soviet citizens had been brought to Yehudi's attention before he left London. One was incarcerated in a mental hospital because of his political views; the family of the other, who had defected, was being prevented from joining him in the West. Normally in such cases – and there were hundreds over the years – Yehudi would write an appeal or sign a petition, but since he was in Moscow he decided to intervene directly on their behalf. He was kept waiting for a meeting until a few hours before his flight and was then treated by the number 3 in the Culture Ministry's hierarchy, Valentin Supakhin, to a stream of invective concerning Western drug degeneracy, Yehudi's tactless intervention and the undoubted guilt of Solzhenitsyn – 'neither a great Russian nor a great writer'. Yehudi had to admit defeat. 'If I have offended you,' he remembered saying, 'it's only because there is no one in the world who would more like to be friends with you.' To John Roberts he expressed his exasperation: 'Have you ever encountered anyone who you feel would murder his mother to get up the next rung of the ladder? Well, I encountered such a person today.'

Two years later, Yehudi had another confrontation with the Russians over the fate of his friend Slava Rostropovich. For its twenty-fifth birthday, the IMC organized a gala concert in Paris. Among the artists who had agreed to take part were Yehudi's Beethoven sonata partner Wilhelm Kempff, and the singers Régine Crespin and Dietrich Fischer-Dieskau. Surprisingly, Rostropovich had been granted permission to come from the Soviet Union. But a few days before the concert Yehudi heard a rumour that the Russian had had a heart attack. He telephoned the cellist's wife in Moscow to commiserate, only to learn that Slava was in the best of health, conducting in Erevan and due back at the weekend. He sent a telegram to Moscow to call the Russians' bluff. Goskonzert, the Soviet artists' agency, responded with a counter offer: the Borodin Quartet would play Shostakovich's latest quartet (presumably the penultimate quartet, No. 14, Op. 142) with the composer present. Yehudi cabled back: 'Shostakovich heartily welcome but we will accept no substitute for Rostropovich.' The Russians ignored this, merely sending a request for official invitations for composer and quartet. Yehudi decided to go over Mrs Furtseva's head and appeal directly to the President, Leonid Brezhnev. (Perhaps he knew that Brezhnev had a soft spot for Slava's wife, the opera singer Galina Vishnevskaya.) In his cable he threatened to publish the recent exchange of telegrams and give the world's press the story of how the authorities were systematically humiliating Rostropovich inside Russia. According to Yehudi this threat to Brezhnev's policy of *détente* saved the day: Slava got his visa that afternoon and the concert went ahead. Ian Stoutzker, a London friend, remembers the scene at the Salle Pleyel in Paris. 'We waited and waited, not believing that he would show up . . . and then of course he did: to see it actually happen was an example of Yehudi standing up for what he thought was right.' In his memoirs Yehudi described Slava's elation: 'He was like a little boy, laughing, shouting, pinching himself to make sure these really were the streets in

Paris.' But he was still under orders not to speak to the media: the Russian member of the IMC's executive, Professor Boris Yarrustovsky, was given responsibility – literally on pain of death, according to John Roberts – for the cellist's good behaviour.

Yehudi implies that Rostropovich left Russia for good at this time but it was several months later, after the humiliation of having a recording of *Tosca* cancelled in midstream, that he and his wife successfully appealed directly to Brezhnev for permission to live abroad for two years; soon after they left the Soviet Union they were stripped of their citizenship. After the death of the equally genial but much more reserved David Oistrakh, in October of the same year, Rostropovich became Menuhin's closest Russian friend.

Yehudi was at the head of the IMC at the time of the third Israeli–Arab War of 1973. When it broke out Yehudi telephoned friends, among them the writer George Steiner, urging them to join him in a public demonstration: 'Ten of us must go at once to the Middle East and camp between the lines. This would initiate an immediate cease-fire.' Steiner ventured the thought that nine of them would swiftly be done away with, leaving only Yehudi's illustrious self in intact solitude. 'The sadness in Yehudi's tone as he rang off made me regret what hint of cynicism or of levity there may have been in my objection.'

A new crisis developed a year later, when UNESCO officially censured Israel for starting archaeological excavation in the sensitive area under the Great Mosque of Jerusalem. John Roberts remembers a meeting of the IMC's Executive Committee at which Yehudi read aloud a letter

from Artur Rubinstein and other great-name Jewish musicians from New York, Paris and London, requesting that Yehudi as President and the whole Executive of the IMC should resign because of a criticism of Israel . . . I won't go into our discussion but we all agreed that if there were problems with UNESCO, it was much more intelligent for Yehudi to use all his good offices to bring about change from the inside rather than all of us abandoning the IMC, which was working positively to help the many musics of the world.

Once again Yehudi found himself locking horns with the Jewish musical Establishment. This time he stuck to his guns and won. He did not resign, though at one time he threatened to, and by working hard behind the scenes with prominent Israelis and UN diplomats, among them UNESCO's Director-General, he persuaded UNESCO to modify its position. His critics included a good friend: Leonard Bernstein.

Their exchange of cables was published in the *New York Times* in February 1975. Bernstein deplored UNESCO's 'politicizing resolutions against Israel'; Menuhin responded by asserting that because of its universal meaning, Jerusalem 'must be treated as a trust for humanity at large and not as the province of a single power'. He followed up his cable with a letter setting out his position:

Just as a musician must be absolutely convinced of his interpretation, or a composer of his creation, so am I, as a friend of Israel, and as a colleague of artists everywhere, obliged to voice an opinion which I firmly believe my colleagues will in fact themselves adopt, for they too are guided by the same concern for humanity at large and for Israel in particular . . . My contention is that this exaggerated condemnation is ill served by the equally exaggerated response of my fellow Jews and will merely obscure the issue . . . The issue is simple: general war or peace; simply: the survival of Israel. This depends on the extent of support which firm, moderate opinion can command in Israel, echoed in the Jewish communities of the world and among the peoples of the world, including Israel's neighbours. Every wise and precious friend is an asset to Israel . . .

. . . If she showed herself prepared to listen to censure and criticism in a mature way (as we musicians always must), Israel would win many friends who now either condemn her out of hand, or who are only limply reluctant to offend their Jewish friends and colleagues. I cannot repeat emphatically enough how important it is for Israel to remain present and represented at all conferences and deliberations. Challenge is endemic through our long history and the dignity to meet it [is] our destiny . . . The only way the Jewish people can put their immense historical experience and perspective to work for the benefit of Jews everywhere, for Israel and for the world, is to apply to others that understanding and compassion that they themselves have rarely received, thus reversing the disastrous chain of events which again threatens to engulf them and the world.

Meetings at UNESCO convened in 1975 by its incoming chief, Amadou M. M'Bow, provided Yehudi with another forum in which to plead for a morality of tolerance and the separation of culture from politics. It was here that one of the most persistent themes of the last twenty years of his life emerged, the need for some kind of parliament that would provide 'voices for the speechless, deputies who represent the fowl of the air, the fish of the sea, the unborn generations'. Initially he wanted UNESCO to be an organization where all cultures, including, for example, Kurds and American Indians, might find expression. When that dream failed to convince UNESCO's bureaucrats in Paris he launched a parallel concept, specifically for Europe, of a Parliament of Cultures,

serving alongside the European Parliament – a Second House, as it were – but not a new bureaucracy. This house would consist of worthy representatives, each with his or her own independent profession, chosen only for specific missions. These individuals would donate their time to a public cause, receiving only nominal compensation. They would act both as a consultative body and a legislative one, for without their approval no governing decisions could be taken.

Such castles in the air were to preoccupy him increasingly in his sixties and seventies. It is easy to scoff but he was ahead of his time in so much else that this political proposal may yet turn out, in the age of the Internet, to have a practical application.

Yehudi's six years as IMC President ended in a collaborative glow after he defused a potentially explosive debate at the 1975 assembly in Toronto. The three Israeli delegates arrived with a statement rejecting the UN's condemnation of their state. Behind the scenes Yehudi was firm: anybody talking politics would be asked to leave. In his opening address he urged delegates to remember that they were not only national delegates but also

musicians representing humanity's cultures. It is our solemn and noble duty to conduct ourselves in a way which can give comfort and hope to humanity at large and as would befit the dignity and dedication of our calling . . . In this spirit I am personally inviting my colleagues from Egypt, Iraq, Syria, Tunis, together with my colleagues from Israel, for a quiet get-together so that we may profit by this unique opportunity of trying to understand each other sensitively and sympathetically. We are free agents; we are musicians. At least we can compose a Middle East federation of cultures and peoples which politically belongs, I pray, to a not too distant future, but which humanly and musically may already be within our reach.

John Roberts remembers that

with the exception of the Iraqi delegate we managed to assemble those concerned in the suite occupied by Yehudi and Diana in the Sheraton Hotel for a private luncheon at which the matter was resolved.

During Yehudi's presidency the IMC established a Musicians' International Mutual Aid Fund. The idea, John Roberts recalls, was that a series of fund-raising concerts given by some of the greatest living musicians would create a fund to be used to help musicians in the Third World. A few years later Roberts visited Beijing to invite the Chinese to join the IMC. On his return he telephoned Yehudi.

I told him about a rehearsal I attended of the Beijing Philharmonic in which a talented young woman violinist was trying to perform the Mendelssohn Concerto on a poor instrument. This led to a discussion on the generally poor-quality musical instruments that Chinese musicians were using. We finally decided to suggest to the Board of MIMAF that an outstanding violin should be given to China for use by outstanding violinists. However Yehudi said, 'I would like personally to pay for half the cost and MIMAF can pay the other half.' There was no end to his generosity. He also sent an oboe to a Chinese oboist who was struggling with an inferior instrument. On International Music Day in Ottawa in 1975 [the first of its kind, initiated by the IMC while Yehudi was President] he refused to take his fee after giving a demanding solo violin recital and asked that the money be give to a worthy cause, so it went to the IMC.

His stock might have been high at the International Music Council, which was essentially a talking shop for idealists, mandarins and hangers on, but at the beginning of the 1970s Yehudi's reputation took a tumble in the hard-nosed professional world of the New York Philharmonic. In March 1971 he was engaged to play the violin, conduct the orchestra and talk to the audience in one of the celebrated Young People's Concerts that were televised on Saturdays from what was then called the Philharmonic Hall at the Lincoln Center. The children's concerts had acquired immense popularity during Leonard Bernstein's time as the Philharmonic's Music Director and since his retirement in 1969 different guest speakers were being tried out in a search for a permanent successor. Among them were Bernstein's protégé, Michael Tilson Thomas, and his older friend Maestro Menuhin – as Yehudi would have been addressed within the orchestra. His topic was to be Béla Bartók and his examples were chosen from the *Concerto for Orchestra* (which he had conducted in New York the previous year with the American Symphony Orchestra). He was to launch the programme by playing the opening of the Second Violin Concerto.

Yehudi had no previous experience in television pedagogy. A series of hour-long educational films he had recently made in England as companion pieces to a book, *Violin: Six Lessons with Yehudi Menuhin,* were dense, didactic and stiffly delivered lectures given to students at his School. He didn't talk into the camera – but a relaxed direct approach to the audience was the essential element in the Young People's Concerts as they had been developed by Bernstein and his television producer Roger Englander in the course of more than fifty shows dating back to 1958. There was a routine and Yehudi had evidently not given himself time to learn it. Moreover the New York musicians had a reputation for being difficult with visiting conductors, but respect for Yehudi's achievements as a musician would have outweighed any potential hostility among the older Jewish members because of his support for Furtwängler twenty years earlier. It was still an exceptionally sticky forty-eight hours for all concerned, as a report by Helen Thompson, the orchestra's Managing Director, chronicles:

Thursday 3–25–71 [dates were given US style, month first]
Received music cue sheet late in afternoon, but there were no word cues.
[Yehudi had listed the musical illustrations he proposed from Bartók's *Concerto for Orchestra* but not the precise words he would speak before he cued the music – the players had the speaker's text attached to their parts.]

Friday 3–26–71
Considerable difficulty for the musicians because they had no word cues . . . Menuhin was not properly prepared and the rehearsal was extremely difficult.
Spent all afternoon in a script session with Menuhin, CBS people and Mrs Menuhin. Script and music running overtime, made a good many changes.
[The overall duration was rigidly controlled: the 'commercial' hour for CBS was not a second over fifty-three minutes. Yehudi was to deliver his script looking into a camera equipped with a teleprompter.]
Some of our staff people then started working about 4:30 on revision of cues and preparing word cues. Mimeographing finished that night, ready for Saturday rehearsals.
[Saturday was tough: a camera rehearsal at nine, a dress rehearsal at eleven (to a full house of children and escorts) and a second performance at two which normally became the mastertape for the subsequent television broadcast.]

Saturday 3–27–71
7:45 a.m. Menuhin, CBS people and Mrs Menuhin and the Teleprompter – considerable problem. He was nervous; she was more or less in command but some significant improvements were made [to the text].
9 a.m. rehearsal with orchestra. It was obvious that the Bartók *Concerto for Orchestra* is far beyond Mr M.'s conducting technique. Orchestra having a tough time but out of respect to Mr M., they worked hard and earnestly. He was extremely nervous, distraught over lack of time he was finding he needed to rehearse the music.
11 a.m. performance. Menuhin stopped and started the orchestra twice on the opening bars of the Concerto for Violin – which sounded dreadful. Then he turned to the audience and said, 'Do you mind if we start this concert again?' Applause. Started again and on we went with fair results. His tempi were unreliable, the orchestra was taking over to hold the thing together and did a remarkable job. Some portions were something of a shambles.
12 to 2. Another script conference and we all decided to do away with his use of the Concerto for Violin as the introductory scene. This relieved Menuhin's nervousness somewhat. Revised various cues, took out some things, shortened some of his comments because he was extending the playing time considerably beyond the original timings . . .
2 o'clock show. Menuhin was much more poised, his verbal comments much improved. Orchestra was marvelous in trying to do the best possible job under the

434

circumstance. Menuhin was conducting without the score, got lost several times, continued beating after the orchestra was finished on some occasions. We thought it was going to be a fairly good production until the last section of the Bartók when he just lost several of the tempi, the orchestra was lost and the playing for a few minutes was a shambles. Roger doesn't know what they can do with it other than try to cut the last section. It's very doubtful that they can splice in that section from the first take. On the first show Menuhin's hair was flopping around wildly. Second show they used hair spray – and the appearance in the two performances is vastly different.

Summation. On behalf of the Philharmonic's reputation, I feel we must help guide the choice of works when these guest conductors are selected for the YP concerts. I attended Menuhin's concert with his own Festival Orchestra which appeared here the week before he was with us. He does quite nicely with the orchestra when he is playing and conducting it in smaller chamber works. He was not properly prepared on the Bartók score, and if he had been, his conducting technique is not up to handling the big orchestra in so complicated a work . . . There is absolutely no sense in putting the orchestra and all the rest of us through this last-minute frenetic program and cue changes!!!!

Yehudi was never invited back to deliver a second Young People's Concert. But the following season he played the Bartók Violin Concerto in the Philharmonic's regular subscription series, as if to prove that his poor showing had been but a momentary aberration.

New York dealt another blow to Yehudi's pride fourteen months later after a collection of his essays and speeches was published under the title *Theme and Variations*. The *New York Times* review by Thomas Lask began gently enough, describing him as a virtuoso with a difference, whose every appearance was an event. Classical music lovers, Lask noted drily, were pleased that Yehudi had been awarded the KBE when the Beatles had had to make do with the MBE, several notches lower in the pecking order. And thus the teasing began:

He has not been afraid to indicate his interest in all things Indian, in organically grown food, in yoga exercises and to declare himself on man and his culture . . . When he and his sister played for Presidents Nixon and Charles de Gaulle, he thought it an excellent time to lecture the two men on the superiority of beauty over material things.

The essays on specific musical topics are praised for supplying 'chewy musical food for thought . . . but when he moves into other realms than music [such as education, world citizenship and architecture] he is no better than the rest of us'. Menuhin is put down as no more than

a well-meaning, idealistic, hopeful and generous spirit . . . whose arguments are so lofty, the language so rhapsodic, the intentions so worthy, the means so nebulous that the essays begin to sound like a Sunday morning sermon. They are agin sin, and who isn't? . . . Although he offers dozens of blueprints for the good life, he never faces up to the mechanics of achieving it . . . His description of Indian life is so utopian, so bland that one senses instinctively that it is too good to be true.

Yehudi is taken to task for over-praising the concept of hereditary monarchy, for describing the English public school as 'the complete microcosm of human society' – a preposterous notion, according to Mr Lask – and for patronizing the Negro as the 'still partly childlike race'. The reviewer is relentless:

Too often the ideas are worn, the analogies misleading, the exhortations super-fluous . . . None of this reflects on Mr Menuhin's music making, but it does rein-force the idea that the best place to listen to him is in the concert hall.

Perhaps because Yehudi had opted for the expatriate life, American journalists tended to be harder on him than did their European counter-parts. A decade later a piece by Joseph McClellan in the *International Herald Tribune* roundly declared that 'for several years now his tech-nique has not matched that of the average graduate of a good conser-vatory but he continues to play to standing ovations'. The insult caused a stir. Among the correspondents who rose to Yehudi's defence was the cellist of the Amadeus Quartet, Martin Lovett, who wrote that 'The man's profound artistry is a wonder of our time.' An equally dis-tressed Frenchman evoked Yehudi's glorious past:

Those of us who were in Paris in 1944 will never forget the concert he gave at the Opéra at which his music became a symbol of the freedom we were at last tasting after four years of occupation.

Yehudi had a generous disposition (and a thick skin) but there were occasions when he was not averse to retaliation. In the aftermath of the UNESCO controversy over Jerusalem he publicly described Artur Rubinstein's account of the affair as a calumny, which in turn prompted the pianist to label Yehudi 'a bad Jew'. The insults flew across the Atlantic, inspiring the theatre director Peter Cotes to write to the London *Times* extolling Yehudi's 'broad, bold and compassionate vision'. Yehudi had already refuelled the flames of Jewish Establish-ment hostility by giving a charity concert after the 1973 Israel–Arab war – in aid of Palestinian refugees. That led to a suspension of his visits to Israel for half a decade; he played with the second-division Jerusalem Symphony Orchestra in 1979 but it was not until 1982,

under the headline 'Menuhin ends boycott of Israel', that he returned
to the Philharmonic, eagerly asserting his enthusiasm for the belea-
guered state at a time when it was under fire around the world for its
intransigence: 'I feel more than ever that this difficult time for Israel is
the time for me to be here. I never add my voice to those condemning
Israel.' A photograph taken at the Wailing Wall a few years earlier,
after the Camp David peace settlement, provides a rare glimpse of him
playing the fiddle while wearing a yarmulka.

From a musical standpoint the 1970s were much less troubled
times. The end of his spell as a festival director did not deter him from
commissioning new works for the violin, although the level of fee he
had to offer could be surprisingly frugal. Camilla Panufnik, the composer's widow, remembers her husband being turned down when he
asked (tentatively, since he was the gentlest of men) whether the £200
he'd been offered to compose a concerto might be increased. But a
Menuhin commission was not to be ignored, so Andrzej Panufnik
wrote a concerto all the same and Yehudi gave the première at the
1972 City of London Festival. When Panufnik said he was not sure he
could complete anything in the short time available, Menuhin smiled
briskly and suggested composing the last movement first: this did the
trick. A panic about its dedication ensued. Panufnik was superstitious:
his most successful compositions had all been dedicated to his wife.
She insisted it should go to Menuhin. 'I wrote to Yehudi about my
dilemma,' Panufnik noted in his memoirs,

and he replied with the utmost grace that of course it should be for Camilla and
that he would dedicate his performance to her too! . . . I was moved to find that
Yehudi had taken the trouble to memorize the whole work. Though our original
intention had been that he should direct the Concerto from the violin [the work is
scored for string orchestra], the cross-rhythms of the fast last movement turned
out to be too tricky and dangerous to risk without a conductor's baton, so in the
end he asked me to conduct the first performance . . . at the magnificent
Goldsmiths' Hall.

A year later Yehudi commissioned the veteran Swiss composer
Frank Martin, a devout Catholic, to write a work to be performed at
the opening of the 1973 IMC conference in Geneva. Yehudi thought
very highly of Martin, describing him as

after Bartók perhaps the most important composer whom I have commissioned
. . . He told me that on receiving the IMC request he had not known what he
would write until one day he found himself in Siena and in the museum there saw

a polyptych of scenes from the Gospel . . . Palm Sunday, the Last Supper, Judas, the Garden of Gethsemane, the Judgement and the Glorification. I told him I was grateful he had spared me the Crucifixion.

It had already been decided that the work would be scored for double string orchestra when Diana, who normally never interfered with Yehudi's commissions, had what she called a brainwave:

I suggested that it be developed in a way that Yehudi could be the Evangelist as well as Jesus [with, as YM later wrote, 'the orchestra supplying apostles, crowd and atmosphere']. I said to Yehudi that if the last movement was to be the Resurrection then it's got to end up on a very high note.

Yehudi bestowed on *Polyptique* a disappointingly bland seal of approval, describing it as 'one of the works of which the twentieth century can be proud to bequeath to the future'. In fact it would make a fine contemplative soundtrack for an Easter television programme (even without a Crucifixion), married to images of the Sienese polyptych that inspired it. Unfortunately the LP recording has been deleted and so far no transfer to CD is available.

Yehudi appeared on British television in the mid-1970s in two unusual programmes produced by the London Weekend Television arts magazine series *Aquarius*. The first was an adaptation of a concert piece by Edwin Roxburgh, for chamber orchestra and narrator, entitled *How Pleasant to Know Mr Lear*. This had already been performed at the Windsor Festival and had the inestimable merit, in Yehudi's eyes, of providing Diana with the star role. She made the selection of Edward Lear's poems with the composer and declaimed them grandly from a golden throne, rather in the manner of Edith Sitwell narrating her own brand of nonsense verse in *Façade*. The show was sufficiently successful for *Aquarius* to follow it up at Christmas 1973 with a world première. This time Roxburgh chose to set a group of love lyrics by the American poet E. E. Cummings. Vincent Price, a star of countless horror movies, shared the deliciously camp narration with Diana. Yehudi was delighted to observe her triumph from the conductor's rostrum.

I had thought I knew Diana through and through; still she managed to astonish me. To see her completely emancipated from subservience, giving herself to the production of the poetry, projecting it, shaping the lines, encompassing a range of emotional, dramatic effect from satire though comedy and bawdy to tragedy, was a revelation.

Menuhin himself had just become something of a television star in

Britain thanks to a guest appearance with Stéphane Grappelli on the 1971 Christmas edition of *Parkinson*. In his memoirs Yehudi wrote that his memorable partnership with the jazz violinist happened virtually on the spur of the moment: 'The BBC rang me one Christmas morning [19 December] and said blandly, "Tonight you are playing with Grappelli."' Michael Parkinson himself remembers it differently. His programme's familiar chat-show format offered impromptu conversations, mostly with showbusiness guests, but Mr Parkinson was (and still is) genuinely fond of music and liked to round off his shows with a world-class performer from the theatre or the light-classical field. He recalls wooing Menuhin for some months and eventually sending a researcher to The Grove to explore suitable topics for a television conversation that would have mass appeal. (Not, therefore, Russia's treatment of Jewish dissidents or the parlous state of housing in India.) The researcher noticed on his desk a record sleeve of the jazz violinist Stéphane Grappelli, famous for his recordings with the Quintette du Hot Club de France. Was he an admirer? 'Not yet,' Yehudi replied. He'd *met* him (presumably at the Bath Festival) but had never heard him play, although he'd certainly like to. Who sent Yehudi that recording remains a mystery, but moving swiftly on this valuable tip, Parkinson and his producer Richard Drewett set up a studio meeting between the two violinists and Max Harris, a gifted composer and arranger.

Grappelli was terrified: 'I'm a fiddle player; he's a *maestro*.' Menuhin for his part was reported to have been apprehensive lest Grappelli 'might be saddled with a useless colleague who had never played jazz and could only remember one tune from the rhythmic point of view: "Jalousie"'. When he and his sisters had taken dancing lessons in New York back in 1936, Gade's 'Jealousy' was the record they used to learn the tango. He knew from his work with John Dankworth that jazz improvisation did not come easily for him but to his eternal credit he decided to give it another try, although Max Harris actually wrote out a great deal of what he was to play in advance of the rehearsal. As he'd shown with Ravi Shankar, Yehudi was an extremely quick learner and he was given a superb group of backing musicians, all well-known British jazz players, to provide the jazz equivalent of a baroque continuo: the broadcast proved to be a big success, prompting several repeat appearances on television. The subsequent EMI recording, the first of many, was in the experienced hands of the pianist Ronald Kinloch Anderson, who had played continuo in the Brandenburg Concertos in 1959 and produced many of Yehudi's subsequent recordings for EMI. But the partnership would never have got off the ground without the instant rapport, both personal and musical, that sprang up between Menuhin and Grappelli, who was eight years the senior and the personification of laid-back Gallic charm. Yehudi wrote that he envied him almost as much as he loved him: he could 'use any theme to express any nuance – wistfulness, brilliance, aggression, scorn – with a speed and accuracy that stretch credulity'. Michael Parkinson remembers the Frenchman exclaiming to him in jubilant mood: 'Three bars into "Lady be Good", who's a *maestro*?'

In the television studio their diverse musical traditions were obvious from their body language. Grappelli always wore colourful shirts and tapped his toe as he played, like a country fiddler at a hoedown. Menuhin discarded his tuxedo for polo and slacks but he faced out to the cameras (and the studio audience behind them) with the disciplined stance of the classical musician and never strayed far from the music stand. Yet listening to the dozens of tracks the duo went on to make – bestsellers for a decade – it's not always possible to tell which violinist is playing, and that's proof enough that even though he still needed the composer Max Harris to guide him, Yehudi had gone a long way, indeed as far as he could, down what he called the 'journey to spontaneity'. His upbringing held him back from total abandon (to appreciate the nature of true jazz one has only to compare Grappelli's sedate duetting with Menuhin to the inspired records he made with the gypsy guitarist Django Reinhardt) but the partnership struck a chord with many millions of British viewers, remoulding Yehudi's image into that of an elevated personality who was also a bit of a 'card' – and this at a time when he might otherwise have fallen from public view.

By his own account he was briefly too much in the public view when he went to Athens in the autumn of 1974. Seven years previously, when the Greek Colonels seized power and forced King Constantine into exile, Yehudi had denounced the overthrow of democracy and stayed away from his home in Mykonos. After the Colonels were forced out, the Menuhins were invited back by the new government as a mark of gratitude for their support. Athens was in ferment over a referendum concerning the future of the monarchy in the restored democracy. (The King was still in Rome: he would have done better to return as soon as the dictators fled.) Through their friendship with the

King's sister, Princess Irene, the Menuhins had become strong supporters of the Greek Royal Family. To Yehudi's mind a constitutional monarchy, the 'non-power above power' as he called it, was the best way to ensure stability during change. He said as much at a press conference, calling for 'evolution not revolution' and throwing his weight behind the monarchist cause – to the evident displeasure of most of his journalist listeners.

At his recital with Louis Kentner next evening he came out on stage to a storm of protesters crying 'Fascist!' 'Apologize!' 'Go home!' The disturbance continued for five minutes, he recalled. 'Kentner sat patiently at the piano and I regarded the uproar before me on the principle that fierce animals should be faced head on and approached.' When the commotion ran out of steam, he addressed the audience, expressing admiration for the students' pioneering resistance to the dictators and explaining that the proceeds of the concert were to establish a scholarship for music students. Then he suggested that they 'get on with the business of the evening and invited the hostile element to a powwow afterwards'. But this was not a Berlin DP camp in 1947; he was on less certain moral ground than he had been with Jonas of Lemberg and nobody stayed to talk. The next day he offered to give a concert for the students who could not afford to attend his recital but on the eve of the referendum the atmosphere was still explosive and the authorities vetoed the proposal. The monarchy was duly rejected and although Yehudi continued to visit Mykonos he made no further attempt to influence the course of Greek politics.

The Menuhins' island home was a simple cottage their musician friend Peggy Glanville-Hicks helped them to find in 1962. A second, more sophisticated house was built immediately above it; this they reserved for themselves, inviting family and friends to use the older building. Yehudi loved the idyllic simplicity of Greek island life. The houses overlooked a tiny harbour and there was a terrace where Yehudi could do his yoga in the early-morning sun. But there was no concealing the march of time on Mykonos: by the 1980s it had been transformed from a quiet backwater to a noisy holiday resort. They rented a jeep to get around the island and employed a local couple to look after them, but ultimately Diana's failing health forced them to leave: walking became something of a trial for her and she had difficulty negotiating the steep path down to the sea; she fell several times, and developed leg ulcers. Mykonos had become too hazardous for a couple approaching their eighties to enjoy and although they both loved their holiday retreat Yehudi eventually insisted on selling it.

That particular disappointment was still two decades in the future, however, when, in 1976, Yehudi celebrated his sixtieth birthday. He had been making conciliatory statements to Diana about taking a sabbatical and did indeed reduce his concert engagements, but as a good American he flew to Washington to perform at the Bicentennial celebrations on 4 July and when the Queen received President Ford at the British Embassy four days later Yehudi and a group of young musicians from his School were there to provide the musical entertainment. A longer summer holiday than usual followed at Gstaad, but such was his compulsion to generate activity that, far from being an opportunity for lying fallow, the sabbatical season proved one of the most creative of his entire life: he founded a new music school in Switzerland, created a new concert organization for young professional musicians in London and hosted what at that date was the most ambitious history of music ever attempted on television, produced by the CBC in Toronto. He even helped to start a new festival.

His friend Sir Edwin Leather had been made Governor-General of Bermuda in 1973 (after the previous incumbent had been murdered, a violent incident that helped to give the Gulf Stream resort a bad name). Yehudi had known Ted Leather many years – he was Chairman of the Bath Festival – and invited him on to the board of the Menuhin School. Prompted by British Airways, who wanted to improve Bermuda's image, Ian Hunter recruited Yehudi to try to start a music festival on the island but they failed; as Yehudi told Leather, 'The place is a cultural wilderness, Ted, it's awful: you must *do* something.' Leather agreed, on condition that if he was successful in setting it up, Yehudi would open the first festival. An insatiable collector of new countries, Yehudi kept his word, giving the inaugural recital with his sister Hephzibah in January 1976. More important in the long run, he also set up the Menuhin Foundation of Bermuda with funds raised at a second concert. This has provided an annual bursary for professional string players from Britain to spend a year in Bermuda 'taking teaching into the schools and providing accessibility for all', to quote a recent Festival programme book. In 1998 Yehudi wrote to express his 'great satisfaction that the (admittedly good!) suggestion I made . . . was lovingly embraced and so enthusiastically adopted'.

The year 1977 saw the creation of another educational venture, a year-round academy for young professional string players in Gstaad. Yehudi saw it as a halfway house to full professionalism, a sort of musical finishing school for gifted musicians who had completed their conservatoire training but still needed insight into chamber music, orchestral ensemble and the performance style of different composers. He wrote that many young musicians find it difficult to marry spontaneity to discipline. Sixteen string players between the ages of seventeen and twenty-six are selected each year from Asia, the Americas and Europe to create a chamber orchestra – the Camerata – which is the performing arm of the Academy. Both are under the leadership of Alberto Lysy. Lysy, born in 1935, had run a similar academy in Italy (where Jacqueline du Pré had been a summer student) and later in the Netherlands, before Yehudi took him under his wing, negotiated substantial Swiss sponsorship and created a framework that survives him to this day.

Yehudi thought of his Academy as a year-round extension of the Gstaad Festival and in 1996 wrote proudly that it had become

a Swiss national institution, supported by the government, by private sources, the town of Gstaad, the canton of Bern and by the Suisse Romande . . . I hoped to bring music in a permanent way to this most beautiful of regions [the Bernese Oberland] . . . I have to confess that I introduced a rather larger bird than the nest can accommodate.

The Swiss company Nestlé has provided one of its residences, Villa Blonay, overlooking Lake Geneva, as a second base for the Camerata's activities in the harsh winter months. The Academy also holds short residencies in Germany, Italy, Spain and even Argentina, Lysy's birthplace. Thus, Yehudi wrote proudly, 'these young students gain a sense of belonging to the world and an understanding of many different countries'. In addition to the trip to China in 1982 already mentioned he led them on tours to Japan and the United States.

Diana Menuhin sparked off the idea behind LMN, Live Music Now!, the eye-catching title Yehudi gave to the organization he established in 1977 to provide work for young professional musicians. She remembers walking through the underpass near Baker Street station in London – she had perhaps been shopping at Yehudi's organic food shop near by – when she heard some solo Bach violin music:

I stopped and there was a boy looking not very well fed, with a cap on the ground. I dropped in some coins and asked whether by chance he'd been trained up the road [meaning at the Royal Academy of Music]. The answer came, yes, and I thought how ghastly, this boy is forced to play for his lunch; he's one of the endless young who are being very well taught and what do they do next? Play in the tunnel!

Yehudi responded to her remonstrances with a scheme he had first dreamed up nearly thirty years previously in New York with his Australian friend Peggy Glanville-Hicks. Her plan, turned down by the Ford Foundation, was to recruit talented young music students and create an organization whereby they could take music to people who would never go to concerts. 'I agreed with her,' Yehudi wrote,

especially after my own experiences during the war, when having played many hundreds of concerts in camps, hospitals and military prisons, I found I learned a great deal . . . this experience was one of the most formative of my life.

In 1977 he convened a meeting of organizations that already arranged concerts in hospitals.

The agents appreciated we were widening the musical public, the Musicians' Union realized we could provide valuable training and waived all union fees for the young artists concerned. The Arts Council gave us its blessing and a [start-up] grant of £5000.

The chosen players have to develop secondary skills as communicators in order to introduce their instruments and their repertoire to audiences for whom classical music is a closed book. Every performer is paid, albeit modestly, and receives adequate expenses. When on tour away from home players are often billeted locally and transported privately. Yehudi was proud of the social purpose behind the movement: 'Organizers become acquainted with musicians . . . and musicians get to know what it feels like to be part of a mining family, or to be sick or dying or to be imprisoned.' He was undoubtedly referring not only to his war-time years but to the visits that his School pupils regularly paid to borstals, psychiatric hospitals, old people's homes and a mining village in South Yorkshire. The strong connection between the School and Live Music Now! was cemented when Virginia Renshaw, who had taught at the School for thirteen years, took over as LMN's Director in 1988. Her predecessor was Sheila Gold, an experienced music officer at the Arts Council, who was recruited in 1979 after LMN's first administrators had failed to make much impact. An equally important appointment was that of LMN's Chairman (in succession to the film producer James Archibald, who died): this was the financier Ian Stoutzker, a keen amateur violinist and collector, who at that time was completing a seven-year stint as Chairman of the Philharmonia Orchestra. Yehudi knew him through a shared passion for violins – Stoutzker had lent him his 'Vieuxtemps' Guarnerius for a year in exchange for the 'Soil' Stradivarius.

Stoutzker remembers that music 'outreach' (to use the educationalists' terminology) was almost unknown in the late 1970s:

At first the administrators of the venues to be visited resisted the idea, one saying, 'Our residents have bingo and television, why should they need musicians?' When these homes accepted musicians, the transformation in the attitude was profound.

New types of venue were constantly approached, among them community centres, schools for children with special needs, homes for the disabled and centres for the blind. Stoutzker enlisted business sponsors and charitable trusts to help pay for the Live Music Now! operation alongside regional arts boards, local authorities and music festivals such as Cheltenham, which often include LMN concerts in their fringe programmes for those too frail to attend the principal events. Sheila Gold's pioneer work led to the establishment of seven regional centres around the UK. The turnover is close on £500,000 and LMN provides work for 250 singers and instrumentalists a year. Today, similar groups flourish in nine countries. Yehudi became a passionate advocate of music as a healing force. Lines from Shakespeare's *Henry VIII* –

> In sweet music is such art,
> Killing care and grief of heart –

were used to introduce LMN's annual report in 1999. As important as music therapy was his ambition for LMN as an instrument for social change:

It has been my dream to bring music back into the everyday lives of people of all ages . . . not only in the home, but also in those places where most of us spend our time, where we work, study, suffer or celebrate, be it in the office or factory, school or prison, parish hall or church.

He was ahead of his time again: nowadays almost every musical organization has its outreach programme and it can sometimes appear as if the attempt to reach parts of society untouched by other means is more important than the basic business of putting on performances in concert halls. But Yehudi's scheme works because it supplies the needs of both the givers and the receivers. Such humanitarian work was acknowledged, often fulsomely, in his lifetime. What was less widely perceived was the effort he put in behind the scenes (as he also did with his School) to ensure that the right people were in place to sustain the day-to-day administration of his vision. He had a knack for picking people out and then making them work much harder than they expected on his behalf. He could be generous with praise and encouragement, too. When Prince Charles, LMN's patron, went backstage after the twentieth birthday concert at the Barbican in 1997, he, Yehudi and Ian Stoutzker spoke personally to every one of the scores of children, most of them disadvantaged in one way or another, who had been taking part in the new works commissioned for the programme.

Yehudi was involved in a plethora of activities in Europe around the time of his sixtieth birthday. His was a world horizon – but it had a consistently British tinge. A Californian childhood had been followed by periods in which different countries of the old British Empire had loomed large in his consciousness: first came pre-war England, land of Elgar and tolerance. Then Australia, through his own marriage (and Hephzibah's) and the warmth of the welcome he had experienced when on tour there in 1935 and 1940. His divorce in 1947 and Hephzibah's move to London a decade later saw the weakening of the antipodean relationship, although he continued to maintain cordial friendships with the Nicholas family on his tours. Ironically, Nola herself settled in London in the late 1960s. On one memorable occasion she and Diana came face to face – at the food counter in Fortnum and Mason's. After the death from a heart attack of her third husband, William Bayard Hawthorne, Nola returned to Australia, dying there in 1978. Yehudi was at the School at Stoke d'Abernon when he heard of her death; he sent a wreath of her favourite gardenias.

If Yehudi could be said to have focused on India and South Africa in the 1950s (two visits each), and on England and its festivals in the 1960s, then in the next decade he turned his attention to Canada, a country that had intrigued him since, when still a boy, he had visited a model farm outside Toronto. (He watched cows being mechanically milked to the accompaniment of classical music and his hatred of Muzak was born.) His friendship with the Canadian Broadcasting Corporation dated back to his 1965 television programme with Glenn Gould and had flourished during his spell at the International Music Council, when the CBC's John Roberts was his right-hand man. Roberts introduced him to a colleague, John Barnes, then Head of Arts, Music and Science programmes at CBC Television in Toronto.

446

Barnes had a dream: he wanted to do for music what Kenneth Clark had done for art in the BBC TV's *Civilisation* series. He teamed up with the American producer Curtis Davis, the former Head of Cultural Programmes for Channel 13/WNET in New York, who had trained as a composer and violinist. They took a gamble and invited Yehudi to join them. 'I readily embraced a project which promised to be as inspiring as it would be fulfilling,' he wrote in the preface to the companion book to the series.

The Music of Man was its title, and it came at exactly the right time for him, just after his six years at the International Music Council. His presidential efforts had been directed towards, as he put it, 'the possibility of encouraging a constructive exchange between peoples representing all varieties and ranges of opinion'. Now television was to improve on UNESCO's diplomatic channels, offering viewers innumerable examples of 'the parallels and reciprocal relationship between folk music and *musique savante*'. Not that it would have been a practical proposition to offer a comprehensive survey of music history: Kenneth Clark, after all, had felt obliged for reasons of time to omit any reference to Spanish art in his thirteen-part series. The Canadians opted for eight programmes, in which Yehudi and his producers (none of whom was a professional writer) provided what he described as

the equivalent of topographical maps showing the position of music throughout the ages, alternating general overall views which reveal long-term trends, cultural interactions and ways of life, with close-ups of particular situations and periods.

The programmes looked handsome and had solid production values. Yehudi cast himself in the role of a 'moderate fanatic', endorsing almost everything he heard around the world with equal enthusiasm. In deference to local susceptibilities, he recorded his links in both English and French.

Inevitably the Canadian-produced script called for a substantial quotient of Canadian music. He played a jazz duet for two violins with Canada's answer to Stéphane Grappelli, Jean Carignan; it had been written especially for them by another French-Canadian, André Gagnon. He met the composer Murray Schafer in a barn crammed with objects emitting sounds halfway between music and noise. With Glenn Gould he held a discussion concerning the merits of recording versus live concerts. Once again he teased Gould: 'Isn't there a risk [with studio work] of losing the sense of life? The sense of risk itself?'

447

But world travel was obligatory for any self-respecting television series. In Senegal he interviewed the poet President Léopold Senghor, failed in an attempt to play the *riti* (a single-stringed instrument with a curved bow) and marvelled at the singing of a black African choir in a setting of the Catholic Mass. He was filmed in the cloisters of Sylos in Southern Spain, the Greek amphitheatre of Delphi, Cape Canaveral in Florida and the courtyards of the Alhambra; he stood in sunshine near Venice's Bridge of Sighs and in freezing rain in Rothenburg. In Vienna he listened to schrammel music in a Grinzing wine café close to Beethoven's summer lodging. In Salzburg he sat at Mozart's keyboard, in the room where the composer had been born. He was seen playing the violin obbligato in 'Erbarme dich' from Bach's *St Matthew Passion* – the very work he had filmed for Paul Gordon in Chaplin's Hollywood studio, thirty years previously. This time the location was the church of Saanen, home of the Gstaad Festival. In Canterbury Cathedral, England, the Accademia Monteverdiana performed a Gabrieli motet, conducted by Yehudi's old friend Professor Denis Stevens. Back in Toronto, Yehudi played the violin obbligato in *Swan Lake* for two of Canada's leading dancers.

Naturally Yehudi had many interesting perceptions to contribute but he was no Kenneth Clark and the series packed little punch on an intellectual level. The book he and Curtis Davis brought out to coincide with the telecasts is bedevilled by its dual authorship. Davis tries gamely to provide a coherent narrative but he is interrupted after almost every paragraph by what the preface describes as Yehudi's 'interpretative statements', which are indicated by vertical line running down the left margin of the text. It is for Yehudi's insights that most people would turn to *The Music of Man* in the first place but too often they go off at a tangent or fall back on generalizations. Thus Mahler's music is lumped together with that of Richard Strauss and airily dismissed as 'the loud echo of this self-confident age of colonial empire, with its delusion of limitless expansion and growth – already nostalgic and therefore possibly more vivid'. But one can't help warming to his account of a visit to a Rolling Stones concert at the Earl's Court stadium in London. (Mick Jagger's rock band had donated a hundred tickets as a benefit for the School.)

We arrived in great style in the huge black car . . . Though we were some distance from the hall, I heard what sounded like a premonition of hell. We edged up the narrow stairs into the arena while the sound grew like a thunderstorm. I wanted to listen for the musical content but for me the sheer volume obliterated that possibility. For the first time I experienced real physical pain hearing music . . . Aural overkill: a sheer sound wall . . . I understood how deliberately the whole madness is engineered. It aims to numb all aware senses, to leave no choice but to surrender and participate. I did neither – I left after ten minutes.

The Music of Man is best approached not as a reference book but as a lucky dip in which a handful of individual treasures are singled out from centuries of musical development. It is enjoyable for many passages of both autobiography and musicology – and for its excellent illustrations. But it lacks the narrative thrust and the humanity that make Yehudi's autobiography such a good read.

Unfinished Journey was the final creative fruit of Yehudi's sabbatical year. Over four hundred pages in length, most of which he dictated rather than wrote by hand, it was published to considerable acclaim in 1977. J. W. Lambert of *The Sunday Times* was captivated, proclaiming that the memoirs were

irradiated by the author's personal voice and distinctive idiom, bubbling with his capacity for joy, his unflagging curiosity about everything under the sun, crammed with descriptive sketches brilliantly lighting up places and people, suffused by an ironic humour.

The book was expanded by a further seventy pages in the year of Yehudi's eightieth birthday, in 1996. There are still a few factual errors (and lacunae concerning his personal affairs) but *Unfinished Journey* is among the most enjoyable musical autobiographies of the twentieth century.

———

Recommended Recordings

Bach: Sonata in C minor (BWV 1017) for violin and piano
with Glenn Gould (piano)
SONY SMK 52688
Recorded: 25 and 26 October 1965, in Toronto
Two of the century's finest Bach interpreters – this is the only recording they made together, although they remained great friends until Gould's sadly premature death in 1982. On the same CD, Schoenberg's *Fantasy*, Op. 47, is a less happy collaboration but Beethoven's G major Sonata, Op. 96, is also recommended.

Walton: Violin Concerto
London Symphony Orchestra, conducted by the composer
EMI 5 65003 2

Recorded: 12–15 June 1969
In Classic FM's eightieth birthday series *Menuhin: Master Musician*, YM chose
the opening melody in the first movement to demonstrate the glorious tone of his
'Prince Khevenhüller' Stradivarius.

Bruch: Violin Concerto No. 1 in G minor
London Symphony Orchestra, conducted by Sir Adrian Boult
EMI 7 62519 2
Recorded: 17 December 1971
YM's fifth and final recording of what today is the most popular concerto in the
repertoire.

Lennox Berkeley: Violin Concerto
Malcolm Williamson: Violin Concerto
Menuhin Festival Orchestra, conducted by Sir Adrian Boult
EMI 5 66121 2
Recorded: April and June 1971
Two concertos commissioned in the 1960s, first heard at the Bath Festival and
much admired by YM.

Niels Gade: *Jealousy*
CD CDM 7 69220 2 – *Yehudi Menuhin and Stéphane Grappelli Play* Jealousy *and
Other Great Standards*
Recorded: 1972 and later
Other CDs of this delightful partnership are devoted to music by George
Gershwin, Irving Berlin, Jerome Kern and Cole Porter.

Andrzej Panufnik: Violin Concerto
Menuhin Festival Orchestra, conducted by the composer
EMI 5 66121 2
Recorded: 1975
This was the last work Yehudi coached at his School, in February 1999.

18 Maestro Menuhin

Conducting in Japan

1981: death of Hephzibah; 1982: death of Moshe; appointed President of the Royal Philharmonic Orchestra; survey of conducting career; 1983: concert for the Pope; move to Chester Square; 1984: conducts La clemenza di Tito *in Bonn, other opera productions; 1985: granted British citizenship, becomes Sir Yehudi; 1987: made OM; 1991:* A Family Portrait *shown on television; foundation of International Yehudi Menuhin Foundation in Brussels; 1993: life peerage; 1996: eightieth birthday celebrations.*

YEHUDI'S VIOLIN PLAYING took on a new zest when in 1978 he succumbed to constant temptation and bought a Guarnerius, the 'Lord Wilton', one of the finest violins ever made by Giuseppe Guarnerius 'del Gesù'. Previously he had always maintained that his constant companions were his Strads while his 'illicit affairs', as he called them, had been with Guarneri violins. His passion for the instrument (and for violin bows) was unbounded: he talked about them lovingly in his CBC television series and wrote several books about how to play and look after them.

Life Class (*The Compleat Violinist* in the US) is described on the flyleaf as the 'thoughts, exercises, reflections of an itinerant violinist'. Published in 1986, it's an engaging self-portrait, edited by Christopher Hope, and includes photographs of Yehudi looking astonishingly youthful in his seventieth year as he demonstrates a variety of yoga exercises useful for violinists. A decade later, in 1996, the year of Yehudi's eightieth birthday, the French publishers Flammarion produced a gorgeously illustrated coffee-table book, *The Violin*, devoted entirely to Yehudi's personal history of the instrument. But the most focused of Menuhin's overlapping books on the same subject is the *Music Guide* he and his fellow violinist Denis Stevens edited for the publishers Macdonald in the late 1970s, one of ten titles in the series.

Over the years Yehudi amassed a valuable private collection of violins and bows. He also commissioned new instruments from present-day makers in many parts of the world, and recorded the Brahms viola sonatas on a modern instrument in 1980. Whenever the opportunity arose he would extol the violin's beauty beyond that of all other instruments. He never had any but harsh words to say about the piano.

Yehudi's many books satisfied a desire to leave something solid for future generations but his recordings were (and still are) the more lucrative medium. When it came to the handful of great violin concertos, he could not compete with his own back catalogue, but he continued to explore new repertoire for EMI and, whatever the carping that might have gone on behind his back concerning his untrustworthy bouncing bow, he could still rise to a violinistic challenge. In late middle age he tackled the Violin Concerto by Delius for the first time, and in the same week in June 1976 (supposedly a sabbatical year!) he shared the limelight with the cellist Paul Tortelier in Delius's even less familiar (but equally luscious) Double Concerto. Two years later, with Delius's former assistant Eric Fenby at the keyboard, he recorded all three Delius sonatas. As somebody who enjoyed anniversaries and was – with good reason – very conscious of the date of his own birthday, Yehudi must have relished the fact that he and Fenby shared the same date: Fenby was exactly ten years his senior.

The name Yehudi Menuhin remained a sure-fire box-office attraction.

Concert appearances with the world's great orchestras, coupled with a distinguished array of classical recordings and the Stéphane Grappelli jazz duets, provided his main source of income. He also continued to give recitals, often with his sister Hephzibah; they recorded the Elgar Sonata in 1978 and toured America once again in 1980. Yehudi persuaded himself retrospectively that he had detected in Hephzibah's playing in her fifties 'a depth and a warmth, an ever-growing dimension'. But she developed cancer of the throat and died, after a long battle, on 1 January 1981. To his intense chagrin Yehudi was not at his sister's bedside, even though he knew that she was by then gravely ill; he wrote in his memoirs that he had a concert engagement and 'the idea of cancelling seemed impossible'. Afterwards he spoke of her as his Siamese soul and wrote to his aged parents that 'her presence remains stronger than ever' but the reality was that when they were not making music he had seen very little of her over the two decades they had both lived in London. She wore herself down with the gruelling work she undertook with the homeless in South London. He worshipped the memory of her as a musical partner but was perhaps made a little uncomfortable by the very practical way – in contrast with his own more lofty approach – that her love of humanity expressed itself. Only a year later his father died after a long illness. Yehudi was in New York to play the Bloch Concerto with the Philadelphia Orchestra under Riccardo Muti. Eleanor Hope remembers that he insisted on going ahead with the concert at Carnegie Hall after he'd been given the news of Moshe's death a few hours earlier, saying his father would have wanted it that way. Marutha told an interviewer that stress, engendered by his extreme views on Israel and the controversy that it had aroused, had brought on the cancer that killed her husband. But obviously old age must also have played a part: Moshe was eighty-eight. He had had a heart problem for many years. Yehudi was equally convinced that his sister had developed cancer because of the stress inherent in the lifestyle she had adopted with her sociologist husband Richard Hauser. Perhaps it was these two recent deaths in the family that led him, in 1982, to admit to himself for the first time his concern for his future as a violinist.

For years he had chosen to avoid the subject of his deteriorating technique. In 1980 an American journalist suggested that wrist problems had affected his bowing. 'Not really,' came the reply. 'It's nothing I haven't been able to overcome and work out.' The interviewer persisted, pointing out that Yehudi was employing a bowing technique that avoided using the bow at the heel, where his wrist control was potentially weak. Yehudi responded with an astonishing attack on his earlier playing style.

The situation can be traced back to the time . . . when I studied with Adolf Busch . . . If you look at the old photographs . . . the position of the bow arm is absolutely atrocious . . . I'm absolutely *aghast* at the position I had at that time . . . the high elbow with a pressure exerted through the first finger and hence, the lack of a proper balance in the bow.

'Enesco never criticized you about this?' asked the interviewer.

Never. The trouble is I played too well . . . I never studied with a pedagogue like [Carl] Flesch . . . at the time I never analysed these things . . . I can now report that I'm working in a totally relaxed frame of mind. And technically . . . in as far as age permits, I feel I'm far better than I've ever been before.

But age was a hard taskmaster. Yehudi continued to practise yoga and give concerts but his bowing arm became more vulnerable and the embarrassments more acute, although there was a conspiracy of silence within his family circle: his son Jeremy remembers, 'It was really a subject one couldn't talk about. As I thought his music-making was always so interesting I decided to disregard the occasional bouncing bow.' Jonathan Benthall, Zamira's second husband, a friendly but objective observer, noted in his diary (at the 1976 Gstaad Festival) that he was 'in a cold sweat out of concern for him'. On 22 August Benthall heard a Beethoven quartet.

Those who know him very well seem to be not in the least concerned about it . . .

23 August: A few more insights into Y's *spiccato* yesterday, in the course of a superb concert of two Brahms sextets. Bruno [Monsaingeon] told me that he avoids playing this way but finds other techniques to replace it, e.g. playing *martélé* with the end of the bow, which Bruno says is more beautiful . . . I suggested to Zamira that perhaps this was rather like a stammer. He finds other ways of playing as stammerers find paraphrases to replace the words they cannot utter.

26 August: [Diana accepted the stammering analogy] attributing the hang-up to his years of marriage to Nola. She says the reason for it is that it has to be done with a perfectly free right hand. I am never to mention the matter outside this house . . . But D contradicts herself because she blamed under-rehearsal for the poor quality of the Beethoven quartet the other day, when no amount of rehearsal would be able to rectify a hang-up or 'stammer'.

2 September: Considerable tension between D and Y continues. She gave him hell yesterday in front of the Princess [of Hesse] . . . because he had left his tails at home. It is hard to forgive the way she lays into him just before or after a concert.

If he has any psycho-technical problems they can hardly get better with these strains upon him.

In the end it was to his assistant Eleanor Hope that Yehudi turned for advice. She had been hired as his secretary in 1975 and proved so effective in running his professional affairs that he eventually decided to leave the Harold Holt agency, where Ian Hunter had looked after him for over thirty years, and make Mrs Hope his personal manager. Most uncharacteristically he announced the decision in a typed letter. Hunter remembers the pain it caused him: 'He said he was so happy that I had got married again. My change of circumstances prompted the thought that it was the moment when we should relax our relationship.' Personal friendship was soon re-established: there is no doubt that Eleanor Hope regenerated his professional life when it was in danger of running into the buffers. (Yehudi was also close to her husband, Christopher, who collaborated on several books with him.)

In March 1982 Eleanor Hope was with Menuhin in Portsmouth for the final of the second International String Quartet Competition he had helped to found. (The first, in 1979, had been won by the outstanding Takács Quartet, with the Endellion in second place.) He confided to her that he was experiencing considerable pain when he played. He told her that one day he would be forced to reorganize his life and that it should be sooner rather than later. They discussed what he called the Heifetz option, which would involve retirement from the concert platform to concentrate on private teaching and public masterclasses. This was unacceptable: he could not face total renunciation of performing in public. He chose instead a gentler re-ordering of priorities: he would not stop playing the violin (he played in private and while teaching even after his official retirement in 1996) but he would cut back on solo engagements and hope to make more appearances as a conductor of symphony orchestras.

Up to this point his experience with the baton had mostly been with small ensembles, but now Eleanor Hope began looking for work with the major orchestras. The New York Philharmonic débâcle in 1971 had been a setback but Yehudi had recently stood in for no less a maestro than the ailing Herbert von Karajan, conducting a cycle of Brahms symphonies with the Berlin Philharmonic, and this had gone well. In May 1982 he took part in the Berlin orchestra's centenary celebrations by conducting the opening of Beethoven's Fifth Symphony – standing on his head! The all-important down beat was indicated by a sharp scissors movement of the legs. Karajan was cross but the orchestra and the audience loved it and television viewers around the world were reminded not only of Yehudi's *chutzpah* and devotion to yoga, but of his availability as a conductor. His German agent, Witiko Adler, was encouraging about the new career; Yves Dandelot in Paris was upset, Eleanor Hope remembers, and Tommy Thompson of Columbia Artists in New York 'not very helpful'.

Neither were the policy-makers at EMI. They had recorded Yehudi conducting a substantial swathe of the baroque orchestral repertoire, including rare symphonies by William Boyce, and they had just extended his violin catalogue with a new recording of the Bach Double – with Jin-Li, a Chinese boy prodigy he brought over to the School – to mark the fiftieth anniversary of the Abbey Road studios in 1981. Later in the decade Yehudi was to record Bartók and Beethoven sonatas with his son Jeremy. (Over a period of fifty years he made no fewer than seven recordings of the 'Kreutzer' Sonata.) But his old company's loyalty did not extend to Yehudi in his new, conducting role: how could he possibly match up to their current stars, such as Klaus Tennstedt? Luckily Simon Foster, the producer of Virgin Classics recordings, recognized Yehudi's potential and invited him to conduct a group of late Mozart symphonies. Ironically, the company was later bought by EMI so these Virgin recordings of Mozart did eventually find their way into the EMI catalogue. (The 1996 *Penguin CD Guide* named Yehudi's versions of Symphonies Nos. 40 and 41, made with the Sinfonia Varsovia, as the best pairing then available.)

The turning-point in his conducting fortunes came during the 1981–82 season when the Royal Philharmonic Orchestra, prompted by Ian Hunter, offered him the post of President. His first engagement with them as a conductor had been 'out of town' in 1975 at the Bletchley Leisure Centre: he followed that up with all-Elgar programme in London that included the First Symphony and the Violin Concerto, with Nigel Kennedy as soloist. He was already making records with them, too, starting in 1979 with Beethoven's Third Piano Concerto, with Jeremy Menuhin as soloist. The RPO's previous President, the composer Malcolm Williamson, had been persuaded to resign following his decision to return, temporarily as it turned out, to his native Australia. Yehudi accepted with the proviso – fought for by

Eleanor Hope – that he would also be guaranteed regular conducting dates. His old friend Antal Dorati, the RPO's Conductor Laureate, smiled wryly as he gave the orchestra's manager, Ian Maclay, a gentle warning: 'The man has no training as a conductor.' Dorati was well placed to make such an assessment since he had given Yehudi his first chance as a conductor back in 1946. And he was right to point out that while Menuhin would make an ideal figurehead as President, he'd had very little instruction in such matters as baton technique or score reading. Yehudi did however take a lesson from Sir Adrian Boult when he was studying Berlioz's *Symphonie fantastique*:

He gave me his own baton, specially designed with a bulbous end wreathed in rubber bands to prevent it slipping from the three fingers supposed to wield it. Sure enough it worked admirably, allowing the fingers to control an immense orchestra with the minimum of tension.

Yehudi was an astonishingly quick learner, but among British musicians he had acquired a reputation for not burning up too much midnight oil on preparation. He wrote that his temperament lay midway between those of his parents. From his father he had inherited prudence, from his mother what he described as 'the repudiation of the forethought that restricts' – in other words, spontaneity. In his conducting role it has to be said that his mother's influence had been dominant. The broadcaster Brian Kay, then a choral scholar, remembers a recording session in King's College, Cambridge, when Maestro Menuhin bounced on to the rostrum with the cheerful greeting, 'Good morning, ladies and gentlemen, and what great classic are we to record this morning?' One of his producers at EMI, Christopher Bishop, recalls the day when Yehudi thanked the band and released it – at a session of baroque music – before the work had been completed. 'Christopher's found another movement,' he told the players a little sheepishly after they'd been called back. But Ian Maclay had no qualms about Yehudi's status as a conductor.

In the right context, his insights into the music transcended everything . . . and he was influential politically. He opened doors . . . He sat next to the movers and shakers and if you could ride on his coat-tails it was well worth while. He had a tremendous inner strength and calmness. I found it disconcerting going into his dressing room before a concert to find him standing on his head in a corner in his underwear doing his yoga, particularly if I had to conduct a conversation with him . . . but he was totally at his ease . . . He had a great affinity for the English repertoire and drew from the orchestra some of the greatest performances in its history. I found him a very considerate man, enormously sympathetic to the needs of the orchestra and the musicians. He would be forever championing the cause of the orchestra, their rates of pay, the value of their work . . . of course he came from a privileged background and lifestyle but that didn't mean he was out of touch.

Whenever possible Yehudi used his influence to help young musicians. Back in 1982, his first presidential venture with the Royal Philharmonic Orchestra was to conduct four concerts featuring young soloists. Three were graduates of his School: the violinists Ralph de Souza and Nigel Kennedy, and the cellist Colin Carr. He had first heard the fourth player, the violinist Tang Yun, in Beijing. He had campaigned to make China a member of the International Music Council while he had been its President, and after John Roberts had been out to prepare the ground he had been invited there in 1979 to give recitals, masterclasses and straightforward advice to literally hundreds of Chinese violinists of all ages who queued up to play for him. The visit caused a considerable stir and he was made an honorary professor of the Beijing Conservatoire, which had not long been re-opened after the Cultural Revolution. (Yehudi reported that the leader of the Beijing orchestra had been imprisoned for ten years 'for daring to disclose an addiction to Western music'.)

He was gratified to find that, independently of his new career in the field of symphonic music, German-speaking countries wanted him as a conductor of opera, primarily of Mozart. As a boy visiting the Salzburg Festival he had been taught to think of the slow movements of Mozart violin concertos as the equivalent of operatic arias. Now he could experience the real thing. He spoke German fluently and to judge from various television documentaries he rehearsed his musicians with slightly more precision in that language than he did in English. German sopranos had a special appeal:

When I was on tour in the United States for the first time, as a boy of twelve, I was deeply in love with Elisabeth Rethberg [the leading German opera singer of the day]. She appreciated the homage although she was about thirty. After that they gradually got closer to me in age.

Irmgard Seefried was actually three years his junior.

In 1981 he conducted *La finta giardiniera* in the rococo splendour of the Cuvilliés Theater in Munich. In 1984 he spent five weeks at the Bonn opera house conducting a new production of *La clemenza di Tito*. In Vienna's Konzerthaus he conducted *La betulia liberata* (KV 118) and

Idomeneo; in Leipzig *Die Zauberflöte* and at Gstaad *Don Giovanni*, with Thomas Allen in the title role. Only *Figaro* among the major Mozart operas eluded his grasp. Soon after the success of *Tito* he admitted to a journalist that one of his few unfulfilled ambitions was to conduct at the Royal Opera in London. The message (backed up by entreaties from Diana) went unheeded in Floral Street.

His last Gstaad opera, conducted in the big tent in the year of his retirement from the Festival, was *The Merry Widow*, but even that was not his final operatic venture. In August 1998, aged eighty-two, he conducted Rossini's *Otello* at the Theater an der Wien in Vienna. He had planned to direct the première but Eleanor Hope persuaded him to withdraw because Diana had fallen seriously ill during the rehearsals – she had to be flown from Vienna to a Swiss hospital in a private plane – and Yehudi was left with insufficient time to learn the long opera. Much as they loved him, the members of the Sinfonia Varsovia were in revolt, protesting that he could not negotiate the long stretches of accompanied recitative in which the work abounds. Nevertheless, when he took over for the third performance on 12 August, *Opera* magazine's Vienna correspondent reported that 'The difference was dramatic. Every phrase was lovingly shaped and coloured and he kept the rhythms purring along.'

In Yehudi's first years as a guest conductor Eleanor Hope accepted relatively low fees for his services, but as concert managements discovered that the Menuhin name, billed purely as conductor, could still fill a hall, she was able to raise them 'over three or four years' to match his very high scale as a violinist. Agents and impresarios are loath to furnish precise figures concerning artists' fees. We have Moshe's figures for the pre-war era. In the 1940s, Yehudi's soloist fee with the New York Philharmonic was known to be $5000 (considerably more than Jascha Heifetz or Isaac Stern). According to the distinguished promoter Victor Hochhauser, a Royal Albert Hall engagement in the same era would attract a fee of a thousand guineas, a not dissimilar figure at a period when the dollar exchange rate was over four to the pound. For Yehudi, Hochhauser remembers, the most important thing was that no other artist should be paid more than he was.

Yehudi remained the RPO's President until his death. He conducted the orchestra in several concerts each year in London, Croydon and Nottingham, where they had a residency. He led them on foreign tours (including several visits to Gstaad as well as to the Czech Republic and the United States) and made many recordings with them, among them Elgar's two symphonies and the *Enigma Variations*. He described the RPO's character as 'ebullient, light-hearted and full of fun . . . their joyous and entertaining post-concert revelry can go on until well into the small hours', yet, wonder of wonders, 'they never arrive for rehearsals the next morning the worse for wear'. He found inspiration in the orchestra's devoted approach to music-making, as John West, the recording producer for Elgar's First Symphony, recalls:

We only had three sessions for a fifty-minute work. After we had finished on the closing day I asked if we could do the link from the *Scherzo* into the *Largo*. I knew he had a plane to catch . . . and he said we needed to finish by one fifteen. So I said, 'No problem', and we started about ten pages before the change of movement and it was wonderful; the orchestra were on top form. We got to the end of the movement and started the slow movement, and suddenly something happened: the music blossomed, it grew and I couldn't stop. It went on and just got better and better, and I could see Yehudi standing on the podium looking at his watch occasionally, conducting wonderfully with his other hand but I thought we must go on as long as we possibly can and we went on some ten minutes into that movement, almost to the end. If you listen to that recording it is quite glorious.

Yehudi was also President of the English String Orchestra (with whom he recorded an entire disc of Bartók's music) and often appeared with the English Chamber Orchestra, many of whose members also formed the nucleus of the Menuhin Festival Orchestra. Abroad he had regular engagements with French symphony orchestras in Paris and in the regions as far afield as Lille and Monte Carlo. The warm personal links he had established in Dresden and Leipzig before the Nazi era led to invitations to conduct the great orchestras of those two cities in the 1980s. In his memoirs he singled out Kurt Masur, then in charge of the Leipzig Gewandhaus, for having helped him with his conducting technique, while in Dresden he celebrated the sixtieth anniversary of his 1929 début with a concert in the newly rebuilt Semper Opera House; at rehearsal he spoke movingly to the players of his deep emotion at being asked back. In 1995 he was in Dresden again, this time with a British orchestra, to conduct the Mozart *Requiem* on a grimmer anniversary, the destruction of the city by Allied bombing in March 1945.

When Antal Dorati died, in 1988, Yehudi took over the presidency of the Philharmonia Hungarica orchestra, which was made up of musicians who had settled in West Germany after the 1956 uprising. He claimed that their interpretation of the Bartók *Concerto for Orchestra* was superior to all others and, as if to efface the memory of his New York Philharmonic embarrassment in 1971, he toured the *Concerto* with them in America, as well as in Russia and the Baltic states. Eleanor Hope says he was particularly popular in Lithuania: he took its chamber orchestra (and the Kaunas State Choir) to many parts of Europe with a semi-staged version of Handel's *Messiah*, over the years conducting it sixty times – a staggering total. Mrs Hope remembers a performance in Vilnius in 1989: the Russians had just left, 'having cut off all the heating, oil and gas. It was bitterly cold and we did *Messiah* and the people stood up for the Hallelujah Chorus!' More extraordinary still was a performance in the Kremlin, immediately after the fall of communism: 'To take that message to Moscow – "You came to us with guns, but we come with music" – was something I shall never forget.'

His closest partnership, sustained over twenty years, was with the Polish Chamber Orchestra, which enlarged itself and changed its name in the 1980s to the Sinfonia Varsovia. The friendship was forged in 1983, when the orchestra was invited to play for the Pope at his summer residence at Castel Gandolfo, an event, as Yehudi put it, 'fraught with emotion and symbolism for all the players'. The programme he chose could hardly have been more ecumenical in character: music by the Catholic Vivaldi, Venice's 'Red Priest', was followed by the Protestant J. S. Bach's 'Erbarme dich' aria, in which an Israeli contralto, Mira Zakai, sang the solo, accompanied by a violin obbligato played by an American Jew. And to round things off there were violin concerto movements by a Viennese Freemason, W. A. Mozart. The concert was held outdoors in a courtyard lit by candles. The Pope sat on a dais in one corner and as they played Yehudi felt a 'passionate current' flowing between the Polish pontiff and the musicians from his homeland. When the music was over the Pope descended from his throne to talk to Yehudi and then blessed in turn each member of the orchestra as they knelt and kissed his hand. Diana remembers the Poles being very moved and weeping copiously. Eleanor Hope observed that when the Pope and Yehudi embraced they looked like Tweedledum and Tweedledee.

Yehudi described the Sinfonia Varsovia as 'utterly tireless, devoted and determined', their playing characterized by 'unflagging rhythm, spellbinding pace and noble intensity – notably in Wagner's *Liebestod*'. At rehearsals there was no hint of the union mentality he deplored in American orchestras; they would work an hour's overtime if necessary and their output was phenomenal. Among Yehudi's symphonic CDs with the Poles (produced and engineered by English musicians, notably John West, Mike Clements and Mike Hatch) was an impressive landmark, the nine Beethoven symphonies, recorded 'live' during a week-long festival in Strasbourg in June 1994. Three years later they recorded all nine Schubert symphonies over a ten-day period, this time in a Polish Radio studio in Warsaw. In another CD of Rossini opera overtures Yehudi conjured from the Polish musicians some dazzling, quick-silver performances; nobody, he thought, could match their *brio*.

The Polish musicians were also committed humanists. In October 1996 Yehudi arranged for the Sinfonia Varsovia to join forces with the embattled players of the orchestra in Sarajevo. They gave a concert together, conducted by Yehudi, in a bombed-out hall. The European Commission and UNESCO were patrons. 'It was a matter of pride to get the German government to supply a plane,' Eleanor Hope remembers.

The connection with Sarajevo remained, as the musicians made friends with one another. Musicians from Sarajevo then came to Gstaad at Yehudi's invitation. He was always building bridges between people . . . having access to orchestras in out-of-the-way places was almost a symbolic thing for him.

The year of the visit to the Pope, 1983, was a momentous one for the Menuhins. Their sons Gerard and Jeremy both got married and they themselves moved into the centre of London. At a farewell concert Yehudi raised £2000 for Highgate's St Michael Church restoration fund but Diana couldn't resist a parting barb: 'I can't pretend the air is as good as it was when we first moved here.' Their new home was a fine Regency house of five storeys, built by Thomas Cubitt in 1838 to a design dating from ten years earlier, at a corner site on Chester Square, Belgravia, a few hundred yards from Lowndes Street, where Diana had been born seventy years earlier. It was a little smaller than 2 The Grove but that didn't matter since their children had long since fled the nest. The rooms were elegantly proportioned and the place was a great deal more convenient for West End stores, theatres and concert halls. Buckingham Palace was just round the corner.

In May 1985 Yehudi became a British citizen – at the instigation of Sir Robert Armstrong, then Cabinet Secretary. This meant he could receive the honorary knighthood he had been awarded twenty years earlier and he paid an official visit to the Queen. 'I've been British ever since I played the Elgar Concerto,' he observed gallantly, when he came face to face with his new monarch; 'I feel as if I have been belatedly baptized.' Two years later he was back at the Palace to receive from Queen Elizabeth an award that was in her own gift to bestow upon artists and intellectuals: the Order of Merit. Isaiah Berlin, Graham Greene and the historian C. V. Wedgwood were fellow members of this most exclusive of intellectual clubs. So was Mother Teresa.

The house in Chester Square was reported in newspaper property columns to have been bought for £425,000. Their former home remained unsold for two years before a buyer was found in the person of the pop star Sting. The asking price had meanwhile dropped by £200,000, down to £650,000. Instead of taking out a bridging loan Yehudi sold his 'Prince Khevenhüller' Stradivarius. (Later in the decade he also parted with the Guarnerius given him by Nola in 1939 – eyebrows were raised by a dealer concerning its authenticity – and his other Stradivarius, the 'Soil', which was bought by Itzhak Perlman.)

Meanwhile Diana lavished all her skills as an interior decorator on their new home and it became a joy to visit, despite a few worrying signs of the onset of hubris: paintings and drawings of Yehudi and Diana lined the walls on the elegant staircase from the dining room up to the first-floor lounge, and the entrance to the conservatory was guarded by twin bronzes of the master and mistress of the house. On the top floor Diana created an airy, spacious music studio, all in wood, which helped provide a welcoming acoustic for the hundreds of musicians who were rehearsed and coached there by Yehudi over the next decade and a half. The grand piano was covered with signed photographs of the great and the good and the walls were crowded with the engravings and prints of Niccolò Paganini that Diana had hunted down for Yehudi in antique shops over the years. (Yehudi had had a soft spot for Paganini since the 1930s and 1940s; playing his music was, he said, like skating into the sunset.) No expense was spared to make the entire house friendly and comfortable: they even installed a lift, remarking accurately, if a little unkindly, that 'many of our friends are so old they need this now'. The cost of the renovations became something of a *cause célèbre* in London gossip columns when it transpired that the Menuhins were suing their builders for almost £200,000 which they claimed they had overpaid on the repairs. In the long run it was money well spent since the lease on the property is now worth several million pounds.

So much of Yehudi's time was still spent on the road that one might be forgiven for doubting whether he fully appreciated what Diana had created for him. He took the trappings of the civilized life for granted: from the age of twelve he had never been without them. But they were no more than a pleasant backcloth, only incidental to his real purpose in life: music. He saw his routine in simplistic terms: 'My life revolves between the two poles, the solitary concentrated work which is an artist's refuge and the social side' – by which he meant, according to a 1984 interview he gave to the *Scotsman*, going to the theatre or talking over dinner with friends such as Lord Carrington, who two years previously had resigned from Mrs Thatcher's Government over the Falklands crisis. His schedules reveal a diversity and complexity of engagements that would have been overwhelming – were it not that travelling was a compulsion. 'He couldn't see blank spaces in his diary,' Eleanor Hope remembers.

They had to be crammed full of *something* and if it wasn't concerts, he was giving interviews or going off to see people or starting new projects. There was a restlessness, a drive in him, that was super-human . . . He was a gypsy: he could never stay in one place, was always on the move, looking to the next project, the next idea.

Here, surely, is the key to the personality of Yehudi Menuhin, provided by somebody who worked with him intimately on musical matters for the final twenty years of his life.

In February 1980, to take an example of his vagabond leanings from the beginning of the decade, he went to Lake Placid in upstate New York to help launch the Winter Olympics. He played in the televised première of *Around the Common Centre* by Lukas Foss, a piano quartet to which Foss added an extra part especially for Yehudi. Orson Welles narrated and Elaine Bonazzi sang; among the other performers was the violinist Edna Michell, who in 1996 was to organize his eightieth birthday concert in New York. Two months later he was talking to the press in London, showing off an electric car called 'Silver Volt' which he had imported after testing it in Florida. Such was his enthusiasm for electric transport that three years earlier he had paid $25,000 for a car unromantically named 'Transformer One'. Eighteen feet long, it weighed $4^{1}/_{2}$ tons and could hardly get up Highgate Hill. The boot was packed with heavy-duty batteries. Eleanor Hope remembers the car well:

He drove around London while bus conductors leaned out of the window and hurled abuse because it went so slowly. He even had an electric bicycle which was made for him specially in Birmingham. But he wasn't a crank – he was a vision-ary. As a young man he made drawings of mobile wings on fighter planes . . . and discussed with scientists the use of magnetic rails for trains, which are in use now on monorails.

But the electric car proved a dream too far. Prudently the Menuhins kept a Ford Cortina in reserve for when the Silver Volt's batteries failed.

In his later years Yehudi transferred his loyalty to the internal com-bustion engine as perfected by the German car manufacturers Audi, a firm with an enlightened policy for arts sponsorship: in Britain it lent its name to a valuable competition for young instrumentalists and provided Yehudi with a comfortable saloon to which he transferred his personalised number plate, YM 44. It was a very gentlemanly agree-ment: Yehudi conducted the occasional concert at Audi's headquarters in Ingolstadt but was not required to endorse the company's famous slogan, 'Vorsprung durch Technik'. (His own technique was hardly the strongest weapon in his conducting armoury.) That he should have enjoyed possessing a personalized number plate might come as a sur-prise: it was a self-indulgence to which distinguished musicians of his generation seemed particularly prone; for many years Sir Georg Solti drove a Mercedes marked GS 20; in the US the same company provided Leonard Bernstein with a saloon which had the plate MAESTRO 1.

A long-term project dates from 1983: he founded the International Violin Competition based in Folkestone, Kent, that bears his name: it is aimed specifically at young artists, being open to violinists of every nationality under the age of twenty-two, with a junior section exclu-sively for under-sixteens. Partly funded by the Regional Development Fund of the European Community, it is held every two years and now-adays alternates between Folkestone and Boulogne-sur-Mer. Shortly before his death Yehudi wrote of his competition's excellent record in discovering talented young violinists and helping them to launch their professional careers. 'The event is also designed', he continued,

to encourage cultural exchange and the development of new friendships. Competitors and their teachers are invited to stay for the whole competition even if they are no longer competing. There are many activities throughout the ten days that give participants the opportunity to meet and learn from one another.

Among the violinists who won early recognition through this inter-national event are Tasmin Little, Isabelle van Keulen and Joji Hattori, who is now its President.

In the same year, 1983, Yehudi was given the Freedom of the City of Venice. He went to receive his award at the time of one of the annual historical gondola processions and seems to have been under the illusion, to judge from his memoirs, that it had been arranged especially in his honour. In 1984 Jacques Chirac, then the city's mayor, honoured him for services to Paris – it was forty years since he had been the first to play at the Opéra after the Liberation – and in 1986 President Mitterrand trumped his rival by making Yehudi a Commander of the Order of the Légion d'Honneur. Almost sixty years had by then elapsed since his first concerts in Europe under Paul Paray. In the same year, 1986, Yehudi arranged a tribute, in Manchester, to the skills of his yoga teacher Mr Iyengar, then sixty-seven. He took to calling him his most important violin teacher – declaring that under his tuition he had finally learned how his body worked.

In 1987 he appeared as soloist in one of the European Community Youth Orchestra's regular tours of major capitals, including Rome, where he made all the right diplomatic noises offstage but revealed on the concert platform the extent to which his bowing arm had deteriorated in a sometimes embarrassing performance of the Beethoven Concerto. In the same year he was invited back to Moscow. In the era of *glasnost* his earlier support for Solzhenitsyn was forgiven and he was able to make music with such luminaries as the conductor Gennadi Rozhdestvensky, his pianist wife Victoria Postnikova and the Moscow Virtuosi under their brilliant violinist leader Vladimir Spivakov.

In 1991 he arranged for this chamber orchestra to be invited to the Davos World Economic Forum, which he personally began attending two years earlier. Economics was hardly one of his specialist subjects but Yehudi was always happy to sit among a gathering of the world's movers and shakers, sharing with them, in the words of the chairman's report, 'his vision of moving from an exploitative world to a world in which we value and protect beauty and culture'. He attended six out of the Davos Foundation's ten meetings in the 1990s, the last only weeks before his death. As high-powered talking shops with no legislative follow-up to complicate matters, they provided a perfect platform to present the ideas that increasingly preoccupied him – among them the need, as he put it, to give voice to the voiceless (the parliament of cultures) and to support what he called humanization against globalization. In 1995 he was a recipient of a Davos Crystal Award for his contribution to cross-cultural understanding. In his acceptance speech, whose transcript reads as if it was delivered impromptu, he expressed his hopes and fears for the future:

My greatest hope for humankind is to learn just a little sense of measure as of proportion, of direction as of serenity: embracing the whole of creation of life in a spirit of courtesy, reverence and respect, dignity and humility. Negatively expressed, it is the elimination of the simplistic form of thought which only accepts black and white rather than the myriad shades of in between. Or that thinking which is brutal or sentimental rather than tenderly strong and delicately passionate: or that travesty of thought which is being persistent by one exclusive prejudice or belief, for there lies total madness . . .

Quite so. Diana no longer undertook the winter journeys; Yehudi's speeches had been sharper when she was at his side to wield the red pencil. But Klaus Schwab, Davos's guiding light, says Yehudi made the delegates feel inspired and that was the point of his being there.

Back in 1989, he had launched a new musico-diplomatic venture that built on his earlier visits to China. The plan was for him to fly to Shanghai to conduct the inaugural concert of the hundred-strong Asian Youth Orchestra, the brainchild of an enthusiastic musicologist from San Francisco named Richard Pontzious. A third of the auditioned players, some of them as young as twelve, were Chinese. The project had abruptly to be scrapped when the Chinese government put down the student rebellion in Beijing's Tiananmen Square, signalling a new era of brutal repression. The orchestra was launched the following year, switching its base to a training camp in Japan. Isaiah Jackson, formerly in charge of music for the Royal Ballet, rehearsed the young players before Yehudi arrived to take them on a tour that also included Taiwan and Hong Kong. Thanks to Yehudi's presence, the orchestra was handsomely sponsored by Far-Eastern businesses and the players were all kitted out in designer uniforms. Relations cooled in subsequent years after Yehudi discovered that other international performers were receiving hefty fees while he worked for expenses and inexplicably was being offered engagements only in minor cities. But back in 1990 many of the young players had literally wept for joy when he arrived to take his first rehearsal.

The year 1990 saw the beginning of yet another musical project, a symposium dedicated to string playing held at Fitzwilliam College, Cambridge. The new venture – public masterclasses for sixteen student quartets and a concert of massed string players at the end of the weekend, conducted by Yehudi – was a spin-off from what had begun as the

Portsmouth Quartet Competition. This had been relaunched in London in 1988 and was thereafter closely linked with the City: competing quartets are housed in the City University's halls of residence and rehearse at the Guildhall School; the Goldsmiths' Hall is the venue for the performances. A foundation was created in 1994 to oversee the competition and symposia and this also organizes chamber-music workshops in schools and links up with an international centre in Fontainebleau. Once again Yehudi found excellent administrators, to turn his vision into reality. The project was born out of a conversation in the mayor's parlour with Richard Sotnick, a lawyer who was Leader of the Council, after Yehudi had given a recital in the city of Portsmouth. Sotnick was Chairman from the outset: the administrator, Dennis Sayer, was a local government officer who took early retirement to run the operation full time. (Both men retired after the 2000 competition, which was won by the Casals Quartet from Spain.) It is an important creation (with a budget of £400,000) to set beside the School, Live Music Now! and the Folkestone violin competition.

When the gossipy *Hello!* magazine interviewed Yehudi at Chester Square in 1989, he obligingly stood on his head for the benefit of the photographer. The interviewer must have been American: 'Sir Menuhin, where do you live most of the time?' was the first question, to which Yehudi replied, 'In hotels and planes.' Earlier that year he gave an interview of a more confessional nature to, of all people, the food columnist of the *Sunday Express*.

Diana calls me 'compost heap'. I have to savour everything – except drugs – in the world until I'm satisfied. You'd think it would apply to sex but the funny thing is, it doesn't. From the age of three I was always in love – a kind of chivalrous devotion to a succession of women I put on a pedestal. Then came Diana, and she has remained on a pedestal . . . She devoted her life to helping me and may have suppressed a lot. It isn't easy to become the servant of another person, but she's managed it in the most extraordinary way.

Yehudi's effusive tribute to his wife came at a time when they were both being interviewed at length for a documentary film profile by one of Britain's best-known chroniclers of the musical world, Tony Palmer. Two hours long, this 'family portrait' was commissioned by Channel 4 and transmitted in April 1991 to mark Yehudi's seventy-fifth birthday. It proved to be a rather unpleasant anniversary offering, in which members of his family were wheeled in one by one to highlight his shortcomings as a father. Zamira looked gracious but gave little away, at one moment pleading with the director to stop pumping her for anecdotes. Krov revealed that he was shunned by his father and step-mother when he came to London in 1958, not having seen them since they left Alma. He felt he was being punished for having stayed with Nola: 'Nothing could be gained by our meeting at the present time,' he'd been told. Gerard, filmed on the porch of the family chalet in Gstaad, inched towards an admission that his father did not take much inter-est in him. (He did not mention his mother, who was away travelling with Yehudi for much of his childhood.) Jeremy is seen squirming at his father's apparent lack of familiarity with the Beethoven piano concerto they are rehearsing together. He refused to be interviewed. According to Palmer, Diana breathed a sigh of relief when she heard: 'Thank God. He would only have come out with all that psycho-twaddle.'

Tony Palmer's thesis was that behind the façade of the great musi-cian a darker story was waiting to be revealed for the first time. He set out to show that Menuhin's saintly exterior was privately flawed by the way he had allowed his mother and his second wife to dominate him. The film purported to be both a family portrait and an impres-sion of Menuhin himself. While it is acceptable to imply that he had weaknesses in his personality – who hasn't? – the effect here was little short of character assassination. Palmer relied heavily on a long and astonishingly hostile interview with Yaltah, which he threaded relent-lessly through the film. Her dislike of her mother (whom she had not seen for over thirty years) and her errors of fact (as an example, she stated that Nola left Yehudi in 1943) are allowed to flow unchecked. Diana makes an equally unfortunate impression. She was filmed with Yehudi in Gstaad, Berlin and Carnegie Hall, New York. Already seventy-five and tending towards the garrulous, she would have done well to follow her son Jeremy's example and hold her peace. Instead, perhaps because she was nervous in front of the camera, she comes over as bossy, querulous, condescending, argumentative and forever intent on sus-taining the proposition, elaborated in her memoirs *Fiddler's Moll*, that Yehudi's violin playing was all at sea until she came to his rescue after the war. He was Humpty-Dumpty and she had put him together again.

Nola emerges as something of an unsung heroine, thanks to some wonderfully evocative colour home movies of her married life, including the carefree honeymoon with Yehudi in Yosemite National Park and the birth of their babies. Palmer points this up by cross-cutting to happy shots of the young couple just after Yehudi has drunk a toast 'to the women in my life', naming only Marutha and Diana. In the film's final reel, Palmer dealt his trump card, introducing the audience to Marutha for the first time. Snippets of Yehudi playing the Elgar Violin Concerto, set against a neutral background without an orchestral musician in sight and Yehudi looking distinctly uncomfortable and a tad embarrassed – are intercut with a hand-held *vérité* scene of Yehudi and his camera crew meeting Marutha at her Los Gatos home. The camera was not eavesdropping: the visit had been arranged for the specific purpose of showing a charming family reunion. The juxtaposition with Elgar was intended, one presumes, to offer some revelation concerning the source of Yehudi's musicality. The effect is a little comic: Marutha at ninety-two comes over as considerably more coherent than some of her descendants and hardly the control freak that the documentary has been nudging viewers to assume.

The film is not in the same league as Palmer's best efforts, such as the studies of Britten, Walton and Stravinsky which had won him a unique hat trick of Prix Italia a few years earlier. Menuhin was a performing musician, first and above all else, but examples of his music-making, both as conductor and soloist (the latter often of fascinating archive footage) are never heard for more than a few seconds at a time. As biography the film is perfunctory, offering no attempt at a chronological framework. It doesn't mention Yehudi's unpopular defence of Furtwängler; the School is relegated to a cursory footnote and Yehudi's countless humanitarian efforts are derided – by Diana, of all people – as being on the level of support for a home for broken-down bicycles. Newsreel footage from 1945 of dead bodies being shovelled into a mass grave at Belsen is used to imply that Yehudi visited the actual concentration camp, which in fact had been destroyed two months before he and Britten arrived.

Palmer's personal charm, and his distinguished track record, seduced Yehudi into agreeing to an exercise that created considerable friction within the family and did his reputation substantial harm. A few weeks later the *Observer*, quoting Palmer, stated that his parents

lived off Yehudi's earnings from the age of nine. When a Hollywood studio offered $2m for Yehudi's life story in 1931, they turned it down because he was already earning more elsewhere.

Yehudi's first reaction after a private screening was said by Palmer to have been positive: 'It's time it all came out.' But frantic memoranda seeking changes were soon being faxed from Japan, where Yehudi had flown to give concerts. They were no doubt prompted by Diana, who had been unable to exercise the editorial control she had applied when Robert Magidoff was writing his biography in 1954. Errors of fact were corrected (or so Palmer claimed in the preface to his book) but the Menuhins had casually ceded control to the director (and to Channel 4) without ensuring legal recourse. Palmer was a clever man but he might not always have resisted the temptation to manipulate his material in the cutting room to suit his own agenda. The Menuhins had been warned concerning his working method: the conclusion must be that hubris got the better of them. The film was televised in many countries and can still be bought as a video.

Within days of the film's transmission Yehudi was able to reclaim the moral high ground. In Israel he was awarded one of the Wolf Foundation's international prizes for creativity in the field of the arts and sciences; with it went an invitation to deliver a speech to members of the Knesset, the Israeli Parliament. The previous day he visited East Jerusalem and several settlements on the West Bank and was appalled by evidence of 'utter ruthlessness' on the part of what he described as the occupying Israeli forces: 'The destruction of villages, the abduction of children, the closing of schools and summary arrests all added up to unnecessary acts of cruelty and violence.' In a school for Palestinian orphans he was equally shocked to find children being taught to hate the Israelis. His idealistic solution to the problem, inspired by long residence in trilingual Switzerland, was a confederation of neighbouring cultures, with Jerusalem becoming a shared capital.

In the Knesset, he told his listeners that he owned a very special title, that of his noble Hasidic ancestor, Rabbi Schneer-Salman: 'As a small child playing the violin my naïve dream was to be able therefore to heal the suffering heart – fulfilling thus a Jewish mission.' (This was a diplomatic variation on another frequently recounted dream from his childhood, that if he were allowed to play his violin in the Sistine Chapel, universal peace would break out.) Having established his rabbinical credentials, Yehudi lectured the parliamentarians on the need to find a solution to the problem of Palestine:

All around us we see pain, anguish and horror – is this not the very moment when we, as Jews, gathered together in Israel, should recognize our supreme destiny: to heal and help?

It is difficult not to admire Yehudi's courage: he was David in the lions' den. The right-wing Israeli government was led by Menachem Begin, who as a terrorist had threatened Yehudi with death forty-two years earlier. And here he was, preaching to them on the need to find a peaceful solution:

Do not calculate your actions out of the darkness of fear, but rather in the bright light of King Solomon's words: 'Let not mercy and truth forsake thee' . . . Whatever the choice of solutions: that of two separate states or the one federated state (which latter would seem preferable and less likely to carry the endemic danger of war) – or again a humiliating conference of the other powers sitting in judgment on Israel – one factor surely must remain: there must be absolute reciprocity, absolute equality, mutual recognition of the dignity of life, respect for each others' traditions and its background – these are the *sine qua non* of peace.

To an audience whose majority were sceptical hardliners, he warmed to his theme of reconciliation:

It is unworthy of my great people, the Jews, who have striven to abide by a code of moral rectitude for some five thousand years, who can create and achieve a land and society for themselves such as we see around us, but can yet deny the sharing of its great qualities and benefits to those others dwelling amongst them.

How proud Moshe would have been to hear such sentiments uttered by his son. Yehudi ended by quoting the Psalmist David:

Let the words of my mouth and the meditations of my heart be acceptable in thy sight, O Lord, my strength and my redeemer.

He gave his prize money to Israeli voluntary organizations providing support and legal protection to Palestinians and education for their children. The next day he drove north over the Allenby Bridge to meet King Hussein of Jordan: 'I shall never forget his heartfelt words when he said that his dearest and greatest dream was for a Semitic federation of peoples.'

Yehudi never made total peace with the Israelis. In January 1998, when Benjamin Netanyahu's Government had begun obstructing the peace process to which it had reluctantly signed up, Yehudi gave what *The Times* called an 'incendiary interview' to *Le Figaro*, headlined, 'Illustrious violinist finds whiff of German Nazism behind politics of the national Right in Israel.' Referring to Israel's claims to the Holy City, he commented that

those who have tried to have Jerusalem for themselves alone have been defeated because this is an eternal city . . . it is extraordinary how nothing ever dies completely; even the evil which prevailed yesterday in Nazi Germany and which is gaining ground in that country today.

'Menuhin is a very weird man' was the response of an Israeli journalist quoted in *The Times*; the Israeli government itself was furious, labelling the interview

a desecration of those who died in the Holocaust. . . . Vitriolic statements . . . do a disservice to the truth [and] reflect on the judgement of anyone who would utter such a shameful remark.

An unrepentant Yehudi was no doubt encouraged when British Jews praised him for speaking out against the intransigent Netanyahu, who was decisively defeated in elections the following year.

Elsewhere in the world, Yehudi was enough of a diplomat for UNESCO to appoint him a goodwill ambassador. He spoke up for the organization itself in 1995 when the Royal Philharmonic Orchestra was invited to play at a gala in San Francisco on the fiftieth anniversary of the signing of the UN Charter. 'I spoke my mind,' he reported the following year in his updated memoirs:

I chided the rich nations of the world for denying the UN their support, called on the USA and the UK to rejoin UNESCO and pleaded for a global conscience towards the world's troubles.

Unfortunately his audience, which he noticed 'rose to its feet as one at the end', was a little thin in top-flight dignitaries – Yehudi mentioned only President Lech Walesa of Poland and Princess Margaret as being present. His wife Diana, nearly eighty-two, had not made the trip but his mother Marutha was in the front row to hear her son speak. She was ninety-nine and was to live nearly two years longer.

In Britain he was invited to join another, less controversial political forum in 1993 when John Major's Tory Government offered him a life peerage. He took the title Baron Menuhin of Stoke d'Abernon and his coat of arms was designed by the Canadian artist Myfanwy Pavelic, a close friend whose 1973 portrait of Yehudi hangs in the National Portrait Gallery. First he discussed his escutcheon with the Garter King of Arms. His list of requirements included violin strings, scrolls and bridges, a wooden plough representing his Swiss canton, a seven-branched Jewish candelabra, a gypsy flag, a globe held between two hands (symbolizing reverence for life) and a litany of Hebrew words such as 'faith', 'hope', 'charity', 'knowledge', 'understanding' and 'wisdom'. With such a panoply of symbols and good intentions one could hardly go wrong.

He made his maiden speech on 26 January 1994, having been presented to the house by his sponsors, Lord Armstrong (the former

Cabinet Secretary) and Lord Jakobovits (the Chief Rabbi). The topic for debate was arts funding. By convention a maiden speech should be brief and non-controversial and Lord Menuhin opened his account rather entertainingly:

My Lords, the cheeky taxi-driver who refused to take me from Portland Place to Highgate Village, saying that it was too far and that it was lunchtime, added insult to injury when he shouted after me as I walked away, 'Has anyone told you how much shorter you look off stage?' That cheeky fellow would have been more than vindicated to observe me here today, perceptibly further diminished even onstage – as I must appear to the serried ranks above me – and, as befits the humility of this 'maiden' of seventy-seven years, an itinerant musician who has fiddled his way through life.

Plenty of lordly chuckles greeted this opening piece of self-deprecation but the rest of his discourse, which ran four minutes over the theoretical maximum of ten, was on the woolly side; indeed his very next paragraph slid into unscripted miasma:

What can so alien a character offer in return for this honour? Perhaps, that long and concentrated discipline demanded by music which harnesses a player to a basic rhythm that at once supports and governs him – giving him a wider view – a wider sense of the myriad fluctuating pulses of all speeds which propel mankind along its tortuous course. Perhaps also a sense of the span of man's works. Might it be the intuitive counterpart of the learned historian's grasp of human destiny?

He embarked on a eulogy of the non-elected second chamber, which was concerned with abstract topics that are none the less, he thought, of 'supreme urgency'. Then he praised the art of good music, claiming as he hit his stride that it fed 'the tangible intangibles which enable us to breathe and to dream'. He warmed to his own rhetoric: 'For man acts according to his visions, be they ideals or simply ambitions. It is those dreams which shape our lives – too often twisted into nightmares by hideous incertainties and fears.' Turning to specifics, he spoke up for an endangered species, the symphony orchestra. A move was afoot to merge several London bands into a 'super' orchestra. 'How could anyone consider reducing, on false premises, such essential and inspiring examples of human achievement?' He had praise for teachers, whose job it was 'to instil into our young not only learning but character, and may I add, compassion, courtesy and creativity in a society wherein the lack of those basic qualities can only encourage crime.' He wanted lottery money (when it came on stream) to be diverted to schools in order 'to channel the wild energies which are now rampant in certain classrooms into better purposes, partly by music and singing'. He claimed rather grandly that 'music is the one art which can create order out of chaos'. He painted a vision of his assembly of cultures ('we are witnessing the proliferation of states and the extinction of cultures') and put in a plea for the government not to follow the Americans but to return to the UNESCO fold. Perhaps in due course, he added, 'I could move one or two resolutions.' (He never did.)

Aristocratic reviews for his début effort rang round the chamber. Baroness Birk hailed the speech as 'quite outstanding in its depth, breadth, substance and in its brilliant presentation'. *The Times*'s lobby correspondent reported that 'the elevated tone and length of his contribution clearly unsettled some peers, save one Lord who snored'. Lord Skidelsky said he had been moved, called it 'profound' and hailed an important contribution to the debate. Lord Palumbo, about to stand down as Chairman of the Arts Council, was more restrained, calling him an idealist and a visionary, refreshing qualities that 'do not always fit easily into the reality of arts funding at the coalface'.

Lord Menuhin spoke only twice more in debates, on the issue of asylum for illegal immigrants and on the benefits of non-conventional medicine. Membership of the House of Lords proved too cumbersome a way to make his views known to the nation. He preferred the equally old-fashioned but less time-consuming medium of the correspondence columns of *The Times,* which published twenty-seven letters from him over fourteen years and politely turned down many more.

Shortly before his eightieth birthday, Yehudi scribbled an *aide-mémoire* to his daughter Zamira. It was intended, when typed up, for the Chairman of the Board of his School, Mrs Barbara Rees-Davies Fisher, who was preparing an appreciation to be included in the programme book of his birthday concert. In Zamira's estimation this document is the nearest approach her father made to a balance sheet, not of his music-making, which he took for granted, but of his recent life. The punctuation has been regularized and the contents annotated and clarified where necessary – but not the stream of consciousness in which he enumerated his achievements:

Here are a few dates for Barbara Fisher's words in programme, April 20.

1 Grandchildren arrival since Lin [born 1964]
   Six grandchildren born since *Unfinished Journey* was published [in 1976]: Dominic and William [Zamira and Jonathan Benthall's sons]; Aaron, 1982

[Krov and Ann Menuhin's son]; and finally Diana's and my three: Nadia, 1985; Petroc, 1988 [Jeremy and Gabriel Menuhin's children] and Maxie, 1990 [Gerard and Eva Menuhin's son, whose full name is Maxwell].

The marriages of his three sons had all been dissolved and none has married again. By way of self-justification he wrote elsewhere: 'My way of life has not allowed me to behave like a "normal" grandfather, just as I found it hard to be a "normal" father.'

2 Establishment of IYMF Brussels to further all my brainchildren YMS, LMN, ESTA, ACE, MUS-E.

Yehudi had a penchant for initials. IYMF stands for the International Yehudi Menuhin Foundation, which was established by royal decree in Brussels in 1991. He had become adept at lobbying for funds in the corridors of Strasbourg and Brussels; the Foundation provided the best way of tapping into European Community funds. Despite its name, which suggests that it administers substantial funds of its own, the foundation is wholly dependent on grants.

The first two 'brainchildren', his School and Live Music Now!, have already been described in some detail. ESTA, the European String Teachers Association, brought together teachers of stringed instruments from all over Europe. Yehudi had been the first Chairman of the British branch, which was founded in 1973 after tireless work by Nannie Jamieson; two great teachers, Max Rostal and Yfrah Neaman, were among its other supporters. He was later elected Life President.

ACE denotes Assembly of Cultures of Europe, a long-standing project of Yehudi's upon which, according to Eleanor Hope, he lavished 'a huge amount of effort' in the 1990s. The idea, as we have seen, was to encourage the expression and projection of cultural identities by the creation of a forum that would be 'giving a voice to the voiceless', such as the Basques and the gypsies. Inspired by the example of the Soviet dissident Andrei Sakharov, for whom Yehudi spoke up and raised funds on many occasions, the project assumed a specifically European dimension. Europe, he believed, 'could only be understood via the diversity of its cultures . . . they should be given a platform where they can express their hopes and responsibilities and bring their contribution to the [European] Union'. Yehudi was later to preside over the Assembly's first meeting, held under the auspices of the European Parliament in Brussels in November 1997. Delegates from fifty cultural minorities attended. Other meetings followed in Lisbon and Barcelona. Yehudi hoped to harness the Internet to encourage informal exchanges of views.

The last of the acronyms was MUS-E. The MUS-E programme aims, according to its Charter, 'to improve the environment of the child by music, arts and all the disciplines necessary to its entire fulfilment'. In his memorandum to Zamira, Yehudi summed up his idea as:

bringing singing and dancing (folklore and social) mime and martial arts to schools ridden by violence – (in each case totally successful) in 9 countries of the European Community.

Since his death the MUS-E movement has been taken up by another three countries. A hundred and fifty musicians are involved around Europe and eight thousand children take part each year, most extensively in Spain. Yehudi believed music to be 'one of the key elements for transforming an atmosphere of fear, hatred, prejudice and crime in schools'. In the mid-1990s he found a willing British apostle in a dynamic singing teacher, Susan Digby, who was carrying out an impressive three-year experiment at the Oxford Gardens Primary School in a tough, multi-racial district of West London. Yehudi visited the school and was photographed leading a group of small children in jumping and clapping games in the playground. But Digby withdrew her organization, Voices, from the MUS-E umbrella after Yehudi announced he wished to add dancing (and later mime and the martial arts) to the regular curriculum. She felt the message would be diluted and the cost of providing instructors prohibitive.

The headmistress of Oxford Gardens, Liz Rayment-Pickard, has no doubt that Voices improved the quality of life at her school, where pupil numbers have almost doubled since the experiment began in 1992. She remembers Yehudi being overwhelmed by the buoyancy and energy he encountered at the school and how he soon had the kids 'eating out of his hand'. He had, she said, a strong vision of a reformed lifestyle for deprived urban children but his own sheltered upbringing, and the solicitations of his second wife, had protected him from reality. Rayment-Pickard attended several MUS-E meetings abroad but felt some of their projects were 'completely potty' and that Yehudi had 'lost the plot a bit' by envisaging too many different activities for schools to be able to cope realistically in a crowded curriculum.

At the time of writing, 2000, there is no British representative on the board of the International Menuhin Foundation – an indication of a certain coolness between the keepers of the flame in England, where the School and Live Music Now! flourish independently, and the Foundation in Brussels which is concerned with Yehudi's more recent 'brain-children'. The Foundation's General Secretary is Marianne Poncelet. In his memoirs Yehudi described her as 'an invaluable personality of real imagination and zeal, who has shown unlimited resourcefulness and determination'. Once again he had found somebody totally devoted to his dreams – and determined to make them come true: her support and friendship were very important to him in the last decade of his life.

The last of the new 'good causes' was described in the next paragraph of the aide-mémoire to Zamira:

The Mozart Funds: to impose composers' and authors' rights on works in the public domain [creating a fund by imposing a levy on performances of non-copyright material such as Mozart] for *preventive* measures against man-made catastrophes – in direct association with the International Red Cross [which is] concerned largely with the catastrophes themselves.

And other projects incubatory.

Yehudi switched to personal matters for his next four highlights before returning to contemplate his appearances on the world stage:

3 My 22 years with Eleanor Hope.
4 My daughter's unbelievable 50th anniversary. She *cannot* be that old!

Zamira was born in September 1939. In April 1996 she was fifty-five.

5 Diana's 80 – our 50 years together.
6 Move to Chester Square.
7 Return to Russia – Gorbachev.
8 Return to S. Africa.
9 Return to Romania with Princess Margherita performing Enesco with RPO [in September 1995].
10 Unforgettable evening of YMS [his School] and Royal Ballet School – a dream of creation, composition and choreography achieved by the children of these two schools *together*.

In March 1995 three School pupils composed ballet scores which were choreographed by Matthew Hart, Lynn Seymour and Gail Taphouse and danced by pupils from the Royal Ballet School, the Royal Academy of Dancing and Elmhurst Dancing School. Sets and costumes were designed and made by students at the Central St Martin's College in London. Sixty young dancers took part. Two more collaborations have since taken place; the most recent, in 1999, involved dancers from five countries.

11 House of Lords
12 My two débuts in the role of addressing parliaments.
A. [5 May 1991] The Knesset when half the audience applauded and the other remained seated. Gidon Raphael said it was the best speech ever delivered in the Knesset. Diana worked on it with me the day before. [Menachem] Begin *had* to proffer his hand – about forty years after he sent me a note threatening my assassination.
B. Sept. 27 1995 addressing the cultural delegates of all fifteen states at a formal gathering of the European Parliament – with the unanimous response to support all three projects I had submitted on behalf of the IYMF.
There may be others – yes [i.e. The House of Lords].
13 Bringing back the Hungary Orchestra – in exile the Philharmonica Hungarica – after being welcomed and maintained by a most hospitable Germany for almost forty years to Budapest in two programmes including a performance of their own great director Antal Dorati's glorious 2nd symphony.
(I have yet to persuade the RPO and the BBC, both of which London orchestras Dorati conducted for many years, to give a memorial tribute concert. *They simply refuse.* You can put that in the programmes, Zamira darling, and *they* can put it elsewhere.)
14 My [1994] recording of the nine Beethoven symphonies with that unbelievable orchestra – my beloved Sinfonia Varsovia – an achievement I have dreamt of nearly all my life.
15 The Queen according me a most delightful personal 'investiture à deux' the O.M. order of merit.
16 Mitterrand according me the second highest order of the Légion d'Honneur with a delightful speech he delivered from memory.
17 Chirac, when Mayor of Paris, at a ceremony at the Hôtel de Ville – the municipal tribute.
18 The [television and live concert] programme 'From the Sitar to the Guitar' – the history in music and dance of the great trek of the Gypsies – the Romanies – from India to Spain both North and South of the Mediterranean over a thousand years which Ravi Shankar and I hosted [in Brussels, in November 1995] – the realization of a lifetime desire to illustrate and make heard the voices of the oppressed. We are now organizing a programme including Africa, Asia, Middle Eastern and European voices of unfavoured cultures and peoples.
I may still have forgotten some – of course *Zauberflöte* in Leipzig, *Idomeneo* in Dusseldorf, the B Minor Mass and so much more.
19 My mother's 100 birthday.
20 Founding and conducting the Asian Youth (superb) Orchestra. Richard Pontzious, initiator and co-founder.
21 (give dates) Freedom of the City of Vienna.
22 Freedom of the City of Budapest
(Ask Eleanor to list German cities – I think 2 or 3.)
23 Freedom of City of Warsaw.
24 Freedom of Venice – that was heaven; procession of Gondolas – regatta, etc.
25 Addressing students and profs – Oxford, Cambridge, Sorbonne, Japanese

university, University of Calif., Berkeley - those are the dates that stick out [in the margin he wrote 'but more'].

26 Conducting in St Petersburg, Tchaikovsky *Pathétique* with the St Petersburg Phil on the very same stage where Tchaikovsky himself conducted the première.
There are probably others.

27 Yes, my 30th Festival festivities in Gstaad (this year my 40th) I have appointed Gidon Kremer to succeed me.

28 Diana's and my first visit to China and my appointment as Honorary Prof to Beijing's Conservatory.
There must still be others.

29 Saddest day, my sister Hephzibah's death.
Such sad days are coming ever thicker as I grow older. Sir Ronald Harris [former Chairman of the School] – and so very many.
Fortunately I am surrounded also with youth wherever I am, and my hopes and ambitions are ever more vested in *their* lives rather than in my own. They also serve to keep me feeling contemporary – the illusion of youth – and I am infinitely indebted to them,
Yehudi

30 ?There must be others!!!!

Recommended Recordings

Handel: *Messiah*
soloists, Kaunas State Choir and the Lithuanian Chamber Orchestra,
conducted by YM
ISS Classics (distributed by IMG Artists) 691112
A live recording, produced by John West, of the complete *Messiah*. YM led sixty performances of Handel's oratorio, many of them semi-staged, in the last decade of his life.

Elgar: Symphonies Nos 1 and 2
Royal Philharmonic Orchestra, conducted by YM
Virgin Classics CUD 5 61276–2
Good examples of YM's affinity with Elgar and his ability to master a truly symphonic canvas.

Beethoven: The Nine Symphonies
Sinfonia Varsovia, conducted by YM
Carlton Classics (5 CDs): 30368 00032/42/52/62/72
Probably the orchestral recordings of which YM was most proud – taken from public concerts given in Strasbourg in June 1994.

Rossini: Overtures
Sinfonia Varsovia, conducted by YM
BMG Conifer 75605 57031
Brilliant playing by the Polish musicians, urged on to breakneck speeds by YM,
who relishes Rossini's wit and sparkle.

19 Final Years

Celebrating Marutha Menuhin's hundredth birthday

1996: eightieth birthday celebrations in London, Stoke d'Abernon and New York; retirement from Gstaad Festival; relations with Zamira, Krov, Gerard and Jeremy; 1997: deafness; 1998: German tour with Sinfonia Varsovia; Australia, viewing of Hephzibah *documentary; 1999: January, speaks at World Economic Forum, Davos; February: last orchestra rehearsal at School; March: annual German tour interrupted by illness in Berlin; 12 March: sudden death.*

YEHUDI'S EIGHTIETH BIRTHDAY celebrations went on for half a year. Prince Charles set the ball rolling on 21 March, a month and a day early, by hosting a spectacular musical party for Yehudi in the ballroom at Buckingham Palace, followed by a banquet in the galleries. Three hundred and sixty people were invited and no fewer than eleven members of various European royal families sat in the front rows, headed by the Queen, the Queen Mother and Princess Margaret. 'Yehudi's heaven-sent talent', Prince Charles declared in his address,

has delighted audiences around the world who have found his playing an expression of the human spirit at its most sublime . . . He is relentless in his pursuit of his vision of music as a reconciler of national differences and comforter of the needy.

Scenes from a new film, *The Violin of the Century*, evoked Yehudi's life as a prodigy. The director, Bruno Monsaingeon, had unearthed some marvellous historic footage and then filmed Yehudi's reactions as he watched this portrait of the artist as a young man. (A professional violinist, Monsaingeon first fell under Yehudi's spell in 1962 when he attended his masterclass at the Dartington Summer School. Bruno became Boswell to Yehudi's Dr Johnson and they made many films together.) The orchestra from the Menuhin School was at the Palace to play Elgar's *Serenade for Strings* under Yehudi's direction; two Russian girls, entrancingly contrasted in their performance styles, were the soloists in Bach's Double Violin Concerto. The concert ended with the clinking of glasses and a spirited rendering of the champagne ensemble from Johann Strauss's *Die Fledermaus*, performed by six young opera singers who had been helped in their careers by Live Music Now.

On 20 April, two days before Yehudi's actual birthday, a handsome eightieth birthday concert was mounted at the Royal Albert Hall for an audience of some 5,500, many of them sponsors and patrons whose generous donations to Live Music Now! and the Menuhin School had already secured them, as a bonus, much coveted invitations to the Buckingham Palace 'birthday bash'. A bright new fanfare by Gareth Wood was followed by an intriguing and touching cantata, *A Hopeful Place*, by Malcolm Singer, a composer on the staff at Yehudi's School who has since been appointed its Director of Music. The text was by Friedrich Hölderlin; it begins:

> We come humbly, as pilgrims, to a hopeful place
> We children are the great hope of the world
> and freedom may still flourish with us!
> Why does freedom only come with age?
> This is not fair!

At this point in the text Singer inserted words recently uttered by Yehudi himself on a visit to South Africa: 'I was born old, and have been growing younger ever since.' The musical forces involved represented many of Yehudi's special interests: the massed children's choirs were trained by Susan Digby of the Voices Foundation; an octet of solo strings was provided by the School, and members of the Royal Philharmonic Orchestra filled the platform to play for their President, who had a busy evening conducting for his supper. Participants in the star-spangled programme included the operatic bass Samuel Ramey, whose link with the occasion was somewhat tenuous (although Eleanor Hope suggests that 'Ol' Man River', which he sang, was one of Yehudi's favourite ballads); Slava Rostropovich, who played Tchaikovsky's *Rococo Variations* to the manner born; and Anne-Sophie Mutter, who gave an exquisite performance of the Mozart G major Concerto, lovingly accompanied by Yehudi and the RPO. The official programme concluded with a vigorous but sensitive reading of Elgar's *Enigma Variations*, after which Yehudi joined his wife in the Royal Box to watch the zany encore, Michael Haydn's *Toy Symphony*, conducted by Yan-Pascal Tortelier with a dazzling array of celebrity soloists performing on tin trumpets, toy drums, ocarinas, warbling birds, penny whistles and even football rattles. The standing ovation that followed was rounded off by the release from the roof of an enormous cloud of red, white and pink balloons. The spirit of the Proms came early that year to the Royal Albert Hall in what was a cheerful and deeply affectionate celebration of the man who had first played there sixty-seven years previously.

The British press and radio also did him proud on his anniversary: Classic FM inaugurated a twenty-part retrospective of his life and music-making entitled *Menuhin: Master Musician*; the interviews he contributed were the inspiration for this biography. But neither BBC Television nor Channel 4 acquired Monsaingeon's *The Violin of the Century* and the birthday passed unnoticed on television – an indication, it should be said, of the planners' changing values rather than of a falling off in the public's affection for Yehudi. In the 1940s and 1950s Menuhin had been very close to the BBC. In the 1960s he was a member of the BBC's Music Advisory Council at a time when it wielded considerable influence. Yehudi's sixtieth birthday in 1976 had been celebrated by the BBC with a party combining elegant performance and high-table conversation televised by BBC2 from a studio mock-up of the Menuhins' music room at The Grove. But in 1996 the eightieth birthday concert was recorded and put on the shelf for transmission as a Christmas attraction, nine months out of date. That the programme included filmed reminiscences from Sir Isaiah Berlin and Sir Peter Ustinov, and a narration by another friend, Sir David Attenborough, made the decision to delay this birthday tribute even more inexplicable.

Down in Surrey another party in Yehudi's honour featured a nine-part *Fantasia on 'Happy Birthday to You'* especially composed by Cheryl Frances Hoad, a cello student, and the festivities ended with a concert in Stoke d'Abernon to which the Menuhins were transported in a large pink Cadillac. Earlier Yehudi planted a birthday oak tree in the meadow between the school and the M25 motorway and cut the symbolic first turf to mark the start of another building development. Two years later, on 19 March 1998, he unveiled a plaque to commemorate the opening of that building, named the White House; it contained three new classrooms, a music studio, a music technology studio, a science laboratory, library, music library, large drama studio and new school office. The solid success of the school – in bricks and mortar as well as musical prowess – was an eloquent rebuttal to a sceptic like Alexander Waugh who later in the year tried to write Yehudi off in *Punch* as a saintly snob, mouthing 'love and peace waffle'. And Waugh was not alone: a colleague in the House of Lords once described Yehudi as 'the third most boring speech-maker' he had ever heard.

Yehudi sailed on, oblivious to such sniping. The birthday-party spirit was rekindled in August in an unexpected quarter, New York, where the 1996 Lincoln Center Festival devoted its closing programme at Avery Fisher Hall to a Benefit Tribute in his honour. In old age Yehudi had become that inexplicable anachronism to Americans, an English milord, but he was a New Yorker by birth and had lived many significant moments in his artistic life there. The extraordinary concert was the brainchild of Edna Michell, an Israeli-born violinist living in New York. She organized an entire evening, fourteen works in all, of world and American first performances by composers as eminent as Lukas Foss, Arvo Pärt, Steve Reich, Poul Ruders and John Tavener. Some were for solo combinations, others small-scale concertos with accompaniment for string orchestra. 'That so many of the world's most eminent composers should have responded is a measure of the love and respect Yehudi enjoys,' commented Curtis Price, the American head of London's Royal Academy of Music. The evening concluded with an entertainment conducted by Yehudi entitled *Cabbages and Kings* by

David del Tredici, designed to employ everybody heard earlier and culminating in a rendition of the egregious 'Happy Birthday' melody.

Yehudi was exhilarated by the warmth of his reception from a full
house in New York. The next day he flew to Switzerland to join the
annual family reunion at Gstaad. He faced another round of tributes,
and a wave of emotion from his normally undemonstrative Swiss
neighbours, when he made his farewell after forty years to the artistic
direction of his modest but world-renowned Festival. Artistic direction
passed to Gidon Kremer; they had played the Bach Double Concerto
in Saanen church the previous August, Yehudi's last solo appearance.

But even at eighty withdrawal from the public scene was not an
option he was prepared to consider. When his daughter Zamira pleaded
with him to slow down and spend more time with his family he
replied, 'Darling, I'd miss the airports . . . Please don't worry about me.
I'm doing exactly what I want to do. I couldn't imagine life without
the whirlwind.' Meetings and symposia inspired by the MUS-E project
and the Assembly of Cultures filled the empty spaces in his engagement
book that according to Eleanor Hope he could not bear to contemplate. There weren't many gaps: in 1996 he conducted a total of 112
concerts. He spent a great deal of time closeted with state presidents
and Council of Europe potentates, lobbying for grants, and could
often be spotted marching down the corridors of power in Strasbourg
and Brussels, where Marianne Poncelet and her secretariat laboured
endlessly in the service of his Foundation.

Zamira was heard to complain, only half in jest, that to be sure of
seeing her father she had to book a date with his secretary weeks in
advance. In a letter to his sister-in-law, Griselda Kentner, written some
years earlier Yehudi had conceded his inadequacy as a father:

Perhaps you are right in saying our children share a sense of unrequited love.
Diana says that I am incredibly impersonal from time to time. I do not feel that
way with Zamira, but that is father to daughter and she is very special, she has a
philosphical streak.

Zamira enjoys a happy second marriage with the anthropologist
Jonathan Benthall, with whom she has two sons, both of whom followed their father (and Menuhin uncles) to Eton, and she has become
closely identified with her father's work: she is on the Board of the School,
where her most urgent task in the new century is to raise money for a
much needed concert hall to stand as a fitting memorial to her father;

she also serves as President of the European Federation of Live Music Now! Her father's strong paternal feeling towards the end of his life can be sensed – through the syntactical chaos – in an undated, handwritten thank-you letter he sent Zamira after she had masterminded a fundraising concert at the Royal Academy's Poussin exhibition.

Dearest Daughter

Bags packed – letters noted to write tomorrow – leaves me momentarily with only one most pleasant task – that of thanking you with all my heart for the most lovely meticulously planned and executed evening of music, good company, conversation and food ever imaginable.

And the décor and the beautiful tables, as much for the eye as for the mouth and stimulus a-plenty for all other senses as well.

A *perfect* gala evening!

Usually being an exemplary wife, mother, stepdaughter – these various roles are not usually found in glamorous style and luxury – but you combine them in good taste and great charm.

I was very proud of my two ladies! My life certainly could not be without ladies! Not quite a Don Giovanni – he has my entire sympathy – even in his recitative he replies totally astonished to Leporello: 'What no women? They are more than bread and sustenance to me!'

I admire men, but I love women – and you Miras are, with Diny [the family name for Diana] the principals!

A very grateful

Daddy

Naturally Zamira welcomed her father's affection but she recognized its limitations.

He had so many ideas that only he could pull off. He needed space and he was lucky enough to have people in his life who gave it to him . . . He would have hated to be thought of as anything but a warm man, but his warmth was for humanity more than for individuals.'

Yaltah Menuhin's psychologist husband Joel Ryce put it in a different way: 'Very few people interested Yehudi. He was interested in *all* people.' But many individuals, from many walks of life, have testified as to how impressed they were by his evident interest in what they were doing; he had the knack of making you think that while he was listening to you, you were truly at the centre of his attention and concern, and that he would not forget you when you left.

His time might have been at a premium but Yehudi was never mean with his money. His eldest son, Krov, had special reason to be grateful for his father's generosity. In his youth he had seemed the antithesis of

Yehudi, a man of action living outdoors, responding more to his Australian Nicholas genes than those of the Menuhins. He volunteered for the US Special Forces (the equivalent of Britain's SAS), served secretly overseas, became a parachutist, a frogman investigating underwater plane crashes and an experienced pilot of both planes and helicopters. When in the early 1970s he turned his back on the military life and decided to become a film-maker, Yehudi lent him $5000 to finance the first of several underwater maritime documentaries, about the life of whales off the coast of Patagonia. Yehudi was 'over the moon', his son remembers, when he saw a rough cut. He paid for the film's music score, by Edwin Roxburgh, and invited Krov and his wife Ann to stay at his Mykonos villa for six months while they worked on the project. Krov Menuhin became one of the most admired practitioners in his specialist field. After he settled in Provence Krov saw his father at least 'twice as often' as he had in previous decades. Yehudi particularly admired the way he brought up his son Aaron.

Of Yehudi's four children, Gerard seems to have had the toughest time coping with the difficulty of being the son of a famous father. After infant years spent mostly in the care of Schwester Marie, he was sent to boarding schools in Switzerland and Germany before spending his teens at Eton College. A spell at Stanford University in California (he discovered he needed to spend five continuous years in the US in order to retain his American citizenship) was followed by an apprenticeship as a film editor, but Gerard found it hard to settle in a career and received financial help from his parents. 'Some of my previous experience', he wrote recently,

has been as a consultant for trade with Albania, as a novelist [*Elmer*, disliked by Yehudi], a production executive at United Artists in New York, a sales executive for International Creative Management (Los Angeles) in Paris and as a film editor in London.

That was many decades ago. Since 1992 he has been working on a European environmental initiative that appealed to his father. He describes it as 'a network of regional centres for training in architectural skills throughout Central Europe'. There are projects in Germany, Hungary, the Czech Republic and Romania concerned with the restoration of half-timbered houses and the preservation of stonework, façades and documents. He visited Bucharest with his father in 1998: there are plans to restore the town house Enesco shared with Princess

Cantacuzène. He is on the Board of Germany's Yehudi Menuhin Foundation. He lived in the family chalet in Gstaad until it was sold after his father's death. These days he visits his mother when he comes to London to collect his son Max for school holidays. His brothers see him from time to time; his sister never.

Jeremy, the youngest son, had more to do with his father than his siblings because of their musical collaborations. He appeared regularly with Yehudi's orchestras as a concerto soloist – 'as an accompanist he was one of the best I've ever had . . . exceptionally sensitive' – and they recorded Bartók and Beethoven violin sonatas together in the late 1980s. 'To play with him was liberating,' Jeremy remembers.

Sometimes what he asked me to do took days, even months, to achieve. I wanted to please him. He often said, 'You're the person with whom I like to play the most.' Once, in my early twenties, we played the First Bartók Sonata at the Festival Hall and I felt something wild emanating from him, as if my youth had somehow freed the oppressed part of him.

Jeremy has kept a diplomatic silence but he must have been deeply hurt when his father supported the appointment of Gidon Kremer to succeed him as the Artistic Director of the Gstaad Festival after his retirement in 1996: it would have been so simple to hand over to Jeremy – then in his mid-forties – and thus keep the family closely involved. Jeremy's musical pedigree was impeccable. He had studied in Paris with Nadia Boulanger and in Vienna with the conductor Hans Swarowsky. And he was a Menuhin. But he had turned down the offer to be involved with Gstaad when his father approached him about the succession some years earlier, believing he was not ready for it. He was not entirely in sympathy with the Gstaad Festival when it expanded into the Festivalzelt, the big tent, in the 1980s: 'I liked it when all the concerts took place in the church and there was no clapping, people just stood up at the end . . . there was a feeling of respect for the building.'

In the autumn of 1998, when Kremer withdrew after only two Festivals – his programmes proving too expensive and too rigorous for Gstaad's summer clientèle – Jeremy lobbied his father again but Yehudi could be ruthless when the future of one of his 'brainchildren' was at stake: he favoured Dmitry Sitkovetsky, who like Kremer is a prominent international violinist with considerable conducting experience. But the appointment was no longer in Yehudi's gift. Sitkovetsky took part in the 1999 Festival (after Yehudi's death) but it was Eleanor Hope who was eventually offered the post of Artistic Director of the renamed 'Menuhin Festival Gstaad'.

Jeremy confided to a journalist that he had earlier been made to feel inadequate by Yehudi's mother, who once wrote him a letter saying, 'How dare you think of yourself as a musician, clinging to your father's coat-tails?' (Marutha was equally hard on Gerard, though he was the only sibling to attend her hundredth birthday.) Jeremy has survived such blows to his self-esteem and is greatly admired by fellow musicians both as a concert pianist and a player of chamber music. It has been announced that he will appear regularly at future Gstaad Festivals, maintaining the presence of the family name. With his father he had made a sort of peace, in which the musical joys they experienced together (their Bartók violin sonata recordings won a Grand Prix du Disque) were compensation for a less than perfect personal relationship:

He didn't have moods; he was either more distant or less distant . . . The things that were furthest removed from personal feelings were all right but . . . it was impossible to have an ordinary conversation with him unless you were talking about one of his projects.

To show your feelings, or even worse to be over-emotional, was to be too Jewish and had to be suppressed. Marutha might have been speaking through her son.

When Yehudi celebrated his eightieth birthday Diana was already eighty-three. Her mind was still sharp but her body was increasingly frail: a party for their fiftieth wedding anniversary in October 1997 had to be postponed at the last moment because of her illness. Her knees grew so weak she was obliged to take to her bed and make excursions outdoors only in a wheelchair. Inevitably she became depressed and sometimes surprisingly bitter about her life. When I was visiting her one afternoon she confided wistfully that she wished she had indulged in what she called an 'amitié amoureuse' when she had had the opportunity. Yehudi, she knew, had had three such relationships during their long marriage. (She asked if I had met 'the lady from Brussels'. I had not.)

On the rostrum Yehudi could still impose his will on the players, and at dinner parties he would perk up noticeably when seated next to a pretty girl, but he, too, was showing signs of encroaching old age. His memory was fallible and secretly he was facing a musician's worst threat to his livelihood: he was going deaf. He employed what John West, his recording producer in the 1980s and 1990s, described as 'super hearing aids' made especially for him – 'but of course he never remembered to put the batteries in the damned things'. Even with his hearing impaired (although certainly not lost altogether, as was rumoured at the time) he continued to spend many weeks of the year on tour with his orchestras. The backstage valeting role first assumed by his father and later by Diana, the 'fiddler's moll', was taken in his later years by an assistant provided by IMG Artists (part of the International Management Group headed by Mark McCormack), which Eleanor Hope had joined as a consultant, taking Yehudi with her. Sometimes Philip Bailey or Timothy Coupland of Yehudi's personal staff would be in charge. The task had not changed over the years: laying out the concert clothes, setting out the framed family photographs in the hotel sitting room, organizing the transport, sorting the mail, checking the spare handkerchief and the concert scores. But the pace of the tours was very different from the leisurely, two-performances-a-week schedule of Yehudi's childhood. When the Sinfonia Varsovia visited Germany in February 1998 they played a concert every night for eight successive days in eight different cities: Duisburg, Braunschweig, Berlin, Hanover, Kassel, Mannheim, Munich and Regensburg. In the second week they appeared in Bremen, Hamburg, Cologne and Marl, followed in the third week by Augsburg and Stuttgart, fourteen concerts in all, spread over only twenty days. (One programme was of Schubert's Symphonies Nos. 8 and 9, preceded by Ptaszynska's *Concerto grosso*; the other featured Schubert's Fourth and Brahms's First. They had recorded all nine Schubert symphonies the previous year in Warsaw.) At the end of each performance Yehudi would climb into the front passenger seat of a large Mercedes and be whisked down the Autobahn, through the night, to the next hotel. He was then two months off his eighty-second birthday.

Trips overseas were given a personal slant whenever possible: he never forgot an anniversary. The return to South Africa in 1995 marked sixty years since his first appearance there. On the fiftieth anniversary of India's Independence he flew to Delhi; his plan to conduct *Messiah* with his favourite Lithuanian choir and orchestra collapsed, but he made the trip all the same – without a concert – in memory of his friendship with Pandit Nehru. In December 1998, he took the School orchestra to Paris to play in the UNESCO hall on another fiftieth anniversary, that of the UN Declaration of Human Rights. Young musicians of fourteen nationalities took part.

In September 1998 he undertook a goodwill mission to Romania with Hungary's Budapest Symphony Orchestra. The countries are uneasy neighbours, so Yehudi picked his encores with care: a Hungarian dance by Brahms and a Romanian folk dance by Bartók. The purpose of the visit was to do further honour to the reputation of George Enesco. The former King, Michael, was at the concert with his fund-raising daughter Princess Margherita. Yehudi retained his penchant for princesses: that this one spoke with a plummy English accent and wore nice frocks was no problem for him. And his energy was phenomenal: after his concert he went off to dinner with the President and later still he and the King attended a midnight show laid on by his friends the gypsies. Next day he flew by private jet (paid for out of his fee) to conduct in the city of Cluj, close to the Hungarian border. Maurice Whitaker, a colleague of Eleanor Hope from IMG, who was travelling with him, noticed that Yehudi's hand luggage was staggeringly heavy on the private flight back to Vienna. It was crammed to bursting with the medals of honour, academic gowns and Romanian panpipes he had been given during his few hours in Cluj.

When Yehudi flew to Australia in October 1998 for a short tour with the Sinfonia Varsovia, Whitaker was with him again. He always admired the way Yehudi would take out his mobile phone to contact Diana as soon as he landed in a new country but this devotion had its drawbacks: at Melbourne they were first off the plane (he always travelled first class) and Whitaker was looking forward to a swift passage through the immigration channel when Yehudi pulled up, took out his phone and, while hundreds of passengers streamed past them, held a long conversation with Diana from the tarmac. The next morning Yehudi's nephew Kronrod, a senior pilot with Qantas, arranged a visit to the airline's flight simulator. Whitaker remembers that Yehudi had a bumpy ride but enjoyed himself hugely. Later that day he attended a party with members of the Nicholas clan, relations of his first wife and his sister's Australian family.

They were given a private screening of a recently completed biography of Hephzibah's life, a devastating documentary by Curtis Levy. While the others sat down, Yehudi stood motionless, close to the television set, throughout the film's ninety minutes. When it was over he turned, hands in pockets, to the members of his family, among them his sister's two sons, who had been deserted by Hephzibah when they were boys. It is an exceptionally poignant film and they were deeply moved. But for Yehudi no expression of personal feeling was permitted. 'There are a few inaccuracies,' he said, 'but they seem to have got the right story.'

The account of his sister's tragic falling away from her bright beginnings is overwhelming in itself, but Yehudi had also come face to face at that viewing with the home movies taken during his visit to Australia in 1940. The happiness in his own face after two years of marriage is clear for all to see, and yet for fifty years, prompted by Diana, he had been writing it off as a youthful indiscretion: 'Yehudi's ghastly mistake'.

He took instant evasive action by entering into a busy round of press and radio interviews to publicize the Australian tour. After giving concerts in Melbourne, Sydney and Brisbane – only four in all; Yehudi didn't want to spend too long away from his sick wife – the orchestra flew on to Kuala Lumpur, where IMG Artists administers the new concert-hall complex. Maurice Whitaker remembers that on the long flight Yehudi became greatly exercised concerning the political trial of Malaysia's former Deputy Prime Minister, Anwar Ibrahim. After reading newspaper reports about the human rights issues it raised, Yehudi was convinced he should call a press conference on his arrival. But many IMG jobs in Kuala Lumpur depended on maintaining good relations with the government so Whitaker was desperate for him not to upset the apple cart. A compromise was reached: instead of talking to the press Yehudi would send a letter of protest to the President. He wrote it overnight and handed it to Whitaker, who diplomatically omitted to deliver it.

The two concerts passed without incident and Yehudi was delighted when he was then driven out to the airport directly from the hall. British Airways had agreed to hold the midnight London plane for him, thus saving a day in his life, and his white Mercedes was escorted, sirens blaring, by a fleet of police motor cyclists. (Did he perhaps look back to the day he was driven in an American jeep from the Paris Opéra to Le Bourget airport in October 1944? Or to himself as a teenager careering around the streets of San Francisco on a fire engine, his sister Hephzibah hanging on for dear life and Yaltah banging on the fire bell?) Delivered punctually to Kuala Lumpur airport, he borrowed money and gave each police outrider a tip – of rather small denomination, Whitaker recalls, but it was the goodwill gesture that mattered.

A week later he was in Brussels for a three-day MUS-E seminar and the sixth annual gala event organized in his name, *Menuhin's Dreams*: the mime Marcel Marceau and the folk violinist Volker Biesenbender (a former pupil of the School) were among the guest artists. Later in the autumn Yehudi conducted his School orchestra in a fundraising concert at Goldsmith's Hall in London, at which John Dankworth and Cleo Laine renewed the links they had forged with Yehudi at the Bath Festival thirty years earlier. The performances of the Bach Double Concerto and Elgar's *Introduction and Allegro* were finely done by any standard. Malcolm Singer recalls the coaching sessions at Stoke d'Abernon for the Bach:

He spent close to four hours working with the orchestra on this fourteen-minute piece. As ever he was gracious, loving and humble before the music, but he was equally fastidious and obsessive to shape each phrase as he believed it should be played. We must have spent more than half an hour working to discover the best articulation for the first five notes of the piece.

Rehearsing the Elgar was equally inspiring:

Virtually no bars in the piece move at the same tempo and his inimitable flexibility of pulse allowed him to stretch and contract phrases like an incredibly cultured rubber band – for everything he did oozed musicality, and creative tempi were often his speciality, forcing one to hear the music in a new way. Everything was always fresh and sparkling as if it had just come from the composer's pen.

A few days later at the Royal College of Music he conducted a playful orchestra of musicians (among them Tasmin Little, Philip Jones and Sir David Willcocks) in the *Toy Symphony* – a ninetieth-birthday-present offering to an old friend, Belinda Norman Butler. There was no chance for a rehearsal and Yehudi, arriving at the last moment, set an excessively slow tempo to which he then adhered slavishly, seemingly unaware of any incongruity as his performers tooted and warbled their way through the minuet at a tortoise's pace. Even at the second reprise he made no effort to jolly things up. In the prevailing mood of frivolity nobody among the performers and party-goers was tactless enough to mention what was perhaps a tell-tale sign that when he was tired – and his fatigue was inevitable in the light of his gypsy schedule – Yehudi's powers of musical concentration could occasionally slip.

He was off at the crack of dawn next day to conduct Beethoven's Ninth in Madrid. There was no sign of waning powers on that occasion, nor in January 1999 at his annual recording sessions in Warsaw.

The engineer for those sessions, Mike Hatch, remembers that

Not all the orchestra spoke very good English so he had to use his musicianship to communicate with them . . . His popularity in Poland was extraordinary. He was firmly of the belief that Poland should be a member of NATO and wrote an article on the subject that was very well received.

At Christmas Yehudi and Diana stayed in Henley-on-Thames. They were well looked after but Zamira, visiting with her own family, found the place desperately depressing, a *de-luxe* old people's home with the word 'END' written all over it. That was something her father could never face with equanimity. She admired the way he balanced care for his ailing wife with his need to go on working: 'We watched helpless while he, week after week, pursued a schedule that a young man would have felt exhausted *looking* at.' She travelled up with him in the new year for a speaking engagement at Churchill College, Cambridge.

The talk was an unforgettable *tour de force* – entirely natural – never losing the thread of his thoughts on life, religion, music, philosophy and education as he spoke standing without a note for one and a half hours.

It proved to be the last 'great occasion' she spent with her father: 'I'll never forget the sight of him surrounded by eager, intelligent faces of the young at the reception afterwards.'

He was on equally good form later in January at the World Economic Forum symposium in Davos, where he conducted a fund-raising concert with the Sinfonia Varsovia and made a surprise appearance, standing in for an expert delayed by a blizzard, in a forum on the vexed subject of pop culture. It was not, however, a topic with which he was closely in touch. His observation that 'we are battered continuously with everything from Muzak to the amplification at Rolling Stones concerts' would have been more appropriate twenty-five years earlier. Television was another out-of-date target: he deplored 'the bewildering succession of images flashed before us on the screen, a world where there are so many markets and where even the weather report seems accelerated'. But his own message rang out clearly: 'We still have our own individual life and we need to live it, to sing it.' Children, he added rather bleakly, 'are born with the gift of creation and we beat it out of them'. He was sending out mixed signals. He was right to stress the value of singing in class as a way of building up self-confidence in young children. But at the very end of the century it did little good to rail in vague terms against the pace of modern life.

Music was Yehudi's natural language and he was on more solid ground at his School, to which he returned several times in February. His affinity with Bartók's music remained intense: he had known the *Divertimento* intimately for forty years and had recently advised the School against tackling it because it would be too difficult for that season's young and inexperienced orchestra. The Director of Music had taken the plunge none the less and invited Yehudi to conduct a rehearsal. 'I need hardly say what a thrilling occasion it was,' wrote Malcolm Singer.

He was obviously delighted with the music-making. As we left the rehearsal he touched my arm and asked mischievously, with that familiar twinkle in his eye, when he was due to conduct it in a concert. When I pointed out that he was not scheduled to do it with us (a fact he knew perfectly well) he said, 'Pity', and then a moment later added rather whimsically, 'Do you think we can do it as an encore?'

A later rehearsal, on 23 February, was devoted to the Violin Concerto he had commissioned from Andzrej Panufnik almost thirty years earlier. Malcolm Singer worked on the outer movements but he wanted Yehudi himself to take the players through the slow movement.

I am not sure why I had the courage to be so insistent but somehow I knew that it was important he did this with us. It is the most elegiac of slow movements and incredibly slow; the semi-breve is marked = 36. I had always wanted to take it slower than the pupils wished to and we had usually compromised over tempo. Yehudi had the courage of his own convictions and took it slower and quieter than you could possibly imagine. It was an exquisitely beautiful and magical moment – the last thing he was to do with the School orchestra.

Earlier that week, on Sunday 21 February, he chaired a meeting arranged by the Jewish Music Heritage Trust, of which he was President. It proved to be a journey into his own past: the main speaker was a friend of his from his UNESCO days, Dr Israel Adler of the Hebrew University in Jerusalem, and the subject was the archive recordings of Russian Jewish folk music recently unearthed in Kiev – the music Moshe Menuhin would have sung as a boy before he left for Palestine. Yehudi shared a memorable evening with three hundred enthusiasts, none of them suspecting that this would be his final appearance in London.

A few days later, on 1 March, Yehudi embarked on another big tour of Germany with the Sinfonia Varsovia. There were to be thirteen performances in eighteen days but because Diana's failing health was ever more worrying, breaks were planned each week so that he could fly home to see her. Nevertheless the tour began, as it had the previous year, with eight concerts on successive nights, again in eight different cities, and with changing programmes chosen from works by Mendelssohn, Prokofiev, Schnittke and Brahms. The tour was to conclude at Freiburg with performances of all four Brahms symphonies in two concerts. The economics of touring a fifty-piece orchestra imposed a tight schedule but mentally Yehudi was ready for it. Physically, too, he seemed on good form and economically (although this was not widely known) he needed his substantial fees to maintain the Menuhin back-up team, the support system for what he called his 'no-profit-making activities' and his family's needs. His lifestyle always involved first-class travel and top hotels but in his personal life he retained a certain frugality, instilled by Marutha as a child; Diana always darned his socks and he would think nothing of turning up for rehearsals in shirts with frayed collars. Eleanor Hope remembers getting a Viennese tailor to run up a replica overnight of a favourite pink shirt from which he could not bear to part. In 1999 he still had no fewer than fourteen people working for him either at Chester Square or in a separate London office. With hindsight one may sympathize with his daughter's opinion that the German schedule was too strenuous for an octogenarian, even one as obsessed with work as Yehudi was. While at Davos he had considered the possibility of postponing the German tour until Diana's health improved but his professional advisers and colleagues felt that conducting was a kind of therapy for him and in any case he had a life-long aversion to cancelling his engagements.

The first week of concerts went ahead as planned. The reviews were uniformly good. 'Dirigenten-Senior mit viel Vitalität' was one headline. 'The old man approached the rostrum with careful steps,' another report noted, 'but from the first down beat his energy and temperament fairly took the breath away.' On Thursday and Sunday, in Cologne and Düsseldorf, the programmes included Alfred Schnittke's Sonata No. 1 for violin and chamber orchestra, a concerto in all but name, in which the soloist was Daniel Hope (Eleanor's son), a rising star among young British violinists in whom Yehudi had long taken a personal interest. Mrs Hope attended the second concert and saw her son score a big personal success: 'Yehudi pushed him out on to the stage to play an encore', she remembers, and for some curious reason Daniel decided to play *Kaddische*, the Jewish prayer for the dead by Ravel. He played it most beautifully and movingly . . . Yehudi was sitting at the back of the stage listening and he said to Daniel afterwards, 'I'm so glad you played that – I haven't played it since I was sixteen', and then proceeded to discuss the fingering.

When she joined them backstage, Eleanor Hope realized that Yehudi was unwell. He insisted nothing was wrong and flew back to London early next morning as planned to see Diana. Mrs Hope sent a message to him through her colleagues in London suggesting that he should see his doctor while he was home. The staff at Chester Square added their concern. Normally it was the state of Lady Menuhin's health that worried them but that morning Yehudi seemed terribly tired and frail. But instead of consulting his GP as Eleanor Hope and his alternative-medicine guru Bob Jacobs recommended, Yehudi merely bought some homeopathic remedies. He had a secret appointment to see a heart specialist on the following Thursday, his next planned return visit to London. He had known for some months that he had a heart problem but was desperate to keep it from Diana. Zamira later advanced the theory that her father was acting recklessly (a fortnight earlier, when he attended the lecture about Russian-Jewish music he had left his coat and hat in the car on a freezing cold day) because 'he thought Diana was going to die and therefore it really didn't matter if he got ill and died too'.

Yehudi was due to fly back to Germany on Tuesday morning. When Nicky the housekeeper went to wake him she sensed something was wrong. Normally he would instantly spring to life but on this occasion he was difficult to rouse; it was clear that he was dreadfully tired. At the airport in Berlin, where he had a concert that evening, he was met by Mrs Hope, who told him she had arranged for a doctor to examine him at the Hotel Bristol as soon as he checked in. 'I don't like the sound of his lungs' was the analysis and Yehudi was admitted to the Martin Luther Hospital. It was Tuesday, 9 March, and a lung infection had been (as the doctor told Zamira later) 'festering' for a good two weeks. His breathing difficulties came from pneumonia and pleurisy in both lungs and fluid on the lungs which was caused by a chronic heart condition. There was substantial insurance against concert cancellation but, as Eleanor Hope put it,

There was no way he was going to cancel. Yehudi only cancelled twice in the twenty-four years that I was with him; he was not going to give up the opportunity of a Brahms cycle.

His concert that evening at the Philharmonie (and one the following evening in Hamburg) were announced as 'postponed' and the Polish orchestra was sent home by train to await developments. Witiko Adler, Yehudi's German manager, set about rescheduling the rest of the tour for the month of May. Maurice Whitaker remembers fetching the Menuhin family photographs from the hotel and setting them out in the hospital room as Yehudi lay on his bed in a medical smock, alternately tapping his chest over and over again and making calls on his mobile telephone. He looked frail but his spirit seemed indomitable. He dictated several letters, including one to the players in the Sinfonia Varsovia, apologizing for having disrupted the tour:

My dear friends,

I was so touched by the beautiful letter written by Ewa on your behalf . . . I am so happy that this is not a cancellation, just a postponement. You all played so wonderfully in the first concerts of the tour and I know they will be even better when we resume work. With heartfelt thanks from your devoted Yehudi Menuhin.

He was not to know that only three days earlier, while he was back in London, the Polish musicians held a long meeting with the IMG management to discuss their wish to broaden their range of conductors. After hugging Yehudi farewell, Maurice Whitaker departed for London with the unneeded luggage of musical scores and concert clothes. He says he will never forget 'the tiled walls and unpleasant décor' of that hospital room in Berlin.

Yehudi was anxious to avoid causing his family unnecessary worry. He hated fuss and sent a fax to his London office saying that his children should not be informed of the nature of his illness: it should be given out that he had bronchitis. When she heard that news Diana found it difficult to believe he was ill: she had had bronchitis twice and never gone to hospital. When Yehudi used his mobile to telephone her he summoned extra strength to speak as normally as possible so that she would not be frightened by his breathlessness. A nurse gave him oxygen to help the brave subterfuge.

For his film-making friend Bruno Monsaingeon he found the energy to scribble a note: 'I always say – that *everything* is possessed of infinity and eternity – as it is transformed – a source of pride and humility –'

Yehudi normally never took antibiotics and his lungs quickly responded to the treatment prescribed by his doctor, Professor Detlef Oltmanns, who expressed optimism that he would make a good enough recovery to be able to return to London quite soon; he would then have to rest for a long time. Witiko Adler and his wife Jutta arrived bearing a gift of his favourite dessert, Rote Grütze (red-currants) with vanilla sauce. He was moved out of the intensive care unit and when Eleanor Hope left him on Thursday evening he was busy with a lengthy and cheerful call to Diana and was evidently feeling much better. But the improvement was illusory. He telephoned Eleanor in distress early on Friday morning, complaining of pain in his back and chest.

I realized there was something desperately wrong. I jumped into a taxi and raced over to the hospital and his heart had given in. But he was still talking and we talked politics while they took a cardiogram and to my dismay I saw there was an almost straight line on that cardiogram but he kept talking right up to the last moment when they took him into intensive care and I said, 'I think they are just going to do a few more tests', and he looked at me with those wonderful blue eyes of his and said, 'Oh, all right', and that was it – he stopped there.

He had suffered a massive heart attack. He fell into a coma caused by the bleeding in his brain. Dr Oltmanns ordered electric shocks to try to get the heart started but Yehudi died swiftly, without regaining consciousness.

Zamira had been reassured by Eleanor Hope's report the previous evening, which made the shock when her brother Jeremy telephoned at around 11 a.m. all the more profound. He had just been told that their father was in intensive care: the doctor thought they should fly out to Berlin immediately. Zamira was packing her bag when Jeremy called again to say the journey was 'no longer necessary'. He was choking with emotion when he telephoned Nicky Caxton-Spencer at Chester Square. His mother could not be given such news over the telephone; it might cause a relapse. Nicky should do it. She had been with the Menuhins for fifteen years; she was like one of the family. Fortunately the family doctor, Peter Wheeler, was at the house and she was able to share the onerous task with him. After Nicky had turned off the television set the doctor broke the news to Diana that her husband was dead. They had been married for over fifty-one years. Still recovering from a stroke, Diana found the death impossible to comprehend and for several days asked when Yehudi would be returning from Berlin.

Within minutes, the news of his sudden death was being flashed around the world. Radio and television programmes broadcast tributes and recordings. Newspapers accorded him the amount of obituary space normally reserved for distinguished statesmen. In London, the *Independent* quoted Sir Adrian Boult's judgement, written in the early 1970s: 'the greatest man in the profession'. The *Guardian*'s Edward Greenfield, a personal friend, wrote that 'from him there shone a searchlight beam, willing the best in everyone'. *The Times* said he was 'touched by the Gods' but could not resist a dig; he was, its obituary suggested, 'famous for the three Ys: yoga, yoghurt and Yehudi'. But its editorial made amends: 'Constantly bubbling with naïve enthusiasm, he espoused a plethora of brainstorming plans for ending starvation, redeeming criminals, preserving the environment, creating world peace.' Itzhak Perlman, who first met him in Tel Aviv when he was a boy, provided a musician's assessment of his violin playing:

He had a wonderful vibrant tone that stayed with him throughout his career – a musicality that just overflowed, a sound that had a pulsing quality to it. It was something that was very definitely his own, that you recognized straight away.

The prevailing tone was epitomized by the critic Michael White:

Mother Teresa apart, it's hard to think of anyone who made a more obvious impact for good in the world, anyone who more persuasively realized the idea of music as a healing art.

After five agonizing days dealing with the bureaucratic paperwork, Eleanor Hope flew home with Yehudi's body. The coffin looked surprisingly large because of the obligatory lead-lining required for the journey from Berlin to London. For the night of 18 March Yehudi returned to Chester Square. The enormous mahogany and brass coffin was placed in front of the fireplace in the dining room. It was open and the death mask taken at the time shows that his expression was calm and beautiful, serenely untroubled. Zamira noted that his bushy, straggly eyebrows were rather more neatly trimmed than usual. He had been dressed in his rehearsal clothes, a black and gold Paisley-patterned shirt and a grey cardigan. His fine hands, so recently at work moulding the music of Schnittke and Mendelssohn, were hidden beneath the folds of white satin in which the seemingly tiny body was wrapped. Around the coffin were piled the masses of flowers that had been arriving at the house throughout the week. Members of the family gathered to say farewell and share their emotions with Diana and the grief-stricken members of the Menuhin staff.

A private funeral service was held next day, 19 March, at the Yehudi Menuhin School in Stoke d'Abernon. The immediate members of the family included Zamira and Jonathan Benthall and their boys Dominic and William, with Zamira and Fou Ts'ong's son Lin; Krov and his former wife Ann with their son Aaron; Gerard with his former wife Eva and their son Maxwell; Jeremy and his former wife Gabriel, with their children Nadia and Petroc and his present partner Daniela – all united by Yehudi's death; Yaltah was there, still mourning her beloved third husband Joel Ryce, who had died the previous summer; also Hephzibah's granddaughter Angela, Marston Nicholas's child, and Mike Gordon, the Nigerian psychology teacher that Hephzibah and her second husband had adopted as an orphan boy in the 1970s. Diana was in her wheelchair, her two sons at her side, positioned discreetly at the back of the assembly hall so few of the mourners could see her, although her distinctive voice occasionally pierced the oppressive silence before the service began.

Eleanor Hope handed out yarmulkas as the mourners entered. Other staff members included the housekeeper Nicky Caxton-Spencer and the archivist Susanne Baumgartner, both devoted colleagues of long service. Yehudi's friends included Queen Sofia of Spain and her sister Princess Irene of Greece, and the wives of two Gstaad neighbours, Prince Sadruddin Aga Khan and the painter Balthus. On a cold grey day, close on a hundred people were seated on eight rows of school chairs. In the middle of the unadorned assembly room stood the coffin, its lid closed now, decorated with thousands of flowers, among them a spray of sweet-smelling lilies. The service began with the young musicians of the school filing in to give a performance (all standing, except the cellists) of the slow movement of the Bach Double Concerto, with two twelve-year-old girls playing the solo parts. For older listeners, memories of Menuhin and Oistrakh in the 1960s must have come flooding in, and of the famous pre-war recording of the Concerto Yehudi made with Enesco when he was still a boy. Seeing the mourners, some of whom were weeping, and the coffin holding the body of the man who less than a month before had been a living presence in their midst, a man who was the very embodiment of music and had been such a vibrant presence at his last orchestral rehearsal, some of the children began to cry, too. None had handkerchiefs.

When he spoke, the officiating rabbi, David J. Goldberg, set exactly the right tone. He said that later in the year the great and the good of the world would gather to honour Lord Menuhin. There would be a memorial service at Westminster Abbey – it took place in June – and a concert at the Royal Albert Hall – it was held in November, on the seventieth anniversary of his London début. But today's was to be a simple ceremony to honour Yehudi the man. The rabbi then began reading the Kaddish in Hebrew, switching occasionally to a fine English translation. He spoke deliberately and with intensity but in a remarkably soft voice, tinged with a Lancashire accent.

The second musical work was the Schubert song 'Litanei', transcribed by Jerzy Lefeld for strings and piano. For the first verse the song was played in unison but in the second the strings were divided to express both Schubert's poignant, noble melody and the divine harmonies he wrote as accompaniment. The sound produced by nearly fifty string players, some of them only eight years old, was overwhelmingly beautiful. Then the rabbi read from a prayer Yehudi had written ten years earlier at the request of the BBC Religious Department. It ended with the following injunction:

May those who survive me not mourn but continue to be as helpful, kind and wise to others as they were to me. Although I would love to enjoy some years yet the fruits of my lucky and rich life, with my precious wife, family, music, friends, literature and many projects, in this world of diverse cultures and peoples I have already received such blessing, affection and protection as would satisfy a thousand lives.

Finally a senior pupil, Sasha Sitkovetsky, played an Elegy on the G string for solo violin, composed for the service by Malcom Singer.

'Sooner or later,' Yehudi had written in his autobiography,

every life must become a death. Sometimes I envy the simple solution of the desert peoples who leave their corpses, wrapped in white, to the attention of the wild animals and the elements . . . The very thought of coffins, churches, fire, of stone slabs and monuments and ceremonies is anathema to me. My preference is for whatever will reunite me most quickly to the sources of life . . . Back to the earth, under a tree or in a river, that is what I choose.

His wishes were respected. The mourners filed out after the coffin. On a bitterly cold and windy afternoon, small groups made their way over the rough grass of the sloping meadow towards the graveside while the pupils, staff and governors hung back near the school buildings. The air was silent save for the hum of traffic on the M25 less than half a mile away. The grave had been dug under the oak tree that Yehudi himself had planted on his eightieth birthday. Diana in her invalid chair was manhandled rather than wheeled over the rough terrain. As she waited for the coffin to arrive she took out a little mirror and defiantly applied a gash of bright red lipstick. She had to be in good order before saying goodbye to 'the old boy', as she had taken to calling him. The pallbearers lowered the heavy coffin into the grave. Prayers were spoken, handfuls of earth thrown down – and a white camellia from Zamira's garden. Last farewells were muttered through veils of tears and little groups stood forlornly, comforting each other as best they could. Diana was silent when she was wheeled away but her eyes stared wildly into space as if she was screaming inside. She could not forgive Yehudi for being the first to depart this world, leaving her horribly alone.

A month after his death the BBC mounted an entire evening of documentaries, discussion and recorded performances on Radio 3 in memory of Yehudi. In her interview Zamira observed that the funeral had been 'desperately sad but also very beautiful'. She added that she had since returned to the School.

I had an afternoon free and I went back, and the children were not there because it was holiday time, and it was extraordinary because the whole of the area around his grave was covered with little brown rabbits. It was particularly poignant for me because his favourite children's story was a book called *The Velveteen Rabbit*, a very charming parable that he read to his children and grandchildren.

The printed order of the funeral service concluded with two passages from Yehudi's autobiography, *Unfinished Journey*:

As a small child, playing the violin, my naïve dream was to be able thereby to heal the suffering heart, fulfilling thus a Jewish mission . . . Ever since I can remember I have tried to relate the beauty of great music to the harmony of life.

I wanted to play the violin . . . anything that one wants to do really well and loves doing, one must do every day. It should be as easy to the artist and as natural as flying is to a bird. And you can't imagine a bird saying, 'I am tired today. I am not going to fly . . .'

The bird would fly no more; Yehudi's long journey was finished at last.

20 Coda

1998

~~~
HAPPY CHRISTMAS
~~~

The last joint Christmas card, 1998

ON WHAT WOULD HAVE BEEN Yehudi's eighty-fourth birthday, 22 April 2000, I had just completed the first draft of this biography. For days I had been plagued by an uneasy feeling that although I had sketched in the principal events in Yehudi's life with a fair degree of chronological exactitude and left the reader in no doubt as to his

myriad achievements both musical and beyond music, I had nevertheless failed to pin down what it was in his character and style that had
drawn me to him in the first place. As I recounted in my introduction,
I took on the role of biographer as early as 1996, when I embarked on
a 20-part radio series with Yehudi for Classic FM. I look back on
those interview sessions with great affection: I would call for him at
Chester Square in my car; he would be wearing his lovely green loden
coat, with the big artist's style floppy hat, his music scores under his
arm ready for a quick study before his next engagement. Once
installed at the radio station he occasionally had difficulty in catching
my question but his voice was always soft and amused as he spun out
his oft-told yet perennially fresh stories of Elgar, Bartók and all the
other great figures with whom he had worked down the years.

Yet something of Yehudi's nature remains elusive. Diana called him
a firefly and part of him was always on the move, defying analysis. In
1984 he confessed to Michael Binyon of *The Times* that he had never
stopped so long in one place as when he conducted *La clemenza di
Tito* in Bonn – a mere five-week assignment. When he told Malcolm
Singer about the fourteen composers who had honoured his eightieth
birthday in New York he commented that the works they wrote were
all rather solemn in character. 'Is that how people think of me?' he
asked wistfully. With a quizzical look that always promised mischief in
the air he went on: 'Don't they realize I'm really a gypsy?'

Perhaps I have paid insufficient attention to the gypsy's twinkling
charm, his perpetual good humour and enduring gentleness. His son
Jeremy might argue that the gentleness was only skin deep, that when
his father was playing Bartók an astonishing vein of aggressiveness
was unleashed. I worked with him on various projects over a span of
forty years and suspect that nobody could be familiar with every
aspect of his personality: 'firefly' is too lightweight a description to do
him full justice. I remember the almost ferocious energy he unleashed
when he conducted the 'Eroica' Symphony at the Barbican.

Was he at heart a spoilt child who always got his own way? His
mother would not have agreed that she spoiled him, quite the contrary,
and his father could point to the broadly liberal outlook he instilled in
the 1930s, inspired by *The Nation* and the *Manchester Guardian*. I
don't know enough about the workings of the mind to evaluate the
suggestion that throughout his life he retained the mentality of a child
prodigy, a proposition that *The Times* leader summed up thus when he

died: 'Menuhin was not one to take the plodding steps of reason, to reach his answers along a well-trodden path. Rather he took the leap of faith.'

On his eighty-fourth birthday, 22 April 2000, I experienced two examples of Yehudi Menuhin's vision, his leap of faith, which permit me to conclude that his achievements will not disappear like those of a burnt-out firefly. On television the BBC transmitted a documentary entitled *Menuhin's Children,* which described an experiment in teaching the violin to eight-year-olds on which Yehudi was personally engaged in his last months. Later the same evening, at the seaside town of Folkestone, the prizewinners in the Yehudi Menuhin International Competition for Young Violinists were taking part in a gala concert. Their judges, also present, included several of the world's most eminent teachers and performers, among them Zakhar Bron, Erick Friedman, Erich Gruenberg and Igor Oistrakh. The outright winner, a twenty-one-year-old Japanese girl named Akiko Ono, had attended Yehudi's school for five years. The second prize in the junior section went to a Russian girl, Alina Ibragimova, fourteen, who is also a pupil at the Menuhin School. Yehudi had worked with them both many times: at Folkestone one felt his spirit hovering happily over the gathering of twentyfour immensely talented young violinists with their families and teachers in support, all assembled in his name. As Alina played the Ysaÿe Sonata dedicated to George Enesco one sensed both the continuation of a very long tradition of violin teaching and the strength of Yehudi's dream: young musicians have come from all over the world to live and make music together at his school and they do so at the highest level of musical artistry.

To my mind the documentary shown that night on television brought home the meaning of what has been lost by Yehudi's death just as powerfully as the grandiose Memorial Service in Westminster Abbey the previous June. On that occasion Prince Charles and Baroness Thatcher had been among the principal mourners; a message was read from the Dalai Lama and addresses were given by eminent speakers representing Christian, Muslim and Hebrew faiths. The music included the slow movement of the Bach Double played by children from the School and a Schubert Mass sung by the Abbey Choir. In the BBC film, made at Stoughton Grange School in North Guildford, we watched Yehudi's other world: he was putting into practice his belief that all reasonably musical children can learn the violin, particularly if they spend a few months doing preliminary exercises with hoops and drumsticks, getting their bodies accustomed to the awkward patterns of motion involved in violin playing before they start on the instrument itself. He was patience personified at the school, quickly establishing a grandfatherly rapport with the twelve selected children and sweetly apologetic when he accidentally trod on a boy's fingers. The children wrote poems about his visits; their parents, who come from many walks of life, expressed themselves in awe. Then suddenly, in March 1999, he was gone and the children were shattered; for most, Yehudi was the first person they knew who had died. 'He was a loving and caring man,' one of them wrote; later they visited the grave at Stoke d'Abernon to say their own goodbyes.

Yehudi's last visit to Stoughton Grange in February had been the most exciting. The children were playing real violins for the first time and he improvised a little tune for them with which to practice bowing and changes of fingering. Rather than abandon the project after his death, work continued under the aegis of his assistant Rosemary Warren-Greene. (As Rosemary Furniss she had been one of the original pupils at the School in 1963; for the group photo she stood on the front step next to Yehudi.) Malcolm Singer worked up Yehudi's little tune into a short concert piece in which the beginners played in unison at the front of the concert platform (to an audience of admiring parents) while the Menuhin School Orchestra from nearby Stoke d'Abernon provided a rich contrapuntal background. Six months after Yehudi's death all twelve Guildford children were still involved in the project. Few of them demonstrated any special aptitude but for Yehudi that was not the point: his last words on the soundtrack were that all the participants would benefit from such an experiment in learning to conquer a craft: 'It will be useful throughout their lives. I don't think they'll ever regret it.'

Few who encountered Yehudi regretted the experience. He served music and his fellow human beings and will continue to be useful (to adopt his modest language) through the institutions he created and the music he brought to life.

'He who makes music in this life makes music in the next.'

from The Talmud, Sanhedrin 91b
inscription carved on YM's gravestone

Diana described Yehudi as Bhodisattva, the mythic figure through whom the
Gods transmit their messages to human beings.

References

Quotations are identified by the first words cited or by summary of topic. When two or more quotations from the same source follow each other with little intervening text, only the first quotation is used for identification. Sources clearly and fully identified in the text are not cited again here. Yehudi Menuhin is identified within the references as YM; the author as HB.

Abbreviations:

CFM	Classic FM interviews with YM, conducted by HB, 1996
FM	Menuhin, Diana, *Fiddler's Moll* (Weidenfeld and Nicolson, 1984)
GO	Menuhin, Diana, *A Glimpse of Olympus* (Methuen, 1996)
MA	Menuhin Archive
MFO	Rolfe, Lionel, *The Menuhins: A Family Odyssey* (San Francisco, 1978)
MS	Menuhin, Moshe, *The Menuhin Saga* (Sidgwick and Jackson, 1984)
UJ	Menuhin, Yehudi, *Unfinished Journey* (Methuen, rev. edn, 1996)
YM	Magidoff, Robert, *Yehudi Menuhin* (Robert Hale, rev. edn, 1973)

Part One: Childhood 1916–1930

1 ORIGINS

5 'The first time I saw her', *MS*, 46.

8 'Under the stairs', *Pittsburgh Jewish Criterion*, 29 May 1931.

11 'One evening', *MS*, 75; Rinder and Persinger, *San Francisco Examiner*, 28 November 1926.

12 'He listened to the music', *MS*, 81; 'Seated on my mother's knee', *UJ*, 18; 'a flat roof', ibid., 13.

13 'The Egg Basket': *UJ*, 14, has the Kavins living at Walnut Creek. This account is taken from *YM*, 21. Moshe says his brother Louis eventually returned from Palestine to live in Petaluma and died there of over-eating (*MS*, 261); 'As we drove along', *YM*, 21.

14 'Americans cannot pronounce', *MS*, 78.

2 THE PRODIGY

16 'I let my gaze', *UJ*, 20; 'An ordinary common Jew', *MS*, 23; Persinger's repertoire: San Francisco Symphony Orchestra Archive.

17 'Yehudi picked it up', *MS*, 80; 'I shall never forget', *UJ*, 21.

18 'When the Registrar', *MS*, 81; 'a regular American school', CFM.

19 'The first one we saw', ibid.; approach to Persinger, *UJ*, 27; 'After a brief period',

Anker's advertisement in a 1929 concert programme; 'His business in life', *UJ*, 25.

20 'Merely holding the violin', ibid., 25–6.

21 'BOY VIOLINIST WINS LAURELS', *San Francisco Examiner*, 10 November 1922.

22 'the latest child prodigy', *San Francisco Chronicle*, 11 February 1923.

23 'We lived there in a tent', *MS*, 82; 'My first challenge', *UJ*, 24; 'spreading a pall', *YM*, 31; Yehudi's parents objected strenuously to such hostile references to Marutha when Magidoff's 1955 biography appeared. One can only conjecture that the information came from Yehudi or his sisters.

24 'a reckless man', CFM; 'We settled down', *MS*, 85.

25 'Had I given him', *San Francisco Examiner*, Anker's letter, 12 February 1928; 'On the contrary', *MS*, 83; YM's hostility towards Anker: YM, interview with HB; Persinger tuning YM's violin: *UJ*, 28; Persinger's career: San Francisco Symphony Orchestra programme book celebrating Persinger's centenary, December 1986. *New Grove* wrongly states that he left the orchestra as early as 1917.

26 'allowed me to beget', *UJ*, 33; 'I shall never forget', *YM*, 36.

27 'I was told to play', CFM; 'We sat spellbound', *UJ*, 28.

28 'He could slide', CFM; 'a little Jewish boy', ibid.; 'a very feeling, sentimental', ibid.; 'kept saying things', ibid.; 'dim and dismal', *UJ*, 38.

29 'a very healthy routine', CFM; 'As far as I remember', *UJ*, 41.

30 'My ambition', Marutha Menuhin, interviewed by HB for Classic FM, 1996; 'If I happened', *UJ*, 28; 'Everything had to be taken', CFM.

31 'Concerts were necessary', *UJ*, 50; 'Hence there were no interviews', ibid.; 'Every year a huge', ibid., 49–50.

33 'Midway through the *Andante*', ibid., 34.

34 disputed value of bursary: ibid., 34; *MS*, 86; 30 March 1925: YM gives 25 March as the date but the newspaper reviews are all dated 31 March; 'Let your pen fly', *San Francisco Examiner*, 31 March 1925.

35 'Now do me a big favour?', *YM*, 53; 'Use your good mathematical head', ibid., 41.

36 'Miserably, Moshe took the belt', ibid.; 'In order to penetrate', CFM.

37 'He offered my parents', *UJ*, 58; 'It was to the many', *MS*, 87; 'I found her emotional', *YM*, 54.

38 'no man has had', *UJ*, 59

39 'terrifying canyon streets', ibid., 52.

41 'The boy played', unidentified press cutting photocopied in San Francisco and dated in error '20 May 1925'; the month should be November or December; 'Kreisler walks on', *UJ*, 54, 55; 'was all subtle emphasis', ibid.

42 'Stagehands and police', concert programme for YM's San Francisco concert, 4 March 1926.

43 'One listens to him', *San Francisco Chronicle*, 5 March 1926; 12 March 1926: surprisingly, neither YM nor Magidoff gave the date in their books.

44 'The auditorium presented', *San Francisco Chronicle*, 13 March 1926; 'Hertz lifted me', *UJ*, 50.

45 Enesco: the common, anglicized spelling of Enesco's surname is adopted here. In France, where he settled, the pronunciation of the final syllable in the Romanian 'Ene*scu*', which sounds like a part of the female anatomy, would have risked provoking vulgar laughter; 'Before a note was sounded', *UJ*, 57.

46 'His innocent childish eyes', *San Francisco Chronicle*, 17 November 1926.

47 'Playing with his eyes closed', *San Francisco Examiner*, 17 November 1926.

48 'Yehudi, Don't Forget', reproduced in *MS*, 97–8.

49 'Sweet master', ibid. (Moshe's version begins, 'Dear Master!')

3 KEEP YOUR EYES ON THE STARS

52 'Enesco sat down', *MS*, 100.

53 'Yehudi has as much to offer me', ibid., 262; 'I have heard your young son', undated letter, MA; 'brought out a high degree', *MS*, 103.

55 'To judge by the concerted gasp', ibid., 101–2.

56 'partners in the business', *MS*, 101; 'I moved at this point', *UJ*, 78; 'What I received', ibid., 70–73.

57 'more or less as a bird sings', ibid., 72; 'I taught him that real art', *San Francisco Examiner*, 28 January 1928.

58 'the smell of damp earth', *UJ*, 77.

61 'It may have been a resentment', *YM*, 76.

62 'asked Yehudi to look out', *MS*, 105.

63 'It astonished me', *UJ*, 82.

65 'Lightning split the sky', ibid., 85; 'My boy, always remember', *MS*, 106.

66 'This little girl', *New York Journal*, 16 November 1927; 'Never having possessed', *UJ*, 86; 'I would just as soon', *New York Evening Post*, 25 November 1927; 'Our children have never been to school', *New York Sun*, 18 November 1927.

67 'Yehudi played so gloriously', Fritz Busch, *Pages from a Musician's Life*, 175–6.

68 'but supported by Busch', *New York Times*, 26 November 1927.

69 'I lived within the bosom', *YM*, 100.

71 'At the end he was still', *New York Evening World*, 13 December 1927.

72 'I couldn't feel the weight', *UJ*, 89; 'My devoted parents', ibid., 91.

73 'Have you heard the story', quoted in *YM*, 93.

74 'The parents of little Yehudi', *Burlington* [Vermont] *Free Press*, 13 January 1928; 'nervous', *New York Times*, 8 January 1928; 'Yehudi did not disappoint', *San Francisco Examiner*, 23 January 1928.

77 'Our philosophy', *San Francisco Call*, 9 July 1928; 'He found harmonic analysis', *YM*, 102.

78 'rather grand and important', sleeve notes for the CD *Yehudi Menuhin: The Early Victor Recordings* (BID LAB 031).

79 'enthralled men who were leading orchestras', *San Francisco Call-Post*, 26 November 1928.

80 'reach the potential', *MS*, 113; box-office 'take': *San Francisco Call-Post*, 9 October 1928.

81 'California has loomed large', ibid., 6 December 1928; 'since he took a quarter-size violin', *San Francisco News*, 6 December 1928; 'Entirely self-possessed', *San Francisco Chronicle*, 6 December 1928.

82 'When they asked me to say goodnight', quoted in *MS*, 116–17; 'Chaplin cancelled all his work', ibid., 119.

84 the 'Bâle' Guarnarius, YM, *The Violin* (Flammarion, 1996), 95; 'constant stretching', *MS*, 120.

85 'Mr Mengelberg took the tempo', *New York Morning Telegraph*, 31 December 1928.

86 'is prevailingly more sensational', *New York Times*, 7 January 1929.

87 'Now you must choose', *UJ*, 95; 'It will be a privilege', *MS*, 123; 'ample and round', *UJ*, 95. For more information on YM's violins, see *YM* (114) and YM, *The Violin*, op. cit., *passim*.

88 'Rumors have reached us', *San Francisco Call-Post*, 9 July 1928; 'The President and the First Lady', *MS*, 124; 'His mother and I believed', *Cleveland News*, 31 January 1929.

89 'Persinger accompanied me', *UJ*, 94; 'Dutifully he fiddled his way', *New York World*, 25 February 1929.

90 'This will never happen', *YM*, 116.

91 'I was keyed up', ibid., 118.

92 'Seeing the anger', ibid., 119; 'Once in every century', *San Francisco Post Enquirer*, 4 December 1928.

4 SWISS FAMILY MENUHIN

96 'He was a child', quoted in *YM*, 123; abridged; 'I marvelled to find', *UJ*, 97–8.

97 Walter on Einstein: Bruno Walter, *Theme and Variations*, 257; YM meets Einstein: CFM.

98 'Now what, Yehudi?', *Berkeley Gazette*, n.d. [presumably April 1929]; YM and *Bar Mitzvah*: YM in conversation with HB, February 1999.

99 'played with electric trains', *MS*, 129; 'to jump in and play it', *UJ*, 99; 'easier to admire', ibid.

100 'excessively coherent', ibid., 100.

101 'an almost silent', ibid., 101; 'a dear good Italian', ibid., 102.

102 'You come to each lesson', CFM; 'As the years go by', *YM*, 138; 'combined scholar-ship with passion', *UJ*, 100.

103 'Yehudi will learn', *MS*, 132.

104 'so that I can accompany you', *YM*, 132; 'a still greater virtuoso', Joseph Brainin quoted in a 1930 Menuhin press release, MA.

105 'If we give in', *MS*, 137.

106 'To Ivor Newton', Ivor Newton, *At the Piano*, 185; 'a mad surge', *Musical Courier*, 30 November 1929; 'went beyond the demands', *UJ*, 122; RCA Victor history: see Roland Gelatt, *The Fabulous Phonograph*.

107 'It seemed to be the grandest thing', sleeve notes for the CD *Yehudi Menuhin: The Early HMV Recordings* (BID LAB 032); 'Fugues by Bach', *New York World Record*, 4 January 1930; 'The former Menuhin', Leonard Liebling, *New York American*, 4 January 1930; YM meets Toscanini: *Los Angeles Times*, 9 March 1930.

108 'A person is either', *YM*, 136; 'the afternoon hour', YM, 'Open Letter', *The Baton*, January 1930.

109 'Every Golus Jew is attracted', *Every Friday*, 17 January 1930; 'To hear Yehudi play', *Detroit News*, 21 January 1930.

110 'Dear friend Mr Hertz', SFSO Archive; 'I looked forward', *UJ*, 116.

111 'It was not a bootlegger's trunk', *San Francisco Examiner*, 27 July 1930; 'We beat the train', *Santa Monica Outlook*, 27 March 1931.

112 'The memory of the hours', *MS*, 139; 'Curiously enough', *UJ*, 118.

114 'I never laughed before', *The Oregonian*, 1 May 1931; 'She was the most wholesome person', quoted in *YM*, 139.

115 'due reflection', *Jewish Journal*, San Francisco, 22 July 1931.

Part Two: Youth 1931–1941

5 JEUNESSE DORÉE

119 'As a family', *UJ*, 106; 'She never hesitated', ibid., 107.

120 'a superb game', ibid., 111.

121 'We carved out', ibid., 108; 'He's got five tutors', *San Francisco Chronicle*, 8 April 1932; 'exciting, cultivated', *UJ*, 110; 'In the Menuhin family', *MS*, 1146; 'silently cherished', *UJ*, 109.

122 'I have never had enough', ibid., 113; 'On the way to the hospital', *New York*

Herald, 23 September 1931; 'YEHUDI UNDER KNIFE ABROAD', *San Francisco Call Bulletin*, 22 September 1931.

123 'with most reverent care', *The Times*, 24 November 1931; YM's concert dress: *New York Times*, 24 November 1931; 'I allow him to play', *Daily Mail*, 21 November 1931.

124 'the two small, fair-haired sisters', *News Chronicle*, 2 December 1931; 'Miracle!', *MS*, 145.

125 'At one moment', Jerrold Northrop Moore, *A Voice in Time*, 188; 'It breaks my heart', letter, dated 1 February 1932, to Chairman, Musicians Emergency Aid Committee; 'Menuhin has graduated', *New York Times*, 24 January 1932.

126 'not in keeping', *Toronto Mail*, 8 February 1932; 'Great music was spoiled', *Atlanta Journal*, 28 March 1932; 'nothing short of', *Minneapolis Star*, 4 March 1932; 'in one upstroke', *St Louis Post Dispatch*, 3 March 1932; 'crowd huge', *Daily Star*, Toronto, 9 February 1932; 'the transcendent genius', *Pittsburgh Press*, 27 February 1932.

127 'Grasping the throttle', *St Louis Despatch*, 10 February 1932; 'a slightly crackly baritone', *San Francisco Chronicle*, 15 April 1932; 'elderly satyr', *San Francisco Eye*, 15 July 1932.

128 'Menuhin seemed to gain', *New York Times*, 19 February 1932; 'He followed Yehudi', *MS*, 146; 'She was by then married', *UJ*, 131.

129 'We are having an ideal crossing', *YM*, 155; 'an atmosphere of activity', *Daily Telegraph*, 18 November 1932; 'They walked the deck', CFM.

130 'There was no effort', *Seattle Post Intelligence*, 25 October 1937; 'as a youthful and pliant performer', quoted in Jerrold Northrop Moore, *Elgar on Record*, 194–5.

131 'Father, this Concerto', *New York Herald Tribune*, 12 November 1932; 'Despite the rich orchestration', CFM, slightly edited.

132 'He was sure', *UJ*, 125; 'arose with great excitement', *MS*, 148; 'I can add nothing', Fred Gaisberg, *Music on Record*; 'We played right through', Ivor Newton, *At the Piano*, 186–7.

133 'All was ease', *UJ*, 126; 'Essentially a music of syllable', ibid., 112; 'My husband has a long career', *MS*, 144.

134 'English music for once', *Morning Post*, 21 November 1932; 'Each thought the cheers', *New York Times*, 21 November 1932; 'robbed of its English reserve', *Sydney Herald*, 26 April 1940; 'This is how I heard', ibid.

135 'I shd. be', quoted in Gaisberg, op. cit.; 'overcome by the "majesty"', ibid.; 'We sat down', *MS*, 149; 'I fear my appearance', *MS*, 148–9.

136 'His human frailty', *Birmingham Mail*, 13 December 1932; 'the head of a man', *Liverpool Post*, 15 December 1932; Toscanini backstage: *The Concert Bulletin*, vol. XXII, May 1933.

137 'We simply must play', ibid.; 'IT MUST BE DONE!!!', *MS*, 150.

138 'Your career is going to be', ibid., 152; 'I played in Germany', *Oakland Post Enquirer*, 27 April 1933; 'everyone has a job', *New Orleans Item*, 26 March 1933.

139 'The young virtuoso's face', *San Francisco Call*, 26 March 1933.

140 'The way that boy plays', Eric Fenby, *Delius As I Knew Him*, 125; 'One felt', Jerrold Northrop Moore, *A Voice in Time*, 197.

141 'for imposing', *Daily Mail*, 1 June 1933.

6 THE WORLD TOUR

143 'gorgeous . . . a wonderful inspiration', sleevenotes for the CD *Menuhin Plays French Masterpieces* (Biddulph).

144 'just to try out', *MS*, 154; 'small but so elegant', CFM; 'He couldn't wait', ibid.; Alpine recital: collated from CFM; *MS*, 154–5, and *Daily Telegraph*, 11 September 1933.

145 'with great admiration', CFM; Candide Prize: *Daily Telegraph*, 24 May 1934.

146 'Someone must make', letter quoted in *MS*, 157; Furtwängler correspondence: ibid.; translation amended by HB.

147 'I refused to play', *Toronto Star*, 31 January 1934.

148 'Dearest Yehudi', letter quoted in the *Daily Express*, 11 December 1933; 'Toscanini sang', *New York Journal*, 5 January 1934.

149 'a half-hour to shave off', *Cincinnati Times Star*, 25 January 1934; 'aeronautics, girls', *Washington Post*.

150 'we musicians', *New York Times*, 5 January 1934; 'unilaterally opposed', *Washington Star*, 4 March 1934; 'In response to an urgent plea', *MS*, 161.

151 'The conductor excused himself', ibid., 160–61; 'We had reached', *UJ*, 128; 'If the maestro', *YM*, 176.

152 'Taught from childhood', ibid., 175; 'Violin playing of the first order', *New York Sun*, 19 January 1934; 'a great concert', *New York Times*, 19 January 1934; 'the greatest violin and orchestra', *Washington Star*, 14 February 1934; 'the violin of the century', *Los Angeles Illustrated Daily News*, 12 April 1934; 'an electrifying', *Philadelphia Inquirer*, 10 March 1934; 'My beloved and adored', letter quoted in *MS*, 162.

153 Toronto critic: *Toronto Globe*, 31 January 1934; 'This is Bach', *YM*, 160–61; the girl's name was Tineke de Werff.

154 tribute to Willa Cather: *UJ*, 131–4; 'I am always up in arms', *Musical America*, 4 April 1934.

155 'small enough', *UJ*, 134.

156 'What still remains', *San Francisco Examiner*, 9 April 1934; 'a redwood estate', *New York Times*, 18 July 1934.

157 'a grand work', sleevenotes for Biddulph CD, LAB 067; 'We were really one person', *YM*, 147; practising in the dark: *New York World Telegraph*, 5 December 1934; 'sometimes pounded', *Minneapolis Register*, 29 December 1934.

158 'two young people', *New York Times*, 19 December 1934; 'but not a quantity one', *New York World Telegraph*, 5 December 1934; 'I was very ashamed', *YM*, 149; 'the devil in the family', *New York World Telegraph*, 5 December 1934.

159 'It will offer', *Pittsburgh Press*, 14 February 1935; 'mechanical civilization', *Buffalo Evening News*, 14 January 1935.

160 'talking, thinking, dreaming', *UJ*, 137; 'a new version', *MS*, 166; $250,000 deal: *Boston Sunday Globe*, 20 January 1935; 'Between Yehudi's art', *MS*, 166.

161 'Down under Yehudi', quoted in *MS*, 166; 'The symphony orchestra', *Melbourne Herald*, 14 June 1935; 'The melancholy thinness', *Melbourne Herald*, 23 August 1935; 'But this is monstrous', ibid.

162 'intellectual and sympathetic', ibid.; 'fresh and young', CFM; 'Subscribers to the first', *MS*, 167; 'You don't ever want', *Melbourne Herald*, 21 August 1935.

163 'for her devotion', *The Advertiser*, Adelaide; 'building a seven-room guest house', *Watsonville Register*, California, 5 March 1936; 'Our children began to raid', *MS*, 167; 'I don't think', *Johannesburg Sunday Express*, 29 September 1935.

164 'Midway through our travels', *UJ*, 139; 'Discerning a form', ibid., 144; 'The Beethoven Violin Concerto', *Johannesburg Sunday Express*, 29 September 1935.

165 'The tour has been', *MS*, 168.

166 'My very dear father!', ibid., 170.

167 'Neither child nor man', *New York Times*, 23 February 1935; 'had taken on', *New York World Telegram*, 24 March 1935.

168 'listened to it', *UJ*, 145.

169 'We do not intend', *New York World Telegram*, 24 March 1936; '29 March 1936', quoted in *YM*.

170 'Menuhin whipped his magic horsehair', *Variety*, 1 April 1936; 'Get the violin', *New York World Telegram*, 28 March 1936; 'Whatever freedom', *YM*, 171; 'monstrosity', *Musical America*, 10 May 1936; 'its nightly scare', *San Francisco Examiner*, 16 April 1936; car blow-out: ibid.

171 'I'll raise fruit', *Watsonville Register*, California, 5 March 1936.

7 ESCAPE FROM PARADISE

173 'no trees or flowers', *UJ*, 146; security measures: *Watsonville Register*, California, 6 March 1936; 'living in a glass house', *Musical America*, 10 May 1936; 'I want you to feel', *MS*, 171.

174 'I buried on that hill', ibid., 172; 'a little, hot, dusty', *UJ*, 145; 'with flowerbeds', ibid, 146; 'happy and carefree', ibid.; $30,000, *MFO*, 179.

175 'I had a sense of style', ibid.; 'Today, Yehudi has made', quoted in *YM*, 175; 'very beautiful', ibid.

176 Cyrano de Bergerac: Yaltah Menuhin, interviewed by HB, 1999; 'crowned by four or five', *UJ*, 149; 'There were hours', *MS*, 173; 'Many were the boys and girls', ibid.; 'I hope he will marry early', *Indianapolis Star*, 4 October 1936; 'We'll take good care', *MS*, 173.

177 'twice as hard', *New Yorker*, 29 January 1938; 'I rather think', quoted in *UJ*, 148; 'would take long walks', *MFO*, 181.

178 'The apotheosis', *Utica Observer Dispatch*, 1 February 1937; 'My first wish', *Erie Dispatch*, 31 January 1937; 'proud of the fact', *Columbus Citizen*, 25 February 1937.

179 Ford concert: *MS*, 174

180 Menuhin children and marriage: *San Francisco Chronicle*, 11 August 1937, and *San Francisco News*, 5 July 1937; 'We call ourselves', *Seattle Post Intelligence*, 25 October 1937.

181 'the work is so great and so beautiful', *San Francisco Chronicle*, 11 August 1937.

182 'a thunderbolt', *San Francisco Call Bulletin*, 11 September 1937; 'Reich forces violinist', *Minneapolis Journal*, 24 September 1937; 'He deliberately streamlined', *Brooklyn Eagle*, 28 November 1937; Goebbels: UP report, 26 November 1937; 'I ask no special rights', *Time*, 23 August 1937.

183 'shocking decision', *Minneapolis Journal*, 24 September 1937; 'Because I am non-Aryan', *Salt Lake Telegram*, 1 October 1937; 'a very weak composition', *New York Times*, 7 December 1937; 'Joachim was protecting', *Boston Transcript*, 1 December 1937.

184 'a tall, straight', *Musical America*, 10 October 1937; 'changes every stitch', *Omaha Morning World-Herald*, 13 November 1937; 'a breath-taking splash', Alexander Fried, *San Francisco Examiner*, 30 September 1937; 'perhaps a finer craftsman', Alfred Frankenstein, *San Francisco Chronicle*, 4 October 1937; 'Yehudi returned', *Washington Herald*, 30 January 1938; 'The time will come', *Los Angeles Times*, 17 October 1937.

185 'a hypnotic effect', *New York Times*, 9 February 1938; Schumann Concerto: *New Orleans Times Picayune*, 12 December 1937; 'Compulsory education', *Cincinnati Post*, 28 December 1937; 'Marriage is not always fatal', *Philadelphia Evening Public Ledger*, 21 January 1938.

186 'Really we can't', *Rochester Democrat Chronicle*, 7 January 1938; 'I have plenty', ibid.; 'I have never written', *Aberdonian*, 24 February 1938; 'Technical difficulties', *Daily Telegraph*, 7 March 1938.

187 'Scotland Yard detectives', *The Times*, 21 March 1938; 'ineffably sweet', *The Sunday Times*, 27 March 1938.

188 'I instantly sensed', *MS*, 182; 'fresh and young', CFM; 'a little, shall we say', ibid.

189 'I knew and my sister knew', ibid.; Nola's boyfriend Ron: letter, undated, to Nola from Shirley Nicholas, née Alcock, George's second wife, and conversation with Mrs Gwynneth Drage, a friend of Nola Nicholas, 31 March 2000; 'Nola is my ideal girl', *Daily Sketch*, 11 May 1938.

190 Nola as violinist: letter from Robert Masters, whose wife Noel played flute in the orchestra; Nola's piano examination: letter, with envelope marked '1935/36?', from Nola to Shirley Nicholas; 'Dear Dad': letter, dated 12 May 1938, from YM to George Nicholas.

192 Pulvermacher family: *MFO*, 191; acceptability of Nola's non-Jewishness: CFM; 'Yehudi has never been Orthodox', *The Age*, 12 May 1938.

193 'produced a portable gramophone', *Daily Sketch*, 12 May 1938; 'a week of', letter, dated 15 July 1938, from Hephzibah Menuhin to Bruno Zirato; 'there is no more romantic background', *MS*, 138; 'marvelled at the shy youth', *YM*, 191; 'disengaged himself', ibid., 213.

194 'one of the prettiest', *Sydney Morning Herald*; 'A Jew who brands', *MS*, 187.

195 'an ice-blue two-piece ensemble', UP report, 26 May 1938; 'but only a violinist', *Cleveland Plain Dealer*, 27 May 1938.

8 MIDSUMMER MARRIAGES

198 Marutha and Nola on the *Ile de France*: anecdotes taken from *YM*, 193–4; 'dark, handsome', *Washington News*, DC, 7 June 1938; 'completely immature', *MS*, 183; 'Why should we', *New York Evening Journal*, 7 June 1938.

199 'Only I was to blame', *UJ*, 152; 'The girl is lovely', *San Francisco News*, 23 June 1938; 'Yehudi's problem', ibid.; 'clasping each other's hands', *San Francisco Call Bulletin*, 22 June 1938.

200 'As a good wife', letter quoted in *YM*, 194–5, and widely reproduced elsewhere; Moshe gave it to the press.

201 'The home movies show',Tony Palmer, *A Family Portrait* (Faber and Faber, 1991), 43; 'plagued', *YM*, 196; 'a remarkable person', *UJ*, 152; 'How little I understood', ibid., 152–3; 'temperamental but marvellous', interview with Nola, *Evening Standard*, 3 March 1939.

202 'Yehudi cannot be persuaded', press release, 2 November 1938; 'I feel that the right', press release, MA.

203 'a dress-collar union', *Time*, 28 November 1938; 'Young Mr Menuhin', agency report, quoted in the *Patriot Ledger*, Quincy, Massachusetts, 1 November 1938; 'I will give up', *Los Angeles Examiner*, 3 November 1938; 'breaking faith', *Los Angeles Herald Express*, 3 November 1938.

204 'first conflict with life's brutalities', *Time*, 28 November 1938; 'They know that their commissions', *Washington Sunday Herald Times*, 6 March 1938; 'sickeningly trashy', *Los Angeles Morning News*, 17 November 1938; 'the same inwardly fully-balanced young artist', *Pasadena Star News*, 19 November 1938; 'I'm a million miles away', *Milwaukee Journal*, 16 January 1939; 'Barbarism may engulf', *Philadelphia Record*, 24 February 1939.

205 'It was the only criminal thing', *Columbus Citizen*, 2 January 1939; 'Yaltah married the wrong man', *Daily Mail*, 2 March 1939; 'wiser and sadder', *Manchester Evening News*, 13 March 1939.

206 'Do not for one single', *MS*, 194–5; 'As regards Nola', letter, undated [March 1939], from YM to George Nicholas; 'I have had to give up', *Evening Standard*, 3 March 1939.

207 'for further research', *Manchester Guardian*, 13 March 1939; 'exactly the same dimensions', *Portland Oregonian*, 31 October 1939; dating of Guarnerius: ibid.; provenance of the Guarnerius, HB's interview with the violin dealer Peter Biddulph, 16 November 1999.

208 'a tall, elegant baby carriage', *UJ*, 153; 'Our Nola is very well', letter, 29 August 1939, from YM to George Nicholas.

209 'I asked the doctor', *MS*, 195.

210 'Heavy-set, tousle-haired', *Fargo, N.D., Morning Forum*, 19 November 1939; 'Moshe failed to sense', *YM*, 198.

213 'A blind man', *Melbourne Herald*, 16 May 1940.

214 'totally inadequate education', quoted in *Hephzibah*, documentary film, directed and produced by Curtis Levy, 1998; 'made no objection', *UJ*, 154.

215 naming of Krov: ibid.; draft tribunal: Los Gatos City Hall, 17 October 1941.

216 'My intentions are', *San Jose Mercury Herald*, 17 January 1941; 'I don't see how', *Fort Wayne Journal-Gazette*, 17 January 1941; 'lacked much of the fire', *San Francisco Chronicle*, 24 April 1941; 'Ten consecutive', *MS*, 198; 'Moi aussi', *CFM*; 'South Americans resent', *Philadelphia Evening Public Ledger*, 15 July 1941.

217 'They have symphony concerts', letter, headed 'Hampshire House', dated 17 July 1941, from Nola to Shirley Nicholas; 'I gave them to Abba', letter, dated 13 August 1941, from Nola to Shirley Nicholas.

219 'The realization of a need', *Los Angeles News*, 13 August 1941; 'glassed-in play-room', *UJ*, 155.

Part Three: Coming of Age 1941–1956

9 MENUHIN AT WAR

224 'a dreary Christmas', *San José Mercury News*, 29 December 1946; 'Through music', quoted in *YM*, 223.

225 'the most cultivated', press release, 16 January 1942, MA; 'The war has brought', letter, dated 23 May 1942, from YM to George Nicholas.

226 AFM dispute: *UJ*, 163. In *MS*,194, Moshe went into the AFM's fight with AGMA in great detail. He described his son's branch as the 'San Francisco Local No. 6'; a newspaper specified Santa Clara County; Yehudi remembered it simply as the 'San Francisco branch'. Yehudi also wrote that a few days later he was making a recording with Adolph Baller until the last moment before an AFM strike call. However the archive suggests that the first recording he made with Baller was not until December 1944; Chicago concert: letter, undated [August 1942], from Nola to George Nicholas.

227 'I do not like seeing him go', letter, dated 10 November 1942, from Nola to George Nicholas; 'a minor affair', *CFM*.

228 'Every day I played', ibid.; *Stage Door Canteen*: Fox Movietone; director: Frank Borzage; producer: Sol Lesser. See *Variety*, 4 February 1943. The soundtrack was broadcast on 2 March 1943 – unless YM made a separate 'live' appearance on that date; the newspaper reports are unclear. YM did not arrive in the UK until 15 March 1943, so he could have done both dates; 'half frozen', *FM*, 29.

229 Wieniawski recording, letter, dated 13 August 1940, from YM to Moshe; 'fitted up a warm jacket', *Huddersfield Daily Examiner*, n.d.

230 reading through new scores, CFM; Dorati's chamber-music evening: *UJ*, 168; Antal Dorati, *Notes of Seven Decades*, 171; 'No other composer', BBC broadcast, 4 November 1945; reprinted in the *Listener*.

231 'He had already drawn up', CFM, edited; 'the necessary changes', Dorati, op. cit., 58; 'He played . . . Bach's', Stevens, *The Life and Music of Béla Bartók*, 99.

232 'I regret', YM and Curtis Davis, *The Music of Man*, 308; 'a test for ears', *New York Times*, 27 November 1944; 'the thrill of knowing Bartók', YM and Davis, *The Music of Man*, 308.

233 'hastening back', *UJ*, 161; 'It was quite an interesting thing', letter included in an undated press release prepared by Moshe, MA.

234 'I was in the steam room', *Pasadena Star News*, California, 14 April 1944; at the end of June: *YM*, 208, states that Menuhin was in England at the time of the D-Day invasion on 6 June 1944 and was on the heels of the American and British forces invading Europe. This is incorrect. YM did not fly to Europe until September. Magidoff also gives 1943 instead of 1944 for Menuhin's Aleutians tour.

235 'The most terrifying audience', CFM; 'Often I would take part', YM, 205; seaweed gathering: ibid., 160.

236 'an entirely Orphic', *Los Angeles Herald Express*, 13 July 1944; 'The months of September and October', draft press release, 26 June 1944, MA; 'They would not allow me', CFM; 'I am very fond', *Orkney Blast*, 15 September 1944.

238 'Between danger zones', *UJ*, 181; 'Thus to carry out', draft press release, 26 June 1944.

239 conditions at the Ritz: *New York Times*, 13 October 1944; Krauss and Karajan in occupied Paris: Hervé Le Boterf, *La Vie parisienne sous l'occupation* (Paris, Editions France-Empire, 1997); 'Allegro molto appassionato!', *YM*, 210.

240 'We had a refresher', Adrian Boult, *Blowing My Own Trumpet*, 121; recital with Landowska: the entire concert was privately recorded and is now available on a transfer to CD.

241 a musical friend of theirs: Diana Menuhin's grandmother, Mrs Harcourt's mother, was a friend of Mrs Koshland, the benefactor (and friend of the Menuhins) who had commissioned Messrs Dennison and Ingerson to design the Ark for her San Francisco synagogue.

242 'We all turned up', Classic FM interview with Diana; 'the most beautiful woman', *UJ*, 176; 'When he told me that', Classic FM interview with Diana; 'Listened to Menuhin', *GO*, 256; broadcast performances: *Radio Times*, 8 October 1944.

243 'Last year, because he stayed', draft press release, 17 October 1944; 'I'd come back from Europe', CFM.

244 'When I first told her', ibid., 39.

10 THE UNEASY PEACE

247 'not specifically American', CFM; 'Against the huge silken drop', Leroy V. Brant, *San Jose Mercury Herald*, 6 May 1945.

248 'when the *Moses* Variations', Gerald Moore, *Am I Too Loud?*, 135.

249 'perhaps my one compromise', sleeve notes for the CD, *Yehudi Menuhin: A Portrait* (Biddulph CD 80 sound track reminiscence 22); 'I chose not to tell him', *GO*, 274; Marie Rambert: ibid., 142.

250 'to bring bliss', ibid., 301.

251 'We stayed the night', Donald Mitchell and Philip Reed (eds.), *Letters from a Life*,

1272; 'the sounds and cries', Tony Palmer, *A Family Portrait* (Faber and Faber, 1991); 'On Friday Menuhin', Mitchell and Reed, op. cit., 1273.

252   'who were difficult to rouse', ibid., 1274; 'in a highly wrought emotional mood', *Jewish Chronicle*, 28 April 1950; shapeless garments: WDR interview, 1995.

253   'Yehudi was nice', Mitchell and Reed, op. cit., 1272; 'Too long has our government', *YM*, 249; Mendelssohn broadcast: Jack Bornoff, interviews with HB, April 2000.

254   'I received a phone call', CFM; 'For several years', reprinted in the *Listener*, 8 November 1945.

255   Nola's visit to Australia with Tony Williams: Zamira Benthall, interview with HB; 'I told him never to use', *GO*, 275; 'Again we found', *FM*, 32.

256   Enforced landing at Karlsbad, information contained in a letter, dated 24 February 1999, from YM to the pilot's son, Mr Patrick Speller, MA; Lidice wreath-laying: CFM and information from the Czech Philharmonic supplied by Mrs Inka Vostresova; Karlsbad stopover, *UJ*, 188.

257   'The Russian soldiers', CFM.

258   'I said I don't want', ibid., 23; 'unassertive and shy', *UJ*, 195; 'shining like a lone good deed', ibid., 376; 'Some of us', Dmitry Paperno, *Notes of a Moscow Pianist*, 54; 'It was not just fantastic playing', 'A Night to Remember', *Sunday Telegraph*, 24 January 1993.

259   Bach Double Concerto: *Newsweek*, 9 December 1945; aerial concert: interview in *San Antonio Light*, 7 January 1946.

260   Furtwängler's infatuation with Griselda: *GO*, 135.

261   'At the very moment', *New York Times*, 6 December 1945; Hitler in Bayreuth: Friedelind Wagner, interviewed in the *New York Times*, 22 February 1946.

262   'a victim of envious', quoted in Ardoin, *The Furtwängler Record*, source not provided. The comment possibly dates from 1949 when Furtwängler was prevented from accepting the conductorship of the Chicago Symphony Orchestra.

263   'a rather flaccid violinist', *Minneapolis Star Journal*, 9 February 1946; 'something essentially cold', *Minneapolis Daily Times*, 9 February 1946; 'silken smoothness', *St Paul Pioneer Press*, 21 February 1946; 'He is not a great violinist', Chicago newspaper, 21 February 1946; 'Other violinists', *San Francisco Commercial News* and *Chronicle* reviews dated 28 March 1946.

264   'I heard none of that', *World-Telegram*, 24 January 1946; 'the most authoritative', *New York Times*, 18 October 1946.

265   conducting lessons with Dorati: *Variety*, 30 January 1946; 'a well-prepared reading', *Dallas News*, 7 April 1946.

267   'astute knowledge', *GO*, 287; marital reconciliation: ibid.; 'The meeting was cordial', letter, postmarked 17 April 1946, from Nola to Shirley Nicholas.

268   'to try to persuade', Zamira Benthall, interview with HB; 'Yehudi may not be', letters, April 1946, from Louis Kentner to Griselda Gould.

269   'It was an Enesco festival', *UJ*, 222.

270   'dense with Jews', ibid., 223; 'Yehudi is nervous', letter, n.d., from Nola to Shirley Nicholas.

271   'a very sweet', CFM; 'I love the early', ibid., edited for clarity.

272   'very ill', *GO*, 287.

273   'He knew there was nothing', ibid., 290; 'My love is of a birth', quoted in *Fiddler's Moll*, 33; 'left a good deal to be desired', *New York Journal American*, 18 October 1946; 'How helpless', *UJ*, 198; 'sick of holding out', letter, n.d., from Nola to Shirley Nicholas.

274   'We would go for walks', *GO*, 290; 'sick of the hassle', Zamira Benthall, interview

with HB; 'I will spend some time', *Denver Post*, 7 October 1946.

275 'purely philosophical', *MS*, 204; 'I couldn't bring myself', CFM; 'Lindsay says', letter, dated 27 January 1947, from Nola to Shirley Nicholas.

276 'His whiskers', *New York Sun*, 7 March 1947.

277 'Under the gaiety', Lewis, *Willa Cather Living – a personal record* (Knopf, 1953), 174; quoted in *YM*; 'You are asking me', *GO*, 298.

278 signing the bill at Pruniers: *GO*, 308; Moshe on Nola's extravagance, CFM; 'She could not leave', *GO*, 306; 'Zamira and Krov are already', letter, dated 17 June 1947, from Nola to George and Shirley Nicholas.

280 'majestic in scope', Ardoin, op. cit., 151; 'a quite wonderful communion', CFM; 'Yehudi said', Classic FM interview with Diana.

281 'If Yehudi doesn't marry', unpublished postcard, William Walton to Griselda Kentner; 'I wasn't even making', CFM.

282 'There were ovations', MA.

283 'Help, give, serve', draft press release, 30 October 1947, MA; 'The rubble', *GO*, 321; 'To play the greatest', *UJ*, 234.

284 'I came down from the clouds', ibid., 234; 'When I read', quoted in *YM*, 247.

285 'D'ya know', *GO*, 324; 'Boos, hisses', *UJ*, 235; Deuppel Centre speech: conflated from *UJ*, 235, and *MS*, 247.

286 'If Menuhin offered us', *Time*, 27 October 1947; 'Lying hideously', *GO*, 326.

287 'the most important event', *Kristeligt Dagblad*, 13 October 1947; 'cleaning away', *GO*, 327; 'I had not the smallest doubt', *UJ*, 203.

288 Yehudi's and Diana's wedding, *FM*, 2–3; 34.

11 LIFE WITH DIANA

291 'in his most Sitwellian', *FM*, 3; 'avoided sex': conversation with HB.

292 'as bare as a set', *FM*, 4–5.

294 'Picture was made', *Variety*, 20 October 1948; documentary film: produced by the Berlin company, Bernd Bauer Verlag; Menuhin was interviewed by HB (in Warsaw, where he was working with the Sinfonia Varsovia).

295 'He has not yet learned', memo by Moshe Menuhin, undated [presumably 1948], MA; 'upon which the standing player', *FM*, 98.

296 'not only in technique', 'T.H.' (?Trevor Harvey), *Gramophone*, May 1949.

297 'dull and fuzzy, *Time*, 14 April 1948; 'His bowing was often rough', *Daily Variety*, 2 April 1948; 'strictly for longhairs', *Variety*, 7 April 1948.

299 *Tulag na Bunso: Manila Chronicle*, 22 November 1948; 'Did you have to add', *FM*, 44–5.

300 'I have never encountered', quoted in Ardoin, *The Furtwängler Record*, 60; 'The protest of American artists', telegram, dated 19 January 1949, from Wilhelm Furtwängler, Chicago Symphony Orchestra Archive; 'and there is also Artur Rubinstein', quoted in Ardoin, op. cit., 61.

301 'to the extent of provoking, *UJ*, 237; 'the route led steeply downhill', ibid., 247.

302 'At eleven thousand feet', *FM*, 31; 'their mindless habit', *UJ*, 249; 'A particularly musically minded insect', *FM*, 48–9.

303 'I was rapidly becoming', ibid., 48; 'spacious, uncomplicated', Ardoin, op. cit., 255.

304 'We are delighted', unpublished letter, dated 7 February 1950, from William Walton to Griselda Kentner; £1000 fee: letter, undated [autumn 1948]; 'strained and rough', *Time and Tide*, 11 February 1950.

305 'With firm mastery', *New Statesman*, 11 February 1950; 'one of its creator's greatest

works', Kennedy, *Portrait of Walton*, 144; 'through our porthole', *FM*, 55.

306 Moshe's potential political role: *MFO*, 201.

308 'Across the path', *The Star*, Johannesburg, 17 February 1950; 'They stood and chanted', *Rand Daily Mail*, 17 February 1950; 'I suggested', *UJ*, 254.

309 'As we drove out', *Harpers Magazine*, November 1957, quoted in *MS*, 214; 'one of the most affecting', *UJ*, 253–4.

310 'I get a greater intensity', *New York Post*, 12 April 1950; 'We shall have to sue you', *UJ*, 255.

311 'He got so excited', quoted in *MS*, 215; 'I can't wait', *FM*, 59.

312 Fiumicino airport anecdote: *MS*, 215.

313 Begin's threat: *FM*, 60, where the telegram is quoted verbatim; 'conjured away', *UJ*, 237; 'It was the first time', *MFO*, 210; professions of Israeli relations: *UJ*, 238.

314 'a meeting of heritage', YM in interview with R. da Costa, *Haaretz*, 7 April 1950; 'I was born a Jew', UP, 12 April 1950; 'I may have inadvertently', *UJ*, 237; $14 ticket price: UP (United Press) report, 13 April 1950.

315 'After a hard day in the fields', *Flair* magazine, January 1951; 'Israel is the most tolerant country', *Jewish Chronicle*, 5 May 1950; 'The people everywhere are working', *San José Mail-News*, May 1950.

316 'would lose his essential characteristics', *FM*, 61–2; 'that the opportunities for action', *UJ*, 239.

317 sympathetic artistry: 'sympathischen Kunstlertums', *Wiener Tageszeitung*, 8 June 1950; 'no one who has not been separated', *FM*, 62; 'picnics in the woods', *FM*, 63.

318 'like some buckle-kneed Rosinante', *FM*, 57; 'a bright little Jewish boy', 1951 press release from YM's publicist at the time, Muriel Francis, MA.

319 'the performer coming back onstage', *UJ*, 342; 'still calculated to reduce', *UJ*, 342; 'He uses dry rice', *Melbourne Sun*, 19 June 1951; 'Always he gives his money', ibid.

320 'We've laughed so much', *NZ Traveller*, 15 August 1951; 'finding much pleasure', *UJ*, 258.

321 'there is no trace of unsteadiness', sleeve notes for the two-CD set *Menuhin in Japan* (BID LAB 162/163).

322 'Nothing is done without purpose', *San Francisco Chronicle*, 7 October 1951; 'bolts of exquisite ancient brocade', *FM*, 70.

12 DISCOVERY OF INDIA

324 'Both are in the minor', preface, Mendelssohn, Violin Concerto in D minor (Peters Edition, 1952); 'lively jesting finale', *New York Times*, 5 February 1952.

325 'utterly delightful', *New York Sun*, 7 February 1952; 'I have fulfilled', *Times of India*, 22 February 1952.

326 Mehta family: Bookspan and Yockey, *Zubin: The Zubin Mehta Story*, 11; 'I thought I was going to meet', quoted verbatim in *FM*, 76, and, in a slightly different wording, by YM in *UJ*, 266.

327 'He took off his Gandhi cap', *FM*, 75.

328 'friend, philosopher and guide', Saaed Jaffrey, *Saaed: An Actor's Journey* (Constable 1998), 42; 'He seemed to be so overwhelmed', BBC Radio 3 interview, April 1999; 'the gentleness of his manner', *FM*, 76.

329 'The raga reflects', introductory essay for the four-CD box set, *Shankar Anthology* (Angel Records, 1995); 'Ravi played magically', *FM*, 77; 'In the course of that merry evening', Antal Dorati, *Notes of Seven Decades*, 172; 'It is like a river', YM and Curtis Davis, *The Music of Man*, 51.

330 'I was taken at four o'clock', *UJ*, 258.

331 'I asked Y how he had enjoyed', *FM*, 87–8; 'should be prepared to go', *Times of India*, 2 March 1952; 'If I was a name to be reckoned with', *UJ*, 259; Mr Iyengar's teaching: B. K. S. Iyengar has published several books including a standard account, *Light on Yoga* (Allen and Unwin, 1968).

332 'to rise from their seats', *Evening News of India*, 5 March 1952; 'There was a small pool', *Sunday Standard*, 2 March 1952; 'wrenched from the navy', *FM*, 80; 'the most energetic musician, *Evening News of India*, 7 March 1952; 'They weren't at all bad', letters, dated 5 and 11 March 1952, from Diana Menuhin to Moshe Menuhin.

333 'The wonderful gesture', quoted in *MS*, 216; 'serene contemplation', *UJ*, 268; 'Its vast size', *FM*, 82.

334 'He comes from here', *FM*, 83; 'Its clearings and pathways', *UJ*, 268.

335 'Until India has sufficient electrical power', quoted in *MS*, 258–9; 'Your visit was an event', ibid., 261; 'yoga promised release', *UJ*, 273; 'If this concert had consisted', quoted in Tim Bullamore, *Fifty Festivals*, 39; 'Wonderfully alive', John Ardoin, *The Furtwängler Record*, 175.

336 'the Yehudi Menuhin who played', *New York Times*, 22 January 1953; 'Menuhin comes of age', *Newsweek*, 2 February 1953.

337 'Violent virtuosity', *Life*, February 1953; 'in his undefining way', *FM*, 94.

338 'After a few tussles', ibid., 96; 'You think you can', Diana Menuhin, Classic FM interview.

339 'In all the luxury', *FM*, 99; 'He was afraid', Diana Menuhin, Classic FM interview; 'We have been kept awake', *Los Gatos Times*, 19 March 1953.

340 'At one point Enesco', *FM*, 105; Enesco's violins: Noel Malcolm, *George Enescu*, 258; the Guarnerius went to Romania and the Santo Serafino was sold at Sotheby's on 16 November 1999 for £65,000; 'This was a greater Menuhin', *Daily Herald*, 26 June 1953.

341 'the constant switching about', *South Wales Echo*, 18 June 1953; '"There, darling," says he', *FM*, 98–9.

342 'Damn me, Menuhin', ibid., 111.

344 'an exquisitely suitable finale', *Bombay Chronicle*, 5 April 1954.

345 'The splendour of that great', *FM*, 110–11.

346 'Didn't I tell you?', ibid., 101.

347 chickenpox: various newspaper reports, 18 December 1954; 'A solitary figure', *Bath Chronicle*, May 1955, quoted in Bullamore, op. cit, 45.

348 'Whom, he soon asked me', *UJ*, 346; 'Y discovered to his fury', *FM*, 115.

349 borrowed concert dress: Diana Menuhin, Classic FM interview, and *FM*, 116–17.

350 death of Alexis: Diana Menuhin, Classic FM interview, and *FM*, 102; 'One cannot help', Adrian Boult (ed.), *Music and Friends: Letters to Adrian Boult*, 160.

351 'fascinating and penetrating'/'a skilfully organized': reviews quoted on the dust jacket of the 1973 revised edition of *MS*; typed memorandum: carbon copy, retained by Moshe, MA.

352 'Perhaps the worst', *YM*, 213; 'You turn your insides', letter, dated 1 November 1955, from Moshe to YM.

353 'Some of us', quoted in *MS*, 220; 'Why not call it', letter, dated 1 November 1955, from Moshe to YM; 'loving but vague', *FM*, 101–2.

354 'too shy to suggest', *UJ*, 207; 'strong in line', Ardoin, op. cit., 175.

Part Four: The Sage of Highgate 1956–1968

13 MOVING TO EUROPE

358 'hoping I would always be', *UJ*, 290; 'voluntarily and very quietly', Eleanor Hope, letter, dated 26 October 1999, to HB; 'for most of the time', *FM*, 9; 'dull old Switzerland', DM in conversation with HB, 25 October 1999.

359 'Most of us were becoming', *World-Telegram and Sun*, 25 October 1961; 'fineness as a person', *Star*, Johannesburg, 31 October 1956.

360 'an excellent black choir', *UJ*, 452'; 'I was obliged to wear', CFM; origins of Gstaad Festival: documents supplied by Gstaad Festival and the Britten–Pears Library.

361 'His identity with the concerto', *Herald Tribune*, 13 December 1957.

362 'a bit of the sparkle', *New York Times*, 13 December 1957; 'The melancholy second movement', *New York Times*, 16 December 1957.

363 $5000 fee: New York Philharmonic Orchestra Archive; 'an impulse', *Saturday Review*, 28 March 1958.

364 'But the gesture reflected', *New York Times*, 13 December 1957; 'a wild, forlorn stretch', *UJ*, 345; 'The prospect of a fascinating journey', *FM*, 146.

365 'We – composers and performers', 'Audiences and New Music', *The Sunday Times*, 19 October 1958; 'At the concert', *UJ*, 349.

366 'It's a rare programme', ibid.

367 'like a huge cowpat', *FM*, 165.

368 'the most liveable country', *UJ*, 207.

369 'My mother had painted over', Anna Massey, interviewed by HB, November 1999; 'In my conception', *Annabel* magazine, June 1983.

14 THE IMPRESARIO

372 'a graceful house', *FM*, 184.

374 orchestral colleagues and conducting skills: CFM.

375 'It was a lovely, vivacious festival', Tim Bullamore, *Fifty Festivals*, 85; 'Not the least of Menuhin's gifts', *Daily Telegraph*, 6 June 1959; 'The choice of venues', Bullamore, op. cit., 54.

376 'an exercise in self-education', *The Times*, 16 May 1960.

377 'I used the curved baroque bow', CFM; 'He was the only man', ibid.

378 'Young as she is', *Bath Chronicle*, 12 June 1961; Jacqueline du Pré: the young cellist can be seen in the photograph of the orchestra on the third page of the inserts between pp. 96 and 97 of Bullamore, op. cit.; 'This passionate and gifted young sprig', quoted in Elizabeth Wilson, *Jacqueline du Pré*, 70; 'Some of the most superb playing', *YM*, 292.

379 'It was a bit mundane', John Dankworth, interviewed by HB, November 1999.

380 'I loved it', Bullamore, op. cit., 67.

381 Malcolm Williamson on Concerto première: Malcom Williamson, interviewed by HB, November 1999; 'A long, serenely expressive', *The Times*, 16 June 1965.

382 *Carnival of the Animals* verses: MA (manuscript).

383 'We learned hardly more', quoted in Bullamore, op. cit., 75; 'Menuhin's début', *Opera*, 1966 Festivals issue, 45; 'secret ambition', *UJ*, 359.

384 'Banging the door', *FM*, 216.

385 'Doesn't matter', ibid., 218; 'The Guildhall mahogany', ibid., 219; 'You're making the greatest mistake', *UJ*, 360.

386 subsidy per capita: Bullamore, op. cit., 77; 'I wanted to make you sweat!', Alexander Goehr, interview with HB, November 1999; 'I remembered the famous recording', Pierre Boulez, interviewed by HB, April 1999.

388 'Menuhin may not be', *Opera*, 1967 Festivals issue, 45; 'Although this is only', *Opera*, August 1968, 667; 'rather anonymous pattern', letter and article quoted in Bullamore, op. cit., 81–2.

389 'I would say the trouble', ibid., 87.

390 *The Soldier's Tale*: John Cox, interviewed by HB, November 1999; the telecast was on 23 August 1968; the author was at that time Head of LWT's Drama, Arts and Music Unit.

391 'by far the most sucessful production', *Western Daily Press*, 28 June 1968; 'in a very dramatic way', quoted in Bullamore, op. cit., 85; 'almost unequalled', ibid., 89.

392 'I've always wanted', *Guardian Weekly*, 14 August 1969; 'Mr Menuhin caught the lilt', *The Times*, 18 September 1969; 'I was expecting', letter, dated 21 November 1999, from Oliver Knussen to HB.

394 'lingering connotations', 'N.S.', *Windsor, Slough and Eton Express*, 2 October 1970.

15 INTERLUDE

397 'A Day in the Life', *FM*, 184–7.

16 THE SCHOOL: UTOPIA IN STOKE D'ABERNON

402 'In the violin world', *New York Herald Tribune*, 1 November 1959.

403 'I studied this boy', *Travel* magazine, October 1962.

405 'a very special place', *The Times*, 8 November 1962; 'Aptly enough', *FM*, 201–2; 'We had many meetings', Ruth Railton, *Daring to Excel*, 343–4.

406 'Just as Sir Julian Huxley', *Sunday Telegraph*, 6 January 1963.

408 'We had a womb', *UJ*, 381; Ronan Magill: interview with HB, November 1999.

409 purchase of YMS building: *YMS Newsletter*, February 1971; 'With his vision', ibid., April 1985; 'He believed in being in touch', ibid.

410 'Music is a way of life', Introduction by YM to Eric Fenby, *Menuhin's House of Music*.

413 'It is at this stage', *The Times*, 1 March 1965; 'partly on a general physical condition', Fenby, op. cit., 116; 'It's done me so much good', ibid., 33.

414 'The rather unreal nature', Nigel Kennedy, *Always Playing*, 13; 'When I was seventeen', *YMS Newsletter*, summer 1998.

417 domestic facilities: *The Times*, 1 March 1965; 'Nobody who witnessed him', *YMS Newsletter*, March 1986.

418 'Yehudi said to me', letter from Nicolas Chisholm to HB, 11 February 2000.

Part Five: 'I Was Born Old' 1969–1999

17 CONFRONTATIONS AND COLLABORATIONS

422 'ambassadors, politicians', *New York Times*, 27 April 1966; *Gramophone* review: April 1966; signed 'TH' (Trevor Harvey).

423 'firmly in the centre of the note', *Gramophone*, October 1969.

424 'My dear, I am at one', Glenn Gould, *Selected Letters*, 87–8. In 1995 Yehudi was the recipient of the international prize established in Glenn Gould's name to honour work in the field of music and television.

425 'I have been singularly ineffective', letter, dated 6 July 1971, from YM to Jack Bornoff, MA; 'My outspoken regret', *UJ*, 291.

426 'would expose the policies', letter, dated 6 December 1999, from John Roberts to HB; 'worked on it under the bedclothes', CFM.

427 'a capitalist plot', quoted by YM in a letter, dated 6 July 1971, to Jack Bornoff, MA.

428 'People would come to me', CFM; 'I noticed Yehudi', letter, dated 6 December 1999, from John Roberts to HB.

429 'If I have offended you', *UJ*, 295; 'Have you ever encountered', letter, dated 6 December 1999, from John Roberts to HB; Rostropovich's 'political' heart attack: Galina Vishnevskaya, *Galina*, 436; 'We waited and waited', Ian Stoutzker, interviewed for BBC Radio 3, April 1999; 'He was like a little boy', *UJ*, 297.

430 'The sadness in Yehudi's tone', George Steiner, funeral oration at Westminster Abbey, June 1999; 'from Artur Rubinstein', letter, dated 6 December 1999, from John Roberts to HB.

431 'politicizing resolutions', *New York Times*, 11 February 1975; 'Just as a musician', MA; reproduced in *UJ*, 304; 'voices for the speechless', *European*, 20 May 1993.

432 'musicians representing', *UJ*, 307; 'with the exception', letter, dated 6 December 1999, from John Roberts to HB; 'I told him about a rehearsal', ibid.

434 'Thursday 3-25-71', New York Philharmonic Orchestra Archive, internal memo from Helen Thompson to Carlos Mosley, General Manager, 29 March 1971.

436 'He has not been afraid', *New York Times*, 25 May 1972; 'Those of us who were in Paris', *International Herald Tribune*, 8 August 1982.

437 'I feel more than ever', *Daily Telegraph*, 22 October 1982; 'I wrote to Yehudi', Andrzej Panufnik, *Composing Myself*, 319–20; the work was recorded in 1975; 'after Bartók', *UJ*, 346.

438 'I suggested that it be developed', Classic FM interview with Diana; 'I had thought I knew Diana', *UJ*, 213; the author was Editor of *Aquarius* from 1970 to 1975 and the director of the Christmas 1973 edition was Brian Izzard.

439 'The BBC rang me', ibid., 274; 'might be saddled', sleevenote for CD EMI CDM 7 69220 2.

440 'use any theme', *UJ*, 274.

441 'Kentner sat patiently', ibid., 308–9.

442 'The place is a cultural wilderness', Bermuda Festival, twenty-fifth anniversary programme book, January 2000.

443 establishment of the Gstaad Academy: *UJ*, 418–19; 'I stopped', Classic FM interview with Diana.

444 'I agreed with her', UJ, 414–15.

445 'At first the administrators', Ian Stoutzker, undated memorandum to HB; 'In sweet music', *Henry VIII*, III:i.

446 1997 Barbican concert: this event was introduced by HB.

447 'Isn't there a risk', YM and Curtis Davis, *The Music of Man*, 293.

448 'the loud echo', ibid., 218; 'We arrived in great style', ibid., 287.

18 MAESTRO MENUHIN

451 purchase date of the 'Lord Wilton': catalogue of violins prepared by Peter Biddulph, MA; Yehudi, wrongly, gave the purchase date as 1972, *UJ*, 313; attitude to violins: Jay Stack, 'A Conversation with Yehudi Menuhin', *New England To-day*, 18 June 1980.

452 *Music Guide* series: the *Music Guides* were republished in 1991 by Kahn and Averill and are still in print.

453 'a depth and a warmth', *UJ*, 433; 4 'the idea of cancelling', ibid.; Bloch concert and Moshe's death: Eleanor Hope, letter, dated 5 May 2000, to HB; 'Not really. It's nothing', Stack, op. cit.

454 'It was really a subject', Jeremy Menuhin, interviewed for BBC Radio 3, April 1999; 'in a cold sweat', diary extracts, courtesy of Jonathan Benthall.

455 'He was so happy', Ian Hunter, telephone interview with HB, November 1999.

457 'The man has no training', Ian Maclay, interviewed by HB, February 2000; 'He gave me his own baton', *UJ*, 369; 'the repudiation of the forethought', ibid., 366; 'Good morning', Brian Kay, telephone interview with HB, October 1999; 'Christopher's found', Christopher Bishop, interviewed for BBC Radio 3, April 1999; 'In the right context', Ian Maclay, interviewed for BBC Radio 3, April 1999.

458 'for daring to disclose', *UJ*, 409; 'When I was on tour', ibid., 404.

459 'The difference was dramatic', *Opera*, November 1998; 'over three or four years', Eleanor Hope, interviewed by HB, November 1999; Victor Hochhauser on YM's fees: BBC Radio 3 interview, April 1999.

460 'We only had three sessions', John West, interviewed for BBC Radio 3, April 1999.

461 'having cut off all the heating', Eleanor Hope, BBC Radio 3 interview, April 1999; 'utterly tireless', *UJ*, 395; 'unflagging rhythm', CFM.

462 'It was a matter of pride', Eleanor Hope, interviewed for BBC Radio 3, April 1999.

463 'I feel as if I have been', *Herald Tribune*, 25 July 1985; property prices: *Ritz* magazine.

464 'My life revolves', *Scotsman*, 22 December 1984; 'He drove around London', Eleanor Hope, interviewed for BBC Radio 3, April 1999.

465 'The event is also designed', brochure for the 2000 Yehudi Menuhin International Competition for Young Violinists.

466 Beethoven performance in Rome: the author directed a telecast of this Rome concert for Italian Television and can vouch for the disappointment.

467 'My greatest hope', communiqué, World Economic Foundation 1995 meeting; all other quotes from YM's Davos speeches supplied by Professor Klaus Schwab, the Forum's director; Asian Youth Orchestra: information from Susanne Baumgartner, then a tour adminstrator, later the Menuhin archivist.

468 'Diana calls me', *Sunday Express*, 16 July 1989.

469 'Thank God', quoted by Alexander Waugh in *Punch*, 21 December 1996.

470 'lived off Yehudi's earnings', Gillian Widdicombe, 'Child's play or purgatory?', *Observer*, 5 May 1991; Palmer film: Tony Palmer's video version of *Yehudi Menuhin* is distributed by RM Arts; *Le Violon du Siècle,* issued in 1996 for YM's eightieth birthday and distributed by EMI Classics, is a more rewarding film from a musical standpoint.

471 'As a small child', typescript of speech delivered 5 May 1991, MA.

472 'I shall never forget', *UJ*, 456; 'those who have tried', *The Times*, 23 January 1998.

475 'the elevated tone', ibid., 27 January 1996; YM's letters to *The Times*: Information Services Manager, News International Newspapers Ltd.

476 'My way of life', *UJ*. 431; ACE: information from documentation provided by Marianne Poncelet, Secretary of the IYMF.

477 YM at Oxford Gardens: Liz Rayment-Pickard, interviewed by HB, February 2000.

19 FINAL YEARS

482 Buckingham Palace birthday celebration: HB was master of ceremonies at this party.

485 'love and peace waffle', 'Menuhin on a Mission', *Punch*, 21 December 1996.

486 'Darling, I'd miss the airports', *Sunday Telegraph*, 31 October 1999; 'Perhaps you are right', ibid.

487 'He had so many ideas', 'Happy to be Daddy's Girl', *Daily Telegraph*, 5 November 1999; 'Very few people interested Yehudi', quoted in Tony Palmer's film, *Menuhin – A Family Portrait*.

488 'Some of my previous experience', letter, dated November 1999, to HB.

489 'as an accompanist', interviewed for BBC Radio 3, April 1999; 'To play with him was liberating', *Daily Telegraph*, 5 November 1999; 'I liked it when all the concerts', interviewed for BBC Radio 3, April 1999.

490 'How dare you think of yourself', quoted in *Daily Telegraph*, 5 November 1999; 'He didn't have moods', ibid.; 'the lady from Brussels', Diana, in conversation with HB.

491 'super hearing aids', John West, interviewed for BBC Radio 3, April 1999.

494 'He spent close to four hours', *YMS Bulletin*, summer 1999.

495 'Not all the orchestra', Mike Hatch, interview for BBC Radio 3, April 1999; 'We watched helpless', Zamira Benthall, interview with HB, April 2000; 'we are battered', World Economic Forum, Davos, 28 January–2 February 1999.

496 'I need hardly say', *YMS Bulletin*, summer 1999; Jewish Music Heritage Trust evening: information from Geraldine Auerbach, Director, Jewish Musical Institute.

497 'Dirigenten-Senior', *Rheinische Post*, 8 March 1999; 'The old man approached the rostrum', *Neue Ruhr Zeitung*, 9 March 1999; 'Yehudi pushed him', Eleanor Hope, interviewed for BBC Radio 3, April 1999.

498 'he thought Diana was going to die', *Sunday Telegraph*, 31 October 1999.

499 'the tiled walls', Maurice Whitaker interview with HB, 11 February 2000; 'I always say', note reproduced (with no explanation) in Bruno Monsaingeon, *Passion Menuhin – Album of a Life*, 191.

500 'I realized there was something', Eleanor Hope, interviewed for BBC Radio 3, April 1999.

501 'He had a wonderful vibrant tone', *Independent on Sunday*, 14 March 1999; 'Mother Teresa apart', ibid.

504 'desperately sad', Zamira Benthall, interview for BBC Radio 3, April 1999.

Bibliography

BOOKS BY YEHUDI MENUHIN

Menuhin, Yehudi, *Violin: Six Lessons* (Faber Music, 1971)
– *Theme and Variations* (Heinemann, 1972)
– *Unfinished Journey* (Methuen, 1977; rev. and expanded edn, 1996)
– *The Violin* (Flammarion, 1996)
Menuhin, Yehudi, and Curtis Davis, *The Music of Man* (Methuen, 1979; pbk edn, 1986)
Menuhin, Yehudi, and Christopher Hope, *Life Class* (US: *The Compleat Violinist*) (Heinemann, 1986)
Menuhin, Yehudi, and William Primrose, *Yehudi Menuhin Music Guide: Violin and Viola* (Kahn and Averill, 1991)

BIOGRAPHIES AND BOOKS ABOUT YEHUDI MENUHIN

Daniels, Robin, *Conversations with Menuhin* (Macdonald, 1979)
Dubal, David, *Conversations with Menuhin* (Harcourt, Brace Jovanovich, 1991)
Fenby, Eric, *Menuhin's House of Music* (Icon Books, 1969)
Magidoff, Robert, *Yehudi Menuhin*, rev. edn with additional chapters by Henry Raynor (Robert Hale, 1973)
Menuhin, Diana, *Fiddler's Moll* (Weidenfeld and Nicolson, 1984)
– *A Glimpse of Olympus* (Methuen, 1996)
Menuhin, Moshe, *The Menuhin Saga* (Sidgwick and Jackson, 1984)
The Menuhin Collection, Sotheby's auction catalogue, 16 November 1999
Palmer, Tony, *A Family Portrait* (Faber and Faber, 1991)
Rolfe, Lionel, *The Menuhins: A Family Odyssey* (Panjandrum Books, San Francisco, 1978)
Yehudi Menuhin 1916–1999: A Celebration, Royal Albert Hall, 6 November 1999, illustrated programme book (72 pp.), edited by Anne Simor

OTHER BOOKS CONSULTED (SELECT LIST)

Ardoin, John, *The Furtwängler Record* (Amadeus, 1994)
Boult, Adrian, *Blowing My Own Trumpet* (Hamish Hamilton, 1973)
– *Music and Friends: Letters to Adrian Boult*, edited by Jerrold Northrop Moore (Hamish Hamilton, 1979)

BIBLIOGRAPHY

Bullamore, Tim, *Fifty Festivals: The History of the Bath Festival* (Mushroom Publishing, 1999)

Burton, Humphrey, *Leonard Bernstein* (Faber and Faber, 1994)

Busch, Fritz, *Pages from a Musician's Life* (Hogarth, 1953)

Carpenter, Humphrey, *Benjamin Britten* (Faber and Faber, 1992)

Dorati, Antal, *Notes of Seven Decades* (Hodder and Stoughton, 1979)

Fenby, Eric, *Delius As I Knew Him* (Icon Books, 1966)

Gaisberg, Fred, *Music on Record* (Robert Hale, London, 1947)

Gelatt, Roland, *The Fabulous Phonograph* (Cassell, 1977)

Gould, Glenn, *Selected Letters* (OUP Toronto, 1992)

Iyengar, B. K. S., *Light on Yoga* (Allen and Unwin, 1968)

Kennedy, Michael, *Portrait of Walton* (OUP, rev. pbk. edn, 1990)

Kennedy, Nigel, *Always Playing* (Weidenfeld and Nicolson, 1991)

Malcolm, Noel, *George Enescu* (Toccata Press, 1990)

Mitchell, Donald, and Philip Reed (eds.), *Letters from a Life: Selected Letters and Diaries of Benjamin Britten*, vol. II: *1939–45* (Faber and Faber, 1991)

Monsaingeon, Bruno, *Passion Menuhin – Album d'une vie* (Textuel/Arté Edition, Paris, 2000)

Moore, Gerald, *Am I Too Loud?* (Penguin, 1962)

Moore, Jerrold Northrop, *A Voice in Time* (Hamish Hamilton, 1976); rev. edn, edited by Fred Gaisberg, *Sound Revolutions* (Sanctuary, 1999)

– *Elgar on Record* (OUP, 1975)

Newton, Ivor, *At the Piano* (Hamish Hamilton, 1966)

Osborne, Richard, *Herbert von Karajan* (Chatto and Windus, 1998)

Panufnik, Andrzej, *Composing Myself* (Methuen, 1987)

Paperno, Dmitry, *Notes of a Moscow Pianist* (Amadeus, 1998)

Railton, Ruth, *Daring to Excel* (Secker and Warburg, 1992)

Roth, Henry, *Violin Virtuosos from Paganini to the 21st Century* (California Classic Books, Los Angeles, 1997)

Sadie, Stanley (ed.), *The New Grove Dictionary of Music* (Macmillan, 1980)

Schneider, David, *The San Francisco Symphony* (Presidio Press, 1987)

Stevens, Halsey, *The Life and Music of Béla Bartók* (OUP, rev. edn, 1964)

Vishnevskaya, Galina, *Galina* (Hodder and Stoughton, 1984)

Walter, Bruno, *Theme and Variations* (Hamish Hamilton, 1947)

Wilson, Elizabeth, *Jacqueline du Pré* (Weidenfeld and Nicolson, 1998)

Chronology

1916   22 April: born New York City, US
1917   Family moves to Elizabeth, New Jersey
1918   Family moves to San Francisco, California
1920   Birth of Hephzibah
1921   First violin lessons with Sigmund Anker (two years)
        Birth of Yaltah
        First performance at a pupils' concert
1922   First appearance at the Civic Auditorium, San Francisco, (playing in a pupils' concert)
1923   Lessons begin with Louis Persinger
1924   First appearance, aged seven, under the auspices of the San Francisco Symphony Orchestra, playing the *Scène de ballet* by de Bériot, accompanied at the piano by Persinger
1925   First full-length solo recital, aged eight, given at the Scottish Rite Auditorium, San Francisco
1926   January: First New York recital, at the Manhattan Opera House
        March: First performance of a concerto (aged nine) – Lalo with the San Francisco Symphony Orchestra, Curran Theater (Persinger conducting)
        December: The Menuhin family sail to Europe for the first time
1927   February: Début in Paris, aged ten; Lalo and Tchaikovsky Concertos
        March: Lessons commence with George Enesco; they continue in the summer in Romania, where he hears gypsy fiddlers
        November: First concerto concert (Beethoven) in Carnegie Hall, New York Symphony Orchestra conducted by Fritz Busch
1928   March: First recordings for Victor
        October: first US concert tour
1929   January: Gift of 'Prince Khevenhüller' Stradivarius from Henry Goldman
        April: Berlin début, playing Bach, Beethoven and Brahms Concertos, Bruno Walter conducting the Berlin Philharmonic
        June: Studies with Adolf Busch (and in summer 1930); the Menuhins establish family home in Basel
        November: début in London at Queen's Hall, LSO conducted by Fritz Busch. First solo recordings with HMV
1931   Family home established at Ville d'Avray, outside Paris; first concerto recording (Bruch No. 1) with LSO under Sir Landon Ronald

1932   Records Elgar Concerto in London with the composer conducting and in Paris the Bach Double Concerto with Enesco

1933   Refuses to play in Germany after Nazis assume power; first duo recording with Hephzibah as pianist

1934   Plays Beethoven Concerto with New York Philharmonic under Toscanini; first US radio network broadcast

1935   'World Tour' visits Australia, New Zealand, South Africa and Europe

1936–37   Eighteen-month 'sabbatical' at new family home at Los Gatos, California

1937   Gives US première of Violin Concerto by Schumann

1938   Meets and marries Nola Nicholas; both his sisters marry (Hephzibah to Nola Nicholas's brother, Lindsay)

1939   War in Europe; birth of daughter Zamira; first tour of South America

1940   Australia: concerts and recordings with Hephzibah; birth of son Krov

1941–42   US enters war; Yehudi is deferred, plays for troops and makes second tour of Latin America

1943   First wartime visit to UK

1944   March: tour of military bases on the Aleutian Islands
June: Plays for Pacific Ocean battle troops in Hawaii
September: Second UK wartime visit, meets Diana Gould, the British ballet dancer and actress
October: plays in Antwerp, Brussels and Paris shortly after their liberation
November: gives the première of Bartók's Sonata for solo violin in New York

1945   April: plays for the inaugural United Nations assembly in San Francisco
June: London, records sound track for Paganini film, *The Magic Bow*
July: with Benjamin Britten plays for survivors of concentration camps at Belsen and in August broadcasts Mendelssohn Violin Concerto from Hamburg
November: first visit to Moscow, friendship with David Oistrakh

1946   January: records Bartók Violin Concerto No. 2 with Dorati
April: conducts the Dallas Symphony Orchestra in a semi-public rehearsal of the *Mastersingers* Prelude by Wagner; YM and Nola begin an unsuccessful, year-long attempt to achieve a reconciliation

1947   January: conducts an hour-long broadcast concert with Dallas SO
August: records Beethoven Concerto with Furtwängler and later appears with him in Berlin; special recital boycotted by Jewish DPs
October: marries Diana Gould in London
December: first full-length music film, *Concert Magic*

1948   Appears for first time at Edinburgh International Festival, soon after the birth of his son Gerard in July

1949   Zurich première of violin and piano sonata by Walton

1950   February: challenges apartheid in South Africa
April: first visit to Israel; it proceeds despite bomb threats

1951   May: with Hephzibah gives first recital in London's Royal Festival Hall

June: visits Australia and New Zealand; discovers yoga
October: first concert tour of Japan
November: birth of son, Jeremy

1952 Concert tour of India in aid of Famine Relief; hears Ravi Shankar and meets yoga teacher, B. K. S. Iyengar

1953 Renounces flying (for eight years) following prominent musicians' deaths in air crashes

1954 Holds first violin classes, at Nadia Boulanger's Academy in Fontainebleau, France; first summer vacation for family in Gstaad

1955 August: death of newly born son Alexis
October: rift with parents following publication of biography by Robert Magidoff; the Menuhins quit their Alma home for Europe

1956 Plays at Johannesburg Festival, his last South African visit until the end of apartheid; back operation forces two months rest

1957 First Gstaad Festival

1958 The family begins two year sojourn on the estate of Bernard Berenson at Villa I Tatti outside Florence

1959–68 Artistic Director (named as such in 1966) for ten years of the Bath Festival; becomes a regular conductor of concerts and recordings (notably, in 1959, the six Brandenburg Concertos by Bach)

1960 The family takes up residence in London at 2 The Grove, Highgate; and at their chalet, Chankly Bore, in Gstaad

1961 Introduces Jacqueline du Pré, aged sixteen, at Bath Festival

1962 Receives Royal Philharmonic Society's Gold Medal; accompanies Margot Fonteyn in *Swan Lake pas de deux* at Bath; acquires summer home on Mykonos

1963 Establishes Yehudi Menuhin International School in London; it moves after a year to larger premises at Stoke d'Abernon, Surrey

1964 Bath: Macmillan's ballet *Divertimento* is danced by Fonteyn and Nureyev to Bartók solo Sonata

1965 Made honorary KBE; appears at Commonwealth Festival, London

1966 Conducts first opera, Mozart's *Così fan tutte* ; performs and records duo improvisations with Ravi Shankar

1967 Leads Bath Festival Tour on North American tour; East meets West concert at UN Assembly

1968 Quits Bath Festival over budgetary problems

1969–72 Joint Artistic Director (with Ian Hunter) of Windsor Festival

1969–75 President International Music Council, UNESCO

1970 Honorary Swiss citizenship awarded by two cantons; at Windsor, conducts première of Knussen's Second Symphony

1971 Supports Russian dissidents in Moscow speech; first duet appearance with jazz violinist Stéphane Grappelli

1972 Publishes essays and speeches in *Theme and Variations*

1973 Gives première of *Polyptique* by Frank Martin – one of several dozen works commissioned by YM over a fifty-year span

1974   Clash with Artur Rubinstein and others over role of UNESCO
1975   Plays at International Music Day, Ottawa; conducts Royal Philharmonic
       Orchestra for first time
1976   Plays at inaugural Bermuda Festival and for President Ford and HM The
       Queen in Washington, at US Bicentennial celebrations
1977   Foundation of Live Music Now and International Menuhin Academy at
       Gstaad; publishes autobiography, *Unfinished Journey*
1978–79   *The Music of Man* television series for the Canadian Broadcasting
       Corporation
1979   Establishes Portsmouth International String Quartet Competition (trans-
       ferred to London in 1988); visits China, named honorary professor of
       Beijing Conservatoire; first recording with RPO (in 1982 he was named
       the orchestra's lifetime President)
1980   Performs at Winter Olympics, Lake Placid, US
1983   Moves from Highgate to Chester Square in Belgravia, Central London;
       conducts Sinfonia Varsovia in concert for the Pope; foundation in
       Folkestone of Yehudi Menuhin International Competition for Young
       Violinists
1984   Conducts *La clemenza di Tito* at Bonn Opera
1985   Assumes British citizenship and becomes Sir Yehudi
1987   The Queen makes him a member of the Order of Merit
1988   Named Honorary President of Philharmonia Hungarica Orchestra
1989   Attends World Economic Forum, Davos, for first time; conducts *Messiah*
       in the Kremlin shortly after the collapse of the Communist regime
1991   Controversial Channel 4 film, *A Family Portrait,* is shown to mark
       YM's seventy-fifth birthday; receives Wolf Prize at the Knesset in Israel;
       establishment by royal decree of the International Yehudi Menuhin
       Foundation in Brussels
1993   Becomes a baron, The Rt Hon The Lord Menuhin of Stoke d'Abernon,
       OM, KCB
1994   Launch of MUS-E in Brussels
1995   Returns to South Africa, conducts *Messiah* with black singers
1996   Final public appearance as a solo violinist at 40th Gstaad Festival; con-
       ducts Sarajevo Peace Concert under patronage of Germany, European
       Commission and UNESCO
1997   First meeting of the Assembly of Cultures
1998   Death of Marutha Menuhin, aged a hundred (Hephzibah died in 1981;
       Moshe in 1982)
1999   12 March: Death in Berlin while on concert tour with Sinfonia Varsovia

Acknowledgements

It was back in 1995 that my friend Michael Bukht, Controller of Programmes at Classic FM, set this project in motion by accepting my proposal for a twenty-part radio series on Yehudi Menuhin's musical life. The programmes were produced by Declan McGovern, who had worked with me earlier in the decade on a Leonard Bernstein series. He cunningly interwove excerpts from the ten hours of interviews with Yehudi's recorded performances and the counterpointing memories of family, friends and fellow musicians.

Over several agreeable lunches at Daphne's, my agent Abner Stein encouraged me to develop a broader treatment of Menuhin's life, suitable for publication, and happily Faber and Faber renewed their faith in me. For close on two years, my editor at Queen Square, Belinda Matthews, has been like Patience on a monument – I've been delivering in instalments – and her colleagues, notably Ron Costley, Charles Boyle and above all Jill Burrows, have kept my spirits up with their enthusiasm when the sheer mass of detail threatened to bog me down. That's one of the remarkable things about Yehudi Menuhin: he inspires affection and commitment, even from beyond the grave. Everybody to whom I turned had a story to tell: for music-lovers, attending your first Menuhin performance is, it seems, like remembering where you were when you heard the news of the Kennedy assassination or the death of the Princess of Wales.

Menuhin's own death came as an enormous shock. I'd like to record my admiration for BBC Radio 3, which immediately organized a comprehensive five-hour memorial tribute, broadcast on what would have been Yehudi's eighty-third birthday, 22 April; I am grateful to Adam Gatehouse and his producer colleagues Andrew Kurowski and Clive Portbury for their commitment to the concept. I must also thank the BBC for permitting me to quote from the many interviews carried out for that memorial programme – it is gratifying to have had both the national classical music radio networks involved with this book at different times! Incidentally, copies of the interview tapes will be deposited in the Menuhin Archive for the use of historians and students.

That Archive is a treasure trove. Literally hundreds of boxes of concert programmes, press cuttings and correspondence await future researchers; I would never have got started had I stopped to read them all – as I mentioned in my foreword, I conceived my task as the provision of an overview, occasionally zooming in to close-ups for crucial episodes in his incredibly active musical life. And thank heavens for enthusiastic critics like Redfern Mason and Alexander Fried who described so eloquently Yehudi's impact on San Francisco audiences in the 1920s!

Press reviews and interviews, not to mention the gossip columns, bring us close to the action, even at three-quarters of a century's remove. In San Francisco I found useful cuttings in the files of the *Examiner* and the Performing Arts Library but it is Moshe Menuhin who most deserves a biographer's gratitude. He built up a monumental collection of scrapbooks crammed with stories of his son's achievements; his account of the family odyssey, *The Menuhin Saga*, is as indispensable for the pre-war days as Yehudi's own autobiography. Diana Menuhin's entertaining description of her life as a fiddler's moll is equally valuable, and over the past four years she has provided answers to many enquiries.

In October 2000, the month this book will be published, Yehudi's younger sister Yaltah moves into her eightieth year. It's been a boon to me that she, too, lives in London. Her recollections of her family are astonishingly vivid. The matriarch, Mrs Marutha Menuhin, greeted me at her Los Gatos home in 1996, when she was close on a hundred years old. She was deaf as a post but very sprightly in her responses once she had grasped the import of my written questions. Warm thanks go also to Yehudi's daughter Zamira and her husband Jonathan Benthall. Yehudi's sons Krov, Gerard and Jeremy Menuhin have also been generous with their time and information.

I must also express appreciation for the kindness offered me by Yehudi's personal staff. Jutta Schall-Emden was the archivist in the mid-1990s. On her retirement she was succeeded by Susanne Baumgartner, who can be relied on to find in a few moments exactly the photo, concert programme or document one is looking for. Nicky Caxton-Spencer, the Menuhins' housekeeper for sixteen years, was always on hand with a smile at Chester Square, while Eleanor Hope, who is based now in Vienna but keeps close to every aspect of Yehudi's artistic legacy, has given me her ringside-seat perceptions of the last two decades of his life.

I have had similar insights from other impresarios close to Yehudi, not to mention recording producers, diplomats, journalists, schoolmasters, violin pupils and fellow musicians. There is no space to elaborate their contributions individually and to those inadvertently omitted I tender instant apologies but here at least are the names of those with whom I have talked: Witiko Adler, Agnes Albert, Peter Andry, Rose Anker, Geraldine Auerbach, Irvine Bartha, Bernd Bauer, Michael Berkeley, William Bernell, Michael Binyon, Christopher Bishop, Pierre Boulez, Richard Bradburn, Simon Campion, Nicolas Chisholm, Francis Coleman, Robert Commanday, John Cox, Malcolm Crowthers, John Dankworth, Colin Davis, Susan Digby, Gwyneth Drage, David Farrell, Peter Feuchtwanger, Lukas Foss, Patricia Foy, Thomas Gayda, Kim Gaynor, Alexander Goehr, Sheila Gold, Carola Grindea, Mike Hatch, Lilian Hochhauser, Victor Hochhauser, Daniel Hope, Eleanor Hope, Albert Howell, Margaret Hubicki, Ian Hunter, Tim Ingles, Brian Izzard, Bob Jacobs, Morris Kahn, Julie Kavanagh, Brian Kay, Oliver Knussen, Anita Lasker, Charles Lister, Peter Logan, Ian Maclay, Ronan Magill, Anna Massey, Lothar Mattner, Bruno Monsaingeon, William Mostyn-Owen, Peter Norris, Carola Oman, Camilla Panufnik, Michael Parkinson, Tony Palmer, Edgar Paltzer, Jack Phipps, Marianne Poncelet, Liz Rayment-Pickard, Max Rayne, Peter Renshaw, Virginia Renshaw, Luke Rittner, John Roberts, Albi Rosenthal, Jack Rothstein, Edwin Roxburgh, Dennis Sayer, Rüdiger Schramm, Klaus Schwab,

ACKNOWLEDGEMENTS

James Schwabacher, Marianne Seymour, Ravi Shankar, Malcolm Singer, Anne Simor, Richard Sotnick, Helen Sprott, Klaus Stadler, Isaac Stern, Denis Stevens, Ian Stoutzker, Jock Sutcliffe, Peter Thomas, Roy Tipping, John Tooley, Wendy Toye, Vincent Tovell, Inka Vostresova, Susana Walton, John West, Maurice Whitaker, Malcolm Williamson, David Wynne.

Archivists of many orchestras, concert halls and musical organizations have furnished important information, notably: the Gedenkstätte Bergen-Belsen, the Berlin Philharmonic (Dr Helge Grünewald was particularly helpful), the Britten–Pears Library (Jenny Doctor), the Czech Philharmonic, EMI (Richard Blackburn), the Gstaad Festival (Carol Würsten), the House of Lords Library, the Israel Philharmonic, the Jerusalem Symphony Orchestra, the London Symphony Orchestra, News International Newspapers Ltd, the New York Philharmonic (Barbara Haws), the Royal Albert Hall, the Royal Philharmonic Orchestra (Louise Chartres and Sarah Lom), the San Francisco Symphony (Larry Rothe) and Eric Wen and Peter Biddulph of Biddulph Records.

Two years ago I was fortunate to meet Alex Milner, then in his last year at Eton and now a choral scholar at King's; he was looking for work experience and he volunteered to sift through dozens of books of memoirs on the look-out for Menuhin references; in the midst of all his music-making he proved a tireless researcher.

Finally I should like to thank my wife Christina, for applying her cool intelligence to each chapter from the first drafts onwards. She knew the Menuhins for thirty years, ever since she arrived in London from Sweden; Diana still calls her my 'Ice Princess'. (See the Christmas card on page 505.) A photographer herself, she helped assemble the illustrations to this book and I couldn't ask for a better second pair of eyes. For all errors and omissions, however, I take personal responsibility.

I hereby express my gratitude to the owners of copyright as follows: to the Random House Group Ltd for permission to quote from *Unfinished Journey* by Yehudi Menuhin (originally published by Methuen); to Diana Menuhin for permission to quote from *Fiddler's Moll* and *A Glimpse of Olympus*; to the New York Philharmonic Archive for permission to reproduce Helen Thompson's report (pp. 434–5); to Sidgwick and Jackson and the executors of the Moshe and Marutha Menuhin Trust for permission to quote from *The Menuhin Saga* by Moshe Menuhin (1984). The quotations from the letters of Benjamin Britten are © the Trustees of the Britten–Pears Foundation and may not be further reproduced without the written permission of the Trustees. Permission has been sought, but the estates have not yet been traced, to quote from *Yehudi Menuhin*, by Robert Magidoff with additional chapters by Henry Raynor (revised edition published in the UK by Robert Hale in 1973).

Index

Figures in italics indicate captions to photographs. 'YM' indicates Yehudi Menuhin.

INDEX

'From the Sitar to the Guitar' TV programme
479
West Meets East (originally *East Meets
West*) 330, 385
Shapeero, Ezra 34, 35, 38, 274
Shawe-Taylor, Desmond 305
Sher, Sara Liba (YM's grandmother) 5, 6, 17
Shostakovich, Dimitri 258, 277, 296, 359
  String Quartet No. 14, Op. 142 429
  Violin Concerto in A minor, Op. 99 357,
    359, 360, 361
Shrine auditorium, Los Angeles 80, 82
Sibelius, Jean 348
  Violin Concerto 339, 348
Sils Maria, Swiss Engadine 134, 157
Simpson, Derek 373
Sinaia, Romania 56, 61–5, 93, 223, 270
Sinfonia Varsovia (previously Polish Chamber
  Orchestra) 456, 459, 461–2, 479–82, 491,
  492, 495, 499
Singer, Malcolm 483, 494, 506, 508
  A Hopeful Place 483
  Elegy on the G string for solo violin 503
Sitkovetsky, Dmitry 489
Sitkovetsky, Sasha 503
Skidelsky, Robert, Lord 475
Sokoloff, Nikolai 108, 122
Solzhenitsyn, Alexander 425, 428, 429, 466
Sophia, Queen of Spain 502
Sotnick, Richard 468
South Africa 142, 158, 164–5, 290, 304,
  307–11, 317, 357, 358–9, 446, 478, 483,
  491
South America 197, 211, 216–17, 290, 301–3,
  307
Soviet Union
  YM's campaign to release dissidents 372
  YM in 254–9, 371, 405–6, 421, 426–9, 466,
    478
Spain: MUS-E organization in 477
Spanish Civil War 194
Spivakov, Vladimir 466
Stage Door Canteen (film) 228
Steiner, George 424, 430
Stern, Isaac 300, 341–2, 344, 459
Stevens, Denis 374, 377, 448, 452
Stix, William 177, 192, 198, 205
Stoke d'Abernon 401, 409, 412, 482, 485, 494,
  502, 508
Stokes, Richard 71, 84
Stokowski, Leopold 26, 152, 159
Stott, Kathryn 413
Stoughton Grange School, North Guildford
  507–8
Stoutzker, Ian 44–5, 429, 446
Stradivarius, Antonio 87
Strafford, Claire, Countess of 408
Strasbourg 476, 480, 486
  festival (June 1994) 462
Strathcona, Lord 389
Strauss, Johann, II 392, 483
Strauss, Richard 95, 448
Stravinsky, Igor 380, 390, 470

Sunday Express 468
Sunday Standard (Bombay) 332, 344
Sunday Telegraph 406
Sunday Times 105, 167, 365, 449
Supakhin, Valentin 428–9
Swint, Curran D. 81, 91
Sydney 161, 162, 212, 213, 343, 493
Szigeti, Joseph 264, 296
Szymanowski, Karol 136
  The Fountain of Arethusa 263
  Myths 62

Tan, Melvyn 413
Tang Yun 458
Tartini, Giuseppe 62
  Sonata in G minor ('Devil's Trill') 63, 75,
    129, 187, 324, 332
Taubman, Howard 336, 362, 364
Tavener, John 485
Tchaikovsky, Pyotr Ilyich 19, 247, 293, 480,
  484
  Sérénade mélancolique 28, 49
  Trio, Op. 50 168, 171
  Violin Concerto 44, 46, 53, 55, 83, 84, 86,
    91, 189, 296, 304, 336, 360
Tel Aviv 312, 314, 501
Telemann, Georg Philipp 361
Teresa, Mother 463, 501
Terinallum 214, 343
Tertis, Lionel 408
Thatcher, Margaret, Baroness 416, 464, 507
Theatre Royal, Bath 375, 380, 383, 390
Theatre Royal, Drury Lane, London 304
Thibaut, Jacques 111, 120, 122, 146, 239, 240,
  342
Thomas, Peter 376
Thompson, Oscar 84, 113
Tibbett, Laurence 64, 203
Time magazine 182–3, 203, 204, 260, 286,
  296–7
The Times 123, 187, 342, 376, 381, 393,
  404–5, 407–8, 417, 436, 472–3, 475, 501,
  506–7
Times of India 331
Tippett, Sir Michael 375, 378, 379–80, 386, 391
Toronto 153, 386, 432, 442, 446, 448
Toronto *Daily Star* 126
Tortelier, Paul 279, 452
Tortelier, Yan-Pascal 484
Toscanini, Arturo 96, 107–8, 113, 119, *119*,
  124, 129, 134, 136, 137, 145, 148,
  150–53, 156, 169, 194, 203, 261, 300,
  307, 310–11, 358
Toye, Francis 134
Toye, Wendy 387, 391
Tredici, David del 485–6
Trinity College of Music, London 381
Tuckwell, Barry 374
Twain, Mark 37, 114

UNESCO 425, 430, 431, 436, 447, 473, 475,
  491, 496
United Nations 385